Children's
Literature
Review

Guide to Gale Literary Criticism Series

When you need to review criticism of literary works, these are the Gale series to use:

If the author's death date is:

You should turn to:

After Dec. 31, 1959
(or author is still living)

CONTEMPORARY LITERARY CRITICISM

for example: Jorge Luis Borges, Anthony Burgess,
William Faulkner, Mary Gordon,
Ernest Hemingway, Iris Murdoch

1900 through 1959

TWENTIETH-CENTURY LITERARY CRITICISM

for example: Willa Cather, F. Scott Fitzgerald,
Henry James, Mark Twain, Virginia Woolf

1800 through 1899

NINETEENTH-CENTURY LITERATURE CRITICISM

for example: Fedor Dostoevski, George Sand,
Gerard Manley Hopkins, Emily Dickinson

1400 through 1799

LITERATURE CRITICISM FROM 1400 TO 1800
(excluding Shakespeare)

for example: Anne Bradstreet, Pierre Corneille,
Daniel Defoe, Alexander Pope,
Jonathan Swift, Phillis Wheatley

SHAKESPEAREAN CRITICISM

Shakespeare's plays and poetry

Antiquity through 1399

CLASSICAL AND MEDIEVAL LITERATURE CRITICISM

for example: Dante, Plato, Homer, Sophocles, Vergil,
the Beowulf poet

(Volume 1 forthcoming)

Gale also publishes related criticism series:

CHILDREN'S LITERATURE REVIEW

This ongoing series covers authors of all eras. Presents criticism on
authors and author/illustrators who write for the preschool
through high school audience.

CONTEMPORARY ISSUES CRITICISM

This two volume set presents criticism on contemporary authors
writing on current issues. Topics covered include the social sciences,
philosophy, economics, natural science, law, and related areas.

ISSN 0362-4145

volume 10

Children's Literature Review

Excerpts from Reviews,
Criticism, and Commentary
on Books for Children
and Young People

Gerard J. Senick
Editor

Melissa Reiff Hug
Associate Editor

Gale Research Company
Book Tower
Detroit, Michigan 48226

STAFF

Gerard J. Senick, *Editor*

Melissa Reiff Hug, *Associate Editor*

Susan Miller Harig, *Senior Assistant Editor*

Motoko Fujishiro Huthwaite, *Assistant Editor*

Sharon R. Gunton, *Contributing Editor*

Lizbeth A. Purdy, *Production Supervisor*
Denise Michlewicz Broderick, *Production Coordinator*
Eric Berger, *Assistant Production Coordinator*
Kathleen M. Cook, Maureen Duffy, Sheila J. Nasea, *Editorial Assistants*

Victoria B. Cariappa, *Research Coordinator*
Jeannine Schiffman Davidson, *Assistant Research Coordinator*
Daniel Kurt Gilbert, Maureen R. Richards, Keith E. Schooley, Filomena Sgambati,
Vincenza G. Tranchida, Valerie J. Webster, Mary D. Wise, *Research Assistants*

Linda M. Pugliese, *Manuscript Coordinator*
Donna Craft, *Assistant Manuscript Coordinator*
Maureen A. Puhl, Rosetta Irene Simms, *Manuscript Assistants*

Jeanne A. Gough, *Permissions Supervisor*
Janice M. Mach, *Permissions Coordinator, Text*
Patricia A. Seefelt, *Permissions Coordinator, Illustrations*
Susan D. Battista, *Assistant Permissions Coordinator*
Margaret A. Chamberlain, Sandra C. Davis, Kathy Grell, Mary M. Matuz, *Senior Permissions Assistants*
Colleen M. Crane, Josephine M. Keene, Mabel Schoening, *Permissions Assistants*
Margaret Carson, H. Diane Cooper, Dorothy J. Fowler, Anita Williams, *Permissions Clerks*

Arthur Chartow, *Art Director*

Frederick G. Ruffner, *Publisher*
Dedria Bryfonski, *Editorial Director*
Christine Nasso, *Director, Literature Division*
Laurie Lanzen Harris, *Senior Editor, Literary Criticism Series*
Dennis Poupard, *Managing Editor, Literary Criticism Series*

Copyright © 1986 by Gale Research Company

Library of Congress Catalog Card Number 75-34953
ISBN 0-8103-0342-6
ISSN 0362-4145

Computerized photocomposition by
Typographics, Incorporated
Kansas City, Missouri

Printed in the United States

CONTENTS

PREFACE

As children's literature has evolved into both a respected branch of creative writing and a successful industry, literary criticism has documented and influenced each stage of its growth. Critics have recorded the literary development of individual authors as well as the trends and controversies that resulted from changes in values and attitudes, especially as they concerned children. While defining a philosophy of children's literature, critics developed a scholarship that balances an appreciation of children and an awareness of their needs with standards for literary quality much like those required by critics of adult literature. *Children's Literature Review* (*CLR*) is designed to provide a permanent, accessible record of this ongoing scholarship. Those responsible for bringing children and books together can now make informed choices when selecting reading materials for the young.

Scope of the Series

Each biannual volume contains excerpts from published criticism on the literary works of authors and author/illustrators who create books for children from preschool through high school. The author list for each volume is international in scope and represents the variety of genres covered by children's literature—picture books, fiction, folklore, nonfiction, poetry, and drama. The works of approximately fifteen to forty authors of all eras are represented in each volume. Although earlier volumes of *CLR* emphasized critical material published after 1960, successive volumes have expanded their coverage to encompass criticism written before 1960. Since many of the authors included in *CLR* are living and continue to write, it is necessary to update their entries periodically. Thus, future volumes will supplement the entries of selected authors covered in earlier volumes as well as present criticism on the works of authors new to the series.

Organization of the Book

An author section consists of the following elements: author heading, author portrait, author introduction, excerpts of criticism (each followed by a bibliographical citation), and illustrations, when available.

- The **author heading** consists of the author's full name followed by birth and death dates. The portion of the name outside the parentheses denotes the form under which the author is most frequently published. If the majority of the author's works for children were written under a pseudonym, the pseudonym will be listed in the author heading and the real name given on the first line of the author introduction. Also located at the beginning of the introduction are any other pseudonyms used by the author in writing for children and any name variations, including transliterated forms for authors whose languages use nonroman alphabets. Uncertainty as to a birth or death date is indicated by question marks.

- An **author portrait** is included when available.

- The **author introduction** contains information designed to introduce an author to *CLR* users by presenting an overview of the author's themes and styles, occasional biographical facts that relate to his or her literary career, a summary of critical response to the author's works, and information about major awards and prizes the author has received. Where applicable, introductions conclude with references to additional entries in biographical and critical reference series published by Gale Research Company. These sources include past volumes of *CLR* as well as *Contemporary Authors, Something about the Author, Yesterday's Authors of Books for Children, Contemporary Literary Criticism, Twentieth-Century Literary Criticism, Nineteenth-Century Literature Criticism, Dictionary of Literary Biography,* and *Authors in the News.*

- **Criticism** is located in three sections: **author's commentary** and **general commentary** (when available) and within individual **title entries,** which are preceded by **title entry headings.** Criticism is arranged chronologically within each section. Titles by authors being profiled are highlighted in boldface type within the text for easier access by readers.

The **author's commentary** presents background material written by the author or by an interviewer. This commentary may cover a specific work or several works. Author's commentary on more than one work appears after the author introduction, while commentary on an individual book follows the title entry heading.

The **general commentary** consists of critical excerpts that consider more than one work by the author being profiled. General commentary is preceded by the critic's name in boldface type or, in the case of unsigned criticism, by the title of the journal.

Title entry headings precede the criticism on a title and cite publication information on the work being reviewed. Title headings list the work's title as it appeared in its country of origin; titles in languages using nonroman alphabets are transliterated. If the original title is in a language other than English, the title of the first English-language translation follows in brackets. The work's first publication date is listed in parentheses following the title. Differing U.S. and British titles of works originally published in English follow the publication date within the parentheses.

Title entries consist of critical excerpts on the author's individual works, arranged chronologically by publication date. The entries generally contain two to six reviews per title, depending on the stature of the book and the amount of criticism it has generated. The editors select titles that reflect the entire scope of the author's literary contribution, covering each genre and subject. An effort is made to reprint criticism that represents the full range of each title's reception —from the year of its initial publication to current assessments. Thus, the reader is provided with a record of the author's critical history.

• Selected excerpts are preceded by **explanatory notes,** which provide information on the critic or work of criticism to enhance the reader's understanding of the excerpt.

• A complete **bibliographical citation** designed to facilitate the location of the original book or article follows each piece of criticism. An asterisk (*) at the end of a citation indicates that the essay or book is on more than one author.

• Numerous **illustrations** are featured in *CLR.* For entries on author/illustrators, an effort has been made to include illustrations that reflect the author's styles as represented in the criticism. Entries on major authors who do not illustrate their own works may also include photographs and other illustrative material pertinent to the authors' careers.

Other Features

• A list of **authors to appear in future volumes** follows the preface.

• An **appendix** lists the sources from which material has been reprinted in the volume. It does not, however, list every book or periodical consulted for the volume.

• *CLR* volumes contain **cumulative indexes** to authors, nationalities, and titles.

The **cumulative index to authors** lists authors who have appeared in *CLR* and includes cross-references to *Contemporary Authors, Something about the Author, Yesterday's Authors of Books for Children, Contemporary Literary Criticism, Twentieth-Century Literary Criticism, Nineteenth-Century Literature Criticism, Dictionary of Literary Biography,* and *Authors in the News.*

The **cumulative nationality index** lists authors alphabetically under their respective nationalities. Author names are followed by the volume number(s) in which they appear. Authors who have changed citizenship or whose current citizenship is not reflected in biographical sources appear under both their original nationality and that of their current residence.

The **cumulative title index** lists titles covered in *CLR* followed by the volume and page number where criticism begins.

Acknowledgments

No work of this scope can be accomplished without the cooperation of many people. The editors especially wish to thank the copyright holders of the criticism included in this volume, the permissions managers of many book and magazine publishing companies for assisting us in securing reprint rights, and the staffs of the Kresge Library at Wayne State University, the University of Michigan Library, the Detroit Public Library, and the Wayne Oakland

Library Federation (WOLF) for making their resources available to us. We are also grateful to Carole McCollough, Coordinator of Children's and Young Adults' Services for WOLF, and to Anthony J. Bogucki for his assistance with copyright research.

Suggestions Are Welcome

In response to various suggestions, several features have been added to *CLR* since the series began:

- Since Volume 3—**Author's commentary,** when available, which presents the viewpoint of the author being profiled.

  —An **appendix** listing the sources of criticism in each volume.

- Since Volume 4—**Author portraits** as well as **illustrations** from works by author/illustrators, when available.

  —**Title entries** arranged chronologically according to the work's first publication; previous volumes listed titles alphabetically.

- Since Volume 5—A **guest essay,** when available, written specifically for *CLR* by a prominent critic on a subject of his or her choice.

- Since Volume 6—**Explanatory notes** that provide information on the critic or work of criticism to enhance the usefulness of the excerpt.

  —A **cumulative nationality index** for easy access to authors by nationality.

- Since Volume 8—Author entries on retellers of traditional literature as well as those who have been the first to record oral tales and other folklore.

  —More extensive illustrative material, such as holographs of manuscript pages and photographs of people and places pertinent to the authors' careers.

- Since Volume 10—Entries devoted to criticism on a major work by a single author.

Readers are cordially invited to write the editor with comments and suggestions for further enhancing the usefulness of the *CLR* series.

AUTHORS TO APPEAR IN FUTURE VOLUMES

Aardema, Verna 1911-
Adams, Adrienne 1906-
Adams, Harriet S(tratemeyer)
    1893?-1982
Adams, Richard 1920-
Adler, Irving 1913-
Aesop 620?BC-564?BC
Anderson, C(larence) W(illiam)
    1891-1971
Arnosky, Jim 1946-
Asbjörnsen, Peter Christen 1812-1885
    and Jörgen Moe 1813?-1882
Asch, Frank 1946-
Asimov, Isaac 1920-
Avery, Gillian 1926-
Avi 1937-
Aymé, Marcel 1902-1967
Bailey, Carolyn Sherwin 1875-1961
Ballantyne, R(obert) M(ichael)
    1825-1894
Banner, Angela 1923-
Bannerman, Helen 1863-1946
Barrett, Judi(th) 1941-
Barrie, J(ames) M(atthew) 1860-1937
Baum, L(yman) Frank 1856-1919
Baumann, Hans 1914-1985
BB 1905-
Beatty, Patricia 1922- and John
    1922-1975
Behn, Harry 1898-1973
Belloc, Hilaire 1870-1953
Benary-Isbert, Margot 1889-1979
Benchley, Nathaniel 1915-1981
Berenstain, Stan(ley) 1923- and
    Jan(ice) 1923-
Berger, Melvin 1927-
Berna, Paul 1910-
Beskow, Elsa 1874-1953
Bianco, Margery Williams 1881-1944
Bishop, Claire Huchet
Blades, Ann 1947-
Blake, Quentin 1932-
Blos, Joan W(insor) 1928-
Blyton, Enid 1897-1968
Bodecker, N(iels) M(ogens) 1922-
Bødker, Cecil 1927-
Bond, Nancy 1945-
Bonham, Frank 1914-
Branley, Franklyn M(ansfield) 1915-
Branscum, Robbie 1937-
Brazil, Angela 1869-1947
Breinburg, Petronella 1927-
Bridgers, Sue Ellen 1942-
Bright, Robert 1902-
Brink, Carol Ryrie 1895-1981
Brooke, L(eonard) Leslie 1862-1940
Brown, Marc 1946-
Brown, Marcia 1918-

Bryan, Ashley F. 1923-
Buff, Mary 1890-1970 and Conrad
    1886-1975
Bulla, Clyde Robert 1914-
Burch, Robert 1925-
Burchard, Peter 1921-
Burgess, Gelett 1866-1951
Burgess, Thornton W(aldo) 1874-1965
Burnett, Frances Hodgson 1849-1924
Burton, Virginia Lee 1909-1968
Butterworth, Oliver 1915-
Caines, Jeannette
Carlson, Natalie Savage 1906-
Carrick, Carol 1935-
Childress, Alice 1920-
Chönz, Selina
Christopher, Matt(hew) 1917-
Ciardi, John 1916-
Clapp, Patricia 1912-
Clark, Ann Nolan 1896-
Clarke, Pauline 1921-
Cleaver, Elizabeth 1939-1985
Cohen, Barbara 1932-
Colby, C(arroll) B(urleigh) 1904-1977
Colman, Hila
Colum Padraic 1881-1972
Cone, Molly 1918-
Coolidge, Olivia 1908-
Coolidge, Susan 1835-1905
Cooney, Barbara 1917-
Cormier, Robert (Edmund) 1925-
Courlander, Harold 1908-
Cox, Palmer 1840-1924
Cresswell, Helen 1934-
Crompton, Richmal 1890-1969
Cunningham, Julia 1916-
Curry, Jane L(ouise) 1932-
Dalgliesh, Alice 1893-1979
Daugherty, James 1889-1974
d'Aulaire, Ingri 1904-1980 and Edgar
    Parin 1898-
de la Mare, Walter 1873-1956
de Regniers, Beatrice Schenk 1914-
Dickinson, Peter 1927-
Dillon, Eilís 1920-
Dodge, Mary Mapes 1831-1905
Domanska, Janina
Duncan, Lois S(teinmetz) 1934-
Duvoisin, Roger 1904-1980
Eager, Edward 1911-1964
Edgeworth, Maria 1767-1849
Edmonds, Walter D(umaux) 1903-
Epstein, Sam(uel) 1909- and Beryl 1910-
Ets, Marie Hall 1893-
Ewing, Juliana Horatia 1841-1885
Farber, Norma 1909-
Farjeon, Eleanor 1881-1965
Field, Eugene 1850-1895

Field, Rachel 1894-1942
Fisher, Dorothy Canfield 1879-1958
Fisher, Leonard Everett 1924-
Flack, Marjorie 1897-1958
Forbes, Esther 1891-1967
Forest, Antonia
Freeman, Don 1908-1978
Fujikawa, Gyo
Fyleman, Rose 1877-1957
Galdone, Paul 1914-
Gardam, Jane 1928-
Garfield, Leon 1921-
Garis, Howard R(oger) 1873-1962
Garner, Alan 1935-
Gates, Doris 1901-
Gerrard, Roy
Giblin, James Cross 1933-
Giff, Patricia Reilly 1935-
Ginsburg, Mirra 1919-
Goble, Paul 1933-
Godden, Rumer 1907-
Goodrich, Samuel G(riswold) 1793-1860
Gorey, Edward 1925-
Goudge, Elizabeth (de Beauchamp)
    1900-
Gramatky, Hardie 1907-1979
Greene, Constance C(larke) 1924-
Grimm, Jacob 1785-1863 and Wilhelm
    1786-1859
Gruelle, Johnny 1880-1938
Guillot, René 1900-1969
Guy, Rosa (Cuthbert) 1928-
Hader, Elmer 1889-1973 and Berta
    1891?-1976
Hale, Lucretia Peabody 1820-1900
Harnett, Cynthia 1893-1981
Harris, Christie 1907-
Harris, Joel Chandler 1848-1908
Harris, Rosemary (Jeanne) 1923-
Haugaard, Erik Christian 1923-
Haywood, Carolyn 1898-
Heide, Florence Parry 1919-
Hill, Eric
Hoberman, Mary Ann 1930-
Hoff, Syd(ney) 1912-
Hoffman, Heinrich 1809-1894
Holland, Isabelle 1920-
Holling, Holling C(lancy) 1900-1973
Hughes, Langston 1902-1967
Hughes, Shirley 1929-
Hunter, Mollie 1922-
Ipcar, Dahlov 1917-
Iwasaki, Chihiro 1918-
Jackson, Jesse 1908-1983
Jacobs, Joseph 1854-1916
Janosch 1931-
Jeschke, Susan 1942-
Johnson, Crockett 1906-1975

Johnson, James Weldon 1871-1938
Jonas, Ann
Jones, Diana Wynne 1934-
Judson, Clara Ingram 1879-1960
Juster, Norton 1929-
Keith, Harold 1903-
Kelly, Eric P(hilbrook) 1884-1960
Kennedy, Richard 1932-
Kent, Jack 1920-1985
Kerr, Judith 1923-
Kerr, M. E. 1927-
Kettelkamp, Larry 1933-
King, Clive 1924-
Kipling, Rudyard 1865-1936
Kjelgaard, Jim 1910-1959
Kraus, Robert 1925-
Krauss, Ruth 1911-
Krumgold, Joseph 1908-1980
La Farge, Oliver 1901-1963
La Fontaine, Jean de 1621-1695
Lang, Andrew 1844-1912
Langton, Jane 1922-
Lasky, Kathryn 1944-
Latham, Jean Lee 1902-
Lauber, Patricia 1924-
Lavine, Sigmund A(rnold) 1908-
Leaf, Munro 1905-1976
Lenski, Lois 1893-1974
Levy, Elizabeth 1942-
Lewis, Elizabeth Foreman 1892-1958
Lightner, A(lice) M. 1904-
Linklater, Eric 1899-1974
Lofting, Hugh 1866-1947
Lunn, Janet 1928-
MacDonald, George 1824-1905
MacGregor, Ellen 1906-1954
MacLachlan, Patricia
Major, Kevin (Gerald) 1949-
Mann, Peggy
Marshall, James 1942-
Martin, Patricia Miles 1899-
Masefield, John 1878-1967
Mayer, Mercer 1943- and Marianna
     1945-
Mayne, William 1928-
Mazer, Harry 1925-
Mazer, Norma Fox 1931-
McCaffrey, Anne (Inez) 1926-
McClung, Robert M(arshall) 1916-
McGovern, Ann
McKillip, Patricia A(nne) 1948-
McNeer, May 1902-
Meader, Stephen W(arren) 1892-1977
Means, Florence Crannell 1891-1980
Meigs, Cornelia 1884-1973
Meltzer, Milton 1915-

Merriam, Eve 1916-
Merrill, Jean 1923-
Miles, Betty 1928-
Milne, Lorus 1912- and Margery 1915-
Minarik, Else Holmelund 1920-
Mizumura, Kazue
Molesworth, Mary Louisa 1842-1921
Moore, Lilian
Morey, Walt(er) 1907-
Naylor, Phyllis Reynolds 1933-
Neufeld, John (Arthur) 1938-
Neville, Emily Cheney 1919-
Nic Leodhas, Sorche 1898-1969
Nichols, Ruth 1948-
North, Sterling 1906-1974
Nöstlinger, Christine 1936-
Ofek, Uriel 1926-
Olney, Ross R(obert) 1929-
Oneal, Zibby 1934-
Ormondroyd, Edward 1925-
Ottley, Reginald
Oxenbury, Helen 1938-
Parish, Peggy 1927-
Peck, Richard (Wayne) 1934-
Peck, Robert Newton 1928-
Peet, Bill 1915-
Perl, Lila
Perrault, Charles 1628-1703
Petersham, Maud 1890-1971 and Miska
     1888-1960
Petry, Ann (Lane) 1908-
Pfeffer, Susan Beth 1948-
Picard, Barbara Leonie 1917-
Platt, Kin 1911-
Politi, Leo 1908-
Prelutsky, Jack
Price, Christine 1928-1980
Provensen, Alice 1918- and Martin
     1916-
Pyle, Howard 1853-1911
Reeves, James 1909-1978
Richards, Laura E(lizabeth) 1850-1943
Richler, Mordecai 1931-
Robertson, Keith 1914-
Rockwell, Anne 1934- and Harlow
Rodgers, Mary 1931-
Rollins, Charlemae Hill 1897-1979
Ross, Tony 1938-
Rounds, Glen 1906-
Sánchez-Silva, José María 1911-
Sandburg, Carl 1878-1967
Sandoz, Mari 1896-1966
Sawyer, Ruth 1880-1970
Scarry, Huck
Scott, Jack Denton 1915-
Seton, Ernest Thompson 1860-1946

Sharmat, Marjorie Weinman 1928-
Sharp, Margery 1905-
Shotwell, Louisa R(ossiter) 1902-
Sidney, Margaret 1844-1924
Silverstein, Alvin 1933- and Virginia
     1937-
Sinclair, Catherine 1880-1864
Skurzynski, Gloria 1930-
Sleator, William 1945-
Slobodkin, Louis 1903-1975
Smith, Doris Buchanan 1934-
Snyder, Zilpha Keatley 1927-
Spence, Eleanor 1928-
Sperry, Armstrong W. 1897-1976
Spykman, E(lizabeth) C. 1896-1965
Spyri, Johanna 1827-1901
Steele, William O(wen) 1917-1979
Stevenson, James 1929-
Stolz, Mary 1920-
Strasser, Todd 1950?-
Stratemeyer, Edward L. 1862-1930
Streatfeild, Noel 1897-
Taylor, Sydney 1904?-1978
Taylor, Theodore 1924-
Ter Haar, Jaap 1922-
Titus, Eve 1922-
Tolkien, J(ohn) R(onald) R(euel)
     1892-1973
Treadgold, Mary 1910-
Trease, Geoffrey 1909-
Tresselt, Alvin 1916-
Treviño, Elizabeth Borton de 1904-
Tudor, Tasha 1915-
Turkle, Brinton 1915-
Udry, Janice May 1928-
Unnerstad, Edith 1900-
Uttley, Alison 1884-1976
Ventura, Piero 1937-
Vincent, Gabrielle
Vining, Elizabeth Gray 1902-
Voigt, Cynthia 1942-
Waber, Bernard 1924-
Wahl, Jan 1933-
Walter, Mildred Pitts
Ward, Lynd 1905-1985
Wells, Rosemary 1943-
Westall, Robert (Atkinson) 1929-
Wiese, Kurt 1887-1974
Wilkinson, Brenda 1946-
Williams, Barbara 1925-
Yates, Elizabeth 1905-
Yonge, Charlotte M(ary) 1823-1901
Zemach, Harve 1933-1974 and Margot
     1931-
Zion, Gene 1913-1975

Readers are cordially invited to suggest additional authors to the editors.

Children's
Literature
Review

Raymond (Redvers) Briggs

1934-

English author/illustrator of picture books and fiction, editor, and illustrator.

Briggs is perhaps the most radical social commentator in contemporary children's literature. Employing engaging characters and poignant wit, he spotlights victims of political power struggles and bureaucracy as well as imaginary people outside the mainstream of society. Many of Briggs's books are satires which manifest the evils of nuclear war, nationalism, governmental incompetence, and social intolerance. He tempers the seriousness of his messages by using a strip-cartoon format together with verbal and visual humor. Among Briggs's most popular works are his accounts of Father Christmas, which depict the universal figure as a crusty but loving individual with human failings and needs. He has also created a wordless fantasy about a boy and a snowman and invented an alternative culture centering on the outwardly repulsive but inwardly enlightened Fungus the Bogeyman, whom the author later featured in a pop-up book. As an artist, Briggs is noted for the accuracy and beauty of his drawings and for his use of color to convey mood.

Critics generally regard Briggs as an accomplished, compassionate, and sometimes powerful storyteller who translates the drama of his stories into detailed pictures which convey a range of emotions. While reviewers agree that most of his books are beyond the full comprehension of the traditional picture book audience, they acclaim Briggs for his unique skill in adapting complex themes into an unpretentious artistic format.

Fee Fi Fo Fum: A Picture Book of Nursery Rhymes and *The Mother Goose Treasury*, works both edited and illustrated by Briggs, received the Greenaway Medal in 1965 and 1967 respectively; in 1974 *Father Christmas* won the Greenaway Medal. In 1979 *The Snowman* was highly commended by the Greenaway Medal committee, received the Lewis Carroll Shelf Award, and won the *Boston Globe-Horn Book* Award for illustration. *When the Wind Blows* was the recipient of the Other Award in 1982.

(See also *Something about the Author*, Vol. 23 and *Contemporary Authors*, Vols. 73-76.)

AUTHOR'S COMMENTARY

[In the following excerpt, Jean F. Mercier interviews Briggs, who comments on his most recent book, Father Christmas, *his artistic training, and his writing and drawing style.]*

The latest book by British author-illustrator Raymond Briggs is on hand to help celebrate the Yuletide season—and in his own very distinctive way. "Father Christmas" (Santa Claus to us Americans), . . . represents the gifted artist's unique blend of fantasy and reality, a personal viewpoint that has made Briggs one of the most popular figures in children's literature since he did the illustrations for "Ring-A-Ring-O'-Roses"—a collection of nursery rhymes—in the early 1960s.

His conception of Saint Nick is by no means the familiar hearty, ho-ho-hoing, happy philanthropist. He is a grumbling, shiv-

ering, entirely human fellow who would much rather stay home and hug the fire on Christmas Eve than dash about the globe with those reindeer. "Blooming Christmas here again," he mutters when the alarm goes off and he spies his calendar. "Blooming soot, blooming chimneys. . . ." But he does his job, just as the man who was the inspiration for the book did his—for the book is really an endearing memoir of Raymond's father, a milkman. "I used to watch him and listen to him get ready to make his rounds," says Raymond. "For all his grumpiness, he was softhearted. Our cat used to drape itself round his shoulders, just like the one in the book."

On the occasion of his first visit to the United States, *PW* interviewed Briggs and learned that all his stories and pictures are personal, based on his own experiences and observations. He told us he had always wanted to be an artist, "forever drawing when I was a kid." He added that he was an only child, happy and terribly spoiled. "When I told my parents I wanted to study art, they agreed at once. Though they were working-class people, they weren't fussed that I didn't want to learn a useful trade."

At 15, Raymond enrolled in the Wimbledon School of Art, with the intention of becoming a cartoonist, specializing in illustrations. "But my teachers told me, and I believed them, that commercial art was very bad, that one had to model oneself on Michelangelo or da Vinci. I felt they were right, then, and it took me some time to get back to my original ideas." . . .

Raymond looks back at the beginnings of his career and credits the influence of two Americans, Roy Lichtenstein and Jules Feiffer, with setting him on the right road again: "Feiffer, for one, reaches a much bigger audience through his cartoon strips than he could have otherwise."

Raymond is different from most people in the children's books field in that he never considers the age of his possible audience. With unequivocal candor, he reports, "Fact is, my publishers got hold of my stuff and they decided it would attract children. I don't work with or near children; don't know much about them, really. I just write and draw to please myself and feel it ought to please others. If it doesn't, too bad; I won't change."

So far his publishers . . . have never seen fit to ask Mr. Briggs to change, and for good reason. His **"Mother Goose Treasury," "Ring-A-Ring-O'-Roses," "The White Land," "Fee Fi Fo Fum"** and others have become popular classics.

Mr. Briggs credits his illustrations for these collections with having given him valuable experience but adds: "I don't like doing pictures for someone who has been digging up old texts. I much prefer doing my own text and pictures."

And he never has any problem with ideas. "I have so many, it's hard to get round to all of them. Usually I work about a year ahead." His recent visit to America has given him plenty of new material, he says, and he's anxious to return. (p. 12)

Jean F. Mercier, in an interview with Raymond Briggs, in Publishers Weekly, *Vol. 204, No. 19, November 5, 1973, pp. 12-13.*

GENERAL COMMENTARY

ELAINE MOSS

Raymond Briggs is a gentle, considerate man, who says quite candidly that he knows hardly anything about children. . . . If his cartoon stories give pleasure to readers of any age, he's happy: "Ten-year-olds at your school like *Fungus*, do they? Gosh. Yes. Good." That he has pierced a rich vein of storytelling that spans young and old is, he would have us believe, more luck than good judgement.

Success in his chosen art form was a long time coming. Four years at Wimbledon studying Renaissance painting. . . . Then two years in the army followed by two at the Slade. The Slade is the home of pure painting, and it was here that Raymond Briggs's talent for painting scenes from the imagination and making them realistic was recognized for what it was. "You are," they said, "illustrator's 'colour' "—and that, Raymond explains, was a term of abuse.

After a few commissions for newspapers, book jackets and advertising Raymond Briggs found himself getting work for children's book publishers, mostly line drawing for series like the early Hamish Hamilton "Gazelles" and "Antelopes". He thought the texts fairly mundane so wrote two himself—*Strange House* and *Midnight Adventure*—both of which, to his utter amazement, were accepted. (p. 26)

When he speaks of his students he is rather gloomy. Colour and photo-realism are all the rage now, and few of them want to work in line. "If you ask them to do more than three pieces of work for the illustration of a story, they have a fit. If you asked for forty-five drawings, they'd think you were mad."

So where will the narrative illustrators in the tradition of Shepard and Ardizzone come from?

Maybe the tradition is dying, or is being translated, by artists like Raymond Briggs, into storytelling through pictures rather than illustrated word narrative. It is too early yet to see the developments of our own time in perspective, but one day the succession in the genre may be traced from the Ardizzone picture books with their thread of bubble talk as counterpoint to the narrative, through the Briggs strip-cartoon storybooks, to the Ahlberg's *Brick Street Boys,* Mark Kahn's *It's a Dog's Life* and beyond. (p. 27)

What [Raymond Briggs] is very serious about is strip cartoon as narrative and the snobbery of the English in refusing to recognize it as an art form—a minor art form—worthy of considered criticism. With the *Father Christmas* books, *Fungus the Bogeyman* and *The Snowman* to his credit (and to his publisher's, for the books were not easy to launch in a market where one head teacher spoke for the multitude when he wrote, "These are not books at all, *merely* strip cartoons"), Raymond Briggs is in a position to attack the prevailing critical silence, which his sales figures challenge.

"If anything becomes part of the folk culture of an age, you can't just pretend it's a lot of rubbish," says Raymond Briggs, referring not to *Father Christmas* or *Fungus* (he is too modest for that) but to Rupert, Peanuts, Tintin, Asterix. He is an inordinate admirer of the early Rupert—"fantastic drawing and marvellous composition"—loves Peanuts, finds Tintin frames remarkably well organized but the text a bit banal, whereas the Asterix texts are full of verbal wit but the frames "so tortuous that I can hardly bear to 'read' them".

The word 'read' applied to pictures is interesting, for children do read pictures in the way Raymond's remarks suggest that he does. . . . In the latest Briggs picture book, *The Snowman*, there are no words at all, but the poignancy of the story—silent like snow—is none the less sharp.

Raymond Briggs really combines in *Father Christmas* and in *Fungus the Bogeyman* two art forms that the British see as separate. *Father Christmas* won the Kate Greenaway Medal but, says Raymond with feeling, it was given to him for the artwork alone, since no one seems to see people like himself and John Burningham as storymakers in the way novelists are, but storymakers spanning two media. Of course the Kate Greenaway is an illustrator's award, but Raymond Briggs found it significant of the prevailing attitude towards art that, as he put it, "Even when I was getting the blessed Medal, the lady giving it said [passing on to the Carnegie winner, Penelope Lively] 'We now come to the *senior* of the two Awards'."

In this Raymond sees a hangover from medieval cultural snobbery, which regarded the painter as a craftsman because he got his hands dirty, and the writer as a superior being, an intellectual, a scholar who kept himself clean. "Fungus, and the Snowman?" I asked. "Perhaps . . . mm . . . Perhaps," said Raymond. (pp. 28-9)

Raymond thought *Fungus the Bogeyman* would really appeal to dropouts—"rather grubby, rather lazy anti-establishment intellectuals, messing about hitch-hiking round the world with their guitars." It does. But it has also caught the imagination of the latent adolescent, of all ages, because it dares to challenge the standards not of decent behaviour (Fungus is a model citizen) but of subjects that can be decently discussed. Eleven-year-old sniggers are now open laughs. A healthy "surface" development? Or an invasion by an adult of the bogeyworld that properly belongs to the eleven-year-old?

The dictionary was a happy hunting ground for Bogey words and ideas, and Briggs found himself reading one from end to end; then, not fully satisfied, he went out and bought the two-volume *Shorter Oxford.* Bogeyology became an obsession and it now fills a whole drawer in his filing cabinet. About a third of it was used in *Fungus,* the rest is stored away for future use.

"But the point about Fungus," says his creator, "is that, like all of us, he wonders what he's alive for. *Fungus the Bogeyman* is about his search for a role. It's really the first chapter in what could become a novel in a sense. Pretentious word for it, but there's no other term. Fungus is going to go on to try to find this role, and his great dream is to do away with this war between the Bogey world and the Surface world and reconcile them to one another. The second book would be about tourism, you see—getting people from the surface to come and look. The Michelin Guide to the Bogey world; but of course it's all a dreadful failure because no one wants to spend a holiday there. Oh dear! Then there's a book on Bogey literature I could do, and one on getting Surface people interested in Bogey trade . . ."

At this point I asked, "Do you think of Fungus as a sad character?"

[Raymond Briggs]: Yes. Very sad, yes.

[Elaine Moss]: Is he real? Does he represent something in all of us?

R. B.: I'm noticing all my characters now are sad old men or, rather, sad middle-aged men, which is what I am probably. [Laughter] Life is sad really but there's always love, which makes life worth living. Fungus has a loving relationship with his wife, which makes it bearable.

E. M.: Do you think failure is sadder than success?

R. B.: I've been terribly lucky.

E. M.: Has it made you happier?

R. B.: No, I don't think so. But I don't know what I'd have been like without it. I might have been miserable and embittered like I was at the Slade when I recognized that I was a rotten painter . . . Only about a handful of my students will make a real success of anything . . . We are educating people beyond their own capacity for fulfilment, which I think is very sad . . .

Of course Raymond Briggs is not a "rotten painter" as anyone who looks at the frames in *Father Christmas,* for example, will discover. The problem is that, critically, very little attention is focused on "mere" cartoons in England.

When Raymond Briggs talks of the cartoon form, of the careful planning he must do to give variety to the picture shapes on the page and to work his story into the number of pages he can use, one begins to see what is involved and how far along the road he has come. But when he begins to expound on new ways of using the medium to convey visual messages to the reader, one senses the excitement of an artist exploring, enlarging his (and our) experience. Suppose, for instance, the tail of the bubble in which the dialogue is encapsulated were drawn right across the face of the character being spoken to, almost obliterating him: he would instantly be recognized as a repressed person. *Gentleman Jim,* Briggs's work in progress,

uses this innovation as well as others. But when the book is published, where is the English-language journal, who are the writers capable of considering it in its world context?

Sadly Raymond goes to his studio and brings back into the living room hugh tomes of criticism from France, Italy or Germany—where magazines like *Phenix, Linus, Alter Alter* flourish—to demonstrate that in other countries cartoon strips are taken as seriously as films, radio plays or light novels; here they are thought of "as a low form of life equivalent to the daily tabloids".

Sad, yes—but not despondent. For after all someone in Britain has at last written an article which suggests that the strip-cartoon techniques of author-artists like Hergé and Raymond Briggs deserve the kind of specialist attention that would bring the best of them out of Bogeyland into the Surface sunshine. (pp. 30-3)

Elaine Moss, "Raymond Briggs," in Signal, *No. 28, January, 1979, pp. 26-33.*

AUDREY LASKI

[There is a] marvellous flood of picture books pouring on into the Christmas quarter. To start at the very beginning, and with a true delight, there is the perfect book for the prereader: Raymond Briggs's exquisite *The Snowman* . . . , perhaps the most eloquent piece of story-telling in pictures since medieval churches were lined with strip cartoons of the Testaments. Briggs also gives us *Jim and the Beanstalk* . . . , with Jim fixing it for a geriatric giant. This should be good for reading aloud. . . .

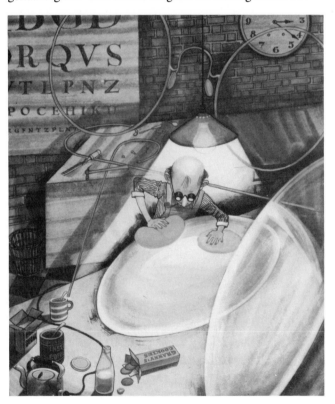

From Jim and the Beanstalk, *written and illustrated by Raymond Briggs. Coward, McCann & Geoghegan, 1970. Reprinted by permission of Coward, McCann & Geoghegan, Inc. In Canada by Hamish Hamilton Ltd. Copyright © 1970 by Raymond Briggs.*

Audrey Laski, "The Goose Is Getting Fat," in The Times Educational Supplement, No. 3358, October 31, 1980, p. 24.*

BOOKS FOR YOUR CHILDREN

If you had to name the illustrator who has most influenced trends in recent children's books, Raymond Briggs would be the most likely choice.

His work can be divided into two distinct halves, his glorious early picture books for very young children seen at their best in the 897 prizewinning illustrations for The Mother Goose Treasury, but it is his lively picture strip books that have been most innovative. He has given a new meaning to the comic format. Raymond Briggs has made comics so respectable that even the most ardent anti-comics parent ("thou-shalt-not-read-that-rubbish") have had to give in.

Father Christmas enchanted them, Fungus enticed them, and Gentleman Jim will bowl them over. Parents as much as children enjoy having these Raymond Briggs books on their shelves. . . .

[Snowman] combines the best of both styles, being a picture strip book without words for younger children. It takes a classic theme, the snowman that comes to life, and transforms it. The boy and the snowman explore each other's world. . . . What is so special about this book is that it does not have a single word to convey all the details of the story, the excitement and adventure, the wonder and magic of it all is there in the pictures. (p. 22)

[Raymond Briggs's] robust pictures full of humour and wit are very appealing to children who like clear colourful outlines, bold images and strong picture relationships with the story. . . .

Each Christmas we feel we have to remind any families who just might not own a copy of Briggs's Father Christmas that it is a vital part of any festive celebration. Don't worry about the weak sequel where Father Christmas goes on holiday, it is full of cliches about the British abroad, just stick to 'himself' grumbling and grunting as he delivers his 'bloomin' presents'. Cliches of a different type feature in his latest tale Gentleman Jim, the everyman figure—the dreamer who works as a lavatory attendant but has designs on better things. . . . Raymond Briggs shows great compassion and understanding of the plight of the underdog in a hostile world, and this rather sad story is his tribute to it. Not a book for very young children (p. 23)

"Cover Artist: Raymond Briggs," in Books for Your Children, Vol. 15, No. 4, Autumn-Winter, 1980, pp. 22-3.

ELAINE MOSS

Raymond Briggs has no sense of the age or range of his readership, which is probably why his cartoon picture books appeal across a wide swathe of readers from five or so to grandparents—and excite both acclaim and disapprobation. A serious artist, with a detached stance that enables him to go deep into the minds of underdogs and present his characters with a humour that is always sympathetic, Briggs has opened up new vistas: on the accepted folklore of Father Christmas, on the alternative society, and on the function of fantasy in the life of the oppressed. (p. 31)

Take a good long look at each frame in [Father Christmas]. Note the variety of sizes, some full page, some long and thin across two pages (as the sledge travels), one L-shaped to accommodate Big Ben as well as the Houses of Parliament; see how Briggs breaks the frame edge with bubble-talk, with the clock (moving on towards Christmas morning), with the shocking pink pinnacles of a paper hat, with holiday brochures—a foretaste of Father Christmas Goes on Holiday. Then give yourself a real treat and study all the details, correct to the last architectural feature of a building or the cross-section of a carrot. . . .

Open [Father Christmas Goes on Holiday] at any page and it will be obvious that neither the language bubbles ('I can tell you what to do with the plume of your blooming tante, mate') nor the situations—on a French caravan site where the old man has diarrhoea or in a Las Vegas nightclub where he hits the big time ('Oh dear . . . keep dozing off . . . getting old . . . bed-time')—are for the very young. But over all, in this cartoon strip book satirizing the joys of foreign travel and its problems for a celebrity, there is a sympathy with naive old Father Christmas trying to behave like the natives, failing disastrously and returning home to the North Pole, his animals, his garden full of weeds, the letters asking for this or that for Christmas. 'Still,' he says to himself, 'at least I've had a blooming good holiday.' Looking at this book afresh, there are distinct signs in it that Fungus the Bogeyman and Gentleman Jim were on the horizon. (p. 32)

By any standards [Fungus the Bogeyman is] an extraordinary book! Astonishing that Briggs, primarily an artist, should have collected files full of esoteric words, misquotable poems, adaptable book titles (Cider with Bogey), phoney physiological features ('Debentures: Bogey dentures curiously bent to allow for the long tongue'), in order to create a believable Bogey world. Astounding that his murky pictures of this grey-green dank alternative world should become the norm for the immersed reader to the extent that pictures of Surface life among the Dry Cleaners look oddly desiccated. Bogey dialogue—'I only wanted to daub you, darkling,' says Fungus to his wife Mildew as they retire to their slime-chilled bed—has become part of many a light-hearted conversation, evidence that it fascinates, compels.

So what is this curiosity that has become a cult? It is not a novel: it is the stage setting for the novel that could have been if Briggs had been given the green light—aha!—for a work of 144 pages in full colour, estimated price £30 a copy! Fungus the Bogeyman as it stands is a guide book to an alternative world, a mirror of Surface society whose lifestyles and values are seen in reverse. But—and this is the big question detractors of Fungus have either overlooked or sidestepped—is this book only the sum of its anarchic jokes, or is it, 'under the Surface', a challenge to our 'civilized' way of life from a species of creature who may live differently but who is gentle, loving, inventive, hard-working and above all able to question the meaning of his drab existence? 'I'm quite happy really,' says Fungus. 'It's just that I'd like to know why.' (pp. 32-4)

Gentleman Jim is the satirical novel in picture strip that Fungus the Bogeyman might have been. It is a heart-breaking but comical story of Bloggs, an under-educated lavatory attendant whose idea of the world outside his white-tiled bolt hole is conditioned entirely by newspaper advertisements, TV serials, pulp adventure fiction and, yes, crude comic strip of the 'BOOM! BANG! .. Donner und Blitzen, Zose verdamt Englanders' variety. Led astray by the prospects of glittering rewards Bloggs tries to put his Mittyesque fantasies into practice—only to land himself in gaol after an unsuccessful impersonation of Gentleman Jim the highwayman (on his donkey) on the M1 where he holds up a police car!

In this brilliant satire Briggs himself holds up the consumer society, bureaucracy and education to ridicule—for where does all this pursuit of super-civilization land poor Bloggs? In prison. 'The Judge says it was for Her Majesty's pleasure,' he meekly tells his wife through the bars, and she replies, 'Yes dear, wasn't that nice.' Any adult interested in the many languages through which we fail to communicate with one another in Britain—Official Bureaucratic, Journalistic Advertisement, High Class Purveyor, Travel Agent Chic, Highfalutin' Legal, Cartoon Comic, Purple Romantic—will have a field day with this book. It must be the only strip cartoon book ever to look at language and make a monkey of it in its debased (as opposed to its demotic) forms. A book to study, laugh at, cry with, enjoy. (pp. 34-5)

Much used, much loved by younger children, **The Snowman** is included [in this discussion of the comic strip] because of the pleasure it can give to anyone of any age and because the purity of the Snowman is the crystalline essence of all of Briggs's heroes, from crusty old Father Christmas with his heart of gold through good citizens like Fungus the Bogeyman to downtrodden Gentleman Jim. (p. 35)

Elaine Moss, ''Raymond Briggs,'' in her Picture Books for Young People 9-13, *The Thimble Press, 1981,* pp. 31-5.

SUZANNE RAHN

It has been called "the nastiest book ever published for children," [see excerpt below by Aidan Chambers for *Fungus the Bogeyman* (1977)] and it stands in a pivotal position among the picture books of the British artist-writer Ramond Briggs. **Fungus the Bogeyman** . . . offers both the most fully developed fantasy and the most outrageous affront to conventional mores of all Briggs's children's books to date. It also marks the midpoint of a philosophic curve Briggs has been tracing from the cheerful confidence of **Jim and the Beanstalk** . . . , to the black despair of **When the Wind Blows**. . . . A close look at **Fungus** reveals the common concerns that tie these two extremes together, and that make the last book a wholly logical development from the first.

Bogies, according to K. M. Briggs's *Encyclopedia of Fairies,* comprise "a whole class of mischievous, frightening and even dangerous spirits whose delight it is to torment mankind." From this basis in folklore, Raymond Briggs has postulated a race of large, blobby, green-skinned beings who inhabit their own underground world. At night (their day), the Bogeymen emerge to carry on their "work"—frightening human beings with mysterious footsteps, scrapings on windowpanes, and an occasional graveyard appearance; they also cause boils. But we see the daily life of Fungus at home too, eating breakfast with his wife and son, bicycling off to work, and stopping off at a pub on the way back. Meanwhile, as an anonymous narrator fills in a complete picture of Bogeydom, lecturing in academic style on Bogey culture, sports, flora, fauna, and anatomy, Briggs utilizes the full subcreative power of fantasy, supposing not only magical powers (as he does in **Father Christmas** and **The Snowman**), but a race of imaginary beings and their entire world.

Fungus is Briggs's most deeply fantastic book for children and his most startling. Indeed, both in form and in content, it could scarcely be better calculated to repel the adult reader—or intrigue the young one.

In form it is what has been called strip-format book, a hardcover book designed like a comic strip to tell a story by means of a sequence of pictures, several to a page, with dialogue inserted inside ''balloons'' and explanatory captions above or beneath the frame. Such children's books have been popular in Europe for decades—the *Tin-Tin* series being especially noteworthy artistically, and *Asterix the Gaul* for its sophisticated humor—but in America the strip-format never achieved hardcover status, and adult disapproval of softcover comics has been widespread since at least the 1940s. Like several other of Briggs's picture books, **Fungus** defies this old prejudice. It looks at first glance like an enlarged comic book with frames, balloons, and captions, though in fact Briggs has modified the traditional format considerably. The color scheme is unusual, being dominated not by primary colors but by soft shades of grass-green, blue-green, and brown in the background, and by the brighter yellow-green of the Bogeymen. Also, a large proportion of his page space is devoted to hand-lettered ''captions'' of extraordinary length that compete with or even overwhelm the pictures; there are actually more words per page than in many older children's books of conventional design.

The real truth of the matter is that **Fungus** requires and stimulates above-average literacy in its young readers. Its reading level is, in general, at least sixth grade. Puns and other varieties of word-play, literary allusions, quotations, misquotations (from authors like Milton, Keats, Shelley, and Tennyson), and obscure English words like ''scran'' and ''dwine'' and ''hodmandod'' are scattered lavishly through its pages. Fungus himself and his family are avid readers; the reader is shown the shelves of a Bogey library which Fungus visits and is even tacitly challenged to recognize the originals of such ''adapted'' titles as *Far from the Madding Bogey, A Portrait of the Artist as a Young Bogeyman*, and *A la Recherche de Bogeys Perdus.* (pp. 5-8)

[**Fungus**] plays games with the reader, . . . for example deleting a picture of a Bogey lavatory with a black square or referring to ''great literary works, such as this book you are reading.''

In fact, this element of game in **Fungus** may be what makes its more esoteric literary devices and allusions intriguing rather than simply incomprehensible to young readers—this challenge to notice and appreciate both visual and verbal detail. And most, though not all, of this detail is placed within their reach; if the adult titles in the Bogey library are obscure, children can still try their wits on the bookshelf of Fungus's son, which contains such favorites as *Anne of Green Bogeys, Tom's Midnight Bogey,* and *The Tale of the Flopsy Bogies.* . . . (p. 8)

Thus, **Fungus** is, among other things, a joke on the adult reader with a bias against the ''antiliterary'' format of the comic strip—or on the child who expects from it an easy-reading experience. Its content, too, is deceptive, arousing prejudices far more deeply rooted than those against comic books, and with equally unexpected results.

The opening scene shows Fungus and his wife Mildew at sunset, just awakening in their Bogeybed:

Fungus: Oooh! What a night that was! This bed has almost dried up!

Mildew: I know, drear. It needs more slime.

Fungus: What a horrible day! Feels quite warm!

Mildew: I hate this time of year. It's so light.

Fungus [retrieving clothes from a trough of water]: Ah! Nice wet dressing-gown and sabots!

Mildew: I'll change the sheets today, drear. The dirt has almost worn off these.

Fungus: I know, love, the smell's all gone. . . .

Even more shocking is the Bogey bathroom, where Fungus plasters his armpits with muck ("just add slime"), and the sink counter contains bottles of Eau de Colon, Femstench Rollon Odorant for Bogey Ladies, Faboge Pus, and Toilet Water. . . . By this point, the adult may already be abandoning *Fungus* in disgust—even before encountering the Bogey family at the breakfast table ("'These flaked corns are still a bit crisp, Mum— not mouldy yet at all'," . . .) or watching Fungus get dressed ("The waterproof layer is not intended to keep the rain out, but rather to keep the Bogeyman's own natural secretions in." . . .) Undoubtedly, the book deliberately violates taboos as thoroughly entrenched in our shower-a-day society as those related to sex, death, and religion—taboos against dirtiness, against smelliness, against virtually all of the "natural secretions" that Bogeymen prize so highly. There is also no doubt that children find these taboos particularly titillating. Is Briggs simply catering to this youthful fascination with innards and excretia?

Some aspects of Bogeydom seem to fit this explanation well enough; others do not. Bogeys do indeed like damp and dirt and smelliness—they call human beings "Drycleaners"—but they are also

> extremely quiet in their movements and in their voices. They never shout and they speak in gentle voices scarcely above a whisper.
>
> Perhaps this is because a lot of their normal aggression is dissipated at work.
>
> At home, they are gentle, shy, and very polite to one another. So. . . .BE QUIET WHILE YOU READ THIS BOOK. . . .

Nothing about this passage seems calculated to appeal to low childish tastes, and it is reinforced by numerous other instances of Bogey quietness and gentleness. Bogey bicycles have "soft, fat tires (for slowness)." . . . Favorite Bogey sports include tiddlywinks—"probably because it is silent and requires no exertion. As with most Bogey games, the object is to achieve a draw," . . . but in angling, the main aim "is to avoid catching fish." . . . The favorite spectator sport is Bogeyball, a relative of soccer, whose object is

> to put the ball into the player's own goal and help the opposing team to put the ball into their goal. . . . Should two players accidentally bump into one another, they will immediately step back and bow formally, emitting a quiet hiss at the same time. . . .
>
> Bogeymen never run or hurry, not even in their games, so the match proceeds with an almost dream-like slow motion.
>
> There is no shouting or cheering. The crowd expresses its approval with quiet hissing. A goal is greeted with complete silence and stillness; many spectators instantly fall asleep. . . .

Contrary to the narrator's own suggestion above, not even at "work" does Fungus display any real aggression. Stolidly going through the motions of a monster, he even wonders whether there is much point in scaring people: "'I wonder if

it does *them* any good?' . . . 'I can't think what else I could do' . . . 'I'm quite happy, really. It's just that I'd like to know WHY . . .'." . . . Such thoughtfulness also seems a part of Bogey nature. Bogey graffiti, for example, "is never scatological. It almost always consists of platitudes or grave philosophical statements." . . . "Silence is deep as eternity—speech is shallow as time" reads one typical inscription. . . .

Bogeydom is not simply our own world turned upside down. On one level, Bogeymen lead lives much like ours; they have families, sleep in beds, use bathrooms, ride bicycles, play tiddlywinks, and so on. It is chiefly in its value system that Bogeydom radically opposes twentieth-century human civilization—not only in matters of hygiene, but in its concept of what the quality of life should be. By presenting this opposition to his readers, Briggs makes of *Fungus* both a plea for tolerance and understanding of creatures different from ourselves and a critique of our own civilization.

Form reinforces content in encouraging tolerance from the reader. The strip-format itself, as well as Briggs's own idiosyncratic deviations from it, must be tolerated, or we cannot even read the book. Then, the minimal storyline, though sequentially-told, is interrupted so continually by notes, diagrams, and explanations that one's reading rate slows almost to the dreamlike pace of life in Bogeydom; thus Briggs coaxes the reader to slow down, to look closely, to reflect on unfamiliar values and mores. The scientific detachment of the narrator, too, helps the reader maintain a kind of emotional neutrality and objectivity; one is asked neither to identify with Fungus nor to feel disgust at him, only to observe and to learn.

This process of mental adjustment may be somewhat different for adults and for children. Adult readers are more likely to find themselves repelled by Bogey love of filth and attracted by Bogey quietness, gentleness, and love of literature, while for young readers adjustment may move in the opposite direction; their attraction to Bogeys as taboo-breakers may help them to accept Bogey quietness, slowness, lack of aggression, and fondness for "grave philosophical statements." In either case, something alien must be accepted along with what is more naturally congenial. And acceptance gradually becomes understanding and even affection; it is impossible to finish the book (if one can finish it) without some fondness for the melancholy Fungus and this race of shy, homely creatures with "very small tops to their heads." . . . (p. 11)

By using imaginary beings (rather than some distant human tribe), Briggs universalizes his theme of tolerance; Bogeymen may be interpreted as another social class, another human race, or another species altogether. The nonhuman possibility predominates in the chart of Bogey anatomy which reveals the Bogeyman's long, coiled tongue ("used for catching flies"), vestigial spinal fin, three nipples, and four stomachs ("They constantly regurgitate their food and rechew it, in the manner of Surface cows.") . . . At the same time, their generally human clothing and way of life permit us to see the Bogeymen as a nonwhite race or a (literally) lower class. Particularly the latter, perhaps. Bogeydom, as we are shown it, is exclusively a working-class world, with no profession depicted beyond those of policeman and librarian; the Bogeymen bicycling up the tunnels to the Surface from their drab rows of houses look very much like a crowd of workers on their way to the factory, while their recreations (pub games, holiday camps, Bogeyball) are those associated with the British lower classes. Raymond Briggs himself came from a working-class family, and one can see a similarity between his milkman-father and Fungus: both

From The Snowman, *written and illustrated by Raymond Briggs. Random House, 1979. Copyright ©*
1978 by Raymond Briggs. All rights reserved. Reprinted by permission of Random House, Inc. In Canada
by Hamish Hamilton Ltd.

have a ''round'' of houses to which they deliver their stock-in-trade while most of their customers are still sleeping.

Briggs's plea for tolerance is interwoven with his critique of human civilization. First, we are forced to realize that Bogeymen are no more repulsive to us than we are to them. We learn, for example, that Bogey horror films feature ''Sunlight, flowers, cornfields, and hot dry beaches with Drycleaners laughing gaily and playing loud music.'' . . . We discover that in Bogeydom teenage rebellion is linked to an unhealthy preoccupation with the ways of humankind:

> These ''drop-ins'' also profess to like bright colours and noise. Ancient gramophone recordings and abandoned equipment have been smuggled in from Surface rubbish dumps and these are used with a total disregard for tradition, custom, and even law. Worse still, some of the more extreme members of the cult began keeping themselves clean, scraping off their protective layers of dirt and slime and taking baths in warm, clean water. . . .

Finally, some pages from a book on *Where to Watch Drycleaners: A Field Guide to Surface Life* show us ourselves as crea-

tures with ''Tiny, malformed ears and tiny noses'' and ''Minute mouths with thick pink lips'' who breed ''in noisy, very crowded colonies. Easily located by noise and smell.'' . . . (p. 12)

Having reached this degree of detachment, we can see human society, too, through Bogey eyes—as not only clean and dry, but loud, shallow, contentious, restless, and horrifyingly violent. Disgusting as they may be by our standards, Bogeys hurt no living creature (see, for instance, their version of ''pig-sticking'' . . .); one cannot even count the boils against them, for they *like* boils. Their only guns are wooden ones—''found to be much more satisfactory, as they are silent and harmless.'' . . . It is ironic, Briggs seems to imply, that we are so repelled by dirt and smelliness and other natural aspects of our own bodies—and so little disturbed by the noise and destruction and brutal aggression of our world.

Viewing *Fungus* as a guided adventure in tolerance and a sharp criticism of contemporary civilization provides a key to the sequence of Briggs's other recent picture books. In *Jim and the Beanstalk,* the boy Jim does not steal the old giant's possessions, but procures him a wig, spectacles, and a set of false teeth that together renew his youth and spirits. Like the Bogeymen, the giant can be interpreted as another race or class or species—one that has been exploited in the past. *Jim* suggests that we can, with fairness and compassion, rewrite the old tale of our own history and repair the injustices done by a former generation. *Father Christmas* . . . , too, is positive in its outlook on human society and its class relationships. Showing in strip-format sequence how Father Christmas spends his very busy and chilly Christmas Eve, Briggs makes him a lower-class hero . . . whose journeying binds all homes together, from the little trailer barely big enough for a bed to Buckingham Palace. Father Christmas works hard and grumbles constantly, yet he can also enjoy the creature comforts of a good dinner, "'nice clean socks,'" and the brandy left out for him by a thoughtful customer ("'Lovely!'"). The final frames, which show him presenting a gaily-wrapped fish and bone to his own cat and dog, confirm the meaningfulness of his role.

A sequel, *Father Christmas Goes on Holiday* . . . , shows Briggs's amused awareness of some characteristic limitations of that same working class that he had glorified in *Father Christmas*. For despite his desire for exotic experiences, Father Christmas proves hopelessly insular and urban, unable to enjoy himself either in France (where the food gives him indigestion), or in the Scottish Highlands (where he catches a dreadful cold). He finally discovers the vacationland of his dreams—in Las Vegas. But there is genuine admiration as well as lighthearted satire in Briggs's depiction of American society at its most absurdly luxurious. Briggs, as a recent visitor to the United States, had been struck by the friendliness and freedom from class-consciousness he found in America, and here—till his money runs out—his working-class protagonist lives like a king.

Fungus comes next in the sequence. Like *Father Christmas*, it is based on the daily routine of work, yet it has an underlying sadness that is absent from the earlier book and points ahead to Briggs's later, darker picture books. Both stories end with the protagonist snug in bed, but while Father Christmas's last action is to give presents and wish the reader too a "'Happy blooming Christmas,'" Fungus's is to question the meaning of his life and work. "'Why am *I* a Bogeyman?'" he demands. "'What are we frightening them for? Does it do any *ultimate good* ? (or even *ultimate bad?*)'." . . . Mildew cannot understand what is troubling him—"'Come along, drear, better get to bed—your brain is overtired'" . . .—and the last frame shows her fast asleep while Fungus lies staring out at us with a great black question mark over his green head. "And so," reads the caption, "we say Farewell to Fungus as he lies awake pondering upon The Significance of His Role in Society, Evolution and LIFE." . . . Overhead a framed quotation from Swinburne—"Even the weariest river / Winds somewhere safe to sea"—may refer (as in its original context) to death as readily as to sleep.

Why this melancholy ending? In this book, for the first time, Briggs seems doubtful about the direction of modern society, and in particular about the fate of those who have no control over it. Bogeydom is at once conspicuously immune to some of the ills of our civilization and prone to others. Fungus's sense of purposelessness and alienation is proverbially characteristic of twentieth-century man. Like many in the post-industrial age, he can no longer find meaning in what he does for a living—only in his family relationships and leisure-time activities. Briggs assigns no blame for this situation—yet. Fungus's unhappiness seems here a merely personal problem, for which his slow-paced, courteous society cannot really be responsible.

Briggs's next picture book, *The Snowman* . . . , was in some ways a reaction from *Fungus;* Briggs himself has confessed

that the reason it contains no words is because he was so tired of hand-lettering long captions [see excerpt below under Author's Commentary for *The Snowman* (1978)]. It is a gentle, fanciful story in strip-format for an even younger age group than the seven- to nine-year-olds most likely to appreciate *Father Christmas*. It is about a snowman who comes to life in the night and takes the little boy who made him on a magical flight to the seaside; here there is no hint of social criticism. Though boy and snowman belong to different realms, they can (unlike Bogeymen and Drycleaners) become friends and share experiences. The ending of this story, like that of *Fungus*, is melancholy: when the boy wakes up next morning, his friend has melted down to a featureless little heap and is gone forever. There is a strong contrast here with the ending of *Jim and the Beanstalk*, another story of a boy's friendship with an alien being; unlike the snowman, the giant survives, happier and healthier than before. Yet again, as in the ending of *Fungus*, no blame can be assigned for what is, after all, the natural fate of snowmen. Sorrow, in both *Fungus* and *The Snowman*, is accepted as an inevitable condition of existence for creatures who think and love each other.

In *Gentleman Jim* . . . , yet another strip-format book, Briggs's outlook darkens further. He returns to his concern with modern society, but the indirect critique of *Fungus* has become a diatribe. Jim is a Walter-Mittyish little lavatory attendant (like Fungus, literally an *untermensch*), none too bright and bullied by every authority figure within reach, who enacts his dream of a more exciting and fulfilling job by becoming a highwayman; despite his obvious and childlike harmlessness, he is thrown into prison at once, and ends up cleaning toilets there instead. Here Briggs's condemnation of the social system is total and unsparing. No one, save his wife and, in one frame, a bookseller, shows even tolerance, let alone compassion, for Jim—not even his own neighbors. On the last page Jim himself identifies his fault: "I got ideas above my station," he says. In a society in which wealth, social standing, and academic qualifications are prerequisites for all the prestigious jobs, the poor, the weak, and the ignorant are ruthlessly forced into the niches that no one else wants. In a society so rigidly bureaucratic that Jim cannot keep a donkey in his yard without getting into trouble with four different officials, the helpless are likely to be ruthlessly punished as well.

From the melancholy doubts of *Fungus*, Raymond Briggs has progressed to complete pessimism in *Gentleman Jim*. The only mitigating factor in Jim's life is that he and his equally simple Hilda love each other, and as the story ends they have been separated by prison bars. And yet there is an even darker level—an ultimate failure of compassion—that Briggs still has to explore.

On the cover of each of Briggs's books since *Father Christmas* is a full frontal, waist-length portrait of its chief character, and through these we can trace a kind of progress in his work. Father Christmas looks tough, sturdy, self-respecting, and, in *Father Christmas Goes on Holiday*, happy. Fungus, on the other hand, looks sad and a little foolish with his tiny, close-set eyes and wide down-curving mouth, despite his bulky body and powerful hands. The Snowman's mouth curves upward in a smile, but his almost featureless round face and sloping shoulders make him seem both innocent and helpless, foreshadowing his naive encounters with modern technology and his final fate. Jim's portrait, in which he is seen at work in the lavatory, is the logical next development. Like all these protagonists, he is rounded in shape, but to even greater extremes; he is no more than half the size of the officials, and his face has become a perfect circle with tiny, sad features and a few wisps of hair. The confidence and strength of character that enabled Father Christmas to cope with the modern world have entirely disappeared. Finally, . . . *When the Wind Blows* departs slightly from the established pattern. Its cover shows a small, round man and wife, closely resembling Jim and Hilda, and in the background a third principal character—a large, black mushroom cloud looming over their heads.

In *When the Wind Blows*, the Briggsian protagonists encounter nuclear war. They pay dutiful attention to newspaper and radio accounts of the current crisis, construct their makeshift fallout shelter according to instructions, survive the blast in it, and, in the last few pages, die slowly of radiation sickness. The book alternates between strip-format scenes of the couple at home, bewildered yet optimistic, and double-page spreads of the juggernaut planes, ships, and bombs that are being unleashed upon them. This is Briggs's final indictment of our society—that it is preparing to betray these little people, these innocents who will go on trusting it to the end.

Gentleman Jim was sold as a children's book, I think mistakenly and out of habit; even the older children who enjoy *Fungus* will not appreciate Briggs's satirization of bureaucratic institutions that they are scarcely aware of, or the savage irony of the ending. *When the Wind Blows*, even more obviously a picture book for adults, has been marketed as such. Thus, in moving from the hopefulness of *Jim and the Beanstalk* to the pessimism of *Gentleman Jim* and *When the Wind Blows*, Raymond Briggs has precisely demarcated one boundary between books for children and those for adults. It lies somewhere between *Fungus the Bogeyman* and *Gentleman Jim*—between an imaginary society gentler than our own and a real society seen through the eyes of its oppressed—and, especially, between sorrow and despair. (pp. 12-17)

> Suzanne Rahn, "Beneath the Surface with 'Fungus the Bogeyman'," in The Lion and the Unicorn, *Vols. 7 & 8, 1983-84, pp. 5-19.*

MIDNIGHT ADVENTURE (1961)

Two boys manage to foil a gang of burglars—a formula much loved by children. One of the few books available for that difficult in-between stage of reading development when picture clues are needed at every other paragraph to sustain concentration. These are some of Raymond Briggs' earliest illustrations and are full of the promise which he was later to develop to such good effect.

> A review of "Midnight Adventure," in Books for Your Children, *Vol. 11, No. 4, Autumn, 1976, p. 6.*

SLEDGES TO THE RESCUE (1963)

Tim and Mary Martin may often have played at milkmen, but one snowy day, when they were trying out brand-new sledges, they really *were* milkmen. When they found Ernie the roundsman stranded at the roadside, exhausted by his hand-cart, they mobilised all their friends in the neighbourhood, organised a most efficient delivery service, and pooled their tips to buy flowers for Ernie's missus. The gaiety of the story is made even better because the story is so probable, its details so good, and its characters resourceful in such a natural way, and the

drawings—those chunky, absorbed boys and girls Raymond Briggs does so well—give the book a special flavour.

> Margery Fisher, in a review of "Sledges to the Rescue," in her Growing Point, *Vol. 1, No. 9, April, 1963, p. 130.*

[*Sledges to the Rescue*] makes a slight, sentimental tale with nothing more than competence in the writing but it can do no harm and might do some good out of season.

> A review of "Sledges to the Rescue," in The Junior Bookshelf, *Vol. 27, No. 3, July, 1963, p. 129.*

JIM AND THE BEANSTALK (1970)

Raymond Briggs has a happily childlike, literal wit. Of course the giant whom Jim finds at the top of the beanstalk uses Gigantoplast—what else? Of course he reads "The Baby Giant's bumper fun book" (although he has Mr. Briggs's nursery rhyme volumes too). And of course, when Jim has provided him with spectacles, false teeth and wig of suitable size from down below, the old giant recovers his appetite and thinks fried boy would be rather nice. In his new role as author Raymond Briggs allows his characteristic humour to show just a little in words that have the matter-of-fact sound of fairy tale:

> Early one morning Jim woke up and saw an enormous plant growing outside his window.
>
> 'That's funny' he said, 'it wasn't there yesterday. I'll see how high it goes', and he began to climb up the plant.

This splendid story gives the artist an opportunity to indulge all his special talents—a beautiful precision of detail, his delight in contrasting big and small and making a design from them, his love of sharp colour (what he makes of that tape-measure!). There's only one disappointment in this superlative picturebook: I do wish Jim's morale-boosting had extended to the old Giant's slippers.

> Margery Fisher, in a review of "Jim and the Beanstalk," in her Growing Point, *Vol. 9, No. 3, September, 1970, p. 1577.*

This is the sort of revival that will delight some people and repel others—except for the spectacle of Jim carrying the giant glasses, false teeth and wig through the streets it's no great shakes either way.

> A review of "Jim and the Beanstalk," in Kirkus Reviews, *Vol. XXXVIII, No. 18, September 15, 1970, p. 1027.*

Raymond Briggs is the most approachable of this formidable trio of Medal winners [Charles Keeping, Brian Wildsmith, and Briggs]. In his new book he gives a neat new twist to the story of Jack and the Beanstalk. . . . A good story, matched with big, flat, rather crude pictures. It should be a winner.

> A review of "Jim and the Beanstalk," in The Junior Bookshelf, *Vol. 34, No. 5, October, 1970, p. 277.*

The story has a nicely rounded conclusion, making it satisfactory for storytelling. Large drawings, alternating in full color and black and white, abound in savory detail; there is considerable humor in the relationship of the proportions of the little boy to the gigantic false teeth, spectacles, and wig.

Virginia Haviland, in a review of "Jim and the Bean-stalk," in The Horn Book Magazine, *Vol. XLVII, No. 1, February, 1971, p. 42.*

This fanciful story is cleverly illustrated. . . . The pictures, multicolored spreads alternating with others in black and white, are well integrated with the text and very amusing. Minor inconsistencies—such as the giant being able to eat beef but not fried boy—may be noticed by a precocious child, but most children will enjoy this picture book—reading, viewing and listening to it.

Kathlyn K. Lundgren, in a review of "Jim and the Beanstalk," in School Library Journal, *an appendix to* Library Journal, *Vol. 17, No. 7, March, 1971, p. 116.*

FATHER CHRISTMAS (1973)

AUTHOR'S COMMENTARY

I can't really remember where the idea for *Father Christmas* came from. An idea comes in almost no time at all, but it is often a year or two before it can be started. Then, with the strip-cartoon method it takes about a year to do, then almost another year before it is in the shops. By then the beginning has been forgotten.

Father Christmas's house is closely based on my parents' house where I lived for over twenty years. I can still remember every detail of it, though often the things I remember are as they used to be long ago. Sometimes I find I have drawn something, and only realise it is a memory *after* having drawn it. I recog-nise it when it appears on the paper and think "Gosh, yes! That's how it was".

Father Christmas's wooden bed is my parents' bed, also the green eiderdown and the bamboo table beside the bed with the double-bell alarm clock on it. My father was a milkman and had to get up very early like Father Christmas. He kept the alarm clock in a biscuit tin so it made more noise and also put it some distance from the bed so he had to get out to stop it. I wanted to have this in the book, but it was too complicated.

I think the character of Father Christmas is very much based on my father. The jobs are similar and they both grumble a lot in a fairly humorous way.

The brown dressing gown is my father's, and the cat on the shoulders is him, too. The cat's head always on the *left* shoulder.

I always remember the outside lavatory with the light coming under the door. Also the little mailed fist holding the toilet roll. The sink he washes at is the sink as it used to be when I was an infant, with the home-made wooden draining board. This was later replaced by the usual boring formica and stain-less steel thing. The red tea caddy with black and gold letters on the green shelf and the green tooth mug were all there, too. The stove in the kitchen is not as it was. We had ones like that in the Army and I've always liked them.

As an art student I drew and painted my mother and father in the kitchen hundreds of times. The green curtains, green painted dresser, blue tiled fireplace. The shaving mirror hanging on the hook by the window. The yellow London bricks outside, the green back door and the cat flap. The country cottage is where I was evacuated in the war, with the red and blue glass

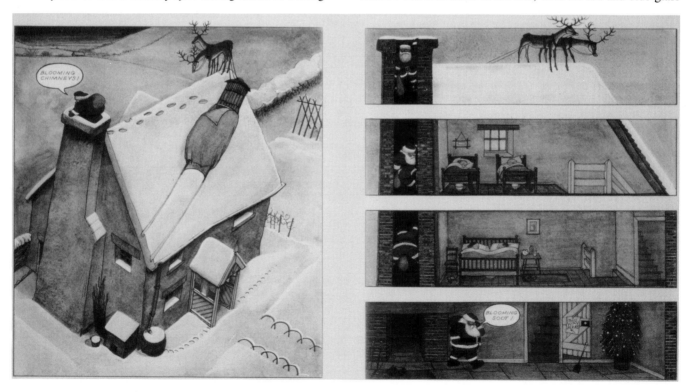

From Father Christmas, *written and illustrated by Raymond Briggs. Coward, McCann & Geoghegan, 1973. Reprinted by permission of Coward, McCann & Geoghegan, Inc. In Canada by Hamish Hamilton Ltd. Text and illustrations copyright © 1973 by Raymond Briggs.*

in the porch, the rain butt and the cream painted stair door with black lock and brass knob.

The modern house is my present house with its hideous pink bathroom and blue Volkswagen van.

The terrace house with cars is again my parents' house—and so on.

I suppose all this helped to give realism to the setting of the fantasy, and gave the book a solid basis.

Most kids when they write say "I liked it best the bit where he was on the lavatory". (pp. 195-96)

> *Raymond Briggs, "That Blooming Book," in* The Junior Bookshelf, *Vol. 38, No. 4, August, 1974, pp. 195-96.*

In demythologizing Santa Claus, Raymond Briggs has created a comic-strip style picture book of the most engaging and affectionate kind, already one of my personal favourites. *Father Christmas* . . . is here shown as a home-loving domestic old gent, all the more attractive for being so than the thunderous, ho-hoing erl-king of legend. This comfortable suburban Falstaff of the fireside who soaks his teeth in a glass at night and loves his dog, his cat and his deers, and mutters about "blooming work", "blooming Christmas" and the "blooming weather" that accompanies the season of good cheer is to my mind infinitely preferable to either the denizen-figure of legend or the pensioned-off old drunkard employed by Walt Disney. In fact, the Briggs version is not just a Father Christmas story, but a hymn of praise to Everyman and his working day, a conception that makes of this quite the happiest, gentlest, and indeed most moving picture book for many a day. It surely will cross all the boundaries of age, sophistication and social background to find for itself a wide and appreciative audience for many a year to come. A Happy Blooming Christmas to you too, Mr. Briggs.

> *Pelorus, in a review of "Father Christmas," in* Signal, *No. 12, September, 1973, p. 163.*

We must thank Mr. Briggs—who obviously knows [Father Christmas] well—for joining the ranks of biographers of the famous and allowing us to meet him 'in the round'. . . .

The pictures, though for the most part small, with meticulous detail, are never so busy as to confuse a small child who will delight in the juxtaposition of Christmas magic with the practicalities of cocoa-making.

This is great for those up to seven or eight, for whom it is intended, and those up to seventy or eighty who grab it.

> *Margott Petts, in a review of "Father Christmas," in* Children's Book Review, *Vol. III, No. 6, December, 1973, p. 170.*

Technically this gorgeous picture-book has no text, but in fact Father Christmas's ballooned exclamations . . . are a text in themselves, expressing what the pictures show in comic detail. . . . The relating of the nursery myth to everyday life is done with sly skill; Father Christmas in the reindeer sledge steers a clever middle course between sentiment and disenchantment.

> *Margery Fisher, in a review of "Father Christmas," in her* Growing Point, *Vol. 12, No. 6, December, 1973, p. 2301.*

Father Christmas (British for Santa Claus) steals the show in one of the most irresistible yuletide books to appear in many years. Stripped of his long-familiar vacuous jollity, commercialism, and sentimentality, he remains, nevertheless, properly corpulent, red-clad, and white-whiskered. And although he is still hard-working and faithful, he can also be grumpy and impatient—in short, thoroughly human. . . . Almost wordless except for the old man's terse comments, . . . the book consists of blocks and panels of full-color pictures which occasionally blossom into dramatic, brilliant doublespreads.

> *Ethel L. Heins, in a review of "Father Christmas," in* The Horn Book Magazine, *Vol. XLIX, No. 6, December, 1973, p. 583.*

There is not much Holy Night about Raymond Briggs' offering. He gives us, in strip form, one day in the life of Father Christmas . . . [until he] is off to sleep with a final "Happy blooming Christmas to you, too!" to a profoundly gratified reader. There was never a Christmas book like this. . . . A gorgeous book, drawn with Raymond Briggs' clarity and virtuosity. Dad and Junior will fight for first look all over the Christmas table, and the delight should last for a good many Christmases to come. (pp. 377-78)

> *M. Crouch, in a review of "Father Christmas," in* The Junior Bookshelf, *Vol. 37, No. 6, December, 1973, pp. 377-78.*

A Christmas book with tremendous appeal for a wide age range: very young children will enjoy the homely, intimate details of this individualistic Santa Claus' Christmas Eve and gift-delivering journey; older ones will appreciate the gently satirical humor in his reluctance to go to work and his gruff, monosyllabic comments throughout; and readers and nonreaders alike will take to the comic-strip structure of the illustrations that carry the load of the narrative. Each small picture is precisely detailed, convincingly well-drawn, and alive with action; the longer and larger frames—including some full-page spreads—offer a lot of visual contrast in size, color, and content. (pp. 595, 598)

> *A review of "Father Christmas," in* The Booklist, *Vol. 70, No. 11, February 1, 1974, pp. 595, 598.*

FATHER CHRISTMAS GOES ON HOLIDAY   (1975)

Raymond Briggs' not-so-jolly elf is still alive and kicking. After poking fun at forced gaiety in *Father Christmas,* . . . Briggs twits English provincialism as his *Father Christmas Goes on Holiday.* . . . The same ill-tempered tourist whether soaking up the sun (and the grape) in *la belle France*, trying his loch in the Scottish highlands, or taking in the tacky splendor of the Vegas strip, culture-shocked Father Christmas is relieved to point his reindeer-powered mobile home toward the North Pole. The comic strip layout may tempt children, but the quips and complaints about French haute cuisine or the classical kitsch of Nero's (read Caesar's) Palace in Las Vegas are for the parents of the picture-book set. (p. 79)

> *Pamela D. Pollack, "Claus-trophobia: Closing in on Christmas '75," in* School Library Journal, *Vol. 22, No. 2, October, 1975, pp. 78-81.**

The use of repeated forays into celebrated holiday spots has provided a neat shape to the book, and the illustrations are as apt, concentrated, engaging and witty as ever. If there seems a slight lack of brio, this may simply be because we can no longer have the pleasure of being *introduced* to Briggs's can-onised but crusty hero.

> *Margery Fisher, in a review of "Father Christmas Goes on Holiday," in her* Growing Point, *Vol. 14, No. 6, December, 1975, p. 2774.*

If you're an adult or older reader, watching Father Christmas sample the mixed pleasures of "La Belle France," chilly Scotland, and ostentatious Las Vegas is sure to elicit a guffaw. But picture-book audiences who first met the crusty old man (he hasn't changed a bit) in *Father Christmas* ... will lose out on the full measure of humor, though studying all those detailed comic-strip scenes will no doubt carry an appeal of its own. Marketed as both a children's and an adult title, with good reason, this cheeky second installment is destined to gather a cult following or at least achieve status as a conversation piece.

> *Denise M. Wilms, in a review of "Father Christmas Goes on Holiday," in* The Booklist, *Vol. 72, No. 9, January 1, 1976, p. 622.*

After his Herculean efforts in presenting the best blooming Christmas book of all time (about 200 pictures compared with 16 in the average picture book) Raymond Briggs might have rested awhile. An invention as gargantuan as this Father Christmas cannot easily be put aside. Public demand and inner compulsion alike insist on further investigation. So here is Father Christmas again. ... A joyous book, its humour and good-humour beautifully sustained, and executed with unflagging craftsmanship. (pp. 80-1)

> *M. Crouch, in a review of "Father Christmas Goes on Holiday," in* The Junior Bookshelf, *Vol. 40, No. 2, April, 1976, pp. 80-1.*

This must be the only book to concentrate solely on what Father Christmas does during the summer, and the results—in comic-strip—are always entertaining. ...

Everyone will enjoy this book, with all its jokes, broad and sly, and its sudden, dazzling effects of a different scenery and travel through huge, lurid skies.

> *Nicholas Tucker, "What Santa Claus Does during Summer," in* The Observer, *October 2, 1977, p. 25.**

FUNGUS THE BOGEYMAN (1977)

Fungus the Bogeyman may well turn out to be the most controversial picture book of the year; but not because the Whitehouse band may beat a few drums about the preoccupation with ooze, ordure, stenches, boils, umbilical cords, triple nipples and other matter so dubious as to be censored off the page.

Raymond Briggs's *Father Christmas* books had explorable pictures, a crisply witty text and a cheery vulgarity which invited the young reader to enjoy very funny and very clear stories; if grown-ups were youthful and sane enough to join in, they were welcome too. The story of *Fungus the Bogeyman* is little more than a thread we follow through the underworld which is Bogeydom. Here live Fungus, his wife Mildew, little Mould and the whole bogey community, relishing the "fetid darkness", dirt, slime and smells; a gentle, attractive folk, delighting in aimless games, tranquil hobbies, much sustained by half-memorized verse. The "plot" traces Fungus's increasing puzzlement about the point of his nightly work—to come up to our world ("the surface") and play bogeyman to us, "the drycleaners".

The puns, comic inversions and minutiae of the dank green realm below our feet should be of immediate appeal to many children: "Pepsomuck gets teeth really black", "Flaked Corns" and "Gripe Nits" for breakfast, cats called Mucus and Pus. But the slim plot and the large areas of explanatory text—no matter how ingenious the layout to the adult eye—may not retain the interest of many children of picturebook age throughout this 40-page introduction to bogey culture.

Even the humour—brilliant and inventive if you dip here and there about the book—may seem intrusive to a child who likes to get on with the story. Much of the parody and wit depends upon allusions to an adult, even a literary, world; and the vocabulary may prove impenetrable rather than extending ("Bogey Graffiti: this is never scatological. It almost always consists of platitudes or grave philosophical statements").

Yet the basic idea *is* very engaging. Those who become addicted to Bogeydom—probably bright and reflective children whose parents share their books with them—will love to return to different pictures and notes, master the bogey language, and even make up Fungus stories for themselves.

> *Geoff Fox, "Drear New Hero," in* The Times Educational Supplement, *No. 3258, November 18, 1977, p. 35.**

[*Fungus the Bogeyman*] is a truly disgusting new character from the creator of the Alternative Father Christmas. As such he's bound to charm the average dirty-minded nine-year-old. ...

[The Bogeyman's] lifestyle, set out and explained in a wealth of footnotes and asides in the customary Briggs comic strip format, is for those who like their jokes laboured. The detail is such that fan clubs are likely to be started where discrepancies and inconsistencies can be hammered out. ... The book deserves to be wildly popular even though the main Bogey pastime would seem to be flogging dead horses.

> *William Feaver, "Slimy Newcomer," in* The Observer, *November 27, 1977, p. 29.**

"Then swill it down with a cup of cold sick", we used to chant in the playground, concluding thus the most loathsome of children's rhymes. To mouth it at all was a sort of dare, particularly for those who just could not stop their imagination attempting to picture what "green snot pie" or "a dead dog's eye" might look like. Now, this famous emetic nonsense stands as one of the epigraphs to Raymond Briggs's *Fungus the Bogeyman;* but it cannot possibly justify such a coprophilous and putrid volume. It is one thing for an author to note that children set out deliberately to make themselves shudder once in a while, but quite another for him to draw out that flirtation with squalor into an obsessive monologue on decay.

What makes this natural history of Bogeydom so peculiarly disgusting, and inappropriate to these pages, is precisely its obsessive quality: the way its anal-erotic preoccupations are relentlessly catalogued by an adult mind. I should explain that the Bogeymen, who live underground, have slimy wrestlers' bodies, and cretinous pigs' heads equipped with vestigial horns and equally stunted Dracula teeth. They are, in themselves, bearable. But they sleep in wet beds (an experience associated by children with shame as well as discomfort), cultivate boils on the back of their necks, and marinade their trousers until they reach a satisfactory level of stink. This is not amusing or engaging (it is a great mistake to think that children are in love with dirt, when they are merely indifferent to it at the messiest of times); and the fact that everything in the Bogey world so mechanically defeats the expectations of the Surface world (gold is a base metal, the object of billiards is to avoid getting the balls in the hole, flowers are cultivated and prized for their etiolation and droop, and so forth) makes for a swiftly cumulative tedium.

But of course it is not the Bogeys themselves who make the book offensive but the implications they raise about Raymond Briggs's own attitude to the fact of living in a human body that has habits, functions and needs. One way of registering horror at these organic processes is to make a horror of them; and this, in the most literal-minded way, is what Briggs had done. Hence the Bogeys' three nipples, three breasts; their bathroom bottles of "Pus" and (much more indicative) "Femstench roll-on Odorant"; and their terms of endearment, expressed at their height by the Bogey poet John Dung:

> Are not your kisses then as filthy,
>   and more,
> As a worm sucking an envenomed
>   sore?

It is a peculiar parent who could take pleasure in reading this aloud to his child; and a peculiar child who did not feel perplexed by his inability to empathize with these new "characters".

From Fungus the Bogeyman, *written and illustrated by Raymond Briggs. Random House, 1979. Copyright © 1977 by Raymond Briggs. All rights reserved. Reprinted by permission of Random House, Inc. In Canada by Hamish Hamilton Ltd.*

Russell Davies, "Ode to Putrefaction," in The Times Literary Supplement, *No. 3949, December 2, 1977, p. 1412.*

I don't agree with the suggestion that the Champion Dirt Collectors are the right customers for this Anatomy of Bogeyland. If you need a strong stomach to assimilate the details of slime, muck and melancholy malice, you also need a certain amount of literary experience to appreciate the misquotations and puns, the grave dictionary definitions (rhyporographs: paintings of mean or sordid subjects—scran: broken vessels; scraps, refuse), the ingeniously oblique derived activities (Drycleaner-watching, visits to the Odeum, Bogeyvision) and, finally, the ambivalence of the whole book, expressed in Bogey's sporadic murmurs of doubt about the validity of his work tormenting humans above ground with boils and night-fears. This is in fact a highly intellectual book—as much non-fiction as fiction, you could say—and the elaborate layout with its speech-balloons, footnotes and lettered text demands a concentration which children under ten are hardly likely to give it. Nor will they necessarily realise the precision of the artwork, the careful drabness of colour, the nicely-calculated appearance of Bogey, the constant visual allusions that provide a satirical undercurrent. If the book is not exactly Swiftean, there is a note of distaste, surely, behind the artist's thorough and skilful exploration of his subject. The legend on the board of a Sandwichman, "Nothing is permanent but Woe", is perhaps a bit more than a misquotation from a Wayside Pulpit. (pp. 3368-69)

Margery Fisher, in a review of "Fungus the Bogeyman," in her Growing Point, *Vol. 17, No. 2, July, 1978, pp. 3368-69.*

Our editor tells me **Fungus the Bogeyman** . . . has reached [America] at last and that it is causing some confusion. Let me try and explain why I think this is one of the most significant children's books to come from England in the last ten years.

To hear some people talk, you'd think the creator of such easily loved books as **Father Christmas** . . . and **The Snowman** . . . had suffered a terrible aberration during which he somehow engineered what has been described to me as the nastiest book ever published for children.

I don't believe in that kind of quirk. I tend to think that when an artist of Briggs's undoubted talent produces something startlingly unexpected and perhaps even disconcerting, he has good artistic reasons for doing so. The best the rest of us can do about it—especially we critical intermediaries (librarians, teachers, academics, and others who take on the self-appointed role of public guide and pundit)—is to try and understand what is going on. In that spirit I look at this extraordinary work.

At first blush I see a book that resembles the picture books for older children, of which we are getting more and more; but then I notice that a very great deal of the text is taken up with a very great number of words, many of which are not exactly commonplace or used in simple ways. I see a book that looks like one of the less salubrious children's comic-strip books. There is a touch of the lurid about it and monstrously outrageous characters apparently performing outrageously slapstick routines. But then I look again—a critical doubletake—and see that the color has been handled with such skill that in the volume's forty pages there are subtly modulated variations of tone, shape, and organization of pictures and that neither color nor pattern are at all crude or tiresome but constantly inventive and refreshing.

Furthermore, the outrageous incidents are only superficially vulgar. They are like the scene (a favorite of mine) in *Henry the Fourth: Part One* in which Hal and Falstaff are comically rude at the expense of the establishment in the shape of Hal's father, King Henry. Far more is going on under the surface—between characters, between audience and characters, and between author and audience—than a first impression suggests. Indeed, it is what is going on under the surface of the broad comedy that really matters.

On a careful reading these Bogey people, too, turn out to be not what they seem. They are kindly, gentle, compassionate, philosophically inclined. While family-loving Fungus goes his rounds of nefarious jobbery—giving us "drycleaners" frights and boils—he is, like so many workmen who have routine lives, pondering the problem of his *angst*. He's happy and cannot understand why. And which of us who are happy don't wonder about it?

What appeals to me most about the Bogeys is that they're literate. Their library is great fun and much valued. The Bogeys are *readers;* wouldn't we have the whole human race that way! Come to think of it, who would *you* rather meet even on a dark night (of the calendar or the soul): Fungus or your local congressperson? I know whom I'd choose any time.

But away with such meanderings. Back, not to Fungus but to The Book. I notice that many jokey games are being played between author and reader, outside, so to speak, the covers of the book. An obvious example: Those blacked-out bits with legends appended like "The Publishers wish to state that this picture has been deleted in the interests of good taste and public decency." Pure Marx Brothers, this; neo-Surrealist. I say no more. Enjoy finding your own examples.

Then there is all that language. Such as: "Scran: broken victuals; scraps, refuse." And: "Weem: a subterranean chamber lined with rough stones." Though a few of these delicious words are Bogey vocabulary, most are included in the unabridged *Oxford English Dictionary*. Far from being a mindless, tasteless picture book, *Fungus* turns out to be a verbally witty construction of language forms, some of which happen to be visual and some of which are fine and vivid words rescued from unhappy neglect. To my mind, the sharpest test of all literature is the question: How far does this book protect, enrich, and imaginatively employ our language? By that yardstick *Fungus* comes out tops.

But let's go on with my catalog of first impressions. Begin where children are, the educators tell us, and lead them on to the unfamiliar, to the more difficult and deepening. *Fungus* looks, I agree, like a discordant comic strip—which is exactly where many children are as readers. (Not a moral judgment, by the way; simply an observation.) And that is how my wife's ten-year-old godson treated it when he was given a copy. He flipped through it and chuckled that devilish muttered laughter that ten-year-olds give off when they think they've got something the adults will hate and they will love. But then he turned to the beginning and started a thorough reading. He was still there, in the same place on the floor, three hours later. A hint that the *O.E.D.* included most of the asterisked "funny" words sent him burrowing for them and provided what I am sure was for him a new idea of what a dictionary can offer.

I know, I know, this is one of those awful appeals to special cases that all of us who deal with children's reading make from time to time in support of our own opinions. But the fact is that in England a great many other special cases have made

Fungus widely popular simply by word of mouth rather than by the adman's publicity. It is becoming no less than a hinge book in children's *affectionate* approach to literature. Valuable, that.

If you total the features that comprise this work, you'll find, I think, that they add up to The Modern Novel. Which means: An interest in the mosaic texture of life expressed in various modes (story, handbook-like explanations, diagrams, documentary reportage, overlays of feeling and perception, running gags, gossip, interior monologue—on and on) rather than in a sequentially told, unwaveringly modulated narrative controlled by a nineteenth-century idea of logic in cause and effect; games being played; the book as Book—as Object—and Fiction as Artifice being constantly drawn attention to and made overtly part of the entertainment. Thus the reader is forced to "handle" the text (pictures and words). You cannot simply lose yourself in it but must match your own wit against the wit of the book's creator.

All literature is only ink on paper; all pictures (even photographs) are only fictions. *Fungus* is an open deception. It pretends to be one thing and is actually another. It pretends to be a picture book but is really a novel. It pretends to be about ugly and unpleasant characters who live in a nasty world, but it is actually about the virtues of our life and the deep ponderings of twentieth-century human beings living in the West. It pretends to be coddish and slapstick; it is actually subtle, serious, and witty. It pretends to be antibook and is actually formatively, lovingly book-bound.

Fungus belongs to the best art movements—especially the literary art movements—of this century. What it offers children who give it close reading is the chance to meet those ideas, the ideas of post-Joycean fiction—which, paradoxically, is a tradition that has always been present in English literature, though it has sometimes been ignored or disliked. Sterne and *Tristram Shandy* belong to it, and Shakespeare is a master craftsman of it when he wants to be.

Fungus is rare as one of those creations which lead children, *in their own terms* yet without losing its integrity and voice, towards an educated understanding, pleasurably gained, of the art of their own time and which give expression to their own ways of seeing. The book deserves all the exposure we can give it; but luckily it will reach out to the intended audience anyway, because once a few children have found *Fungus*, their own telegraph system will rapidly pass the news to all of them.

What I hope is that Briggs will go on displaying his talent in books that press the form as vitally and energetically as *Fungus* does for many years to come. (pp. 99-103)

Aidan Chambers, "Letter from England: 'Fungus' Encore," in The Horn Book Magazine, *Vol. LVI, No. 1, February, 1980, pp. 99-103.*

A friendly indigenous teenager or two can be of great assistance to those of us who try to stay in touch with the shifting patterns of adolescent folkways.

One of my favorite informants is Lisa Gray, a fourteen-year-old gamin who sometimes sings and performs eccentric dances. . . . Lisa studies creative writing in a special UCLA class for the superbright and is an articulate and helpful book-discusser.

Not long ago Lisa and I sat down at the kitchen table over cups of coffee and piles of books to talk about laughing. I had given her a wildly divergent selection of recent books that were intended to be funny, and now we were ready to anatomize the adolescent funny-bone.

"As a not-so-typical teenager," I said, indicating the stack of books in the middle of the table, "which of these do you think is really funny?" (p. 456)

I handed her my own favorite, the book that I had called "the YA goody of the year," *Fungus the Bogeyman* by Raymond Briggs. She picked it up with two fingers.

"Oh help!" she yelped. "From the very beginning with this I was *grossed out!* And he kept up with it, and all it did was get grosser, and grosser, and *grosser!* There was too much of it for me. A lot of younger guys even in seventh grade would like this though—the whole seventh grade is taken up with grossness—fart jokes and burp jokes and all that. But kids wouldn't stick with it because of the detail on the pages, the literary quotes, and the subtleness of some of the jokes."

I suggested that maybe teenagers like to laugh at stories about things they don't dare to do. "Yes," she agreed, "the more outrageous the incident and the more it applies to them, the more they're going to like it."

It occurred to me that maybe I like *Fungus* because I was always afraid to burp in the seventh grade. But I didn't tell Lisa. (p. 457)

Patty Campbell, in a review of "Fungus the Bogey-man," in Wilson Library Bulletin, *Vol. 54, No. 7, March, 1980, pp. 456-57.**

THE SNOWMAN (1978)

AUTHOR'S COMMENTARY

The Snowman was done as light relief from the muck and slime of *Fungus the Bogeyman*. . . . Like most artists, I always have a backlist of ideas waiting to be used. The ideas come in a moment, but each one takes a year or two of work to become a book. *Fungus the Bogeyman* took over two years and involved a lot of research into the vile depths of Bogeydom. Also, after the wordiness of *Fungus,* it was a change to do a completely wordless book. So, no muck, no slime, no research, no words. And, above all, no hand lettering!

People have often said that my preliminary drawings for a book are better than my final ink and color work. Consequently, in *The Snowman* I used pencil crayons in the hope of letting the crayoning evolve from the penciling. I wanted to avoid the abrupt change that takes place when a brutal black pen line is scratched on top of a quiet pencil drawing. So there is no ink line or paint in the book; it is all crayon.

The setting of the book is based on my own house and garden, which is in Sussex at the foot of the South Downs, a few miles from Brighton. In the book the snowman and the boy fly over the Downs to Brighton, then over the Royal Pavillion, which was built by George IV. Contrary to what some reviewers have said, it is *not* Moscow, and *not* the Kremlin! (pp. 96-7)

Raymond Briggs, "For Illustration: 'The Snow-man'," in The Horn Book Magazine, *Vol. LVI, No. 1, February, 1980, pp. 96-7.*

Incomparably sweet, touching and funny, Briggs's wordless book tells a story with all the depth and breadth of a novel.

The pictures in creamy, soft pastels show a small boy making a snowman twice his size and sporting a friendly face, hat and scarf. The huge fellow stands in the yard until mum tucks her son into bed. Then he slips out of the house and invites the snowman in. They have a good time as the little host introduces his guest to the marvels of TV, the sleeping parents with their teeth in a cup, among other things, and the snowman clowns around in the father's clothes. Then it's turnabout when the giant takes the boy on a fantastic flight over the countryside and through a whirling snowfall to faroff places. At the flush of dawn, the snowman flies his friend home and they part. The final scene in the morning is indescribably touching.

A review of "The Snowman," in Publishers Weekly, *Vol. 214, No. 15, October 9, 1978, p. 76.*

In the most delicate sequence of colour and line, in pictures that suggest the very texture of snow, Raymond Briggs uses strip-picture techniques to tell the story of two friends for whom adventure is clearly coloured by instant affection. . . . The inevitable disappointment next morning is not over-dramatised; indeed, the whole book is a striking example of what simplicity can encompass if it is allied to an exact vision of textures, climate, landscape and the open, unaffected feelings of a child.

Margery Fisher, in a review of "The Snowman," in her Growing Point, *Vol. 17, No. 4, November, 1978, p. 3425.*

How Briggs could have made such a warm book out of such a cold subject is remarkable. Unlike his sharp, clearcut images in *Father Christmas* . . . , these have the hazy softness of air in snow, mostly created with long strokes of colored pencil. . . . The innocence and joy of [the boy and Snowman's] spree make all the more poignant a last small picture of the boy discovering his melted friend in the morning light. But the experience is one that neither he nor young "readers" will ever regret or forget.

Betsy Hearne, in a review of "The Snowman," in Booklist, *Vol. 75, No. 5, November 1, 1978, p. 474.*

Unlike *Fungus the Bogeyman,* this book *will* appeal to children and parents alike. . . . Raymond Briggs has treated his subject in a gentle, sympathetic way with muted colours and soft, snowy backgrounds, abandoning his rather garish, brash *Father Christmas* style. The whole treatment of the book resembles the snow itself, and this approach succeeds in no uncertain manner. If a book can be described as "lovable", then this is it.

A review of "The Snowman," in Book Window, *Vol. 6, No. 1, Winter, 1978, p. 13.*

The Snowman is a good example of an idea conveyed by visual images alone. It presents a rare kind of relationship: a child and an adult (fancifully depicted as a snowman) who exist on equal terms. There is a role reversal at the beginning; the child guides the "adult" through new experiences. But these friends are clearly equal in the way they enjoy each other's company and delight in new discoveries. . . .

Without the help of a single word, the book contains a narrative, two distinct characterizations, and a poignant theme. Briggs uses either full-page illustrations or a group of rectangular spaces, distributing colors and shapes consistently in each drawing and creating a low-keyed effect with closely related tones and soft-textured lines. His uniformly controlled style produces a warm surface on the page and a calm, matter-of-fact aura.

Olga Richard & Donnarae MacCann, in a review of "The Snowman," in Wilson Library Bulletin, *Vol. 53, No. 8, April, 1979, p. 576.*

This is without question one of the outstanding picture books of this year and perhaps of all times. Briggs's tale has the power to probe deep into a child's imagination. The book is limited only by the mental processes available to the reader. Highly recommended for all ages. (p. 92)

A review of "The Snowman," in Catholic Library World, *Vol. 51, No. 2, September, 1979, pp. 91-2.*

GENTLEMAN JIM   (1980)

Raymond Briggs has in this book produced another character as likely to become a cult figure as *Fungus the Bogeyman*. . . . A child's book? I doubt it. It is a most scathing and brilliant commentary of the present day social scene and as such it is the best thing that Briggs has done. Young children probably would not understand a lot of it, adults will only too well. Let's hope the book makes people think hard about its message which is a very powerful one and pathetic too. In this book Briggs uses comedy to get his message across the way Charlie Chaplin did in his films and the result is a most moving and poignant commentary on life. Sensitive adults could well end up in tears! Please do read it—it can teach everyone a great deal.

Margaret Walker, in a review of "Gentleman Jim," in Book Window, *Vol. 7, No. 2, Spring, 1980, p. 22.*

The philosophical conclusion of this story is that it is safer not to try to realise a dream: the social conclusion is that bureaucracy is invincible. With two such massive statements, and with the literary puns and analogies that swing the narrative along, the book seems to sit squarely in a teenage and adult readership. The deep sadness of the book is communicated through lavatory-attendent Jim's wistfully innocent face and through his pathetically literal attempts to move out from underground to the seemingly romantic careers of a marine, artist, cowboy or highwayman. Impeccably selected detail, balanced structure, balloons which reveal the hero's painful naïveté, an ingenious change of style and format to mark the change from drab actuality to passionate fancy—these are concomitants of a book which once more shows Raymond Briggs as a novelist working within the picture-book format. (pp. 3708-09)

Margery Fisher, in a review of "Gentleman Jim," in her Growing Point, *Vol. 19, No. 1, May, 1980, pp. 3708-09.*

Raymond Briggs's largest cartoon book describes the Walter Mittyish fantasies of a meek little lavatory attendant and his fight against faceless bureaucracy. But faceless bureaucracy is rather a thankless subject for a cartoonist. Jim himself and Hilda, his currant bun of a wife, are drawn with minimal features, and the characters in the story tend to become a gallery of stereotypes. Reviewers have murmured politely that this book is one for the adult shelves, but the satire would have to be sharper and more inventive to compete with some of the talented cartoonists for adults now being published. . . .

Like other passages in the book [Jim's reverie on the subject of "Ex-ectives"] shows too heavy a reliance on a weakish text. Pictures tend to be subordinated to words, despite some glowing set pieces. There is a sad lack of zest in this book, though perhaps zest should not be looked for in a story which begins in a public lavatory and ends in a prison.

Myra Barrs, "Anomie in Dreamland," in The Times Educational Supplement, *No. 3336, May 23, 1980, p. 29.**

Raymond Briggs has found a hero to follow his Father Christmas, and found him, somewhat surprisingly, in the Gents'. . . . Mr. Briggs handles the strip-cartoon format brilliantly. Every one of the hundreds of tiny pictures is beautifully composed, and the tone and the humour are consistent throughout. The book is as immaculately stylish as Gentleman Jim's toilets. (pp. 166-67)

M. Crouch, in a review of "Gentleman Jim," in The Junior Bookshelf, *Vol. 44, No. 4, August, 1980, pp. 166-67.*

Raymond Briggs's previous picture book, the wordless *The Snowman,* ended on a note of consolatory, sustaining melancholy. Briggs's ability to confront loss and the transience of joy in a picture book without either sentimentalizing his themes or depressing his readers made the book an extraordinary achievement, and makes *Gentleman Jim,* which will appeal more to the over-eights than the under-fives, even sadder. Gentleman Jim is a barely literate lavatory attendant, whose attempts to act on his tawdry daydreams . . . bring him into inevitable and tragic conflict with authority. The full poignancy of the situation is, however, missed by Briggs's denying Jim full adulthood. The text is lengthy and the jokes, visual and verbal, somewhat knowing. The book will no doubt add to Briggs's growing cult following among adults, but it requires from the child reader an unlikely ability to distance himself from the story's simple and pathetic hero.

Gentleman Jim is a despairing book. . . .

Neil Philip, in a review of "Gentleman Jim," in British Book News Children's Supplement, *Autumn, 1980, p. 12.*

WHEN THE WIND BLOWS   (1982)

AUTHOR'S COMMENTARY

[In the following excerpt, Richard North interviews Briggs, who relates how he was inspired to write When the Wind Blows *and how he has reacted to the finished work. North concludes by comparing Briggs to Edward Ardizzone.]*

[Raymond Briggs,] acclaimed children's writer and illustrator, has elevated his eyes from the bogeys and slime of one of his earlier creations (the glorious *Fungus the Bogeyman*), and discovered instead—the apocalypse.

From *Fungus the Bogeyman* to his latest, even bigger seller, *When the Wind Blows,* wherein the unimaginable is imagined and drawn, is quite a step. It has taken a popular writer away from his quiet subversion of the nursery . . . out into the big bad world. "I thought when I finished it that it couldn't possibly be for children", says Briggs, a quiet fellow who doesn't at first seem a particularly doomy sort. "It was so depressing". And so *When the Wind Blows* was destined for the adult list of his career-long publishers, Hamish Hamilton. And it got

From When the Wind Blows, *written and illustrated by Raymond Briggs. Schocken Books, 1982. Reprinted by permission of Schocken Books, Inc. In Canada by Hamish Hamilton Ltd. © 1982 by Raymond Briggs.*

adult reviews, as well as garnering, "It is *really* good" from Tony Benn, and a note from Mrs Thatcher that she hopes to read it at her next holiday. . . .

"But we found it went into the children's bookshops and started selling there too, to my surprise". It is now required reading for hep teenies, and is also—I happen to know—going down a storm in a well-bred rural prep school for girls. Briggs has ways of crossing barriers. . . .

In case you've been on Mars (which will not be a bad spot to be if Mr Briggs' vision comes to pass), the book is about an amiable pair of people of the kind that there will be no more of. They are stoutly and sweetly working class. Decent, quiet, loyal people who expect rather little of life, and get it. But they have each other, and this is portrayed in a way which perhaps comes with sad ease to Raymond Briggs, who lost both his parents and his wife within a few years of each other.

[James] Bloggs has already proved himself a bit of a dreamer in *Gentleman Jim*. . . .

"I tried to keep him out of the next book, but he kept turning up", says Raymond Briggs. And so it is nice Mr and Mrs Bloggs who endure the nuclear holocaust that fades their gums and wobbles their teeth and makes them bleed and their hair

fall out, with only *Protect and Survive* between them and irradiation. . . .

"I hadn't thought about these things much" says Raymond Briggs. "But there was a *Panorama* one Monday, and a television crew came the next day to do a thing with me and we were talking about the Bomb and so on, and one of them said, 'there's your next book'". And so his regular eighteen-month cycle of gestation and production produced the fearsome comic epic.

"I wasn't really a CND [Campaign for Nuclear Disarmament] sort of person at all", says Raymond Briggs. "I wasn't when I started the book, and I wasn't even when I finished it." He has become more convinced of the case for nuclear unilateral disarmament as he has read books like *The Fate of the Earth* . . . , which discusses the results, globally, to the ecosystem of a possible nuclear war. Now he has given some copies of the book to CND for them to sell, and he is increasingly feeling that he ought to join up formally. He has, in short, been radicalized. . . .

Raymond Briggs' vision of the world is beautifully rooted in Englishness. He was a child of the war: the explosions in his drawings, both of shells and of dreams, come from the Pathe

News and boys books. He doodled Lancasters, and knew all about blazing an orange heart to a WHAAM of ack-ack fire. . . .

On his shelf, though he says it is there from admiration rather than slavish devotion, is a book on Ardizzone (probably the only rival to Briggs in the recent past): the portly Edwardian could never have put aside the world of claret and seaside holidays for long enough to have created the inside-out world of slime's-nice, warm's-a-bore that Briggs made in *Fungus the Bogeyman*. But Ardizzone and Briggs meet well enough in their affection for people, and in the poignancy of the foibles and daydreams. It's just that Briggs has had some of the optimism, knocked out of him (in a thoroughly modern way: Ardizzone, for instance, knew battle fronts, and Briggs doesn't). But things have got more peculiar since the days when the Hun, and evil, was all we had to fear. Now man has his own Promethean might to manage. "We have all this technology" says Raymond Briggs, "But we haven't grown enough to match it".

Richard North, "Cartoon Apocalypse," in The Times Educational Supplement, No. 3441, June 11, 1982. p. 41.

[Raymond Briggs' latest strip book] is not a children's book at all. Gone is the cosy, nostalgic Father Christmas, but instead we have Mr. and Mrs. James Bloggs . . . facing up to the crisis of a nuclear attack. Through the tale of an ordinary retired couple it demonstrates the ignorance of most people and the pathetic attempts made by the authorities to inform and advise. A disturbing book, which the publishers have sent to every M.P. and every member of the House of Lords. Not to be given lightly even to the most questioning of teenagers, who, whilst they need to have the truth, need also to have a sense of hope and purpose.

A review of "When the Wind Blows," in Books for Your Children, Vol. 17, No. 2, Summer, 1982, p. 21.

In a way, we should have seen it coming. The realism of Raymond Briggs's comic-book-style children's books was a hint. Father Christmas as member of the working class, cursing the "blooming snow" up there at the North Pole (**"Father Christmas"**) or basking luxuriously in the sun at Caesar's Palace in Las Vegas (**"Father Christmas Goes on Holiday"**): this should have warned us that Mr. Briggs does not believe in sentimental fairy tales.

Yet his new book, **"When the Wind Blows,"** still comes as a terrific shock. It starts with the book's cover, which shows a roly-poly working-class couple—it could be a shaved Father Christmas putting a comradely arm around his cleaning lady—standing in front of a nuclear mushroom cloud.

It grows at the beginning of the comic-strip story that follows, as an elderly pensioner named James Bloggs comes home to his cozy rural cottage for lunch after a morning of reading the papers in the public library, and tells his wife, Hilda, "They say there may be a pre-emptive strike, dear." "Oh, not *another* strike," says Hilda, bringing James his sausages and chips. "It's wicked. I'd have them all locked up. Blessed Communists." "It's not that sort of strike, duck," says Jim. "It looks as if there's going to be a war, dear."

You tell yourself that Raymond Briggs must be kidding us as an announcement comes over the Bloggs's radio about "the

deteriorating international situation . . . warning the country . . . preparations are under way . . . outbreak of hostilities . . . fallout shelters . . . three days time. . . ." You're sure he isn't going to go through with it, as James tells Hilda, "We'd better commence the construction of the fallout shelter immediately, dear. We must do the correct thing," and Hilda puts her best cushions in plastic bags to protect them from any radioactive dust.

And then, sure enough, with the simple eloquence of a blank double-page spread, whose horrifying whiteness shades gradually on the following pages to pink, then red, then crimson and then back to the dark green and brown of the Bloggs's shelter, punctuated finally by a word balloon containing a simple, monstrously understated "Blimey!"—Armageddon comes, and we are in a place to which no picture book has ever taken us before.

I suppose that in this unexplored land almost any touch of satire runs the risk of seeming heavy-handed. That may be why I worried over the digs that Mr. Briggs resorts to in the wake of the end of civilization. In the wake of the ultimate catastrophe, James Bloggs continues to fret over whether he is following "Govern-mental specifications" to the letter, as if the British welfare state could succeed where all else has failed. Hilda goes about her routine of dusting and mopping, but wonders why she is feeling "all hot and shivery."

Together, they pass the empty time by reminiscing about the last war ("Yes, it was nice in the war, really") and speculate what they will do if a German soldier should show up: "Oh no, sorry. That's last time. I *keep* forgetting. It's the Russkies, now." Hilda complains that "There was blood when I went to the toilet this morning." "Yes, me too," says James. "Piles, that is, Humanoids. A common complaint in middle-aged people like ourselves. I'll pop down the chemists when the crisis pales into insignificance—get some of those suppositories." Humor has rarely been blacker.

It may be too much, or it may simply be that I was nervous in the presence of such an audacious project. One wants it to work. Yet somehow one can't believe that it is going to work. It seems bound to deteriorate into a message. Besides, Mr. Briggs can't possibly kill off these dumb, lovable people, can he? Yet how in the scorched and barren world is he going to get them out of their predicament?

In the end—and it *is* the end—the book does work, despite the vaudeville comedy and heavy-handedness. Using the simple materials of comic-book art, Mr. Briggs has fashioned a statement about the incomprehensibility of nuclear war that is more eloquent in its way than Jonathan Schell's "The Fate of the Earth." In the end, alone and dying in their dark little shelter, James and Hilda decide to pray. ("Who to?" asks Hilda. "Well, God, of course.") They stumble around the 23d Psalm, the wedding ceremony and other scriptural clichés, then give up. "That was nice, dear," says Hilda. "I liked the bit about the green pastures." "Oh yes," answers her husband. "Into the Valley of the Shadow of Death . . . rode the Six Hundred. . . ."

Christopher Lehmann-Haupt, in a review of "When the Wind Blows," in The New York Times, September 14, 1982, p. C7.

Two recently released books attempt to answer an obvious need to present nuclear war in terms intelligible to young people. *Hiroshima No Pika* and **When the Wind Blows** present much of their information on war as pictures and the rest as simple text. Neither is for very young children, however, and *When the Wind Blows* is aimed, one guesses, for, at the youngest, a teenage audience.

Hiroshima No Pika by artist Toshi Maruki is the true story of a mother and child in Japan in 1945 who flee from the atomic blast that has reduced their home to rubble. (pp. 39-40)

Maruki presents the inhuman destruction as gently as possible and in human terms, so that what is stressed is an individual's courage and responsibility.... [The] conclusion a child might draw is that preventing another use of atomic weapons is something children and grownups should work to achieve. All is calculated to avoid freezing the young reader in miserable helplessness.

When the Wind Blows is another matter entirely. It would make devastating reading for anyone so young or innocent as to lack a protective cynicism.... The tone of the narrative is bitterly ironic. Following government safety guidelines is of course useless; common sense is useless; good cheer is useless; optimism and bravery are mere self-delusion. Hilda and Jim Bloggs are chirpy, plump, common-sensical little figures. Like all cartoon figures they have the seeming innocence of animals, which makes their betrayal and death all the more heartbreaking....

This is not really a book for teenagers about nuclear war, any more than *Macbeth* is a play for teenagers about government. Young people read the one, however, and they might as well read the other, provided there is somebody around to discuss the book with and make sense of the reading.

Both these new titles are excellent, and both will meet a real need. But no book can provide an adequate approach to a subject so hideous.... If we allow our children to read one of these books we had best be prepared with whatever antidote to new-born horror we can provide, for anything less than a strong show of active opposition to our doom will merely augment our children's sense of helplessness. (p. 40)

> *Penelope Mesic, in a review of "When the Wind Blows," in* Bulletin of the Atomic Scientists, *Vol. 39, No. 2, February, 1983, pp. 39-40.*

From England, a shocker.... Three times the pattern of the format is broken by a dark, foreboding double-page spread: a space missile is launched, a malevolent black shape looms in the ocean, and the shadows of bombers move across a cold gray sky. For all its sardonic humor, the book is tough and grim, focused on its message and effective in conveying that message despite the details that slow the pace but ramify the concept that many—if not most—of us are uninformed and unprepared in the event of nuclear war.

> *Zena Sutherland, in a review of "When the Wind Blows," in* Bulletin of the Center for Children's Books, *Vol. 36, No. 6, February, 1983, p. 103.*

The allusions, exaggerations, humor are all terribly British: "After all, you don't get a Nuclear Bomb every day of the week, do you?" The woman is, typically, more uninformed than her spouse, but in their very ordinariness, their passivity in the face of destruction, they typify the masses (ourselves included).

This graphic vision of the end of days is powerful in its simplicity and will provoke much serious discussion when used programmatically. Implied, of course, is a strongly anti-nuclear arms position. Highly recommended.

> *Esther Nussbaum, in a review of "When the Wind Blows," in* Voice of Youth Advocates, *Vol. 6, No. 2, June, 1983, p. 101.*

Can you envision a child's picture book on the outcome of nuclear warfare? I couldn't until I saw Raymond Briggs' book....

Briggs provides a stark visual explanation of the Bloggs' predicament. The colors in the cartoons progress from vivid hues in the beginning to washed-out hues toward the end.

Though its content and format could be controversial, this book is a necessary item for any junior or senior high school which includes nuclear issues in the curriculum.

> *Eileen Binckley, in a review of "When the Wind Blows," in* The Book Report, *Vol. 2, No. 2, September-October, 1983, p. 55.*

FUNGUS THE BOGEYMAN PLOP-UP BOOK (1982)

There are four 1982 pop-up titles which could well become classics. **Fungus the Bogeyman Plop-Up Book** ..., with its murky jokes and slimy humour, is one [; the others are *Giorgio's Village* by Tomie de Paola, *Lavinia's Cottage* by John Goodall, and *The Crocodile and the Dumper Truck* by Ray Marshall and Korky Paul.] ... **Fungus** will probably appeal to teenagers as a cult book, but also to young children and, no doubt, a large number of childish adults. It has a crudeness which is rather breathtaking, but as a complete book it works.

> *Linda Yeatman, in a review of "Fungus the Bogeyman Plop-Up Book," in* British Book News Children's Supplement, *Autumn, 1982, p. 3.*

[**Fungus the Bogeyman Plop-up Book**] is an ingenious sequel to Raymond Briggs' first **Fungus** book with which the young delight in disgusting their elders. A feat to wonder at, but without the gloriously detailed slimy horrors of the original.

> *A review of "Fungus the Bogeyman Plop-Up Book," in* The Times Educational Supplement, *No. 3464, November 19, 1982. p. 36.*

Fungus is already a cult figure with many teenagers and adults, and his fans will be delighted to find there are plenty of slimy jokes spread liberally throughout this new book. Perhaps the most unpleasant (a compliment in Fungus terms) is the Umbilical Cord which Bogeymen use 'to discharge noxious stomach gasses into D. C. bedrooms'. Fungus as a Plop-Up has the look of a classic in the making for it has been thought through by Raymond Briggs and [paper engineer] Ron van der Meer to the finest details and will attract an ageless public who have a sense of humour and can enjoy a sick joke too. (p. 32)

> *Linda Yeatman, "Paper Engineering—A New Art Form," in* Books for Your Children, *Vol. 17, No. 3, Autumn-Winter, 1982, pp. 32-3.* *

THE TIN-POT FOREIGN GENERAL AND THE OLD IRON WOMAN (1984)

If anyone was going to come on bowling antinationalist googlies from the Nursery End it would be Raymond Briggs. Briggs has inventively extended the children's books repertoire into more radically different zones than anybody else. Only he would spot the nursery-tale elements in the Falklands saga: the

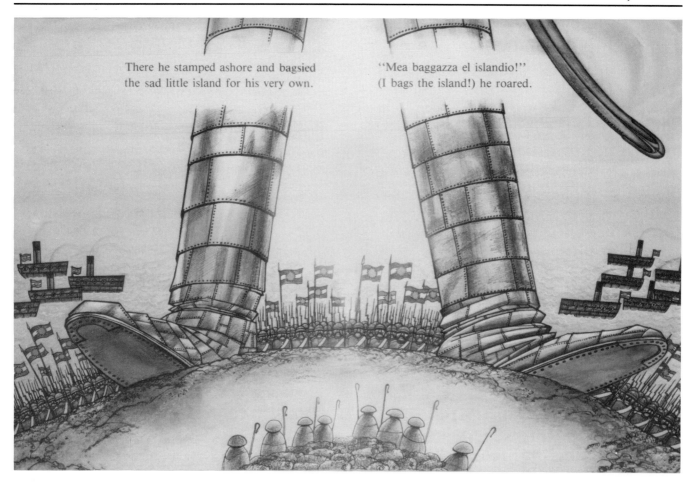

There he stamped ashore and bagsied the sad little island for his very own.

"Mea baggazza el islandio!" (I bags the island!) he roared.

From The Tin-Pot Foreign General and the Old Iron Woman, *written and illustrated by Raymond Briggs. Little, Brown, 1984. Copyright © 1984 by Raymond Briggs. All rights reserved. Reprinted by permission of Little, Brown and Company.*

"sad little island" peopled by harmless shepherds locked into folk-tale rhythms ("mutton for breakfast, mutton for dinner, mutton for tea"), a dour scenario gratuitously worsened by a greedy Wicked Foreign General and then by the sour, equally grabby Old Woman who resists him.

The implied reader for this tale is, evidently, the small child—in appearance very like the little boy who had the friendly adventures with the snowman in Briggs's marvellously gentle *The Snowman* . . .—who is to be found on the last page of *The Tin-Pot Foreign General* looking on as flowers are laid on a grave ("And the families of the dead tended the graves"). This child, or a child like him, is one who, Briggs knows, can take the nastier truths—at least, he can if he's kept up with Briggs in the *Fungus the Bogeyman* books.

Grisliest truth of all is that fairy-tales were right all along about grown-ups. The Tin-Pot General and the Old Iron Woman are just as untrustworthy as "The Recruiting Sergeant" or "Giant Bonaparte" in the nursery rhymes Briggs so cannily illustrated in *The Mother Goose Treasury*. . . . Which is to say that adults behave as selfishly and cruelly as unrestrained children. "I bags the island", cries the Wicked Foreign General. "It's MINE. MINE! MINE! MINE! I bagsied it AGES ago!", ripostes the Old Iron Woman; "I bagsied it FIRST! DID! DID! DID!" Nor is it any consolation that the Bogeyman flying our flag is nastier and more terrifying than the General flying the

other side's colours. With their large and putrescent tongues they are about as hideous as each other, but, it has to be conceded, she is far more dynamic than he is, altogether a more excited and exciting leader, with her astoundingly agile buttocks zestfully beckoning to her troopers as she sits astride the gunship headed for the little island.

None of this horror, though, not even the slight whiff of misogyny that hangs about it, will be too much for the little reader who has stayed with Briggs's grimmer visions and visuals up until now. The telling indications of politics' slipperier contradictions (the General's sword is stamped "Made in Birmingham"; suddenly the Iron Woman has plenty of cash available for warfaring) are only footnotes to Briggs's anti-nuclear volume *When the Wind Blows*. . . . The anti-religious note ("and everyone went to Church and Thanked God")is routine in Briggs's texts (the good Bogeys, we learnt ages ago, dislike vicars and like to "do" them; the disabling of Gentleman Jim and his missus began when they only got Bible and Prayer-book out of their schooling). The ships sailing now this way, now that towards the little island, and the guns firing now from this side now from the other, are merely updated Grand Old Duke of York stuff. What will extend the young reader's moral and political education beyond *When the Wind Blows,* is the use of a more grown-up cartoon style to depict the horrific effects upon the fighting soldiers of the little island warfare. The vociferously colourful, broad-brush style in which the Tin-

Pot General and the Iron Woman are drawn—apt to their declared unreality and the brash rhetorics that sustain them—suddenly gives way towards the end of the book to a softer, impressionistic, style, showing men being shot, drowned, burned, blown to bits, returned home in a vast box of dead bodies or "with parts of their bodies missing". Unlike those fantasy heroes of Jim, "they were all real men, made of flesh and blood. They were not made of Tin or of Iron".

Such sobering thoughts demand, and get, their sobering images. And neither the reflections—which are, of course, partisan, slanted, biased, ideologically clear-cut in their wry pacifism—nor the accompanying images can be thought of by anybody familiar with Briggs's work as a betrayal of a previous talent nor as a significant deviation from the previous directions of his work. Briggs has been making his young readers progressively more alert to the awfulness of war for some time now (and they rather admire this directed earnestness). He has long tried to give voice and identity to a repressed class of small-time victims—adults pitiably like children, the good bogeys, children themselves. So it's only natural that he should seek to make us mindful of that war's throng of unsung amputees. "But the soldiers with bits of their bodies missing were not invited to take part in the Grand Parade, in case the sight of them spoiled the rejoicing. Some watched from a grandstand and others stayed at home with their memories and their medals."

Valentine Cunningham, "The Recruiting Sergeant Goes Further," in The Times Literary Supplement, *No. 4253, October 5, 1984, p. 1139.*

[In *The Tin-Pot Foreign General and the Old Iron Woman*], Raymond Briggs continues the anti-war protest that he made so tellingly in *When the Wind Blows*. . . . This bold and bitter allegory of the Falklands conflict, however, is slightly less successful in putting across its message than its subtle and tender forerunner. Briggs is so anxious to point out the tragically destructive ramifications of nationalism that he oversimplifies certain facts. He neglects, for instance, to mention that many (probably most of?) the "poor shepherds" on "the sad little island" so much wanted to get rid of "the tin-pot foreign general" that they welcomed the determination of "the old iron woman" to "bagsy" back their country, even though this might ultimately mean people would be shot or maimed or drowned. Nevertheless this book will deservedly be influential, and appreciated by adults as well as children. One can only be grateful that Briggs has decided once again to use the tremendous power of his pictures to explode the concept that any group or nation can ever "win" a war. (pp. 22-3)

Mary Cadogan, "Animal Antics," in Books and Bookmen, *No. 350, November, 1984, pp. 22-3.**

Raymond Briggs has written a moving, necessary and bitter story in *The Tin Pot Foreign General and the Old Iron Woman*. . . .

Raymond Briggs does his book and his little (and not so little) readers a great injustice in rendering the Iron Woman and the Tin Pot General in such a literal and crude manner. She is an ugly, iron-plated monster, he is made of tin pots. It is easy for children to believe that these hideous, robot-like creatures could cause such horror to happen. It would mean far more if they were to feel that quite normal looking human beings, not so different from the grown-ups they know, could wreak such havoc. This awareness might help to develop a distaste for violence from early childhood.

A review of "The Tin Pot Foreign General and the Old Iron Woman," in The Economist, *Vol. 293, No. 7370, December 1, 1984, p. 110.*

Those who are already familiar with Raymond Briggs's chilling account of nuclear attack upon Britain in *When the Wind Blows* . . . will know what to expect, but quite a number of people will be very cross indeed at this further example of the artist's growing disenchantment (disgust is perhaps a better word) with violence in the modern world.

To be angry, however, is to miss the point entirely. Whatever feelings one may have or have had about the war in the South Atlantic, the satire in these pages is piercing and brilliant. . . .

Raymond Briggs's superbly drawn pictures remind us vividly that the art of angry satire is not entirely dead, and that the bubble of pomposity can be pricked. Whether one agrees with the artist's view or not, the publication of this searing book can only be a healthy sign, and does not in any way belittle or call into question acts of individual heroism. Indeed, the unspoken question underlying his book is quite simply: to what extent do the bravery and endurance of ordinary men and women redeem the bombast of political and military leaders? There are no easy answers, but Briggs's book provokes serious thought about one.

Victor Neuburg, in a review of "The Tin-Pot Foreign General and the Old Iron Woman," in British Book News, *January, 1985, p. 47.*

"Nationalism is an infantile disease. It is the measles of mankind," says Albert Einstein, and Dr. Johnson concurs, "Patriotism is the last refuge of a scoundrel." With epigrams from these two luminaries, Raymond Briggs begins his book on one of the three things—religion, sex and politics—that adults are advised not to discuss in polite society and that children are least interested in reading about.

It is a befuddling book. The title conjures up memories of nonsense masterpieces like *The Owl and the Pussycat* or famous fables like *The Tortoise and the Hare*. But this is not a book of nonsense and, more to the point, it is not a fable.

The title also refers to Argentina and England—the book, I'm told, is a best seller in Great Britain—and the story tells of a "sad little island" at the bottom of the world, on which no one lives but a few poor shepherds and their sheep. There is a Wicked Foreign General who "was not real. He was made of Tin Pots." In the illustrations, this general's body is tin, topped with curling mustachios; a bomber jet is clenched between tin teeth. His enemy, "an old woman with lots of money and guns . . . made of Iron" is shown with exposed rump, and with breasts which fire cannons and explode fireworks. She is dressed in iron high heels, garters, and a scant pair of iron panties. Colors for these illustrations are lurid primaries.

True to expectation, the Tin-Pot Foreign General lands on the sad little island and "bagsies" it. The Old Iron Woman, eyes drawn in mesmerizing concentric rings, opens her iron breasts from which pour gold coins. She buys boats, and heads to the island. "BANG! BANG! BANG!" go the guns of the Tin-Pot Foreign General and the Old Iron Woman, as surely as the ducks on Old MacDonald's farm go "quack quack here" and "quack quack there."

We turn the page and face a powerful change. "Some men were shot." "Some men were drowned." "Some men were burned alive." On five consecutive pages appear human soldiers in subtle, sensitive, black-and-white drawings. These are not political sketches nor editorial cartoons; they look more like genuine war-correspondence material: simple, quick pencil or conté crayon exercise of a corpse sinking quietly in the ocean, a lacerated human form on fire.

Returning to the action, the Old Iron Woman's soldiers win out over the Tin-Pot Foreign General's soldiers, of course, the island is a shambles, and the bodies of the dead and maimed soldiers are returned home. "After this, there was a Grand Parade to celebrate the Great Victory and everyone went to Church and Thanked God." On the penultimate page, the two styles of art come together in a simple pencil sketch of the family of a one-legged veteran sitting in the parlor before a television, from whose screen radiate the electric reds and blues of the hypnotic face of the Iron Lady, grinning in glee. The families of the dead, we are told on the last page, "tended the graves."

The issues of war and peace are not new to children's books, nor is concern with picture-book treatment of adult themes. Last year Dr. Seuss's *The Butter Battle Book* had reviewers, consumers, and professionals up in arms, as it were, over using a picture book to show a stalemate nuclear confrontation, without suggesting that reasonableness, humanism, or sheer political ingenuity might release some of the pressure. Two years earlier, there was [Toshi Maruki's] *Hiroshima No Pika,* a full-color expressionistic recollection of the Hiroshima bombing, told from a child's apolitical perspective. Natalie Babbitt, in the *New York Times Book Review,* citing some of the problems of picture-book treatments of adult themes, concluded that "you would not hang Picasso's *Guernica* in the nursery."

The problem with these books lies in their reliance on a form which is unsuitable to their themes. Dr. Seuss is an adept fabulist and fabler. His *Horton Hears A Who* is a stirring call for the right to exist as a minority culture. The story works because the form of the fable is honored, the story is shaped with tension and resolution, and the moral is stated, in true fable fashion, loudly and clearly and often: "A person's a person, no matter how small." The very small person, hearing this from the protective shelter of an adult lap, can appreciate the sentiment because it has something to do with the story as well as with life as a child.

Seuss's *Butter Battle* and Maruki's *Hiroshima,* and even more Briggs's current book, are commentaries on society's behavior, not on the behavior of individuals. As such, although compelling, they may not be suitable for young children. A fable must have a moral, implicit or explicit. It needn't have *morals,* necessarily, but it must have a moral. . . .

The Tin-Pot Foreign General and the Old Iron Woman is a fable without a moral; a fantasy in which the mythical creatures are portrayed pornographically and in color, the human creatures in soft pencil. It is powerful, chillingly conceived, and painstakingly executed. But who is it for?

The book may be taken up by adults, who can postulate for themselves the unstated moral, if they want one, or bear to live without it if they choose. Middle-school children may look at the book, if they're not too big for their britches. But small children? How will they respond to the Iron Woman? Or to the shifts in style of artwork, or the subtle and sophisticated messages behind them? Children may throw the book across the room. Too bad, too bad. There is a place for this very book in our society, despite the horrendous imagery. But the book isn't for young children, not as the incomplete fable it is—not yet. Old MacDonald's farm will become Animal Farm all too soon.

Gregory Maguire, in a review of "The Tin-Pot Foreign General and the Old Iron Woman," in Boston Review, *Vol. X, No. 4, September, 1985, p. 27.*

Margaret Wise Brown

1910-1952

(Also wrote as Golden MacDonald, Juniper Sage, and Timothy Hay) American author of picture books, poet, reteller, editor, and translator.

Brown is recognized as an important pioneer of concept books for preschoolers. The author of more than ninety picture books including such classics as *Goodnight Moon, The Runaway Bunny,* and the "Noisy Books", she expressed a sensitive awareness of the emotional and intellectual development of the young child. Brown's involvement in storytelling as a student at the Bank Street College of Education convinced her of the need for a body of stimulating nursery-age books, a field neglected by publishers of the 1930s. She subsequently wrote and published anthropomorphic tales which incorporate poetry, fantasy, and realistic topics such as occupations and animal behavior. Most notably, her works reflect innovative experiments in such areas as sense perception, size comparison, and audience participation. Written from a child's perspective, Brown's books convey the warmth of maternal love, the need for independence, and an appreciation of nature. Her texts, with their reassuring themes, instinctive rhythm, and comfortable repetition of phrases and ideas, continue to delight children three decades after her death.

Reviewers applaud Brown's strength as a poet while acknowledging her techniques as a storyteller. Though her tales are sometimes thought to be slight, they are repeatedly praised for their musical cadence, childlike humor, and uncondescending simplicity.

(See also *Yesterday's Authors of Books for Children,* Vol. 2; *Contemporary Authors,* Vol. 108; and *Dictionary of Literary Biography,* Vol. 22: *American Writers for Children, 1900-1960.*)

AUTHOR'S COMMENTARY

Writing for children is an exciting field in which to be working today because it is still pure. It is the only field of writing where something tried for the first time, provided it works on children, is welcomed with open arms. Of course it is a field full of whimsy and money mongering and inferior images, but the real thing is always welcome—Sense or Nonsense—because children under six will recognize it.

It is not hard to trace an interest in children's books through a love of the English language. I don't think I am essentially interested in children's books. I'm interested in writing, and in pictures. I'm interested in people and in children because they are people—little primitive people—keener in some ways than they themselves will be later on. And, I am interested in simplicity. In children's books all these combine.

The first thing I can remember that started my curiosity and amusement in children was a story of Miss Susie Blair's, about a little boy who used to walk around murmuring to himself: "Miss Nancy Owl walked down the street with her eyes full of tears." A year or two after College, as luck would have it, I ran into what seemed an unexplored field—the field of very young picture books for children under five. It is still a large

and fascinating field and still relatively unexplored because no one dares to be simple enough. Much is needed that doesn't exist. A book for a child under five years of age is a colorful medium. For a picture book is like a still life or a very short play or a static ballet where the only action is in the turn of the pages, the start at the beginning and the stop at the end, the timing and the pace of the whole book, the long, slow rhythms and the sudden jumps of the writing itself.

I dream some of my stories—never have any idea at the beginning of a story of what the end will be and usually take from 15 to 20 minutes to write one down. Then I sometimes take a year or more to try the story on children and listen to it and make sure the words fall true and that the story isn't too long or too short and that I haven't included too much of the nonsense that someone who is no longer a child is apt to put into a children's book. Timing in picture books, as in everything, is of the essence.

As for the "Noisy Books," their design and creation came right from children themselves—from listening to them, watching them and letting them into the story when they were much too young to sit without a word for the length of time it takes to read a full-length story to them. I mean three and two-year-olds. Dogs will also be interested in the "Noisy Books" the first time they hear them read with any convincing suddenness and variety of whistles, squeaks, hisses, thuds and sudden silences following an unexpected ''BANG''! Children wrote those books and I was merely an ear and a pen. And also by some accident, one who shared their pleasure or inattention with them.

Anyway—this all becomes very abstract as the basis of all design will become if you talk about it too much. I do not remember many books when I was a child. At that time I was too busy. ''The Song of Roland,'' the story of ''The Golden Fleece,'' ''Black Beauty,'' ''Beautiful Joe,'' ''Peter Rabbit'' and ''Snow White'' were all true to me and ''Aladdin'' was the most exciting of all the fairy tales.

It did not seem important then that any one wrote these stories. They were true. And it still doesn't seem important! All this emphasis today on who writes what seems silly to me as far as children are concerned. That is why I use so many names— ''Timothy Hay, Juniper Sage, Golden MacDonald, Hurricane Jones, Daisy Clover, Pussywillow Brown.'' What does it matter what name you use? All I want to do is to write a story that seems absolutely true to the child who hears it and to myself. True as ''Hansel and Gretel,'' true as ''Brer Rabbit,'' true and wonderful as Aladdin and his wonderful lamp. Maybe it takes a couple of hundred years of story telling to sift out the symbolism and purity of such tales. I have written about sixty-four books for a younger level, and I keep writing them because I like to make them up or maybe because I can't stop when they are so badly needed. (pp. 1, 14)

But, before anyone goes into the field of writing, let them have already fallen in love with Chaucer's affectionate naming of all the things in his world about him; Shakespeare's pounding rhythms and certain meanings and some of Wordsworth for his simplicity—Dr. Janney—''The light as of a single star when only one is shining in the sky.''

If you want to make money, open up a Grocery Store. For the problem of writing is the same for any age—to be utterly simple, and as clear cut as the fine King James English. . . . And also to appreciate Susie Blair's story of the little boy still murmuring to himself along the Scottsville Road—''Miss Nancy Owl walked down the street with her eyes full of tears.'' (p. 14)

Margaret Wise Brown, ''Writing for Children,'' in Hollins Alumnae Magazine, *Vol. XXII, No. 2, Winter, 1949, pp. 1, 14.*

GENERAL COMMENTARY

BRUCE BLIVEN, JR.

[Margaret Wise Brown holds] solid claim to the title of World's Most Prolific Picture-Book Writer. . . . (p. 59)

Writing for young children looks easy. An entire book may contain 300 words of text, or even less. The words are simple. It is not as easy as it looks, however, because children are a merciless audience. An author of picture books may fool publishers and adults some of the time; the unavoidable test is what happens when the child hears the story. Most of Miss Brown's 53 books, put to this trial, are a rollicking success. Her ''noisy books'' (*The City Noisy Book, The Country Noisy Book, The Seashore Noisy Book* and *The Indoor Noisy Book*) are written in sounds and questions that bring the child into the story. They concern a small sightless dog, Muffin, who trots around hearing noises: an automobile's ''awuurra awuurra,'' an airplane's ''rrrrr,'' a frog's ''Jugar jugarum,'' a vacuum

cleaner's ''mmmzzmmmmmmmmmm'' or the hush of a very quiet custard. Nothing could be more fascinating to a four-year-old than listening to his parents' struggles with the vocal demands of the text or more hilarious than the books' surprise questions: ''It began to snow. But could Muffin hear that?'' (pp. 60-1)

[One] of Miss Brown's writing principles [is] that it is valuable to appeal to *all* the senses of a very young audience. Five-year-old children, she maintains, reach a peak of sensory awareness and she therefore likes the challenge of writing for them. After five, she says, the average child's perception, especially in touch, taste and smell, begins to dull. ''Once in a great while,'' Miss Brown says, ''a five-year-old retains his awareness and then he becomes either a painter, a writer or a poet.'' (p. 62)

''A picture book,'' Miss Brown says, ''must be dramatic, and much of the drama is in turning over the pages.'' One dramatic device, recurrent in the collected Brown works, is contrast. The biggest noise on the street, the fire engine, is immediately followed by the sound, if any, of the sun shining. The foghorn is followed by the flutter of little birds' wings, the whistle of the ocean liner by a sailboat sailing by. Miss Brown also thinks a book should include at least a couple of words too big and cumbersome for her youthful listeners, a theory which drives many child psychologists, teachers and librarians, professionally committed to safe and sane age-level word lists, into shocked outrage. Miss Brown loves to tuck in words like ''sanctimonious'' and ''ruminating,'' phrases like ''by the incredible velvet that grows on your nose, you are a rapscallion cat.'' ''I once read a book in French to the Threes,'' says Miss Brown with a note of triumph in her voice. ''They couldn't understand a word. They loved every syllable.'' (p. 64)

Bruce Bliven, Jr., ''Child's Best Seller,'' in Life Magazine, *Vol. 21, No. 23, December 2, 1946, pp. 59-62, 64, 66.*

ELLEN LEWIS BUELL

The indefatigable Miss Brown has added two more volumes to that long bookshelf which bears her name. **''Two Little Trains,''** for 4-to-7-year-olds is probably the more enduring of the two. One little train was a streamliner, carrying a little boy; the other was a little old train carrying a girl and assorted livestock. Their parallel (and curiously simultaneous) trip across the continent is described in infectious rhythms—some of them reminiscent of ''The Lonesome Road''. . . .

''My World'' is for the very youngest onlookers and listeners of 2 to 4 who will recognize in the snug bunny home many of those first objects which they are learning to call by name. There are ''my car, Daddy's car,'' ''My soap, Daddy's soap'' and so on. Obviously, this isn't very sturdy stuff, but the book does furnish a pleasant mnemonic device while interest lasts. . . .

Ellen Lewis Buell, ''Trains and Bunnies,'' in The New York Times Book Review, *December 18, 1949, p. 12.*

MARCIA WINN

These three utterly enchanting books [**''The Peppermint Family,'' ''The Dream Book,''** and **''The Quiet NOISY Book''**] for the 4 year old set are reviewed in a group because all were written by Margaret Wise Brown, poet, songwriter, and author, whose books for children unfailingly have distinction. In all three are combined the gravity, the dreams, and the bright scintillant humor of childhood. Each is an exceptional book. . . .

My own favorite of the three is **"The Quiet NOISY Book,"** but, while the 4 year old on whom I tried all, likes it and **"The Dream Book"** as well, it is **"The Peppermint Family"** (who had a baby named Chocolate with a peppermint bassinet and a peppermint rattle) that she demands to hear and see over and over again.

> *Marcia Winn, in a review of "The Peppermint Family," "The Dream Book," and "The Quiet NOISY Book," in* Chicago Tribune, *Part 4, November 12, 1950, p. 4.*

ELLEN LEWIS BUELL

Taken together [**"Where Have You Been?"** and **"Pussy Willow"**] resemble one of Miss Brown's familiar counterpoints: there is a great big book and there is a very little book—or, at least, comfortably little. And like many of her other books these both deal with the world of small creatures illuminated with a pleasant kind of nonsense. The little book, **"Where Have You Been?"** is the more appealing and more childlike. Here are crisp little verses about a frog, a toad, a bunny and other familiar animals. They are the kind of poetry which young children learn by heart without knowing it and they are also easy reading for beginners. . . .

"Pussy Willow" is a big picture book about a gray kitten who searches all through the year for his namesakes, the pussy willows. The animals whom he questions answer according to their own ways of life, which isn't very helpful, nor is it very helpful, either, when Pussy Willow discovers finally that "Everything that anyone would ever look for is usually where they find it." The charming word sounds and imagery don't quite carry the slight theme.

> *Ellen Lewis Buell, "Small Creatures," in* The New York Times Book Review, *February 17, 1952, p. 34.*

LOUISE S. BECHTEL

In her new Little Golden Book [**"Mister Dog"**], Miss Brown tells of a dog "who belonged to himself." We think we have seen Crispin's Crispian, and we are sure that if he lived in a house like this one, he would keep house, cook, dine, sleep, just as he does here. It is a charming turn of affairs for a dog to bring home a boy, and we think very small boys will love both story and [Garth Williams's] pictures. It is silly, gay, sunny, doggy, and comfortable.

For **"The Noon Balloon,"** we cannot work up much enthusiasm. A little cat goes off on a balloon ride, and that's all there is to it. . . . [The] story has little point.

> *Louise S. Bechtel, in a review of "A Child's Good Morning," "Mister Dog," and "The Noon Balloon," in* New York Herald Tribune Book Review, *November 16, 1952, p. 3.*

LOUISE S. BECHTEL

[In **"Sleepy ABC"**] Miss Brown invents charming rhymes offering pleasant ideas for the very small child on his way to bed. Most of the ideas are yawning, dreamy, listening. We like "U is for nothing Under the bed." . . .

[**"The Sailor Dog"** is a] very real little dog book. "Born at sea, in the teeth of a gale, the sailor was a dog, Scuppers was his name." . . . Here is a very small child's idea of a sea venture, told through the medium of a most lovable dog. . . . It is the special treasure among the new Little Golden Books.

What a contrast is . . . [**"The Hidden House"**] about Miss Brown's own beloved "hidden house," her little white farm in the heart of the city. We doubt that children will like this quiet description and disappointing ending.

> *Louise S. Bechtel, in a review of "Sleepy ABC," "The Sailor Dog," and "The Hidden House," in* New York Herald Tribune Book Review, *May 17, 1953, p. 10.*

ELLEN LEWIS BUELL

Margaret Wise Brown's too-early death last November deprived the children's book field of one of its most original and prolific writers. Of her more than seventy published books for very young children some were, inevitably, tenuous and some were repetitious, but at her best she was inimitable. . . . Of the four most recent there is none which quite measures up to **"The Noisy Books"** or **"Wait Till the Moon Is Full,"** but each has a measure of Miss Brown's characteristic imagination and unpredictable humor.

The narrative of **"The Duck"** is skillfully fashioned around Ylla's photographs of a brash young duck who is equally intent upon seeing the world and being seen. . . . Miss Brown has endowed the duck with personality and points up his encounters with hippopotamus, chimpanzee, rooster and puppy with amusing dialogue.

"The Hidden House" tells of a little boy's discovery of one of those tiny relics still to be found if one looks hard enough among the skyscrapers of New York. It is every youngster's house as he would like it to be—private, cozy, furnished with the everyday objects which a very young child delights in recognizing. Here once again Miss Brown showed her awareness of what is important in the early years of life. . . .

The same feeling for domestic details is ingeniously combined with adventure in **"The Sailor Dog."** Scuppers, the seagoing hero, manages to make himself comfortable whether aboard ship or cast away in Crusoe style. For all its brevity this nonsense tale has a swing to it. . . .

In **"The Golden Bunny"** poetry and prose are intermingled in that distinctive fashion which has helped make Miss Brown's books so popular with the nursery set. This is a big, thin picture book of eighteen stories and verses about rabbits. For the most part, the so-called stories are little more than sketches of mood and atmosphere. The most memorable parts of the book are certain haunting little verses and the pictures by Leonard Weisgard.

> *Ellen Lewis Buell, "A Duck and Others," in* The New York Times Book Review, *May 17, 1953, p. 24.*

LOIS PALMER

[Margaret Wise Brown's] directness, her use of color and sound and of reality and the imaginary—with sometimes a happy blending of the two—have made many of her books long-time favorites for which children ask again and again. It is very probable that [**"Whistle for the Train,"** **"Three Little Animals,"** and **"David's Little Indian"**] will also be cherished additions to a child's library.

"Whistle for the Train," will be enjoyed by all young children, but it is an especially good find for the 2 and 3-year-olds, for whom too few books are written. This is the story of a busy little train going steadily on its way, told with nice onomatopoeic clickety-clack sounds and with gentle, firm warnings to animals and children to stay off the track. (pp. 48-9)

"Three Little Animals" stars three furry, bearlike creatures of the woods. Fascinated by the world of people just beyond their home, they dress up in human clothes or an approximation thereof and join the crowd. It is a lonely experience because they don't recognize each other in their new clothing. All ends happily when a wind blows away their hats; they return to their rightful place in the woods. . . .

The story of **"David's Little Indian"** has an unusual and particularly pleasing theme. The little Indian—no bigger than an ear of corn—whom David discovers is named Carpe Diem, and "seize the day" is just what these two do with great mutual enjoyment. For them each day has a special meaning—Day of the Moon in the Day, Day of the Birds' Flying Away—and so on until the wonders of the changing season have been noted. There is an appreciation for the excitement of each one as it happened. . . . (p. 49)

> Lois Palmer, "Trio," in The New York Times, November 18, 1956, pp. 48-9.

MARGOT DUKLER

[**The Noisy Books**] are probably one of the best-known series of children's stories. They all tell the story of a little dog named Muffin who heard things, all kinds of funny, different things. They appeal primarily to the younger levels of pre-schoolers, from two to four years.

The success of these books lies in three things: (1) the warm and sweet character of "the little dog Muffin," (2) the chance for active and involved participation, which is not gratuitous, but really necessary to the story, and (3) the illustrations. . . .

In these stories, the children identify with Muffin. He is good, he is sweet, he has the usual troubles that young children have, he gets colds, he gets presents, he eats lunch. Such a simple life is the life of the young child. The world around him is just beginning to take on new meanings, and there is much for him to learn. He learns some of it with the help of Muffin, whose specialty is listening and hearing whimsical, wonderful things. (p. 7)

The opportunity for participation really "makes" these books. Anyone sitting in on a group listening to one of these stories is amazed by the intense interest and involvement; one teacher notes that even though her children all know the ending, they wait eagerly to hear it read and resent anyone's giving it away before the proper time. There is perhaps no more suspenseful thing in the life of a two-year-old (figuratively speaking) than waiting to see just what it is that is coming up the stairs to Muffin's room:

Was it a little bug coming to see Muffin?	NO
Was it an elephant coming to see Muffin?	NO
Was it a soldier?	NO
Was it a duck?	NO
Was it a clown with a firecracker?	NO
What could it be?	
It was the cat, of course.	

In the **Winter Noisy Book,** Miss Brown is more poetic, still whimsical:

And then he heard a little noise . . .
soft, soft, soft in the growing darkness.

What could it be?	
Was it a big balloon going up to the moon?	NO
Was it the sound of something brittle and shining and full of air breaking into a hundred little golden pieces?	NO
Was it a big butterfly flying through the night?	NO
Was it someone telling a secret?	NO
What do you think it was?	
It was the snow falling out of the sky, of course.	

And Muffin caught a snowflake on
his little black nose and ate it up.

This is lovely writing, coming from inside a person who still shares many of the child-world secrets and thoughts. This is here-and-now mixed with a lot of imagination and creative ability, and it comes out first-rate.

The **Muffin** books present no unusual situations, no threatening problems, they provoke no great anxieties. They take the usual, and make it unusual, by the merest twist of language. They do what a good book should do—they throw new light on a familiar aspect of life. (pp. 7-8)

> Margot Dukler, in a review of "The Noisy Books," in Elementary English, Vol. XXXV, No. 1, January, 1958, pp. 7-8.

LOUISE SEAMAN BECHTEL

[Bechtel was a distinguished critic and editor of children's literature as well as a friend of Brown. The following essay is based on a speech given by Bechtel commemorating the opening of the Margaret Wise Brown Collection at the Westerly Public Library in Westerly, Rhode Island.]

What do writers care most about? My answer would be two simple things: first, that they continue to feel a joy in the act of writing; second, that their work be published so that possibly it may live. Margaret Wise Brown was one whose joy in writing was most obvious to all who knew her. She wanted her books published even more than most writers because she conceived them as picture books and couldn't wait to see the picture part completed. She had that satisfaction to a remarkable degree, with the added joy of huge sales which told her she had delighted many children. . . .

Probably humor or fantasy is all one can use who is asked to explain what drives one to publish from four to eight books a year, when it is not financial need. Her inner ambition was to write adult poetry, of which she left a great hoard, all unpublished. . . . She was adult and sophisticated in many ways, yet she never lost the special sensory acuteness of childhood nor a present sense of the real and the dream worlds of her childhood. (p. 173)

At school and college she was chiefly interested in experimental writing and in reading "new" writers. After college she took a short story course at Columbia but said she gave it up because she "couldn't think up any plots." That she was more a poet than a storyteller is obvious in most of her children's books.

Chance suddenly led her into a field of writing she had never considered. She heard of a truly experimental writing group, a class conducted by Lucy Sprague Mitchell at the Bank Street School, then called "The Bureau for Educational Experiment.'' Her very first work there made her happy. She said, ''Experimenting in writing for children is so much less *precious* than doing it for grownups.''

The brilliant Mrs. Mitchell who ruled over ''69 Bank Street'' was the sort of creative person who analyzed writers shrewdly and helped many besides Brownie to find themselves. I often visited her writing classes to criticize or to advise about publication. After one of them Mrs. Mitchell said to me, ''That Brownie bears watching. She is a poet, and really knows small children.''

At Bank Street, Brownie could tell stories to various age groups of children. . . . She took down stories told by children at the Little Red Schoolhouse and said they were ''a revelation of spontaneity, of imagination and of language.'' So she studied lower age levels' ''to find how and when this creative vitality started.'' (pp. 174-76)

Soon she met young William Scott and his partner John McCullough, who were starting a new firm to publish new kinds of books for the ''neglected'' nursery-age child, the age of their own children. She was their first official editor, and author of their first book *Bumblebugs and Elephants*. . . . Printed on stiff cardboard, its ''big and little'' creatures still delight the very youngest. . . .

In 1939 came Brownie's and Scott's first big sales success, *The Noisy Book.* We met the little dog Muffin, with his bandaged eyes, guessing at city things about him by their sounds. A child must guess, as Muffin does, before you turn the page. Thousands of parents found out how their youngest children were all attention for a book they had to talk back to. . . . So a series was started which now has seven titles, all nursery classics. . . . When interviewed about them, Brownie once said that they were intended ''to make children give honest sensory responses, not take them from a page without thinking.'' (p. 176)

During the war, I once met her for lunch at the Museum of Modern Art. . . . I told her I was against her using pseudonyms—''Golden MacDonald'' and ''Juniper Sage''—that they didn't hide her real name from anyone. She gleefully announced a third one, ''Timothy Hay,'' but *he* had only one book, *Horses.* She claimed that each name had a different personality, and publishers didn't like having so many books a year under one name. Probably I told her that success was ruining her.

Be that as it may, ''Golden MacDonald'' wrote some of Brownie's best books. . . . What child could resist *Red Light, Green Light* . . .? What adult could fail to buy *Little Lost Lamb*. . . . Whatever the ''alias'' used on them, these books surely will live as Brownie's.

As ''Juniper Sage'' she collaborated with Edith Thacher Hurd, a friend of the Bank Street days, on that startling book *The Man in the Manhole: and the Fix-it Men*. . . . A new edition has appeared recently, taking children again under city streets to see the mysteries that bring them light, heat, and water. Brownie and Mrs. Hurd also did together the Little Golden Books about firemen, miners, policemen, etc., bringing those heroes to the level of very small children, weaving facts into brief, amusing stories.

Brownie's first Simon and Schuster book was a ''big'' one, *The Golden Egg Book*. . . . It was the essence of spring and a most welcome new version of the Easter bunny idea. It was a great success. . . . (p. 177)

My own firm favorite of [her eighteen Simon and Schuster books] is *Mister Dog,* ''the dog who belonged to himself.'' . . . Dog lovers of all ages chuckle at the details in *Mister Dog* and at the very essence of dogginess in this lovable book. The touch of genius is in creating a small boy who also ''belongs to himself,'' as all little boys realize they do, while they laugh at the pretend boy who lived with a dog.

Brownie could write anywhere and on any old scrap of paper, in an airplane, in the station wagon in front of her grocer's. But of course her homes were important to her books. (p. 178)

[She] bought an old house on the Maine island called Vinal Haven, twelve miles out to sea from Rockland. There she had spent several summers in childhood. . . . In its attic studio, she told me, she felt as if living in treetops, wonderfully alone with the sounds of the sea, ''wanting to think hard but happy just in being.'' The magic of the place, its dramatic changes with mists and tides, seeped into her. No words or ideas about it seemed worthy of it; she waited and waited. ''Suddenly I had the thought that it is such a relief, when we are adults with the bewilderingly gigantic world around us, to remember that we knew, as children, that the world is as big as the part of it we really know.''

So she slowly wrote and rewrote *The Little Island,* with its kitten who learns that the island is both part of the great world and a world of its own. . . . [This book] captures the magic of all islands. (pp. 178-80)

One day [Brownie] showed me her ''Diary,'' kept in an old book with a worn Florentine leather cover. ''What's in it,'' she said, ''isn't facts of my life, but other matters. Dreams— I have wonderful dreams—and I put down interesting colors, and faces, and places. A few stories—here are some told me by children at a school in Harlem. Maybe I'll use them some day, but not as they are here, the children wouldn't like that. They want words better arranged than their own, and a few gorgeous big grownup words to bite on. Most children are so wonderful. After being with them I decide that almost no stories they have are good enough for them. I mean, of course, very small children. One can keep trying new ways to release their own feelings and imaginings.'' (p. 180)

[*The Runaway Bunny*] is a treasure for young mothers to read aloud and for young eyes to look at over and over. Brownie said she was ''using the repeated cadences of an old French love song, transferred to the real world of a small child.'' It has sold on and on. Less popular, but still being reprinted, is *The House of a Hundred Windows* . . . , introducing fifteen modern paintings to children. Each was a window in a magical house where lived only a cat. At the end, ''It was up to the cat!''—whether or not he would go out the door and never return, a mind-stretching question. (pp. 181-82)

And oh! the fun I had with *The Little Fur Family*. . . . Do you remember it, all bound in rabbit skin, in a little box with a hole to show that little fur stomach? That box alone made a kindergarten class roll on the floor with laughter. I had to read it to them over and over. . . . (p. 182)

Of thirty-eight illustrators of her work, Mr. Weisgard has been her most frequent collaborator, with twenty-two titles. His are the books with the most varied styles and moods—he can be funny, real, magical; he can evoke beautiful places, create appealing children and creatures. . . . Clement Hurd, with his power to make the present world both real and touched with magic, and his special understanding of small children, comes next with ten titles. Garth Williams, in nine books, brings to life unforgettable creatures, expressive, wonderfully funny and appealing, always real animals. All three artists were superbly able to fulfill Brownie's book plans and to supplement them with their own different sorts of imagination. But she was in a very real sense a collaborator with each artist, discussing her own layout, their sketches, and all details. When a picture was finished, sometimes she changed some words in the text to fit it better. She generally "pulled out" the best work of every artist. She was always eager for collaborators with "new" styles, such as Lucienne Bloch, Dahlov Ipcar, Symeon Shimin, E. Slobodkina, Marc Simont, Remy Charlip.

An artist whose work Brownie greatly admired and was proud to have illustrate her words was the French-Mexican Jean Charlot. He did *A Child's Goodnight Book* in 1943 and made a larger, revised version of it in 1950. With all his forceful strength and bold design, he still captured the humor and tenderness of the text and took the poetic suggestions a leap further. (pp. 182-83)

Mr. Scott wrote in 1938: "The tremendous success of her books is due to a rare quality: sure emotional insight into the realities of a young child's world bounded by the here and now." With equal discernment, he wrote in 1955: "All her books have an elusive quality that was Margaret Wise Brown. . . . [They have] simplicity, directness, humor, unexpectedness, respect for the reader, and a sense of the importance of living." (pp. 183-84)

In the early days a publisher once asked Brownie, "Have you another manuscript you can show us?" She replied: "I have a big drawer full of them. I dream them up in twenty minutes, then polish some of them for a year." A person who is creative in this way (and I think most truly creative people are prolific) is not apt to be self-critical, that is, as to relative values of separate pieces of writing. Brownie believed in the criticism given her by children themselves. She would often try out manuscripts and finished books on children she knew in various homes and in schools. This way of testing books is far from infallible. But anyone who has seen small children make a beeline for her books knows that, with her, it worked. (p. 184)

The last words should be her own:

> A book can make a child laugh or feel clear-and-happy-headed as he follows a simple rhythm to its logical end. It can jog him with the unexpected and comfort him with the familiar, lift him for a few minutes from his own problems of shoelaces that won't tie and busy parents and mysterious clock-time, into the world of a bug or a bear or a bee or a boy living in the timeless world of story. If I've been lucky, I hope I have written a book simple enough to come near to that timeless world.
>
> (p. 186)

Louise Seaman Bechtel, "Margaret Wise Brown, 'Laureate of the Nursery'," in The Horn Book Magazine, *Vol. XXXIV, No. 3, June, 1958, pp. 173-86.*

MAY HILL ARBUTHNOT

The style of [Margaret Wise Brown's] books was cadenced, the goal was to stimulate the sensory preceptions and awareness of young children.

The Noisy Book . . . was a pioneer in this awareness school of writing. It was followed by several more *Noisy* books. Then there was a series contrasting bigness and littleness. The hero

of *The Little Fisherman* caught little fish and the big fisherman caught big fish, and so it went with *The Little Cowboy* and *The Little Farmer*. Of all these innumerable picture books, . . . two will probably outlive or at least outdistance in popularity all of the others. These are *Little Lost Lamb* and *The Runaway Bunny*. The former tells a real story about a shepherd boy and his dog who retrace their steps up a dangerous mountain after dark to find a lost lamb. . . . *The Runaway Bunny* is a delightful talking-beast tale. . . , with the nearest approach to humor that Margaret Wise Brown ever made. . . . Her contribution lies chiefly in her sensitive perception of the child's sensory responses to the big booming confusion of the world. Her cadenced style comes close to poetry now and then, but her attempts at verse never quite reach poetry. (p. 427)

May Hill Arbuthnot, "Here and Now," in her Children and Books, *third edition, Scott, Foresman and Company, 1964, pp. 426-75.*

ETHEL L. HEINS

Anyone who has ever eavesdropped on small children absorbed in unself-conscious play knows about their fascination with sounds and their flair for mimicry. Dramatizing and giving shape to sounds in all their exciting, endless variety, [*The Noisy Book*]—which featured an irresistible little black dog—openly invited participation. The response of young children was ecstatic. . . . [But its text,] which emphasized emotion rather than conventional punctuation, was viewed with suspicion by many librarians and book reviewers. Yet, the *Noisy Books* in battered, seedy-looking copies on my grown-up children's bookshelves are eloquent reminders of their special place in my family's literary history. (pp. 646-47)

[*Country Noisy Book*] tells how Muffin was put into a box and sent on a train journey. Once again [as in *The Noisy Book*] he was unable to see anything, but he heard strange, new sounds: "*dong-dong ding-dong*" and "*[p]ocketa pocketa pocketa pocketa.*" Reunited with his family in the country, the dog heard the boisterous daytime noises of nature and the quiet rustic sounds of night. Back home in the city in *Indoor Noisy Book* . . . , Muffin had a cold and had to stay in his room all day. Meanwhile, the subtle sounds of domesticity drifted up to him. . . .

[The *Winter Noisy Book*] celebrated the season's own indoor and outdoor sounds. The little dog lay before the fire, listening to people cracking nuts and popping popcorn; he heard the roar of the wind and the snapping of icy branches. The contour and pattern of the four books are the same: suggestive noises for children to echo, tempting interrogation, deliciously ridiculous possibilities, and a final revelation. . . . [They] are enormously welcome. . . . (p. 647)

Ethel L. Heins, "A Second Look: 'The Noisy Books'," in The Horn Book Magazine, *Vol. LII, No. 6, December, 1976, pp. 646-47.*

BARBARA BADER

In the short span between the publication of her first work in 1937 and her early death in 1952, Margaret Wise Brown wrote more than ninety picturebooks (some of which appeared posthumously). A few, issued both before and after her death, utilized stories previously published, for she also wrote herself (or adapted or translated) a half-dozen story collections—a judiciously simplified Uncle Remus, for one—and, beginning with the ubiquitous *Another Here and Now Story Book*, contributed to others. She wrote stories too for *Good Housekeeping*, and for *Story Parade* and other children's magazines; and

Then slowly a grey wetness came in the air
and Muffin couldn't see very far. What was
that greyness?

Far off in the fog Muffin could hear:

        Whoooo
        Whoooo
        Whoooo
        Whoooo
What was that?

And he could hear:
   lapping slapping
       slap lap lap
against the side of the boat.
      What was that?

Brown worked closely with artist Leonard Weisgard to produce over twenty books, including a Caldecott winner, The Little Island. The Seashore Noisy Book *was third in the "Noisy Book" series, which first prompted their collaboration. From* The Seashore Noisy Book, *written by Margaret Wise Brown. Pictures by Leonard Weisgard. Harper & Row, 1941. Copyright 1941 by Margaret Wise Brown. By permission of Harper & Row, Publishers, Inc.*

as her interest in children's records grew, she wrote songs for her stories and stories in song; right along she wrote poetry. . . .

Four, five, seven of her books appeared a year, of several sorts at various prices from assorted publishers; a long extravagant profile ran in *Life* [see excerpt above, 1946] and Margaret Wise Brown became famous, the first author of picturebooks to be recognized in her own right. The first, too, to make the writing of picturebooks an art.

Maybe **When the Wind Blew** . . . was submitted to Harper by a friend unbeknownst to her, as reported in *Life,* and maybe it wasn't; Ursula Nordstrom simply remembers taking it on— one of her first selections as an apprentice editor—because "children like sad stories." And, wrote its author: "In **When the Wind Blew** I took a plot of Chekhov, about a very sad and bitter man trying to drown a fly in an ink blob and then suddenly deciding to save its life and by that one small gesture feeling better; and I tried to make a sad story for children, believing that many of the graver cadences of life are there at any age."

An old, old lady is "all by herself in the world because she was so old everyone had forgotten her, and the children and the new people in the world didn't even know . . . she was alive." But she is not alone, she has seventeen cats and one little blue grey kitten who follow behind her when she goes to bathe in the ocean and mew for breakfast when they get home. (p. 252)

To be sick with no one to tend you, to lie in bed shivering with the wind howling outside and whistling through the cracks ("and her toothache was all that there seemed to be in the world"): to a child it is sadder than starvation, which is unimaginable—as any suffering is closer and sadder than death— and sad rather than frightening, the way extreme danger is. If only "she had a hot water bottle to put against her jaw to soothe the ache that was there." And then she hears a click click purr, purr, click purr near her ear, and feels something warm along the side of her face ("What could it be?") and finds the little blue grey kitten—"Just as good as a fur-covered hot water bottle." (pp. 252-53)

[**The Dead Bird**] is and is not like **When the Wind Blew;** for one thing, it is and is not a sad story.

"The bird was dead when the children found it," it begins; "But it had not been dead for long—it was still warm and its eyes were closed." The children feel for the beat of the bird's heart, and find none; the body grows cold and stiffens—"That was the way animals got when they had been dead for some time—cold dead and stone still with no heart beating." They are sorry it's dead and can't fly again, and glad they found it "because now they could dig a grave in the woods and bury it. They could have a funeral and sing to it the way grown-up people did when someone died."

The funeral follows, with a song to the little dead bird, and some crying "because their singing was so beautiful and the ferns smelled so sweetly and the bird was dead." A stone is placed on the spot and flowers planted round; "And every day, until they forgot, they went and sang to their little dead bird and put fresh flowers on his grave."

That children are naturally sympathetic and naturally egocentric, eager to emulate adults and fond of ceremony, ardent and quick to forget, was not Margaret Wise Brown's discovery; but understanding it well—recognizing too that the first dead thing encountered by most children is a bird—she is able to deal with death directly and, for them, honestly and immediately. Sorrow is expressed without embarrassment, joyfulness without shame; and a small child cannot but be comforted.

It is likely, too, that the clinical signs of death are meant to be a practical help to him. . . . *The Fish with the Deep Sea Smile* (deepest when he's smiled himself off a hook) is dedicated to Lucy Sprague Mitchell and it too has its purposes; but it has also several stories about "Sneakers, That Rapscallion Cat" that later turned up in a book of their own, another large group—some of them poems actually—designated as **"Sleepy Stories,"** and, throughout, what Margaret Wise Brown was to refer to shortly as "interludes."

> There is another form I wonder about for five-year-olds. I call it an interlude, it is not a story with a plot, it isn't very long. It is somewhere between a story and a poem, a dwelling on some theme in words, a recreation of some experience. It is the thing some five-year-olds do in their own writings. I have tried to do it in **'The Wonderful Day,' 'The Dead Bird,' 'The Pale Blue Flower'**; and perhaps **'The Children's Clock'** and **'Christmas Eve'** are only long interludes or incidents rather than real stories. Whether this is a good form for children's writings I am not sure. I think, because it is a quiet and simple form it might be, if it is read to a child at the right time.

What she is describing tentatively and exploratively is of course the form she was to make uniquely her own in picturebooks.

In the offing too, anent 'themes' and 'experiences,' was attention to those "graver cadences of life" which—Brown had intended to say apropos of *When the Wind Blew*—"escape the scientific labeling and age leveling of the materialistic psychologist." . . . Though she would always stress her indebtedness to her Bank Street training and to Mrs. Mitchell, *When the Wind Blew* represented for her "a protest against Bank Street doctrine"—an impertinence of a sort, and then by extension a declaration of independence from all strictures.

As of 1944 she had turned out for Harper—all the while doing *Bumble Bugs*, the **"Noisy Books"**, *The Little Fireman—The Streamlined Pig* (sheer silliness), *The Polite Penguin* ("Manners seem unreasonable and no use evading it"—MWB), *Night and Day* (with Leonard Weisgard—to be "the most beautiful book we had ever done"), *Don't Frighten the Lion* (the Rey zoo caper), *Little Chicken* (who discovers that "some wanted to play with him, and some didn't"), *SHHhhhh . . . BANG: a whispering book* ("She liked the idea of children going into a library and asking for *SHHhhhh . . . BANG*"—[Ursula Nordstrom]), *Black and White* (an allegorical conflict), *The Big Fur Secret* (unbeknownst to adults, "animals don't talk"), *They All Saw It* (the Ylla album), *Horses* (by "Timothy Hay"); and

in their midst, fresh and melodious and sure, *The Runaway Bunny.* (pp. 253-55)

[This book] is a game of hide-and-seek, with the child taking the lead; a fledgling's challenge and a mother's response in kind; rebellion and unfailingly, reassurance. . . .

The carrot [given to the bunny by his mother at the end of the book] was an afterthought, flashed from Maine—a fillip after the measured rhythm back and forth, and an anchor, the daily bill of fare. But if an afterthought, not an accident: knowing that food and bed stand for security to small children, Brown regularly led her firemen and bunnies to one or the other or both. For all its eloquence, nothing becomes *The Runaway Bunny* more than that last snap of carrot. (p. 256)

[*Little Fur Family* is a] little fur book for small hands to hold (cheeks to rub, arms to cuddle) with the smallest of stories, about being, just being, a little fur child. He goes out to play in the wild wild woods and wild grass tickles his nose and makes him sneeze . . . *kerchoo;* and his grandpa comes *thump thump thump* and says "Bless you," and sneezes too. "Bless you," says the little fur child. He catches a fish and throws it back in the river, catches a bug and throws it back in the air, catches "a little tiny tiny fur animal, the littlest fur animal in the world"—like the littlest last best babushka in a Russian nesting egg—and puts it back gently in the grass. The sun goes down, the sky grows wild and red, and the little fur child runs home—to his mother and his father . . . and a snug sleepy song. In *Little Fur Family*, Margaret Wise Brown wrote, she only dared to be very simple; and as an entity it is as inevitable in its way as a wooden totem pole or a marble fish.

It is also a dear little funny book—funny because "a little tiny tiny fur animal, the smallest fur animal in the world," is funny, especially skedaddling to a hole in the ground; and a little tickly-nose sneeze is, and a grandpa sneeze. . . . (pp. 256-57)

[Garth Williams illustrated several of Brown's books, including *Little Fur Family*.] With Clement Hurd, he was to give shape to Margaret Wise Brown's tenderest, most private work for children, her look-alike animal world.

She would start thinking, she wrote early on, "of the small animal dignity that children and puppies and shy little horses struggle so hard to maintain," of "the wonder and surprise at the world" of a kitten by itself for the first time; and stories would come. She took to likening the mechanics of writing for small children—"the sudden starts and stops, the sounds and silences in the words"—to writing for a puppy or a kitten. ("Dogs," she attested, "will also be interested in the **'Noisy Books'** the first time they hear them read with any convincing suddenness and variety of whistles, squeaks, hisses, thuds and sudden silences following an unexpected 'BANG!'") And *My World*, the child/bunny book very like our next, *Goodnight Moon*, had its origin, she said in a talk, in the life of her own dog.

> . . . My dog has a world that I am a part of and more often no part of—a very certain world in which he has his home, in which he has himself, in which he has night and day, and hot and cold, and his poor little dinner that only comes once a day—his own dear door, and his own dear dish and his own dear rugs—his own dear me and his own dear cat that he chases across the fence whenever he gets sight of it.

So every child has his own world. His dear
day, his dear shoe, his dear self, his own dear
sun that he sees every day, his own dear stars
that he sometimes sees at night; his own dear
pillow, his own dear bed, his own dear everything in the world that he knows. . . .

In *Goodnight Moon,* it is the close of day, and a room first
brilliant with light darkens at each color opening as, outside,
the moon rises and brightens the sky. . . .

> In the great green room
> There was a telephone
> And a red balloon
> And a picture of—

Here, as Dorothy White [in *Books before Five*] remarks, "one
should turn the page," but her daughter wasn't ready. "'You
haven't said about the rabbit on the bed.' She held the page
down and went round the room pointing out all the things I
hadn't said." Then on to a picture of "The cow jumping over
the moon" and "three little bears sitting on chairs" . . . .

To interrupt the text is to do violence to it, and Mrs. White
correctly points out that the intervals between page turnings
are apt to be long when the pictures offer much to look at and
a child has much to say. To give primacy to delivering the
text, on the other hand, is to do violence to the child. Margaret
Wise Brown, one suspects, would say to let the specific rhymes
go and rely on the rhythm and reiteration to carry over, as they
do. (p. 258)

Praising the pictures, Dorothy White speaks of the text as
"inferior . . . the barest commentary"; and notes that her daughter
"has very much more to say about the book than the author
has." Exactly. In saying less, the author allows the artist [Clement
Hurd] to say more, and the child to find more—to find the old
lady knitting (the author doesn't say that), the cats playing with
the yarn (or that), the extra blanket, the slippers, the fire. But
why are we looking so hard? Because "In the great green
room / There was a telephone / And a red balloon. . . ." And
would we be listening so intently were it not a 'great green
room,' a 'telephone,' and a 'red balloon'—a real telephone,
mind you, beside the child bunny's bed.

Of all of Margaret Wise Brown's writings, *Goodnight Moon*
is probably the most abstract in form and concrete in substance;
the closest to Gertrude Stein and to the utterances of children;
the most circumscribed and, as put into pictures, the most
difficult to exhaust. What about that mouse, for instance, in-
habiting a room in a house? accepted by the family, untouched
by the cats? (But they are rabbits, we remind ourselves, wavering.) For all the dear mittens and socks, the great green
room is at the last—a mystery.

It is risky to interpret any variation in the course of Margaret
Wise Brown's work as a change, to decide that she did—or
meant—first this, then that. She liked to say that she wrote
her stories down in twenty minutes and polished them for two
years or more; writing constantly, she had numerous manuscripts out on approval; and . . . earlier work was apt to turn
up at any time, either in a new form or newly published.
Moreover . . . she had by 1937-38, when she was just beginning, so many definite interests and ideas that the compara-
tively few years of her writing career could not absorb them.
It is just because she followed different leads simultaneously
that her work shapes up, as it were, in parallel columns.

But in the books closest to the lives of children, the ones about
child animals, there is in the late Forties a noticeable shift,
intentional or not, from security as a theme, and toward one
form or another of independence—whether the freedom to go
out after dark or, finally, the freedom to be oneself.

A little raccoon is impatient to see and know the things of the
night. "Wait," his mother tells him, *Wait Till the Moon Is
Full*. Wondering and questioning, growing "quietly fat," grad-
uating from pull toy to rubber ball to sailboat, he waits as the
moon grows bigger too; and then, baseball and bat at the ready,
a new cockiness in his talk . . . , he gets the answer to all his
wants . . . "the moon is full." (pp. 259-60)

Songs are interlarded, songs that are part nonsense, part nature-
lyric—where before, as in *Little Fur Family,* a lullaby might
be sung at the close (or, elsewhere, a song appended). It was
more and more important to Brown, this writing of songs, of
poems to be sung; but alongside some of her picturebook texts
the poems meant as such are weak tea. She wrote poetry, it
could be said, except when she tried to; when she was writing
naturally, the way a child does, not in standard forms (fatal to
child poetry too). Or when—call it poetry or lighthearted verse—
she was just rhyming or alliterating, relishing the sound and
swing of words. . . .

Wait Till the Moon Is Full succeeds, then, in spite of the poems—
because wanting to go out at night is as deep-seated as wanting
to be safe in bed, and the exchanges between mother and child
raccoon have a sweet and comic ring of truth. The extent of
the dramatic realism was new; the extent of the resemblance,
that is, to the familiar thrusts and feints of family life. . . . [In]
The Runaway Bunny, the conflict is formalized and allegorical.
In a sense—Margaret Wise Brown's chief sense—*Wait Till the
Moon Is Full* is about the night and "all things that love the
night" (a carryover from her earlier *Night and Day*) but implicit
in the little raccoon's assertive "I want," his mother's re-
straining, assuring "Wait," is the conflict of wills inherent in
growing up. (p. 260)

Three Little Animals is a big book but otherwise a successor,
of a sort, to *Little Fur Family*. Three little fur animals live
together happily "in their own little warm animal world in
their warm way. But the world of people was over the hill and
the little animals naturally wondered what that world was like."
Donning the garb of a proper gentleman, the first sets out, and
then the second, dressed like a lady (yes, like). The little one
has no clothes so he has to stay behind until, lonesome, he
makes himself some things to wear. . . . But, as the first two
have already discovered, out in the world clothes are a cover-
up ("everyone thought they were people") and the little one,
too, is lost in the crowd. . . . (p. 261)

Comes a big wind, blowing everyone's hat off, "And the three
little animals saw each other's fur ears and they knew they
were not like other people. So did the people." Off they run,
throwing their togs to the wind, until they reach their home in
the woods where they belong—"For they were little animals!"

The state of nature vs. the republic of man, or, in Fifties'
terms, individuality vs. conformity, *Three Little Animals* cannot be read other than as a parable of some sort; c. 1970, as
an example of dropping out and doing your own thing. But
whatever one finds in it, there's no escaping the pox on people—
while animals ("in their warm way") are simple, happy, affectionate: wouldn't it be better to be one?

Brown didn't usually juxtapose the two worlds. Seeing the child world and the animal world as one, she ignored adults—the larger human world—except as parent-figures. In *Little Fur Family* there is no world of people over the hill, seen or unseen; as far as they and we are concerned, they are the people, and their way is the natural way. But turn Arcady into a suburb of Chicago and their simplicity becomes innocence, and they in turn become gallant or pathetic—Three Little Animals and the Great Grim World, it could be called. (pp. 261-62)

Meanwhile she had ideas about incorporating art—the art of the museums—in picturebooks, and so *The House of a Hundred Windows* . . . appeared, with paintings by Ryder and Audubon, Henri Rousseau, Ernst, Chirico, Tanguy—a mix of modern and near-modern masters—showing through the windows. She was still interested in giving young children "a form to put their own observations into," per the "Noisy Books" and the result . . . [was *The Important Book*]: "The important thing about the wind is that it blows. You can't see it, but you can feel it on your cheek, and see it bend trees, and blow hats away, and sailboats. BUT THE IMPORTANT THING ABOUT THE WIND IS THAT IT BLOWS."

She was writing verse—after "I like bugs. / Black bugs, / Green bugs, / Bad bugs, / Mean bugs, / Any kind of bug . . ."(*The Fish with the Deep Sea Smile*), the group of riddling rhymes that comprise *Where Have You Been?* . . . . Best reply: the mouse's "To see if the tick / Comes after the tock / I run down the clock." . . . [In *Christmas in the Barn* and *The Little Fir Tree*], Brown and [Barbara] Cooney manage a trim, snug simplicity appropriate to the audience and the occasion.

[Brown] was launched on the songs and musical stories; and the best of the musical stories, *The Little Brass Band,* was performed publicly as well as recorded, and later became a book. There were other records derived from books or published poems: *Wait Till the Moon Is Full,* two about Mittens, and a dozen or so more.

The First Story started as a musical story, turned into a story without music . . . ; a new version of Eden (first girl finds first boy), it meant a great deal to her. So did *The Dark Wood of the Golden Birds,* another allegory, in the form of a prose poem, *about* enchantment and *about* devotion; and consequently bloodless. (pp. 263-64)

Once, explaining what she wanted in her work [see excerpt above in Author's Commentary], Brown recalled a story she'd heard about a little boy who used to walk around murmuring to himself, "Miss Nancy Owl walked down the street with her eyes full of tears." Enough said then, it suffices now. (p. 264)

Barbara Bader, "The Emotional Element," in her American Picture Books from Noah's Ark to the Beast Within, *Macmillan Publishing Company, 1976, pp. 241-64.*

MICHAEL PATRICK HEARN

Perhaps one has to have grown up with Margaret Wise Brown's picture books to truly appreciate her art. Early on my father read to me *The Wind in the Willows, A Christmas Carol,* and *The Yellow Knight of Oz* rather than *Little Fur Family, The Runaway Bunny,* and *The Golden Egg Book;* so I learned to regard any Margaret Wise Brown title as just another "baby book." However, countless little children have adored *Goodnight Moon,* many obstinately refusing to go to sleep until after the reassuring refrain, "Goodnight room / Goodnight moon / Goodnight cow jumping over the moon. . . ." Children's book

authors, artists, child psychologists and college professors also have confessed their love for her books. . . .

From the start, Brown was an experimental author and editor. An admirer of contemporary Russian and French picture books, she developed techniques of composition similar to those introduced by Kornei Chukovsky, Samuil Marshak and other early Soviet writers for children. She also succeeded in getting Gertrude Stein to write the unconventional *The World Is Round.*

What Brown thought the trade needed most were books for the very young. She believed that they should be told about familiar sights, sounds and smells, and that fairy tales, myths and legends should be postponed until the children were older. Her own short, simple, plotless texts are generally not stories. She called her form the "interlude": "somewhere between a story and a poem, a dwelling on some theme in words, a recreation of some experience." By introducing mood, sentiment and ancedote into the American picture book, Brown inspired the "conceptual" school, which includes Charlotte Zolotow, Ruth Kraus, Beatrice Schenck De Regniers and Alvin Tresselt, many of whom, like Brown, have also been editors. These authors tend to treat literature as therapy, trying to meet some specific emotional need of the child.

Like the Children's Television Workshop, Brown experimented in her own "literature lab." She tested each element of the text and art of a picture book on groups of two-to-four year olds; only that which met the full approval of these small judges went into the published version. Consequently, as her publishers advertised, each title was "custom-made for its eventual users." Such a method of composition does seem a bit calculated: however, Brown had a redeeming wit and love of words, elements generally lacking in the work of the majority of her successors.

Perhaps Brown's greatest gift as a writer was her rare ability to involve the child in the storytelling. "The child grasps the 'plot' in the first few pages," a publisher's blurb typically described one of her books, "so that he can 'read' the story through the pictures. This makes it uniquely his own—a book that no one has to help him read." Brown believed that the picture book should have the power to "jog him with the unexpected and comfort him with the familiar" [see excerpt above by Louise Seaman Bechtel dated June, 1958]. What has especially endeared her work to parent and child alike has been her quality of reassurance. Most of her picture books conclude with a bedtime scene—the hero or heroine, like the listening child, soon to be lost in dreams.

Not everyone was impressed with either Brown's ability or her prolificness. Anne Carroll Moore of the Children's Room of the New York Public Library pooh-poohed her early books; *The Horn Book* did not review them. Brown was not the typical children's book writer, and she did have her contradictions. Although she made her living by writing about kitties and puppies, her favorite sport was "beagling," a vicious pastime in which a pack of beagles are sent out after an Oklahoma jack rabbit. "Well," she once admitted, "I don't especially like children either. At least not as a group. I won't let anybody get away with anything just because he is small."

Michael Patrick Hearn, "Margaret Wise Brown: Comforts of the Familiar," in Book World—The Washington Post, *November 11, 1979, p. 16.*

LEONARD S. MARCUS

Margaret Wise Brown remains a legendary figure among children's book writers and editors, . . . a companionable voice and presence—by turns broadly mischievous and lyrically comforting—to millions of nursery-age children in this country and around the world; and, not least of all, a boon to the parents of the very young. . . .

Much of what Margaret Brown published in her lifetime was not, for that matter, particularly good. Always experimenting, she was often content to throw off a few sparks in a promising direction. But a full dozen or more of her books are and will remain classics. Working at a time (much like the present) when illustration was considered the greater part of bookmaking for the young, she demonstrated, as Barbara Bader has said [see excerpt above, 1976], that writing for very young children can also be an art. . . .

She wrote in a furious sprawling longhand, at times with a swan's plume or blue heron feather.

Contests of wits exercised and delighted her. As William R. Scott and Company's children's book editor in the late 1930s and early '40s, she "fought, bled and died over a comma" in editorial meetings, much to her satisfaction. . . .

[Brown believed that to] write picture books well one had to love "not children but what children love." (p. 74)

Friends did not know her to labor over a manuscript, and many story fragments hastily scribbled on the backs of hotel envelopes, shopping lists and budgets attest to her susceptibility to bolts from the blue. But Margaret Brown worked out elaborate dummies for many books (occasionally pasting on a cut-out of the Caldecott Medal for good measure), and impressed coworkers time and again with her dedication to and knowledge of her craft. It may be, as Clement Hurd has said, that she worked "all the time," turning an image or sentence over in her mind. . . . [She] withheld many manuscripts from publication for years, waiting to be sure of each word. Even so, some of what she did publish might have benefited from such second or third thoughts. . . .

The Runaway Bunny, Little Fur Family, Fox Eyes are all hunting stories in which the power of the strong over the weak—which all children are acutely aware of—is freely acknowledged. She identified herself in her writing with both parties to the hunt: the artist-adult seeking mastery over the materials of art and existence and the animal-child, wild, unhindered, intensely alert yet at times in urgent need of protection. She wrote well for young children not only because she had studied their behavior at the Bank Street School but because she had remained essentially one of them. (p. 75)

As both a Harper and Golden Book author (a dual identity anomalous enough in the eyes of some critics to have left still-lingering doubts as to the seriousness of her artistic intentions); as Scott's editor during the first years of the house's existence and as its best-selling author; and as a friend and advisor to numerous other gifted children's book artists—among them Clement and Edith Thacher Hurd, Esphyr Slobodkina, Garth Williams, Jean Charlot and Leonard Weisgard—Brown contributed immensely to the American children's book field in every conceivable way.

There is widespead agreement among editors working today that, for all the second- and third-rate manuscripts she also published during her brief, intensely prolific career, no writer since Margaret Wise Brown has so often achieved a voice and vision so knowingly alert to the sensual immediacies and actual concerns of persons newly aware of the world beyond their toes. More recently, Maurice Sendak has provided children

with a potent means for confronting in imagination their innermost fantasies. Brown, writing for the most part for still younger listeners and readers, offered children the emotionally secure and solid ground on which such inner explorations can alone safely proceed.

In 1952, . . . Margaret Brown published *Mister Dog,* informally completing a major cycle of her work. Earlier picture books, especially *The Runaway Bunny* and *Wait Till the Moon Is full,* epitomized, as Barbara Bader has said [see excerpt above, 1976], various stages in a child's gradual growth toward selfhood. *Mister Dog,* the story of winsome "dog who belonged to himself," was her fable of self-possession realized. (p. 76)

> *Leonard S. Marcus, "The Legend of Margaret Wise Brown," in* Publishers Weekly, *Vol. 224, No. 4, July 22, 1983, pp. 74-6.*

CLAUDIA LEWIS

The picture book, Margaret Wise Brown once said, should have the power to "jog the child with the unexpected and comfort him with the familiar" [see excerpt above by Louise Seaman Bechtel dated June, 1958]. This thought-provoking statement I found as I was putting together some of my recent ideas on both writing for young children and reviewing and evaluating children's books. It opened up for me a new path to explore.

The "unexpected"? I looked through that great favorite, *Goodnight Moon,* to see if Margaret Wise Brown was following her own prescription, and it was easy to see that she was, even in a book for a child as young as 2. In this story the little rabbit in the bed says goodnight to all those comfortable, familiar things on page after page, . . . then suddenly there is an entirely blank page, "Goodnight nobody." Here is the unexpected jog for the 2-year-old. In the **"Noisy Books"** the jog for the child or reader of any age comes in the inventiveness of the thoughts. In *The Quiet Noisy Book,* for instance, the quietest noise in the world might be "quiet as a bird's wing cutting the air," quiet as "butter melting," or as "a new leaf uncurling." (p. 198)

> *Claudia Lewis, "Searching for the Master Touch in Picture Books," in* Children's literature in education, *Vol. 15, No. 4 (Winter), 1984, pp. 198-203.**

WHEN THE WIND BLEW (1937)

"When the Wind Blew," is a story for little children that has poetic quality, color and rhythm. "Once," it begins, "there was an old, old lady, and she lived by the side of the ocean, all by herself." She had seventeen cats and one little blue-gray kitten. . . . How the seventeen cats and the blue-gray kitten helped their old friend out of her difficulties is explained in a way that will be thoroughly satisfactory to little children, and the musical flow and repetition of the text make it an admirable story for reading aloud. . . .

Beginners in reading will enjoy this as well as the 4 to 6 year olds.

> *Anne T. Eaton, "—And Seventeen Cats," in* The New York Times Book Review, *October 3, 1937, p. 10.*

This is definitely not up the writer's standards. . . . [It has] a so-so story. The book's small size is appealing to the little ones, but its contents have no appeal. There is really no point in the story. So what if the old woman had a toothache!

Connie Kuhn, in a review of "When the Wind Blew," in Children's Book Review Service, *Vol. 6, No. 4, December, 1977, p. 31.*

["**When the Wind Blew**"] is a book well paced for little children. . . . Its easy plot and simple characters—numerous feline and one human—fit admirably within the space of a young child's attention.

Ann S. Haskell, in a review of "When the Wind Blew," in Book World—The Washington Post, *December 11, 1977, p. E4.*

THE FISH WITH THE DEEP SEA SMILE (1938)

AUTHOR'S COMMENTARY

This book is an attempt to write of a child's reality, the things that seem important to a child of five, six, or seven—nonsense that children can recognize; getting lost and getting found; being good and being bad; shyness and loneliness and the sheer joy of living. Wonder at the colors and smells and sounds of the world so fresh to their brand new senses; the importance of the seasons. This book hopes to touch their imaginings and to suggest imaginings in the realm of a child's reality.

Margaret Wise Brown, in comments from the dust jacket to her The Fish with the Deep Sea Smile, *E. P. Dutton & Co., Inc., 1938.*

The best introduction to this book of stories for five-to-eight is to . . . read "**The Wonderful Kitten.**" I say this not because I like cats, but because it has caught, in a surprisingly direct way, the feeling of being very, very young and not in the least helpless. Babies may be weak, but they seldom realize that they are. On the contary, to them every yawn is something accomplished, something done; every step, when they get so far, is a new proof that they have single-handed—or footed—brought about the conquest of gravity.

>   There it went again.
>
>   Hic.
>
>   He looked at all his brothers and sisters. But there they were all curled up, sound asleep. What could that noise be?
>
>   Hic-up. This time the little kitten shook all over when the noise came.
>
>   "Why, it's me!" said the little kitten. "What a wonderful kitten I am. I can Yawn some, Sneeze some, Purr some, Hear some, Crawl some, and HIC-UP."

That is but a bit of it; you get the idea. It is a thoroughly sound idea. I wish all the rest of the stories were as good: this is a product of the Writer's Laboratory on Bank Street of this city, and the portentiousness that hangs about such undertakings gets into several of these productions. But there are tales enough to furnish a book's worth of pleasure to a very small child—a four-year-old, for instance, who likes to hear about things all about her, in her own world. It is, to my way of thinking, more interesting to the general public, and more useful to the everyday parent, than other examples of the Here-and-Now school of thought that I have seen since its earlier period.

May Lamberton Becker, in a review of "The Fish with the Deep Sea Smile," in New York Herald Tribune Books, *May 1, 1938, p. 14.*

[Brown's] tales bear the earmarks of having been tried out with boys and girls and show that she understands children's interests. Stories originating in this way are of great value; on the other hand, they sometimes lack the spontaneity of the tale told for the love of storytelling, the tale which is simple not because the author is consciously holding himself down to the capacities of a child of a certain age, but because it deals with situations and a way of life that are childlike, direct and unsophisticated.

The tales in this volume vary considerably in interest. "**The Wonderful Kitten**" describes with real imagination and a touch of humor the very first experience of a week-old kitten, but the best and liveliest story in the book is "**The Steam Roller Fantasy**," in which the author seems to forget everything but the fact that she is telling a rollicking tale of an absurd adventure which yet has the logic of genuine nonsense. A book which mothers and teachers will be glad to add to their list for reading aloud.

Anne T. Eaton, "A Book of Tales," in The New York Times Book Review, *May 22, 1938, p. 10.*

THE STREAMLINED PIG (1938)

A nonsense picture-book story that younger children, boys especially, will find lots of fun. The ingredients are appealing. There is a small boy, a farm with a fat pig, a gray donkey, and a buffalo; and there is a flood with everyone rescued in streamlined airplanes. Pig is the hero of the rescue, making a parachute landing that streamlines the kinks right out of his tail.

Marjorie F. Potter, in a review of "Streamlined Pig," in Library Journal, *Vol. 63, No. 15, September 1, 1938, p. 656.*

One of the few really American picture story books I have seen that has any charm is "**The Streamlined Pig.**" Miss Brown . . . is an author and an editor to be watched with interest. She knows well what sort of ridiculous pretending small children like.

Louise Seaman Bechtel, in a review of "The Streamlined Pig," in The Saturday Review of Literature, *Vol. XIX, No. 4, November 19, 1938, p. 18.*

NOISY BOOK (1939)

AUTHOR'S COMMENTARY

[In the following excerpt, Brown discusses how she and illustrator Leonard Weisgard collaborated on Noisy Book, *the first of a series on loud and soft sounds.]*

As a result of our first conversation [Leonard Weisgard and] I realized that my feelings were chiefly those of an author who was looking for an artist who wanted to do something for very young children that had never been done before. At a subsequent luncheon Leonard told me of his father taking him around London and recording the street noises and cries for him on a phonograph record, at which we both agreed that shapes could suggest sounds, and that maybe a book of sounds could be done for children—the two, three and four year olds who were

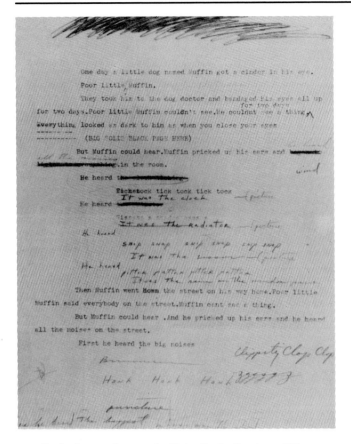

Revised typescript page for Noisy Book. *Courtesy of Westerly Public Library, Westerly, RI.*

hearing these sounds for the first time—in which the shapes behind the objects making the noise could suggest the sound.

I rushed back to my desk at the Writers Laboratory at 69 Bank Street and wrote the first sketch for the first *Noisy Book*. . . . [The next morning I] went through every group in the nursery school trying to see what this book written in the form of questions would mean to the children of different ages and what questions they might ask which could be included in the book. I listened carefully to the sounds the children made in answer to the questions, listened to the timing to judge the length of the book, revised my original sketch and that same afternoon handed Leonard the manuscript. (pp. 40-1)

Then came weeks of testing words and pictures with the children. . . . I deleted the "Honk Honk" of my own first childhood memories of automobile horns and put a three-year-old's well heard correction into the text "A WRurrrrrra." Spell that one, if you can.

So we made the first *Noisy Book*. . . . And to this day that book has increased in sales every year much to Leonard's and to my astonishment. We knew how it worked on children but we didn't think grownups would like it. (p. 41)

> Margaret Wise Brown, "Leonard Weisgard Wins the Caldecott Medal," in Publishers Weekly, *Vol. 152, No. 1, July 5, 1947, pp. 40-2.*

Two generations of American children have already enjoyed participating in the simple sequence of this nursery book. . . .

A small dog whose bandaged eyes are under treatment uses his ears to identify sounds. Small children can respond first in echoing the verbal equivalents of a sneeze, a fly, a clock, and then in answering rhetorical questions about a small, unidentified squeak ("Is it a policeman . . . a garbage can . . . an aeroplane"). The whimsical approach may seem a little heavy now but the invitation to the young to share the dog's experience should still be accepted with some enjoyment.

> Margery Fisher, in a review of "The Noisy Book," in her Growing Point, *Vol. 16, No. 9, April, 1978, p. 3295.*

COUNTRY NOISY BOOK   (1940)

A two-year-old will have fun with this book and so will the parent or nursery school teacher who shares it with him. . . . It tells of a little dog's trip to the country and suggests all the noises he hears along the way, the clickety clack of the train and the drrr of an airplane. At first the country seems quiet, but then all kinds of interesting noises come to the little dog's ear: chirp chirp, baa baa, jugar jugarum, eek eeeek. But at last "Muffin fell asleep and he didn't hear any more noises. Not even the wind."

> Marjorie F. Potter, in a review of "The Country Noisy Book," in Library Journal, *Vol. 65, No. 18, October 15, 1940, p. 877.*

["**The Country Noisy Book**"] starts, as all good stories of travel should, with the first exciting noises of a train's departure, blending into the rhythmic clickety clack, pocketa pocketa of the wheels as it gets under way. . . . Once arrived, [Muffin] is kept busy and happy, as his followers will be, discovering and identifying the [sounds he hears.] . . .

[The] sounds are as faithfully transcribed as ingenious author and printer can make them. The text, with its crisp sentences and many interrogations, demands response from small listeners and thus not only increases perceptivity of a sense too often neglected for that of sight but insures a lot of fun for those of an age who would rather, and generally do, make a lot of noise than do anything else in the world.

> Ellen Lewis Buell, "Country Sounds," in The New York Times Book Review, *January 19, 1941, p. 10.*

THE COMICAL TRAGEDY OR TRAGICAL COMEDY OF PUNCH AND JUDY   (1940)

Whatever its positive or negative values, "Punch and Judy" has through three centuries become a rightful heritage and it could scarcely have had a livelier presentation in book form than this one.

Margaret Wise Brown has adapted it in swinging sentences, with plenty of hits and runs, but no errors, and with rolling verses set to the tune of "For He's a Jolly Good Fellow." In this version, contrary to the usual one, Punch out-thumps all comers, even the devil, remaining triumphantly alive to the very end.

> Ellen Lewis Buell, "An Old Favorite," in The New York Times Book Review, *December 22, 1940, p. 11.*

THE POLITE PENGUIN (1941)

The little Penguin, who hailed from a mannerless South Pole, learned to be polite only after advice and encounters almost as baffling as were Alice's instructions from the Red Queen. The Penguin was willing and anxious, but also like Alice he was literal-minded and argumentative, and he found the Raccoon's lessons in etiquette as confusing as many a child finds the explanations of well-meaning but inexplicit parents. . . .

Nevertheless [the Penguin] finally understood what the Raccoon meant when he said that consideration is the basis of politeness, and so will the youngsters who have laughed their hilarious way through antics and dialogue which are as unexpectedly logical as they are absurd.

> *Ellen Lewis Buell, "A Penguin's Education," in* The New York Times Book Review, *December 7, 1941, p. 10.*

BRER RABBIT: STORIES FROM UNCLE REMUS (1941)

[Margaret Wise Brown in her ***Brer Rabbit***] explains diplomatically that she has omitted the preambles and internal chat so that children may enjoy the stories without interruption. She has also modified the dialect slightly and has simplified where she felt it was necessary for "children of all English-speaking countries, . . . all the children, black and white, who do not understand in this day the Gulla dialect of Uncle Jack or the local dialects of the Georgia Negro in the days before and just after the Civil War". But she insists (and italicises her words) that *"All revision has tried to be faithful to the tone and rhythm of the stories and to the desired emphasis of the Negro storyteller behind the story, to the cadence and musical timing of his art"*. The emphasis on the imaginary but essential storyteller is important and despite some abbreviations and alterations in spelling and word, the twenty-four tales she has chosen do retain the spirit of the original. (p. 3260)

> *Margery Fisher, in a review of "Brer Rabbit," in her* Growing Point, *Vol. 16, No. 8, March, 1978, pp. 3260-61.*

THE RUNAWAY BUNNY (1942)

There is a rich background to this up-to-date, affectionate picture-book. The student of folksong recognizes a baby's variant of the old chansons in which a persistent suitor follows the elusive beloved through successive changes of form—reminding one of less affectionate duels of magicians in the Arabian Nights. That duel now becomes a duet between mother and baby. There are rabbits, but a human baby at once identifies himself with the bunny, who said to his mother, "I am running away," to which she replied: "If you run away, I will run after you, for you are my little bunny."

> *May Lamberton Becker, in a review of "The Runaway Bunny," in* New York Herald Tribune Books, *March 15, 1942, p. 6.*

There is a definite nursery rime quality in [***The Runaway Bunny***]. . . . Small children will find the rhythmical repetition irresistible and will undoubtedly amplify the story with ideas of their own.

> *A review of "The Runaway Bunny," in* The Booklist, *Vol. 38, No. 15, April 15, 1942, p. 311.*

Peter Rabbit sort of story, done in simple text. . . . Rhythm and beauty of dialogue between Mother Bunny and her baby make authentic poetry of a little prose book that may well become a very-small-child's classic.

> *Siddie Joe Johnson, in a review of "The Runaway Bunny," in* Library Journal, *Vol. 67, No. 8, April 15, 1942, p. 368.*

There have been an enormous number of talking-beast stories for two- to six year-old children in the last several decades. . . . One of the best of these stories is Margaret Wise Brown's ***The Runaway Bunny***. . . . The word pattern goes on like a song. . . . (p. 233)

> *May Hill Arbuthnot and Zena Sutherland, "Modern Fantasy," in their* Children and Books, *fourth edition, Scott, Foresman and Company, 1972, pp. 210-77.**

This charming paperback is the embodiment of maternal love. . . . It is a simple story, glowing with tenderness and love which makes it a most comforting and attractive book for young children.

> *Margaret Walker, in a review of "The Runaway Bunny," in* Book Window, *Vol. 5, No. 3, Summer, 1978, p. 14.*

[***The Runaway Bunny***] is an extraordinary fantasy about the constancy of parental love. It can be appreciated by all ages and on many levels. Even very small children can follow the simple story. . . . Adults will see in this story parallels with Francis Thompson's *The Hound of Heaven*, for this story, too, suggests the constancy and pervasiveness of God's love for each member of creation.

> *A review of "The Runaway Bunny," in* New Catholic World, *Vol. 222, No. 1328, March-April, 1979, p. 92.*

NIGHT AND DAY (1942)

Picture book of two cats, one who loves the day and one who loves the night. The white cat learns to overcome her fear and to love the sounds of the night. Full of sensory details—of which every child is aware. . . . Should prove useful to parents who wish to cure their children of fear of the dark. Recommended.

> *J. Ethel Wooster, in a review of "Night and Day," in* Library Journal, *Vol. 67, No. 16, September 15, 1942, p. 796.*

There has been an increasing tendency to consider other senses than sight this year, in books for young children. . . . This one calls for ears as well as eyes, but it has a special value in warding off fear of the dark in children as young as four. . . . It ends "You see how the world is quiet. The world is all our own at night. It belongs to us, and to all things that love the night." . . . It makes a blackout seem beautiful and there's no reason why a little child should not be encouraged to see that it really is.

> *May Lamberton Becker, "All Sorts of Little Stories," in* New York Herald Tribune Books, *November 15, 1942, p. 30.*

THE NOISY BIRD BOOK (1943)

Here we find, in a brief text . . . , many of the best known birds, with the less familiar pelican, stork and wild turkey and finally the American eagle. . . . [The] thread of story which represents little dog Muffin coming upon one bird after another as he chases a rabbit, has the merit of action and surprise (though it may be a trifle confusing to little children to find the woodpecker apparently living next door in the forest to the now extinct Great Auk).

It is unfortunate, however, that in order to bring this book in line with its predecessors, **"The Country Noisy Book," "The Seashore Noisy Book," "The Indoor Noisy Book,"** the author should have chosen such a misleading title, for though each has its characteristic call and song, surely no one can think of the humming bird, cardinal, goldfinch and chickadee as *noisy birds*. If this series is to go on indefinitely a number of small children may grow up without being able to distinguish between a *noise*, which may or may not be loud, and *noisiness*.

> *Anne T. Eaton, "Muffin and the Birds," in* The New York Times Book Review, *February 28, 1943, p. 10.*

Little dog Muffin and his human family went to the woods listening and looking for birds. Many came to their notice and, at the end, the great American eagle flew across the sun. This strikes a slightly false note in otherwise good book, distinguished by careful writing . . . , though not wholly accurate information.

> *Elizabeth Schmidt, in a review of "Noisy Bird Book," in* Library Journal, *Vol. 68, No. 6, March 15, 1943, p. 249.*

SHHHHHH. . . . . .BANG, A WHISPERING BOOK (1943)

[SHhhhhh . . . Bang! is a] very clever little book for quite young children. Teachers, parents, librarians, and others who read aloud will love scope of the thing—from whisper to shout! And children will thoroughly sympathize with the hero, who brought delightful noise into a silent town.

> *Siddie Joe Johnson, in a review of "SHhhhhh . . . Bang!" in* Library Journal, *Vol. 68, No. 9, May 1, 1943, p. 364.*

BIG DOG, LITTLE DOG (1943)

Picture books that ask questions to which a very little child can instantly and correctly reply have a double purpose in the nursery. They entertain him, of course, but they also give him a chance to take part and thus build up his sense of importance. For instance, here is a big dog and a little dog. . . . "One was the father and one was the son. Which one was the father? Of course! That is the way it was." So they each had a dish, big and little, with bones to match, and when they went for a walk through the city the big dog saw everything that was interesting to a big dog. . . . But the little dog noticed little things that moved; he also barked at everything that moved, big or little, but nothing barked back until he met another little dog, floppy-eared and appealing. They played together, and the big father dog watched them, and all this time the little reader speaks up as the occasion requires, goes "sniff-sniff" and "yap-yap" and generally co-operates.

> *May Lamberton Becker, in a review of "Big Dog, Little Dog," in* New York Herald Tribune Weekly Book Review, *May 16, 1943, p. 10.*

There is in this rhythmic tale of two Kerry Blue terriers a fine feeling of experience gauged just right for the age which considers a walk down the street to be the height of adventure. . . .

[The meeting with another little dog provides] the climax for a wholly successful expedition and to a tale which little children will find most satisfying for its variety of detail, which at that age amounts to valid experience. . . . [The] text has a patterned swing which makes it good fun to read aloud.

> *Ellen Lewis Buell, "Terrier and Son," in* The New York Times Book Review, *May 30, 1943, p. 12.*

A CHILD'S GOOD NIGHT BOOK (1943)

A little book that succeeds in its aim—to be a kind of lullaby in prose. It is meant to be read before bedtime to small children to make them feel sleepy and safe. The night comes, everything goes to sleep; the fish in the sea, the birds, the rabbits, the sheep—"sleepy sheep." The repetition on each page is restful and effective. Finally we reach the "sleepy children" and a prayer—like a benediction. (pp. 25-6)

> *Joan Vatsek, in a review of "A Child's Good Night Book," in* The Saturday Review of Literature, *Vol. XXVI, No. 46, November 13, 1943, pp. 25-6.*

Of all the books prepared to meet the demand for bedtime stories to send a child to sleep, this one seems to me not only the most beautiful but likely to be most effective. . . . The text is a simple, rhythmic statement that everything is going to sleep. . . . The child will likely tuck his head under his arm like a bird, cuddle like a sheep, close his eyes as one after the other of his friends is doing. . . . A moving little book, it is serene in thought and in execution.

> *May Lamberton Becker, in a review of "A Child's Good Night Book," in* New York Herald Tribune Weekly Book Review, *November 14, 1943, p. 12.*

General idea of this book, that night is coming and everything is going to sleep, is of interest to a child of three years old and younger. In selection of material there is too much of the unfamiliar for so young a child.

> *Bernice W. Bell, in a review of "A Child's Good Night Book," in* Library Journal, *Vol. 68, No. 20, November 15, 1943, p. 962.*

Books for the "read aloud" times for the youngest children—as a preface to morning and afternoon rest periods and for just before bed—serve many good purposes. Entertainment is basic, of course, but along with that go the enlarging of horizons, the translation of impressions into ideas, the linking of the child with the outside world. . . . Then, too, books that become well loved supply the first step toward reading. . . .

An excellent example of multiple values is Margaret Wise Brown's **"A Child's Good Night Book."** Here, in simple, rhythmic words, is a picture of all the world going to sleep as night falls. In itself it is a sleep-making text, and by covering the child's whole horizon conveys the idea of all things quieting down.

Lois Palmer, in a review of "A Child's Good Night Book," in The New York Times Book Review, November 28, 1943, p. 20.

A gentle, rhythmic text, in the somnolent style for which this author is well-known, tells the sleepy-stories of friendly animals and machines in a lovely book designed to ease heavy-lidded toddlers to sleep. . . . [The] children stop thinking, whistling and talking, say their prayers and go to sleep too. A prayer—more for Mother than child—ends the book.

A review of "A Child's Good Night Book," in Virginia Kirkus' Bookshop Services, Vol. XIX, No. 15, August 1, 1951, p. 387.

[In] *A Child's Good-night Book* which [my daughter] Carol quickly christened her 'sleepy book', we have discovered a little classic, one with that uncloying sentiment to be found sometimes in French films. (p. 10)

A Child's Good-night Book opens with a double-page picture illustrating these words. 'Night is coming. Everything is going to sleep. The sun goes over to the other side of the world. Lights turn on in all the houses. It is dark'. Over the page it continues with birds, 'the little fish in the darkened sea', and rabbits and kangaroos all going to sleep. 'The sheep in the fields huddle together in a great warm blanket of wool'. As text this may seem simple enough. Indeed unless one has made one's way through second-class children's books filled with lumpy prose, one might not appreciate the quietly measured pace, the rhythmical placid style of this devisedly 'sleepy book'. (p. 11)

Dorothy White, "Two to Two and a Half," in her Books before Five, Oxford University Press, 1954, pp. 1-18.

LITTLE CHICKEN (1943)

For very little children who like to take part in a story by asking and answering questions, this tale of a very little chicken adopted by a nice soft rabbit is good for repeated use. . . . The rabbit, deciding that his pet needs society, sends him out to play with other animals. The little chicken meets lady-bugs, caterpillars, sparrows, beavers, butterflies, a tired old man, a porcupine, a bear, a monkey and a duck. . . . Would this one or that one play with the chicken? You ask the listener. The answers are obvious: the story ends with the chicken asleep in his foster parent's warm fur. It makes a good bedtime book.

May Lamberton Becker, in a review of "Little Chicken," in New York Herald Tribune Weekly Book Review, December 26, 1943, p. 5.

[*Little Chicken* is] one of Margaret Wise Brown's lesser works—in itself, a loose amalgam of motifs and phrasings from some of the more auspicious. First we have the dependent/protective relationship between the little chicken and the Rabbit. . . . Then the Rabbit decides to go for a long, long run—leaving the shy little chicken to try to find someone to play with. Not always rationally, some do [want to play] and some don't. . . . A wispy little conceit . . . and not really worth reviving.

A review of "Little Chicken," in Kirkus Reviews, Vol. L, No. 13, July 1, 1982, p. 729.

Brown's genius is evident in all the stories she created . . . and certainly in this sweet adventure that has entranced and taught

children since 1943. . . . In her simple story, the author subtly plants a seed that can help children understand themselves and others.

A review of "Little Chicken," in Publishers Weekly, Vol. 222, No. 1, July 2, 1982, p. 55.

BLACK AND WHITE (1944)

I can't see this—it's a *tour de force* that doesn't come off. A trick book for which the lame reason would be no reason at all to small fry. . . . [In] a far-fetched text, the story is told of the black man who spurned everything not wholly black, until a snow storm left a white snow lady in his house, and he fell in love with her and they were married and lived happily ever after. A neat little juvenile problem of miscegenation! Humor far-fetched. And definitely not geared to picture book age sense of fun, as I know it.

A review of "Black and White," in Virginia Kirkus' Bookshop Service, Vol. XII, No. 9, May 1, 1944, p. 216.

A rather unusual picture story book of a black Welshman who wanted everything about him black. . . . But mysteriously one night white things began coming into his dreams and into his life, and he was much happier thereafter with everything white and black. The book has quite an original touch, different from most of our picture books. . . . Recommended.

Marian A. Webb, in a review of "Black and White," in Library Journal, Vol. 69, No. 13, July, 1944, p. 607.

RED LIGHT, GREEN LIGHT (1944)

A "safety book" and a good one. There's lots of humor in the text which follows the adventures of animals, cars, jeeps—coming from their "homes" each morning, and going through the day safely because they obey the signals.

A review of "Red Light, Green Light," in Virginia Kirkus' Bookshop Service, Vol. XII, No. 19, October 1, 1944, p. 448.

Slender as [the story] may seem . . . , something in both words and . . . [Leonard Weisgard's] pictures, sets up the right overtones. Children at this age feel them, though they do not put them into words. In these quiet pages, wondering as little children do, [they see] what is going on outside while they are sleeping. . . . There is a real idea in the simple words. . . .

May Lamberton Becker, in a review of "Red Light, Green Light," in The New York Times Book Review, October 15, 1944, p. 6.

The brief text has a pleasant rhythmic quality: its chief value is to hold together the unusual pictures through which a child unconsciously gains a sense of the world beyond his doorstep, a world secure and protecting when safety laws are obeyed.

Anne T. Eaton, "Stop and Go," in The New York Times Book Review, January 21, 1945, p. 21.

WILLIE'S WALK TO GRANDMAMA (1944)

"How will I know when I get to your house?" asked Willie. "Look inside and you will see me there," answered Grandmama on the telephone. Practical-minded adults may object to Willie's walk alone through city streets and open country, but the four- to eight-year-olds will take Willie's adventures to their hearts as they did *Runaway Bunny*.

> *Florence W. Butler, in a review of "Willie's Walk to Grandmama," in* Library Journal, *Vol. 69, No. 19, November 1, 1944, p. 937.*

HORSES   (1944)

A mother horse took her little horse to the circus where they saw all the sights. Text is very slight. Book's appeal would be to picture-book age.... "Fact" statements given about each picture would not concern children for whom book is apparently intended.

> *Alice M. Wetherell, in a review of "Horses," in* Library Journal, *Vol. 70, No. 1, January 1, 1945, p. 36.*

THE HOUSE OF A HUNDRED WINDOWS   (1945)

Orchids to Margaret Wise Brown for experimenting with an idea.... Picture book age will pore over it; a bit older will want the text read to them; and even above nine will find it the ideal introduction to famous paintings, carefully chosen with appreciation of child interest. The little cat is quite content to stay inside his house and look out through its hundred windows, because from these windows he can see beauty, excitement, danger, humor and tranquility captured for him by famous artists,—Rousseau, Ryder, Chirico, Audubon, Tanguy, etc. No hackneyed selections here, but a high level of quality.... A quaint little story, not *too* sugar-coated which does bring fine art to small persons.

> *A review of "The House of a Hundred Windows," in* Virginia Kirkus' Bookshop Service, *Vol. XIII, No. 7, April 1, 1945, p. 159.*

This is not the first book to introduce painting to children but it is, so far as I know, the first addressed to a very young audience, and an original one it is....

Such a forward-marching step toward the enjoyment of art deserves applause even though one may not wholly endorse its total result. The emphasis in this collection of fifteen pictures is mainly upon contemporary art, with a strong dash of surrealism. That is reasonable enough, since a child's imagination often transcends our adult literalness and there is much here to stimulate the fancy. Yet it is doubtful if some of these paintings are truly distinguished examples of our age....

> *Ellen Lewis Buell, "Feline Art-Lover," in* The New York Times Book Review, *May 6, 1945, p. 18.*

THE LITTLE FISHERMAN, A FISH STORY   (1945)

[A book] about a big fisherman and a little fisherman both of whom sailed boats. Delightful text which tells what these fisherman do and how they do it. Little sailors with little ropes, little buckets and little hammocks will appeal to children from first picture book age on to six or seven.

> *A review of "The Little Fisherman," in* Virginia Kirkus' Bookshop Service, *Vol. XIII, No. 17, September 15, 1945, p. 420.*

A four-year-old gets at once contrast in size, so dramatic at that time of life....

We are told that children collaborated on the scenario; for this there is internal evidence, as it repeats just enough to please and ends on a laugh.

> *May Lamberton Becker, in a review of "The Little Fisherman," in* New York Herald Tribune Weekly Book Review, *November 11, 1945, p. 8.*

LITTLE LOST LAMB   (1945)

The parable of the lost sheep appears in a new version for the picture-book age in this smoothly flowing narrative of a shepherd boy and his errant black lamb. The full-page pictures ... [by Leonard Weisgard] are lovely in color and evocative of the changing moods of the story.

> *Ellen Lewis Buell, in a review of "Little Lost Lamb," in* The New York Times Book Review, *December 23, 1945, p. 10.*

LITTLE FUR FAMILY   (1946)

No question but what this will sell, but the perceptive customer for children's books will find it a disappointing book from an author who has written real childhood classics, like the *Noisy* books.... [The] rather affected story of the wild wood adventures of the little fur child seems pointless.

> *A review of "Little Fur Family," in* Virginia Kirkus' Bookshop Service, *Vol. XIV, No. 19, October 1, 1946, p. 489.*

This is a little tiny book in a box on whose cover is a lifelike picture of a little fur child. It is impossible not to stroke its stomach, as this is real fur.... The book inside has a slip cover of rabbit fur.

This is, of course, a stunt, causing one who knows the edition to be large to question in advance whether the story will be worth so many rabbits. But it proves to be rhythmic and soothing, repeating words such as warm and soft in telling of a little fur child, who went for a walk in the forest, whose fur mother gave him his supper and whose fur father joined in singing him to sleep....

This tiny little book with its gray fur cover ... sounds the way it feels, like something soft as one goes to sleep.

> *May Lamberton Becker, in a review of "Little Fur Family," in* New York Herald Tribune Weekly Book Review, *October 28, 1946, p. 8.*

The story of one day's happenings in the life of the bear family is simply told in a rhythmic prose that is pleasant to read aloud and will please young listeners. The illustrations by Garth Williams add much to the enjoyment of the book.

> *A review of "Little Fur Family," in* Bulletin of the Children's Book Center, *Vol. V, No. 3, November, 1951, p. 20.*

Margaret Wise Brown, a prolific writer of tone poems about realistic topics, could also weave gentle fanciful stories. Her *Little Fur Family* ... doesn't have much plot, but the pleasant lines are memorable. They convey the bliss of a group of creatures unknown to zoologists:

> There was a little fur family
> warm as toast
> smaller than most
> in little fur coats
> and they lived in a warm
> wooden tree.

This is word magic to capture any child's fancy, even those who aren't interested in fanciful narrative. (pp. 194-95)

> *Sam Leaton Sebesta and William J. Iverson, "Fanciful Fiction," in their* Literature for Thursday's Child, *Science Research Associates, Inc., 1975, pp. 177-214.**

THE LITTLE ISLAND (1946)

[This is the] story of a little island in the ocean, and the changes that come to it during the four seasons, of the lobsters and gulls and spiders and seals who visit it and of a special visitor who came and learned that he and the island were attached to the rest of the world. An imaginative, charming book, with a bit of unnecessay preciousness.

> *A review of "The Little Island," in* Virginia Kirkus' Bookshop Service, *Vol. XIV, No. 20, October 15, 1946, p. 522.*

This little island may have been off the seacoast of Bohemia, in a word. But in the midst of the sea it was itself and none other.... [One] day a little cat, come along with a picnic, says "it is as little as Big is Big." "So are you," replies the Island; the kitten jumps into the air and for the moment is a little fur island itself. "But I am part of the world", it insists, "and the island is cut off from the land". "Ask any fish," says the contented island, and you see under water how the island and land are one. All this in . . . brief melodious text. . . .

[There] is more in this than you need expect very little children to get; some of them will, even more quickly than grownups, but for most six year olds this will be just a series of lovely pictures [by Leonard Weisgard.] . . . Later, when the comics are faded and forgotten, something may bring to mind this book and as it comes back it will open.

> *May Lamberton Becker, "Witch, Doll, Cats and Angels," in* New York Herald Tribune Weekly Book Review, *November 10, 1946, p. 10.**

Lovely pictures and brief poetic text describe for young children what it is like on a little island—what lives and grows on it, how the weather and the seasons affect it. Because there is no real story the book will be meaningless to many children; for the imaginative child the book will hold magic and beauty. (pp. 89-90)

> *A review of "The Little Island," in* The Booklist, *Vol. 43, No. 5, November 15, 1946, pp. 89-90.*

["The Little Island"] was very personal to Brown: She spent long summers on just such a closed-in island off the coast of Maine. But in its mushy lyricism, its recourse to verbal exchanges between the little island and a little kitten, it hasn't the inevitability of her tighter, purer work. (p. 66)

> *Barbara Bader, "A Lien on the World," in* The New York Times Book Review, *November 9, 1980, pp. 50, 66-7.*

THE MAN IN THE MANHOLE AND THE FIX-IT MEN (with Edith Thacher Hurd, 1946)

One of the most successful and original books of the season—and a MUST for small boys' Christmas lists, particularly small boys in the city, boys (and girls too) who are endlessly curious about what's going on above, below and on the city streets. This book goes about minding everybody's private business,—the hole in the roof, the cracked plaster, the leaky pipes, the telephone wires, the wrecked taxi, the road needing repair—and perhaps most fascinating of all, the loose joint way under the street where the man in the manhole goes. In prose that sings, . . . this book should jump right off the counters. . . . [The author] has a fascinating, lilting text, and has made a book that lends itself to story and play.

> *A review of "The Man in the Manhole and the Fix-It Men," in* Virginia Kirkus' Bookshop Service, *Vol. XIV, No. 20, October 15, 1946, p. 521.*

Story and pictures [by Bill Ballantine] are full of life and action and will stimulate good play activity for the child who plays alone or for groups of children. This book is a must for children three to seven.

> *Lois Palmer, in a review of "The Man in the Manhole and the Fix-It Men," in* The New York Times Book Review, *November 10, 1946, p. 42.*

Some of the types of work performed by repair men in a community are presented in brief text. . . . There is some useful information, although the tone of the writing is unnecessarily coy. . . .

> *A review of "The Man in the Manhole and the Fix-It Men," in* Bulletin of the Children's Book Center, *Vol. X, No. 14, December, 1956, p. 55.*

THE BAD LITTLE DUCKHUNTER (1947)

Nature gangs up on the little duck hunter, and makes his day in the duck blind an utter failure. The mother duck nips him, the mosquitoes bite him, the wind blows his hat away, the clouds rain upon him and he ended the day with a conviction that there's no fun in going duck hunting. Nonsense tale . . . —the background is a trifle off the line of child experience or interest but the development gives it some measure of general appeal.

> *A review of "The Bad Little Duckhunter," in* Virginia Kirkus' Bookshop Service, *Vol. XV, No. 5, March 1, 1947, p. 127.*

[With] rhythmic repetition this sportsman's misadventures proceed until at last, reckoning them from his refuge in a hollow tree, he asks himself: "Why shoot?" Why indeed, think all the little animals, as they gather around this reformed character—and if this is a moral tale it is a good moral. . . .

> *May Lamberton Becker, in a review of "The Bad Little Duckhunter," in* New York Herald Tribune Weekly Book Review, *March 16, 1947, p. 7.*

The 4's, 5's and 6's will find this delightfully silly, which is the way they like their stories. Once again Miss Brown has shown her ability to choose the right, simple words to make the plot clear, weaving into the story the color, sound and motion of poetry.

> *Lois Palmer, in a review of "The Bad Little Duck-hunter," in* The New York Times Book Review, *March 16, 1947, p. 26.*

THE GOLDEN EGG BOOK (1947)

"**Golden Egg Book**" is a wonderful gift for Eastertime. The story of the lonely bunny who found an egg and the lively duck who finally hatched from it is simple and charming. This is a picture book for the youngest children. . . .

> *Frances C. Darling, in a review of "Golden Egg Book," in* The Christian Science Monitor, *March 25, 1947, p. 11.*

[This is] one of Miss Brown's slighter tales. But what there is of it is told with the author's special gift for the sound of words and the heft of a sentence, and within its narrow structure it holds a sense of satisfaction. . . . This is not only a distinguished picture book but also a very happy one.

> *Ellen Lewis Buell, in a review of "The Golden Egg Book," in* The New York Times Book Review, *March 30, 1947, p. 40.*

GOODNIGHT MOON (1947)

Little children will love this going to sleep book—a really fresh idea by a talented and prolific author. . . . In a soft sing-song, here is a bunny saying goodnight room, goodnight moon, goodnight to all the familiar objects in the softly lighted room. . . . [This] is a good buy, from quality of text and [Clement Hurd's] pictures—and most of all, idea.

From Goodnight Moon, *written by Margaret Wise Brown. Pictures by Clement Hurd. Harper & Row, 1947. Copyright 1947 by Harper & Row, Publishers, Inc. By permission of Harper & Row, Publishers, Inc.*

> *A review of "Goodnight Moon," in* Virginia Kirkus' Bookshop Service, *Vol. XV, No. 13, July 1, 1947, p. 334.*

The sound of the words, the ideas they convey and the pictures combine to lull and reassure when bedtime and darkness come. The rhythm of the little story is like the sing-song of disconnected thoughts with which children so often put themselves to sleep, and should prove very effective in the case of a too wide-awake youngster.

> *Virginia H. Mathews, in a review of "Goodnight Moon," in* The New York Times Book Review, *September 7, 1947, p. 35.*

In these days of hurry and strain, a book for little children which creates an atmosphere of peace and calm is something for which to be thankful. Such a book is "**Goodnight Moon**". . . .

An ideal bedtime book with its rhythm, its atmosphere of cozy security, its poetry and childlike imagination.

> *Anne Thaxter Eaton, in a review of "Goodnight Moon," in* The Christian Science Monitor, *September 30, 1947, p. 14A.*

A go-to-sleep book for the parents' collection; there may be some doubt, however, in the minds of parents as to whether the book will induce drowsiness or merely provide the small child with further ideas for prolonging bedtime.

> *A review of "Goodnight Moon," in* The Booklist, *Vol. 44, No. 4, October 15, 1947, p. 74.*

Sleepy stories have a special place in nursery equipment, as every mother knows. This one combines a softly repeating, rhyming text with pictures for the most part in full color, together creating an atmosphere of going to sleep so contagious that the eyelids of a reviewer may begin to droop if he is writing on a warm day. . . .

Remembering how for years I have put myself to sleep, when needed, by going over the names of the guests at the Kenwigs's evening party in "Nicholas Nickelby" or the articles of furniture in a room described in "Sketches of Boz," I can testify that the principle involved in this cozy little book is sound.

> *May Lamberton Becker, in a review of "Goodnight Moon," in* New York Herald Tribune Weekly Book Review, *October 26, 1947, p. 10.*

[In **Goodnight Moon**], a preschool classic, a [build-up] sequence occurs. A very young rabbit says "good night" to the objects in his room. . . . Then, when the pattern is firmly established, the text suddenly turns antic. "Good night nobody!" it exclaims—to a blank white page. After that the pattern resumes, creating both relief and pleasure as after a deep breath taken. The withholding creates the tension, the completion allows release; the balance between these elements is almost palpable. (pp. 38-9)

> *Joan W. Blos, "Getting It: The First Notch on the Funny Bone," in* School Library Journal, *Vol. 25, No. 9, May, 1979, pp. 38-9.**

THE FIRST STORY (1947)

In the tradition of the poetic, wondrous fantasies of Oscar Wilde fairy tales, here is a dreamy, rather tiresome story of the "world before anyone knew anyone else". A little girl wanders about learning that she is not a squirrel, or a cat, or a fish, or a horse, but a little girl. And she meets a little boy who has had trouble convincing the fox that he is not a fox, and the goat, and the wolf, and the hog, too, that he is a little boy. So they met, and grew up and ''their children knew each other. . . . down to this day''. Miss Brown's lovely poetic prose is here and the pictures of Marc Simont. . . . capture the timeless quality. . . . The story may cause some confusion . . . in the small mind that has learned of the origin of the world through Bible stories.

> *A review of ''The First Story,'' in* Virginia Kirkus' Bookshop Service, *Vol. XV, No. 15, August 1, 1947, p. 392.*

A poetic, dreamy, other-worldly telling of how things might have been just after the Creation. . . . This one is for a rather special child, to be sure, but it will delight the right audience. (p. 132)

> *Rosemary C. Benét, ''Children's Books: The Story Still Counts,'' in* The New Yorker, *Vol. XXIII, No. 42, December 6, 1947, pp. 130-48.**

THE WINTER NOISY BOOK   (1947)

[*Winter Noisy Book*] is another story of Muffin, the little dog with the expanding consciousness, and like its predecessors it is original, beautiful, funny, and composed with every possible awareness of what a child would like said next. Margaret Wise Brown . . . is, in our opinion, tops among writers for the very young. . . . She has miraculously retained the perceptiveness which most of us lose in the second grade, and her flair for the instinctive rhythms of a child's attention is extraordinary. We endeavored, in a somewhat heavyhanded way, to analyze her methods—how she knew when to ask a question and when to answer; how she knew when to be stark and when to pile on the adjectives; when to appeal to her customers' tenderer emotions and when to set them rolling in the aisles. We gave it up. Miss Brown's talent is in a class by itself, and figuring it out would be like taking a master's degree in leprechauns. (pp. 142, 144)

> *Jane Cobb and Helen Dore Boylston ''One Child at a Time,'' in* The Atlantic Bookshelf, *a section of* The Atlantic Monthly, *Vol. 180, No. 6, December, 1947, pp. 142, 144.**

THE LITTLE FARMER   (1948)

Margaret Wise Brown's *Big and Little Series* needs no introduction. This is a day out of the life of the Big Farmer, who had a big farm, with everything big on it, and of the little farmer who had things in the scale a child would want. Here again comes the final dream where the big farmer dreams a little dream and the little farmer dreams a big dream. Hop-o-my-thumb psychology holds true consistently, and children are beguiled by the theme.

> *A review of ''The Little Farmer,'' in* Virginia Kirkus' Bookshop Service, *Vol. XVI, No. 3, February 1, 1948, p. 46.*

Miss Brown regales the youngest set with the story of the great big farmer and the very little farmer who live side by side. It is not a highly varied pattern, except for the paradox at the end, being a kind of antiphony of rhythmic repetitive prose describing the actions of the two protagonists which differ only

in proportion, but it is eminently suited to 2- to 4-year-olds who are very conscious of size in a world they never made.

> *Ellen Lewis Buell, in a review of ''The Little Farmer,'' in* The New York Times Book Review, *April 11, 1948, p. 30.*

It is not the scant plot that arrests the attention but rather the ever-appealing contrast of the big farmer who has everything big and a little farmer with everything little. Miss Brown has managed to convey a sense of wonder at the elements which are too big for either of them. Recommended for ages 5-7.

> *Florence W. Butler, in a review of ''The Little Farmer,'' in* Library Journal, *Vol. 73, No. 8, April 15, 1948, p. 656.*

THE LITTLE COWBOY   (1948)

The opinion here is unanimous—we don't like this book! Any part of it,—text by the gifted and industrious Margaret Wise Brown, and pictures by Esphyr Slobodkina. Contrapuntal treatment of a routine big and little pattern—Big Cowboy and Little Cowboy, big boots, little boots, big hat, little hat, big pony, little pony, big cows, little cows and so on. Somehow this theme is wearing thin, and the handling in this book suggests a thoroughly adult concept in plays on words, and so on, with little to appeal to the picture story age the format suggests.

> *A review of ''The Little Cowboy,'' in* Virginia Kirkus' Bookshop Service, *Vol. XVII, No. 5, March 1, 1949, p. 107.*

In ''**The Little Cowboy**'' Miss Brown follows the familiar, successful pattern of ''**The Little Fisherman**'' and ''**The Little Farmer**,'' contrasting in rhythmic phrases the size, equipment and feats of a big cowboy and a little cowboy. It seems, in comparison to the directness and robustiousness of [Lois Lenski's] ''Cowboy Small,'' a little thin. Nevertheless, 3-to-7-year-olds will take pleasure in the swing and the sound of the text, which describes a day on the range with gusto.

> *Ellen Lewis Buell, ''Home on the Range,'' in* The New York Times Book Review, *April 24, 1949, p. 34.**

Here the wild West is brought to three and four-year level, pistol, lasso, round-up and all. The story is pure action, as it should be with this subject, yet over all the active words, partly because of the rhythm and repetition, partly from the bits of song, there hangs an atmosphere of gayety and of poetry.

> *Louise S. Bechtel, ''Two More Books for Honor,'' in* New York Herald Tribune Weekly Book Review, *May 8, 1949, p. 8.**

WONDERFUL STORY BOOK   (1948)

A Big Golden Book collection of Margaret Wise Brown's poems and stories, forty two of them, and good stories they are, bearing rereading even if you've had them before. Animals, airplanes, trains, birds, fishes, imaginative stories, and fanciful ones balanced by down to earth might be true stories. Some have made place for themselves as junior classics already,—*The Terrible Tigerr, Fifteen Bathtubs, The Fish With The Deep Sea Smile*. . . . [This is] a book which will afford extensive pleasure. . . .

A review of "Wonderful Story Book," in Virginia Kirkus' Bookshop Service, Vol. XVI, No. 8, April 15, 1948, p. 195.

If there is even one very small child in the family, this isn't just a book, it's an investment. Try reading any of these . . . tiny stories and poems to a child too small to read for himself, and see how often you'll have to read it again. A few have already proved their quality—"**The Terrible Tigerr**," for instance, or the one about the little boy who had access to fifteen bathtubs and would go no further than the garden hose—but your auditor will like the one about the kitten that could yawn some, sneeze some, purr some. . . . Or Bunny No-Good who warned 1,100 other bunnies about the fox. . . . Well, any of them.

May Lamberton Becker, in a review of "Margaret Wise Brown's Wonderful Story Book," in New York Herald Tribune Weekly Book Review, May 23, 1948, p. 6.

This generous collection reveals both the strength and the weakness of Miss Brown's writing for young children. A few of these . . . are so tenuous that they would blow right off the page were it not for the author's characteristic manipulation of words and rhymes. The sum total, however, is on the credit side. The nursery set will revel in the adventures of a little girl who got a steam roller for Christmas, laugh over "**Fifteen Bathtubs**" and rejoice in "**The Little Girl's Medicine**," all of which show a close understanding of the young child's desires and interests. The majority of the poems, which deal with animals, the seasons, the weather, are lovely in sound and in their evocation of sense perceptions.

Ellen Lewis Buell, in a review of "Margaret Wise Brown's Wonderful Story Book," in The New York Times Book Review, June 27, 1948, p. 20.

"**The Terrible Tigerr**" who would eat only four-year-old meat and "**The Fish with the Deep Sea Smile**" who was finally caught only to escape still smiling are high points of this book. "**The Polite Polar Bear**" who apologized nicely before eating his victims and "**The Little Steamroller**" who flattened all who came into his path (including teachers and policemen) will delight the vicarious juvenile delinquent.

Some of the poems could have been dropped and there are a few extra adjectives around, but on the whole it is an entertaining and varied collection. Most of the pieces are short enough to be read aloud before the light is put out.

A review of "Wonderful Story Book," in The New Republic, Vol. 119, No. 23, December 6, 1948, p. 32.

[This is] a bonanza of the late author's inimitable inventions. Among the stories and poems is Brown's classic "**The Steam Roller**." . . . Brown's uncanny ability to write as if she were a child herself makes all the entries delightful and unforgettable.

A review of "Margaret Wise Brown's Wonderful Storybook," in Publishers Weekly, Vol. 227, No. 18, May 3, 1985, p. 73.

WAIT TILL THE MOON IS FULL   (1948)

The mystery and wonder of nighttime is presented here in a way to sharpen the awareness of the very young child and to dispel any fears of it which the more timorous may have. The story, so brief that it is scarcely more than a prose poem, concerns a baby raccoon who had never seen the night. His mother said, "Wait till the moon is full," and as the raccoon's curiosity grows about the color and shape of the night he questions her about it, learning about it in a kind of reverse Socratic system. This is very slight, but the words, the rhythm and the mood have a great deal of charm and humor. . . .

Ellen Lewis Buell, in a review of "Wait till the Moon Is Full," in The New York Times Book Review, November 14, 1948, p. 5.

[*Wait till the Moon is Full* has] a text unexceptional for this author. The story tells of a little raccoon who wanted to go out at night and "see the moon—and see the night—and know an owl—and how dark is dark?—and listen to the Whippoorwill—and stay up all night and sleep all day" etc. (A familiar sound, eh?). And he does it. Simple and nice.

A review of "Wait till the Moon Is Full," in Virginia Kirkus' Bookshop Service, Vol. XVI, No. 22, November 15, 1948, p. 598.

[A] must is *Wait Till the Moon Is Full*, by Margaret Wise Brown. . . . This is her best story so far, but it is the delectable drawings of Garth Williams that really make the book. The combination is irresistible. (p. 221)

Blanche Jennings Thompson, in a review of "Wait till the Moon Is Full," in The Catholic World, Vol. 168, No. 1005, December, 1948, pp. 221-22.

Everything about this book seems just right. The title is intriguing; children will like it. Story has a lilt and gaiety and tender appeal. . . . One of the outstanding books of this year. Highly recommended.

Marian A. Webb, in a review of "Wait till the Moon Is Full," in Library Journal, Vol. 73, No. 22, December 15, 1948, p. 1825.

A classic American picture book first published in 1948 and dedicated to all things that love the night. . . . This is a children's book of real quality which, like its author, deserves to be much more widely known in Britain.

A review of "Wait till the Moon Is Full," in Books for Your Children, Vol. 13, No. 2, Spring, 1978, p. 5.

THE IMPORTANT BOOK   (1949)

A perfect book for very small children, one that will go on long after the printed word has been absorbed, for the text establishes a word game which tiny children accept with glee. The text is a series of word songs, the child's first conception of poetry, dealing simply and repetitively with each object pictured, whether grass or sky, an apple, shoes, rain, or what have you. Children go on from there, picking out the important thing about other familiar objects around. . . . This is tops—with us.

A review of "The Important Book," in Virginia Kirkus' Bookshop Service, Vol. XVII, No. 10, May 15, 1949, p. 252.

Again this interesting author and [the artist Leonard Weisgard] give us something fresh, different, thoughtful and beautiful.

Their big Easter-egg book is a great favorite, and their book about the little island, more subtle, is equally loved by children. Now they offer the pre-school child and whoever will look with him and talk with him a conversation with pictures about many familiar things, in order to decide what is the most essential word applying to each one. . . .

You are pulling up a shade, or looking at the back of a door, or rushing alone through wind or snow; and never another child, only you, looking and looking.

You are allowed to disagree with what is important, and you will. Most important of all is that the game can go on with many more "things" than are on these pages.

> *Louise S. Bechtel, in a review of "The Important Book," in* New York Herald Tribune Weekly Book Review, *May 22, 1949, p. 14.*

It is difficult for adults to see everyday objects as children see them. They have been using spoons and shoes for so long that these are just spoons and shoes. . . . But to children, spoons . . . [and shoes are] new experiences.

Margaret Wise Brown with her unusual perception of what children think and feel puts into words for them the pleasure-giving qualities of such everyday but exciting objects as an apple, a daisy, the sky, the grass. Each quality is described simply and each story developed slowly. The refrain "it is important" occurs on each page, and what is important becomes a game which reader and listener share. . . .

For three-to-seven-year-olds the book offers much to think about. . . .

> *Lois Palmer, "Everyday Things," in* The New York Times Book Review, *July 17, 1949, p. 22.*

This is a fresh and stimulating book to interest a child in the world around him, but to this reviewer at least, the dogmatic text is a disappointment. If only Margaret Wise Brown had written questions instead of flat statements.

> *Frances C. Darling, in a review of "The Important Book," in* The Christian Science Monitor, *September 13, 1949, p. 10.*

MY WORLD   (1949)

Very small children will identify themselves with the white bunny and his awakening sense of his own world, and the things in it that are his, with willing concession to his parents' possessions. . . . Without actually writing her text in verse, Margaret Wise Brown gives it a sort of rhythm that has a natural lilt.

> *A review of "My World," in* Virginia Kirkus' Bookshop Service, *Vol. XVII, No. 17, September 1, 1949, p. 463.*

This "very young book" takes "me," a bunny, through a happy day and night in a little boy's or girl's world. As a parent reads the few words chosen so well, the pictures [by Clement Hurd] offer much to point at and to linger upon, that is "just like me." Both author and artist are adept at knowing the child's love of recognition of familiar things: they use the familiar with the added magic of gentle humor and poetry. Beyond the intention of fun and happy recognition, the book offers that sense of security in talking about his own world which so comforts the very small child. . . .

The end has the typical M.W.B. touch: "Your world. My world. I can swing right over the world." . . . Then, for two tiny postscript pictures: "My tree. The bird's tree." And, "How many stripes on a bumble bee?"

> *Louise S. Bechtel, in a review of "My World," in* New York Herald Tribune Book Review, *November 13, 1949, p. 6.*

This new book by the same combination who did **Goodnight Moon** is unfortunately not its equal in either text or illustrations. Some of the text is delightful, such as "My bed. Mother's bed. I go to sleep when my story is read. When my prayers are said and when my head is sleepy on the pillow." But most of it is forced as if the author were searching desperately for a rhyming word to complete the thought. . . . Children will, however, undoubtedly have lots of fun putting themselves in the place of the bunnies as they go through the familiar, everyday activities. This book would probably be useful in helping little children distinguish between "yours" and "mine", but it does not seem really worthwhile enough to justify wholesale library or nursery school purchase.

> *A review of "My World," in* Bulletin of the Children's Book Center, *Vol. III, No. 1, December, 1949, p. 2.*

Similar in theme and treatment to **Runaway Bunny** and **Goodnight Moon**. A little rabbit compares his possessions with those of his parents. Idea is good and, in the main, well handled, although a few of the verses seem a bit silly.

> *Marian Herr, in a review of "My World," in* Library Journal, *Vol. 74, No. 21, December 1, 1949, p. 1827.*

TWO LITTLE TRAINS   (1949)

A picture book about two trains that traveled through rain and snow, under tunnels and over mountains to the West. Such a book has definite possibilities for use as the basis of a discussion about trains and train trips, and the rhythmic prose and repetition will be appealing to children. (p. 2)

> *A review of "Two Little Trains," in* Bulletin of the Children's Book Center, *Vol. III, No. 1, December, 1949, pp. 2-3.*

The author and the artist [Jean Charlot] swing along zestfully through the journey of a big streamliner and a "little old train" going West. The breezy, rhythmic prose will probably have four- to seven-year-old children stamping around the room. (p. 166)

> *Katharine T. Kinkead "The Children at Christmas Time," in* The New Yorker, *Vol. XXV, No. 41, December 3, 1949, pp. 162-88.**

This is one of those clever, pseudo-primitive picture-books which are liked nowadays in the States and which seem to me often to be quite pointless. The text . . . is thin, rhythmic stuff, pretentiously artless. . . . There is no story to speak of.

There is a glimmering of an idea in the book which might be good, but it is clouded with sophisticated self-consciousness.

> *A review of "Two Little Trains," in* The Junior Bookshelf, *Vol. 24, No. 4, October, 1960, p. 211.*

A PUSSYCAT'S CHRISTMAS (1949)

The idea is one that will appeal at the two and three year old level—of what the little cat thinks about the excitements of Christmas, the rattly paper, the tempting ribbons, the irresistible Christmas tree ornaments. Done in . . . a rhythmic, repetitive prose patterned text, which reads aloud beautifully.

> *A review of "A Pussycat's Christmas," in* Virginia Kirkus' Bookshop Service, *Vol. XVII, No. 23, December 1, 1949, p. 653.*

In "A Pussycat's Christmas" Margaret Wise Brown evokes the smells, the sounds, the glittering lights of Christmas Eve as experienced by a small but observant cat. The sounds are especially effective. The rustle of tissue paper, the tinkle of baubles, the deep hush of a snowy night are conveyed in prose which will please the ears of 3-to-6-year-olds.

> *Ellen Lewis Buell, in a review of "A Pussycat's Christmas," in* The New York Times Book Review, *December 4, 1949, p. 42.*

THE COLOR KITTENS (1949; also published as *The Color Kittens: A Child's First Book about Colors*)

Very slight story of two kittens who experimented with colors in an attempt to make green paint. The story is too slight to hold the interest of pre-school children and the mixing of colors is probably beyond the experience of most of them. The book should have some value for beginning art classes. Of particular value is the naming of colors in connection with common objects that are those colors.

> *A review of "The Color Kittens," in* Bulletin of the Children's Book Center, *Vol. III, No. 4, March, 1950, p. 27.*

Any young child who has played with colors—with crayons, paint, Easter egg dyes—is immediately interested in the color kittens' problem: "making green." And every child enjoys the rhythmic, rhyming text [and] the quickly shifting word pictures. . . .

> *Elizabeth Doak, in a review of "The Color Kittens: A Child's First Book about Colors," in* The Horn Book Magazine, *Vol. XXXIV, No. 4, August, 1958, p. 258.*

As a parent who has read Margaret Wise Brown's **The Color Kittens** . . . more times then he would willingly recall, this reader can affirm that it is a book impermeable to time.

> *Thomas Lask, in a review of "The Color Kittens," in* The New York Times Book Review, *November 2, 1958, p. 51.*

THE DARK WOOD OF THE GOLDEN BIRDS (1950)

[**Dark Wood of the Golden Birds** takes] us away to a magic wood and a small boy who braved it to bring back to an old man the song of the golden birds. Since the facts of Miss Brown's life are pretty well known to librarians, suffice it to say that she considers writing for children a challenge that it would take a poet, scientist, or a dreamer to be clear and simple enough to meet.

> *Louise Davis, in a review of "Dark Wood of the Golden Birds," in* Library Journal, *Vol. 75, No. 8, April 15, 1950, p. 632.*

When two artists like this artist with words and Leonard Weisgard join forces there should be occasion for exultation. But this time we feel that they have gone too far into a rarified atmosphere remote from child interest. There's even a subtle aura of fear engendered—and never clarified in the story of the forest from which comes the music of golden birds, into which people who venture never return or else return speaking an unknown language. An old man shelters two wayfaring children, and keeps for them the magic of the forest and the song. But when they want to enter the wood he breaks the charm by saying he cannot hear the song and the birds are unreal. He becomes ill; the boy goes into the forest; and when ultimately he returns, the magic is there again but the mystery remains illusive. Somehow it doesn't come off.

> *A review of "The Dark Wood of the Golden Birds," in* Virginia Kirkus' Bookshop Service, *Vol. XVIII, No. 12, June 15, 1950, p. 331.*

[This] is a parable of the poetry and beauty of life, of the courage and faith which are needed to find them and of the insensitivity which comes to those who deny their reality. Now, important as is this theme, the first duty of a parable is to be interesting as a story. This one seems to me too tenuous, to subtle to convey its message effectively.

> *Ellen Lewis Buell, "A Parable," in* The New York Times Book Review, *July 9, 1950, p. 22.*

This is one of those special odd books that took a bit of courage on the part of the publisher, who knew well that the modern allegory is a form not too welcome. Its little boy and girl have the pathos of the old babes in the woods; yet their story is imaginatively modern. It can be taken as a lovely fairy tale for the younger reader, or used as a gift for those much older who will realize its implications.

Such an unusual little book is well worth its rare flight of imagery. Quietly its green pages, with mysterious trees and drifting, unnamed children, take hold of the imagination. All of us, even children, know our particular dark woods, and may be glad to be reminded that our courage in piercing them could have [a reward like the boy's].

> *Louise S. Bechtel, in a review of "The Dark Wood of the Golden Birds," in* New York Herald Tribune Book Review, *July 23, 1950, p. 8.*

A fanciful tale with a mystical quality that will be lost on the very young reader for whom it is intended. The way in which so many elements are left in a misty, unresolved state will also prove unsatisfactory for them. Teen-age girls who are at the stage of great appreciation of poetry and the super-romantic will probably read the book with enjoyment.

> *A review of "The Dark Wood of the Golden Birds," in* Bulletin of the Children's Book Center, *Vol. III, No. 9, September, 1950, p. 53.*

THE DREAM BOOK: FIRST COMES THE DREAM (1950)

Another experiment with the dream-theme, with a mood enchantment in . . . word-rhyme, but without the careful coordination and direct appeal to children of *Who Dreams of Cheese?*

Brown at an early age. Courtesy of Westerly Public Library, Westerly, RI.

. . . Again the author's rhyme is simple, unforced, artless. However, the theme here slides off the pleasant circular track at times with a sophisticated aside—"toward such a world comes first the dream". Comes at this point, we think, a yawn.

> *A review "The Dream Book," in* Virginia Kirkus' Bookshop Service, *Vol. XVIII, No. 18, September 15, 1950, p. 556.*

An attempt to create a mood for the very young child. The sections in which the animals are dreaming are not too bad but when the author brings in man's social progress starting with the dream that precedes each step then the ideas become too complex to have any meaning for the pre-school age level. . . . Not recommended.

> *A review of "The Dream Book: First Comes the Dream," in* Bulletin of the Children's Book Center, *Vol. IV, No. 2, January, 1951, p. 11.*

THE QUIET NOISY BOOK (1950)

Another addition to the Brown-Weisgard book a month partnership. This time a puppy hears a slight sound and goes through the list of things it could be but isn't until he finally realizes

it is day breaking. A whole lot of nothing and all for $1.50. Not recommended.

> *A review of "The Quiet Noisy Book," in* Bulletin of the Children's Book Center, *Vol. III, No. 10, October, 1950, p. 59.*

The new **"Noisy Book"** has been awaited with extra curiosity. How could it be quiet? But the inventor of Muffin comes through: she is exploring "very quiet noises." After Muffin had been asleep all night, quietly something woke him up. You have your choice of a lot of very quiet guesses, and funny ideas about how quiet they are. At last, you know; it was the sun coming up; it was the new day. This is all a very pleasant increase of the small child's powers of listening. It does not integrate the dog Muffin with its idea, as did the first **"Noisy Book,"** but it is interesting, charming, well worth a "quiet" hour with a small child on your lap. The questions in the **"Noisy Books"** always delight this age.

> *Louise S. Bechtel, in a review of "The Quiet Noisy Book," in* New York Herald Tribune Book Review, *November 12, 1950, p. 16.*

THE PEPPERMINT FAMILY (1950)

Much ado about peppermint in an amorphous picture book, possibly evolved in haste—a great disappointment from this author who has made so many fine contributions to children's literature. Mr. Peppermint goes to the North Pole (for no apparent reason) and the Peppermint baby is born. Mrs. Peppermint sends a letter to the North Pole for a name ("Chocolate Peppermint" is the choice), and Mr. P. returns home to see the baby. This is an unsuccessful joining of unmatched parts only superficially united in the peppermint device.

> *A review of "The Peppermint Family," in* Virginia Kirkus' Bookshop Service, *Vol. XVIII, No. 19, October 1, 1950, p. 606.*

Any ordinary man who departed for the North Pole on a pleasure trip and casually answered the announcement of the birth of his son with "Home soon. Just one more fish and polar bear" would be despicable, but not Mr. Peppermint. He, after all, thought of the perfect name for the child. Children 3-6 will love this imaginative, fanciful tale written easily and rhythmically. . . .

> *Elaine E. Beatty, in a review of "The Peppermint Family," in* Library Journal, *Vol. 75, No. 20, November 15, 1950, p. 2016.*

THE SUMMER NOISY BOOK (1951)

The joys of hearing familiar names and lovely satisfying sounds mark the constant appeal of the *Noisy Books,* and the . . . illustrations by Leonard Weisgard contribute to the buoyant confusion of clatters, rustles and booms. Little Muffin, the dog, was introduced to summer as he heard the birds, the clippety clop of the horse, the ding dong dingle of the cow bells, the jug a rum of the frogs and all the symphony of the countryside, ending with the giant rumble of a thunderstorm. Noises unexplained tease the young listener on to the next page. . . . [The] whole production is an exhilarating sense experience.

A review of "The Summer Noisy Book," in Virginia Kirkus' Bookshop Service, *Vol. XIX, No. 21, November 1, 1951, p. 631.*

Another addition to the greatly beloved ["**Noisy Books**"]. . . . Highly successful in conveying sound through text and pictures. Greatest use will be with the preschool group. . . . Recommended for wide purchase.

Margaret E. Martignoni, in a review of "The Summer Noisy Book," in Library Journal, *Vol. 76, No. 21, December 1, 1951, p. 2019.*

You might think that Muffin, the ever-listening Scottie of the **"Noisy Books,"** would have heard every noise in the world by this time. It is true that some of the sounds he hears in **"The Summer Noisy Book"** are the same as those in **"The Country Noisy Book."** The basic pattern is similar, too: the trip to a farm, the investigation of new sounds, explained in a game of questions and answers which invites young listeners to join in the fun. Yet in this book Miss Brown has shifted her emphasis. The impact of the country noises is stronger and there is here a sense of life beginning as spring moves into summer.

Ellen Lewis Buell, "Sounds of Life," in The New York Times Book Review, *December 9, 1951, p. 42.*

The words used to describe the sounds are not always accurate representations and several would require an expert mimic to give them any meaning for the child. The book would be more successful with a child who is already acquainted with the sounds than with one to whom the country is an unknown place. Not recommended.

A review of "The Summer Noisy Book," in Bulletin of the Children's Book Center, *Vol. VI, No. 1, September, 1952, p. 3.*

FOX EYES (1951)

This is a strange tale, and to me disappointing. The sly fox upsets animals and children by merely peeping at them. He goes to sleep and forgets what he has seen. But those whom he has upset don't know that he forgets. This the publishers call "a wry little fable, directed against unnecessary self-consciousness and unnecessary feelings of guilt." Oh dear, oh dear! . . . [To] our minds it is neither reasonable nor amusing for children.

Louise S. Bechtel, "One Author, Many Artists," in New York Herald Tribune Book Review, *November 11, 1951, p. 34.*

Each [animal and child] feels that the fox has somehow caught him out . . . and readers too get the eerie feeling that this all-knowing eye is ubiquitous. But it all comes to nothing when " . . . the fox just yawned . . . and went to sleep. . . . For, of course, the fox could never remember the next day what he had seen the day before." But the words and [Garth Williams's] pictures have generated so much watchful apprehension that this news comes less as reassurance than as let-down. And to be further toyed with at the turn of the last page—"But no one knows that but the fox"—is merely disconcerting.

A review of "Fox Eyes," in Kirkus Reviews, *Vol. XLV, No. 8, April 15, 1977, p. 421.*

A new generation of young readers should welcome this reissue of an old favorite by an author who still maintains her hold, despite her death over two decades ago. Brown's knack for spinning a simple story has just begun to merit the appreciation she deserved long ago.

Ruth M. Stein, in a review of "Fox Eyes," in Language Arts, *Vol. 54, No. 6, September, 1977, p. 684.*

[*Fox Eyes* is a] captivating story. . . . Pictures and text enhance each other in this enchanting tale which is characterized by a subtle touch of humor.

Fox Eyes lends itself to several classroom applications: being read aloud by the teacher; dramatization; discussion of the animals' conduct and worries; and discussion of the habits of the forest dwellers. Information concerning the animals' habits, camouflage, and environment is accurate and could provide useful ecological facts for study.

A review of "Fox Eyes," in The Reading Teacher, *Vol. 31, No. 5, February, 1978, p. 576.*

PUSSY WILLOW (1951)

[A] story that reads quite delightfully as a round the season pattern of growing things—this should prove a special Easter item, and a good all year round gift item. The idea of the slender thread of story is an original one. A tiny kitten that doesn't grow any bigger and that doesn't seem to have any family is sure he's kin to the pussywillows. He was born into a Spring world—and then suddenly the pussywillows disappeared. And he looked until he found them again—a whole year later. . . . Purists (and this includes many small inquiring minds) will be bothered by the lonesomeness of the kitten and his not growing. Even his relief when he finds his pussywillows again—just where they'd been before—isn't enough quite to offset the sadness of disappointment in the months between. On an adult level the book has great appeal.

A review of "Pussy Willow," in Virginia Kirkus' Bookshop Service, *Vol. XX, No. 3, February 1, 1952, p. 67.*

[The] amiable conclusion may give the nursery age a chuckle, if they see how it matches the answers given the kitten by each creature during her search. Adults will not be impressed.

Here are this popular author's usual airy logic, sense of the beauty of the visible world, and lovely prose rhythms. . . . [The story] has not the impact of gay surprise that made the big **"Golden Egg Book"** such a success, but it is a happy new Easter item.

Louise S. Bechtel, in a review of "Pussy Willow," in New York Herald Tribune Book Review, *March 30, 1952, p. 10.*

WHERE HAVE YOU BEEN? (1952)

In winsome verses . . . —a book tiny children with that early awareness of repetition of sound and rhythm will claim as their own. Familiar creatures such as cat—bird—squirrel—fish—mouse and so on appear in verses asking questions—"Where have you been?" And the answers have odd quirks of humor "To see if the tick comes after the tock"—the kinds of things that bring chuckles to the youngest readers.

A review of "Where Have You Been?" in Virginia Kirkus' Bookshop Service, *Vol. XX, No. 3, February 1, 1952, p. 67.*

A happy gift for the nursery age, [**"Where Have You Been?"**] combines the talents of an author and an illustrator [Barbara Cooney] widely loved. It is so appealing that many over six will "collect" it, besides the parents and other adults who will be asked to read it over and over. At four or five, it will prove a fine "pre-reader," with its big type and repetition.

A review of "Where Have You Been?" in New York Herald Tribune Book Review, *May 11, 1952, p. 21.*

[This rhymed text] retains its appealing simplicity. There's a sound of old nursery rhymes here. . . . Toddlers will find the characters identifiable and the musical repetition comfortable.

Betsy Hearne, in a review of "Where Have You Been?" in Booklist, *Vol. 78, No. 14, March 15, 1982, p. 956.*

THE NOON BALLOON (1952)

Magic combination of names—with Leonard Weisgard as illustrator—but a story that seems to this reader rather pointless from two who know better. Absurdity plus—as a small cat takes refuge from the bothersome mice in a balloon and goes sailing across the world. What he sees and how he decides he has had enough doesn't make a sure story to hold the small fry.

A review of "The Noon Balloon," in Virginia Kirkus' Bookshop Service, *Vol. XX, No. 17, September 1, 1952, p. 545.*

This book has rhythm and beauty, soft as rain water, in both text and pictures . . . and stands the real test of any book: the text is good without the pictures. It is as peaceful a story as floating along in a balloon must be. Libraries and families should both have it.

Phyllis Fenner, in a review of "The Noon Balloon," in Library Journal, *Vol. 77, No. 18, October 15, 1952, p. 1817.*

Miss Brown, who is an expert at describing the impact of new experiences upon the five senses, isn't quite as brilliant in her imagery as usual and her story is a bit disjointed. Nevertheless, she has captured in her prose the slow, drifting motion of the balloon, a quality which makes this a good book to read just before bedtime.

Ellen Lewis Buell, "Old-Fashioned Cat," in The New York Times Book Review, *November 16, 1952, p. 41.*

A CHILD'S GOOD MORNING (1952)

Just as **"A Child's Good Night Book"** curves and flows in soft sleepy rhythms, these words and [Jean Charlot's] pictures are gaily alert, promising a wide-eyed, beautiful day. The blend of imaginative text and arresting pictures should bring pleasure and interest to any wide-awake nursery audience.

Irene Smith, "Waking Up," in The New York Times Book Review, *November 16, 1952, p. 38.*

Simple, rhythmical text describes the coming of day from the first light of dawn through the awakening of the birds, the animals, and finally the children. . . . A very slight but pleasant introduction to environmental concepts for the pre-school child.

A review of "A Child's Good Morning," in Bulletin of the Children's Book Center, *Vol. VI, No. 4, December, 1952, p. 30.*

Though obviously intended as a companion volume to *A Child's Goodnight Book,* this is . . . less harmonious in concept.

While Jean Charlot is busy interpreting the mood of the awakening world with startling lithographs, . . . Margaret Wise Brown patters along in her inevitable rhythmic prose in which mood is expressed largely through exclamation points. Nevertheless, a *must* book for the picture-book age.

Mary Strang, in a review of "A Child's Good Morning," in Library Journal, *Vol. 77, No. 21, December 1, 1952, p. 2074.*

CHRISTMAS IN THE BARN (1952)

The story of the Nativity has been retold in verse for very little children. . . . Miss Brown's phrases are musical and evocative, but because she omitted all religious significance her version loses point and drama unless it is amplified by a grown-up.

Ellen Lewis Buell, in a review of "Christmas in the Barn," in The New York Times Book Review, *December 7, 1952, p. 50.*

Published in 1952 to unanimous praise, this is one of Brown's enduring gifts to readers young and old. . . . Lyrics describe the Nativity as Joseph and Mary shelter in a barn,

> In the sunset of the west.
> And a star rose
> Brighter than all the stars in the sky.

A review of "Christmas in the Barn," in Publishers Weekly, *Vol. 228, No. 7, August 16, 1985, p. 71.*

SLEEPY ABC (1953)

There is a reassurance in these alphabet verses which ought to send a child off to bed with the feeling that all is well. As in many of the late Margaret Wise Brown's books, the familiar, domestic aspects of a child's life are combined with a poetic sense of the larger world. Thus "M is for Mother, who tucks you in tight," "N is for the dark and starry night." There is, too, the comfortable anticipation of the next day—"X is for all the things you can play."

The sound effects are pleasantly soporific. . . .

Ellen Lewis Buell, "Bedtime Song," in The New York Times Book Review, *February 15, 1953, p. 26.*

An ABC book designed for use at bedtime. The text has an uneven rhyme scheme and rhythm, and the choice of words does not always make sense. Too slight and too uneven in quality for the price. . . .

A review of "Sleepy ABC," in Bulletin of the Children's Book Center, *Vol. VI, No. 7, March, 1953, p. 50.*

Wonderfully enfolding, world within world, alphabet sayings for bed time. Margaret Wise Brown's imagination captures, quite completely, the sleepy, dreamy, goodnight feelings of the young with definitions like "A is for Aaaah when a small kitten sighs", "I is for me who is going to bed", "V is for visions that dance in your head".

> *A review of "Sleepy ABC," in* Virginia Kirkus' Bookshop Service, *Vol. XXI, No. 5, March 1, 1953, p. 147.*

THE GOLDEN BUNNY AND 17 OTHER STORIES AND POEMS (1953)

Bunnies, bunnies—all sorts of bunnies, going about their bunny busyness in a world of bunnies. Golden Bunny, best loved bunny in all the world, who got lost in the cool green woods, but was found by his big warm mother and made safe again in his home in the hollow tree. Silly Bunny who shouted, "Fire! Fire! Fire!" at the woods in the fall, the blazing red flowers, the red sun, and the red moon. And Rabbit who ran softly about the forest at sundown telling the animals to go to sleep. These and others romp thru 18 little stories and poems, not forgetting **"A Bunny's Hungry ABC,"** which make up this enchanting Easter offering. . . . The quiet magic of the late Margaret Wise Brown's singing phrases have a perfect complement in Leonard Weisgard's [illustrations.]

> *Polly Goodwin, "Bunnies, Bunnies," in* Chicago Tribune, *Part 4, April 5, 1953, p. 10.*

A collection of imaginative rabbit tales, made half fancy and half real by Miss Brown's rich, suggestive turns of phrase that can take young readers right inside the cover of the book to a different stream or meadow as each page is turned. . . . Perfect for Spring.

> *A review of "The Golden Bunny," in* Virginia Kirkus' Bookshop Service, *Vol. XXI, No. 8, April 15, 1953, p. 261.*

THE HIDDEN HOUSE (1953)

Tucked away in the midst of big city skyscrapers is a little house in **"The Hidden House,"** . . . which a little boy discovers when he crawls through a hole in the fence one day. There is a "Goldilocks" flavor to the story as the boy explores the house and finds smoke up the chimney, tiny flames in the fireplace, the smell of chicken brewing on the stove, clothes hanging in the closets. . . .

There is a wonderful surprise ending to this quiet story told in Miss Brown's inimitable style.

> *Ruth C. Barlow, in a review of "The Hidden House," in* The Christian Science Monitor, *May 14, 1953, p. 13.*

The climax comes when the occupants, "two wild Indians," return. The use of the adjective "wild" to describe Indians who just happen into a story for the picture-book age is pointless, and, indeed, the story lacks originality and any special charm.

> *Viola K. Fitch, in a review of "The Hidden House," in* Library Journal, *Vol. 78, No. 11, June 1, 1953, p. 1006.*

LITTLE FRIGHTENED TIGER (1953)

The book is gay and amusing, with a tiger who will appeal especially to small boys of nursery age. But we wonder whether the effect will really be cheerful. For this baby's parents cured him of fearfulness by showing him how all creatures are afraid, the elephant's afraid of a mouse, the whale afraid of a ship, etc. It turns a scary little tiger into a brave one, but we do think the little tiger's song should have ended "I'm a BIG tiger, inside." The proof that just being a tiger is enough has not been given. It always was atmosphere rather than logic which was the strong point of this writer, and for the nursery age this jungle . . . is good.

> *Louise S. Bechtel, in a review of "Little Frightened Tiger," in* New York Herald Tribune Book Review, *October 4, 1953, p. 12.*

Parents finding themselves hard pressed to explain the last line in the story "[he] was not afraid of anything, except himself," might quickly divert young attentions to Leonard Weisgard's lavish pictures. . . . It is Mr. Weisgard who carries the book.

> *Mary Lee Krupka, "Timid Tiger," in* The New York Times Book Review, *November 15, 1953, p. 43.*

Here a salutary lesson is taught, I think, by showing that fear isn't too important, because everyone is afraid of something. . . . So, if you have timid youngsters in the house . . . that cling to Mummy too much, this is for you. As a matter of fact almost any boy or girl under five would be amused by it, and if it fills a deeper need, so much the better.

> *Margaret Ford Kieran, in a review of "Little Frightened Tiger," in* The Atlantic Monthly, *Vol. 192, No. 6, December, 1953, p. 97.*

THE SAILOR DOG (1953)

This new edition of a 1953 publication should be a bestseller. It's a collaboration by the late Brown and illustrator [Garth] Williams, two of the most honored people in children's literature. . . . With her genius for writing as though she were a gifted child, the author creates a charming, believable tale about Scuppers, who can't rest until he's back on the bounding main. Leaving home, he turns down offers to ride in a car, train, subway, etc., but eagerly gets aboard a dandy sailboat. The sea dog's story becomes heady excitement, what with a shipwreck, rebuilding his boat on a deserted island, then visiting an exotic land—but never happier than when he's skimming over the waves in his tidy craft.

> *A review of "The Sailor Dog," in* Publishers Weekly, *Vol. 220, No. 13, September 25, 1981, p. 88.*

WILLIE'S ADVENTURES: THREE STORIES (1954)

A tiny trilogy by a skillful hand has its own quiet quality and forms three imaginative openings into the world of small boy adventures. In the first, incredulous Willie . . . awaits a new pet cat, wondering the while about all the things it could have been. The second sees him finding things for his pockets and the third going on a walk to his grandmother's in the country. Miniscule meanderings, winsome and fetching in the right way.

> *A review of "Willie's Adventures," in* Virginia Kirkus' Bookshop Service, *Vol. XXII, No. 7, April 1, 1954, p. 231.*

Willie telephoned his grandmother who lived in the country. "I would like a little animal for my very own," he said. Their conversation, and Willie's dreams of what will come, are priceless. And what a name Willie chose for his animal—"Grandcat." . . . [In his second adventure,] Willie's experiments and decisions are delightful; so is Father's surprise contribution at the end. . . .

Miss Brown's special genius is at its best in this chunky, gay little book, equally good to read to four-year-olds, or for beginning readers. She recognizes the small boy's innate manliness and the wide range of his thoughts, and adapts them to the simple drama of each tale without sentimentality or condescension.

> *Louise S. Bechtel, in a review of "Willie's Adventures: Three Stories," in* New York Herald Tribune Book Review, *May 16, 1954, p. 8.*

The last story, previously published separately under the title, **Willie's Walk,** has long been a favorite with pre-school and kindergarten children, and the two new stories will appeal to them just as much. All are told with Miss Brown's sure sense of how to reach little children.

> *Jennie D. Lindquist, in a review of "Willie's Adventures," in* The Horn Book Magazine, *Vol. XXX, No. 4, August, 1954, p. 246.*

WHEEL ON THE CHIMNEY (with Tibor Gergely, 1954)

A simply told story of the annual nesting of the storks and their migration between Hungary and Africa. First there is one stork, then there are two, then four—in a cycle that begins once again on the last page of the book. The author's characteristic rhythmic lines of text and [Tibor Gergely's] brilliant pictures together make this a distinguished contribution to the picture-book age.

> *Virginia Haviland, in a review of "Wheel on the Chimney," in* The Horn Book Magazine, *Vol. XXX, No. 5, October, 1954, p. 325.*

A simple tale, this story of the flight of the storks, but a moving and compelling one in its unerring directness and beauty of movement. . . . A beautiful and mind-widening book for children of any age.

> *Rosemary Livsey, in a review of "Wheel on the Chimney," in* The Saturday Review, *New York, Vol. XXXVII, No. 46, November 13, 1954, p. 67.*

The fascination of storks, in legend and reality, has held the imaginations of many of us from childhood on. Mr. Gergely felt it, remembering well the storks of his childhood in Europe. Miss Brown saw his wonderful paintings and collaborated on a text. So we have one of the most striking picture books of the year, a book of far countries and of the ways of these huge, beautiful birds. It makes a rare gift for children of about four to eight. . . .

The gently informative words are a properly brief and simple accompaniment to the wonderful, detailed pictures. . . .

> *Louise S. Bechtel, in a review of "Wheel on the Chimney," in* New York Herald Tribune Book Review, *November 14, 1954, p. 4.*

THE LITTLE FIR TREE (1954)

[A] different sort of Christmas tree story. . . . It is a very slight story, with a rhythmic repeat pattern, following the seasons' round. A little boy is lame and ill, and each December his father digs up a little tree from a meadow where it feels forlornly alone, plants it in a tub, and takes it for the Christmas season and the months following, to his boy's bedside. And in the Spring he takes the tree back to its meadow, to grow a little bigger. Then one year he doesn't come for the tree, and just as Winter without Christmas seems desolate, the little boy, grown strong and well, comes with his friends to the tree. A new story to read aloud—and one the little folks will enjoy.

> *A review of "The Little Fir Tree," in* Virginia Kirkus' Bookshop Service, *Vol. XXII, No. 22, November 15, 1954, p. 751.*

The climax is as expected—a happy one, to be sure—but the quality of the book lies in its beautifully evoked feeling of the seasons as the tree grows and waits and in the little verses and songs, set to familiar tunes, which punctuate the narrative.

> *Ellen Lewis Buell, in a review of "The Little Fir Tree," in* The New York Times Book Review, *December 5, 1954, p. 54.*

Another Christmas story by Margaret Wise Brown. . . . Three songs, with their music, are included, of which the words in "O come little milkcows" are to be noted. It is charming, though not Miss Brown at her best.

> *Louise S. Bechtel, in a review of "The Little Fir Tree," in* New York Herald Tribune Book Review, *December 19, 1954, p. 7.*

One of Brown's studios in Maine. Courtesy of Westerly Public Library, Westerly, RI.

SEVEN STORIES ABOUT A CAT NAMED SNEAKERS   (1955; also
published as *Sneakers: Seven Stories about a Cat*)

All but one of these tales about a ''rapscallion cat'' have appeared in print before, but they were well worth reissuing in
a book of their own. Born in a barn, the white-pawed black
hero becomes a house cat. He gets into mischief, discovers the
sea, reaches the city by stowing away in a suitcase, and learns
that urban living has its compensations. And in the end he
returns to the country.

Nothing could be simpler, yet everything seems exciting or
funny or poetic, everything is touched with a sense of wonder,
because the late Margaret Wise Brown happened to be at least
a bit of a genius.

> *Dan Wickenden, in a review of ''Seven Stories about
> a Cat Named Sneakers,'' in* New York Herald Tri-
> bune Book Review, *May 15, 1955, p. 16.*

Sneakers has that special gusto with which Margaret Wise
Brown endowed nearly all her animal characters and his small
adventures . . . should be equally good for beginning readers
or bedtime listeners.

> *Ellen Lewis Buell, in a review of ''Sneakers,'' in*
> The New York Times Book Review, *July 10, 1955,
> p. 17.*

Margaret Wise Brown's gift for writing with warmth and simplicity has made some of her books classics, and the same
qualities are to be found in these seven stories. . . . However,
some admirers of her later work will find this book a little
talky, a little less polished, even perhaps a little dated. (Was
it really possible in 1955 to take for granted a household that
included a cook?) . . . Yet despite these drawbacks, some kids
will still respond to these stories about the kitten Sneakers. . . .

> *Georgess McHargue, ''Sneakers,'' in* The New York
> Times Book Review, *January 20, 1980, p. 30.*

A long-awaited reissue of a book much loved by younger readers. . . . The writing shows some of Margaret Wise Brown's
most remarkable qualities—her sense of timing, her warmth
of feeling, and her sure instinct for the simplest, most effective
language.

> *Ethel L. Heins, in a review of ''Sneakers: Seven
> Stories about a Cat,'' in* The Horn Book Magazine,
> *Vol. LVI, No. 1, February, 1980, p. 79.*

THE LITTLE BRASS BAND   (1955)

What better way to acclaim the new season's junior books than
with the soaring reveille of **''The Little Brass Band''** . . .? [Its
author] has been an effective writer for children, addressing
them simply and directly and leaving them with the same sense
of forthright accomplishment that they feel in such kindergarten
classics as the ballad of the King of France—who marched up
the hill and then marched down again—or the story of the little
engine that could.

> *Olive Deane Hormel, in a review of ''The Little Brass
> Band,'' in* The Christian Science Monitor, *November
> 10, 1955, p. 1B.*

Slight story based on the Young People's record of the same
name. Early in the morning members of the little brass band
come over the hill to gather in the village, where they play a

concert and then go their separate ways as night falls. . . . A
mood story that will have little meaning except, perhaps, to
children who are acquainted with the record. (pp. 90-1)

> *A review of ''The Little Brass Band,'' in* Bulletin of
> the Children's Book Center, *Vol. IX, No. 9, May,
> 1956, pp. 90-1.*

YOUNG KANGAROO   (1955)

One of the loveliest animal books of the fall is this picture
story about a creature always appealing to small children, whether
in books or at the zoo. The informational text is written with
that special charm and knowledge of the listening child that
characterizes all the work of Margaret Wise Brown. The facts
are woven into a gentle, simple story. . . .

This is a specially lovely little book that will be treasured in
discriminating homes and welcomed in nursery schools.

> *Louise S. Bechtel, in a review of ''Young Kanga-
> roo,'' in* New York Herald Tribune Book Review,
> *November 13, 1955, p. 4.*

Imagine a baby kangaroo, peeping from his mother's pouch
as he sails high over the long grasses of Australia. A baby
kangaroo growing up, smelling, seeing, tasting field grasses
for the first time.

That's what this startlingly beautiful book is about. It's striking
for its simplicity. Beautiful because Margaret Wise Brown
made the ever new and exciting experience of growth the theme
of this story. . . .

The young kangaroo's life is exciting because it is real and
warm and important—not because of manufactured conflicts
or injected problems. It seems as exciting and fresh as nature. . . .

A five to nine year old boy or girl should find a reading brings
him close among the long grasses of Australia, feeling and
nibbling with the baby 'roo—a clean and refreshing experience.

> *Mary Handy, in a review of ''Young Kangaroo,'' in*
> The Christian Science Monitor, *December 29, 1955,
> p. 7.*

Although this is longer than many of Miss Brown's books, it
has her characteristic feeling of love and understanding for
baby creatures, and even very young children will enjoy hearing
it read aloud. It is a book to be used with older children in
nature classes, too. . . .

> *J. D. Lindquist, in a review of ''Young Kangaroo,''
> in* The Horn Book Magazine, *Vol. XXXII, No. 1,
> February, 1956, p. 34.*

In spite of the frequent use of colloquialisms and slang, there
is a certain charm to [*Young Kangaroo.*] . . . Print, sentence
length and vocabulary indicate fifth grade reading level, but
the general appeal will be to younger children, for whom the
book will need to be read aloud.

> *A review of ''Young Kangaroo,'' in* Bulletin of the
> Children's Book Center, *Vol. X, No. 7, March, 1957,
> p. 86.*

Very few nature books for children deal in a straightforward
factual manner with their subject, while at the same time limiting the technical vocabulary. *Young Kangaroo* gives all the

necessary information about kangaroos and is at the same time vital and interesting. Most of the story is told from the point of view of the baby kangaroo and this brings home the points forcefully.

> *V. Millington, in a review of "Young Kangaroo,"*
> *in* The School Librarian and School Library Review,
> *Vol. 10, No. 2, July, 1960, p. 184.*

HOME FOR A BUNNY (1956)

Violets, wind flowers, Dutchman's breeches and other early wildflowers, form the background for a very young rabbit's search for a home. He investigates those of the robins, the frog, a ground hog and inevitably finds the proper one with his own kind. Admittedly this is one of the late Miss Brown's lesser legacies, but it has her inimitable lyric quality and a feeling of quest and homecoming which should be very satisfactory to the young.

> *Ellen Lewis Buell, "Ten Plus One," in* The New
> York Times Book Review, *April 1, 1956, p. 18.**

BIG RED BARN (1956)

The late Margaret Wise Brown's warm touch makes this more than just another animal farm book for three-to-six-year-olds. The old black cat says "Meow," the tiger tom cat says "Yeow," the cow says "Moo," the bantam rooster "Cock-a-doodle-doo" in popular and approved fashion.

But also there is an elemental sense of the part the day and the night, the moon and the sun outside the big red barn play in the world's life and the life of growing animals in particular.

Rosella Hartman's sensitive illustrations . . . increase the simple dignity. With most children growing up in towns and cities away from farms nowadays, a picture book like this has special importance in the library of the very young.

> *Mary Handy, in a review of "Big Red Barn," in* The
> Christian Science Monitor, *May 10, 1956, p. 17.*

Softly colored pictures and brief rhyming text introduce familiar farm animals in a fresh and quiet way. There is no story and no action; the animals are merely accounted for as they go about their business in and around the big red barn from dawn to dusk. Not essential but pleasing to the very young and useful for first and second grades.

> *Helen E. Kinsey, in a review of "Big Red Barn,"*
> *in* The Booklist, *Vol. 52, No. 20, June 15, 1956, p.*
> *438.*

DAVID'S LITTLE INDIAN: A STORY (1956)

[Even if *David's Little Indian*] were the only [book Margaret Wise Brown] had ever done we would be the richer for having read it. . . . It is a successful expression of that elusive art of living each day and enjoying it to the utmost. To children it will be a story as warm as a hearthside and to adults, a measure of the success with which they have followed the principle of the little Indian, whose name was Carpe Diem.

> *A review of "David's Little Indian," in* Virginia
> Kirkus' Service, *Vol. XXIV, No. 20, October 15,*
> *1956, p. 784.*

["David's Little Indian"] appeals to another side of the small child's nature, to his sense of wonder and joy at the beauties of the world around him. David finds a tiny Indian, "no bigger than an ear of corn." Together they look at the world. The little Indian names the days: "the day the crocus blooms," "the day of the dark branches," "the day of the white daisies," "the day of yellow leaves falling," and many besides. . . . It is another kind of growing-up book, a growing-up of the spirit.

> *Margaret Sherwood Libby, "Davids," in* New York
> Herald Tribune Book Review, *November 11, 1956,*
> *p. 12.**

WHISTLE FOR THE TRAIN (1956)

A little black train comes down the track—stand back! Clickety Clack! By simple, repetitive rhyme the child follows the course of the train; through encounters with a cat, a dog, a bunny, a cow, a bumble bee, and finally an automobile. They always stand back. We cannot imagine a better way for the tiny tot of one to four to learn important lessons in safety than to have this read to him—and he will love it.

> *Olive Deane Hormel, in a review of "Whistle for the
> Train," in* The Christian Science Monitor, *November
> 1, 1956, p. 11.*

The rhythm catches you immediately as you open this picture book for the very young. . . Then there is a sharp change in rhythm as the little train must halt, and a final return to the "clickety clack" as the little black train disappears "on the long steel track". . . . Both text and [Leonard Weisgard's] pictures have a most childlike appeal. Out of the simplest and most familiar ingredients, these collaborators have made a fresh, new and appealing picture book to give joy to the eye and ear.

> *Margaret Sherwood Libby, in a review of "Whistle
> for the Train," in* New York Herald Tribune Book
> Review, *November 18, 1956, p. 5.*

THE DEAD BIRD (1958)

Several little children decide to give a suitable burial to a dead bird one of them finds. They put fresh spring flowers on the grave and sing a short song. A most natural little picture book about a natural experience which most children have if they live where there are birds, grass and flowers. . . . Some adults may think this morbid, but children from 4-6 will not feel so. Recommended.

> *Elsie T. Dobbins, in a review of "The Dead Bird,"*
> *in* Library Journal, *Vol. 83, No. 8, April 15, 1958,*
> *p. 1278.*

Margaret Wise Brown recaptures an incident from her own childhood in this picture book. It is not only a book about death but more about life as seen through the eyes of children—innocent, intense, poetic—for children in their simple directness are poets. (pp. 40-1)

> *Maria Cimino, in a review of "The Dead Bird," in*
> The Saturday Review, *New York, Vol. XLI, No. 19,*
> *May 10, 1958, pp. 40-1.*

[*The Dead Bird*] describes that poignant moment when a child first meets death. This very real, very gentle book will comfort small children because it is so true to their feelings and actions at such a time. There are no "answers" about death. . . . The adult who reads it aloud will say to himself, "That's just how it was with me. I didn't talk about it with any grownup either. And after a while, I forgot, too." (pp. 189-90)

> *Louise Seaman Bechtel, in a review of "The Dead Bird," in* The Horn Book Magazine, *Vol. XXXIV, No. 3, June, 1958, pp. 189-90.*

An experience common to childhood is here presented with simplicity and beauty in picture book form. . . . Neither morbid nor sentimental, this is an excellent handling of the subject of death in which all young children have a natural interest.

> *A review of "The Dead Bird," in* The Booklist and Subscription Books Bulletin, *Vol. 54, No. 19, June 1, 1958, p. 567.*

The first book of its kind to be accepted for young audiences, [*The Dead Bird*] specifically describes the physiological manifestations of death as well as the burial services the children accord the dead bird. The story is somewhat impersonal; the bird is not a pet but simply a dead bird found in the path. . . . The language is at the level of the early grades in school, or even preschool, but describes clearly what is happening. It also communicates that part of the process of mourning is also being glad to be alive. As the children conduct a funeral, they sing to the bird. They cry because it is dead, but they are glad that they can participate in this ceremony. And their tears are as much in response to the beauty of their own singing and the fragrance of the flowers as they are for the death of the bird. . . .

[The funeral in Mildred Kantrowitz's *When Violet Died*] is a more realistic one for children who have had actual experience with a loved one's death. *The Dead Bird* serves better for children who have not been inimately involved in a death. (p. 78)

> *Masha Kabakow Rudman, "Death and Old Age," in her* Children's Literature: An Issues Approach, *D.C. Heath and Company, 1976, pp. 69-112.**

Unanimously named one of the most important contributors to children's literature, the late Brown was particularly honored for this sensitive story. . . . The unadorned, natural description of the adventure makes it an ideal way to help small children understand what death means.

> *A review of "The Dead Bird," in* Publishers Weekly, *Vol. 216, No. 22, November 26, 1979, p. 53.*

NIBBLE, NIBBLE: POEMS FOR CHILDREN   (1959)

Down into the cool green world of the sea, filtered through the shadows of a patch of reeds, or high on a trembling branch, Margaret Wise Brown invites the young reader. In this posthumous collection of poems, mainly dealing with nature—birds, animals, and fish—simple rhyme schemes and relaxed meters evoke all the delight in the simple eloquence of nature which the author so amply perceives. . . . [The poems express an] easy and evocative grace.

> *A review of "Nibble Nibble: Poems for Children," in* Virginia Kirkus' Service, *Vol. XXVII, No. 21, November 1, 1959, p. 811.*

[The] verses share the child's point of view. This ability to put herself in the child's place was the great gift of this author. . . . There is a very thin dividing line between Margaret Wise Brown's rhythmic prose and these unselfconscious imaginings in verse,

and both have the happy ability to stimulate the imaginations of the youngest children. Surely this newest book will be greatly enjoyed.

> *Margaret Sherwood Libby, "The Joy of Poetry, that Begins in Delight and Ends in Wisdom," in* New York Herald Tribune Book Review, *November 1, 1959, p. 2.**

Leonard Weisgard's fine green animals . . . [in] **"Nibble Nibble,"** give a more forceful impression of how the "green stemmed world" looks to a bug's eye than the words of the poems themselves. Too often the poems express nature imagery in familiar and rather too solemn language, and in our household, at any rate, this book was only a mild success.

> *Walker Gibson, "Some Like the Tinkle of the Rhyme, Some Can Leave It Alone," in* The New York Times Book Review, *November 1, 1959, p. 2.**

[Of this collection of 25 poems] 14 are here published for the first time. Many others appeared in **"The Fish With the Deep Sea Smile."** These are nature poems and, while few are highly imaginative, most have the freshness and charm of the living things of which they tell. The cadence of the verses, too, should delight younger children.

> *Patricia D. Beard, in a review of "Nibble Nibble," in* Junior Libraries, *an appendix to* Library Journal, *Vol. 6, No. 4, December, 1959, p. 40.*

The best selections are, for the most part, the older poems; most of these express with rhythm and imagination the wonders of nature within a frame of reference comprehensible to the very young. The new material is not quite as good as the old.

> *Zena Sutherland, in a review of "Nibble Nibble: Poems for Children," in* Bulletin of the Center for Children's Books, *Vol. XIII, No. 5, January, 1960, p. 79.*

THE DIGGERS   (1960)

Digging is a universal pastime of small children. In this book, which progresses from the dog burying his bone in the garden to the mighty steam shovel preparing a giant railway tunnel, the activity of digging is explored. Written in a simple vocabulary with a definite and persuasive rhythm . . . , this book should have an immediate appeal to the bucket and shovel brigade and the budding "sidewalk superintendents".

> *A review of "The Diggers," in* Virginia Kirkus' Service, *Vol. XXVIII, No. 3, February 1, 1960, p. 85.*

The text is sometimes in rhythm and sometimes in prose, jumping from one digger to another. The last part of the book is concerned with making a tunnel through a mountain and has more coherence. . . . Rather pointless book. Not recommended.

> *Doris M. Blasco, in a review of "The Diggers," in* Junior Libraries, *an appendix to* Library Journal, *Vol. 6, No. 9, May, 1960, p. 46.*

FOUR FUR FEET   (1961)

A definitely new school approach has been used in **"Four Fur Feet."** . . . To view some of [Remy Charlip's] circular illustrations, the book must be turned sideways or upside down.

Peculiar? No more so than Miss Brown's verse, which describes the wanderings of an unknown animal (we see only his legs) around the world in such passages as: ''Then he walked into the country / on his four fur feet, / his four fur feet, / his four fur feet / . . . and heard the cows go moo—O.'' My children look at me so patronizingly when I read them books like this!

> *George A. Woods, in a review of ''Four Fur Feet,'' in* The New York Times Book Review, *Part II, May 14, 1961, p. 4.*

A slightly delirious little book, with real charm and individuality. . . . It is not logical, nor even the best of Margaret Wise Brown's writing. . . . It is also a slight infant mystery, because the owner of the four fur feet is never identified. . . .

> *Alice Dalgliesh, in a review of ''Four Fur Feet,'' in* Saturday Review, *Vol. XLIV, No. 29, July 22, 1961, p. 36.*

ON CHRISTMAS EVE   (1961)

A poetic, childlike, and unhackneyed Christmas picture tale which captures the intense excitement of four children who lie awake a long time on Christmas Eve and at length cannot resist getting up after one of them suggests, ''Let's go down to touch the tree and make a wish!''

> *Virginia Haviland, in a review of ''On Christmas Eve,'' in* The Horn Book Magazine, *Vol. XXXVII, No. 6, December, 1961, p. 544.*

A beautiful book that captures the feeling of delicious anticipation felt by children who are celebrating Christmas—or of a child in any culture or of any religion who knows that the coming hours will bring wonder. The text is quiet yet it catches the bated-breath quality of quietness that precedes excitement.

> *Zena Sutherland, in a review of ''On Christmas Eve,'' in* Bulletin of the Center for Children's Books, *Vol. XV, No. 7, March, 1962, p. 107.*

THE STEAMROLLER: A FANTASY   (1974)

[There is] one book with the [Christmas] theme having an irrepressible charm—**''The Steamroller''** . . . , a fantasy written by Margaret Wise Brown. This author, of course, has been long gone to where only the very best children's authors go. . . . In the tale little Daisy is given a big, black steamroller for Christmas with which she promptly flattens animals, autos, adults and school chums. . . . We aren't supposed to have that sort of stuff in children's books? We did; we do. No child has ever been corrupted by a runaway steamroller. Besides, there is a surprising and logical resurrection engineered by Daisy. ''And off she went home to Christmas dinner.''

> *George A. Woods, ''Bang Bang, Balthazar,'' in* The New York Times Book Review, *December 1, 1974, p. 8.*

[This fantasy] has obvious current appeal, but it couldn't be farther from a made-to-order liberation message. In fact *The Steamroller* barrels right through all grown-up notions of suitability to waken children's buried dreams. . . . It's an exhilarating ride, and the uneasiness that must inevitably go along will be appeased when, after Daisy jumps out and sends the steamroller across the field in order to avoid squashing her

friends, her parents give her a steam shovel with which to scoop all her victims up and back into shape. . . . [Needless] to say this leaves a vehicle like *A Train for Jane* [by Norma Klein] coughing up dust—or more appropriately, flattened to a shadow.

> *A review of ''The Steamroller,'' in* Kirkus Reviews, *Vol. XLII, No. 24, December 15, 1974, p. 1297.*

Get off the road everyone! Here comes Daisy in her great big Christmas gift, a real steamroller. Brava! Well told, . . . and just the kind of ''Girl Loves Machine'' book we have been waiting for. A fantasy for all seasons.

> *Enid Davis, ''Picture Books: 'The Steamroller','' in her* The Liberty Cap: A Catalogue of Non-Sexist Materials for Children, *Academy Press Limited, 1977, p. 56.*

ONCE UPON A TIME IN A PIGPEN AND THREE OTHER MARGARET WISE BROWN BOOKS   (1980)

It would have been better to let these four stories remain unpublished. Some humorous phrasing is the only asset of the flat title story. **''A Remarkable Rabbit''** uses cunning to escape four species of woods creatures who attack him simultaneously, but the philosophical tone of the ending is jarring. The unpolished, poetic **''Quiet in the Wilderness''** seems a mere germ of a story idea, similar in cadence and subject matter to Brown's **''Noisy Books.''** **''The Gentle Tiger''** is a cub whose mother, with illogical reasoning, teaches him humans' manners. None attain the quality of Brown's best stories. . . . [Ann Strugnell's] drawings almost redeem the text, but a magnificent castle has been built on quicksand.

> *Sally Holmes Holtze, in a review of ''Once Upon a Time in a Pigpen and Three Other Stories,'' in* School Library Journal, *Vol. 27, No. 3, November, 1980, p. 58.*

A book of new stories by Margaret Wise Brown, nearly 30 years after her death, is like a retired champion's return to the ring: The legend is not at risk, but will the magic hold? (p. 50)

We can never be certain just what a writer thought of a particular unpublished manuscript. We can never be sure, especially in the case of a writer like Brown, who died suddenly, which ones she had set aside as unworthy, which she intended to polish, which she might have sent off in the next morning's mail. But we can wonder, on the basis of her own obervations, if she would have conceived of these stories published together, and in a book which presents them back to back, in picture book form.

The title story is about ''a little pig who wouldn't eat''—''no, he wouldn't gobble. He wouldn't snuffle. He wouldn't root. He wouldn't eat. Because he wasn't hungry.'' Reasonable enough, and recognizable. To placate his loving, ''perhaps too'' loving mother, he professes a desire for exotic foods (''A bee, and some pine needles, and a red geranium . . .''); and when they're procured and presented to him, he laughs and says he was only fooling: He's ''not hungry,'' in truth. It's very like a story in Brown's first collection, also about an ornery pig, which she pronounced amusing but ''inconsequential.'' And, like every story here, it's illustrated literally, in elaborate naturalistic detail totally at odds with the silly, playful text.

The second selection, **"A Remarkable Rabbit,"** features another little rabbit who runs away—his mother is napping, "not thinking about her remarkable little rabbit." He falls into a hole; is captured by its assorted denizens, a frog, a snake, a worm and a porcupine; and, thinking quickly, escapes and skedaddles home. The lesson, iterated by his Mother: "You can always get yourself out of [holes]. You are a Remarkable Rabbit." A wildlife misadventure, for building a child's confidence. **"Quiet in the Wilderness"** presents us with a descriptive, evocative, plotless text—which summons forth the many sounds that break the wilderness quiet. **"The Gentle Tiger,"** like **"Once Upon a Time in a Pigpen,"** is whimsy, a little tiger's schooling in proper, dignified tiger behavior. The pictures show lots and lots of cavorting, disporting tigers.

In each case a slight, thin tale, clever at best, is burdened with sumptuous, dramatic illustrations. Stories that differ in tenor and nature—except that all have primarily oral, not visual values—take on the same charged aspect. With every particular enlarged upon, there is nothing for children to imagine or discover. Adults may be beguiled by the plenty into thinking there's something here. What Margaret Wise Brown had to give to children, however, was not empty excitement but a lien on the world—their own pleasures magnified, their thoughts and feelings distilled. (p. 67)

Barbara Bader, "A Lien on the World," in The New York Times Book Review, November 9, 1980, pp. 50, 66-7.

These four newly uncovered animal tales have more than Brown's well-known child-centered style and story. They have a poetic ring, surprisingly witty elements, and a sense of rightness. Each has sly humor, each can stand alone. (pp. 570-71)

Judith Goldberger, in a review of "Once Upon a Time in a Pigpen and Three Other Stories," in Booklist, Vol. 77, No. 8, December 15, 1980, pp. 570-71.

Eric Carle

1929-

American author/illustrator of picture books and reteller.

Carle is internationally recognized for his colorful picture books which introduce instructional concepts to children making the initial transition from home to school. Focusing on educational and emotional needs, his more than twenty-five works range from pre-reading exercises to stories that teach the life cycles of plants and insects. Carle's formats—folding books, board books, pop-up books, and books with cutouts and movable parts—invite preschoolers to play with the pages as well as look at them. Considered an outstanding artist for the young, Carle often utilizes a distinctive collage technique which lends a childlike appeal to his pictures. His succinct texts contain repetition and an easy rhythm appropriate for small listeners. Carle is best known for *The Very Hungry Caterpillar*, a work considered among the most innovative contemporary picture books. The tale of a caterpillar's metamorphosis into a butterfly, the book includes a series of holes made ostensibly by the caterpillar as it eats through fruit and other foods. As with many of Carle's works, *The Very Hungry Caterpillar* combines scientific fact with humor and fantasy. Carle also retells Aesop's fables and the fairy tales of the Grimm brothers and Hans Christian Andersen in a style that often departs from traditional versions.

Critics hail Carle for his originality, wit, and instinctive understanding of his audience. Although he is occasionally faulted for weak plots, Carle is praised as an exceptional author, artist, and book designer whose bright, textured pictures and whimsical storylines make learning pleasurable.

Carle has won many national and international awards for his books.

(See also *Something about the Author*, Vol. 4; *Contemporary Authors New Revision Series*, Vol. 10; and *Contemporary Authors*, Vols. 25-28, rev. ed.)

Photograph by Sigrid Estrada. Courtesy of Eric Carle

AUTHOR'S COMMENTARY

My father was that rare specimen, a non-competitive man. We used to go for long walks in the countryside together, and he would peel back tree bark to show me what was underneath it, lift rocks to reveal the insects. As a result, I have an abiding love and affection for small, insignificant animals. (p. 14)

I am very interested in education. . . . I think that's got a lot to do with my own experience of school. There are two major traumas in anyone's life, being born and going to school for the first time. These days we're trying to make birth easier and more natural, we're having relaxed Leboyer-style births instead of gleaming, technological operating theatres. I have always wondered if we couldn't do the same when it comes to children starting school.

The transition for me from home to school was horrible, and I want to make that transition better and easier for children by providing them with books which help to 'sweeten' the educational process. I make things which are half book and half toy, things a child can touch and feel as well as look at.

But there is something else. So many "learning" books for the young leave out the emotional side of life. I want to keep it in. There is a feeling, an emotional level quite consciously in each of my books. The emotion and feeling were all left out of my education in Germany, and that's why I think it's so important for me now. I also think of myself as an entertainer now. I didn't use to, I concentrated more on the educational aspect of my work. But entertainment is an important part of books for the young. (p. 15)

> Eric Carle, "Authorgraph No. 32: Eric Carle," in *Books for Keeps*, No. 32, May, 1985, pp. 14-15.

GENERAL COMMENTARY

DELORES R. KLINGBERG

Carle's main concern is the child in transition between home and first grade. He equates home with "warmth, play, and protection," while he feels school is represented by "schedule, abstraction, and learning." Consequently, Carle "attempts with [his] books to make [the] transition from one to the other easier." His books are superb examples of this underlying goal, as each one beautifully reveals his genuine concern for and understanding of the young child. Perhaps this interest has been stimulated by his own children to whom he appears devoted.

However, I feel his concern for early childhood education undoubtedly reflects the frustrations of his own childhood. In fact, Carle states, "I strongly believe that the period before and after my transplant from the United States to Germany had caused conflicts in the preschool and first grade area in me which remained hidden until the opportunity and insight presented themselves. Through my work with Bill Martin [whose works contained Carle's first illustrations], an unfinished area of my own growing up had been touched."

Carle's technique of illustrating with collage was demonstrated through a three-step process that Mr. Carle created for me. He begins with tissue papers, which are commercially available in about forty shades, and proceeds to give these papers more interest by painting over them with acrylic paints. He then uses rubber cement to paste down the tissue papers and applies "a little bit of colored crayon here and there . . . and sign!" While he made it appear quite simple, I find his technique subtle, and each detail entirely engrossing. His strikingly bold illustrations are a delight to the eye. (pp. 447-48)

Eric Carle's belief that children enjoy learning is continually reflected in his picture books. Each book offers the young child an exciting lesson in counting, or reading, or some other early childhood concept such as letter recognition, days of the week, and seasons. Each reveals his total dedication to the child in transition between home and the first grade. His personal philosophy is revealed in all of the works—personal struggles as a young child during a difficult adjustment period represent victories for today's young child who is fortunate enough to be exposed to his works. Carle's international reputation as an outstanding artist and designer is well-deserved, as his books provide enjoyment skillfully intertwined with worthwhile learning experiences for the young child. (p. 452)

> *Delores R. Klingberg, "Profile: Eric Carle," in* Language Arts, *Vol. 54, No. 4, April, 1977, pp. 445-52.*

ANN K. BENEDUCE

[Editor-in-chief of Philomel Books, Beneduce has been Carle's editor since 1968.]

[Eric Carle] is not only an original artist, he is also deeply interested in the emotional, aesthetic, and intellectual growth of children—in stimulating their natural creativity and their joy in learning. That seems like a heavy burden to deliver in a simple picture book, but that *is* what makes his books so distinctive. His bold, clear designs appeal strongly to children—but, as they say, it takes the practiced hand to make the simple gesture—and though his books look simple, much careful thought goes into the concepts and how they will affect the child who reads and views them. In addition to being a fine artist, he is a loving, caring, and very joyful person, and these qualities come through to the children who read his books. Also, his books transcend language—they are popular all over the world. (p. 52)

> *Ann K. Beneduce, "Invention and Discoveries," in an interview with Leonard S. Marcus, in* The Lion and the Unicorn, *Vols. 7 & 8, 1983-84, pp. 47-63.*

1, 2, 3 TO THE ZOO (1968)

["**1, 2, 3 to the Zoo**" gives us many of the same animals as Edna Mitchell Preston's "Monkey in the Jungle"], in ascending numbers, on their way to the zoo in open box cars (the

From 1, 2, 3 to the Zoo, *written and illustrated by Eric Carle. The World Publishing Co., 1968. Text and illustrations copyright © 1968 by Eric Carle. All rights reserved. Reprinted by permission of Philomel Books.*

better to count them, my dears). Mr. Carle also draws with sophistication but this often works against him—e.g., when intricate patterns of monkey tails and snake coils make his beasts almost impossible to tally.

> *Selma G. Lanes, in a review of "1, 2, 3 to the Zoo," in* The New York Times Book Review, *November 3, 1968, p. 69.*

With only numerals for text—one to each large doublespread—and with large animals, as richly colored as Wildsmith's, to be counted, the well-produced oversized volume is indeed a satisfactory counting book. There is considerable humor—the hippo's yawning mouth, the giraffe doubled over to examine a miniature mouse, the playfully gymnastic monkeys, and the rhythmically twined snakes. Each species rides in one car of the zoo train, and each pair of pages carries a recapitulation of the numbers, symbolized by a lengthening train along the bottom of the spread—from the engine pulling only the elephant car to a long train, containing a ninth car with nine snakes, shown under the picture of ten exotic birds. It all winds up with a procession of ten blank cars under a zoo filled with all the animals. Unstrained and effective. (pp 40-1)

> *Virginia Haviland, in a review of "1, 2, 3 to the Zoo," in* The Horn Book Magazine, *Vol. XLV, No. 1, February, 1969, pp. 40-1.*

Eric Carle has filled his "**1, 2, 3 to the Zoo**" . . . with superb paintings of animals, bold, lively, handsome, spreading over big double-spread pages. His elephant is all magnificent power, his giraffes a precision of delicacy, his monkeys a tangle of liveliness. This is a book to grow with its owner. The tiny mouse lurking in every picture may remain invisible to the smallest reader and, as the title implies, the book is waiting to teach the art of counting.

> *Adele McRae, "Crayoned Morality Plays," in* The Christian Science Monitor, *May 1, 1969, p. B2.**

A train transports one elephant, two hippos, three giraffes and so forth to the zoo: seven seals lolling indolently on bunks in their compartment, and eight giddy monkeys looping tails in theirs are perhaps the finest, though five burnt umber bears run them close. No reluctant mathematician is likely to withstand for long the charms of this incomparably rich and gaudy counting book.

A review of "1, 2, 3 to the Zoo," in The Spectator, Vol. 222, No. 7351, May 16, 1969, p. 656.

You make your own story with *1, 2, 3 to the Zoo*. The pictures adroitly plot the journey of a train taking on a different passenger at each stop. . . . To the element of surprise (which animal will get on next?) is added an attractive cumulation; at the foot of each page the train appears drawn in miniature, growing in length as each new truck is added. There is, as well, a mouse appearing in a different (safe) place in each picture. The bright exuberant colour is never improbable but just gay enough to suggest that the animals are enjoying their ride.

Margery Fisher, in a review of "1, 2, 3 to the Zoo," in her Growing Point, Vol. 8, No. 2, July, 1969, p. 1349.

This wordless picture book dates back to 1968 and shows more obviously the influence of England's Brian Wildsmith than Carle's more recent illustrations do. The basic idea, however, is original and a cinch to attract tiny tots. Pictures in full, riotous colors and dazzling shapes glamorize numbers, as related to a train carrying animals to a zoo. First comes the chugging, old-fashioned locomotive and a flat car with "1 Elephant," followed by cars with different creatures, all the way to "10 birds." There is great animation in the scenes featuring the impatiently padding "4 lions," the playful "7 seals," etc., as well as in views of the balloon man and happy children waiting, with their parents, to welcome the travelers to their new home.

A review of "1, 2, 3 to the Zoo," in Publishers Weekly, Vol. 221, No. 5, January 29, 1982, p. 67.

THE VERY HUNGRY CATERPILLAR (1969)

AUTHOR'S COMMENTARY

[The holes in *The caterpillar*] are a bridge from toy to book, from plaything, from the touching to understanding. No wonder that we speak of 'grasping' an idea. In the very young child the thought travels mightily fast from fingertips to brain. This book has many layers. There is fun, nonsense, colour, surprise. There is learning, but if the child ignores the learning part, let him, it's OK. Someday he'll hit upon it by himself. That is the way we learn. I would like to make childhood something special and joyous, something that the child does not want to get over with fast, something that immunises him from such warnings as 'time to grow up', 'be mature' and 'don't act like a child'.

"From Hungry Caterpillars to Bad Tempered Ladybirds," in Books for Your Children, Vol. 13, No. 2, Spring, 1978. p. 7.

[Of the three picture books reviewed, which also include John Burningham's *Mr. Gumpy's Outing* and Janet Burroway's *The Truck on the Track*,] Eric Carle comes nearest to producing a satisfying work of art which is entirely accessible to its audience. His very hungry caterpillar eats his way through a week-full of colourful pages and then, after a well-earned sleep in his cocoon, undergoes a beautiful transformation. The biblio-

graphical gimmickry—the pages have caterpillar-sized holes through them—should not distract from this artist's considerable achievement. He displays great virtuosity and assurance in producing a book which is at once beautiful and charming.

A review of "The Very Hungry Caterpillar," in The Junior Bookshelf, Vol. 34, No. 6, December, 1970, p. 347.

In a very humorous way, this book tells the story of a caterpillar's life-cycle, from egg to butterfly. He eats through a great many things on the way—one apple on Monday, two pears on Tuesday, and so on, to a list of ten exotic items on Saturday—and the book's delight, and originality, lie in the way in which these cumulative items are shown. . . .

The text is brief and simple, and has a satisfying cumulative effect that neatly matches the pictures, which are large and bold, in brilliant colours and crisp forms set against the white page, mainly achieved by the use of collage. This book has a direct appeal, true simplicity, and a strong play element that will endear it to the hearts of all children from about eight downwards. Their elder brothers and sisters, not to mention their parents, will find delight in it too, for such an outstanding book has a universal appeal.

John A. Cunliffe, in a review of "The Very Hungry Caterpillar," in Children's Book Review, Vol. 1, No. 1, February, 1971, p. 14.

Occasionally one comes across a book which enchants by its originality and also its professionalism; here is one such. From the first delightful spread showing a moonlit leaf on which reposes a small egg, through each stage of over indulgent feeding undertaken by the caterpillar to the last pages of the book showing a glorious butterfly, this book is a joy, and not only for those very young who will adore the colours and shapes of the illustrations, but also their elders who will relish the wit with which the author makes his point. One final recommendation: you can follow his mistakes hole by hole, literally.

Gabrielle Maunder, in a review of "The Very Hungry Caterpillar," in The School Librarian, Vol. 19, No. 1, March, 1971, p. 93.

With wit and originality, Eric Carle develops the eternal metamorphosis theme, using the caterpillar. His strong shapes have rich and interesting textual treatments; color rings through the book in a commanding and complex manner.

Carolyn Horowitz, in a review of "The Very Hungry Caterpillar," in Top of the News, Vol. 27, No. 4, June, 1971, p. 431.

[*In 1975, Dorothy Butler published* Cushla: A Case Study, *a thesis which documents the development of a severely handicapped New Zealand child. She later expanded* Cushla: A Case Study *into the well-received* Cushla and Her Books. *The following excerpt, originally published in* Signal *in January, 1977, focuses on Cushla's positive response to* The Very Hungry Caterpillar.]

The Very Hungry Caterpillar has probably made more impact on the New Zealand public than any other picture book in the last ten years; it has certainly had record sales. Cushla encountered it just before she turned three years, and echoed the reaction of thousands of other three-year-olds who immediately demanded, "Read it again". It is easy to see what this book has; it is harder to understand the exact nature of its superlative appeal. It certainly has form, unity, colour and climax, and it lists delectable foods that children enjoy. Adults approve of its built-in nature lesson (the stages from caterpillar to "beautiful butterfly" are faithfully documented) and its unobtrusive counting slant—"On Monday he ate *one* apple but he was still hungry. On Tuesday he ate *two* pears"—and the opportunity it presents for painless learning of the days of the week. (pp. 50-1)

> *Dorothy Butler, in a review of "The Very Hungry Caterpillar," in her* Cushla and Her Books, *The Horn Book, Inc., 1980, pp. 50-1.*

A common plot in the most simple of picture storybooks is often that of presenting a familiar reality with memorable language and illustrations thus allowing the reader to experience it with a fresh perspective. Eric Carle's unique rendition of the life-cycle of the butterfly in **The Very Hungry Caterpillar** is particularly effective in design. It provides the child reader a visual representation of the developing plot. The pages get larger as the caterpillar eats more and grows bigger until . . . the double-page spread of his emergence as a beautiful colorful butterfly concludes this excellent picture storybook. This imaginative way of visually representing the simple, repetitive text allows the child who does not read yet to "read" this book through its pictures, thus "seeing" the sequence of events laid out by the illustrator and designer of the book. (pp. 163-64)

> *Margaret Matthias and Garciela Italiano, "Louder than a Thousand Words," in* Signposts to Criticism of Children's Literature, *edited by Robert Bator, American Library Association, 1983, pp. 161-65.**

THE TINY SEED (1970; British edition as *The Tiny Seed and the Giant Flower*)

["**The Tiny Seed**"] seems an ideal introduction to the cycle of the seasons for small eyes and ears. Beginning with the autumn flight of an undersized flower seed, this imaginatively conceived tale of nature's purposeful prodigality unfolds like an Alfred Hitchcock suspense tale.

> *Selma G. Lanes, in a review of "The Tiny Seed," in* The New York Times Book Review, *Part II, November 8, 1970, p. 53.*

The Tiny Seed ridiculously and inappropriately assumes the proportions of a folk hero when it outlasts its larger, stronger comrades to become a towering flower. Swept along by the wind until they fall, then struggling to emerge through the ground as plants which will eventually blossom, the seeds participate in an autumn-to-autumn Odyssean voyage beset by natural, animal and human enemies. . . . Superseed alone survives all these trials (and presumably proves the old adage about the best things coming in small packages); once the weakest flier as well as the latest bloomer, it now gets its growth in a big way, ends up taller than the surrounding trees and houses, and finally sends out its own seeds. This book does feature large, clear print, good-quality paper, stunningly colored pictures. But the text is a disastrous hybrid; the product of a synthesis of unoriginal, unexciting fantasy and misleading explication. . . . Naturally curious—and literal-minded—children can take their intrinsically fascinating natural phenomena straight, however, and this exposition, with its absurd incidents and statements (e.g., "But the tiny seed lies very still and the mouse does not see it."), will confuse rather than enlighten readers. (pp. 32-3)

> *Diane G. Stavn, in a review of "The Tiny Seed," in* School Library Journal, *an appendix to* Library Journal, *Vol. 17, No. 4, December, 1970, pp. 32-3.*

An introduction to the drama of seed travel and growth, this is a delightfully imaginative presentation of the perils befalling a tiny seed's travelling campanions on the journey to a suitable spot for winter rest, spring germination and growth. By accepting the whimsy one readily accepts the exaggerated journey and colossal growth achieved by a tiny seed in a single season. The concepts are good and the strong, but tasteful use of color adds much to the attractiveness of this book.

> *Frances Sherburne, in a review of "The Tiny Seed," in* Appraisal: Children's Science Books, *Vol. 4, No. 2, Spring, 1971, p. 9.*

Seeds travel not only by air, but also by water, by sticking to the fur of animals, and in other ways. The text in this picture book about seed dispersal is not nearly so colorful or descriptive as the illustrations. Although there is action, the script lacks flavor. There is some question as to whether the story would hold the attention of pre-schoolers.

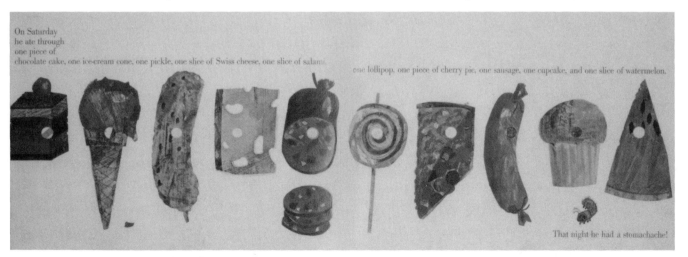

On Saturday he ate through one piece of chocolate cake, one ice-cream cone, one pickle, one slice of Swiss cheese, one slice of salami, one lollipop, one piece of cherry pie, one sausage, one cupcake, and one slice of watermelon.

That night he had a stomachache!

From The Very Hungry Caterpillar, *written and illustrated by Eric Carle. Copyright © 1969 by Eric Carle. All rights reserved. Reprinted by permission of Philomel Books.*

Judith E. Trenholm, in a review of "The Tiny Seed," in Appraisal: Children's Science Books, *Vol. 4, No. 2, Spring, 1971, p. 9.*

Cutting across the zoological and biological oddities with which picture-book artists are apt to regale their young viewers, Eric Carle uses extra-natural colour and scale to illustrate the simple facts of germination and growth in plants.... The circumstance of the plant's excessive growth introduces a touch of fantasy that bridges the gap between botanical fact and the bold swathes of colour and graphic formalism of the pictures. The lesson could hardly be clearer than it is in visual terms; with pictures so dashing and explicit, the brief text seems hardly necessary. (pp. 1741-42)

Margery Fisher, in a review of "The Tiny Seed and the Giant Flower," in her Growing Point, *Vol. 10, No. 1, May, 1971, pp. 1741-42.*

Eric Carle builds each of his books around a single idea, some truth of nature. In his new story he shows the fate of a seed which survives where each of his brothers founders.... There is less humour than we have had from this talented artist, but the pictures are dramatic and lovely. Each of the wide openings gives great pleasure with its richly coloured and textured painting.

M. Crouch, in a review of "The Tiny Seed and the Giant Flower," in The Junior Bookshelf, *Vol. 35, No. 3, June, 1971, p. 160.*

PANCAKES, PANCAKES! (1970)

[*Pancakes, pancakes*] is distinguished by torn-paper pictures emphatic in shape and brilliant in colour which light up a cumulative story in an old tradition. Jack wants a pancake for breakfast so Mother sends him to the mill to get the corn ground, gives him whole corn to feed the hen who lays an egg, sends him to milk the cow and stoke the stove and then shows him how to mix the ingredients and toss the pancake. The only point on which Jack needs no instruction is when it comes to the eating. Humour and a scrap of information are nicely mixed and the picture-book approach puts condescension out of the question.

Margery Fisher, in a review of "Pancakes, Pancakes!" in her Growing Point, *Vol. 9, No. 6, December, 1970, p. 1641.*

The review of this picture book needs an exclamation point after every sentence, for it's a "hey, look!" and a "hey, listen!" book. Look at the bright pictures of tissue paper collage! Listen to the fast words that tell a cumulative tale listing all the people and things that contributed to the pancakes Jack had for his breakfast! And for good measure, learn how *you* can make pancakes!

A review of "Pancakes, Pancakes!" in Publishers Weekly, *Vol. 198, No. 24, December 14, 1970, p. 39.*

Eric Carle has the lightest touch with an instructional theme. After making counting and natural history into fun, he now turns to cookery. Jack wakes at dawn with a pancake-sized appetite. But his mother believes in going back to first principles. After cutting the wheat, grinding the corn, collecting an egg from the black hen and milk from the cow, churning the butter, collecting fuel and jam, he has a belated breakfast—

round about suppertime. The pictures are gay and exuberant and full of the cheerful, accurate detail that children like.

M. Crouch, in a review of "Pancakes, Pancakes," in The Junior Bookshelf, *Vol. 35, No. 1, February, 1971, p. 21.*

The tissue paper collage is bright and gay, but the story moves slowly, despite the modicum of interest in food-from-source, due in part to the stiff style of writing and in part to the lack of any accelerando in the plot.

Zena Sutherland, in a review of "Pancakes, Pancakes!" in Bulletin of the Center for Children's Books, *Vol. 24, No. 8, April, 1971, p. 119.*

DO YOU WANT TO BE MY FRIEND? (1971)

Imaginatively conceived and beautifully wrought, this is a perfect picture book for a small child. Containing but seven words—those of the title—it offers a splendid opportunity for a pre-reader, with a little initial help, to create his own story based on the brilliantly colored, wonderfully expressive pictures. We first meet a lonely little mouse asking, "Do you want to be my friend?" of a large tail swishing high above him. When the mouse discovers, on the next page, that the tail belongs to a grazing horse, indifferent to his plea, he continues his quest, proceeding hopefully from unfriendly alligator to lion, hippo, seal, monkey, peacock, fox, kangaroo, and giraffe until he finds a just-right friend. Drama and suspense are furnished by a villain who slithers unnoticed but in plain view across the bottom of each page until he reveals his true nature in an exciting climax.

Polly Goodwin, in a review of "Do You Want to Be My Friend?" in Book World—The Washington Post, *Part II, May 9, 1971, p. 4.*

The idea is not new, but it is nicely executed, and small children can enjoy the fun of guessing what's on the next page. The illustrations, bold against white space, are reminiscent of Munari's in composition and humor.

Zena Sutherland, in a review of "Do You Want to Be My Friend?" in Bulletin of the Center for Children's Books, *Vol. 24, No. 11, July-August, 1971, p. 167.*

The title question at the beginning and the simple answer at the end are the only words in a book that nevertheless tells a complete, satisfying story.... An earnest, almost clinical Note to Parents and Teachers states that the book "has been designed to be a very first step toward real reading.... Specially planned for the prereading child, [it] teaches basic skills of reading readiness. The ingenious placement of the pictures shows the child the correct direction in which to turn the pages ... instilling the idea of linear sequences ... on which to build correct reading habits." Children, fortunately, will be unaware of such blandishments; of real consequence, however, is the cumulative visual delight in the striking beauty of color and design.

Ethel L. Heins, in a review of "Do You Want to Be My Friend?" in The Horn Book Magazine, *Vol. XLVII, No. 4, August, 1971, p. 374.*

Each turn of the page in this ingenious, all but wordless picture book affords surprise, suspense, and repeated pleasure for the viewer.... The design of the book is imaginative, the bold, vividly colored illustrations instantly captivating, and the story satisfying.

> *A review of "Do You Want to Be My Friend?" in*
> The Booklist, *Vol. 68, No. 2, September 15, 1971,*
> *p. 108.*

A delightfully amusing book, which is based on an illustrative trick that will fascinate all young children. . . .

This is an outstanding picture-book; rich in colour and texture; bold and clear in design; witty and original in conception. Children from eight down will enjoy it immensely.

> *John A. Cunliffe, in a review of "Do You Want to
> Be My Friend?" in* Children's Book Review, *Vol.
> I, No. 6, December, 1971, p. 189.*

This handsomely illustrated picture book which encourages the young child's imagination and language development was designed to teach basic reading readiness skills. . . . Despite the absence of words, this book provides a definite plot, subplot, hero, and an antagonist, as Little Mouse looks for and finally finds a friend. (p. 451)

> *Delores R. Klingberg, "Profile: Eric Carle," in*
> Language Arts, *Vol. 54, No. 4, April, 1977, pp.*
> *445-52.*

THE SECRET BIRTHDAY MESSAGE (1972)

In the field of coloured picture books for infants, the name of Eric Carle is becoming synonymous with originality, imaginative ideas and sound colour illustration. His latest title continues his theme of creative play books in the form of one of the more traditional topics of interest to children—the secret message, where pictures, signs and symbols take the place of words. . . . Whilst there is not the humour and coincidental instruction of **The Very Hungry Caterpillar** and **Do You Want to be My Friend?**, nevertheless Eric Carle has chosen a subject which will have wide appeal to children, who will enjoy the page by page progression to a satisfactory climax, as in the previous books. Play books of this kind are by no means new, but Eric Carle has added a fresh dimension which is at present fulfilling a need in a field where there is a dearth.

> *Edward Hudson, in a review of "The Secret Birthday
> Message," in* Children's Book Review, *Vol. II, No.
> 3, June, 1972, p. 73.*

Categorized as a Very-First-Step-to-Learning-Book, the international author-illustrator's latest work for preschoolers is intended to teach pattern recognition, the concept of following a map, and what *up, down, below, in,* and *through* mean. The *modus operandi* for accomplishing this is a slight story revolving around Tim's Secret Birthday Message: a message with key words deleted and depicted by simple shapes in order to lure the reader through pages shaped and cut out to match the symbols in the message. At the end of the cryptic message, the young reader is rewarded by discovering Tim's universally lovable present, and can then retrace on the final two-page spread the route Tim supposedly took. The book should be fun; instead it is a laborious exercise with an unimaginative and forced conclusion. The joy and the color that sparked **Do You Want to Be My Friend?** are missing—and the loss is grave.

> *Sheryl B. Andrews, in a review of "The Secret Birth-
> day Message," in* The Horn Book Magazine, *Vol.
> XLVIII, No. 4, August, 1972, p. 360.*

Eric Carle is God's gift to the Pre-School Playgroup storyteller. He has just the right touch, the precise relationship between word and picture, the simple directness and the touch of mystery. . . . [**The Secret Birthday Message**] is beautifully done and deserves the inevitable success in store for it. (pp. 218-19)

> *M. Crouch, in a review of "The Secret Birthday
> Message," in* The Junior Bookshelf, *Vol. 36, No. 4,
> August, 1972, pp. 218-19.*

The style is different, the colours more sophisticated, the line more impressionistic, than the author's first success, **The Very Hungry Caterpillar.**

From Do You Want to Be My Friend? *written and illustrated by Eric Carle. Thomas Y. Crowell Co., Inc. Published in 1971 and protected by the Berne Convention. All rights reserved. By permission of Harper & Row, Publishers, Inc.*

Mr Carle uses the method of an illustrated code, which one comprehends by symbols leading on to the discovery of a special 'Birthday Present'. By the artful use of simple black symbols, denoting moon, star, stairs, rock, etc., and accompanying these with pages shaped to match each symbol, the reader follows a fascinating trail to discover his gift. But all is then not over, for Mr Carle cleverly ensures that the book will be read over and over again, by challenging the reader to find his way back through the maze. Impossible to limit the delight of this book to any age. Suffice it to say that the colours will delight the youngest, the puzzle enchant the toddler, and the adult like me will be diverted by the ingenuity of it all.

> *Gabrielle Maunder, in a review of "The Secret Birthday Message," in* The School Librarian, *Vol. 20, No. 3, September, 1972, p. 285.*

THE ROOSTER WHO SET OUT TO SEE THE WORLD (1972; British edition as *Rooster Sets Out to See the World*)

Eric Carle's simplicity of text and gorgeous designs are disguises for a firm educative purpose. He always has a point to make and a valid one too. This time he has made a counting book, and he has integrated the arithmetic in the fabric of his story. Rooster goes for a walk on his own. He picks up friends as he goes and the party progresses arithmetically. Then things go badly, and company by company his friends withdraw until only he remains. The sums are presented pictorially in the corners of the page, a useful accompaniment but no distraction from the splendours of his powerfully designed and exquisitely drawn coloured pictures. Mr. Carle is still the best of all artists for the very young and he continues to grow from book to book. (pp. 301-02)

> *M. Crouch, in a review of "Rooster Sets Out to See the World," in* The Junior Bookshelf, *Vol. 36, No. 5, October, 1972, pp. 301-02.*

A simple, very simple, story is also a device for elementary addition and subtraction. . . . The illustrations are very handsome—the rooster and his friends all larger than life in the beginning until circumstances reduce them to more lifelike proportion—and the endpapers are charming. But the artist's paint-and-collage technique is almost too familiar; his animals could just as easily have come out of Brian Wildsmith's barnyard.

> *Sidney D. Long, in a review of "The Rooster Who Set Out to See the World," in* The Horn Book Magazine, *Vol. XLIX, No. 1, February, 1973, p. 37.*

A brilliantly colored picture story that does double duty as a counting book. Each of the oversized . . . pages has boldly stylized animal paintings full of action and humor—reminiscent of Brian Wildsmith at his best. . . . The book coaxes individual drill through attention-holding pictures along with a simple and amusing bedtime story. (pp. 1992-93)

> *Lillian N. Gerhardt, in a review of "The Rooster Who Set Out to See the World," in* Library Journal, *Vol. 98, No. 12, June 15, 1973, pp. 1992-93.*

A VERY LONG TAIL: A FOLDING BOOK; THE VERY LONG TRAIN: A FOLDING BOOK (1972)

["**The Very Long Train**"] is a "folding book"—a long, accordion-pleated poster full of boxcars. A very smart blue, orange,

and green engine leads the way, followed by a car with one rhinoceros, a second with two elephants, and so on, down to the next-to-last car which contains a rather motley collection of ten fish. The numbers and names of the animals are printed on the back. Artist Carle's illustrations are as charming and cheerful as ever, but the book was just too "educational" for me.

> *Jennifer Farley Smith, "Books Popup, Fold Out, Push Down," in* The Christian Science Monitor, *October 4, 1972, p. 10.**

The tail, curled up on the first panel and attached to a head that appears on the last, stretches along the bottom of the ten intervening "pages" which become a kind of bargain basement frieze in wild Wildsmith-y colors of an unimaginatively represented hippopotamus, lion, seal, monkey, peacock, and kangaroo. The train, between blue engine and caboose, is a series of open cars filled with animals of the same hackneyed ilk. This might do to decorate the top of the picture book cases if there were not so many picture books with more attractive covers and more rewarding contents.

> *A review of "A Very Long Tail (A Folding Book)" and "The Very Long Train (A Folding Book)," in* Kirkus Reviews, *Vol. XL, No. 20, October 15, 1972, p. 1183.*

Popular in Europe (where it is called a *leporello*), the folding book is relatively new to present-day American children's book production. These two examples, made of sturdy cardboard with plastic slipcases, are attractive enough to be used as murals, or for bookcase decoration, and durable enough to be played with on the floor; but their versatility is legitimate: These books can also be spread out and read as very simple picture stories. Because books of this kind fold out, with each picture connected to the previous one, the artistic demands are almost all visual. It is a genre particularly suited to this artist's brilliantly colored collage-paintings.

> *Sidney D. Long, in a review of "A Very Long Tail: A Folding Book" and "The Very Long Train: A Folding Book," in* The Horn Book Magazine, *Vol. XLIX, No. 3, June, 1973, p. 257.*

I SEE A SONG (1973)

The author-illustrator gets A + for inventiveness and effort here but only C − for results. He has created a violinist who invites his audience to "Come, listen, and let your imagination see your own song." Striking and rich color paintings make up the rest of the book, supposedly visions induced by music. Unfortunately, they are just too abstract to suggest much emotion to children. Mr. Carle's pictures are, as usual, of rare artistry but without real substance this time.

> *A review of "I See a Song," in* Publishers Weekly, *Vol. 203, No. 21, May 21, 1973, p. 50.*

Lovely to look at, but insubstantial, a picture book that has an introduction but no text consists of brilliantly colored collage designs and patterns. The introduction is made by a violinist, and the pictures are meant as an expression of his music in color and form, a conception that might be successful were the music audible. Some of the shapes are recognizable, others are abstract, and there is no sequence, although some of the pictures are related (bud to flower, flower bursting into full bloom) and all seem to be in celebration of nature—although this may have to be explained to small children. Enjoyable as art, but no story or focus.

> *Zena Sutherland, in a review of "I See a Song," in* Bulletin of the Center for Children's Books, *Vol. 27, No. 4, December, 1973, p. 59.*

Eric Carle, among the most successful of all picture book artists and one who excels in combining instruction with delight, here tries something new. A fiddler takes his bow and begins to play. He plays a song, and it appears first as isolated notes of colour, then as cascades of patterns, some of them anthropomorphic but mostly abstract. They build up into complex masses, and then fade away. The exhausted fiddler, himself strangely transformed by the experience, bows and walks from the platform. A strange book, just a little like Wildsmith but without Wildsmith's disciplined imagination. One can see that the artist needed to get the book out of his system, but I hope that it will remain an isolated phenomenon.

> *M. Crouch, in a review of "I See a Song," in* The Junior Bookshelf, *Vol. 37, No. 6, December, 1973, p. 386.*

A violinist drawn in black-and-white who poetically evokes reader participation ("I see a song. I paint music. I hear color. . . . Come, listen, and let your imagination / see your own song.") provides an overture to this otherwise textless picture book. From the moment his bow touches his violin, brilliant color explodes forth in the form of abstract finger and spatter-paint collages. These ever-changing shapes reflect moods, feelings, and dream-like states. Designed for children to look at and react to and for stimulating their artistic sensibilities, this will be as successful as the author's award-winning *Do You Want To Be My Friend*. . . .

> *Gail Abbott Furnas, in a review of "I See a Song," in* School Library Journal, *an appendix to* Library Journal, *Vol. 20, No. 8, April, 1974, p. 48.*

HAVE YOU SEEN MY CAT? (1973)

The artist's wonderfully colorful and imaginative pictures make the book a feast for the eyes and, incidentally, educational. Showing a small boy searching for his lost cat, the story takes the reader to various parts of the world where he is introduced to different members of the feline family. The boy finds a lion, a bobcat, a tiger, a cheetah, a jaguar and a Persian cat. But only when he returns home does he find his own missing pet and the babies she has had while he was away. It took a lover of cats and a fine artist to create this lovely book for the preschooler and beginning reader.

> *A review of "Have You Seen My Cat?" in* Publishers Weekly, *Vol. 203, No. 24, June 11, 1973, p. 154.*

Eric Carle stays right in the forefront by reason of his powerful designs, his original ideas and his mastery of extreme simplicity. . . . As always with this artist an educational idea is also very good fun, and presented with great beauty. The book is just right for play-group presentation, and it will also bring a good deal of enjoyment to the home.

> *M. Crouch, in a review of "Have You Seen My Cat?" in* The Junior Bookshelf, *Vol. 37, No. 4, August, 1973, p. 240.*

Here we have yet another of the follow-through picture books which Eric Carle does so well. Through the medium of a boy looking for his own very ordinary domestic cat, the author-illustrator introduces young children to all the principal members of the cat family: lion, tiger, cheetah, puma, bob-cat and leopard. . . . All are easily identifiable. Whilst Eric Carle has not always been completely successful in developing some of his original ideas for picture books for the young, this one which has some positive educational content can be recommended for the three to six-year-olds.

> *Edward Hudson, in a review of "Have You Seen My Cat?" in* Children's Book Review, *Vol. III, No. 4, September, 1973, p. 108.*

Vividly colored collage illustrations, effective against the clean, blank background, picture a small boy in search of his cat. . . . All of the members of the cat family that are shown are identified on the endpapers, so that the book has some usefulness as well as being attractive and having game appeal. Since the boy asks a desert nomad, and various others from other lands, this is not a realistic story, and certainly it is not very substantial as information, but it nicely combines fact and fun in very attractive form. (pp. 38-9)

> *Zena Sutherland, in a review of "Have You Seen My Cat?" in* Bulletin of the Center for Children's Books, *Vol. 27, No. 3, November, 1973, pp. 38-9.*

Child-like collages rich in color and texture partially compensate for an excessively slight story of a boy searching for his lost cat who is not shown until the story's end. . . . Finally, they are reunited; however small children may not realize from the confusing melee of cats pictured on the last spread that the giant feline belongs to the boy and that the other cats who surround her are the newborn litter.

> *Margaret Blue, in a review of "Have You Seen My Cat?" in* Library Journal, *Vol. 98, No. 20, November 15, 1973, p. 3438.*

MY VERY FIRST BOOK OF COLORS; MY VERY FIRST BOOK OF SHAPES; MY VERY FIRST BOOK OF NUMBERS; MY VERY FIRST BOOK OF WORDS (MY VERY FIRST LIBRARY) (1974)

As reviewers we shy away from the mass-produced, super-market-distributed stiff-board books with push-pull tabs which pop up cartoon characters, tell-time books with movable clock hands or I-can-zip-my-fly volumes under the guise of an early-childhood education. Most are of momentary fascination, of dubious value and disappointing durability. But you have to be careful; you never know when you're fondling another "Pat the Bunny."

All of the foregoing is a not-too-devious way of getting your attention directed to four books created and illustrated by Eric Carle called **"My Very First Library."** . . .

[**"My Very First Book of Colors, Numbers, Shapes, Words"**] are Cadillac compacts of early learning. Spiral-bound with stiff pages split sideways, each book's purpose is to have the child 2 to 5 years old match colors, numbers, shapes or words to corresponding objects in the bottom half of each page. A swatch of red, for instance, matches the fire engine; in the **"Numbers"** book two black squares and the numeral "2" matches the two lusciously-colored bananas; in **"Shapes"** the black oval mates with the eye; and in **"Words"** the heavy block-printed word "fish" is right for pisces. Try one—you'll come back for all.

George A. Woods, "Early Learning," in The New York Times Book Review, *October 20, 1974, p. 8.**

[Of the four books in the set, *My Very First Book of Colors*] is the weakest, flawed by the fact that some pictures have colors that don't quite match: the deep purple umbrella doesn't fit the almost-magenta square or the black one, the turquoise background for a picture of a snowman is neither the blue nor the green shown. It's a sound concept, however, and the illustrations are lovely; the book about shapes is even more intriguing, with solid black shapes on one set of pages, and bright matching pictures on the other: a diamond-shaped kite, a triangular wigwam, a half-circle of watermelon.

.   .   .   .   .

[In the same format], and with the small appeal to a child's detective instinct and curiosity, [*My Very First Book of Numbers* and *My Very First Book of Words*] are for slightly older children. The numbers book uses no digits, but has small black blocks on the upper pages, in order from one to ten. The bottom pages are not in order, but have six lemons, one pineapple, nine cherries, et cetera, giving the child a concept of sets. The book of words is even more advanced, requiring children to be able to identify the letter symbols before matching them to the pictures of cat, boy, girl, car, fish, and so on. All in all, a very attractive way to learn.

Zena Sutherland, in a review of "My Very First Book of Colors," "My Very First Book of Shapes," "My Very First Book of Numbers," and "My Very First Book of Words," in Bulletin of the Center for Children's Books, *Vol. 28, No. 10, June, 1975, p. 159.*

ALL ABOUT ARTHUR (AN ABSOLUTELY ABSURD APE)   (1974)

A very captivating original ABC book which combines woodcuts and colored photographs to make visual recognition of letters more realistic. The woodcuts are of the animals Arthur meets in his travels across the USA. The letters photographed are familiar signs found on walls, street signs, sweaters, and trucks. The alliterated descriptions of the animals may be over the heads of the younger set, but they will love the sounds. One cannot go wrong by adding this to the picture book collection in the school or public library.

Margaret M. Nichols, in a review of "All about Arthur (An Absolutely Absurd Ape)," in Children's Book Review Service, *Vol. 3, No. 3, November, 1974, p. 17.*

For all those convinced that there are already enough ABC books and that any new ones are simply repeats of those done before, here is a noteworthy book. Feeling alone, Arthur sets off on a journey through the alphabet during which each new letter finds him in a different city making the acquaintance of some other animal. From Baltimore to Yonkers, the author/illustrator uses tongue-twisting phrases to depict the various forms each individual letter can take. The animals, represented by black woodcuts typical of those appearing in Carle's earlier books, are combined with color photographs of each letter as it might be seen on some everyday object—a sign, a truck, and even a sweater. I think the person reading the verses aloud will enjoy it almost as much as the listener, but practice first because it is quite a mouthful.

Barbara Dill, in a review of "All about Arthur (An Absolutely Absurd Ape)," in Wilson Library Bulletin, *Vol. 49, No. 3, November, 1974, p. 240.*

This alphabet book, better suited to children's listening, looking, and vocalizing fun than to their learning the alphabet, includes such complex words as absurd, befriended, eccentric, inquisitive, and quaint-looking. Humor and variety are the winning points; each page sports a stylized, black-and-white woodcut of an animal in collage with color photographs of its letter taken from street signs and trucks, plus a sentence that uses words beginning with the letter. The loose theme of Arthur the ape's visiting different cities to meet animal friends connects the sentences into a kind of story. Sounds and rhythms invite reading aloud and audience participation after the longish sentences become familiar.

A review of "All about Arthur (An Absolutely Absurd Ape)," in The Booklist, *Vol. 71, No. 5, November 1, 1974, p. 287.*

[Each animal that Arthur meets] has an extravagantly alliterative description . . . that should amuse children because of the appeal of absurdity. There's no liaison, simply a cataloging, but the combined appeals of interesting pages, each of which has a large photograph of a letter from a signboard, nonsense, and animals should be attractive as well as instructive to the audience for alphabet books.

Zena Sutherland, in a review of "All about Arthur (An Absolutely Absurd Ape)," in Bulletin of the Center for Children's Books, *Vol. 28, No. 5, January, 1975, p. 74.*

[If a child] is actually learning his alphabet, would the trendy *All About Arthur* ("In Glasgow he got to meet a graceful gazelle, Gladys. Gladys was glad to go with a groovy group.") meet his needs, either graphically or grammatically? The lettering is as way-out as the style; it's the Pow! Wham! Sock-it-to-you—save-them-from-illiteracy, Sesame Street school which is fine for the spiritually-impoverished, under-privileged American, but not a likely choice for a British Mummy who wants to help her offspring to master the ABC.

Gillian Freeman, "For the Very Young?" in The Spectator, *Vol. 234, No. 7659, April 12, 1975, p. 443.**

"People who perpetrate poetry are peripatetic, potty and prolix". That odd bit I recall from a long-ago facetious invocation of apt alliteration's artful aid and, of course, one knows how easy it can be to alliterate substanitally yet fall short of total reality. Arthur's adventures, from A to Z, or from Aberdeen to Yattenden, naturally sound a dubious note here and there: "Near Newport he met a nutty nightingale wearing a necktie. His name was Nathan". But what fun it is whether it comes absolutely good or not. The accompanying illustrations are a combination of delicacy and splendour. The letters, photographed in situ in any old location, even off brick walls and packing-cases, confirm the general notion of a creative mind at work.

A. R. Williams, in a review of "All about Arthur," in The Junior Bookshelf, *Vol. 39, No. 3, June, 1975, p. 172.*

From All about Arthur (An Absolutely Absurd Ape), *written and illustrated by Eric Carle. Franklin Watts, 1974. All rights reserved. Reprinted by permission of the author.*

ANIMALS AND THEIR BABIES (1974)

The ultimate master of the play-group situation is Eric Carle. No one knows better the value of strong, clean drawing and simple melodious words. Mostly he has tucked his didacticism into the jam of a good story. In *Animals and Their Babies* the lesson is directly stated. I prefer his former method, but this at least enables him to draw a series of endearing animal studies, beautifully stylised and equally accurate. They should give immense pleasure, and sharpen young eyes to an understanding view of nature.

> *M. Crouch, in a review of "Animals and Their Babies," in* The Junior Bookshelf, *Vol. 38, No. 6, December, 1974, p. 333.*

A collection of pictures of animals and their young, with a few basic facts about their lives on facing pages, this seems an uneasy mixture of picture-book and natural-history. The pictures are in Eric Carle's familiar collage style; well designed and in attractive colours: but, are they good natural history? Some of them could be misleading to a child, who might be led to believe that baby elephants, for example, are coloured a variety of shades from bright blue to turquoise! This is all very well in a picture-story book, but surely not in a book that presents itself as giving factual information in its text. . . . Much as I admire the work of Eric Carle, I see no point in this book, and no good use for it.

> *John A. Cunliffe, in a review of "Animals and Their Babies," in* Children's Book Review, *Vol. IV, No. 4, Winter, 1974-75, p. 143.*

THE MIXED-UP CHAMELEON (1975)

Kid-style crayon illustrations, a departure from Carle's usual sophisticated paper collages, make a cheery book that is a good reiteration of the "you are better off being yourself" idea. The tricky bit of die cutting which undoubtedly contributed to the fat price . . . serves as a gimmick for reinforcing color naming skills. Carle is better represented in picture book collections by his *Rooster Who Set Out To See the World* . . . in which the illustrations are more attractive, and there is also a clever built-in number skills device.

> *Merrie Lou Cohen, in a review of "The Mixed-Up Chameleon," in* School Library Journal, *Vol. 22, No. 4, December, 1975, p. 41.*

With Eric Carle's *Mixed-up Chameleon,* the tempo builds up to breakneck speed. The whiplash of his crayoned line drives one breathlessly from page to page. The apparent casualness with which Mr Carle scatters his dynamic coloured scribbles upon smooth, snowy pages is deceptive: he knows all about designing books; the hallmarks are present in an impeccable relationship of type and illustration.

Tony Dyson, in a review of "The Mixed-Up Chameleon," in The School Librarian, Vol. 24, No. 1, March, 1976, p. 30.

The mixed-up chameleon is the product of Carle's observation of a chameleon and his wondering "what if the chameleon could change more than just its color," coupled with his experiences demonstrating to children how a book is made. With the children, Carle works on a book of favorite animals. As the children suggest animals, he draws. However, as requests pour in so fast, only the most characteristic parts are drawn, and these parts become strung together with hilarious results. This unusually illustrated book, with exuberant crayon drawings, is not only a lesson in colors, drawing, observation, and recall, but also a lesson in values as the chameleon discovers it is best to be oneself. (p. 452)

Delores R. Klingberg, "Profile: Eric Carle," in Language Arts, Vol. 54, No. 4, April, 1977, pp. 445-52.

In this colorfully illustrated story of self-acceptance, the chameleon's desire to be more impressive is one any small child can share. Though the text is brief, the lesson is clear. Vivid illustrations show all the imagined changes the chameleon undergoes.

Sharon Spredemann Dreyer, in a review of "The Mixed-Up Chameleon," in her The Bookfinder, a Guide to Children's Literature about the Needs and Problems of Youth Aged 2-15: Annotations of Books Published 1975 through 1978, Vol. 2, American Guidance Service, Inc., 1981, No. 114.

[*Carle revised both the text and illustrations for* The Mixed-Up Chameleon *in 1984. The following reviewers compare the 1984 edition to the earlier version of the book.*]

Carle has replaced the heavy-lined, childlike, scrawled colors with crisp, appealing collages and has streamlined the text. The cutaway pages have been retained, and none of the humor has been lost. The simpler text results in a smoother flow, and children will enjoy the resulting repetition. For example, where the 1975 edition read, "If I could be like a fox, then I would be smart. Instantly it had a fox's fluffy red tail." Now it simply says, "I wish I could be smart like a fox," with the illustrations showing the fluffy red tail.

Barbara Elleman, in a review of "The Mixed-Up Chameleon," in Booklist, Vol. 81, No. 6, November 15, 1984, p. 442.

Collage illustrations characteristic of much of Carle's work are showcased in this reissue of *The Mixed-Up Chameleon*. . . . The collages mimic the form and relationship to text of the original crayon drawings but the bold colors of the original have been muted and in doing so have helped focus readers on the ever-changing composition of the mixed-up animal. In addition to the new illustrations, the text has been tightened in this revision. In both editions, the illustrations enhance and complement the text, but in this revision, the illustrations have become an integral part of the story, adding information not stated. A chance to compare and contrast the two editions will give older readers some insight into the writing and editing process and the role of illustrations in picture books. A book that's sure to remain a perennial favorite.

Sharron McElmeel, in a review of "The Mixed-Up Chameleon," in School Library Journal, Vol. 31, No. 4, December, 1984, p. 68.

ERIC CARLE'S STORYBOOK: SEVEN TALES BY THE BROTHERS GRIMM (1976)

The common way to tell a fairy tale today is the old way, not by improvising but simply by retelling it with variations. Since the famous stories are now transformed into picture books, often written by illustrators with their minds on the pictures, the words are necessarily fewer, shorter, plainer, meant for younger children who may never discover for themselves the original magic of the masters. On the other hand, brevity has its virtue. "**Eric Carle's Storybook**" . . . retells seven tales by the Brothers Grimm with clarity and no long-windedness. Sometimes he changes events for the better. In general Eric Carle, a vivid illustrator, is less gruesome and terrifying, more easy and genial than Grimm. (p. 28)

Helen Bevington, "Once Upon a Time and Ever After," in The New York Times Book Review, November 14, 1976, pp. 28, 50.*

The best buy of the season. Seven tales from the brothers Grimm; and grim and grisly most are—even the full-color collage and paintings. I love children's books in which the people and surroundings look as dirty as they are in real life,

From Eric Carle's Storybook: Seven Tales by the Brothers Grimm, *retold and illustrated by Eric Carle. Franklin Watts, 1976. All rights reserved. Reprinted by permission of the author.*

and in which the author isn't afraid to have a frightened man shout, ''Oh my God!''

> *William Cole, in a review of ''Eric Carle's Storybook,'' in* Saturday Review, *Vol. 4, No. 5, November 27, 1976, p. 36.*

[The seven tales by Grimm] have presumably been chosen for their strong situations. They are illustrated in vibrant colour, the text being skied above dominant art-work and occasionally overlaid by it. The near-grotesque style is as forceful as Lilo Fromm's, faces and figures posed with a consciously rustic stolidity against patternings of leaves, grasses, stonework in lieu of light and shade.

> *Margery Fisher, in a review of ''Eric Carle's Storybook,'' in her* Growing Point, *Vol. 15, No. 7, January, 1977, p. 3052.*

Eric Carle's boldly colored, dramatic illustrations lend added excitement and beauty to these favorite folk-tales. The profusion of large, bright pictures might lead one to select this book for the very young, but it is best reserved for those who are not likely to be disturbed by severed heads, corpses, monsters, and such. These short tales are full of dialogue and action, making them ideal for dramatizing.

> *Jean Mandelbaum, in a review of ''Eric Carle's Storybook: Seven Tales from the Brothers Grimm,'' in* Children's Book Review Service, *Vol. 5, No. 7, February, 1977, p. 63.*

Eric Carle's versions are written with simplicity and clarity. They are good vehicles for reading aloud and the vocabulary and sentence structure are quite suitable for the child who has just moved off a reading scheme.

The real glories of this book, however, lie not only in the pleasing production but also in Eric Carle's superb illustrations: inventive, imaginative and with their obviously sumptuous colour very well reproduced, they give a unique flavour to a most pleasing and worthwhile book. (pp. 35-6)

> *Dennis Hamley, in a review of ''Eric Carle's Story Book: Seven Tales Told by the Brothers Grimm,'' in* The School Librarian, *Vol. 25, No. 1, March, 1977, pp. 35-6.*

Carle's brilliantly colored pictures, handsomely designed but occasionally cluttered with detail, dominate his simplified retellings of the Grimm tales. The style of the adaptation does not always keep the cadence of traditional material (''Let's fix the mean old thing,'' says a robber in **''The Three Golden Hairs,''**) although it has more vitality than some adaptations.

> *Zena Sutherland, in a review of ''Eric Carle's Storybook: Seven Tales by the Brothers Grimm,'' in* Bulletin of the Center for Children's Books, *Vol. 30, No. 8, April, 1977, p. 124.*

THE GROUCHY LADYBUG   (1978; British edition as *The Bad-Tempered Ladybird*)

With chutzpah that far surpasses its miniature stature, the Grouchy Ladybug flies off in quest of an opponent to cut down to size. Whether confronted by a bee's stinger or a hyena's teeth, the ladybug taunts each animal (from a beetle to an elephant) with the rejoinder, ''You're not big enough!'' (How often have children heard *that*?) Finally, a whale's tail flicks the bellicose

bug back where it began, on its own leaf. The finger paint and collage illustrations—as bold as the feisty hero—are satisfyingly placed on pages sized to suit the successive animals that appear (one is cut in the fan shape of the whale's tail). Tiny clocks show the time of each enjoyable encounter, with the sun rising and setting as the action proceeds. (pp. 44-5)

> *Kathy Coffey, in a review of ''The Grouchy Ladybug,'' in* School Library Journal, *Vol. 24, No. 6, February, 1978, pp. 44-5.*

Fans of Eric Carle's **''The Very Hungry Caterpillar''**, one of the most original and appealing picture books ever, will be delighted to hear of his latest book, **''The Bad-Tempered Ladybird''**. . . . Mr Carle makes his own rules. His caterpillar ''ate'' real holes in the pages; his ladybird encounters a series of creatures, from wasp to whale, to accommodate whom the pages gradually become wider, from an inch onwards, until the whale takes several pages and finally slaps the pestering insect with his tail—a cut-out one. Size and time are dealt with subtly, but this book is chiefly a pleasure to read and to look at, with its cross and good-natured ladybirds who agree to share their aphid feast, and its deep-toned illustrations of animals.

> *Caroline Moorhead, ''Animal/Animal, Animal/Human,'' in* The Times Educational Supplement, *No. 3269, February 3, 1978. p. 45.**

A colorful natural history story that contains an astonishing number of concepts. Ladybugs and their customary breakfast of aphids are the taking-off point, but also included are concepts of size with just the right amount of cumulative repetition, and the passage of time diagrammed clearly on a clock face—I wish it had been a slightly larger one. The gentle moral, that bad manners get you nowhere, is an additional bonus.

> *Brigitte Weeks, in a review of ''The Grouchy Ladybug,'' in* Book World—The Washington Post, *February 12, 1978, p. G4.*

Ever felt like fighting, but not enough to risk getting beat up? Then you'll empathize with **''The Grouchy Ladybug,''** a bad-tempered insect who'll win your heart, but not before she gets your goat. . . .

Eric Carle, who wrote the story and did the imaginative art work, deserves an award for one of the most evocative last lines in a children's book: ''The fireflies, who had been sleeping all day, came out to dance around the moon.''

> *Madora McKenzie, ''Long Island, N.Y., Crocodile Finds Happiness under a Bed,'' in* The Christian Science Monitor, *May 3, 1978, p. B8.**

Carle's story is about a ladybug, but he also manages to get across the idea of bullies being cowardly (if one stands up to them) and to introduce the concept of comparative size. . . . The pages are set back, graduated in size, and the concept of time is also introduced, with a nice twist at the end; whereas other creatures were encountered on the hour, it takes almost an hour just to fly past the whale. A fresh approach is developed with ingenuity, and the bold, colorful paintings are particularly effective, with larger and larger print used as the size of the pages increases.

> *Zena Sutherland, in a review of ''The Grouchy Ladybug,'' in* Bulletin of the Center for Children's Books, *Vol. 31, No. 10, June, 1978, p. 155.*

The Very Hungry Caterpillar turned out to be one of the landmarks of the post-war picture-book, and this makes the artist a marked man. Everything that Mr. Carle does now has to stand up to this sort of comparable examination. This is hard on him, and he cannot always maintain the standard. *The Bad-tempered Ladybird* has all his characteristics, a bold use of collage, strong colour contrasts, the application of genuine natural science to a comic theme, a little bibliographical trickery. What it lacks perhaps is spontaneity. The text is well planned, and uses repetition effectively. It locks in with the pictures admirably. One only misses the memorable quality of the artist's other work. So too with the art-work: the designs are set admirably on the page. They are at once strongly stylized and based on natural forms. They do not provoke the uncontrollable chuckle. A good book by anyone's standard, but a little below the best of this best of picture-book makers. (pp. 248-49)

> *M. Crouch, in a review of "The Bad-Tempered Lady-bird," in* The Junior Bookshelf, *Vol. 42, No. 5, October, 1978, pp. 248-49.*

SEVEN STORIES BY HANS CHRISTIAN ANDERSEN   (1978)

Carle simplified seven stories by the legendary Dane, thus making them more accessible to young readers. But the author-illustrator's paintings—ornamenting and revealing episodes on each page—are the book's chief allure. The pictures are in glorious colors, meticulously detailed and full of spirit. Some are full of fun, as well, such as those that show what happens in **"Big Klaus, Little Klaus"** when a poor but canny fellow gets the better of a bully. Scenes of haunting magic illustrate **"The Wild Swans"**. . . .

> *A review of "Seven Stories," in* Publishers Weekly, *Vol. 214, No. 7, August 14, 1978, p. 70.*

These seven stories retain the framework of Andersen, but many descriptive passages have been cut and some episodes either altered or eliminated. The Carle retellings are readable and the illustrations carry the reader through the text, but the format makes the book look easier than it is. If you buy versions of classics which have been cut or retold, this may be a good choice. I strongly suggest, however, that readers be told that these are changed and that fuller translations are available.

> *Annette C. Blank, in a review of "Seven Stories by Hans Christian Andersen," in* Children's Book Review Service, *Vol. 7, No. 4, December, 1978, p. 34.*

The short, stark sentences, deficient in rhythm, convey meaning well enough, but while the style may suit the robust humour of **"Great Claus and Little Claus"**, it hardly conveys the subtle melancholy of **"The Travelling Companion"** or **"The Wild Swans"**. The book must rest on the illustrations. In these, the Egyptian motifs used for **"The Bog King's Daughter"** and the heavily grotesque rendering of demons and human characters, seem to have little to do with the spirit of Andersen. (pp. 3457-58)

> *Margery Fisher, in a review of "Seven Stories by Hans Christian Andersen," in her* Growing Point, *Vol. 17, No. 5, January, 1979, pp. 3457-58.*

Eric Carle is one of my favourite picture book makers, but he is no favourite of mine when he turns his attention to Andersen. If any text should be safe from tampering it is surely this. Story and image and word are so closely entwined, so totally inter-

dependent that even a master of words, which Mr. Carle is not, touches these tales at his peril. What a pity, for Mr. Carle is here drawing at his best, with real perception as well as technique. The book is carefully designed, with excellent colour, . . . but I will perhaps not be alone in refusing to countenance a book which has so fundamental a flaw.

> *M. Crouch, in a review of "Seven Stories by Hans Christian Andersen," in* The Junior Bookshelf, *Vol. 43, No. 1, February, 1979, p. 26.*

Is there an unwritten code which requires every illustrator to produce a Grimm, an Andersen and a Mother Goose book? Carle has shortened and modernized three familiar tales and four which are not usually included in standard collections. Unfortunately, this simplification makes the tales choppy and difficult to read aloud. . . . However, in spite of the limitations of the text, it is simple enough for third graders to read independently and the book is full of bright, bold full-color illustrations which appear on almost every page and enhance the folk-humor that abounds in the stories.

> *Dona Helmer, in a review of "Seven Stories by Hans Christian Andersen," in* School Library Journal, *Vol. 25, No. 6, February, 1979, p. 38.*

WATCH OUT! A GIANT!   (1978)

The colours are striking and vibrant. Eric Carle has once again created a memorable picture book with all the humour and excitement first associated with *The Very Hungry Caterpillar*. The cut pages allow the reading children to explore every possible avenue of escape with the children of the story. It also introduces the youngest child to the marvellous world of fairy tales.

> *Anne Reilly, in a review of "Watch Out! A Giant!" in* Book Window, *Vol. 6, No. 2, Spring, 1979, p. 14.*

Bold colors and ballooned captions fill the pages of an oversize book, telling the story of two children who wander into a giant's garden. The giant captures them and brings them home; the children use a series of trapdoors, jars, boxes (all cutouts in the pages) to seek an escape route—and end on the giant's plate. Abruptly, the last opening—the giant's mouth—leads them directly to their own front door. The pictures have vitality, the subject's appealing to children, but the text seems contrived to make use of the cutout device and the ending is weak.

> *Zena Sutherland, in a review of "Watch Out! A Giant!" in* Bulletin of the Center for Children's Books, *Vol. 32, No. 8, April, 1979, p. 131.*

Eric Carle has made a name as one of the more imaginative of the three-dimensional bookmakers. His pictures 'do things' as well as presenting images, and no one could be a more ardent admirer of *The hungry caterpillar* than myself, for I have seen children of all ages drawn to its holes and flaps as to a magnet. However, invention must always progress and Mr Carle's talent seems to be in search of something new, but there is nothing here that he has not done before and, to my mind, done better. The fold-out patches do not work as a part of the story—in itself a feeble affair—they merely provide a diversion; once they have been worked there is nothing else to be seen, no text of value, and little visual excitement.

Just then two people walked by.
"If I could only..."
But before the chameleon finished that thought it saw a fly.
The chameleon was very hungry.
But it was terribly mixed up. It couldn't use its tongue.
It couldn't catch the fly.
"Oh, if I could only be myself!"

From The Mixed-Up Chameleon, *written and illustrated by Eric Carle. Thomas Y. Crowell Co., Inc., 1975. Copyright © 1975 by the Berne Convention. All rights reserved. By permission of Harper & Row, Publishers, Inc.*

Gabrielle Maunder, in a review of "Watch Out! A Giant!" in The School Librarian, *Vol. 27, No. 2, June, 1979, p. 127.*

Once more, Eric Carle has created an exciting book with holes in it, though even the logic of fairytale or dream is stretched a bit hard as a box-lid on one page appears as a book-page on the next, and a jar-lid as a face! The author intends this to contain elements of the world of fairytales to introduce the very young to their various elements, especially straightforward acceptance of fantasy. Any "toybook" is fun, particularly when illustrated in deep jewel-colours with mysterious dark areas. . . . The text is all balloon-commentary by the children and by the sun, whose humorous remarks cushion the sudden shocks— And yes, perhaps this may serve to allay secret fears from traditional fairytales.

M. Hobbs, in a review of "Watch Out! A Giant!" in The Junior Bookshelf, *Vol. 43, No. 4, August, 1979, p. 193.*

TWELVE TALES FROM AESOP (1980)

Carle has selected twelve of his favorite fables and retold them in a simple style. Best of all, he illustrated them in his inimitable style, with bright, splashy colors that are sure to attract and appeal to a new audience. Each tale gives good advice

without sermonizing. Another treasure from an outstanding artist.

Vee V. Garry, in a review of "Twelve Tales from Aesop," in Children's Book Review Service, *Vol. 9, No. 7, February, 1981, p. 53.*

Carle has acted here as a true storyteller, adding some of his own wisdom and color, a fact that will please some and dismay others. Whatever adults feel, these versions of Aesop's tales, together with Carle's vibrant color illustrations, should prove popular with young listeners. The blackbird in **"The Blackbird and the Peacocks"** vainly displays his attached peacock feathers while gliding about on ice skates, while the families in **"The Frog and the Ox"** stroll past each other in turn-of-the-century garb. **"The Wolf and the Lamb"** is pastoral in text only: a dramatically powerful, tuxedoed wolf plays sweet tunes on his flute for the lamb, who sits on a chair, wearing a long, filmy dress and bonnet. Carle chooses to reward the grasshopper for his musicianship in **"The Grasshopper and the Ants"**: an ant takes the hungry fiddler in and they make a party out of food, song, and company. For each one-page story, there is a full-page picture, giving audiences plenty to gaze upon while they listen.

Judith Goldberger, in a review of "Twelve Tales from Aesop," in Booklist, *Vol. 77, No. 12, February 15, 1981, p. 807.*

Each retold fable is faced by a full-page picture that combines collage, gouache, and crayon in vivid colors, handsome in composition but rather crowded at close range. The fables are retold in adequately simplified style but often diverge from the standard version and lack the summary tag that is the hallmark of the genre. In **"The Grasshopper and the Ants,"** for example, there is no penalty for the former's summer laziness; in **"The Fox and the Crow"** Carle has added a small fox whose hunger prompts his mother to trick the crow into dropping food; and in **"The Wolf and the Lamb"** the story is quite changed. The characters are all shown as animals in clothing in the illustrations, which—while they are most attractive pictures—makes them less forceful in depicting animal characteristics than are the animal figures of the Eve Rice adaptations of the fables, also simplified for younger children.

> *Zena Sutherland, in a review of "Twelve Tales from Aesop," in* Bulletin of the Center for Children's Books, *Vol. 34, No. 7, March, 1981, p. 125.*

Interesting textures (painted collage) and well designed full-page illustrations outshine the retellings of Aesop facing them. Looking like Dracula, a wonderful bat in striped trousers and shrouding cape stalks in purples, grays and blues under a full moon. A mouse rests his elbows on the floorboards, under which a committee discusses belling the cat (asleep on a couch over the mousehole). But some illustrations are inappropriate for the text, viz. the **"Lion and the Mouse"**; **"Wolf and the Lamb"** (more like a deb at a dance); or **"Wolf and the Dog"** (one can't imagine this high-heeled, flounce-skirted, ice-cream-eating lady chained outside a house). Texts are sometimes overelaborate, as in **"Fox and the Crow,"** even though one is entranced by the crow's juggling his schnaps and sausage in a tree. It's good Carle, but poor Aesop—the same age group can better be served by A. T. White's *Aesop's Fables* (Random, 1964) or R. Spriggs' *Fables of Aesop* (Rand McNally, 1975).

> *Ruth M. McConnell, in a review of "Twelve Tales from Aesop," in* School Library Journal, *Vol. 27, No. 9, May, 1981, p. 54.*

THE HONEYBEE AND THE ROBBER: A MOVING / PICTURE BOOK (1981)

In the past several years, the number of pop-up books being published each season has grown considerably. The first for this year is **"The Honeybee and the Robber"** by Eric Carle. . . . His new story, contained in this "moving/picture book," concerns the perils a honeybee faces as she goes about gathering nectar—a bird, a fish and a frog all try to eat her for breakfast—as well as an encounter with a bear bent on stealing honey from the hive. . . .

Mr. Carle slathers on the colors a bit too lavishly at times, but he does impart considerable scientific information. The real genius of the book is in the paper engineering. The reader can work the tabs in and out so that the bee moves his wings, stinger and tongue at the same time, the bear can cross his eyes as the bee stings his nose, a flower opens its petals for a descending bee, and the bear, chased by a swarm of bees, can be sent galumphing off. Popping up in the center of the book is a gorgeous multihued butterfly.

> *George A. Woods, in a review of "The Honeybee and the Robber: A Moving/Picture Book," in* The New York Times Book Review, *February 22, 1981, p. 31.*

After the pop-ups, we now have the moving picture book and what a fascinating one it is. Children can follow the honeybee on her search for nectar and her return to the hive where she frightens away a bear who is hoping to steal some honey. Turn to the back of the book and there find a mass of information for adults and children keen to learn more about bees. This is very useful for answering the awkward questions that children delight in asking! The book owes much to the genius of Eric Carle but almost as much to those who did the paper engineering and how fitting it is that they are named. This is a really outstanding book in every sense and everyone concerned in its production deserves the highest praise. Do look out for it.

> *Margaret Walker, in a review of "The Honeybee and the Robber," in* Book Window, *Vol. 8, No. 2, Spring, 1981, p. 16.*

This may be too fragile for a library collection, but it's not by any means a run-of-the-mill pop-up book, since the oversize pages are vivid with color in Carle's distincitve style of combined painting and collage. . . . Not a strong story, but a handsome book; facts about bees are given in a final section that may be useful but that seems gauged for older children (both because of the small print size and vocabulary) than those to whom the book will have its chief appeal. (pp. 166-67)

> *Zena Sutherland, in a review of "The Honeybee and the Robber," in* Bulletin of the Center for Children's Books, *Vol. 34, No. 9, May, 1981, pp. 166-67.*

The Honeybee and the Robber is an informational picture book, but just barely. Bees and their habits are described in detail on the back endpapers. The rest of the book includes a conventional adventure tale and some popular gimmicks—a pop-out butterfly and several levers that activate the characters when pulled.

The narrative offers several suspenseful moments. A bird and a fish nearly swallow the honeybee, and when a bear threatens the hive, the feisty bee leads the charge that scares him off. A plot needs this tension, and also the audacity of a minute hero confronting a giant mischief maker. Economy in style and story line add a further degree of vitality.

Carle is basically an illustrator. He uses many-toned colors and, in a painterly manner, creates a quivering, animated effect on every surface. There is little attention to the relation between color and specific objects in nature. He applies paint in layered, scrapped, rubbed, spotted, and streaked patterns, achieving a pleasing sense of depth, as well as a playful manipulation of the color. The stark white background and scissored shapes also enhance the three-dimensional illusion. (pp. 770-71)

> *Donnarae MacCann and Olga Richard, in a review of "The Honeybee and the Robber," in* Wilson Library Bulletin, *Vol. 55, No. 10, June, 1981, pp. 770-71.*

Right from the first Eric Carle has used the form of a book to reinforce his argument. He did it in **The Very Hungry Caterpillar,** and here he is again, having fun with bees, bears and other creatures of the wild and sharing his delight in form and colour with a delighted audience. Fish leap and frogs blink at the touch of a lever, a colourful butterfly jumps right out of the page, and the unfortunate bear crosses his eyes in anguish when the honeybee fights off his attack. All this is in Mr. Carle's most dynamic manner. He is a master of the art of selection, missing no important detail but always keeping his designs clean and elemental. Such books can hardly expect a long physical life, especially when they are as tempting as this, but the 'machinery' is reasonably sturdy.

> *M. Crouch, in a review of "The Honeybee and the Robber," in* The Junior Bookshelf, *Vol. 45, No. 4, August, 1981, p. 143.*

The resolution of my problem of how to consider this book came in its very last paragraph where full (and justified) credit is given to 'the skill of the paper engineers' who made the pictures 'work'. Everything moves easily and sturdily, and the central *coup de théâtre* showing a suspended butterfly is magnificent. Inevitably though, one comes back to the textual deficiencies—so thin, so inconsistent (swerving between didacticism and anthropomorphism), so inadequate, that this cannot be said to be a book. Why, I wonder, was it not presented as a series of paper sculptures with accompanying notes for adults (they're already in the appendix)? Then it could be used, as I feel it will be in any case, by teachers with children, rather than by children reading by themselves.

> *Gabrielle Maunder, in a review of "The Honeybee and the Robber," in* The School Librarian, *Vol. 29, No. 3, September, 1981, p. 225.*

CATCH THE BALL!; LET'S PAINT A RAINBOW; WHAT'S FOR LUNCH? (1982)

This set of board books has vibrant color and simple design, but falls short of the mark. In *Catch the Ball* and *What's for Lunch,* the die-cut pages have movable parts that are not easily manipulated; in *Let's Paint a Rainbow,* the colors are unlike those of a real rainbow. There are many excellent illustrations, but the counting and color themes in these books are weak.

> *Emily Holchin McCarty, in a review of "Catch the Ball," "Let's Paint a Rainbow," and "What's for Lunch," in* Children's Book Review Service, *Vol. 11, No. 4, December, 1982, p. 31.*

Storytellers usually know what to expect when a narrative encourages direct, vigorous participation from a preschooler. A

From The Very Busy Spider, *written and illustrated by Eric Carle. Philomel Books, 1984. Text and illustrations copyright © 1984 by Eric Carle Corp. All rights reserved. Reprinted by permission of Philomel Books.*

text that reads, "What's for lunch? A Coconut? No, thank you. Apples? No, thank you," and so on with ten fruits will inspire a spirited performance from the child but may prove monotonous to an uninitiated adult. *What's for Lunch?* . . . is a toy book with a cardboard monkey swinging on a real rope, sliding through a hole in each cardboard page. The child gleefully manipulates the monkey figure while shouting, "No, thank you," at the appropriate moments, and then, "Yes, please!" when the monkey's banana appears.

Carle's designs are witty and well executed. Colors are layered, glazed, scratched, sponged—whatever can be done with a wide-ranging palette to animate a surface and sharpen clarity. Then the artist makes cutouts from this material, keeping the shapes simple in contrast to the richly textured color. These pasted-on silhouette shapes have a mixture of long, curved edges (in tree limbs) and short, angular edges (in small, decorative fruits)—a pleasing combination for the eye. . . .

[*Catch the Ball!*] features a monkey, a lion, and eight other ball players. Each beast has a convincing posture and shape despite the simple collage treatment.

A seal passes to an elephant a ball that is attached to a real rope. The elephant sends it through a hole in the page to a deer and so on, until a kangaroo catches the ball in its pouch. Some of the tale's rhymed couplets are awkward, but they are rhythmic enough to blend with the snappy, energetic images.

> "Throw it here,"
> said the DEER.
> "Where? Where?"
> asked the BEAR.
>
> (pp. 590-91)

> *Donnarae MacCann and Olga Richard, in a review of "What's for Lunch?" and "Catch the Ball!" in* Wilson Library Bulletin, *Vol. 57, No. 7, March, 1983, pp. 590-91.*

THE VERY BUSY SPIDER (1984)

In 1968 Eric Carle's greatest invention, the Very Hungry Caterpillar, ate his way through one apple, two pears, three plums then on to a cup-cake, one pickle, one sausage and one slice of water-melon. The pun on "eating its way through" may sometimes be lost on children but the visual and tactile delight of the little caterpillar holes in each food and fruit has given lasting pleasure and has helped make the book into a classic. The simplicity of its structure is an additional lure. From "In the light of the moon a little egg lay on a leaf" to the final spread of the beautiful butterfly, the Very Hungry Caterpillar is developing.

In *The Very Busy Spider* there is a similar, almost more obvious progressive theme. "Early one morning the wind blew a spider across the field. A thin silky thread trailed from her body." The thread trails from the left to the right-hand page as the spider begins to spin her web. Different animals on the farm try to distract her but she keeps at it and, when night falls in beautiful blues and greys, the web is complete, the pesty fly which has been irritating the other animals is caught and the spider sleeps. "It has been a very, very busy day."

The simplicity of the text with its question and refrain ("The spider didn't answer. She was very busy spinning her web"), the aesthetic pleasure of each collage animal, and the satisfyingly finite ending make this a soothing book for the very young. The "multi-sensory" factor—the web and the fly are both raised so that they can be felt—is obviously of value to the visually handicapped, as they can follow the making of the web and the catching of the fly. It is also fun for a child being read to. The book is difficult to use with a group, however, since it is impractical for them all to follow the thread with their fingers. The story, even with its deliberate and careful introduction of colours, animals and animal noises, is a shade too slight to repay much reading. *The Very Busy Spider* is good-looking book but it lacks the very special magic of *The Very Hungry Caterpillar.*

> *Julia Eccleshare, "Following the Thread," in* The Times Literary Supplement, *No. 4278, March 29, 1985, p. 351.*

Although the story this tells is slight and has a repetitive pattern, the book should enchant children because the fine lines of the spider's web, as it grows, are raised just enough from the page so that they can be felt and because the collage illustrations are so bright in colors and perky in forms. (pp. 161-62)

> *Zena Sutherland, in a review of "The Very Busy Spider," in* Bulletin of the Center for Children's Books, *Vol. 38, No. 9, May, 1985, pp. 161-62.*

The author/illustrator of *The Very Hungry Caterpillar* has created a book so special that it may well exceed the popularity and lasting appeal of his caterpillar classic. The raised illustration in this exceptional book will not only captivate children with normal sight, but will enthrall sightless children. This is a *Charlotte's Web* for younger children. An undisputed candidate for the Caldecott Award.

> *Margaret M. Nichols, in a review of "The Very Busy Spider," in* Children's Book Review Service, *Vol. 13, No. 11, June, 1985, p. 114.*

Dare one go out on a limb and predict an instant classic? This good-looking picture book has just the ingredients to make that happen. Its pictures are strong and inventive, yet strikingly simple; its story has a disarming ingenuousness and a repetitive

structure that will capture the response of preschool audiences. Of special note is the book's use of raised lines for the spider, its web, and an unsuspecting fly. Both sighted and blind children will be able to follow the action with ease. The story isn't really a story, but rather a charming depiction of a spider spinning her web. . . . Carle's pictures are simple but astute compositions that rely on textures and shapes for their interest. Dappled and streaked collage pieces form the various animals, all of which sit against white backgrounds. The spider's web spins out in a framed enclosure that balances nicely with the open space. Visually and verbally, this is a winner.

> *Denise M. Wilms, in a review of "The Very Busy Spider," in* Booklist, *Vol. 81, No. 19, June 1, 1985, p. 1398.*

Bright, splashy endpapers in an abstract expressionist style effectively introduce a multisensory story which follows the progress of a persevering spider as she tries to build a web in spite of distracting invitations proferred by a variety of familiar farm animals. The text is designed as a series of questions, each followed by a repetitive statement describing the spider's activity. . . . The pattern is consistent throughout; the mnemonic sequence practically guarantees audience participation. The strong rhythms are matched by the bold shapes of the animals, suggested through vivid collages. A tactile experience, an effective counterpoint to this visual stimulation, is provided by the gray repoussé shapes of fly, spider, and web—the growth of it from simple line to complex design parallels the cumulative structure of the text. The skillful integration of the three elements—tactile, visual, and onomatopoeic—sets this book apart as a beautifully executed work for the very young that satisfies the needs of both visually handicapped and sighted children without losing its artistic integrity. An imaginative, much needed book which should be a popular choice for libraries, schools, and homes.

> *Mary M. Burns, in a review of "The Very Busy Spider," in* The Horn Book Magazine, *Vol. LXI, No. 4, July-August, 1985, p. 435.*

Ellen (Schaffer) Conford

1942-

American author of fiction and picture books.

One of the most popular authors of realistic fiction for middle-graders and young adults, Conford is best known for her humorous books about contemporary teenagers growing up in suburbia. Her stories, which usually employ current settings and focus on female protagonists, stress the warm relationships of these characters with their parents and friends. Capitalizing on droll everyday situations familiar to her readers, Conford combines amusing observations of human nature and social interaction with themes concerning identity, romance, and success; her lively style includes generous amounts of dialogue and wit. In addition to her books for young people, Conford has created picture books which stress such simple lessons as the importance of individuality.

Critics praise Conford for her perception and her ability to entertain. Applauding her skill with natural dialogue and characterization, reviewers commend Conford's understanding of young adults and her sympathetic treatment of their problems. Although some critics note that Conford loses appeal when she treats more complex issues and that her plots are occasionally weak, most appreciate the humor, optimism, light tone, and relevance of her works.

Conford has won several regional child- and parent-selected awards.

(See also *Something about the Author*, Vol. 6; *Contemporary Authors New Revision Series*, Vol. 13; and *Contemporary Authors*, Vols. 33-36, rev. ed.)

AUTHOR'S COMMENTARY

I write books about people who don't take drugs, don't need abortions, don't have physical disabilities, don't suffer in an environment of urban blight, and don't swim far out of the mainstream of society. In short, I write books about things that could or do happen to 75 percent of the kids I know who face the normal problems of growing up in a middle-class suburban environment with parents who care about them, and, in many cases, understand them.

Frequently, humor appeals to us because of a certain recognition; we see people in situations we've been in, reacting in the very same way we reacted, and we laugh because we recognize both the situation and the reaction.

In my visits to schools and in letters I receive from my readers, I find children who respond to my books on just that basis. . . .

And when children recognize and identify with the characters in your books, they endow you with all sorts of mystical abilities to know and understand their inmost feelings.

"But how do you *know*?" one girl asked me. "How do you know just how I feel?"

Try and explain to a fifth-grader that you were once a fifth-grader too! Children tend to think they're unique, and that no one has the thoughts, hopes, dreams and fears that they do.

No one knows how they suffer the pangs of growing up, no one realizes how they think or what they wish—not even other children, let alone adults. When they read about someone whose hopes and fears correspond to theirs, they are often amazed and relieved to find that they are not alone. They are reassured to discover that they are "OK."

Of course, I'm not writing primarily to provide this reassurance, nor am I qualified to fulfill the psychological needs of preadolescents; if some of my writing happens to hit the emotional target, I think that's great, but it's not the main thing I aim for.

What I am trying to do is to write entertaining, realistic books for a television generation. I think that always in my subconscious as I write is the hope that my book will be entertaining enough to wrest a child away from the TV set for a couple of hours. I try to achieve this by making my books fast-paced, long on dialogue and short on great chunks of unbroken paragraphs of narrative description and above all, that key word, entertaining.

I don't write to pound home a message, or to teach a lesson, or to convert kids to a particular point of view. I want to write books that are fun to read, books that will help children to realize that there is such a thing as reading for pleasure, and that books do not merely inform and teach, but *amuse*.

Ellen Conford, "Nobody Dies in My Books," a promotional piece by Little, Brown and Company, 1977.

GENERAL COMMENTARY

JOHN G. KELLER

We sat in a pleasant if nondescript midtown restaurant. Most of the other luncheon patrons had left, yet we lingered over our coffee.

"Yes, I do understand, John, but I also feel quite strongly that you've got to know your own limitations," she said.

I nodded in partial agreement but thought to myself, "Yes, but not if those self-declared limitations stop you from growing."

The speaker in this case was author Ellen Conford, a very clever, very intelligent young writer of children's books whose reputation as a writer children like to read and who teachers, librarians and parents like to have children like to read, is growing at a steady rate. And I was the Editor of Children's Books for Little, Brown and Company. Ellen Conford's remark and my reaction to it has come to symbolize for me . . . the healthy tension that exists in the relationship between one writer and her editor as they work toward the goal of producing the best books for children that they can.

Of course, every relationship must have a beginning and I think you might be interested in my view of the way Ellen Conford became one of Little, Brown's most popular authors of books for children. (p. 791)

[When I first started reading unsolicited children's book manuscripts] I seemed only to come upon dreary little stories told in trochaic tetrameter, all of which had anthropomorphic animals, vegetables, or minerals who were somehow different and who didn't wish to be ("The Little Diamond That Didn't Shine," "The Fuzzy Squirrel Without a Tail," etc. etc., ad nauseam). Imagine my relief—my joy—when after two months during which I thought I'd never find an author worth publishing I came upon a funny and fresh manuscript about a young, unprepossessing possum who couldn't seem to catch on to the knack of hanging by his tail. The manuscript did have one to two scenes that I felt were overly long but, on the whole, I liked it immensely and I especially liked the dialogue, which was consistently amusing and never became cute.

"Are you hurt?" asked his mother anxiously.

"No more than usual," sighed Randolph. "I don't think I broke any bones."

His father shook his head. "I just don't understand it. Your mother and I can hang by our tails; your brother Eugene can hang by his tail; your sister Geraldine can hang by her tail. It's the most natural thing in the world to sleep upside down."

To show Randolph how easy it was, Geraldine went back up the tree. She scurried out onto a limb, hung upside down, and sang "Pop Goes the Weasel!" as she swung by her tail.

"Would you like to hear 'Mary Had a Little Lamb'?" she asked.

"Nobody likes a show-off," sulked Randolph.

The dialogue, while subdued, was in essence what I heard going on all the time in my suburban household; the book turned out to be *Impossible, Possum;* and the author who seemed to be the answer to my prayers was, of course, Ellen Conford. . . .

Everything about *Possum* worked right. In a field where it often takes several books before the market begins to know and trust an author, this first book exceeded our expectations. Blessed by witty and imaginative drawings by Rosemary Wells, it was chosen one of the best books of the year by the influential *School Library Journal* and went on to sell in very respectable numbers. (p. 792)

I thought of myself as the most fortunate of editors and, when a second funny picture-book text was delivered by Mrs. Conford I was most pleased. *Why Can't I Be William?* was a grass-is-always-greener story, which I asked another young talented artist, Philip Wende, to illustrate. Mr. Wende did a fine job, but after he sent us his final illustrations he phoned me to say in essence that while he really liked the story when he read it, when he came to illustrate he found that the characters really didn't do very much but talk. And darn it—it was difficult to create interesting illustrations of people just standing around talking. Needless to say, I did not pass on Mr. Wende's comments to Mrs. Conford. But the more I thought about it, the more I came to think that he might have put his finger on a possible weakness of Ellen Conford as a writer of picture books. She did tend to emphasize dialogue—sometimes at the expense of scenes that were easy to illustrate.

But what fine dialogue it was! Here is Jonathon, the hero, and his mother having a confrontation in a supermarket:

Jonathon's mother stopped her shopping cart in the middle of the aisle.

"Listen, Jonathon," she said sternly. "You are not William and I am not William's mother, and I don't know *any* mother who doesn't say no sometimes."

"Yes you do," said Jonathon. "You know William's mother. She never says *no*. She lets William buy anything he wants in the store. Ask William if you don't believe me."

Jonathon wondered why his mother closed her eyes and sighed.

"Jonathon," she warned, "I'm getting very tired of this discussion."

"I'm not tired of it," Jonathon said.

"Well, I am, and I'm finished talking."

"That's okay," said Jonathon. "I'll just talk some more."

"No you won't!" his mother said in a very loud voice. Jonathon noticed that all of a sudden it was very quiet in the store.

"How come all those people are looking at us?" he whispered.

"They are wondering," said his mother very softly, "when I am going to lose my temper and spank you."

Sound familiar? I know many seven-year-olds and their mothers who recognize the dialogue and the emotions at once. Nonetheless, the exchange *doesn't* give an illustrator much to go on.

Well, what to do? I had wished for a good writer and had luckily found one. How could I tell her that after all perhaps her talents might be better used in an area outside that of picture books—say, novels for the nine- to twelve-year-old age group? Nothing ventured etc., so I wrote to Ellen and gingerly suggested the idea. After such a letter gets into the mails, I always expect to receive either an irate phone call or the kind of return letter that makes my secretary sigh and roll her eyes heavenward as she puts it in the in-basket. My fears in this case were unfounded. Ellen wrote me one of those letters that brighten one's day. To summarize:

> Although it will mean that I must put aside (temporarily) the six sequels to **Possum**—*The French Lieutenant's Possum, Valley of the Possums, Thus Spake Impossible Possum*, etc. etc., I think the idea a fine one. After all, how many picture book ideas can I deluge you with? And I have a nifty idea. Roughly, it's about a girl who thinks she's a loser. I don't want to say more than that right now. I'll think about it some more and get back to you with an outline and one or two chapters.

It was a lovely letter and it was my introduction to Victory Benneker, the very appealing girl who was to become the heroine of **Dreams of Victory**. Ellen wouldn't tell me a thing about **Dreams of Victory** while she was writing it. She is a writer very much in touch with her own emotions about writing. And, as she explained to me later, during the writing, if I had said that the idea was good rather than that it was superb, a thing of beauty and a joy forever, she would have become so discouraged that the writing would have stopped.

When the manuscript did arrive, I couldn't wait to see if it worked. I put aside whatever I was doing at the time and began to read. Good news—I loved it. Victory, the girl who loses the class election by a landslide so daydreams of being the first woman President; Victory, who is picked to play the lowly part of Litter in the class play but who dreams of being a famous actress, seemed to me to have been picked up bodily from suburban USA and plunked down in the pages of this manuscript. She talked and behaved in her own unique way but she had enough in her of the little girls who often swarmed through my house that I knew that they and—if there were any justice—the adults who recommended that certain books be bought for children would love her. And to make my feelings about the book even more positive, Ellen Conford had done wonders with the relationship between Victory and her parents. It was very refreshing in this day when so many writers who do books for children paint their adult characters as either villains or fools to read Mrs. Conford's manuscript, in which parents and children spoke to each other in what I can only describe as the flip-without-being rude, always concerned and usually loving way that I heard around me as I interacted with my own family. (pp. 792-94)

Suffice it to say that Mrs. Conford made me sympathize with Victory and care what happened to her and her parents. The book was funny and true and once again Ellen Conford had written the kind of book I had wished she would! I knew that now she had found the most proper setting for her gift of writing

dialogue. The critics, I'm happy to report, agreed. **Dreams of Victory** was widely and well reviewed and began to sell well immediately.

Once she has the basic idea for a story, Ellen Conford writes quickly. Her plots are, of course, all different but I feel that in the work she has done so far, her themes have been similar: Believe in yourself. You are worthwhile and have something to contribute. You may have a problem, but we all have problems and, basically, life is good and people care what happens to you. This kind of optimism is never in her hands sticky-sweet and her young readers respond positively to what she has to say. So, when not too long after **Dreams of Victory** was finished, Ellen told me another long novel was about to be sent to me, I was very pleased.

Within the week I had had the pleasure of getting to know Felicia Kershenbaum, the heroine of **Felicia the Critic**. If Victory were unsure of herself, Felicia was a little too sure she knew what was right for herself and everyone around her. She never hesitated to let others know their shortcomings, yet she couldn't seem to understand why her criticisms met with hostile reactions. Her mother, trying to help, introduced her to the idea of constructive criticism but even that didn't help. Felicia soon discovered that any sort of criticism—even when it is offered with the best intentions—can put people off. When she makes a list of the things wrong with her cousin's wedding and reception, which is held in the Lagoon Room of Trader Phil's Shangri-La Restaurant (Mrs. Conford does know, doesn't she?) and it falls into the hands of the mother of the bride, Felicia finds herself in very hot water indeed. Felicia does work her problem out to her own satisfaction, and this reader loved the book. I really did, and yet . . .

And yet I began to want more. Ellen Conford had shown that she could write both picture-book texts and novels for older readers; she had, to borrow a sports reporter's terminology, all the moves. However, when her third novel, **Me and the Terrible Two** arrived I began to want to ask for something more in her writing. Dorrie, the me who meets the terrible two, is an attractive and amusing girl, but I felt that I really didn't know much about her when she wasn't coping with the twin boys with whom she tangles during the course of the book, and the ALA Booklists' review of **Felicia** had begun, "Ellen Conford's latest misfit is Felicia. . . ." Latest? That made it sound like Ellen had written twenty novels instead of only a few. Could it be something was needed to make her writing *really* live for years to come?

I then took my step in the process of changing from editor to a character like the fisherman's greedy wife who couldn't let a good thing be. Ellen Conford had come into my professional life when I needed to work with a good, solid writer. She had changed the kind of writing that brought her initial success and did it partially at my request. The new books were very good, but I was beginning to think she should enlarge the scope and depth of her writing.

I knew that Ellen, for all the funny and positive things she had said and written to me during the course of our relationship, had to be approached cautiously when changes were suggested in her work. (pp. 794-95)

I had by this time read the first draft of her fourth novel, **The Luck of Pokey Bloom** and in it I had found a theme that I thought would illustrate my new thesis well. The main narrative thrust of the book concerns Pokey's attempt to win something—anything—in one of those enter-by-mail contests; yet the book had another theme I thought was worthy of fuller exploration. Pokey, a vivacious ten-year-old, cannot understand why her older brother, who was such a pal last year, now spends long hours lying on his bed staring at the ceiling, making phone calls so personal that he takes the telephone into the hall closet, and in general seems to want Pokey out of his life. As she stands firmly anchored in her childhood, Pokey watches as her brother drifts away from her and into the often choppy waters of adolescence, and it was this sense of failing that I felt could be explored more deeply. Felicia and her sister, Marilyn, fought in *Felicia the Critic*, but the fights were there almost for comic effect. In *The Luck of Pokey Bloom* the author had presented the reader with a heroine as spunky as the other girls she had written about, but had shown her to be more vulnerable and had made the reader get involved with that vulnerability. It was this chord in the novel that I wished Ellen to develop even further.

Not to my very great surprise, Ellen knew immediately what I wanted for the manuscript, but she had a few trenchant words of her own to add to the discussion.

"John, I know what you mean about the book, and I'll try to magnify that theme in some places. But I think you have to understand something about me as a writer. I am not Dostoevski. I am not even Paul Zindel, and what's more, I don't want to be. It would be wrong for me as a writer to try and turn my talent into something it isn't. You've got to know your own limitations; and I think I know mine. I won't be overly modest. I have talent, but I think that above all it is a talent to entertain. I have absolutely no message to get across to my readers. Well, perhaps not NO message, but the reason I write books is not to get kids to think the way I do about life. There's enough of that neo-Victorianism going on in children's books right now without me adding another shrill voice to the pack. So while I think you're a super editor and a nice person, please don't ask me to write in a way that will make me feel uncomfortable. First of all, I couldn't and, second, even if I tried it, you'd probably contract for a book that would wind up one big flop."

As Ellen spoke I relearned that most valuable lesson, which an editor forgets at his peril. Let the writers write and if you can help them to clarify *their* style and *their* ideas, fine. But, never, *never* try to force the writer into the mold of what you want him or her to be. Don't project your aspirations for a writer onto his work, unless he agrees with those hopes. Once again the fisherman's wife stood abashed.

But not for long. I had only one question for Ellen that afternoon and the answer to it will, I think, affect her career as a writer. By saying that we know our limitations don't we often concoct self-fulfilling prophecies? For Ellen Conford to declare too firmly that she knows the limits of her talent may she not impose those limits on a talent that is larger and more multifaceted than she knows?

Ellen Conford is young and she is bright and despite the fact that at that luncheon in New York she told me something I should heed, I still feel that it is up to me as her editor to poke at her work a bit here and prod at it a bit there in the hopes that such action will cause an atmosphere between editor and author full of the kind of healthy tension that will enable the author to do her best work.

Who knows if I am right? All I do know is that I received another funny letter from Ellen the other day and in it she said that she was at work on another novel. This one is meant for an adolescent audience, but she wouldn't tell me any more about it. (pp. 795-96)

My hunch is that I'm going to like the new book very much, and when it finally reaches print, I bet you will too. (p. 796)

John G. Keller, "Ellen and Me or The Editor as Fisherman's Wife," in Elementary English, *Vol. 51, No. 6, September, 1974, pp. 790-96.*

IMPOSSIBLE, POSSUM   (1971)

All possums hang by their tails—all except Randolph, a young possum with an embarrassing problem. But clever sister Geraldine comes up with a solution to dispel Randolph's fears and to give him confidence in himself. There is, of course, a message, but Ellen Conford has cleverly disguised it with humor and imagination. Combined with Rosemary Wells's witty drawings, **"Impossible, Possum"** becomes a delightful story that will charm young children.

A review of "Impossible, Possum," in Publishers Weekly, *Vol. 200, No. 5, August 2, 1971, p. 64.*

WHY CAN'T I BE WILLIAM?   (1972)

"'Why can't I be William?'" is Jonathon's lament when he protests bathing, eating brussels sprouts, and going to bed early. Jonathon tells his mother that William is not burdened with these undesirable duties, but a visit to William's house proves that he is not as lucky as Jonathon thinks. Unfortunately, although the story begins entertainingly, the abrupt end is flat. Lively illustrations [by Philip Wende] are not enough to redeem the unsuccessful story.

Jill Brandenfels, in a review of "Why Can't I Be William?" in School Library Journal, *an appendix to* Library Journal, *Vol. 19, No. 6, February, 1973, p. 57.*

What child hasn't thought enviously of the advantageous situation enjoyed by a friend? . . . Jonathon's mother was getting a bit tired of hearing about William, and she took Jonathon along when she went to visit William's mother. And that's how Jonathon discovered that William envied him: for having a brother, for living in a house rather than an apartment, for having a dog. Also he had needed dental work and could no longer have all the candy he wanted. Hmm. Not so bad, Jonathon decided, not to be William. . . . [The illustrations are] light in mood to echo the tone of the writing; the story has an amused rather than a didactic message, and both the exaggeration of incident and the lively dialogue concerning a familiar situation should appeal to children.

Zena Sutherland, in a review of "Why Can't I Be William?" in Bulletin of the Center for Children's Books, *Vol. 26, No. 9, May, 1973, p. 136.*

DREAMS OF VICTORY   (1973)

Either Ellen Conford has as much imagination as her heroine Victory Benneker, or she has a good memory for what it's like to be one of those mousy, undistinguished kids who aren't nearly so uncommon as they, in their loneliness, believe themselves to be. Victory not only gets a scant six votes when she runs for class president, but she's a wallflower at her friend's coed party, flubs the role of litter in her school play and is even afraid to ride the Ferris wheel at the town carnival. . . . [In] her fantasies Victory is always a credit to her name—whether she's winning the Miss America pageant, making her Presidential acceptance speech, uncovering a spy ring, or distributing a million dollars to her envious schoolmates. Unlike Victory's teacher, we couldn't give an A + to that composition on ''Imagination'' which finally wins her some recognition but Victory herself gets high marks for her spirited, often humorous battle against the agonies of being ordinary.

> *A review of ''Dreams of Victory,'' in* Kirkus Reviews, *Vol. XLI, No. 4, February 15, 1973, p. 186.*

[What] Victoria has is imagination, and what she can do, she discovers, is write about it. The dialog is amusing, the class characters alarmingly familiar, and Vicky's relationship with her parents delightful—two adults and a child who can laugh at each other and themselves.

> *Barbara Joyce Duree, in a review of ''Dreams of Victory,'' in* The Booklist, *Vol. 69, No. 18, May 15, 1973, p. 904.*

A sorry imitation of Thurber's wonderful ''Walter Mitty,'' the girl heroine of this book is incongruously named Victory. She's a loser at everything and so, of course, takes refuge in daydreams. . . . The humor is flat and there are no surprises; every single incident is predictable, including the anticlimactic end.

> *A review of ''Dreams of Victory,'' in* Publishers Weekly, *Vol. 203, No. 25, June 18, 1973, p. 70.*

Ellen Conford has written a satisfying first-person story that is true and funny. . . . Any young reader who, like Victory Benneker, does not have the longest blondest hair in the class or who is apt to be given the part of Litter in the pollution play will love her dreams. They make a simple and successful book.

It is part of a genre. As a fledgling writer Victory is only one of a number of scribbling young heroines in books for young people. Scratch an adult writer and you are likely to find the child writer inside. Thus a book drawn from memories of childhood may have the feeling of smaller boxes nested inside larger boxes: the adult writer writes about the child writer who will grow up to become an adult writer who will write about. . . .

> *Jane Langton, in a review of ''Dreams of Victory,'' in* The New York Times Book Review, *June 24, 1973, p. 8.*

One dream of victory among children's librarians involves having a sufficient number of titles to suggest when middle graders ask for another one like Judy Blume's popular *Tales of a Fourth Grade Nothing.* . . . This can help to serve. The narrator, sixth grader Victory Benneker, is amusing in a situation comedy setting (middle class suburbia) and in her self-deprecating way of reporting the facts of her life. . . . (p. 2191)

> *Lillian N. Gerhardt, in a review of ''Dreams of Victory,'' in* Library Journal, *Vol. 98, No. 13, July, 1973, pp. 2191-92.*

The fiasco episodes are ruefully funny, the classroom scenes amusing, and the conversations between Vicky and her parents especially deft; while the focus is on the situation rather than the plot, there is enough action in the catalog of small failures to sustain interest, and many children can empathize with Vicky as a character.

> *Zena Sutherland, in a review of ''Dreams of Victory,'' in* Bulletin of the Center for Children's Books, *Vol. 26, No. 11, July-August, 1973, p. 169.*

FELICIA THE CRITIC (1973)

Felicia Kershenbaum has every bit as much imagination as Victory Banneker . . . , but Felicia channels hers outward into what is meant to be constructive criticism. . . . [With] an ego-boosting finale and a lot of major and minor catastrophes along the way, *Felicia the Critic* is stronger in traditional story values and structure than the episodic *Dreams of Victory*. But Conford, who is better at monologue and quick satirical sketches than sustained action, seems less at home with the more gregarious, confident Felicia. As a result, there is somewhat more formula and less conviction here, though Felicia is sure to receive good reviews from her critical peers.

> *A review of ''Felicia the Critic,'' in* Kirkus Reviews, *Vol. XLI, No. 21, November 1, 1973, p. 1199.*

Fresh, entertaining, and percipient in the manner of Beverly Cleary's fiction and Jane Langton's books about Grace Jones, this contemporary story looks at Felicia's problems—with her peers, with her older sister who is attempting sophistication at thirteen, and with other relatives. Felicia is by nature more than ordinarily observant and critically outspoken. But although she hands out some well-planned ''constructive criticism'' to the traffic policeman, to the butcher, to her Aunt Celeste (a writer of children's books, one of which Felicia confidently reviews), and even to the radio weatherman, Felicia must refrain from making suggestions to ''in'' members at club meetings if she is to be tolerated. It all adds up to a deft, sympathetic portrait of a real child—a loner aware of the obtuseness and supercritical responses of other people. A better developed book than the amusing *Dreams of Victory* by the same new author of children's books.

> *Virginia Haviland, in a review of ''Felicia the Critic,'' in* The Horn Book Magazine, *Vol. XLIX, No. 6, December, 1973, p. 591.*

Felicia the Critic is a light, ephemeral thing whose conclusion is somewhat ambiguous. Felicia is a young girl whose orientation is toward problem solving of a practical sort. The question the book asks is whether criticism is good. The answer is that criticism is sometimes good and sometimes bad, but the author, Ellen Conford, does not draw the line as clearly as it might be drawn. She seems to believe that one should not be critical if criticism may prove embarrassing. Surely we should wish other criteria than this, for criticism, even at Felicia's level, stems from the impulse to order the disorderly, to create proper proportion, to make just the unjust. I do not find it the least bit humorous that Felicia should finally write the President telling how the country might be made better. Of course carping criticism or personal criticism should be discouraged, but the implication that one should endure rather than risk embarrassment by criticizing (though in truth not a *clear* implication of the book) seeks the basest conformity. (p. 232)

> *Donald B. Gibson, ''Fiction, Fantasy, and Ethnic Realities,'' in* Children's Literature: Annual of the Modern Language Association Seminar on Children's Literature and The Children's Literature Association, *Vol. 3, 1974, pp. 230-34.**

The success of such a book depends very much upon the reader's reaction to Felicia. The touch is light and the episodes briskly told, but moments that are intended to amuse perhaps simply irritate: it could well be that the older the reader is, the less sympathy he will have for the central character. The letter to the President at the end, however, is a hilarious idea. The mind boggles at the possible contents.

> *David L. Rees, in a review of "Felicia the Critic," in* Children's Book Review, *Vol. V, No. 2, Summer, 1975, p. 59.*

Felicia The Critic comes some way after Louise Fitzhugh's *Harriet the Spy* but it is a lively book with some entertaining characters, particularly the awful friends who form a secret society and Felicia's sister Marilyn who wants to change her name to Désirée.

In a series of disconnected incidents Felicia, who has decided to be a constructive critic when she grows up, learns that people don't much enjoy being criticised; one hopes she will learn by the end of the book that she may sometimes be wrong herself, but she doesn't. In the final episode, the organisation of a disastrously mistimed carnival, she only learns to keep her mouth shut. It is a very American book—bologna on rye, peanut butter, sneakers and slickers—but we are probably mid-Atlantic enough for this not to confuse the children, and it is a nice undemanding book.

> *Dorothy Nimmo, in a review of "Felicia the Critic," in* The School Librarian, *Vol. 23, No. 3, September, 1975, p. 228.*

With the same sure powers of observation and understanding that her earlier titles show, Ellen Conford draws real youngsters in action. The story indicates that difficulty in getting along at home may well carry over to school and other spheres in life. The resolution is realistic for the age portrayed and the present state of our knowledge about human behavior. (p. 4)

The relationship between freely giving your opinions and upsetting others' feelings is explored here as a vital part of getting along well in your family. The need for a degree of tact in treating others as well as the emotional peril to oneself if tact is not exhibited is shown concretely. This familial dependence is extended to close friends as well. As a corollary, the book suggests that truth generally prevails, but that the personal cost must be borne if that is what one pursues. (p. 6)

> *Diana L. Spirt, "Getting Along in the Family: 'Felicia the Critic'," in her* Introducing More Books: A Guide for the Middle Grades, *R. R. Bowker Company, 1978, pp. 4-7.*

ME AND THE TERRIBLE TWO (1974)

Haskell and Conrad, the terrible twins just divorced by their father (as they put it) who move in next door to Dorrie, have the disadvantage of replacing her best friend Marlene who has moved to Australia. Even in themselves though they are nuisance enough. . . . But Dorrie is pleased when other girls accept her as a friend, and when Haskell is assigned to the Children's Book Week committee of which Dorrie is made chairman, they work so enthusiastically together on their storybook newspaper that the project brings them not only teachers' praise and local fame but what looks like a warm and lasting friendship. Unlike the heroines of last year's *Dreams of Victory* and *Felicia the Critic,* Dorrie has no particular qualities that make her easy to

remember, but she puts enough spirit and mild humor into the first person telling of her unremarkable adventures to attract a respectable audience.

> *A review of "Me and the Terrible Two," in* Kirkus Reviews, *Vol. XLII, No. 7, April 1, 1974, p. 363.*

This, the best of Conford's three recent junior novels (**"Dreams of Victory"** and **"Felicia the Critic",**) is unique, owing nothing to Walter Mitty or "Harriet the Spy". In a first-person narrative that seems effortlessly written, and "grabs" the reader from page one, heroine Dorrie Kimball tells the wryly funny story of her period of adjustment to twin boy neighbors she's determined to hate. During these same weeks Dorrie is also realizing her own creative potential. Compilers of "Outstanding Children's Books of 1974" lists should include this title—and libraries will want several copies.

> *Joyce W. Smothers, in a review of "Me and the Terrible Two," in* Children's Book Review Service, *Vol. 2, No. 11, July, 1974, p. 103.*

Conford again successfully uses first-person narrative for this book about Dorrie, a middle grader with a less one-sided character and more common set of problems than her counterparts in *Dreams of victory* . . . and *Felicia the critic*. . . . Good fun with obvious appeal. (p. 1252)

> *A review of "Me and the Terrible Two," in* The Booklist, *Vol. 70, No. 22, July 15, 1974, pp. 1251-52.*

Single-theme, realistic stories about contemporary girls and their problems—usually told in the first person—have proliferated in recent years. One readily understands the popularity of such books since they usually make few, if any, intellectual demands on the reader; and occasionally the writing is buoyed up with genuine humor. The author in previous stories presented a day-dreaming heroine and a hypercritical one; now she has written about Dorrie, a sixth-grader, who not only loses her best friend when the family next door moves to Australia, but must be plagued by the new incumbents. . . . The book is appealingly full of school happenings, zippy repartee, and plenty of preadolescent witticisms.

> *Ethel L. Heins, in a review of "Me and the Terrible Two," in* The Horn Book Magazine, *Vol. L, No. 4, August, 1974, p. 375.*

The book isn't strong on plot, but it doesn't need to be; it moves along at a good clip, the characters firmly drawn, the dialogue natural and often funny, and the committee project and classroom scenes entertaining.

> *Zena Sutherland, in a review of "Me and the Terrible Two," in* Bulletin of the Center for Children's Books, *Vol. 28, No. 4, December, 1974, p. 59.*

JUST THE THING FOR GERALDINE (1974)

Geraldine is a young possum whose talents do not seem to lie in the direction her parents had hoped they would. . . . Dancing proves to be a total disaster; she does not do well in weaving, either; and a course in sculpture finds her aptitude in that area to be just about nil. However, what Geraldine does best and enjoys most is to hang by her tail from the branch of a tree and juggle a few acorns. Although her parents continue to encourage her in more "feminine" endeavors, it is her brothers who finally help her find "just the right thing" to make her happy—Geraldine's Juggling School. This is a gentle story. . . . It should touch a note of familiarity with most children, both in the various familial relations and in the frustrations of one who knows what she wants but is detained from achieving it because of the desires of others.

Barbara Dill, in a review of "Just the Thing for Geraldine," in Wilson Library Bulletin, *Vol. 49, No. 3, November, 1974, p. 241.*

[In **Impossible, Possum**], Conford used little Randolph's peculiarly possumy problem, his inability to hang by his tail, to demonstrate her human point about confidence. Here, his sister Geraldine's difficulties . . . are less well adapted to the nature of her species, although they might be just as recognizable to young readers. And when Geraldine's family finally stops pushing her and allows her to do what she does enjoy and is good at . . . , Geraldine is apparently unable to let it go at that. Instead, to general approval, she makes a sign announcing "Geraldine's Juggling School"—indicating to us at least that she's already been pressured past being able to just relax and enjoy it. . . . [But, if this sounds like carping,] you might as well try it—for Conford's sympathetic picture of a hassled child. . . .

A review of "Just the Thing for Geraldine," in Kirkus Reviews, *Vol. XLII, No. 21, November 1, 1974, p. 1144.*

That well-intentioned parents are not always the best judges of their offsprings' talents is the central thread of an animal fantasy which features an engaging family of possums. The adults envision daughter Geraldine as graceful, housewifely, or artistic—meanwhile ignoring her self-taught skill at juggling. . . . Her ingenious solution, readily applauded by her family, is a lighthearted tribute to feminine independence.

Mary M. Burns, in a review of "Just the Thing for Geraldine," in The Horn Book Magazine, *Vol. L, No. 6, December, 1974, p. 688.*

THE LUCK OF POKEY BLOOM   (1975)

With incidents so slight they are forgotten almost as soon as they're read, this novel is no more than a temporary diversion. But if the story isn't memorable, it does provide a few giggles as it tells of a girl's pipe dreams. Pokey is an inveterate contestant. No flack—offering a radio, a dreamhouse or greenbacks—escapes her attention. When Pokey finally wins a prize, after many defeats, she learns that the victory is not a matter of luck but the result of her own efforts. We must add that the story would be more effective if Ms. Conford could leave verbs alone instead of tricking most of them out with inessential modifiers.

A review of "The Luck of Pokey Bloom," in Publishers Weekly, *Vol. 207, No. 19, May 12, 1975, p. 66.*

[**The Luck of Pokey Bloom**] is well-crafted, fast-paced and freshly imagined; Pokey's tribulations and triumphs are the warp and woof of a richly comic, thoroughly believable, contemporary family story.

Mary M. Burns, in a review of "The Luck of Pokey Bloom," in The Horn Book Magazine, *Vol. LI, No. 4, August, 1975, p. 380.*

The threads of the plot are Pokey's luck (she wins fourth prize in one contest) and Gordon's peculiar behavior (first love) but the story is told in such a blithe style no stronger plot is really needed; the several episodes involving Pokey's friends are amusing, but this is above all a warm family story, with good parent-child relationships, firm characterization, and smooth dialogue.

Zena Sutherland, in a review of "The Luck of Pokey Bloom," in Bulletin of the Center for Children's Books, *Vol. 29, No. 2, October, 1975, p. 24.*

The all-consuming desire of a scatterbrained girl to win "big" prizes is the one heavy-handed joke that provides the foundation of this novel. Pokey's mother and other female characters are unstereotypically independent and assertive—a positive feature, but in truth, the only one. Although Pokey and her friends unite to fight off a group of boys who harass them, no positive messages emerge from the encounter. They beat off the boys but then neglect to complete their clean-up project which, in any case, was materialistically motivated.

At the end of this trivial tale, Pokey wins a transistor radio (learning nothing in the process), brother Gordon recovers from his case of puppy love, and yet another author sends out the word that young people are ridiculous and not to be taken seriously. (pp. 135-36)

"The Luck of Pokey Bloom," in Human—And Anti-Human—Values in Children's Books: A Content Rating Instrument for Educators and Concerned Parents, *edited by the Council on Interracial Books for Children, Inc., Racism and Sexism Resource Center for Educators, 1976, pp. 135-36.*

DEAR LOVEY HART: I AM DESPERATE   (1975)

When a freshman, the daughter of the school guidance counselor, is assigned to write an anonymous lonely hearts column for the school newspaper, all sorts of outrageous possibilities come to mind. But Carrie Wasserman, alias Lovey Hart, is basically a sensible girl (Dad objects to her advice but it's better than some guidance counselors give), and Conford chooses to exploit only the gentler ironies and obvious humor of the situation. . . . Unabrasive, genuinely likable . . . though it's hard to imagine why Lovey Hart was such a circulation booster.

A review of "Dear Lovey Hart: I Am Desperate," in Kirkus Reviews, *Vol. XLIII, No. 20, October 15, 1975, p. 1182.*

An imaginative story is delivered in swift prose that should win more fans for the popular author and, incidentally, put across some essential points with neat understatement. Carrie Wasserman works on her school newspaper, the *Lincoln Log*, and her friend Chip persuades her to undertake an advice-to-the-lovelorn column, an addition he feels will perk up circulation. . . . The column is a success until Carrie begins to get flip with people seeking help with real problems. Then "Lovey" becomes a target for readers looking for revenge and the fat is in the fire. The action and the story culminate in an unexpected confrontation, with all concerned learning some hard lessons.

A review of "Dear Lovey Hart: I Am Desperate," in Publishers Weekly, *Vol. 208, No. 16, October 20, 1975, p. 74.*

Just like the advice column launched in the school paper, Conford's latest novel starts out promisingly enough but soon backfires.... Conford's problem is that she bypasses a potentially funny set-up and opts for the easy out: her plot and characters seem to have been lifted straight from a '50's sit com—pesky kid sister, nice guy next door, best friend mooning over a young male teacher, and, of course, good-looking (sigh!) upperclassman who Never Notices Her. Although written with Conford's usual briskness, readers can snatch the same clichés on TV reruns.

> Jane Abramson, in a review of "Dear Lovey Hart, I Am Desperate," in School Library Journal, Vol. 22, No. 4, December, 1975, p. 58.

A potentially corny story is whipped into shape with humorous situations, funny dialogue, and perceptive first-person narrative under the competent pen of Ellen Conford. Although not as rib-tickling as **Me and the Terrible Two** ..., the believable characters, warm family relationships, and satisfying ending make this fun.

> Barbara Elleman, in a review of "Dear Lovey Hart, I Am Desperate," in The Booklist, Vol. 72, No. 9, January 1, 1976, p. 624.

The story is written in lively style, convincing as the writing of a young person, but frequently a bit on the cute side, as when Carrie repeatedly uses "Quarterback or cornerback" to show her ignorance of football. The book is also weak in structure, with a single situation extended to considerable length.

> Zena Sutherland, in a review of "Dear Lovey Hart, I Am Desperate," in Bulletin of the Center for Children's Books, Vol. 29, No. 8, April, 1976, p. 123.

THE ALFRED G. GRAEBNER MEMORIAL HIGH SCHOOL HANDBOOK OF RULES AND REGULATIONS: A NOVEL (1976)

Conford's episodic trifle about a girl's first year in high school (tenth grade) is amusing enough for those who haven't read it all elsewhere.... With some girl-type romance at the end and some contemporary references to computer scheduling and coed dorms, it's essentially an updated, female variation on a familiar Max Shulman theme.

> A review of "The Alfred G. Graebner Memorial High School Handbook of Rules and Regulations," in Kirkus Reviews, Vol. XLIV, No. 7, April 1, 1976, p. 404.

Ellen Conford combines nostalgic humor and fact. Can you remember when? High School and the pain of it all? ... It takes years and a good sense of humor to compile the days gone by and come up with **AGGMHS Handbook of Rules and Regulations**. Here is a book we all thought about writing at one time or another but never got around to.

Undoubtedly, we have all shared many of the same experiences in days gone by. Somewhere along the line the Handbook forgot to mention: Why don't computers understand why a schedule should be changed? Or what does a student do when she falls madly in love with a teacher? Why is the good guy never elected? Or what happens if a boy gets placed in the optional Home Ec rather than Shop? And no Handbook ever mentions how to handle an upperclassman who makes a pass. So what do you do for a friend who is constantly changing

religions in order to observe religious holidays, instead of attending school? ...

The ideas and situations retold in this book can best be enjoyed by parents and teenagers. The story contains most of its hilarity in the first three chapters. The last few are more like a high school book report. Even so, one can not help but enjoy the humorous way in which Ellen Conford presents each situation.

> Barbara J. Eisenhardt, in a review of "The Alfred G. Graebner Memorial High School Handbook of Rules and Regulations," in Best Sellers, Vol. 36, No. 4, July, 1976, p. 126.

My junior high school readers thought this a hilarious picture of the high school scene.... Conford is able to blend what could be, and often is, stereotypical material into a fresh, fast-paced story. Boys may be put off by a lack of male main characters, but if they're looking for a contemporary, funny story, this may please them.

> Sheila Salmon, in a review of "The Alfred G. Graebner Memorial High School Handbook of Rules and Regulations," in Children's Book Review Service, Vol. 4, No. 13, July, 1976, p. 111.

[As in **Dear Lovey Hart, I Am Desperate**], Conford is dealing with high school life here, but her familiar flippant style feels forced and her situations seem less realistic than in her tales involving younger children. The book is divided into chapters which are designed to correspond roughly with appropriate quotations from the rule book on student government, tardiness, phys. ed., etc. This structure, while clever and occasionally amusing, weakens the continuity of both plot and character development. Conford is still entertaining however, and her fans will be anxious to read her latest.

> Diane Haas, in a review of "The Alfred G. Graebner Memorial High School Handbook of Rules and Regulations," in School Library Journal, Vol. 23, No. 1, September, 1976, p. 130.

[Conford's] accounts are lively, but the dialogue occasionally verges on cuteness, and some of the characters (Julie's brother, his girl, the assistant editor of the school paper) seem overdrawn. Despite the lack of a story line, the book has two appeals: familiar situations and humor.

> Zena Sutherland, in a review of "The Alfred G. Graebner Memorial High School Handbook of Rules and Regulations," in Bulletin of the Center for Children's Books, Vol. 30, No. 2, October, 1976, p. 23.

AND THIS IS LAURA (1977)

Though rich and talented, Laura's family has a Brady Bunch typicality, nevertheless twelve-year-old Laura feels "ordinary" compared to the scientist and best-selling author (parents), budding actress (sister), musician and whiz kid (brothers) who surround her. But when Laura suddenly starts receiving vivid glimpses of the future, she feels special after all.... As might be apparent, Laura's access to her visions becomes a little too easy to convince even willing believers, and Conford adds no new wrinkle to her psychic theme; the routine tie-in with Laura's feelings of inadequacy only results in an overlong closing conversation with her parents reassuring her that they love all their children for themselves and not for their talents. But the story reads effortlessly, with a school play serving Laura as a more realistic testing ground, Dennis's constant recitation of TV commercials providing well-cued laughs, and enough easy interaction with family and friends to keep things moving. (pp. 284-85)

> *A review of "And This Is Laura," in* Kirkus Reviews, *Vol. XLV, No. 6, March 15, 1977, pp. 284-85.*

The Conford touch of snappy dialogue and lively narrative overrides credibility gaps around what triggers off or controls Laura's visions. There is a refreshing cheerfulness in the family and friends' relationships, while the subject hits the bull's-eye for popular appeal. (pp. 1418-19)

> *Barbara Elleman, in a review of "And This Is Laura," in* Booklist, *Vol. 73, No. 18, May 15, 1977, pp. 1418-19.*

The author writes convincingly about Laura's psychic powers, and she writes in a vigorous, informal style that includes a good ear for dialogue; the characters are firmly drawn; the parental acceptance of Laura's psychic ability is credible; the one weakness of the book is in the ending: while Laura is comforted by her parents' praise, nothing really happens.

> *Zena Sutherland, in a review of "And This Is Laura," in* Bulletin of the Center for Children's Books, *Vol. 30, No. 11, July-August, 1977, p. 173.*

The validity of ESP is not questioned (it's just a trendy peg on which to hang a familiar message), but the story is lively, fast-paced, and written in natural dialogue (including an occasional "hell" or "dammit").

> *Susan Davie, in a review of "And This Is Laura," in* School Library Journal, *Vol. 24, No. 1, September, 1977, p. 124.*

Lively family and junior-high-school atmosphere, with clever effervescent dialogue and credible action. Good ethical viewpoints, too. Girls 9-12 may ponder a teasing question: Was Laura really psychic, or did coincidence enter into many of her successes?

> *Ethna Sheehan, in a review of "And This Is Laura," in* America, *Vol. 137, No. 18, December 3, 1977, p. 406.*

EUGENE THE BRAVE (1978)

Yet again, Conford forces her characters to sigh, warn, gasp, almost anything but *say* their lines. Once more, she burdens an otherwise bright and charming story with piled-on adjectives and adverbs. The third of the adventures of the Possum family stars little Eugene who upsets the household by refusing to sleep in the daytime and forage for food at night because he's afraid of the dark.

> *A review of "Eugene the Brave," in* Publishers Weekly, *Vol. 213, No. 7, February 13, 1978, p. 127.*

The youngest member of Conford's possum family, Eugene is suddenly afraid of the dark. And sister Geraldine, to the surprise of no one who remembers *Impossible Possum*, is no help. When brother Randolph suggests that "Maybe there will be a nice bright moon out," Geraldine pops in with "I think it might rain." . . . Nevertheless (and again, in character) it is Geraldine who cures Eugene, first conditioning him with small fake scares and then, in the process, falling into a deep hole

("There might be snakes. . . . There might be poisonous spiders") from which Eugene, to everyone's admiration, must rescue her. Geraldine's remedy is par for the picture-book course, but the style of execution, like the earlier peskiness, is all her own.

> *A review of "Eugene the Brave," in* Kirkus Reviews, *Vol. XLVI, No. 8, April 15, 1978, p. 432.*

Immune to his family's insistence on the way nocturnal animals normally live, a young possum finally overcomes his fear of the dark when going to the rescue of someone else. Eugene's discovery of his own bravery is set down as whimsically as are the illustrations [by John Larrecq] of this funny tale.

> *Sharon Spredemann Dreyer, in a review of "Eugene the Brave," in her* The Bookfinder, a Guide to Children's Literature about the Needs and Problems of Youth Aged 2-15: Annotations of Books Published 1975 through 1978, *Vol. 2, American Guidance Service, Inc., 1981, No. 175.*

ANYTHING FOR A FRIEND (1979)

Wallis has been uprooted many times as her father accepts job transfers. Coming to yet another new school, Wallis is convinced that she will never have friends or stability. When she becomes involved with the class wheeler-dealer in hosting a seance, she allows herself to be open and friendly—and she does make friends. . . . Conford captures kids' language and perceptions. The book is funny and yet makes some astute observations about the social structure of a classroom. Buy it—they will like it.

> *Barbara Baker, in a review of "Anything for a Friend," in* Children's Book Review Service, *Vol. 7, No. 12, Spring, 1979, p. 117.*

A child victim of the corporate transfer circuit, Wallis Green finds that once again she faces making friends in a new school. . . . Wanting desperately to be friends with the inner clique, she rebuffs a fat, unpopular girl called Ruth the Doof and allows herself to be drawn into classmate Stuffy's scheme to write fake love letters to Ruth from their teacher. Wallis also agrees to a séance at her home . . . , [hoping] to gain friends for herself. Events take unexpected turns, making Wallis look carefully at her own actions; when her father announces another transfer she is able to meet the news with more confidence in her own ability to cope and adjust. This emotional transition is left vague, but the author does deal with a common problem in our mobile society in a convincing and empathic way, using large doses of humor and a lively style to uplift the realistic situation. (pp. 1217-18)

> *Barbara Elleman, in a review of "Anything for a Friend," in* Booklist, *Vol. 75, No. 15, April 1, 1979, pp. 1217-18.*

It's too bad that Ellen Conford seems to be losing her light touch. In this latest growing-up go-round you almost have no choice but to take her whiney, pain-in-the-neck heroine as seriously as she does herself. . . . At least Conford is no moralist, and despite her heroine's less-than-noble bid for popularity, she does allow Wallis her hour with the in crowd—that is, until Daddy breaks the news of their imminent move to the West Coast. Then too, realistically, the class misfit remains to the end a rather boring leech. Don't go looking for sharp insights about the tricky business of being or getting a friend, but the close observations of pre-teen pecking order and grade-school protocol will probably elicit painful nods of recognition.

A review of "Anything for a Friend," in Kirkus Reviews, *Vol. XLVII, No. 9, May 1, 1979, p. 518.*

The trouble with the book is that having limned a novel that probes with humor and compassion the adolescent social scene, Conford has sacrificed any depth by ignoring its potential for the sake of a superficial, facile read. Blume's *Blubber* (Bradbury, 1974), for a slightly younger audience, has a poignancy entirely missing in this.

Marjorie Lewis, in a review of "Anything for a Friend," in School Library Journal, *Vol. 26, No. 1, September, 1979, p. 132.*

WE INTERRUPT THIS SEMESTER FOR AN IMPORTANT BULLETIN (1979)

Here is Carrie Wasserman, frosh heroine of *Dear Lovey Hart, I Am Desperate* . . . , a year older but just as witty, earnest, and insecure. . . . Conford's comfortable humor finds perfect exposure in, among other things, a hilarious scene at an elegant dinner party during which Carrie gets drunk, and two exquisitely plotted incidents during which a tape recorder is planted and then retrieved. Right up there with the author's *Alfred G. Graebner Memorial High School Handbook of Rules and Regulations* . . . for laughs and a good story, and a fitting though predictable sequel to . . . *Lovey Hart.*

Marjorie Lewis, in a review of "We Interrupt This Semester for an Important Bulletin," in School Library Journal, *Vol. 26, No. 1, September, 1979, p. 154.*

[Although] Conford's story is disjointed in places and misses an opportunity to zero in on investigative reporting issues, the love angle is real and Carrie and Chip do evolve a more meaningful relationship.

Barbara Elleman, in a review of "We Interrupt This Semester for an Important Bulletin," in Booklist, *Vol. 76, No. 2, September 15, 1979, p. 117.*

Although there is much talk of freedom of the press and responsibility in reporting, the book has a rather old-fashioned air because of the preoccupation with boys and romance. But the fast, funny dialogue, the characterization of Prudie as *femme fatale,* and Carrie's self-mocking, humorous attitude towards life and her problems make the book light and amusing.

Ann A. Flowers, in a review of "We Interrupt This Semester for an Important Bulletin," in The Horn Book Magazine, *Vol. LVI, No. 1, February, 1980, p. 59.*

Carrie Wasserman, who got into hot water her first year on the *Lincoln* (High) *Log* (*Dear Lovey Hart, I Am Desperate,* . . .), is so nearly wiped out as a sophomore news-hound that it's hard to imagine what debacles Conford has in store for her junior and senior years. There's a nice little warm-up exercise in which Carrie has trouble writing interviews to suit boyfriend and editor-in-chief Chip. But the real trouble begins with the appearance of sweet-talking, sensational-looking, oh-so-Southern Prudie Tuckerman. Chip flips; and Carrie decides to give her all to reporting—also hoping, of course, to get Chip back. He's gunning for a big exposé of the school lunch program, and already has a low-level informant ("Cottage Cheese," lest

you miss the story's point); but Carrie plants a tape recorder in the office of the supervisor—and gets what sounds to the over-eager kids like evidence of a rake-off. . . . The paper comes out headlining the "scandal"; supervisor Mr. Fell understandably explodes . . . ; and, to the kids' total discredit, Chip's "Cottage Cheese" turns out to be a discharged employee making false allegations. In the fallout, Prudie proves faithless and, more remarkably, Carrie and Chip aren't sacked from the paper. But the exaggeration—of Southern man-eating *and* investigative reporting—makes this a frivolous item all around, even as a latter-day teenage romance.

A review of "We Interrupt This Semester for an Important Bulletin," in Kirkus Reviews, *Vol. XLVIII, No. 4, February 15, 1980, p. 221.*

A friendly indigenous teenager or two can be of great assistance to those of us who try to stay in touch with the shifting patterns of adolescent folkways.

One of my favorite informants is Lisa Gray, a fourteen-year-old gamin who sometimes sings and performs eccentric dances. . . . Lisa studies creative writing in a special UCLA class for the superbright and is an articulate and helpful book-discusser.

Not long ago Lisa and I sat down at the kitchen table over cups of coffee and piles of books to talk about laughing. I had given her a wildly divergent selection of recent books that were intended to be funny, and now we were ready to anatomize the adolescent funny-bone.

"As a not-so-typical teenager," I said, indicating the stack of books in the middle of the table, "which of these do you think is really funny?"

"Well," she said, "I had to put these in categories, because kids go through stages. For *my* stage right now, I'd have to choose this one." She picked up *We Interrupt This Semester for an Important Bulletin* by Ellen Conford. "It was funny, but it wasn't *real* funny. Just sort of amusing. I like her style of writing—it's fresh and you want to keep up with it, turn the page to find out what's happening. The funny things were the capers the kids got into, and the things they said to each other—they were just kind of silly in a junior-high way."

Lisa had serious feminist objections to the plot: "I didn't like what happened to this girl; I didn't like her desperation. The whole book is about her trying to get this guy, like that's the most important thing in life. Even though she's a good reporter on the school paper and writes well, she turns everything around just for this guy. And then in the end she takes him back after he's messed around with this empty-headed blonde! I said to myself, 'That's *it!*' "—she slapped her hand flat on the red tablecloth—" 'I ban this book in my library for that!' Because this does happen, and this is like offering a step-by-step example of how to carry it out."

Patty Campbell, in a review of "We Interrupt This Semester for an Important Bulletin," in Wilson Library Bulletin, *Vol. 54, No. 7, March, 1980, p. 456.*

In one very funny incident, Carrie—who tells the story—describes her reactions when the southern belle gives a dinner party complete with drinks, which Carrie isn't used to; like much of the book it's humorous, but it's better than a dozen lectures on drinking. If the book has a flaw, it's the pervasiveness of the flippant humor, but readers should enjoy Conford's good ear for teenage banter and her understanding of adolescent concerns.

> *Zena Sutherland, in a review of "We Interrupt This Semester for an Important Bulletin," in* Bulletin of the Center for Children's Books, *Vol. 33, No. 8, April, 1980, p. 148.*

THE REVENGE OF THE INCREDIBLE DR. RANCID AND HIS YOUTHFUL ASSISTANT, JEFFREY (1980)

Coping with a class bully . . . is a constant threat for frail-looking 11-year-old Jeffrey Childs, whose mother is a sports reporter. Dubbed "childish" by his prime antagonist, Jeff retreats to his notebook, where he and the imaginary Dr. Rancid concoct magnificent schemes to eliminate the Dewey Belascos of the world. . . . The Dr. Rancid adventures add an extra imaginative dimension to Concord's crisp narrative, which, as usual, is peppered with lively and realistic dialogue and action.

> *Barbara Elleman, in a review of "The Revenge of the Incredible Dr. Rancid and His Youthful Assistant, Jeffrey," in* Booklist, *Vol. 76, No. 16, April 15, 1980, p. 1201.*

Jeff, eleven, is cowed by the bullying of Dewey Belasco, a classmate who's much bigger than he; he's embarrassed when Dewey taunts him in the presence of Coco Siegelman, the nicest girl in the class. Jeff secretly writes when he's alone, and he puts all of his resentment toward Dewey and his admiration for Coco into the rambling Walter Mitty-ish novel about Dr. Rancid; the novel excerpts are interpolated periodically throughout the text and, while mildly amusing, do little to further the story. While defending a smaller child, Jeff gets into a fight with Dewey and, to his surprise, becomes instantly popular. The book has warm relationships within the family (mother a sports editor, father described as working in the city) especially in parental understanding when Jeff finally talks about his fear of Dewey; the writing is competent, but the story seems—in part due to uneven pace, in part to the Dr. Rancid excerpts—overextended.

> *Zena Sutherland, in a review of "The Revenge of the Incredible Dr. Rancid and His Youthful Assistant, Jeffrey," in* Bulletin of the Center for Children's Books, *Vol. 33, No. 9, May, 1980, p. 169.*

With his slender build and young features, Jeff is a prime target for the jibes and ribs of a confirmed bully like Dewey Belasco. . . . When [Jeff] finds that his reluctance to tell his father about his weakness was unnecessary, his father informs him of a similar incident from his childhood. The advice which his father offers (that "Everybody is a coward about something") is supported by logic and the simple rules of survival. A funny and fast moving variation on Stolz's *Dog on Barkham Street* (Harpers, 1960), modernized with liberated as well as understanding parents. (pp. 67-8)

> *Steve Matthews, in a review of "The Revenge of the Incredible Dr. Rancid and His Youthful Assistant, Jeffrey," in* School Library Journal, *Vol. 27, No. 1, September, 1980, pp. 67-8.*

With consistent unself-conscious wit, the author raises an old theme to a new level of freshness and originality; the dialogue is terse and effervescent, and the first-person telling full of wry humor. (pp. 518-19)

> *Ethel L. Heins, in a review of "The Revenge of the Incredible Dr. Rancid and His Youthful Assistant, Jeffrey," in* The Horn Book Magazine, *Vol. LVI, No. 5, October, 1980, pp. 518-19.*

SEVEN DAYS TO A BRAND-NEW ME (1981)

Conford varies a smitch the plot she has worked several times in stories meant for readers like her heroine Maddy in this novel. "The God of Locker Assignments" has put her next to a dream man, Adam, in their high school corridor, but Adam doesn't seem to notice Maddy, and she's too timid to speak to him. She pins her hopes on a self-help book that promises to make her a splendid person within a week. Meantime, Terence continues his friendly overtures to her, and Adam begins studying with Mary Louise. How all this works out is described in a novel with the substance of cotton candy, the dialogue phrased in Conford's style, supposedly expressions of characters who grumble, demand, mutter, moan pitifully, etc., more than they speak.

> *A review of "Seven Days to a Brand-New Me," in* Publishers Weekly, *Vol. 219, No. 3, January 16, 1981, p. 77.*

Conford's ability to make everyday events interesting and amusing has failed in this book: elements that worked before and were good for a few chuckles really bomb here. Maddy, with her endless daydreams, is not a character readers come to know. Unless you need a complete set of Conford, pass this one up.

> *Harriet McClain, in a review of "Seven Days to a Brand-New Me," in* School Library Journal, *Vol. 27, No. 7, March, 1981, p. 155.*

The theme of teenage ugly duckling is a constant in adolescent literature, since most teens feel themselves to be something less than swans, and Conford has often shown her ability to handle this bit of fluff with dash and wit. . . . Conford's lightness carries off this potentially lugubrious and old-fashioned plot with cheerful assurance, to make a book that will be gobbled up by junior high girls.

> *Patty Campbell, in a review of "Seven Days to a Brand-New Me," in* Wilson Library Bulletin, *Vol. 55, No. 7, March, 1981, p. 530.*

Lighthearted and bubbly, the story is highly appealing, and Conford effectively bolsters her somewhat slim plot with witty comments, funny dialogue, and a natural tone. Situations are believable and characters have enough shading to give them warmth and life.

> *Barbara Elleman, in a review of "Seven Days to a Brand-New Me," in* Booklist, *Vol. 77, No. 13, March 1, 1981, p. 926.*

Utilizing the too familiar cultural artifacts of daily life in the American suburb (running shoes, self-help books, shopping malls) Conford has created another sure-to-be popular, younger YA novel. Maddy, our average, plain protagonist leads a normal teenage life and therefore is at the point of despair. Alas, a gorgeous but non-aggressive Adam Holmquist captures Maddy's heart but Maddy can't talk to him because of lack of confidence, adolescent gawkiness, fear, or all of the above. How can she get Adam to notice and reciprocate her love?

Little does she know Adam is a past stutterer with his own problems in the communication department. . . .

A few clever lines and a few corny jokes extremely similar to those told by the kid sister in Danziger's *Can You Sue Your Parents For Malpractice?* keep a semblance of movement in the plot from the girl talk cafeteria scenes to the totally absurd locker scenarios and back. Although my review copy is an advance proof and has no cover art, I suggest this one be ordered immediately.

> *Barbara L. Gottesman, in a review of "Seven Days to a Brand-New Me," in* Voice of Youth Advocates, *Vol. 4, No. 1, April, 1981, p. 32.*

Basically, this is a girl-meets-boy story, but it's balanced by the warmth of the relationships between Maddy and her friends and the less frequent but equally affectionate exchanges between Maddy and her mother. Above all, it's the lively style, especially in the dialogue, that makes the book enjoyable.

> *Zena Sutherland, in a review of "Seven Days to a Brand-New Me," in* Bulletin of the Center for Children's Books, *Vol. 34, No. 9, May, 1981, p. 168.*

TO ALL MY FANS, WITH LOVE, FROM SYLVIE   (1982)

Sylvie Krail, 15, abandoned by her mother and sexually harassed by foster dads, runs away to Hollywood to pursue a movie career. When her wallet is stolen on the Greyhound bus in Dugan, Indiana, she is rescued by an itinerant Bible salesman, Walter Murchison, who offers to drive her to L.A. . . . By Kentucky, Walter has rationalized his feelings of lust as love and proposes marriage. He drives to Las Vegas, but Sylvie walks out on him. Broke and confused, she is befriended by UCLA student Vic, who works in Vegas during the summer. He helps her to see how hungry she is for love from anyone and how that need feeds her desire to become a star. Sylvie ends by calling Child Welfare in New York City. The plot is exciting and fast-paced. The characters are sympathetic and real, though Vic is a little too pat (preparing for a career in psychiatry, he just happens to be the one Sylvie meets when she's ready to fall apart). Scenes are not sexually explicit, though there are references to Sylvie's ample proportions, and she does admit to and fear her confusing sexual feelings for her last foster dad. Too bad Conford didn't set this down in the present. Her memories of James Dean, Velveeta cheese and crinolines may not mean much to today's 15 year olds. Regardless, it's a good story.

> *Symme J. Benoff, in a review of "To All My Fans with Love, from Sylvie," in* School Library Journal, *Vol. 28, No. 6, February, 1982, p. 87.*

Typifies your basic YA plot of unhappy adolescent with absent parents. Adding insult to injury, Sylvie has had, not one, but three foster fathers who have attempted to sexually abuse her. Not much new here. The saving grace of the novel is the theme of confusing sex with love. The vulnerability in these feelings is experienced by many adolescents. This book expresses that it is perfectly normal and O.K. to confuse sex with love. It stresses the idea that the young person does have a choice. Conford seems to be tackling more "grown up" problems than getting the date you want; yet it seems that she has lost her sense of humor along the way. (p. 29)

> *Maureen Ritter, in a review of "To All My Fans with Love, from Sylvie," in* Voice of Youth Advocates, *Vol. 5, No. 3, August, 1982, pp. 28-9.*

IF THIS IS LOVE, I'LL TAKE SPAGHETTI   (1983)

I usually like Ellen Conford, but these nine short stories are just plain silly. They do deal with subjects dear to young girls' hearts—dieting, talking on the phone, finding a date, parent problems, etc., but the approach to each falls flat. I kept expecting to find one that I liked and never did. My young readers, however, liked the book, saying that it was "funky" and that they would recommend it.

> *Jennifer Brown, in a review of "If This Is Love, I'll Take Spaghetti, and Other Stories," in* Children's Book Review Service, *Vol. 11, No. 9, April, 1983, p. 92.*

Beginning frenetically and continuing at a nearly hysterical pitch, these nine stories deal with the anguish of being a teenager, mostly from a facile viewpoint. . . . Three of the stories stand apart, legitimate efforts to address teenagers' constant search for self. In the title story, a young woman decides that if she is to diet, it will be for herself, not for her unrequited love. In **"Loathe at First Sight,"** the romantic love-hate paradox is portrayed with more depth than other stories provide. It's true that these stories will be lapped up greedily by some young adults, but the overall lack of descriptive texture and character depth presented here is less than we have come to expect of Conford. For more thoughtful anthologies which give adolescents a bit more credit for intelligence, try Mazer's *Dear Bill, Remember Me* (Delacorte, 1976) or Konigsburg's *Throwing Shadows* (Atheneum, 1979). (pp. 121-22)

> *Carolyn Noah, in a review of "If This Is Love, I'll Take Spaghetti," in* School Library Journal, *Vol. 29, No. 8, April, 1983, pp. 121-22.*

All but one of these nine bright stories spring from the pangs of a teenage girl caught in the throes of romance. With a wink and a smile, Conford playfully spins out some familiar scenes and syndromes to their logical—or sometimes delightfully illogical—conclusions. Some of the situations are stock, but well-tuned dialogue and a sure sense of character compensate. . . . There is nothing sobering here, only a little light entertainment; but it's rendered with a wit and appealing ease that's not easily dismissed.

> *Denise M. Wilms, in a review of "If This Is Love, I'll Take Spaghetti," in* Booklist, *Vol. 79, No. 15, April 1, 1983, p. 1031.*

Ellen Conford is funny again, sometimes wickedly so, in this collection of nine short stories. Using a variety of snappy styles and titles that turn tricks of their own, she sends her heroines into battle against plates of spaghetti, a minirock star, a double-crossing boy on a double date and more. . . .

Ellen Conford's only disappointing story, unfortunately the first, is **"If This Is Love, I'll Take Spaghetti,"** in which her one-liners give way to preaching about weight and self image.

The short story—ironic, at times satiric and poignant—is too little used in young people's books. Mrs. Conford succeeds with stories grounded in human sensitivities and brightened by her sure knowledge of what makes people laugh.

Patricia Lee Gauch, in a review of "If This Is Love, I'll Take Spaghetti," in The New York Times Book Review, *April 17, 1983, p. 28.*

Look up the word "*exemplum*" in any good literary dictionary and you will find that, as a literary form, the *exemplum* went out with plate armor. Having reached its high point in the fourteenth century, it declined in the face of increasingly sophisticated literary taste and exists now only in the marginal literature of the oral homiletic tradition. This is, of course, not strictly true. The *exemplum* enjoyed great popularity as a television genre in the 1950's and one frequently finds it in children's literature today. The prevailing notion that *exempla* are no longer written seems to derive from the *ars gratia artis* tradition—if one subscribes to this idea, then *exempla* are, by definition, not literature. Furthermore, the schools of literary criticism that dominate American graduate education encourage the apprentice critic to suppress his moral response to the content of the work in favor of an objective examination of the form.

What, then, is the critic to do with *If This is Love, I'll Take Spaghetti,* a collection of nine *exempla,* here called "stories," for the middle-class adolescent girl? As short stories, these pieces are of remarkably high quality. Each short piece (the entire collection may be read in a couple of hours) is a gem of characterization, packed full of wry humor and topical allusion, and conveyed by a spare narrative style, plenty of wonderfully believable dialogue, and profound sympathy for the hapless heroine. But for the *exemplum,* all these features are merely vehicles for the moral, and it is here that I must take exception to Conford's collection. These pieces convey two explicit morals—Mother Knows Best and Happiness Is a Boyfriend—and one implicit moral—that the norms of suburbia are unquestionable—and that's not what I want *my* daughters to learn from literature.

Lois Bragg, in a review of "If This Is Love, I'll Take Spaghetti," in Best Sellers, *Vol. 43, No. 2, May, 1983, p. 73.*

Nine short stories about adolescence address such topics as dieting, telephone addiction, and first love, with the incisive wit and snappy dialogue characteristic of the author's earlier novels, such as *Dear Lovey Hart, I Am Desperate* and *The Luck of Pokey Bloom....* Each of the stories concludes with an unexpected twist—not unlike the surprise ending popularized by O. Henry. Yet, despite similarities in tone and style, variety is provided by differences in structure, perspective, and theme. Several of the selections, like the title story, employ the current confessional mode of narration; **"What Do I Do Now?"** is written as a series of questions and responses between a shy, love-smitten teenager and a newspaper columnist for the love-lorn; both the monologue, **"I Hate You, Wallace B. Pokras,"** and **"Loathe at First Sight,"** a dialogue that would be an effective choice for oral interpretation, recall the rapierlike wit of Dorothy Parker; and **"The Girl Who Had Everything,"** a jewel of a tale—and perhaps the most successful of all—would be a provocative vehicle for exploring ethical questions and the use of irony in fiction. The appealing collection demonstrates the author's versatility with the genre and her ability to isolate those monumental events and problems which dominate a teenager's life but which in retrospect become minutiae. (pp. 309-10)

Mary M. Burns, in a review of "If This Is Love, I'll Take Spaghetti," in The Horn Book Magazine, *Vol. LIX, No. 3, June, 1983, pp. 309-10.*

LENNY KANDELL, SMART ALECK (1983)

Eleven-year-old Lenny is a budding comedian whose greatest desire is to make people laugh. Unfortunately, his humor is not appreciated by his mother, who labels him a smart aleck, and his teacher, who thinks of him as a daydreamer. His sense of humor gets him into trouble when he damages his aunt's fur (it makes a great wild animal) and trips the school bully, who vows to get even. In addition to the wonderful characters and humorous situations, the story gives an excellent picture of its 1946 setting—Saturday films, complete with cartoons, newsreels and serials; friend Artie's interest in "It Pays to Increase Your Word Power;" and Lenny's eventual acceptance of the fact that his father's death in World War II was not the result of heroic action but rather a freak accident. The story has action and tension followed by a satisfying resolution. Children looking for a funny story will find it here—and will probably want to try out some of Lenny's jokes on their friends.

Kathleen Garland, in a review of "Lenny Kandell, Smart Aleck," in School Library Journal, *Vol. 29, No. 9, May, 1983, p. 70.*

One of the novel's dramatic points is the revelation that Lenny's father died not fighting, but accidentally aboard ship. Conford's handling of Lenny at this junction is the story's weakest point: Lenny suddenly acknowledges he knew that family secret—a fact that lacks credibility in light of Lenny's previous thoughts of his dad as a hero. The novel still moves well, however; Conford's light touch allows an ease that readers will appreciate.

Denise M. Wilms, in a review of "Lenny Kandell, Smart Aleck," in Booklist, *Vol. 79, No. 18, May 15, 1983, p. 1212.*

It is 1946 (with lots of little reminders); Lenny Kandell's father was killed in World War II; and Lenny, eleven, dreams of becoming a professional comic. His comic lines (Conford has either found a period treasury or has been saving them up for years) are appreciated by his best friend Artie, and Lenny in turn admires the vocabulary of Artie, who is Increasing his Word Power via the *Reader's Digest....* [The climax of the story] brings out Lenny's feelings about his father, who wasn't quite the war hero Lenny has pretended. With the father angle providing a little needed ballast, the story is sympathetic and entertaining; fortunately Lenny is even funnier when he's not doing his act.

A review of "Lenny Kandell, Smart Aleck," in Kirkus Reviews, *Vol. LI, No. 11, June 1, 1983, p. 619.*

Life with Lenny is turbulent, dramatic, and humorous. Like the heroes of the Saturday afternoon movie serials he and Artie attend in 1946, Lenny courts disaster but always emerges in time for the next episode.... But to the relief of his widowed, perpetually worried mother, his professional and emotional triumphs bring about a latent, yet clear-eyed, awareness of reality. A brisk tempo and an entertaining picture of boyhood in the forties complement the predicaments, jokes, and comic patter that keep Lenny squarely on center stage. Lenny and Artie, a study in friendship, are a pair to call back for an encore.

Nancy C. Hammond, in a review of "Lenny Kandell, Smart Aleck," in The Horn Book Magazine, *Vol. LIX, No. 4, August, 1983, p. 442.*

YOU NEVER CAN TELL (1984)

Conford's latest is a frothy romance in which a teenager's crush on a soap opera star suddenly becomes a reality. Sixteen-year-old Katie, along with the rest of her classmates, is galvanized by the news that Thad Marshall, who plays swaggering, sultry Brick Preston on "Lonely Days, Restless Nights," will matriculate at Long Island's North High School, since his character is about to be killed off on the daytime series. Katie dumps her nice but unexciting boyfriend, Rob, and devotes herself to a thrilling fantasy romance with Thad that, incredibly, comes true. Problem is, Katie is more attracted to Thad's TV identity than to his real-life persona; to her joy, Thad behaves increasingly like Brick as their relationship progresses. . . . The action revolves (literally) around Katie's circular musings about Thad/Brick's chameleon like personality, but Conford's wisecracking, witty patter masks the shortage of plot developments. Most impressively, Conford cheerfully capitalizes on her story's tenuous probability, instead of burdening it with too much rationalization. As this popular author well understands, suspension of disbelief is half the fun. (pp. 587-88)

> *Karen Stang Hanely, in a review of "You Can Never Tell," in* Booklist, *Vol. 81, No. 8, December 15, 1984, pp. 587-88.*

[It] is Thad who sees clearly what Katie does not; it isn't Thad she loves but the cavalier Brick. Thad tells Katie when he leaves how bitter it has been for him, just before he leaves town, but in a brief postscript, she gets a message from him that indicates they may meet again . . . you never can tell. This has good style, excellent relationships within Katie's family (Thad's home life is a disaster) and believable characterization; it is weak in plot and pace. (pp. 102-03)

> *Zena Sutherland, in a review of "You Never Can Tell," in* Bulletin of the Center for Children's Books, *Vol. 38, No. 6, February, 1985, pp. 102-03.*

WHY ME? (1985)

Hobie tells a slightly-slapstick but very funny story about the pitfalls and pinnacles of his young adolescent love life. Secretly yearning for the ripe charms of classmate Darlene, Hobie rejects the persistent advances of G.G. who is one of the class brains, but "She looked exactly the same from the back as she did from the front." Hobie finally brings himself to give Darlene one of the poems he's been writing and is stunned by her enthusiastic reception; she begs for more poems, he gets confident enough to demand kisses as inspiration. Readers will probably see through Darlene's duplicity long before Hobie does: she's telling her friends the poems are from the star athlete that she adores. By then Hobie has begun to appreciate G.G. who is looking more svelte and sophisticated—but he's missed his chance, G.G. is by now firmly attached to Hobie's best

friend, and all that our hero can do is lie low and plan to catch her on the rebound. This doesn't really go anywhere, but it's capably written and consistently amusing.

> *A review of "Why Me?" in* Bulletin of the Center for Children's Books, *Vol. 39, No. 2, October, 1985, p. 24.*

The interactions of these three besotted characters [Hobie Katz, G. G. Graffman, and Darlene DeVries] form a comic romance of sorts, and Hobie winds up realizing that there is more to love than lusting after good looks. Conford keeps everything light and breezy thanks to an ear for natural dialogue and a well-developed sense of humor. All members of this trio get their just rewards, particularly Hobie, who by the time he wakes up to G.G.'s charms, may no longer be in the running for her affections. A nice bit of comedy from a practiced hand, this should quickly click with the popular read set.

> *Denise M. Wilms, "Why Me?" in* Booklist, *Vol. 82, No. 4, October 15, 1985, p. 334.*

A perceptive look at the love triangles of young adolescents by a skilled author of humorous fiction. . . . Conford shows affection toward her hero and also incorporates all the accouterments of adolescent social life—the mall, the movie theater, school, delivered pizzas, all the while poking fun at the proliferation of self-help books.

> *Therese Bigelow, in a review of "Why Me?" in* School Library Journal, *Vol. 32, No. 3, November, 1985, p. 95.*

STRICTLY FOR LAUGHS (1985)

Joey Merino and her longtime best friend Peter Stillman both have dreams. Joey longs to be a comedienne, while Peter wants to make it big on radio. A chance comes for both of them when Peter gets a three-week, late-night stint at his uncle's radio station. Joey hopes this will be a big career break as well as an opportunity to move Peter from pal to boyfriend. But when Peter turns up for the gig with pretty Dinah Smythe, an undiscovered folksinger, on his arm, Joey is angry on several fronts. The action moves at breakneck speed, and Joey's one-liners spin out continuously. As with the jokes of most comedians, if you don't like one, you may like the next, and much of the humor here is the laugh-out-loud variety. Conford also pulls off a neat characterization trick as she develops Joey from a seemingly overbearing loudmouth into a girl whose sensitivities and sensibilities will have readers rooting for her. Consequently, the book's ending, which sees all of Joey's dreams beginning to come true, is sweetly satisfying.

> *Ilene Cooper, in a review of "Strictly for Laughs," in* Booklist, *Vol. 82, No. 4, October 15, 1985, p. 334.*

Lorenz B(ell) Graham

1902-

Black American author of fiction and nonfiction and reteller.

Graham is respected as one of the earliest writers for young people to portray black American and African characters and cultures realistically. He is perhaps best known for his "Town" series—*South Town, North Town, Whose Town?,* and *Return to South Town*—which focuses on the struggles of teenager David Williams and his family as they fight overt prejudice in the South and more subtle racism in the North. Structuring these books around David's efforts to become a doctor and return to the South to serve his people, Graham presents David's search for black identity in a predominantly white society while outlining the injustices that befall him; throughout the "Town" quartet, however, Graham promotes tolerance, respect for the individual, and the hope that blacks and whites can live together successfully. Formerly a missionary and teacher in Liberia, Graham also retells familiar Bible stories for the very young in a Liberian English dialect noted for its resonance and musical beat. Five stories from Graham's initial collection, *How God Fix Jonah,* were later reprinted as individual picture books. In addition, Graham has written *Tales of Momolu, I, Momolu,* and *Song of the Boat,* three stories with an African setting which stress strong intergenerational relationships, especially between Momolu and his father. Graham is also recognized for creating a well-documented biography of abolitionist John Brown, the first one for children in over thirty years.

The majority of critics hail Graham's Bible stories for their power, freshness, and universality while commending the "Momolu" tales for their expression of positive values and their authenticity—both in background and in Graham's informed presentation of changing African socioeconomic conditions. The "Town" series is especially regarded for its timeliness, sensitivity, and inclusion of diverse viewpoints. Reviewers note that Graham's works have contributed to interracial understanding and have heightened the social consciousness of young readers.

Graham has received awards for both his body of work and individual titles.

(See also *Something about the Author,* Vol. 2 and *Contemporary Authors,* Vols. 9-12, rev. ed.)

AUTHOR'S COMMENTARY

[The following excerpt is taken from a speech Graham delivered at the National Language Arts Convention in Los Angeles in 1971.]

This is an important occasion. The National Conference of Language Arts in the Elementary School challenges all of us, and an invitation to address this group adds responsibility to the challenge. Here we are discussing the creative process in writing novels for children. In other sections the conference programs "new avenues for language through literature" and I observe such fascinating phrases as "appreciating our pluralistic society" and "appreciating different cultures."

Courtesy of Lorenz B. Graham

Now, this is exactly what my writing is all about. . . . The creative process in writing for children as I see it, and for me, has been a gathering of ideas, experiences, and emotions, bringing them together, some coming in as solids, some as liquids, some as gases, some as spiritual essences of ideas, yes, as dreams and hopes and fears. They have all become a part of my conscience. They pour forth in a small stream of one scene behind the other. (p. 185)

I have just heard a writer say that from her early childhood she knew she was going to be a writer. She also stated that she does not feel she is writing to carry a message or to prove a point. Regarding her method, this writer prepares an outline and during the writing period she spends certain regular hours at the desk. (pp. 185-86)

Perhaps I came from another planet.

I had no idea that I might become a writer until I was an adult. Everything I write tries to carry a message. I never start with an outline, and I cannot follow a schedule of working hours.

As a child I had no idea that I would ever be able to write a book. I never dreamed I would create anything in writing which people would like to read. For one thing I was considered not a very bright child. Not one of my teachers observed, or reported, a spark of talent in me.

And I did start wanting to write because I had an idea which was consuming me. Today by this same idea I am impelled and compelled to put things on paper.

I will go back.

While in college I had an opportunity to go to Africa to teach at a small mission school called Monrovia College. I left the class room believing that I would be able to help the poor benighted Africans, that I could bring light to the dark land, and that I could open the door to a new life for the ignorant people. I was due for a rude awakening. Shortly after I arrived in Liberia I realized that the people of Africa were so very, very much like people in other lands. Each one was unique in some ways and each one held possibilities and hopes and fears and needs. In time I realized that I had accepted an image of African people which had been presented in the form of moving pictures and the books which I had read. I began to wonder about books which described Africans honestly and I wondered why I had not read these books while I was in the United States. When I sought them I found that there were no such books. I found there were no books written about African people as people. There were books describing Africans as wild animals, as anthropophagical mysteries, as poor heathens groping for the light, as savages wandering in primeval darkness. There were no books describing them in the way that I came to know them, as people living in families and groups, in towns and cities, moving within the bounds of customs and laws which were community recognized and community fashioned. At that point I began saying that someone should write some decent books and let the world, and especially my American world, know that the Africans were people. I talked this to those about me, to other teaching missionaries, to government people, and to whom ever else would stop to listen. It seemed that no others had time or inclination to do such writing. It was then that I decided that since it needed to be done and since no one else would do it, I would write. I would write books which would make Americans know that Africans were people.

This was my beginning.

After returning to the United States and observing what we call our American race problem I realized that there were but few books about American Negroes, as we used the term at that time, or black people as we say now. There were precious few books which described black people in America as people. This was continuation of my great idea and so I am now engaged, very purposefully engaged in trying to write books with a purpose. I am trying to say that people are people.

Please do not dismiss this theme as being academic, accepted or recognized by everybody.

Of course we will say that everyone knows that people are people but we cannot say that we know this with our hearts or shall I, in the vernacular, say we do not know it in our gut. We know it with the head; none would deny it, but most of us feel that we are people and the others are something else. We are people but they are foreigners, or they are Africans or they are communists, or they are Negroes or they are honkies. We willfully get away from acceptance of the fact within our full consciousness.

To this end I write.

I choose to write about black people, black people in America and in Africa. Most of my novels have been short and they are written for young people. I hope that my readers will accept these characters and recognize them as people. Each character is unique. They are shown with different ideas, and with different ideals, and with differences of ability. They are from one another different in many ways but the differences are not merely that of skin. All of my books are written with a purpose.

About the particular methods from which my creativity comes I might feel a bit embarrassed to admit that I do not have a pattern for writing. My pattern it seems is no pattern. At the beginning of a novel I have ideas about some people and some problems. I know quite a bit about the characters who are going to be there. These characters are drawn more or less as composits of people whom I do know or have known. Now knowing the characters I sort of set them on course moving toward their problems. I see them and I watch them and I record their actions. I do not feel that I am making them do anything. Rather I am watching them. I am listening to them. I am trying to understand them. I write down what they are doing and saying and I describe what they are feeling because I do feel with them. And perhaps this accounts for something within my writing which some people criticize but which I will not give up.

The people who are my central characters do have hope. Now in the American scene today are problems of mountainous proportions, war, narcotics, speed-up and inflation, poverty and affluence. Many of the popular writers see their central characters going down in defeat, perhaps amusingly, sometimes tragically, often desperately. I see my characters as coming through. They go over the dam and they are rescued. They are shot and they see others fall. They may go to jail but when they are freed they wash with strong soap and cleanse themselves, and they work to overcome. I am writing for young people and I am trying to establish with them the idea that in every man is potential, and there is need for struggle and courage and movement toward definite goals.

Recently a college student made an analysis of my books and he said that they were not realistic in that I seem to think that if one tried hard enough and persisted long enough one could succeed.

"But," said the student, "this not the way life is."

Now, I say that, "If this is not the way life is, then I am indeed a fool, for I verily do believe that while disaster may come upon any of us at any time, I yet believe that if we choose wisely and if we work steadily and skilfully we can succeed." I recognize that there are times when just the not giving up is success.

A favorite quotation of mine is from one of my own books, the words of my favorite character, David Andrew Williams in **North Town**. He says, "I've learned that what ever happens you don't just quit! You keep going forward, pushing, driving, you don't quit."

This statement goes with almost every letter I write for it is printed as a line at the bottom of my letter head.

Now I could not close this presentation on the creative process in writing for children without reference to something else I am trying to insert into my writing. I do hope that readers will recognize it. It is the wide spread of differences within each culture group. In Africa I found that the African children were not all the same. And in your classroom, your school, all of your children will not be the same. This goes much deeper than consideration of the color or the ethnic group or the economic-social status. Within every classroom there will be many differences in ability, in degree of inspiration, in emotional feel, and in quantity of hope. But in every child will be, sometimes buried deep, the spark of creative urge.

The teacher has the great privilege of locating and helping to bring to flame that spark.

We must not presume. We must not prejudge. We must not for God's sake presume that because of the child's background or race we know the gift he has been given. I am often amused to observe that in spite of the myth many black children cannot sing.

I make reference to this in one of my books. The boy David Williams tells his mother about Becky Goldberg.

"She's all right," he says. "At the rally she played the guitar, and we sang spirituals, and, you know, that gal knew the words better than I did."

Becky also played the part of Mary, mother of Jesus in the Christmas pageant.

I am sure the creative talent is everywhere. The gift falls like drops of rain on the hills and in the valleys, and the distribution is not uneven in Beverly Hills and in Watts.

All of us use the language arts. All of us use our unique creative processes in the language arts. All of us can help others recognize and develop their God given abilities to create and to succeed. (pp. 186-88)

> *Lorenz Graham, "An Author Speaks," in* Elementary English, *Vol. 50, No. 2, February, 1973, pp. 185-88.*

GENERAL COMMENTARY

LOIS BELFIELD WATT

These Bible stories, [*Every Man Heart Lay Down, God Wash the World and Start Again,* and *A Road Down in the Sea,*] told in the direct rhythmic speech of Liberians newly come to the English language, are separately edited now from a collection made and published some years ago. The first of these new editions is the story of Jesus' birth, the second is about Noah and the Flood, while the third tells how Moses found safe passage through the Red Sea. The idiom will be unfamiliar and sometimes startling to many American children, but it transmits the essence of poetry and of deep religious feeling. The text in each case is stronger than the pictures, but the books can provide a moving experience with several dimensions.

> *Lois Belfield Watt, in a review of "A Road Down in the Sea," in* Childhood Education, *Vol. 48, No. 1, (October, 1971), p. 29.*

BINNIE TATE

Lorenz Graham is one black author with integrity who still writes largely from an outdated point of view. Although in *I, Momolu* ... the African perspective is evident, Graham's perception of the "white hope" continues in *Whose Town.* ... (p. 43)

His writing reflects his inability to see beyond the protective vision of an integrated or assimilated society. Today's minority tastes are changing. (p. 44)

> *Binnie Tate, "In House and Out House: Authenticity and the Black Experience in Children's Books," in*

The Black American in Books for Children: Readings in Racism, *edited by Donnarae MacCann and Gloria Woodard, The Scarecrow Press, Inc., 1972, pp. 39-49.**

MYRA POLLACK SADKER AND DAVID MILLER SADKER

In a series of three books published between 1958 and 1969, Lorenz Graham traces the plight of the Williams family as they try to enter America's mainstream. The first of the series, *South Town* ..., reflects the overt forms of racism inflicted upon the Williams family: low pay, separate churches and schools, verbal and physical abuse meted out by white citizens as well as white police officials. David Williams cannot understand how the American Dream is being denied them, nor can David's father, who recalls the sacrifices blacks and whites made together during the war. "By God, if we fight together and die together, we'd ought to be able to live together."

The violence and abuse of *South Town* prove to be too much for the Williams family, and they move to North Town. *North Town* ... confronts the family with the problems of an integrated society. At school David is officially treated courteously, but he is not fully accepted. He survives a run-in with the police and acquires a white friend, who teaches him to play football. Just when things seem to be working out, Mr. Williams is hospitalized, and David is forced to go to work to support the family. Because of the talents of a sympathetic Jewish surgeon, Mr. Williams is nursed back to health. By the book's end the American Dream seems within grasp. David is a football star with plans to be a doctor, his father is back at work, and his family is living in their new house. All the hopeful expectations for the Williams family and the nation at large seem to be summed up by David as he is playing football. He looks up from the football field and he can see in symbols the success of an integrated society: "but the late afternoon sun had broken through the clouds lighting a row of American flags silhouetted against the sky. David knew that his father was there, and Jeanette. ... He could not pick out faces, white or black or brown, but he knew they were all there. This, he thought, was like America."

But in the last book of the three, *Whose Town?* ..., we see that many questions have not been answered. Racial strife once again occurs. As in *South Town,* there is trouble with the police, and the simple integration theme of *North Town* is questioned as David searches for his role as a black man in a white society. *Whose Town?* has more a black identity theme than an integration theme.... (pp. 137-38)

Although the struggle against racism is a theme in all three books, David's dream does undergo modifications in the last book of the series, *Whose Town?....* In *Whose Town?* black frustration is apparent, and the integrationist theme is questioned. In this volume David Williams is no longer gazing into the football stands, seeing neither black nor white, but only Americans.

In his last year of high school David is beaten up by some white youths, and the police falsely charge David with assault. As a result of this fight, David's friend, Lonnie, is shot by a white man. The anger building up in David is fueled when his father and many other Negroes are laid off at the local foundry. Such events lead David to a heightened awareness of black pride, and he considers the more militant goal of separatism. But like Lou in [*Soul Brothers and Sister Lou*], David finally chooses a moderate position. (p. 146)

Myra Pollack Sadker and David Miller Sadker, "The Black Experience in Children's Literature," in their Now Upon a Time: A Contemporary View of Children's Literature, *Harper & Row, Publishers, 1977, pp. 129-62.**

KENNETH L. DONELSON AND ALLEEN PACE NILSEN

Lorenz Graham brought realistic black characters to young adult literature. If *South Town* . . . with its characters seeking a better life in the North seems dated today, *North Town* . . . is still believable as it moves the Williams family and son David, the major character, into conflict with both whites and blacks. *Whose Town?* . . . brings David more problems as he sees his best friend shot by a white man. Graham's books probed for answers but did not provide any easy ones. (p. 163)

Kenneth L. Donelson and Alleen Pace Nilsen, "1940-1966: From Certainty to Uncertainty in Life and Literature Courtesy of Future Shock," in their Literature for Today's Young Adults, *Scott, Foresman and Company, 1980, pp. 141-79.**

RUDINE SIMS

[*In* Shadow and Substance: Afro-American Experience in Contemporary Children's Fiction, *Rudine Sims conducts a survey and analysis of 150 examples of contemporary realistic fiction about Afro-Americans published from 1965-1979. Sims contrasts social conscience literature addressed to non-blacks, books with a "melting pot" theme, and a third group where the characters, settings, and perspectives are Afro-American. In the following excerpt, she concentrates on those works where Afro-Americans survive racism and discrimination.*]

[These books] are in one sense the other side of the coin from the social conscience fiction. A major part of the focus is on conflicts between Blacks and whites, but in contrast with the social conscience fiction, the conflict is viewed from the perspective of the Afro-Americans. A further contrast to the social conscience fiction is the lack of focus on racial integration as a goal of Afro-Americans. The goal of the characters in these books is to achieve their own ends—such as survival, landholding, education, a sense of independence—in the face of racism, discrimination, violence, and other misuses of white economic and political power.

Surprisingly few in number (five in this survey), these books were preceded by older "achieving-against-the-odds" books, such as Jesse Jackson's *Call Me Charley* (New York: Harper and Row, 1945), and Hope Newell's *A Cap for Mary Ellis* (New York: Harper and Row, 1952). This group might also be larger if it included the entire set of Lorenz Graham's "town" books—*South Town* . . . [*North Town, Whose Town?, and Return to South Town*]—which follow David Williams and his family from David's adolescence through his return to his hometown to set up medical practice. Only one representative title of that set, *Whose Town?,* is included. (p. 55)

As a group, these books tend to celebrate the courage and determination of Afro-American families and individuals who are faced with racism, oppression, or violence. Their responses range from riots to boycotts, to use of the legal system, to desperate last-ditch individual stands. *Whose Town?* and *Sneakers* (Shepard, 1973), both set in northern cities, affirm the idea that while Blacks must take responsibility for their own lives, Blacks and whites must learn to coexist—that people must be judged as individuals. *Whose Town?* suggests that many of "the Negro's" problems could be solved by education, hard work, and right living and, further, that the struggle is not

Black against white, but people against evil and hate. Still, the focus is not on being accepted in a white cultural milieu. (p. 56)

Rudine Sims, "Culturally Conscious Fiction: Reflections of Afro-American Experience," in her Shadow and Substance: Afro-American Experience in Contemporary Children's Fiction, *National Council of Teachers of English, 1982, pp. 49-78.**

TALES OF MOMOLU   (1946)

From far-away Liberian Africa come these unusual stories of a boy who grows to learn the things every boy needs to know and wants to know. Through stories of great charm and individuality, we come to know Momolu's family, his brave strong father, Flumbo, who is respected and learned, and other important people of the tribe. A pet monkey, a severe chief, a new friend, all have lessons of bravery, courage, respect. Moral tales with no oppressive taint of preaching. Fine values, colorful, well told.

A review of "Tales of Momolu," in Virginia Kirkus' Bookshop Service, *Vol XIV, No. 16, August 15, 1946, p. 387.*

These stories, collected while the author was visiting mission schools in Africa, show that the problems of growing up are essentially the same, whether one lives in an American community or at the edge of the jungle. Ten to 12 year old boys everywhere will understand Momolu's need for recognition and will enter wholeheartedly—and somewhat enviously—into the accounts of his daily life, here graphically presented in text and [Letterio Calapai's] pictures.

Elizabeth Hodges, in a review of "Tales of Momolu," in The New York Times Book Review, *February 2, 1947, p. 32.*

HOW GOD FIX JONAH   (1946)

Out of a period of work with a missionary in Monrovia, Liberia, Lorenz Graham has gathered twenty-one Bible stories as told in the idiom of the West African native. As Mr. Graham says, the stories must be spoken to be appreciated fully—true of all folklore—but some pleasure and a faint insight into the life of a slightly known people can be got from the printed page.

Perhaps this insight seems obvious because the stories are familiar to us in their early English versions. Reading **"God Wash the World and Start Again"** or **"Samson He Weak for Woman Palaver,"** we get a new perspective not only on the Bible story's essence but on the people who have drawn it out. In a similar manner, some years ago, we had a more sophisticated, literary treatment in "The Green Pastures." But where that method, although based on established concepts, allowed for much extravagance of invention, Mr. Graham's tales are lean, unpretentious and to the heart of the matter.

It should be interesting for Bible students to compare the original stories with these versions as recited by contemporary West Africans to villagers who cannot read books. But unfortunately for the student of folklore, Mr. Graham has not made quite clear whether the stories are verbatim transcriptions from the story-tellers. He says they "are set down as an African lad might tell them to his friends." Nor does he say whether the stories derive from oral readings of the Bible by missionaries or from Sunday School simplifications. This need not, however, detract from enjoyment of the jaunty idiom of such phrases as "Nineveh be one wa-wa place" (wa-wa meaning wild and wicked), or "He come to Sodom Town and Sodom stink." Or Pharaoh's edict in the story of Moses: "The boy picans [children, as pickaninnies] in every Hebrew house must die. The Hebrew mommies self must kill them"; and the narrator's comment: "You think so law can make a mommy kill she child?" . . .

Although printed in verse lines, the stories can hardly be considered altogether poetry. There are isolated passages of poetic feeling here and there, and some of the structural elements of poetry—repetition, parallel phrases and clauses, and certainly rhythmic variety. In the story of Samson and Delilah a four-line refrain occurs throughout which is strongly reminiscent of American Negro folk song. And the story of Lot and his wife (**"She Got Hard Head You Know"**) also uses a four-line refrain but less successfully in its lyric-dramatic effect.

> Hubert Creekmore, "'God Wash the World'," in The New York Times Book Review, December 8, 1946, p. 34.

SOUTH TOWN   (1958)

[South Town *received the Child Study Association of America Award in 1958, an honor referred to in the following excerpt.*]

[*South Town*] is an admirable choice, and in this day of heightened racial tensions, a courageous one. There is, in the moving picture of Negro children growing up in a South where the survival of mores of a slave era color attitudes and points of view, an authenticity, an integrity that could only come from experience, understanding and widsom. As a story, it may seem to lack pace and drive; occasionally both plot and style often limping; but always the essential idea and the realized characters and issues come through.

> A review of "South Town," in Virginia Kirkus' Service, Vol. XXVII, No. 7, April 1, 1959, p. 272.

[*In the following excerpt, Mrs. F. S. Straus, chairman of the Child Study Association of America Children's Book Committee, comments on* South Town.]

South Town presents to young teenagers the problems of Negro families and of both white and Negro children growing up in the South today. With sensitivity and keen insight, the author depicts the everyday life of Negro families in a small Southern town, their work and play, and the tensions that may arise between them and their white neighbors. The situations that grow almost imperceptibly out of small incidents, the hostilities and also the loyal friendships, are handled with realism but without melodrama. Mr. Graham has rendered a real service in giving our young people this timely and moving picture of the difficulties as well as the strengths and courage in people of all races which may be drawn upon to help solve these vital race relations problems. (pp. 28-9)

> Mrs. F. S. Straus, in an extract from a speech presented at the 16th Annual Conference of the Child Study Association of America on March 16, 1959, in Library Journal, Vol. 84, No. 8, April 15, 1959, pp. 28-9.

The centre point of this book concerns the life of a white and a coloured family in a small town in the Southern United States. The author attempts to do justice to both sides and their problems—the blacks, who wish to free themselves from the guardianship of the rich white people, and the white family, who

must first get used to the need for learning and the rise of the negroes. . . .

The book is not intended as an indictment; the author, a coloured priest who has worked for many years in the southern states tries with his story to contribute to a better understanding of the mentality of the negro. He succeeds in this due to his objective and impressive style of writing.

> A review of "South Town," in Bookbird, No. 1 (March 15, 1964), p. 30.

[For] the most part adolescent novels about racial strife published during the 1950s opted for accommodation. In *Hold Fast to Your Dreams* a Negro girl works to become a ballet dancer and her talent alone overcomes white racism. (In a biographical note the author, Catherine Blanton, states that "if we could know all the people of the world as our next door neighbors, our problems could be quickly solved in friendly disagreement.") In *South Town* the white racist reforms and a white doctor states that "progress is being made all the time. . . . In spite of what happened last week, things are better now than they were; and in some places, I understand, you might be very comfortable, and the children could grow up to forget this." . . . Thus, the message for Negroes in these novels tends to be "pull yourself up by the bootstraps" and whites will grant acceptance; for whites the moral is to treat people as individuals and learn that "they're just as good as we are." (p. 237)

> W. Keith Kraus, "From Steppin Stebbins to Soul Brothers: Racial Strife in Adolescent Fiction," in Young Adult Literature in the Seventies: A Selection of Readings, edited by Jana Varlejs, The Scarecrow Press, Inc., 1978, pp. 235-44.*

NORTH TOWN   (1965)

A logical successor to the author's **South Town** and much the better written book. It centers around aspects of racial prejudice that seldom get balanced attention in juvenile books: that the North has extreme inequities; that prejudice works actively both ways fueled by fear; that there is a divisive social structure among Negroes; and that the issue of race and rights is always present for a Negro. It is the story of Dave Williams and what his life was like during his first year away from the small Southern country town of his birth. Like any other country boy he faced the problem of city slickers among his peer group with the additional burden of being black. Circumstances continually forced him to find out just how many rights he had and just how far they went—in school, on the job and among his fellow Negroes. His family is very well drawn, particularly his father. . . . Dave is a sympathetic, average sort of boy and his predicaments are made into a story of mature insight with real appeal.

> A review of "North Town," in Virginia Kirkus' Service, Vol. XXXIII, No. 5, March 1, 1965, p. 249.

Several different Negro points of view are clearly delineated [in **North Town**] and this is the main strength of the novel. Too often, books dealing with important social issues oversimplify the attitudes of the participants. Though the plot is often smoother, the story is commonly weaker.

In this book, we find that David cannot believe that the Negro will be given a fair deal in North Town. . . . After David has his hearing before a juvenile judge, who recognizes his innocent involvement in the theft of a car and releases him, the youth cannot accept the fact that his initial appraisal was wrong. . . . In spite of his feelings, David develops a sincere friendship with one of the white students. David tries to speak, in the white boy's behalf, with one of the Negro crew leaders at the factory where he works so as to help his friend get a job. The violent reaction stuns David:

> I say NO! . . . I wouldn't give a poor white man a crust a bread if he starving or a drink of water if he burning in hell . . . you better get some sense and just cause you up North don't think you going look out for the white boys and they going look out for you. They ain't.
>
> (pp. 6-7)

David finally comes to the realization that not all whites are "out to get the Negro," he understands that though prejudice is exceptionally widespread, there are also a great many white people who will treat him as just another person.

The book displays a complex group of social problems for our examination and permits the reader to understand not only what the different points of view are, but why the various people have come to act as they do.

The author does not directly deal with the attitudes of the whites in North Town. We can only draw somewhat hazy implications from their actions in some of the less important incidents. The only other fault with the book is that the characters are not too well drawn. The author has to have his characters make small speeches, on occasions, to spell out what their attitudes are. You know the participants in the story more as case histories than as individuals. . . . Despite these shortcomings, *North Town* is a book definitely worthy of attention, and it does a good job of delineating several of the different Negro points of view on racial problems, as they are encountered in the north. (p. 7)

> *Phyllis Cohen, in a review of "North Town," in* Young Readers Review, *Vol. I, No. 8, April, 1965, pp. 6-7.*

You can if you prefer, read this book as the story of a colored family from the South who move north to a city such as— well, I think of Detroit, Mich. Ostensibly Lorenz Graham is writing about a father, mother, a boy in high school, his younger sister, and describing what happens to them in health and in sickness, in school and in sport, in the factory and in the home. This is the history of every poor family, white or colored, in the United States today. The book describes a slice of our country, the land we inhabit. If the story isn't always pleasant, existence is rarely pleasant for the poor who struggle but often don't quite make it. Possibly Mr. Graham felt he was writing about integration. I regard his canvas as much larger. Not a great book, perhaps, but a good one, the job of an honest, knowledgeable reporter.

> *John R. Tunis, in a review of "North Town," in* The New York Times Book Review, *April 4, 1965, p. 22.*

The writing style is a little flat, but is straightforward; characterization is good, the plot is rather pat at the end of the story. The strength of the book is in the candid portrayal of a spectrum of reactions, among David's classmates in particular: Buck, who is a snob, Alonzo, who is always suspicious, and Jeanette, who is intelligently objective in her assessments of people and of situations.

> *Zena Sutherland, in a review of "North Town,"* Bulletin of the Center for Children's Books, *Vol. XVIII, No. 9, May, 1965, p. 129.*

[*North Town*] exemplifies the good and bad about children's books. . . . It is as current as Selma, Ala., yet try as he will, Mr. Graham cannot transcend his theme—the difficulties of a Southern Negro boy adjusting to life in a Northern environment. Mr. Graham or the publishers started with an idea. But the idea was fragmented and shattered into hundreds of subideas so that the plot line is lost, and the argument, whatever it is, becomes repetitive. Occasionally, it sounds as if Gunnar Myrdal were writing it. Here, perhaps, one ought to face the simple fact that a child might read with greater profit a straightforward biography of the Rev. Dr. Martin Luther King Jr. than a "story" which is really no story because there is no ending, no happy ending nor unhappy ending.

> *Arnold Beichman, "Please! Let's Skip the Seminar," in* The Christian Science Monitor, *May 6, 1965, p. B6.**

So many times stories about interracial problems are spoiled for ages 11-14 because of the author's conscious lecturing and subconscious setting up of straw figures or stereotypes. This pitfall is avoided in *North Town*. . . . In this well-balanced book, Negro author Lorenz Graham hits straight from the shoulder and shows that not all misunderstandings and prejudices are necessarily on one side or the other.

> *Ethna Sheehan, in a review of "North Town," in* America, *Vol. 112, No. 26, June 26, 1965, p. 899.*

I, MOMOLU (1966)

The difficulties a boy faces when he realizes the advantages of some aspects of civilization and finds these in conflict with the traditional values of his family and society is a fairly popular theme especially in books about underdeveloped countries. It is extremely well-handled here. The development of the boy Momolu is shown with more than the usual subtlety and his relationship with his conservative father Flumbo is particularly well defined. Flumbo associated soldiers with killing and determinedly considered them his enemies even though the Liberian army was primarily concerned with projects to modernize and develop the country with its large primitive areas. He was angered by Momolu's interest in the soldiers and destroyed one of their uniforms. As "punishment" Flumbo and Momolu had to come to Cape Roberts and then to stay at the army barracks. There are some well-focused glimpses into Liberian life (both good and bad) and the father's and son's reactions are well portrayed. The subject isn't quite as vital as Graham's other books, but this is one of the better stories available on modern Africa.

> *A review of "I, Momolu," in* Virginia Kirkus' Service, *Vol. XXXIV, No. 16, August 15, 1966, p. 834.*

The contemplative, introspective treatment of Momolu's experiences lacks appeal for children, but the story is valuable for its enlightening picture of life in modern Liberia and the impact of modern industrialization on ancient tribal customs.

> *A review of "I, Momolu," in* The Booklist and Subscription Books Bulletin, *Vol. 63, No. 6, November 15, 1966, p. 376.*

One book that is sure to meet with approval by boys and girls alike is *I, Momolu* . . . ; it will find favor especially with those who have read and appreciated the author's books, *South Town* and *North Town*. Graham writes convincingly and sympathetically of 14-year-old Momolu's growth from boyhood to responsible manhood. (p. 314)

The reader is caught up in Momolu's excitement at hearing a radio for the first time, his fear at riding in a truck, and his amazement at seeing an airplane at close range. As Eleanor Branch, a ninth-grade student . . . said, "I think this book is very interesting because you never know what's going to happen."

In addition to its theme of understanding those who are different from us, *I, Momolu* has the added strength of being extremely well-written, at times almost poetic:

> "Now I have seen." Momolu was satisfied. "And I know our life is better. I would never leave it."
>
> Flumbo smiled. "Wait," he said. "You cannot judge by what you see in one day from the waterside or by what you smell. Let your heart lie down. Your mouth may yet sing another song". . . .

(pp. 314-15)

Because of the restraint with which it is written and because of the vividness with which Graham depicts the maturation of Momolu, the novel will appeal to senior high school students who are reluctant readers, who are interested in modern Africa, or who, because of changing conditions, are experiencing the tug away from family and tradition. Its interest for junior high school students would extend to all intelligence groups as well as all cultural and socio-economic groups. (p. 315)

> *Geraldine E. LaRocque, "Book Marks: Books That Open Doors to Understanding," in* English Journal, *Vol. 56, No. 2, February, 1967, pp. 314-20.**

A story of modern Liberia that will seem most important for the picture it gives to today's changing Africa. Action is not lacking, however, for fourteen-year-old Momolu, son of a rice planter in the bush, is the unwitting cause of fighting between villagers and soldiers and, thus, of his and his father's imprisonment in the nation's capital. These scenes are drawn with a perception that reveals the unstable relationships between conservative, peace-loving tribesmen and the new government. Other telling incidents indicate the influence of missions, of modern technology, and of American-born Liberians on the uneducated natives. The treatment of individual characters, the bushman's courtesy and hospitality, Momolu's filial respect and his generosity on behalf of his father, strengthens the impact of the book. (pp. 71-2)

> *Virginia Haviland, in a review of "I, Momolu," in* The Horn Book Magazine, *Vol. XLIII, No. 1, February, 1967, pp. 71-2.*

I, Momolu, is a notably vivid picture of the social forces at work in present-day Liberia. The characters are not without dimension, but one feels them to be the victims rather than the manipulators of their environment. From the isolated town of Lojay, Momolu and his father travel to the coast to appear before the Commissioner at Cape Roberts. With them they bring ten precious bags of rice, a fine the father must pay for his inhospitable treatment of government soldiers visiting Lo-

jay. The journey ends in a fiasco, for Momolu loses the rice in the river. A taste of the truly horrible local jail and the dirtiness and venality of the city dwellers are disillusioning experiences for the boy, while the father is bitterly confirmed in his opposition to the ways of civilization. Paroled in the care of a benevolent army captain, who treats them with respect, they participate in a road-building excursion back to the interior. Momolu is soon caught up in the toil and excitement of the road-building and concludes that study and knowledge alone can bring a mastery of the new wonders in the land. His father comes to see that the new ways are not incompatible with the old.

The relationship between father and son is true and touching, even as one recognizes the symbolic purpose of the author. The action is often submerged in descriptive detail, but there is much of value in the graphic and lively panorama. At the end one speculates less about Momolu's future than the captain's road, busily advancing into the primitive wilderness.

> *Houston L. Maples, "African Tales," in* Book Week— World Journal Tribune, *April 9, 1967, p. 18.**

A quiet story . . . , the book gives a good picture of rural and urban patterns in modern Liberia, and it gives a touching picture of family loyalty, especially of the relationship between father and son. It is a slow-moving story, however, partly due to the sedate writing style, partly to the restrained pace of the story line.

> *Zena Sutherland, in a review of "I, Momolu," in* Bulletin of the Center for Children's Books, *Vol. 21, No. 1, September, 1967, p. 6.*

WHOSE TOWN? (1969)

The question posed by the title—*whose town* is North Town, everybody's or only the whites?—is one of many troubling responsible, reasonable David Williams; combined, they register the quandary of the middle-class colored (a term used throughout the book) a few years back. Whether teenagers today will be impressed, as David is ultimately, by the minister's injunction not "to support or endorse hatred and evil" on either side (here directed against inflammatory prophet Prempey Moshombu on the Negro side) is central to the reception of the book since it has little impact purely as fiction: the style is plodding, the people stiff, the developments talked out. In the course of David's unwarranted run-ins with the law—he's accused of aggression by a bully who's jumped him, named attacker by a gas station attendant who's killed his friend—the ugliness of prejudice is projected, and, in the normal course of events, David notes, for instance, that he would never have made the college prep curriculum if he hadn't first made the football team. He sees, too, the cost to family solidarity when his father is laid off and his mother has to go to work as a domestic. As a catalogue of the consequences of racism it comes closer to reality than it does as a critique or a criterion, and it's less successful than *South Town* or *North Town* as a story.

> *A review of "Whose Town?" in* Kirkus Reviews, *Vol. XXXVII, No. 8, April 15, 1969, p. 452.*

Here is a book that is both an exciting story and a skillful conversion of a sociological situation into fiction. No young reader could fail to be enlightened by it. I hope that parents, teachers and librarians will take note of it.

David Williams is the 18-year-old son of a Negro family which has moved recently from the rural South to North Town. They have prospered, own their house, the children are in school, the father is employed, and David, who has a part-time job, plans to go to college. They have made their way and future prospects are good. At the Carver Community Center David listens to the Reverend Moshombo, a Negro leader, speak on Black Power. Through this lucid and not intemperate address, the author sets up a brief but comprehensive statement of the Negro's situation, past and present. Against this background the narrative unfolds.

After a party at a neighbor's house, David and his friends go to a drive-in for hamburgers. As David picks up their order he is deliberately bumped by a drunken white youth. A fracas starts and police are called.

With this beginning the author takes us with relentless and logical precision through every aspect of the White-Black confrontation: prejudice, deprivation, poverty, revolt, violence that includes bloodshed, burning, killing, and a mob riot. The author spares his boy from the worst and most frightening consequences of his increasing involvement. But the reader's apprehension is never relaxed. What the reader endures for a few hours Negro parents must fear for a lifetime.

Graham chooses a style which at the outset seems to run counter to the prevailing informality. But clarity is his object, and the almost formal style becomes a powerful support to the ordered substance of his narrative.

> *Alice Hungerford, in a review of "Whose Town?" in* Book World—The Washington Post, *May 4, 1969, p. 3.*

A social commentary and discussion starter rather than a stylistic show-piece. . . . While the weakness of this timely book lies in the tendency of the message to overshadow the plot, its strength lies in its pertinence to life today, and this will draw the appreciation and recognition of young readers.—(pp. 2509-10)

> *Barbara S. Miller, in a review of "Whose Town?" in* Library Journal, *Vol. 94, No. 12, June 15, 1969, pp. 2509-10.*

[In] this book the author considers questions of black pride and black power. . . . Although David is at the center of [the] events, . . . his role is almost that of a detached observer. He listens with equal attention to the angry words of black-power advocate Reverend Moshombo and the moderate councils of his family's pastor, Reverend Hayes. He wonders if his father is an Uncle Tom. He encounters white men who display every conceivable attitude toward blacks: sympathy, condemnation, hatred and scorn, fear, fairness and respect. His black friends and acquaintances exhibit as great a variety of attitudes toward whites. He wonders if it is still possible to be both an American and a black man. The power of the book resides in the range of ideas that the author represents to the reader. The characters are symbolic, drawn a little larger than life. David's struggle to find his role in our society, to determine if he should consider "which side was right" or "only which side was black," represents the struggle of every Negro "to take his rightful place in America as a man." (pp. 416-17)

> *Diane Farrell, in a review of "Whose Town?" in* The Horn Book Magazine, *Vol. XLV, No. 4, August, 1969, pp. 416-17.*

As in his other "Town" novels, the author stresses the debilitating effects of discrimination and the need for courage and restraint in facing problems involving racial inequality. He emphasizes that extreme measures rarely achieve their purpose, but instead often aggravate the situation. The solid relationships in the Williams family are well portrayed, as are David's positive and admirable values and loyalties. (pp. 59-60)

> *John T. Gillespie, "Understanding Social Problems," in his* More Juniorplots: A Guide for Teachers and Librarians, *R. R. Bowker Company, 1977, pp. 51-74.**

EVERY MAN HEART LAY DOWN (1970)

As the blurb on the jacket says, "this is the story of the birth of Jesus, in the speech patterns of African people newly acquainted with English." The words, the illustrations [by Colleen Browning], African in mood, are so strong and beautiful that they are also universal. "In the storyteller's language, when a man's heart lay down he was at peace." In your reviewer's blunter language, if you don't find the universal appeal in this rare book, you don't deserve Christmas.

> *A review of "Every Man Heart Lay Down," in* Publishers Weekly, *Vol. 198, No. 8, August 24, 1970, p. 64.*

From an earlier collection, **How God Fix Jonah**, "a spoken song . . . in the idiom of Africans newly come to English speech," a song that ennobles the Nativity in facing God with one small boy, one small pican. . . . In contrast to the rhythmic resonance and the brusque imagery of the telling, the illustrations are eclectic exercises. . . . They detract—but the song of the small pican, the self-chosen Saviour, carries its own simple beauty.

> *A review of "Every Man Heart Lay Down," in* Kirkus Reviews, *Vol. XXXVIII, No. 17, September 1, 1970, p. 949.*

This story of the birth of Jesus is illustrated with pictures that, unfortunately, are not equal to the rhythm and force of the text. . . . [The] writing is beautifully direct and natural, especially the passage dealing with Mary's marriage and continued virginity; in traditional American and European versions of the nativity, this is always brushed over to the bewilderment of many children. "Now Mary be new wife for Joseph / And Joseph ain't touch Mary self / So first time Joseph vex. / But God say / 'Nev mind, Joseph, / This be God palaver.' / And Joseph heart lay down." Some children will have difficulty understanding the dialect and will need assistance on the first reading. After that, they will be carried along by the cadence and the images. (p. 150)

> *Marilyn R. Singer, "The Making of a Humbug: Christmas Books for 1970," in* School Library Journal, *an appendix to* Library Journal, *Vol. 17, No. 2, October, 1970, pp. 147-51.**

This African version of Jesus' coming to earth is told with great dignity, vitality, and simplicity. The African speech patterns and the striking pictures give a new meaning and beauty to the timeless story.

> *Elizabeth Minot Graves, in a review of "Every Man Heart Lay Down," in* Commonweal, *Vol. XCIII, No. 8, November 20, 1970, p. 198.*

[At first look, **"Every Man Heart Lay Down"**] seemed to be a children's book, but now I have my doubts. . . . [The story] tells of the birth of Jesus in African pidgin English. Yet to appreciate the charm of dialect one must first have a sure grip on one's own language. So this delightful presentation may help adults see a beautiful old story with fresh eyes. Children, however, may simply conclude that these Africans talk funny, like all foreigners.

> *Oona Sullivan, in a review of "Every Man Heart Lay Down," in* The New York Times Book Review, *November 29, 1970, p. 38.*

One book out of two score and more of this fall's Christmas books for children that I've read or leafed through, shines, compelling and endearing, above the rest. It's *Every Man Heart Lay Down* . . . , in which Lorenz Graham retells the story of the birth of Jesus in the idiom of Africans newly come to English speech, its title deriving from the storyteller's language—"when a man's heart lay down he was at peace." As we read how God's heart "no lay down" when he looked at the world where people "no hear My Word" and "no walk My way," and then see how "God's one small boy—Him small pican" grieved for the people and offered himself for them so that "Bye-m-bye they savvy the way," we cannot but respond to the moving quality and universal meaning of this spoken song. . . .

> *Polly Goodwin, in a review of "Every Man Heart Lay Down," in* Book World—Chicago Tribune, *December 20, 1970, p. 3.*

A ROAD DOWN IN THE SEA   (1970)

Give in to the drama—this could be a play: the story has inherent dynamism; Graham's "sharper images" are visual; his sounds swell integrally as they echo "the idiom of Africans (Liberians) newly come to English speech." Solemn yet relaxed, the lines combine a sense of the numinous with the earthy in fine timing: when the parting of the waters opens a road down in the sea, "The people fear to go / But Moses lead / And one man go behind / Then two, then three, then plenty more, / And all the people follow through / And no man wet him foot." But for the illustrations [by Gregorio Prestopino], a book that enjoins participation; and, regardless, a mightily suggestive resource.

> *A review of "A Road Down in the Sea," in* Kirkus Reviews, *Vol. XXXIX, No. 2, January 15, 1971, p. 50.*

[The] strong, handsome, primitive paintings . . . complement the rhythmic beat and dramatic economy of the text. Retold in the manner and with the imagery of Liberian story-tellers, this is simple yet evocative prose-poetry with a folk quality that lends the familiar story from Exodus about Moses and the parting of the waters of the Red Sea unusual vitality.

> *Della Thomas, in a review of "A Road Down in the Sea," in* Library Journal, *Vol. 96, No. 8, April 15, 1971, p. 1493.*

A good way to learn to speak a foreign language is to imitate the way a foreign speaker speaks English. You get a feeling for his thought pattern and idiom that way, and you learn how to hold your mouth and face and even body. Imitating him in your own language, you feel like him; and, feeling like him, you get to understand him.

"Sway with the rhythm of the storyteller. Feel the beat of the drums," the introduction to this fine book tells us, and in the English of a Liberian African we hear how Moses led the Children of Israel out of the land of Egypt and down the road that the Red Sea opened up:

> When Pharaoh come he see the road
> He see the Hebrews marching on.
> He never see such things before
> He don't know God.

We read the sweet bold language more excitedly than if it were a foreign language, because it is our everyday English that is being enriched for us. Looking at the story of Exodus in this new way gives us a feeling of being African.

> *M. B. Goffstein, in a review of "A Road Down in the Sea," in* The New York Times Book Review, *August 22, 1971, p. 8.*

GOD WASH THE WORLD AND START AGAIN   (1971)

Since Old Testament is as young as ever, and as packed with epic drama, it can be retold in countless ways. Here's a vernacular spectacular, a tale told in primitive English that is right on target—a kind of homing pidgin. It's the speech newly acquired by African boys forty years ago . . . ; and it tells how an African Noah built, stocked, and sailed his ark. The rhythm echoes the tom-tom's patter, rumble, grunt:

> First time God made the world . . .
> First time Him heart lay down
> But bye-m-bye He look and see
> The people no be fit to hear Him Word
> And things what walk be bad too much
> And God want try again.

> *Neil Millar, "Timeless Tales Retold," in* The Christian Science Monitor, *May 6, 1971, p. B4.**

[Lorenz Graham] retells the story of Noah in the speech patterns of African people becoming acquainted with the English language. This verse poem gives emotion and dimension to the relationships between the human characters and God, but the illustrations [by Clare Rumano Ross] do not possess the same stirring quality. Perhaps the text alone could be read aloud to convey the imaginative use of language. (p. 58)

> *Jeanne McLain Harms and Lucille J. Lettow, "A Flood of Noah Stories: A Concern about the Retelling of Old Stories," in* Top of the News, *Vol. 40, No. 1, Fall, 1983, pp. 56-61.**

DAVID HE NO FEAR   (1971)

From *How God Fix Jonah*, the fourth story-into-book—the fourth sonorous, stern, stirring chant in Liberian English. "David don't humbug nobody / And most times nobody don't humbug David. / When he mind the sheep him heart lay down / . . . / He play him harp / He sing." "Bye-m-bye the war palaver catch Judah country"—"David self no be a man / So he stay by and mind the sheep . . ."; "Bye-m-bye the word come back / The word say war go bad for Judah"—"But David, he no fear. / . . . / He put rock in him sling / He turn it all about and round and round / The giant coming close / The sling leggo. / Hmmmmm. . . . . . Bop!" Regrettably, no such implosive momentum graces the competitively hyperbolic woodcuts [by Ann Grifalconi]; as before, this is the better to listen to without looking—the best to singspeak aloud, your own self or in chorus.

> *A review of "David He No Fear," in* Kirkus Reviews, *Vol. XXXIX, No. 17, September 1, 1971, p. 941.*

In an introduction, the artist tells how the Bible stories were brought to Africa by missionaries; and "As they were retold by Africans, they took on the imagery of the people." The story of the boy David and his victory over the giant is told in a distinctively African way, yet the words retain the strength and timelessness of the language of the Bible. (pp. 603-04)

> *Sidney D. Long, in a review of "David He No Fear," in* The Horn Book Magazine, *Vol. XLVII, No. 6, December, 1971, pp. 603-04.*

Children will enjoy sharing aloud this fourth Bible event described in the compelling idiom of Liberian new speakers of English.... Poetic language reinforces the tale of that time when "the war palaver catch Judah country / And all the mens must go," and vividly recalls Goliath's arrogance soon brought low by David's straightforward confidence-plus-sling. The woodgrained illustrations add to the overall impact of strength with humility.

> *O. Robert Brown, Jr., in a review of "David He No Fear," in* Childhood Education, *Vol. 48, No. 4, (January, 1972), p. 205.*

HONGRY CATCH THE FOOLISH BOY (1973)

[This] is a dramatic, compelling retelling of the tale of the prodigal son. Told in the speech of African schoolchildren just beginning to learn English, the words are rhythmic with a poetic cadence which almost begs to be spoken aloud. Having taught for a time in Liberia, West Africa, Lorenz Graham has recreated the story with freshness and new appeal.

> *A review of "Hongry Catch the Foolish Boy," in* Instructor, *Vol. LXXXII, No. 9, May, 1973, p. 75.*

This poetically flowing African version of the story of the Prodigal Son originally appeared in Graham's collection, *How God fix Jonah.* Beautiful to read aloud, it is also interesting as a variant that conveys a sense of the African storyteller's rhythmic patterns.

> *A review of "Hongry Catch the Foolish Boy," in* The Booklist, *Vol. 69, No. 22, July 15, 1973, p. 1073.*

[The story of the Foolish Boy or the Prodigal Son] resembles its predecessors in offering a fresh insight into well-known material through evocative imagery and pulsating, rhythmic language. Pithy, but never arch, certain of the lines are vivid, subtly ironic commentaries on human nature: "The boy have plenty friends / He have plenty fun / Bye-m-bye money finish." Unfortunately, the illustrations [by James Brown, Jr.] tend to dominate rather than complement the essential simplicity of the narrative.

> *Mary M. Burns, in a review of "Hongry Catch the Foolish Boy," in* The Horn Book Magazine, *Vol. XLIX, No. 4, August, 1973, p. 369.*

Another of Graham's fresh, vigorous Biblical retellings in the African idiom.... The illustrations in *Hongry Catch the Foolish Boy* incorporate much authentic detail but Brown's use of African designs in gray as background on every page makes the layout appear confusing. The yellow and purple on alternating full-page spreads are garish and out of kilter with the stark simplicity and swift pace of the parable. Nevertheless, Graham's retellings are satisfying to read aloud, and their rhythmic speech and vivid metaphors invite participation and appreciation.

> *Dorothy de Wit, in a review of "Hongry Catch the Foolish Boy," in* School Library Journal, *an appendix to* Library Journal, *Vol. 20, No. 1, September, 1973, p. 57.*

SONG OF THE BOAT (1975)

[Both Leo and Diane Dillon's] graceful illustrations . . . and the resonant African English that distinguished Lorenz' Bible tales . . . make a stirring occasion of the boy Momolu's discovery, in a dream, of the perfect tree . . . for Flumbo, his father, to carve into a new canoe, replacing one broken by an alligator.... [Even] without the Biblical ballast of Lorenz' previous volumes, something of Momolu's culture lives here. (pp. 1179-80)

> *A review of "Song of the Boat," in* Kirkus Reviews, *Vol. XLIII, No. 20, October 15, 1975, pp. 1179-80.*

In this delightful tale, Lorenz Graham captures the magical quality of West African legend. He depicts the close village and family relationships, where every significant individual act is witnessed by the community. Here is understated, affectionate, deep respect of son for father, and quiet, unerring sustenance from wife and mother.

The most striking feature of this story is that the unique quality of African folklore is evoked through a poetic style. Mr. Graham uses the "pidgin" spoken throughout English-speaking West Africa, and his rendering of this language is authentic. He uses repetition and rhythm to suggest the tonality and rhythmical beat of African languages. He tells the story with sensitivity and simple beauty.

It might have been helpful if the author had informed his readers that the story is set in Liberia. (Momolu is a Liberian version of the name Mohammed, and Flumbo is a name from the Kpele people and their language is typical of that country.) Also, a brief glossary might have assisted the young reader in interpreting such expressions as "This time" (now), "make it" (allow, may) and "small chop" (snack). (pp. 5-6)

This is a satisfying story for children. (p. 6)

> *Joyce Arkhurst, in a review of "Song of the Boat," in* Interracial Books for Children Bulletin, *Vol. 6, No. 7, 1975, pp. 5-6.*

Told in the folk speech of West Africa, the story of Flumbo who goes in search of a new canoe resonates with language so strong and rhythmic that it elevates the simple adventure into a hero quest. Setting out with his son Momolu, "Flumbo look him small boy. / He say, 'The road I walk be long. Oh, / It be long past the legs of my small boy.' / Momolu look up and he say, / 'Elephant cross big hill; / Goat cross big hill same way.'" Eventually Momolu dreams of finding the gum tree from which they will carve the canoe, and on his awakening, the two seek and find it. And after the priests call the spirit of the tree, "Flumbo did make fine canoe, fine past all canoes!"

The author has already produced a series of beautiful, well-crafted picture-book texts—this one is even more subtle than the others; but he has never had an illustrator who so captures the spirit of his work as do the Dillons. . . . Like the text, the woodcuts feel indigenous to Africa, but, at the same time, both text and pictures retain a universal element. (pp. 584-85)

> *Anita Silvey, in a review of "Song of the Boat," in*
> The Horn Book Magazine, *Vol. LI, No. 6, December, 1975, pp. 584-85.*

RETURN TO SOUTH TOWN   (1976)

An earnest look at the New South through the eyes of David Williams who returns with his M.D. to the town that persecuted his uppity father some years before. Dr. Williams' plan to set up a rural practice is sure to be opposed by the town's other doctor, Harold Boyd, chief of the local memorial hospital and scion of the family that ran the Williamses out of the area. But the trouble doesn't come to a head until a plane crash gives Boyd a melodramatic excuse to accuse Williams of practicing without the state license that Boyd's old boy friends have conspired to delay. Until then, Williams spends his time renewing old acquaintances and musing over how things have changed—or not, as the case may be—in the company of his sociologist sweetheart who grafts her class analyses onto the black/white ones of Williams' South Town friends. The plot sloughs along awkwardly and Williams, whose only visible characteristic is sincerity, isn't as dynamic as he might be. Still, Williams' manifest good intentions may prompt readers to be patient with his expository professional manner. (pp. 738-39)

> *A review of "Return to South Town," in* Kirkus Reviews, *Vol. XLIV, No. 13, July 1, 1976, pp. 738-39.*

The further struggles of David Williams to overcome racial prejudice may interest fans of Graham's [*South Town, North Town,* and *Whose Town?*]; however, this is a badly flawed novel that cannot stand on its own. Now a young doctor about to finish his residency in New York, David returns to his repressive hometown to decide if he should set up his practice there. However, the real purpose of his return is to provide a framework for Graham's observations on the status of race relations in the present day South (despite surface changes, Graham still finds the old prejudices at work). Several episodes of medical rescue which feature David as the hero, a romantic interest with a college sociology teacher, and an attempt by Harold Boyd, his old childhood antagonist, to prevent his licensing all serve primarily as jumping off points for an endless stream of sociological platitudes uttered by symbolic see-through characters who will offend even the least sophisticated readers.

> *John F. Caviston, in a review of "Return to South Town," in* School Library Journal, *Vol. 23, No. 1, September, 1976, p. 133.*

[In *Return to South Town,* every] problem is eventually solved. The text moves slowly, and the writing style is not distinguished, but the book gives a good picture of life in a small southern town today and of the changes that have occurred in recent years.

> *Zena Sutherland, in a review of "Return to South Town," in* Bulletin of the Center for Children's Books, *Vol. 30, No. 3, November, 1976, p. 42.*

It's a shame the nostalgic 60's type of books don't appeal to the youth of the 70's. Though it is evident that Mr. Graham's

intentions are honorable, he has lost touch with the current scene, thus creating a book that will not be read by today's teens. The saga of life in South Town has lost its appeal.

> *James S. Haskins, in a review of "Return to South Town," in* Children's Book Review Service, *Vol. 5, No. 4, December, 1976, p. 37.*

[Compared to Robbie Branscum's *Johnny May* and Linda Cline's *Weakfoot,*] **Return to South Town** is by far the most effective. Its weakness—a severe one though practically its only weakness—is its flat made-for-television style, its typical new-South setting and two-dimensional characters, each representing a hue in the spectrum of 1970's race relations. Real situations were never so clear, so complete, so balanced, and so happily resolved—in a word, so plastic. The protagonist's girl friend, a junior college teacher, speaks her intention to do "a study of the changing attitudes among black and white people in the South". . . . **Return to South Town** is such a study disguised as fiction, an optimistic but clear-sighted account of changing racial attitudes. The book is good fare for non-Southerners interested in the South, a fair sketch of residual racism overcome; and young blacks may well emulate Graham's protagonist, as the character named Junior does in the story. Graham's generalizations are healthy. (p. 259)

> *William H. Green, "A Harvest of Southern Realism," in* Children's Literature: Annual of the Modern Language Association Seminar on Children's Literature and The Children's Literature Association, *Vol. 7, 1978, pp. 255-61.**

JOHN BROWN: A CRY FOR FREEDOM   (1980)

The record of John Brown's life, set down without shaping or comment, drama or elaboration. (Thus Graham summarizes Brown's free-stater crusade in Kansas: "He won in several battles. Sons John Jr. and Jason were arrested, imprisoned, and finally released. John Jr. lost his mind and for a short period seemed to be quite helpless. In the next year attacks on free staters continued. . . .") In this manner, Graham brings Brown from birth in 1800 to 1855 in the first 50 pages; the remaining 120 take him from Kansas to preparations for Harpers Ferry, the raid itself, and his execution in 1859. The narrative is frequently broken up with quoted descriptions, tributes, and comments from people who knew and met Brown. Graham gives little attention to such questions as Brown's personality and his effect on history, noting merely that "John Brown has been described as a fanatic and a madman," then quoting contemporary observers who attest to the contrary. In an introduction, Graham makes the fuzzy statement that Brown's life "did indeed help to make this country what it is today," and he promises that reading about Brown will help us understand problems of racial inequality today. However, no parallels or applications are brought out in the text. This is neither the rousing life story nor the provocative inquiry that Brown might inspire. However, as an easy-reference chronicle it will serve.

> *A review of "John Brown: A Cry for Freedom," in* Kirkus Reviews, *Vol. XLVIII, No. 22, November 15, 1980, p. 1470.*

The inclusion of John Brown's eloquent trial speech, eulogies about him by Frederick Douglass, Emerson and others, and a powerful description of the effects of his ill-fated raid on Harper's Ferry make this book a must. The first few chapters which trace the many moves of Brown and his family and his growing abhorrence of slavery are on the dry side and many YAs may need a push to propel them into the more exciting depiction of the raid and its aftermath.

> *Judith Geer, in a review of "John Brown: A Cry for Freedom," in* Voice of Youth Advocates, *Vol. 3, No. 5, December, 1980, p. 42.*

Graham reveals his subject as an impassioned man with a worthy, lifelong cause, yet a person with characteristics that caused some people to proclaim him mad. This biography leaves no doubt, however, that John Brown's activities were a significant factor leading to the Civil War. The writing is not always free flowing and at times seems to rely unexcitingly on detailed, formal reporting based on primary sources. Basically, though, Graham presents an interesting account, with a minimum of fictionalization, interpreting historic matters for a better understanding of the subject.

> *Judith Goldberger, in a review of "John Brown: A Cry for Freedom," in* Booklist, *Vol. 77, No. 12, February 15, 1981, p. 809.*

There are things to criticize in this biography of John Brown, but outweighing any flaws is the fact that the only other children's book about this fascinating person was written 30 years ago. And information about this man—brave enough to fight and die for his religious/moral belief in Black-white equality—is generally unavailable to young readers.

The prevalent myth, nurtured by all U.S. history textbooks, is that Brown was a wild fanatic. This book will do much to counter the myth. Brown's years of work planning for the Harper's Ferry raid involved dozens of prominent leaders of the day. Nothing of this, nor of his moving and dignified trial statements, are known to most Americans. I, for one, was impressed with the statement made by Frederick Douglass after Brown's death: "His zeal in the case of my race was far greater than mine. I could live for the slave but he could die for him." The reverence Brown inspired in Ralph Waldo Emerson, William Lloyd Garrison and many others is eye-opening.

Certainly, young people of all colors should learn more about such a man—and about his dedicated followers. However,

teacher or parent may have to encourage readers to stay with this book through its early pages. Some of it is dull, difficult or overly detailed. Often maps are used; just as often they are called for, but missing.

Quite unintentionally, the lives of poor white women are exposed by some of the historical material. We learn that, "A year after Dianthe died, John married again. His new wife, Mary Day, was only seventeen years old at the time, but she cheerfully took on the task of mothering the five Brown children. In the years that followed, Mary Day Brown added seven sons and six daughters to the family." Musing on what choices young Mary must have had for her to be "cheerful" about taking on five children, I found myself thinking about her as I read about the family's moves from place to place, clearing land, building houses. She was there nursing the sick, cooking, washing and cleaning, and being poor and pregnant. Her story might be another book.

Meanwhile, welcome to this book-in-hand, and let us hope it will encourage more books about Brown and some about the interesting men who fought along with him. (pp. 18-19)

> *Lyla Hoffman, in a review of "John Brown: A Cry for Freedom," in* Interracial Books for Children Bulletin, *Vol. 12, No. 3, 1981, pp. 18-19.*

A compelling biography takes John Brown from a religious childhood through marriage and parenthood to Kansas, where the controversial abolitionist is set on the road that ends at Harpers Ferry. Graham allows Brown's actions and words to speak for themselves. A plethora of evidence succeeds in dispelling the myth of madman and fanatic as popularly pictured. Brown's prophecy regarding slavery—"'The end of that is not yet'"—pertains as much to our time as it did to his. The book sheds light on problems which whites and blacks face more than a century after Brown's execution. Contemporary photos and drawings lend drama to a life that reads like fiction. (pp. 594-95)

> *Ruth M. Stein, in a review of "John Brown: A Cry for Freedom," in* Language Arts, *Vol. 58, No. 5, May, 1981, pp. 594-95.*

June Jordan

1936-

Black American author of fiction and nonfiction, poet, and editor.

Jordan provides black youth with literature relative to their lives in setting, theme, and language. Noted for the skillfulness and originality of her writing techniques, she employs Black English, a language she finds beautiful, respectable, and a means of expressing racial pride. Jordan's realistic fiction, poetry, and biography for elementary school readers focus on historical and everyday topics, and her works maintain an optimistic tone despite their often impoverished settings. Her young adult books include the acclaimed short novel, *His Own Where*, centered on two teenage lovers searching for a secure future in Harlem, and *Dry Victories*, an informal account of human rights legislation in the Reconstruction and Civil Rights eras. These works portray a grimmer picture of racism and poverty, but still convey Jordan's characteristic insight into the feelings and concerns of her audience.

Reviewers praise Jordan for the emotional depth, clarity, and realism that enrich her books. While there is some controversy concerning the appropriateness of sexual expression and pessimism in her works for older readers, critics consistently applaud Jordan's creative language and poetic style, as well as her ability to speak to all races.

***His Own Where* was selected as a National Book Award finalist in 1972.**

(See also *Contemporary Literary Criticism*, Vols. 5, 11, 23; *Something about the Author*, Vol. 4; *Contemporary Authors*, Vols. 33-36, rev. ed.; and *Dictionary of Literary Biography*, Vol. 38: *Afro-American Writers after 1955, Dramatists and Prose Writers*.)

Courtesy of June Jordan

AUTHOR'S COMMENTARY

Love is life force. I believe that the creative spirit is nothing less than love made manifest. I see love as the essential nature of all that supports life. Love is opposed to the death of the spirit. Love is opposed to the death of the dream. Love is opposed to the limiting of the possibilities of experience. When we run on love; when we move and change and build and paint and sing and write and foster the maximum fulfillment of our own lives; when we foster a fulfillment of other lives that look to us for help,, protection, or clues to the positive excitement of just being alive—then we make manifest the creative spirit of the universe, a spirit existing within each of us and yet infinitely greater than the ultimate capacities of any one of us.

I think of the amazing fact that tiger lilies in a field will bloom, wild as they grow, exactly on the same day as wild tiger lilies several miles away. There is an orderliness, a perpetual inclination to grow, to become manifest from an invisible beginning—a perpetual impulse to expand and to transform—that seems to me the essence of being, even perhaps the irreducible purpose of being. By nature, whether we are children or tiger lilies, it seems that our essence, our purpose, does not imply harm to other elements of the world. Neither tiger lilies nor children threaten the rain, or the bees, or the rivers of the world. And it seems to me that love—that serious and tender concern and respect for the nature and spontaneous purpose of other things, other people—will make manifest a peaceable order among us, such that fear, conflict, competition, waste, and environmental sacrilege will have no place. That is what I believe.

What I know is that the creative spirit is real—beyond you or me. In my own life as a poet, and in the lives of many of my students, it has happened more than once in a while that an entire poem or a completely formulated fictional character will be *given* to you. This kind of event by no means represents the mainstay of your productivity, but it does occur often enough to keep you humble. It helps you realize that the creative spirit is as much a process depending upon your receptivity as it is one depending upon willful conjuring or projection of visual, oral, or verbal concepts—for which you like to feel proudly responsible.

In my work as an artist, I always seem to be about a most sobering task—the task of survival for myself and for those who may carry what I offer to them into their own lives. Because we coexist on a planet long defiled by habits opposite to the creative spirit, habits opposite to love, it seems to me that the task of surviving, and the task of providing for the survival of those who are not as strong as I am, is a political undertaking. Vast changes will have to be envisioned and pursued if any, let alone all, of us will survive the destructive traditions of our species. Enormous reversals and revisions of our thinking patterns will have to be achieved somehow, and fast. To accomplish such lifesaving alterations of society, we will have to deal with power. We will have to make love powerful. We will have to empower the people we love; so that they can insist upon the validity of their peculiar coloring, gender, ethnicity, or accidental economic status; so that they can bloom in their own place and time like the tiger lily, beautiful and free.

So far, I have been looking at the creative spirit, or the rational and imaginative manifestation of love, in a general way. How should we see this spirit function in relationship to children?

I know of nothing more important, more difficult, and more purely loving than the nurture of children—be it as a parent, as a teacher, or as an artist wishing to serve them well. Children are the ways that the world begins again and again. If you fasten upon that concept of their promise, you will have trouble finding anything more awesome, anything more extraordinarily exhilarating, than the opportunity and obligation to further a child into his or her own freedom. At the same time children depend on you or me for more than we can easily or comfortably imagine. Like it or not, we are the ones—we who think we know, who believe, who remember—who shape a great part of what they will, in their turn, think they know, or remember, or believe, or expect. We are the ones who feed, clothe, and train them to stay away from fire, or dolls, or Chinese food, or the vigorous climbing of apple trees. In addition, children rely on us for their safety, for their sense of safety, of being in or out of their element, of being capable of solving whatever problems come up, or of being incapable and helpless. We, the large ones, possess a degree of power over the lives of children that we ourselves would find inconceivable and unspeakably tyrannical in any other context.

And yet, we mostly wear this power as some divine right not to be questioned, not to be wrestled with as one would wrestle with an angel for the sake of one's soul. Or, we try to minimize and trivialize power by limiting our concepts of our function to those of discipline or of boundless hugs and kisses. Or, we pretend we don't have power. In the name of what we mistakenly call freedom, we exert ourselves as little as possible beyond meeting relatively middle-class notions of creature needs. Or, we pretend that we do not have power because we look at ourselves, and see the horrendous shameful mess that is our international legacy to our children. And we think, "God, I don't know, kid. Don't ask me."

Regardless of how we view the power and responsibility that we hold vis-à-vis children, that power and responsibility remain—an incomparable, profound, and inexorable opportunity to bless or to curse their lives, to open or to seal their willingness to trust, to explore, and to create.

One abiding characteristic of these little people, the children of our lives, is their unabashed sobriety. Whether they are playing house or practicing how to say "Thank you," whether they are doubling up with giggle fits of laughter or of extremely felt joy, children are serious. They do not pretend to make-believe, or to laugh, or to howl out the hurt and discomfort of the moment. Whatever the feeling, the act, or the so-called game, when compared with the rest of us, the child is supremely unequivocal in her or his commitment to that moment of being.

As a consequence, particularly young children are what we term "literal." I remember when my son refused to return to school after his lunch hour at home one afternoon because—as I finally persuaded him to confide in me—the teacher had told him that he was adorable. Because the word was unfamiliar to him, because her manner was not clearly and simply loving, he felt himself in limbo. Only after I had explained the meaning of adorable, and also the meaning of folks who say supposedly nice things that they do not entirely feel, only then was he ready to enter her dominion again.

Another way of expressing this is to say that whatever happens to someone as a child, whether it is a beating or a picture book, it will happen without meeting defense, without encountering a barrier to its potential impact for good or ill.

In childhood we live through days and nights of singularly direct apprehension, singularly vulnerable passage through uncensored experiences. Let me give you two different illustrations of this, both of them personal. Last night, thanks to the kindness of Ann Golden, I reread "The Ugly Duckling." The version in my hands was *The Complete Fairy Tales and Stories of Hans Christian Andersen,* translated by Erik Haugaard. I wanted to reread the story because two days ago Ann Durell referred to it as a great story. Even as she made that judgment, my heart rebelled.

My memory of "The Ugly Duckling" was different. I remember being given it one night as my parents prepared to go out for the evening, leaving me with an unknown adult, a baby-sitter. Abandoned as I felt, I took the little book into my crib (I believe I was somewhere between two and three years old at the time). And I read and I studied the drawings of that story. Infamous night. In the bastardized version that I held in my hands—undoubtedly the same candy store version now available for 49 cents—the ugly duckling was ugly because it was black and smaller than the rest of the brood, a runt. As I was black, or dark skinned compared with both of my parents, and smaller than my parents, smaller than most kids my age, even smaller than my cousin who lived with me (four years my senior), there was no route that I could find for escape. I *was* the ugly duckling. And, moreover, I was ugly for reasons I could neither control nor change. Reading that story I met my doom. For the first time I acquired a sense of myself as ugly, as not belonging, as wrong. You know, a sense that even now I must struggle to overcome. That wound was severely crippling and intense.

Well, it was quite extraordinary to discover last night that the original version of "The Ugly Duckling" has nothing to do with color: Actually the duckling was larger than the rest of the brood because it was, indeed, a swan. It was quite extraordinary to discover that I agree with Ann Durell; I think it's a great story because now I can see a wonderful meaning to the tale: You will be beautiful when you do not try to be something you are not. When you are true to yourself, then you will become like a swan released in the grace of natural and spontaneous purpose.

Here is a second illustration of the vulnerability of the child. This is a poem that my son Christopher wrote when he was nine.

All of Us a Family

The day will come
When people will come
Red, yellow, black, and white.

A family they'll be
And a family tree.

Oh, and the day will come
When a black leader can stand
In safety,
Knowing that all others
Are his brothers
And sisters in the family of man.

At the least that was his response to the assassination of Martin Luther King, Jr. A terrible wistfulness that no one would possibly deny as to its authenticity. And here is a poem that Christopher wrote one year later, when he was ten years old.

I've Seen Enough

I've been through Africa,
I was there when Solomon was claimed king,
I was best man to Cleopatra,
I've seen the death of a million men in Japan
When that treacherous bomb was dropped.
Surely I can say
I've seen enough.
What more proof need I tell you?
Must I tell you that I bore the cross
On which Jesus Christ was crucified?
I've seen enough.

Now you have a brief but factual testimony to the emotional and intellectual makeup of a two-year-old and a ten-year-old. These are random examples of the vulnerability and of the serious character commonplace to the children whom we frequently dismiss as cute or childish—by which we mean not serious and inconsequential. It is for little people of such possible response that we frequently put together toys and books about nothing at all, or toys and books that inherently we would despise for ourselves because they are silly, or pointless, or fiendish. What do we have in mind when we give a little girl a three-dimensional replica of a kitchen stove that does nothing at all? What do we have in mind when we give a child a book that means absolutely nothing, a book serving no purpose, not even the wonderful one of enlivening a sense of delight? It is with these ideas about the creative spirit, about love, about children, and about a world we need to redeem for their sake (as well as for our own) that I approach the subject of children's literature.

I do not believe that I am alone in these views. It does not surprise me that when we grownups encounter a special friend or a lover whom we really want to cherish, we often head for the children's section of a bookstore. There we will look for still another copy of *The Little Prince* or *Winnie-the-Pooh*. And why? Not because we were regularly given materials of such love in our childhood, of such respect and tender and serious regard, but because we wish our childhood had been filled with such materials, because we now know deeply that we wanted and we needed to have such love abundant to our days.

And so we give these allegedly "children's" books to each other. In so doing we say, "I care about you. I love you. And because I love you, I think about you. I think about what may hurt you, what may make you happy, what may make you feel ugly or small, and what may make you feel competent, interesting, and safe." For what both *Winnie-the-Pooh* and *The Little Prince* have in common, after all, is the depiction of little people as serious, capable, worth knowing, and worth knowing about. In both stories the writing, by any criteria, is

superlative. It is not Goosey-Poosey, Cocky-Locky garbage. It is a suitably serious and literate and lovingly inspired piece of writing that requires no apology, no explanation. And so it will not surprise you to hear that I regard considerations of the usefulness and the craft of children's literature as integral to the creative spirit.

If there is no love between you, as St. Paul has written, then you labor in vain. And if your love is not useful, if your love is not respectful, if you do not extend yourself in the manifestation of love to make your offering as beautiful and as perfect as you possibly can, then you are lovers in vain. We cannot hope to serve well the needs and potential of our children otherwise. I celebrate the existence of *The Little Prince* and of *Winnie-the-Pooh*. I celebrate the existence of the Racism and Sexism Awareness resolution adopted last year by the ALA and the similar resolution that was adopted by the National Council of Teachers of English. I look at the children's books from the People's Republic of China—books such as *The Red Army Women's Detachment*—and find in these offerings an enviable literature that takes children seriously and the question of our survival seriously.

When I turn to my own work, when I consider my opportunities to serve the lives of children and my own future life simultaneously, then I think about purpose: What will be the use of my work? And then I think about craft: How can I best present this offering so that my purpose may have the best chance of its achievement? What I would like to achieve, regardless of the particular story or poem, is to offer a child respect and the belief that there are ways to creatively handle whatever may be the pain or the social predicament of his or her young life. I believe that he or she can and will discover, or else invent these ways.

I want to say to children: I love you. You are beautiful and amazing, regardless of whether you are—and precisely because you are—black, or female, or poor, or small, or an only child, or the child of parents divorced. When you love yourself truly, you will become like a swan released in the grace of your natural and spontaneous purpose. I want to say to children: Let us look at hunger, at famine around the world, and let us consider how you at five years of age and me at 41 can and must elimate this genocide, this terror. I want to say to children: Let us look at tiger lilies blooming, and learn from them how to cherish our own form, orderliness, and freedom. And I want to say to children: Tell me what you think, what you see, and what you dream so that I may hope to honor you. I want these things for children because I want these things for myself and for all of us. Because unless we embody these attitudes and precepts as the governing rules of our love and of our political commitment to survive, we will love in vain, and we will certainly not survive. I believe that the creative spirit is nothing less than love made manifest. And I deeply hope that we can make love powerful, because otherwise there will be no reason for hope. (pp. 161-65)

June Jordan, "June Jordan," in Wilson Library Bulletin, *Vol. 53, No. 2, October, 1978, pp. 161-65.*

WHO LOOK AT ME (1969)

"I am black and alive and looking back at you. / . . . Although the world / forgets me / I will say yes / AND NO!" Proud and provocative, this is a single poem written in many different voices, touching on black experience in a gentle surprise of phrase. The punctuation is casual, the syntax slippery, the impact quite remarkable, especially if the poem is read aloud by a person who's "together." . . . Most of the themes have been approached by other black poets—the uniqueness of black culture, weary defiance toward white hypocrisy and shallowness; here, those feelings spring out again, refreshed via a slight mismatch of terms ("the midnight of the winter"; "a hungerland of great prosperity"; "the grieving fury of his life"; "the pocket deadly need to please"). There are a few stylistic rough spots (e.g. excessive alliteration) and one or two lines are impossibly abstruse. Altogether, though, it has a distinguished stance and a presence of its own. (pp. 863-64)

> *A review of "Who Look at Me," in* Kirkus Reviews, *Vol. XXXVII, No. 16, August 15, 1969, pp. 863-64.*

Opposite the title page of **"Who Look at Me"** is a painting simply entitled "Portrait of a Gentleman." The gentleman is black. June Jordan's book suggests all black Americans are as unknown as the anonymous early 19th-century artist and his subject. . . .

By intermixing 27 paintings of black Americans from colonial times to the present with an original, understated but intense poem that comments indirectly on the paintings and enhances their meaning, she has given children a splendid opportunity to "begin unlimited embrace of human life."

Her text begins with a question: "Who would paint a people black or white?" The implied answer is that centuries of derogatory generalizations about Negroes have done precisely that. . . .

The accompanying poem reveals its unity through repeated words, and themes and records with psychological deftness the evolution of the black man's racial pride. In it Miss Jordan says pithily to whites, "To begin is no more agony than opening your hand." She cautions them "I am black alive and looking back at you." . . .

[Each] section of poetry has lines that we must remember.

> *James A. Emanuel, in a review of "Who Look at Me," in* The New York Times Book Review, *November 16, 1969, p. 52.*

[*Who Look at Me*] is not wholly successful, for the poem lacks coherence and continuity. It is a somewhat disjointed collection of poetic images. The poet's words have their greatest impact when coupled with one or another of the paintings, when they explore or define or comment on the mood or truth or idea that the artist tried to convey. . . . It is harder to grasp the sense of what the author is saying on pages that are blankly white except for a line or two of verse: "These times begin the ending of all lies / the fantasies of seasons start and stop / the circle leads to no surprise / for death does not bewilder / only life . . . can mystify. . . ." Not an easy poem by any means, but one over which to pore and ponder; a strong, impassioned, splendid statement. If her intent was to startle the reader into truly seeing the faces of black America, the author succeeds powerfully. (pp. 47-8)

> *Diane Farrell, in a review of "Who Look at Me," in* The Horn Book Magazine, *Vol. XLVI, No. 1, February, 1970, pp. 47-8.*

"Who look at me," is a phrase repeated throughout; the "me" stands for the author, her black family, her family of black people extending throughout history. She writes of experiences, of feelings, and of past history shared by black people

in poetry of exquisite depth. . . . The paintings and poetry fit so well together that it's virtually impossible to determine which element was assembled first. Miss Jordan . . . has authored a book of exceptional integrity, insight, and beauty. It will have visual and emotional impact on readers of all ages and races as it implores them to discover others—to look at and see.

> *Susan E. O'Neal, in a review of "Who Look at Me?" in* School Library Journal, *an appendix to* Library Journal, *Vol. 16, No. 6, February, 1970, p. 89.*

[These poems] vary in strength and passion but . . . speak, on the whole, with piercing clarity of the pathos, beauty, pride, and anger in Negro lives. . . . The author, young and black, has interpreted some of the paintings rather narrowly, so that the poems cannot quite stand alone, but these are in the minority, and the quality of the writing is consistently compelling.

> *Zena Sutherland, "Reviews of Books: 'Who Look at Me'," in* The Best in Children's Books: The University of Chicago Guide to Children's Literature, 1966-1972, *edited by Zena Sutherland, The University of Chicago Press, 1973, p. 218.*

HIS OWN WHERE   (1971)

AUTHOR'S COMMENTARY

[*In the following excerpt,* Publishers Weekly *interviews Jordan, who comments on her conception of Buddy, the protagonist of* His Own Where, *her concern with environmental change, and her views on Black English.*]

["**His Own Where**" is] a sensitive teenage love story of Buddy and Angela, which also becomes a "survival manual for the young people who confront the hopelessness of the ghetto." Miss Jordan incorporated some of her ideas on environmental redesign in the story e.g.: Buddy's musing that unoccupied skyscrapers should be inhabited by poor people at night and wrote the story, both dialog and stream of consciousness, in "black English."

"Buddy acts, he moves. He is the man I believe in, the man who will come to lead his people into a new community," she says. Miss Jordan firmly believes that only the people living in these ghettos can truly make changes to improve their environment.

"All of the concepts suggested in '**His Own Where**' were governed by the principle that they should really be possible," she contends. "They should cost no more money than anyone who is truly poor could afford. They would really depend on will, rather than on material resources, and not only would these ideas affect the immediate block where you live, but they would also change the big city concept. All these proposals are feasible—nothing that Buddy undertakes in the book is impossible."

Miss Jordan considers the love between Buddy and Angela an important aspect of the book. She feels the real struggle is to remain capable and willing where love is concerned even though one is the victim of so much hatred. "This is a shout—a testament to survival and some suggestions on how to assure that survival for all of us."

Speaking about the consistent use of black English in "**His Own Where**," Miss Jordan says: "Anyone who will care about Buddy and Angela, or truly know them, must take them on those terms. This is the way they speak."

Miss Jordan believes that black English is as expressive a language as any other dialect. "It can be a harsh statement, a loving statement. It can also be a means of art, art as something that does not disfigure or diminish what is real, but enhances it," she said.

"I object to the many books where black English is used only in dialog, and almost always in the context of violence and brutality—the bestial events that are inevitable among suffering peoples. In **'His Own Where'** the reader can fully participate and respond, without contending with a narrator who removes himself from the characters." (pp. 60-1)

An interview with June Jordan, in Publishers Weekly, *Vol. 201, No. 8, February 21, 1972, pp. 60-1.*

A book of inestimable beauty. Like June Jordan's other writings, including the long poem **Who Look at Me** . . . , it is written in a very personal and unorthodox idiom—a kind of cross between Black English and stream-of-consciousness. The story lives in the streets of Brooklyn where two teenagers share a growing love. Buddy Rivers, 16, is virtually on his own: his mother ran off years ago and his father is dying after an accident. Suspended from school by a myopic principal for a minor incident . . . , he has only Angela, just 14, to count on. Meeting at the hospital where her accusing mother is a nurse, "they become the heated habit of each other"—he walks her home at night. But her parents are distrustful, calling her wild, and after her father beats her, she is assigned to a solemn public shelter—in effect, homeless. What usually turns tawdry or melodramatic in pulp magazines (and often sour and ugly in life) is here allowed a hoping time. With little money, his fine initiative, and a belief in each other, they move into a deserted building near a cemetery, His Own Where. It's kind of creepy . . . but it is a haven. It could be, of course, a highly perishable happiness but such thoughts have no part in this brave and gentle love. Despite the odds against them—their ages, their limited resources, their talk about having a child—they seem to have a chance; they *have* to try, and most young readers will recognize this impulse while seeing their vulnerability. Some may question the appropriateness of such matters for teenagers; many will welcome it. In a scant 90 pages, a rich and moving experience from a rare talent.

A review of "His Own Where," in Kirkus Reviews, *Vol. XXXIX, No. 18, September 15, 1971, p. 1021.*

[June Jordan] knows the abandonment of this age. It is a limbo between childhood and young adulthood, where the void is so great as to be unbearable. It is true here that the mind often stammers for language and the heart only responds to song— to the radio. . . . Angela, at 14, trying to understand Buddy, tells him, "Tune the dial to what you want." There must be bridges if we are to reach our young. **"His Own Where"** promises to be one.

The language moves freely, violating syntax to get to deeper levels of meaning. We get into the mind's eye of Buddy; with a rhythm matching his Black lifestyle, we see him in heroic proportions. At first the speech patterns might seem to create a barrier for the reader, but not for long. They are not offensive, not meant to set apart. Little is past tense. There is present, active present and future. This gives a reeling effect, a running action, a telescoping of reality. . . . (p. 6)

Sarah Webster Fabio, in a review of "His Own Where," in The New York Times Book Review, *Part II, November 7, 1971, pp. 6, 34.*

[Jordan] uses the language of the ghetto, but expands it, combining words and phrases of dialect in a stream-of-consciousness style that attempts to remove the barrier between words and experiences. The result achieves a striking immediacy. . . . Although the obvious irony of [Buddy and Angela's] situation is not commented upon until the last line of the book—when the author intrudes and the spell is broken—much of the underlying tension is created by the juxtaposition of images of life and death. The author controls the language carefully, however, and her images never seem melodramatic or contrived. The craftsmanship of the book . . . becomes more apparent with each rereading.

Sidney D. Long, in a review of "His Own Where," in The Horn Book Magazine, *Vol. XLVII, No. 6, December, 1971, p. 620.*

This novel is no cop-out pseudo-case study of a confused kid or of kids "in trouble." Buddy's not guilty, hostile, mixed-up and ineffectual, or prodded on the road to self-discovery by a well-meaning adult. He really loves Angela (for how long is an adult concern) and the two of them can't wait to make a baby and share love with it (what its precise future will be is also not their concern now). Buddy's reactions are rarely clichéd: he sees a hospital as a clean place staffed by concerned people, not as a cold, sterile building; far from wanting solitude for his father, he's glad the dying man at least has a semiprivate room so that he won't meet death alone. The boy's resourcefulness, talent, sensitivity and courage, as well as certain of his escapades in school and elsewhere, are really those of a mythic hero, not a 16 year old. Yet he's so firmly grounded in the modern Manhattan street scene that it's impossible to dismiss him as an unreal or unbelievable character. This is largely due to Jordan's uncanny ability with words. She combines free verse and prose, uses black speech, abandons end punctuation marks. She almost always uses the present tense to describe situations and feelings. The result is a reader-absorbing stream of consciousness effect, a superbly individual vision of "the living" which readers will recognize from their own where. (pp. 64-5)

Rosalind K. Goddard, in a review of "His Own Where," in School Library Journal, *an appendix to* Library Journal, *Vol. 18, No. 4, December, 1971, pp. 64-5.*

Poetically written, this is a sensitive love story for young people. (p. 58)

The active fact of the love relationship is important, but the author adeptly shows physical needs as being intertwined with emotional needs. Although many see this as a problem novel, the issue of sexuality is not presented as a problem. The two young people move naturally toward closeness. Their hope lies in their feelings for each other and the hope for a baby expressed by Angela in the end.

This book presents love and sex in a natural way. It is also important because the love story is told through Black characters and with a rhythm of blackness in the language. (pp. 58-9)

Binnie Tate Wilkin, "The Individual: 'His Own Where'," in her Survival Themes in Fiction for Chil-

dren and Young People, *The Scarecrow Press, Inc.,*
1978, pp. 58-9.

[*His Own Where*] is, by the author's own suggestion, a latter
day revision of *Romeo and Juliet,* though the story ends precariously happily for the young lovers who are together and
trying to have a baby. Indeed, this is precisely what is wrong
with the book: Buddy and Angela, the hero and heroine, are
sixteen and fourteen, respectively. They are the characters the
reader obviously identifies with. To propose as role models a
fourteen year old girl and sixteen year old boy who are flying
in the face of reality by setting up bizarre housekeeping in the
brick shed of a cemetery along side the Interboro Parkway in
Brooklyn is, I think, an act of social as well as literary irresponsibility. (p. 118)

There seems to me to be a deep contradiction between Jordan's
strident nationalism whose linguistic expression is her insistence on Black English, and the absurd conclusion of her novel.
A writer who styles herself a literary champion of her people
by insisting on the sovereignty of their language is certainly
not doing them a service by presenting this unrealistic scenario
for emulation. Whether or not black working class families
agree with Jordan's evaluation of their language, they do not
want their young teenage daughters and sons setting up shop
and starting families of their own. One might, I suppose, explain the novel by assuming that the entire story is a kind of
projected fantasy of Buddy and Angela. But fantasy or not,
this book is intended to be read by teenagers who can "relate"
to it through its language as they cannot to Shakespeare's *Ro-*
meo and Juliet because of its archaic Elizabethan English. . . .
And what they read of is the possibility of escape from the
grim world of oppressive adults—child abusing parents, high
school principals, and licentious nuns.

Furthermore, the language and ideas of the book are often too
abstract and as far from being realistic as is the conclusion of
the story. In fact, I would bet it is as hard for children to read
Jordan's prose as it is for them to read Shakespeare's. The
ellipses in the sentences seem more often poetic license than
omissions characteristic of Black English. The narrator, who
is never identified but who, nevertheless, arbitrarily tells the
story in the dialect, begins:

> You be different from the dead. All them tomb-
> stones tearing up the ground, look like a little
> city, like a small Manhattan, not exactly. Here
> is not the same.

> Here, you be bigger than the buildings, bigger
> than the little city. You be really different from
> the rest, the resting other ones. . . .

The mental gymnastics one must engage in in order to appreciate the metaphor of the tombstones as skyscrapers or the pun
on "rest" and "resting" do not seem worth it when one must
wrestle with Jordan's elusive and sometimes impenetrable prose
as well. Furthermore, while one may intellectually sympathize
with the miserable lives of Buddy and Angela, it is still objectionable to aggrandize their solution through language which
attempts to transform it into the sublime.

Perhaps this is harsh, but sections of the book remind me that
Jordan knows better. The dream sequences in the novel are
eloquent, if utopian, portraits of necessary transformations of
society. She knows what must be done to change things so
that Buddy and Angela need not live as they do. Yet nowhere
does she suggest it is possible for them to fight the oppression

of racism, the ultimate author of these two young people's
woe. (pp. 120-21)

> *Ellen Tremper, "Black English in Children's Lit-*
> *erature," in* The Lion and the Unicorn, *Vol. 3, No.*
> *2, Winter, 1979-80, pp. 105-24.**

DRY VICTORIES (1972)

Written in the form of a black English dialogue between two
teenage boys, a look at those two times "that still be hanging
us up bad": Reconstruction and the Civil Rights era. . . . [The]
whole is not so much history as an emotional reaction against
it, which leaves us still turning to an "list of other books you
can check into" to dig out the facts and feeling that it's "About
time to do something." Ms. Jordan talks of "taking the facts
up front," and the book's value certainly lies in its likelihood
of reaching kids who wouldn't be caught near those dry, sober
reappraisals which have sprung up in the last few years. Her
pessimistic conclusion—that the victories of Civil Rights were
as empty as those of 100 years ago—will certainly be controversial, and in the end even Jerome and Kenny become mired
in the author's sense of futility—"And here we been, for hours.
Just like everybody else. Talking. Just talking." Nevertheless,
a bitter, often eloquent cry of despair.

> *A review of "Dry Victories," in* Kirkus Reviews,
> *Vol. XL, No. 14, July 15, 1972, p. 809.*

Kenny and Jerome "Tak[e] Care of Business" (TCB) well:
they provide dates and statistics; discuss civil rights legislation
enacted on everything from voting to housing and such figures
as Charles Caldwell and Martin Luther King . . . and point up
important events. . . . [The] natural dialogue of the two boys
provides an excellent, unique teaching tool for casually in-
forming kids about history.

> *Rosalind K. Goddard, in a review of "Dry Victo-*
> *ries," in* School Library Journal, *an appendix to*
> Library Journal, *Vol. 19, No. 3, November, 1972,*
> *p. 68.*

Looking on Reconstruction and the civil rights era as "dry
victories" giving blacks neither economic freedom nor equality
this is an unconventional, informal view of revisionist history. . . . A provocative alternate historical perspective with
browsing interest and of particular appeal to readers acquainted
with the author's other works.

> *A review of "Dry Victories," in* The Booklist, *Vol.*
> *69, No. 9, January 1, 1973, p. 449.*

There's so much right about **"Dry Victories"**—the two characters, who are alive, funny, bitter, cool; the magnificent selection of photographs . . .—that it's a shame the book isn't
completely successful.

The fault here is that while the problems are stated clearly, the
conclusions are hazy. Miss Jordan says voting isn't "where
it's at"—that civil rights are meaningless without the "economic bases of freedom." Yet nowhere does she deal with the
forces that have served to maintain, or at least permit poverty.
For example, Reconstruction failed, not because President Grant
was "bored," but because, as John Hope Franklin wrote, the
South was taken over by Northern industrial interests, destroying chances for radical alternatives such as land reform and
redistribution of wealth. The Poor People's Campaign didn't
collapse because President Grant was "bored." It listens in-

tently to those interests that support Right to Work laws and call social welfare socialism.

"Dry Victories" ends with the boys hoping that "parents and them other folk" will . . . "do something." But what has obstructed that "something," or what it should or could be, is never spelled out.

> *Janet Harris, in a review of "Dry Victories," in* The New York Times Book Review, *February 11, 1973, p. 8.*

FANNIE LOU HAMER **(1972)**

The difficulty of maintaining a deft balance between historical fact and imaginative invention is well illustrated in such picture-book biographies as "Marian Anderson" by Tobi Tobias, **"Fannie Lou Hamer"** by June Jordan, and Louise Meriwether's "Don't Ride the Bus on Monday: The Rosa Parks Story." . . .

Oversimplification is a necessary evil in books for younger readers (8 to 10). But in their eagerness to win sympathy for these extraordinary black women, the authors have abandoned objectivity—and, at times, accuracy—altogether. Dastardly villains are white; arch-heroines are black.

Miss Jordan, a talented poet, seems to be deliberately discouraging white children from reading her story.

> *Jennifer Farley Smith, "New Biographies for Children: 'What's the Author's Angle?'" in* The Christian Science Monitor, *February 7, 1973, p. 10.*

Born in 1917, the youngest child in a family of twenty, . . . Fannie Lou soon learned how to be busy. At six, she picked thirty pounds of cotton in return for the Bossman's treat [of food] . . . ; the end of the sixth grade she finished school permanently and began working a twelve- to fourteen-hour day. But there was love and pride and faith as well as hard work, first with her mother and father and then with her husband. And from that love, pride, and faith came her determination in 1962 to help with the black voter registration in Mississippi. Beaten, jailed, homeless because of her activities, Mrs. Hamer, through the aid of Martin Luther King, won national sympathy for herself and her cause. Ultimately, her perseverance led to the formation of The Freedom Farm Cooperative, a six-hundred-forty-acre spread of Mississippi farmland. Using a starkly simple prose style, the author has achieved maximum effect with a minimum of detail. She creates for younger readers a true people's heroine in a chronicle of the triumph of one woman's confidence in herself and in her race.

> *Mary M. Burns, in a review of "Fannie Lou Hamer," in* The Horn Book Magazine, *Vol. XLIX, No. 2, April, 1973, p. 151.*

An eloquent, short biographical profile of a spirited black woman. . . . Jordan's simple, clear portrait captures Fannie Lou's essence and her roots. . . . [For] units on the South, women, and/or black history, this is a timely introduction to an active, dedicated, loving woman.

> *Rosalind K. Goddard, in a review of "Fannie Lou Hamer," in* School Library Journal, *an appendix to* Library Journal, *Vol. 19, No. 8, April, 1973, p. 67.*

Yes, this book is short and slight . . . and the illustrations [by Albert Williams] are pale and soulless, unlike their subject or

the vivid, vigorous language of the text. But happiness is the first full-length book about so great a woman as Mrs. Fannie Lou. Read on, children.

> *Alice Walker, "Can't Hate Anybody and See God's Face: 'Fannie Lou Hamer'," in* The New York Times Book Review, *April 29, 1973, p. 8.*

[June Jordan] has written a comprehensive biography of Mrs. Hamer. The book is valuable not only for its historical content; more important, it shows Mrs. Hamer's love for humanity, which gave her the resilience to challenge a whole system of oppression. The book does not create a fantasy in relating the life of a Black leader or present historical inaccuracies.

This is reading material appropriate for children from four to nine years old. If youngsters have not reached this reading level, the story should be read to them.

> *Norma Rogers, in a review of "Fannie Lou Hamer," in* Interracial Books for Children, *Vol. 5, No. 3, 1974, p. 4.*

NEW LIFE: NEW ROOM **(1975)**

Where'll they put the new baby? Momma, Daddy, Rudy (10), Tyrone (9), and Linda (6) are already crowded in a project flat. With great gusto, the solution is found during a family discussion—Linda will move out of the livingroom and into the big bedroom with the boys. When Momma leaves for the hospital, Dad and his friend move the furniture and leave the kids to arrange things which leads to a lot of mess, some fights, but finally an arrangement which suits everyone. Dad's own contribution is bright paint, humor, understanding, and ice cream. A warm and loving story that doesn't sacrifice style for simplicity, this will touch a responsive chord with newly independent readers—and adults who read it to them.

> *Marjorie Lewis, in a review of "New Life: New Room," in* School Library Journal, *Vol. 21, No. 9, May, 1975, p. 48.*

The children's often ingenious, strictly child-like solutions form a warm, albeit suspiciously violence-free, happening in which the process is the main thing. Jordan's easygoing, amusing narrative reveals a partly ordinary, partly idealized family that readers can enjoy for their good times.

> *A review of "New Life: New Room," in* The Booklist, *Vol. 71, No. 20, June 15, 1975, p. 1075.*

June Jordan has turned a common, realistic problem into a fun story. . . .

The reading is fun, too. The furniture is "pushed, pulled, lifted and turned" as it "bumps, slides, rolls, bangs and rocks." The painting project becomes a merriment of "spilling, dabbing, dripping, streaming and splashing." The words give a pulse to the action which matches the exuberant energy of the children in setting up their new life together.

The vibrations in this gem of a book are good and warm. . . .

> *"Human Values in Children's Books: 'New Life: New Room'," in* Human—And Anti-Human—Values in Children's Books: A Content Rating Instrument for Educators and Concerned Parents, *edited by the Council on Interracial Books for Children, Inc., Racism and Sexism Resource Center for Educators, 1976, p. 168.*

June Jordan has written a lucid narrative. . . . (p. 824)

The father's suggestion of the parents switching rooms with the children, and the practical imaginative manner in which the children are led into the solution is the only strong point of the book.

Despite the existence of a moment of fun the children portray in painting the windows and rearranging their furniture, the book holds little else to capture and hold the interest of a young reader.

The underlying moral of the "will and the way" may or may not be ascertained by a child. (p. 825)

> *Ruby Martin, in a review of "New Life: New Room,"*
> *in* The Reading Teacher, *Vol. 30, No. 7, April, 1977,*
> *pp. 824-25.*

[*New Life: New Room*] is well-written and cozy, if a bit too optimistic. It offers traditional sex roles for children: little sister is already knee-deep in housekeeping toys and feminine attitudes. She is mocked at first for this by her brothers, who later resign themselves to her toys and interests. Nonetheless, the book is a worthy addition to easy reading shelves.

> *Enid Davis, "Easy Readers: 'New Life: New Room',"*
> *in her* The Liberty Cap: A Catalogue of Non-Sexist
> Materials for Children, *Academy Press Limited, 1977,*
> *p. 97.*

KIMAKO'S STORY   (1981)

Seven-year-old Kimako sits on the stoop of her apartment building and watches the world go by. When a neighbor asks her to walk his dog for a week, Kimako advances beyond her stoop to explore her neighborhood. In her own words, she offers her observations of the small and everyday sights and sounds of the city. . . . Jordan captures the ingenuous impressions that belong to the state of childhood.

> *Marilyn Kaye, in a review of "Kimako's Story," in*
> School Library Journal, *Vol. 28, No. 1, September,*
> *1981, p. 110.*

Without sounding any emotional depths, but remembering how the most ordinary and grubby occurrences can be interesting curiosities to a kid, Jordan gives us a glimpse of Kimako's world and its restrictions, how she feels about it, and how any kid feels about being cooped up.

> *A review of "Kimako's Story," in* Kirkus Reviews,
> *Vol. XLIX, No. 3, December 1, 1981, p. 1465.*

[*Kimako's Story*] focuses on her environment, a New York City neighborhood that is busy, friendly, and heterogeneous. . . . This gives a picture of a bright child and of her enthusiasm and curiosity; it may be limited in appeal because it does not really tell a story that has structure and development.

> *Zena Sutherland, in a review of "Kimako's Story,"*
> *in* Bulletin of the Center for Children's Books, *Vol.*
> *35, No. 7, March, 1982, p. 132.*

Kimako strikes instant empathy in the reader and maintains it with her matter-of-fact description of her daily life. . . . Ingratiating details, recounted with a child's bland imperturbability are brought into sharper focus by the excellent illustrations [by Kay Burford].

> *Helen H. Shelton, in a review of "Kimako's Story,"*
> *in* Childhood Education, *Vol. 58, No. 4 (March-*
> *April, 1982), p. 258.*

[June Jordan] gives an authentic picture of a 7-year-old inner-city black girl at work and play. Kimako's world, as Miss Jordan presents it, is essentially the same as the world of suburban children. Because Kimako has witnessed so much, however, she seems an unusually perceptive child. . . .

Although she and her baby brother are brought up in a one-parent household, that is not the focus of the book. Instead, we're pulled into Kimako's immediate concern—which is how she copes with boredom now that her mother is working and she is housebound. Television is an option, but a dull one to Kimako. Instead she studies poetry in a puzzle book she receives. Kimako finds the puzzles stimulating and fun. The little teasers are truly novel. . . .

Poem Puzzle No. 3: "If somebody don't know how to jump—, / He must be lazy or he must be a—."

Miss Jordan renders Kimako's enthusiasm for these puzzles so delightfully that her little book could end at this point, but she treats us to more. . . .

Children are sure to be charmed by this natural little girl and her inner-city world.

> *Brenda Wilkinson, in a review of "Kimako's Story,"*
> *in* The New York Times Book Review, *April 18,*
> *1982, p. 38.*

(Jennifer Carolyn) Robin McKinley

1952-

American author of fiction, reteller, and editor.

McKinley brings an intuitive awareness of adolescence, an enthusiastic knowledge of classic fantasy, and an imaginative writing style to her romantic fairy tales and heroic fantasies. She achieved literary acclaim with her first two original novels, *The Blue Sword* and *The Hero and the Crown*, which powerfully depict two past eras in the imaginary desert kingdom of Damar. Inherent in McKinley's works is the young adult's struggle for identity and self-esteem, coupled with explorations of love and romance. Her protagonists are strong-willed females who sometimes function within the traditional male role: it is Harry and her ancestor Aerin, for example, who win their princes and save Damar from evil forces. A Tolkien enthusiast, McKinley has also borrowed from the Arthurian legends as well as Celtic and Norse myths for the "Damar" books. Her adaptations include a novel-length rendition of "Beauty and the Beast" and two fairy tales from the Grimm brothers.

Critics consistently applaud McKinley for her strong characterizations, which they feel bring depth and distinction to her works. While some of her books are faulted for including excessively detailed descriptions, almost all reviewers agree that McKinley writes absorbing stories and infuses them with a vivid sense of magic and place.

***The Blue Sword* was a Newbery Honor Book in 1983 and *The Hero and the Crown* received the Newbery Medal in 1985.**

(See also *Something about the Author*, Vol. 32 and *Contemporary Authors*, Vol. 107.)

GENERAL COMMENTARY

TERRI WINDLING AND MARK ALAN ARNOLD

It was necessary, perhaps inevitable, that Robin McKinley would become an important writer of our generation—prominence being one of the few social strata amenable to a woman with so much talent and personality. (p. 406)

[While] she claims to be a cynical misanthrope, Robin populates her novels and stories with some of the most civilized, decent, honorable, and well-rounded heroes and villains in modern fiction. She eschews not only helpless heroines and hapless swains but also the one-dimensional, rotten-to-the-core villains of other fantasies. More than adventure, more than romance, more even than her determination to write stories about "girls who do things," her tales are about honor—which is perhaps the key to the "real" Robin McKinley, just as the complexity and vividness of her created worlds resonate from the strength and vibrancy of her own life . . . .

It was in Maine that she wrote her first book, *Beauty: A Retelling of the Story of Beauty and the Beast*, which—like all her books—quickly gained a wide readership in its young adult hardcover edition and in its adult fantasy paperback publication. "I don't write 'children's books,'" Robin says; "I write my books for anyone who wants to read them." . . .

It was in Boston that she wrote *The Door in the Hedge*, her wondrous collection of original and retold fairy tales. (p. 408)

The Hero and the Crown was written while she was living with us in New York City, in a run-down section of Staten Island overlooking the bay and the lights of Manhattan, and she attributes the particular gruesomeness of Aerin's battle with the dragon to the daily stresses and dangers of living in an urban slum. . . .

Robin once told us that an odd—but typical—goal of hers is to become, forty or fifty years hence, "one of those cranky, literary old ladies—the kind who absolutely terrifies young writers." A matter of simply refining attitudes into mannerisms? No, Robin's "cranky, literary old lady" must be a person who, by constantly striving to excel and grow in the years and novels to come, earns a steady elevation from prominence to fame. Having known Robin for five years, we can attest that she has the talent, perseverance, and vision to secure a lasting place in literature. (p. 409)

> *Terri Windling and Mark Alan Arnold, "Robin McKinley," in* The Horn Book Magazine, *Vol. LXI, No. 4, July-August, 1985, pp. 406-09.*

BEAUTY: A RETELLING OF THE STORY OF BEAUTY AND THE BEAST (1978)

A captivating first-person fantasy novel that explores and expands some of the compelling elements of the original tale while leaving others untouched. The realistic characterization of Beauty (not as a victim but as a stubborn, self-taught scholar) and her father and sisters as a family is well integrated with the magic of the Beast; McKinley writes vivid settings of city, country, and castle, all of which serve as strong background to draw readers into the deepening relationship between Beauty and Beast. Several important questions quiver at the end—why were Beauty's sisters so blatantly changed from hostile, as in de Beaumont's original version . . . , to loving, and how has the Beast erred to incur his terrible enchantment in the first place? The book has a style and holding power all its own, however, and offers enjoyment to casual readers on the one hand and fields for thought and comparison to those who delve further.

> *Betsy Hearne, in a review of "Beauty: A Retelling of the Story of Beauty and the Beast," in* Booklist, *Vol. 75, No. 2, September 15, 1978, p. 222.*

The prototype of fantasy in the Western world is the fairy tale. Robin McKinley's *Beauty* is a retelling of the story of Beauty and the Beast, written in a realistic style that turns it into an adolescent identity novel. As Bruno Bettelheim points out in *The Uses of Enchantment*, this fairy tale has deep mythic and psychological symbolism: "The magical transformation which love achieves: Mature love and acceptance of sex make what was before repugnant . . . become beautiful." Or perhaps Beauty, as the psyche or soul, by transferring her love from her father to the Beast, represents the socialization of the id by the superego.

McKinley has made several changes in the story that reveal her insensitivity to these deeper meanings. Beauty is not beautiful, but the typical YA ugly duckling. Her sisters, on the other hand, are beautiful and loving, not evil. Beauty returns from the Beast's castle not to visit her dying father, but to tell her sister that her missing lover still lives. And like all lonely teenagers in YA novels, she has a confidant—her horse—and her relationship with this beast blurs the importance of her relationship with the other Beast.

Nevertheless, it's hard to keep a good story down, and the magic shines through. The homely scenes in the forest cabin as Beauty and her family try to make do after the father's business failure make a nice foil for her life of glittering luxury in the Beast's castle, where her every whim is gratified by invisible servants. And of course all fairy tales have those great happy endings.

> *Patty Campbell, in a review of "Beauty: A Retelling of the Story of Beauty and the Beast," in* Wilson Library Bulletin, *Vol. 53, No. 3, November, 1978, p. 273.*

McKinley's novel-length retelling of "Beauty and the Beast" incorporates no shift in viewpoint, no special perspective (Freudian or whatever), no witty embroidery, or extra dimension of any sort. It's simply a filling out of the story, with a few alterations.... McKinley doesn't seem to have done any speculating about Beauty's (or anyone's) motivation, but contents herself with providing background detail, elaborating on the descriptions of the enchanted castle, getting the plot from here to there via reasonably diverting sequences of events, etc. But she does accomplish all of this with some success. Those little incidentals detailing *how* things come to pass do keep the story flowing pleasantly even for readers already acquainted with its outline. If McKinley doesn't bring Beauty and her family to memorable life, she does give them separate personalities, situations to respond to, and a stage on which to interact. And her choice of a tale for such treatment couldn't be more fortunate; it's a natural for girls who have outgrown fairy tales but not the sort of romance that this one embodies.

> *A review of "Beauty," in* Kirkus Reviews, *Vol. XLVI, No. 23, December 1, 1978, p. 1307.*

The characterizations in this gentle, even pretty version of the folk tale are strong. The aura of magic around the Beast and his household comes surprisingly to life; even Bessie and Lydia, the "rustlings," speak and make themselves felt.... The real magic in the story, however, is the writer's deft handling of the enchantments—in her descriptions of the path opening through the forest, the forest itself, and the myriad of details in the magical castle. The fantasy is nearly always convincing and compelling, except for a somewhat jumbled time problem. Beauty, for instance, reads (in the Beast's enchanted library) books from several time periods, including *The Faerie Queen* and *Le morte d'Arthur;* she rereads the *Iliad* (which she knows well). But she also reads books not yet written, such as the works of Kipling, Dickens, Browning. She also reads 20th-century novels and cannot comprehend the idea of the motorcar or the telephone. Yet, Beauty drops an occasional "okay" in her conversation as if she were an American contemporary. Except for this rather jarring note, the adventure and tenderness come through. The book is sure to attract young adult readers—and some old ones too.

> *A review of "Beauty: A Retelling of the Story of Beauty & the Beast," in* Choice, *Vol. 16, Nos. 5 & 6, July & August, 1979, p. 668.*

[McKinley] does not so much flesh out the classic story as add to it a plausible if somewhat anachronized background.... **Beauty** in its opening chapters shows both the charm and the tendency to hand-wringer plotting of other books written by people who have read heavily in nineteenth century literature. In its closing scenes, it rings down the curtain rather hastily after announcing the troubles are over, rather than showing them resolved for some visible reason. But all this is to make less of a good book than has been made of it by a cult readership which calls it a great one.

Peter S. Beagle is quoted on the cover as having been moved and enchanted. For once, I find myself in substantial agreement with a cover quote. I was not moved to transports, nor was the enchantment a dazzling one. But as gentle fantasies go, **Beauty** is a warm and essentially innocent spell of quiet reading; a book whose author clearly had a defined idea of what beauty is, and set out to evoke it. That is not a mean ambition, nor did McKinley ever abandon it. Worse could be said about an author and her work; much more worse than better.

> *Algis Budrys, in a review of "Beauty," in* The Magazine of Fantasy and Science Fiction, *Vol. 62, No. 5, May, 1982, p. 36.*

[**Beauty**] extends the fairy-tale 'Beauty and the Beast' by a novelistic approach to characters and by a lavish attention to setting and social detail, so that it becomes a romance set in a neutral period in an anonymous country, about a merchant's family who live in the south and consider the north a barbarous, spirit-haunted land.... [In Beauty's] struggles against fear, and against her own diffidence, she is puzzled by the voices of invisible servants whose overheard phrases, chorus-like, offer clues to the girl's emotional growth. It is a strange, absorbing narrative, squarely concrete and domestic in one way, haunting and oblique in another. A touch of coyness now and then is soon forgotten as the story unwinds, familiar yet touched with new perceptions and offering new views of romantic encounters. The reinterpretation of fairy-tale could hardly go further.

> *Margery Fisher, in a review of "Beauty," in her* Growing Point, *Vol. 22, No. 4, November, 1983, p. 4160.*

THE DOOR IN THE HEDGE (1981)

McKinley again uses a style that proved successful in retelling "Beauty and the Beast" ... in these shorter, somewhat less compelling elaborations of four other fairy tales. The author's leisurely pace lingers (too long for most young readers) to evoke vivid scenes, resulting in imaginative if lengthy descriptions. This allows time, however, for character development, which she brings off with graceful acuity and attention to individual idiosyncrasies. Those with a penchant for romantic fantasy will enjoy "**The Stolen Princess,**" the story of a girl whose twin sister is kidnapped (at age 17) to be the bride of the prince of fairyland and whose daughter meets a similar fate; "**The Princess and the Frog,**" the tale about a kindly maiden who finds her true love when she helps an enchanted frog; "**The Hunting of the Hind,**" in which a princess tracks down a golden hind when others have failed and releases it from an evil spell; and "**The Twelve Dancing Princesses,**" in which a soldier follows the king's daughters beneath the ground to discover where and why they wear out their dancing slippers.

> *Barbara Elleman, in a review of "The Door in the Hedge," in* Booklist, *Vol. 77, No. 12, February 15, 1981, p. 810.*

Robin McKinley tells two original stories here, **"The Stolen Princess"** and **"The Hunting of the Hind,"** and retells with a sure touch two others, **"The Princess and the Frog"** and **"The Twelve Dancing Princesses."** She knows her geography of fantasy, the nuances of the language, the atmosphere of magic where running deer become beautiful maidens and frogs handsome princes. She develops the personalities of her characters fully, makes their motives plausible, their actions convincing. The characterization of the soldier in McKinley's rendition of **"The Twelve Dancing Princesses"** does much to enrich that story. This collection should interest readers of all ages who never tire of wizards and fairyland.

> *Alice Digilio, in a review of "The Door in the Hedge," in* Book World—The Washington Post, *April 12, 1981, p. 9.*

[In **"The Princess and the Frog"**] characters have been added—particularly the evil Prince Aliyander—providing narrative interest and emotional tension. The fully developed rewriting of **"The Twelve Dancing Princesses"**—perhaps the finest imaginative invention of the book—is a novella which follows the bare bones of the familiar story but adds subtlety, complexity, and suspense to what is only tersely stated in Grimm. Like a musical theme and variations the telling is full of digressions and decorations—arpeggios of ideas and of language—that add new depth to an old tale. All four stories are linked by a leisurely richness of expression and by their motifs: the temptation of fairy magic versus the joyful acceptance of human mortality and the immutability of love in the face of enchantment. (p. 434)

> *Ethel L. Heins, in a review of "The Door in the Hedge," in* The Horn Book Magazine, *Vol. LVII, No. 4, August, 1981, pp. 433-34.*

If only there were a door in this prickly prose. After cutting away the brier patch of narration and description, there remains very little real action and less dialogue in these [stories]. . . . McKinley has left her stamp on the Grimm tales [**"The Princess and the Frog"** and **"The Twelve Dancing Princesses"**] by plainly demarcating the good and the evil. In **". . . Dancing Princesses"** the princes and their underground domain are clearly demonic, while the princesses are under compulsion to elude their would-be discoverers and continue the nightly dance (unlike the original, in which there is some suggestion that it is the princes who are bewitched and the princesses dance voluntarily to release them). The frog prince now has a brother who is the agent of his metamorphosis and the torment of the princess, who is much too sweet and wise to renege on a promise or ever, ever to dash the creature against a wall (but then her name is Rana, Latin for frog). All this is meager, simplistic fare not made any richer by the hollow psychological observations, the meaningful looks and tacit understandings between characters, or the relentless descriptions. One forces one's self through, expecting a rewarding glimpse of marvels, only to come out on a parking lot. No doubt the author wanted to weave magic, mystery and wonder, but, for all her embroidery, this is a threadbare tapestry.

> *Judith A. Barber, in a review of "The Door in the Hedge," in* School Library Journal, *Vol. 27, No. 10, August, 1981, p. 77.*

Robin McKinley wrote that marvellous evocation of a remote and perilous world, **The Blue Sword.** Those who willingly surrendered to the magic of that book—and who could not?—must beware of too great anticipation of [**The Door in the Hedge**], which, while full of individual and characteristic touches, is an altogether slighter work. (p. 141)

[The two original stories spring] from a thoroughly digested appreciation of the folk tradition. The two folktales—'**The Princess and the Frog**' and '**The Twelve Dancing Princesses**'—are not straight retellings. Not only do they fill in all the colour and detail that the folk-tale leaves out, they give an altogether new interpretation to what were straightforward tales of enchantment. There are dark forces at work in these magical kingdoms. There are sinister elements too in the two original stories, one of which deals at considerable length with the theme of changelings, the other with the quest of the Golden Hind. In both of these stories I felt that the resolution scarcely justified the big build-up, but there was much excitement and wonder on the way. Some adult readers may feel that the writer is being rather too conscious a craftswoman. At times she seems intoxicated by the heady delights of her own prose. Fine writing it is, certainly, and sometimes wise too, but there is rather a lot of it. More than anything else I wonder who is going to read this book. Not the small children attracted by the magical subjects, who will surely be defeated—as will most parents who volunteer to read aloud—by the elegant complexity of the sentences and the artificial cadences of the dialogue. Romantic teenagers are probably the most likely audience, and geriatric readers who remember Andrew Lang (to whom Robin McKinley refers in her dedication).

For my part I am waiting for Robin McKinley to take me back into the wonderful world of Damar. (pp. 141-42)

> *M. Crouch, in a review of "The Door in the Hedge," in* The Junior Bookshelf, *Vol. 48, No. 3, June, 1984, pp. 141-42.*

The language is archaic, formal and consciously beautiful, the names echo the elvish names of Tolkien, Alora, Gilvan and Linadel, and the characters are beautiful too. They float around like so many Burne Jones models twined in art nouveau drapery. Fantasy can be used to state what cannot be stated or to reveal what must at the same time remain hidden but here I feel it is used as embroidery, simply because it is so pretty. The princesses are all as good as gold, the kings and queens as noble and tender as one could possibly wish, and the princes gallant, nay dauntless, in their quests. The stories should appeal to really dreamy romantic girls, and there is nothing wrong with escapism, is there? (pp. 137-38)

> *Dorothy Nimmo, in a review of "The Door in the Hedge," in* The School Librarian, *Vol. 32, No. 2, June, 1984, pp. 137-38.*

THE BLUE SWORD (1982)

[**The Blue Sword**] is a zesty, romantic heroic fantasy with an appealingly stalwart heroine, a finely realized mythical kingdom, and a grounding in reality that enhances the tale's verve as a fantasy. Kidnapped from a remote Homelander outpost by Corlath, king of the old Damarians (who, it is rumored, possess mysterious powers), Harry Crewe soon learns that, possessed of untrained power herself, she is destined to follow in the footsteps and under the protection of a legendary female warrior who generations before had led the Damarians into battle against their enemy. McKinley sparks her narrative with marvelous portrayals of Narknon, a hunting cat that adopts Harry, becoming a true companion, and of the magnificent native horses—particularly in scenes of Harry's warrior training as well as those of her riding, first for the sheer joy of it and finally riding into bloody battle against an evil, powerful, nonhuman force. The author has obviously modeled her Homelander ("Outlander" to the Damarians) civilization on that of Britain's far-flung empire of yore, but she is more comfortable with her evocation of the exotic Damarian culture that, taken together with the sword-and-sorcery elements, makes her narrative soar. The first in a projected series and a treat for fantasy lovers.

Sally Estes, in a review of "The Blue Sword," in Booklist, *Vol. 79, No. 3, October 1, 1982, p. 198.*

[*The Blue Sword*] places the epic battle of good and evil alongside the adolescent struggle to achieve a meaningful adult identity.... Corlath exemplifies his people—strong, fiercely independent, achingly romantic. Harry is a less intense but equally attractive character with tremendous courage and fortitude strengthened by a sense of humor. Although the narrative does not surge forward with the power it might, the measured pace in no way diminishes a fine novel of high adventure. The author hints at old tales, emphasizing the depth of her understanding of the heritage and the force of fantasy, at the same time creating a new language, a new landscape, and a new people—all unforgettable.

Amy L. Cohn, in a review of "The Blue Sword," in The Horn Book Magazine, *Vol. LVIII, No. 6, December, 1982, p. 660.*

On one level, Harry's story is curiously appealing for the number of paragraphs and their sentences which begin, "She ..." or "Her ...," and go on to describe a most human activity or thought not expected in a tale of fantasy but marked by the aspirations of Harry Crewe, like atomic number. On another level, the fantasy world of Damar resembles the obligations and measured alternatives available in a —"Knock, knock"— world less distant: "Harry struggled out of some of the oddest dreams she'd ever had into a dim and foggy reality full of bumps and jolts."

These different levels of reading, often distracting or annoying when treated by a less able writer, mingle with an attractive knowingness and generosity of spirit, of suggestion, of story, making for a comeliness of what may be the underlying polemic and yet no disruption of the story: "'I don't like my dreams—and I ... suspect that I am supposed to pay attention to some of my dreams.'"

"Their voices caused other sleepers to stir ..."

Among these lovely pages of mysterious names, swords, and distant battles, among all the action, bravery, mystical tongues and fantasy, a natural reconciliation is played out much as it is resolved in duller lives, and Harry bears a child.... (p. 446)

The Blue Sword is a story and a time which makes me look forward to its futures.... (p. 447)

Russ Williams, in a review of "The Blue Sword," in Best Sellers, *Vol. 42, No. 11, February, 1983, pp. 446-47.*

Readers of *The Blue Sword* will have Kipling, inevitably, at the back of their minds, but the author will have to excuse those who are also reminded of the Ethel M. Hull tradition of Sheik and abducted maiden—not just because of the actual event but also because the change from hostility to love, tactfully and smoothly traced, is the element which will probably commend the book to the mid-'teens as a richly satisfying read.... Each reader of this substantial, romantic tale will make a personal decision about its most significant aspect—whether it is the wide range of emphatically described scenes of chivalric warfare, memorably linked with richly depicted scenes of mountain and river, or the barely expressed, sharply suggested moods with which Harry and Corlath approach one another, or the ambiguities of good and evil inherent in the three-cornered conflict and in the attitudes of the diplomats and soldiers who try to establish honest contact with the races under their protection. Whether they read the book as political allegory or adventure-romance, their interest is likely to be keen, for this book from America is a most compelling piece of fiction. (pp. 4069-70)

Margery Fisher, in a review of "The Blue Sword," in her Growing Point, *Vol. 22, No. 1, May, 1983, pp. 4069-70.*

I found the first two chapters of Robin McKinley's book very hard going. With the entry of Corlath the action brisks up and never relaxes. If the reader tires it is not through tedium but through the relentless pressure on his emotions.

In the blurb the publisher makes a comparison with Kipling, and at times one might be on the North-West Frontier engaged in a difficult phase of the Great Game. But this is not India and the Raj but Damar, a land and a culture invented by the author. Such inventions are not to be lightly undertaken. What Ms. McKinley gains from it is liberation from the confines of reality and freedom to create a new history and new mores.... Good stuff this, and very exciting as described with the writer's formidable exuberance and intensity, but I couldn't help thinking that she could have done equally well with a real scene and a real place in Earth history.

However, it would be unworthy to quibble. This is a fine story of action, with a strong sense of morality underlying the excitement. I am not sure if we quite believe in Harry but she is drawn with subtlety. Corlath the king is rather too good to be true but his Riders, his bodyguard and inner cabinet, are done with lively individuality. Above all the wild scenery, and the feeling of joy in physical action, are conveyed most convincingly. We feel the heat and the terrible killing wind from the pass through which the Northerners must come. (pp. 172-73)

M. Crouch, in a review of "The Blue Sword," in The Junior Bookshelf, *Vol. 47, No. 4, August, 1983, pp. 172-73.*

[*The Blue Sword*] does right many of the things I've found done wrong in much recent fantasy. It is set in an imaginary world, but a pseudo-Victorian one, rather than the standard-issue textureless Middle Ages. This gets it several points right there. McKinley has a good sense of the outdoors. And she knows horses. Again, many points ahead of the average fantasy writer.

But I couldn't finish this one. Admittedly, I got about three-quarters of the way through, and was even entertained for the first half, before another, even more serious (if just as common) failing became overwhelming. The book is just too *comforting*. The heroine, an ill-adjusted adolescent, is carried off by magic-working nomads. She has quite a good time. She doesn't get homesick. She isn't afraid after the very beginning. The nomads are all very *nice*. And sure enough, she quickly becomes the center of attention, a champion honored by the nomads, a legendary heroine. *Of course* there is a secret about her which gives her unusual powers. . . .

It's all very perfunctory. The element of wish-fulfillment is too nakedly visible. McKinley is a skillful writer without doubt. This book will appeal to some audiences, particularly teenaged girls, but it left me fidgety.

> *Darrell Schweitzer, in a review of ''The Blue Sword,'' in* Science Fiction Review, *Vol. 12, No. 3, August, 1983, p. 46.*

THE HERO AND THE CROWN   (1984)

This splendid high fantasy is a prequel to *The Blue Sword.* . . . Aerin, the somewhat embarrassing offspring of the Damarian king and a witch-woman from the demon-haunted North, is snubbed and mistreated at court until she begins to prove her worth to the realm by discovering a lost formula for an ointment to protect the skin from dragon fire and then by singlehandedly killing the dragons that are destroying the kingdom. Two spine-tingling dragon-killing scenes, with perhaps the most vivid and realistically described fire-breathers in all fantasy, bring her into near-fatal confrontation with the hideous Black Dragon, whose severed head later supplies imaginative surprises and delicious nastiness. Ultimately Aerin is taken in hand, trained and wooed by a refreshingly unconventional wizard, just in time for her to stand by her people in their worst crisis. McKinley misses a couple of dynamite dramatic possibilities with regard to unpleasant relatives who disappear without getting their just desserts, but no matter. Aerin's story is still superb, filled with tender moments, vivid characters, satisfying action and sparkling dialogue. . . .

> *Lyle Blake Smythers, in a review of ''The Hero and the Crown,'' in* School Library Journal, *Vol. 31, No. 2, October, 1984, p. 169.*

Once again, McKinley's battle scenes are galvanizing and her romantic ones stirring, her characterizations have vitality, and her way with animal characters makes them distinct individuals without losing their animality. As much a romance as heroic fantasy . . . , this and *The Blue Sword* can be read independently, but, taken together, they enrich each other—and the reader as well.

> *Sally Estes, in a review of ''The Hero and the Crown,'' in* Booklist, *Vol. 81, No. 3, October 1, 1984, p. 211.*

Over the last several years, Robin McKinley has been quietly molding a world of fantasy—the kingdom of Damar and its environs—which is sure to thrive and outlast the majority of the current rather vast crop of kingdoms. . . .

I don't really consider this a children's book, except in the sense of those classics often referred to as such which are simply fine works accessible to young people. *The Hero and the Crown* is an excellent, gentle fantasy which in a literate and subtly understated fashion draws upon traditional arche-

types evoked in similar works to forge something uniquely the author's own. It is inevitable that McKinley's name will become increasingly prominent in the literature of imagination.

> *Paul Granahan, in a review of ''The Hero and the Crown,'' in* Best Sellers, *Vol. 44, No. 10, January, 1985, p. 399.*

Magic swords, trials by fire and water, dragon slayings—such is the stuff of traditional heroes' mythical quests. **''The Hero and the Crown''** puts a refreshing wrinkle in the familiar plot and gives these tasks to a captivating young heroine.

Aerin . . . is a charmingly unprincess-like princess. Shy and clumsy, she seems to lack most of the skills the royal family takes for granted. . . . But she more than makes up in courage and creativity what she lacks in courtly airs and graces. . . .

The author writes a sonorous, deliberately repetitive prose that, in its somber rhythms, evokes the sounds of Middle Earth as well as of ancient bards. It sustains the otherworldly atmosphere she painstakingly creates through the judicious use of arcane and invented words like ''hathor'' and ''sorka,'' restrained descriptions and interior monologues. An example: ''She remembered with a little shiver that she was no longer quite mortal, and the shiver was not for the knowledge but for the pleasure it now gave her, the first pleasure it had ever given her, that she might look forward to seeing Luthe again some-day.''

In this haunting fantasy of spells and sorcerers, long-lost amulets and primeval struggles between good and evil, Miss McKinley borrows liberally from J. R. R. Tolkien, the Arthurian legends, Celtic and Norse mythology—and even ''Star Wars'' symbolism. . . .

[Miss McKinley has] created an utterly engrossing fantasy, replete with a fairly mature romantic subplot as well as adventure. She transports the reader into a beguiling realm of pseudomedieval pageantry and ritual where the supernatural is never far below the surface of the ordinary. For those who like fantasy fiction, as I do, **''The Hero and the Crown''** succeeds.

> *Merri Rosenberg, in a review of ''The Hero and the Crown,'' in* The New York Times Book Review, *January 27, 1985, p. 29.*

[*The Hero and the Crown* is] as richly detailed and elegant as a medieval tapestry. . . . The culture depicted in *The Hero and the Crown* is less technologically sophisticated than that of the first book; the topography of the countryside differs dramatically. Yet the two novels are similar in the epic proportions of the plot which intertwines classic confrontations between good and evil with an adolescent's search for identity and yearning for self-fulfillment. . . . In the tradition of the romance-legend, [Aerin's] way is far from smooth; each step is an increasingly severe test of her fortitude and dedication; the choices are not easy; the price of victory is high, as the wizard Luthe indicates when he invests her with the Blue Sword. The revelation that she is no longer quite mortal is particularly sobering, yet the reconciliation of her old loyalties with newly awakened emotions is handled thoughtfully, delicately, and realistically: ''It was not that she left what she loved to go where she must, but that her destiny, like her love, like her heritage was double.'' The flavor of ancient legend permeates the style without overpowering the plot; places and characters are described with the authority of someone who is revisiting familiar scenes. Vibrant, witty, compelling, the story is the stuff of which true dreams are made. (pp. 59-60)

Mary M. Burns, in a review of "The Hero and the Crown," in The Horn Book Magazine, *Vol. LXI, No. 1, January-February, 1985, pp. 59-60.*

Simply and gracefully written, major and minor characters come alive as the reader shares their sorrow, despair, love and triumphs. Aerin is a strong and independent woman whose success is also a result of her pride and stubbornness. The story moves swiftly through Aerin's schooling and early adventures toward a compelling and unexpected climax. Blending the best of Sword and Sorcery with the Brothers Grimm, this novel is even more accomplished than *The Blue Sword.*

Rebecca Sue Taylor, in a review of "The Hero and the Crown," in Voice of Youth Advocates, *Vol. 7, No. 6, February, 1985, p. 338.*

TALES FROM THE JUNGLE BOOK (1985)

McKinley presents three early chapters from Kipling's classic describing the boyhood of Mowgli, the Indian boy raised by wolves. Simplified and stripped of the songs that originally began and ended each chapter, this version will be more accessible and attractive to a younger audience than the original. Although the prose is smooth and confident and the plot is intact, the richness of Kipling's language and the depth of emotion are diminished, perhaps inevitably, by adaptation.

Carolyn Phelan, in a review of "Tales from The Jungle Book," in Booklist, *Vol. 82, No. 2, September 15, 1985, p. 135.*

Dhan Gopal Mukerji

1890-1936

Indian-born American author of fiction and reteller.

Mukerji was the first writer of Indian descent to interpret Hindu folklore, epic poetry, and philosophy for English-speaking children. He is best known for his animal adventure *Gay-Neck, the Story of a Pigeon*, which describes a carrier pigeon who participates in the First World War and later travels to a lama's monastery to be cured of battle wounds and psychological scars. Like Rudyard Kipling, with whom he is often compared, Mukerji wrote narratives containing graphic descriptions of animal life. These works vividly recreate the ceaseless struggle of the jungle while representing the details of nature lore that fascinate children. In his retellings of the moral and religious stories his mother taught him—which range from nursery tales to the classic epic *Ramayana*—Mukerji developed a unique style which combines the simple directness of the Indian vernacular with the beauty of formal English prose. Themes such as the virtue of self-control, the renunciation of power, the bond between human beings and other living creatures, and the healing power of prayer and meditation permeate his books, which are recognized for providing intimate glimpses of an exotic world.

Hailed for writing poetic prose in the finest English literary tradition, Mukerji is praised as an author who made the spirit and wisdom of India accessible to children. Although some reviewers have questioned whether the mysticism of his stories is of interest to young readers, most critics acknowledge Mukerji's sincerity, skill as a storyteller, and respect for his audience and subjects.

Mukerji was awarded the Newbery Medal in 1928 for *Gay-Neck*.

AUTHOR'S COMMENTARY

The book I love most, and have dedicated to my mother, is **"Hindu Fables,"** more than one of which I heard from her own lips. Because it is the simplest of my works I dedicated it to her memory. (p. 11)

The little **"Hindu Fables"** I told in English to my mother's grandson who was born in America. My boy heard them again and again until he was seven. By that time they had become clear enough to deserve being set down in writing.

This transcribing Hindu cradle-tales from Indian folk-speech into modern English is an arduous task, if not an insoluble problem. First of all, today there is hardly any current folk-speech in the English language outside of slang. In the time of Queen Elizabeth, the folk-language of Britain must have been wonderful. India, who still lingers in the Seventeenth Century, has a marvellous common-speech. If in manufacture the English-speaking world has moved on from the hand-loom to industrialism, in the matter of story-telling it has passed from folk-lore to slang and realistic fiction.

On the contrary, in Hindusthan we are still trying to preserve the spinning wheel, and folk-utterance. Now, as a translator of my people's matchless speech I had a hard time discovering

UPI / Bettmann Newsphotos

in the English of our Twentieth Century folk an idiom picturesque and direct enough to convey the very simple art of the Orient. Slang is too direct. The so-called picturesque English prevalent in the Senate and the Congress is too involved. At last, worried almost to despair, I tried to invent an arrangement of words that would translate at least a bulk of the grace and directness of my native tongue. My solution of this problem has been the chief preoccupation of all my works.

There was another thing that I had in mind, too: namely, to convey the wisdom of life that Indians are taught by parents through folk-tales. You will notice in my **"Fables"** two kinds of morals stressed. The first is a useful every-day business moral, and the second is the transcendental morality through which men find God. The former stresses the science of surviving in our struggle against the unfair bully and the brute. The latter insists that after we have overcome a conscienceless adversary we must eliminate all materialism from our lives and make an effort to find God.

What has been made explicit in the **"Fables"** remains implicit in all the other books. In every one of my books hides a lesson. **"Kari, the Elephant"** is the history of a practical, as well as spiritual, relationship that a Hindu is taught to establish between man and the four-footed beasts.

"Hari, the Jungle Lad" contains the statement that man must understand and reverence all nature. He must not admit any

127

conflict between nature and civilization. In order to achieve this end, I had to fall back on many persons' experiences with which **"Hari, the Jungle Lad"** is replete.

Now we come to **"Gay Neck"** which some people call my best work. Most of it is a record of my experiences with about forty pigeons and their leader. Alas, as I went on writing the book I had to go beyond my experiences, and had to draw upon those of the trainers of army pigeons. Anyway, the message implicit in the book is that man and the winged animals are brothers.

The work that I consider the most valuable juvenile book that I have written is **"Ghond the Hunter."** In it I have sought to render the inmost things of Hindu life into English. It has been the ambition of my life to put into the hands of American boys and girls about sixteen years old a document that will portray the living soul of a Hindu boy. I hope boys and girls between sixteen and eighteen can be persuaded to read **"Ghond the Hunter."**

Last of all, **"The Chief of the Herd."** How did I think of it? An American friend suggested the central idea of the book. Then as I meditated on it, from day to day the Hindu ideal of a leader and leadership thrust itself to the foreground. At this stage a third thing entered the story of the Chief. This turned out to be the most important matter in the book. In fact, it is so important that I must discuss it at length.

Today in America we are eager to train a generation of leaders. America must produce titanic men and women who will leave their imprints on the pages of Art, Philosophy, Religion and Science. We should plan to rear a generation who will lead us towards those heights. At this writing I feel as if I discern the faces of a coming group of leaders among the children who are playing in the prairies, in the cities, and in the mountains of North America. To them I am sending out the story of Sirdar in **"The Chief of the Herd"** in order to suggest to them what the life of a leader is in the jungle, that laboratory of Nature where she has solved that problem. They should know the ideals and habits that go to make a natural leader. A holy man of modern India has said, "Character is the sum total of habits." The habits that our children are forming today will largely determine the character of their leadership tomorrow.

I am afraid **"The Chief of the Herd"** is an ambitious book. It does aim to speak of leadership to boys and girls of any age between seven and seventeen. Whether the book has missed its mark, I shall leave to my young friends to decide.

In the meantime, let me repeat that behind each one of my books the reader will discover a moral. I believe that there is no point in writing for the young, if one has no ethical convictions to set forth before them. We, their elders, must sincerely express our conclusions both moral and spiritual before the young. To examine and appreciate our ideals is one of their rights.

Any worth-while work of art, whether the Buddhist Jataka Tales or Aesop's Fables, each group, was composed by ancient story-tellers in order to "teach the wise conduct of life" to the boys and girls, as well as to the adults of their time. What nobler example can we moderns follow than the ones set forth by the teachers of Greece and India?

Art for art's sake, stories without morals can be the ideals of those who do not take the craft of juvenile story-writing seriously. Children of every race want to hear and examine mor-

als, provided they come out of a story as simply as fruits from a living tree.

In recent months I have received letters from India about the decline of story-reading among the young. Not only that, one correspondent has gone so far as to intimate that India has no juvenile literature. What a statement in a country of the Jatakas, the Panchatantra, and the Katha! India has the largest body of juvenile literature in the world. (pp. 11-15)

Because our tales have been preserved orally, no literary man thinks of calling it literature, which is not its fault. At a single glance one can see that some of the very best literature of many lands has come down to us by word of mouth. Untold generations have memorised and chanted the Rig and other Vedas. Homer's epics were recited from memory centuries before they were committed to writing. In Southern India even to this day one hears the Sanskrit Ramayana chanted by girls of good families. As for the Ramayana of Tulsidas one can hear all of it many times over from different persons in Northern India.

Like the priceless gems already mentioned the best juvenile stories have been orally preserved in India. There one can find innumerable children who cannot read and write yet; they have heard and memorised the fables of the Hitopodesha, the Indian model for La Fontaine, and many of the Jatakas, the Indian equivalent of Aesop and the Biblical parables in one.

It is better to teach the young the tales by word of mouth than to make them read mediocre stories written by the so called modern juvenile-artists. These men resemble genius in nothing but their fecundity.

In the province of Bengal, which I know most intimately, a child hears stories from three kinds of story-tellers. His nurse and his mother begin the process at home. Elders known and unknown to the young can frequently be seen telling stories under the shelter of a vast banyan. Then there are the Kathakas of the temples and the minstrels in the streets. In my own case all my knowledge and my ability to recite from the Ramayana and the Mahabharata, two of the greatest epics of mankind, I owe to those three sources. My inference is that because stories were told to me, I in turn developed the habit of story-telling.

The art of story-telling which is the predecessor of story-writing comes from the East. The travel of Indian fables to Europe and the rest of the world has been conceded by all competent scholars. Take the "five Tantras": it is said the Panchatantra has been translated into more alien tongues than Shakespeare.

Let us not forget that the fables called Panchatantra are told by parents, friends, and teachers in India to the young. Very few of us read them.

About four years ago when Professor Arthur Ryder brought out his new translation of the Panchatantra for the young of the United States of America the demand for it exceeded more than a dozen editions in one winter. In passing I might add that Ryder's is the only translation that carries over into English the poetry and excellence of the original. However, the Panchatantra has proven that our juvenile literature can be most popular among the American young.

In the presence of such glaring evidence to the contrary, to exclaim that we have no adequate juvenile literature in India is blasphemy. Our literature is so beautiful that for centuries it has captivated our people. Because we have been charmed by it we have taken the pleasant trouble of memorising it generation after generation. Very few countries in the world today can show such high appreciation of classical literature as we possess. And our greatest source of pride lies in the fact that our classical tales are our folk-tales. This indicates the height that folk-culture can achieve. There is no other folk-culture which can surpass that of India.

In my introduction to **"Rama, the Hero of India,"** I have made it clear that our great epics do not remain imprisoned between the covers of a printed work; but travel by word of mouth from person to person, and from age to age. Their styles influence the living speech of the day while their heroic episodes mould the character of the race by showing the triumph of the true over the false—Satyameva Jayate. (pp. 16-18)

[It] is my constant wish that the boys and girls of America should benefit from the ancient lores of India. (p. 18)

I hold that until a nation appreciates the common culture of another nation it will not be able to understand the value of international peace. We need peace between nations, because peace alone can augment the forces of true culture. If we know early in life how good our neighbor's culture can be, we shall think twice before we decide to destroy it by warfare. Of the many agencies working for international amity, appreciation of the cultures of other races is a very potent one. And this appreciation should be made into an art and a habit of the young of every land. (pp. 18-19)

> *Dhan Gopal Mukerji, in an introduction to his* Bunny, Hound and Clown, *E. P. Dutton & Company, Inc., 1931, pp. 11-19.*

GENERAL COMMENTARY

THE JUNIOR BOOKSHELF

In 1928 the Newbery Medal was awarded to a young Hindu of high caste who . . . had written a number of books for children. He had written them in a prose that had a beauty reminiscent of the great English masters, and he had written of a world where animals are endowed with human, spiritual qualities; where the virtues of meditation, kindness, loyalty, self-control and renunciation of power are extolled. He pictured the fierce life of the jungle, its great and small beasts, its expressive silences; the contrasts of its climate and the beauty of the Himalayas at dawn. He re-told the fables familiar to him in childhood, with their wisdom, humour and mischief.

Dhan Gopal Mukerji remains the best interpreter of the East that Western children have had, and though his books have never had the great popularity in this country which they appear to have had in America, they will continue to be read if our children are given the opportunity of reading them and, perhaps, if they are suitably introduced. They probably need such introduction before they will be accepted by appetites that have been fed on thrills and more thrills. (p. 129)

> *A review of "Gay Neck," in* The Junior Bookshelf, *Vol. 2, No. 3, May, 1938, pp. 129-31.*

RUTH HILL VIGUERS

Dhan Gopal Mukerji brought very special attributes to his interpretation of the Indian jungle. First of all he himself was a child of the jungle. His home was on its edge. His mother taught him not to fear it or its creatures, and the holy men, while he was still a little boy, took him into the jungle at night to watch till dawn, and taught him that the animals were his brothers. So he grew up a friend of the jungle dwellers. When

he was a young man he came to America where he received a western education, became a lecturer and married. After twelve years' absence he returned to India, where the urgency of his childhood memories demanded expression in books that would make India better understood by American boys and girls. His first book, *Kari the Elephant* . . . , is the story of an elephant in captivity and the young boy who cared for him; his second, *Hari the Jungle Lad* . . . , tells of a boy's life in the jungle and of his learning the laws and ways of the jungle to fortify him against the "risks of book learning." It is full of fascinating stories of beasts and of a boy's growing in knowledge of them and in accord with them. Other books followed—*Jungle, Beasts and Men* . . . , *Ghond the Hunter* . . . , *Chief of the Herd* . . . , all of which were drawn from his childhood love and knowledge of the jungle and which point up reverence for all nature and the spiritual relationship which the Hindu is taught to establish between man and beast.

In *Gayneck* . . . he used a wider canvas than in any of his other books. It is the story of a carrier pigeon which has sweep and excitement, beginning with its setting in Calcutta, and thence across the Himalaya Mountains and to France during the war. The classical English with which Mr. Mukerji was equipped when he first came to America is reflected in the writing of his books. There is beauty in his language and his unique style, and certain ornate passages create a harmonious setting for the moral precepts woven through the stories, the prayers for serenity and the wisdom which heals hate and fear. (p. 534)

> *Ruth Hill Viguers, "One World in Children's Books: Stories of Other Lands and Peoples," in* A Critical History of Children's Literature: A Survey of Children's Books in English from Earliest Times to the Present *by Cornelia Meigs, Anne Thaxter Eaton, Elizabeth Nesbitt, and Ruth Hill Viguers, edited by Cornelia Meigs, The Macmillan Company, 1953, pp. 524-38.**

ELIZABETH SEEGER

No stories make a more immediate and profound appeal to children than the stories of India. This, I believe, is because there is no other mythology or folklore that represents, as the Hindu does, the whole development of human life, from the lowest form of consciousness to the highest. It runs the whole gamut of human experience and there is food for every taste: humor, unlimited adventure, all the intricacies of relationship and conduct, and profound truth. For this is not a primitive literature to be relegated to the schoolroom or the scholar's shelves; by some miracle mythology, which is usually the product of early intuition, grew up in India when wisdom was already mature and folklore went on and still goes on voicing that wisdom in a thousand different fancies and parables.

In the ancient epics of India, in marked contrast to those of the West, virtue is extolled and the life of the spirit is of supreme importance. The great stories of Europe, because they are primitive and often barbarous stories, abound in instances of adultery, murder, greed, trickery and revenge, in which gods and heroes do not hesitate to take their parts. Not so in the East. Virtue retains its original meaning; it is manhood and strength and its attainment is high adventure. Rama, the hero of one of the epics—he who bent and broke the bow of Shiva, who built a causeway from India to Ceylon and defeated the demon-king of Lanka—is also the pattern of virtue, virtue born of self-control and the practice of meditation and prayer. The principal themes of the great story are the generous loyalty of four brothers, the renunciation of power, the love between husband and wife, the devotion of the divine monkey, Hanuman, and the triumph of the high gods over the powers of evil.

Even the animals of folklore practice religion and know the value of sacrifice, for India is wise and cannot help teaching. Her folklore, when it is not sheer amusement at the vagaries of mankind, is parable. . . . (pp. 53-4)

It is because of the great range of human adventure, the wisdom and nobility contained in these stories that they are still living, after thousands of years of life, in the hearts and on the lips of a whole people. They are sung and acted in villages, recited by the priests, told to children by their mothers and nurses. Their idealism has never been surpassed nor even reached and so they are ever new. And for the same reason they appeal immediately to children, American as well as Hindu. For any one who has had to do with the feeding of young minds knows that nothing, except perhaps the length of words, needs to be diminished to suit a child's taste; the difficulty is in finding material great enough to meet his expectancy. Here is such material, plentiful and of infinite variety. And is the culture of India not our rightful heritage? America came out of Europe and Europe out of Asia; in the homeland there is treasure stored up by our Aryan ancestors for us and for our children. But, because thousands of years and thousands of miles intervene between them and us, an interpreter is needed.

American children have found in Dhan Gopal Mukerji an interpreter after their own hearts. . . . Though he spoke to hundreds of adult audiences and though he wrote books that are probably the best and most intimate interpretations of Hindu life to adult readers, his first book was for children and the majority of his books, a dozen or so, are children's books. But since he gave his best to children, never underestimating their capacity to understand, his writings are immensely enjoyable to all ages.

He retells in lovely language the stories that he was told as a child, tender fables that could have come only out of the heart of wisdom, funny stories that only millennia of worldly experience could have invented, that tickle children's mischief-loving humor. In *Rama* and in *The Master Monkey* he makes one of the great epics readable to children. He makes familiar to them the figures that are revered by every one in India. He acquaints them with the delightful and inimitable monkey, Hanuman, who is now the presiding deity of gymnasia and athletic games. For him a seat is still prepared at village plays based on the life of Rama, because his spirit is dedicated to the worship of his master and so wherever Rama is praised, there Hanuman loves to come.

Quite as valuable as these books are the ones in which Mukerji, out of his own experience, tells of the daily life of India. In *Ghond the Hunter, Gay-Neck, Kari the Elephant* and others, he pictures for us his own boyhood and the life he saw about him or knew through friendships. Through these books one gains, directly and intimately, a knowledge of the life of a household of high caste and that of a village with all its varied activities; we are shown the astounding contrasts of Indian landscape and climate, Himalayan sunrise after the quick dawn, the fierceness of jungle life unknown to our temperate lands, the silver oppression of the rains. Gay-Neck's master, who is Mukerji himself, an eager, highly-sensitive lad, took him down the Ganges, to the foot-hills of the Himalayas, into the jungle and to a Buddhist lamasery where the bird was healed of fear. In several books the chief character is bird or beast who lives with man in that close understanding that comes with a mellowed civilization and long experience.

He was a lucky child who ever heard Mukerji speak. At the school that his son attended as a small boy he used to talk occasionally to the children. No matter what subject he may have started with, he ended invariably in the Indian jungle where his listeners most wanted him to take them. Speaking always as to equals, reciting occasionally a sonorous Sanskrit line, he held them spellbound as he told them what Hindu children are taught about fear and about meditation. They learned that an animal is pursued because he emits an odor produced by his fright, that a fearless creature goes unharmed by its fiercest enemy as a holy man can sit undisturbed on the floor of the jungle. He talked to them about silence and the difference between it and mere stillness and they sat with him in a silence that none of them, probably, had ever heard before. They trusted him readily because he was sincere with them and he took them into his confidence to the point of making them his collaborators, telling or reading them the stories as he wrote them, testing his skill by their approval. *Gay-Neck* was written in Brittany where every afternoon he read to the children who gathered about him on the beach the chapter he had written in the morning. (pp. 54-6)

Whatever attraction or affinity brought him and kept him here, where his spirit often suffered, the West has gained immeasurably by his coming and India cannot have lost by having so eloquent an interpreter among us. Fortunately much that he brought to us is treasured between the covers of his books and can be forever kept. (pp. 57-8)

Elizabeth Seeger, "Biographical Note: Dhan Mukerji and His Books," in Newbery Medal Books: 1922-1955, *edited by Bertha Mahoney Miller and Elinor Whitney Field, The Horn Book, Inc., 1955, pp. 53-8.*

JUNGLE BEASTS AND MEN (1923)

A quality of childlike directness in the prose of Dhan Gopal Mukerji gives to his writing an undoubted power. By the fewest and simplest of strokes, a mood is created—and nothing is done to destroy it because nothing is done to embellish it. The effect is achieved immediately; the background is sketched in with a fine economy and the vivid action is projected across it in broad outlines. If one examines the style in detail, one finds practically no features of unusual distinction; the phrasing is unstudied and the structure of the narrative is elementary. But the mood is there, and consequently these tales of panic and death, of magic and miracle and mystery, come to the reader with their freshness unimpaired.

L. B., in a review of "Jungle Beasts and Men," in The Freeman, *Vol. VIII, No. 194, November 28, 1923, p. 287.*

This fine writer about Indian animals has written . . . a volume of stories, one called *Facing the Tiger in the Jungle* which gives quite a different idea of the jungle from that in books by white hunters and wardens. The author is recalling an incident when, as a boy, he and a friend went on pilgrimage to the Himalayas and suffered a dangerous interruption to their journey. In a short space the author has given a piercingly real picture of the jungle and those who are native to it.

Margery Fisher, in a review of "Jungle Beasts and Men," in her Growing Point, *Vol. 5, No. 1, May, 1966, p. 728.*

HARI, THE JUNGLE LAD   (1924)

In telling imaginative tales of a native boy in an Indian jungle Mr. Mukerji may not be challenging the obvious comparison, but there is definite reason to infer that he would relish having us all discover that a Bengali, too, can work magic, and in English, with these materials.

No such discovery is warranted by **"Hari,"** his second book of the kind. Up to a certain point he has the powers of magicians; he is a fluent storyteller, he writes with charm, his style and narration are at ease within the requirements of writing for children. But his invention is utterly naïve. On me—and, I should expect, on wideawake readers ten years old—the hunting adventures of Hari and his father fail to work, because they are merely "steep" in the Münchausen way; there have been no exploits to match some of them since the Baron's. And though tales like these are not, of course, to be judged with a literal mind, yet when their content is natural, their method reminiscence and their medium versimilitude, one may fairly ask regard for the limitations of woodcraft, animal behavior and game shooting.

> *Harry E. Dounce, "In the Jungle," in* The Saturday Review of Literature, *Vol. I, No. 15, November 8, 1924, p. 259.*

[*The following excerpt is taken from a review of several books, including Padraic Colum's* The Island of the Mighty. *Leonore St. John Power begins her review by quoting Colum on his collection of stories—"They tell of nothing but youth's appearance and youth's adventure"—then uses the same quote in part to describe Mukerji's* Hari, the Jungle Lad.]

In **"Hari, the Jungle Lad,"** "youth's adventure" is perhaps not of . . . signal importance, but it is none the less interesting and absorbing to the children who follow it. The author, Dhan Gopal Mukerji, is himself familiar with the jungles of India, and he pictures tiger hunting, elephant tracking, the rush of floods, the battle of man with beast, in a manner that is convincing and thrilling.

> *Leonore St. John Power, in a review of "Hari, the Jungle Lad," in* The Outlook, *Vol. 138, No. 11, November 12, 1924, p. 410.*

A remarkably vivid story of life in the jungle of India where Hari is taken by his father, a famous hunter, to learn its ways and its mysteries. The atmosphere of this fascinating unknown life is admirably balanced by the sustained interest in the plot—the search for Kari the lost elephant.

> *A review of "Hari, the Jungle Lad," in* The Booklist, *Vol. 21, No. 4, January, 1925, p. 158.*

GAY-NECK, THE STORY OF A PIGEON   (1927)

To every minute circumstance of the marvelous birth and training of this beautiful pet, Mr. Mukerji has brought the boy's understanding, respect and affection for animal life which characterized his earlier stories, **"Kari the Elephant"** and **"Hari the Jungle Lad,"** but in **"Gay-Neck"** he has gone further and has written a story with an international motif, which is sure to appeal to many older readers as well as to boys and girls. Chitra-griva [Gay-Neck], he tells us, was the gifted son of a tumbler and a carrier of most noble family who was considered the most beautiful pigeon of her day. . . .

The story, itself, carries such a novel thrill of adventure and wealth of Eastern color that one regrets that the author did not make a non-stop flight from India to France. Pausing to point a moral with the pictorial imagination alight is not a good thing to do in any story book. **"Gay-Neck"** has originality and vitality enough to survive its too insistent teaching, but it would have been a stronger book if fuller confidence had been placed in the imagination of the reader.

Following every great war there seems to be a determined effort to clear the decks for the next generation by telling children what to *think*, as well as what to *do*. This has always seemed to me, and at no time more so than at present, both dangerous and unfair. The mind and heart of a child should be as free to grow and expand naturally as we have at last learned his body must be if he is to attain full stature. If he wants to share anybody's conclusions he must come to them by his own road and in his own good time. Children's books are essential equipment for playgrounds of the mind to a degree that they respect the integrity of the individual child, and the independence of his judgment. In short, propaganda and special pleading of any cause have no rightful place in their story books.

Character, incident, the color and feel of strange or familiar countries, and the release of the author's personal relation to childhood in general and his own in particular, are determining factors in the longevity of children's books. Mr. Mukerji has invested his story with all of these to an unusual degree, but I think he has made a premature demand upon the emotional reaction of his readers by the introduction of human concern which force his flying hero to carry heavier freight than any pigeon should. Since the book is one that will have a stronger appeal for children over ten than for the younger ones, judicious skipping and the vitality of Boris Artzybasheff's fine drawings will release Chitra-griva to take first place as a carrier pigeon.

> *Anne Carroll Moore, "A Pigeon's Life Story," in* New York Herald Tribune Books, *August 21, 1927, p. 8.*

The art of domesticating pigeons goes back thousands of years in India, and the birth, training, and mating of Gay-Neck, his experiences in the jungle with Ghond, "the greatest hunter in Bengal," and their work together in the Great War, where "death coiled and screamed like a dragon and crushed all in its grip," is a tale as unusual as it is beautiful. . . .

So much is written yearly that might be classed (in tabloid lingo) as twaddle for tots that it is a genuine pleasure to recommend that this absorbing story be given to children, and any one else who is interested in bird-lore.

> *A review of "Gay-Neck: The Story of a Pigeon," in* The Outlook, *Vol. 147, No. 5, October 5, 1927, p. 156.*

A new book by the author of **"Kari, the Elephant,"** will be sure of a welcome from a wide circle of all ages. This story of **"Gay-Neck"** . . . is more fascinating even than the adventures of Kari, partly because the material is so fresh. We had heard from Kipling and others a good deal of the habits of elephants, but we do not remember any previous animal story books about pigeons, with the exception of "Chico." Add to this a plot full of hair-breadth escapes on the part of the clever pigeon from hawks, eagles, and airplanes, and equally hair-breadth escapes from tigers and elephants on the part of his young master, and you have the material for a real "thriller" that will please the taste of even effete little movie fans. But unlike its movie counterparts, this story is told in Mukerji's excellent style, vivid, but thoughtful, with a good bit of Indian philosophy thrown in. Only once in a while are we conscious that Mukerji is using a tongue not his own, as when he says, ''Let me give you just a slight picture of our setting,'' but for the most part he puts many of our native writers for children to shame. Listen to this bit of description:

> The stillness was intense—like a drum whose skin had been so stretched that even breathing on it would make it groan. I felt hemmed in by the piercing soundlessness from every direction. Now and then like an explosion came the crackling of some dry autumn leaves as a soft-footed wild cat leaped on them from the branch of a tree not far away. That sound very soon sank like a stone in the ever rising tide of stillness. . . .

We can thoroughly recommend ''Gay-Neck'' to American youths, philosophy and all.

Mary Gray, ''The Saga of a Pigeon,'' in The Saturday Review of Literature, *Vol. IV, No. 12, October 15, 1927, p. 214.*

The first part of the book is devoted to [Gay-Neck's] training by the boy who owns him, guided by Ghond, a famous hunter. There are descriptions of escapes from hawks and human enemies and accounts of accidents, which in the hands of a lesser writer might make dull reading but as Mr. Mukerji relates them are fascinating and unusual. There are jungle excursions with Ghond, providing glimpses into the curious ways of wild creatures in their native haunts. *Gay-Neck* . . . is not strictly scientific. Part of the first section of the book permits Gay-Neck to relate one of his adventures which the boy and the hunter did not see. The second part of the book is devoted to World War I, and again the pigeon tells part of the story. The war seems more dreadful when it is described from the standpoint of a confused and terrified bird. Gay-Neck, although injured, gets his message through and brings honor to the Indian army. After the war, the bird is cured, but he will not try to fly. Ghond, too, is sick with fear. For the healing of his friends' hate and fear, the boy journeys with Ghond and Gay-Neck to a lamasery high up in the Himalayas. The old lama gives them a meditation on courage which they are to say twice daily for Ghond and Gay-Neck. After ten days in the high mountain retreat, meditating faithfully, Gay-Neck flies again and Ghond is freed of his fear. The book ends with:

> . . . Think and feel love so that you will be able to pour out of yourselves peace and serenity as naturally as a flower gives forth fragrance. Peace be unto all!

This excursion into the mysticism of the Far East is baffling to most American children, and the literal-minded shy away from it. The more thoughtful ought to be able to look at the religious philosophy of the East as they looked at the religion of Dobry [in Monica Shannon's *Dobry*] . . . or Dawn Boy [in Laura Armer's *Waterless Mountain*] . . . with interest and respect. But as a matter of fact, it is too remote from their experience to seem anything but ''queer'' to the average children. This is their own word for it: ''It's a queer story,'' they say, ''and pigeons aren't very interesting.'' Probably the continual shift from the first to the third person is another cause of confusion and also contributes to the sense of queerness. So, despite the Newbery Medal, *Gay-Neck* is an unpopular

book. This is a pity because it contains some thrilling adventures beautifully related, and the philosophy could be explained by an adult.

Perhaps this book belongs to special children, to homes, or to religious education. The idea that hate and fear breed their own poisons, which include sickness and more fears, is, after all, an idea common to many religions. So is the reverse idea that God, or goodness, or love, is a source of increasing strength and power. The adolescent can grasp such ideas, but they are undoubtedly too abstract for children. *Gay-Neck* need not be dropped from lists of recommended juveniles, but adults should know in advance that it belongs to children fourteen years or older. It is a book which needs to be read aloud, perhaps, and discussed bit by bit. Or it might be used as one book in a series of books for a class discussion of comparative religions. (pp. 443-44)

May Hill Arbuthnot, ''Animal Stories: 'Gay-Neck','' in her Children and Books, *Scott, Foresman and Company, 1947, pp. 443-44.*

[*Gay-Neck, the Story of a Pigeon*] received the Newbery Medal nearly fifty years ago. . . . [The] story is told from three viewpoints: the pigeon's owner, the old hunter, and from Gay-Neck's point of view in ''the grammar of fancy and the dictionary of imagination.'' This technique of shifting narration sometimes makes the story difficult to follow. The theme of the book is as modern as the challenges of the moment, that courage and love may be communicated to others to overcome the hates and fears of life. (p. 511)

Charlotte S. Huck and Doris Young Kuhn, ''Books for Special Interests,'' in their Children's Literature in the Elementary School, *second edition, Holt, Rinehart and Winston, Inc., 1968, pp. 507-44.**

Gay-Neck has become a period piece since it was awarded the Newbery Medal in 1928. I hope nobody will try to judge the book according to modern ideas about animals in fiction; it must be read in its own right. . . . The author's respect for animal life pervades the book and makes poetry of his musings on life in general. There is a serene sensitiveness in his descriptions of the bond between pigeon and youth in this grave and beautiful book.

Margery Fisher, in a review of ''Gay-Neck,'' in her Growing Point, *Vol. 8, No. 7, January, 1970, p. 1464.*

GHOND, THE HUNTER (1928)

This is not only a fascinating animal story, but it is much more than that. It reflects the spirit of the jungle and the animal life there in a most convincing way. It also reflects the whole history of man in India. By reading it one gains an understanding of Hindu civilization and philosophy, but it is not technical or abstract. The author knows how to tell a story. He says, ''But the abstract grows from the tree of boredom; monotony hangs like a fruit from its every bough, . . .'' The narrative is personal and is effectively told. The quiet strength and wisdom of the author are evident all through. . . .

This is truly a great story of the jungle and its inhabitants, the tiger, the cobra, the python, the mongoose, the elephant, the birds, and the human animals. The author is not only a hunter, he is a poet who loves beauty. The story is in prose, but it is poetic prose. The literary value, in the opinion of a naturalist, is much above that of the average juvenile book. (pp. 518-19)

> *Clyde Fisher, in a review of "Ghond the Hunter,"*
> *in* The Saturday Review of Literature, *Vol. V, No.*
> *21, December 15, 1928, pp. 518-19.*

HINDU FABLES, FOR LITTLE CHILDREN (1929)

From the fables the author heard during his childhood he has selected ten whose characters, the animals of the jungle, reveal the humor and wisdom of the East. . . . These fables are much longer than those of Aesop or La Fontaine and are not as simple as the Jataka tales retold by Babbitt.

> *A review of "Hindu Fables, for Little Children," in*
> The Booklist, *Vol. 25, No. 10, July, 1929, p. 400.*

There are monkeys and crocodiles in Dhan Gopal Mukerji's **"Hindu Fables"** . . . , a book that comes a little further up the age-scale and is the first this distinguished author has made for very little children. The animals in it are remembered from tales told him by his nurse in India, and have something of the same delicate individuality one finds in the friends and playmates of Brer Rabbit; there are good Indian rabbits here, too. I think St. Francis of Assisi would have liked Mr. Mukerji's animals.

> *May Lamberton Becker, in a review of "Hindu Tales,"*
> *in* Outlook and Independent, *Vol. 152, No. 10, July*
> *3, 1929, p. 392.*

THE CHIEF OF THE HERD (1929)

To write a book a year, to keep the style alive and suggestive and to achieve a result that stands out from one's other efforts is no mean feat. There appears this year from the pen of Dhan Gopal Mukerji a slender volume which seems to me quite the equal of its predecessors, **"Ghond the Hunter"** and **"Gay-Neck, the Story of a Pigeon."** In **"The Chief of the Herd"** he recounts in vivid fashion the adventures of Sirdar, the leader of a herd of elephants, together with distinctive conceptions of his mate Rhada, whom Sirdar liberated from captivity and possessed after a bitter struggle with Kumar, a rival bull; of Ajit, the wise and venerable one, and of Bahadur, the son of Sirdar. Each of these deserve specific mention, for it is more than the fiction of personality that gives them distinction. Rather it is their relation to each other as individual members of the herd.

Thus at the outset let it be said that **"The Chief of the Herd"** is not simply another animal story. Those authors who can invest Fido with human capacities without making of Fido an unnatural prig are few and far between. Dhan Gopal Mukerji is among their number. His success lies in large measure in the fact that in the telling of the tale he slips without notice from the ego of Sirdar, Ajit or Radha, now to the person of Ghond the Hunter, and again to his own natural role as expositor of the ways of the jungle. . . .

Somewhere in **"Ghond the Hunter"** occurs the question: "Have you ever heard Silence?" This query follows hard upon a description of the meditation of Ghond wherein is described the curious medley of tones and pitches that characterizes the slightest sounds of the jungle in the ear of one who listens. At the height of Ghond's concentration it is related that "Silence . . . is full of tongues." This passage is but an example

of a quality of creative receptivity which exists vividly in the work of Dhan Gopal Mukerji.

The imaginative man in the depths of the jungle, on the peak of a mountain or a speck in a vast plain becomes unconsciously attuned to the peculiar circumstances of his situation. And paradoxically in the depths of meditation he is keenly alive and responsive to those same circumstances. In such a condition the happening of the most natural event, the flight of a bird, the cheep of insects, or the call of a wild elephant is etched into the core of his being. Time and again the writing of Dhan Gopal Mukerji bears evidence of this mood, at once receptive and creative.

Furthermore, in this condition the mind of man devises the most simple (in the best sense of that much abused word) of its conclusions. It moves almost intuitively from some half imagined premise to an enlightened result. Here the sophisticated are likely to be led astray. They will dismiss the reflections of the author on the life of this herd of Hathis as sentimental moralizing. In this wise will they miss the depth of his insight, the accuracy of his observation and the slow maturity of his thought.

"The Chief of the Herd" is written in the beautiful language and unusual style that is the author's own. Let us look at the Himalayas through his eyes. He says:

> Seen from this elevated plane, the Himalayan peaks looked superb. Above the immediate verdant foothills the white summits, instead of flaming into red at sunset, were wrapped in violet, silver, purple and carmine. Every sunrise the ranges crouched at the threshold of heaven like lions of amethyst.

There is a wealth of watching in back of these words.

> *Dudley Cammett Lunt, "The Wisdom of Elephants,"*
> *in* New York Herald Tribune Books, *September 1,*
> *1929, p. 6.*

There is always a fascination about the jungle, particularly if the knowledge of it is gleaned through a book that brings it vividly before one. Mr. Mukerji has done a splendid piece of work in **"The Chief of the Herd."** One gains information on elephants in such a way as to make the reader feel a tremendous admiration for those mighty, trunk-waving beasts, which most of us only see in a circus or zoo. The inviolable rules of leadership, the keen perspicacity of those worthy of the right to leadership, are brought out in a telling fashion, while descriptions are meticulously effective. We see vividly the elephant approaching the water, hearing the "sickening shiver of leaves" and realizing the python is there. "I was certain of it by the trembling echo that creased the stillness of the water." In that brief sentence there is conveyed all the quiet abhorrence of a scene with a serpent in the foreground. The chapters dealing with the flood that overtook the elephants and of their actions at that time are singularly stirring, and to balance these there are quiet, delicate passages, pellucid and poetical.

> *Mary Graham Bonner, in a review of "The Chief of*
> *the Herd," in* The New York Times Book Review,
> *October 6, 1929, p. 34.*

[*Chief of the Herd*] is another outstanding book of the year for boys and girls. In its pages, life in the jungle is re-created by a man whose stories are known for the delicacy of their touch and the sensitiveness of their perception. In the jungle, Sirdar is born. In the jungle he grows up, learns to live and eventually becomes leader of his herd. It is a book to place beside *Gay Neck*. . . . And for boys and girls who enjoy animal stories there could be no better choice. (pp. 308-09)

> Helen Ferris, in a review of "Chief of the Herd," in The Bookman, New York, Vol. LXX, No. 3, November, 1929, pp. 308-09.

It is impossible to agree with the publishers' estimate of *Chief of the Herd*. . . . We should like to see the chief feeding the souls of his herd as well as their stomachs, but only one who has achieved the author's intimacy with elephants may claim such a favour. The stories give us no feeling of reality, and surely *hati* is an unusual form to give the elephant's name.

> A review of "Chief of the Herd," in The Spectator, Vol. 143, No. 5290, November 16, 1929, p. 731.

The descriptions of scenery are full of colour, and the story has dramatic turns—the fight between Sirdar and Kumar, his second in command, the charge of the herd through the encircling line of howdah elephants, the moonlight raid on the village, the great flood which came down from the hills and swept the jungle life before it. The tale is told in the third person; but it cannot quite escape the difficulties of every attempt to get inside the thoughts of the brute creation. The descriptions appear at times as a confusion of two planes, as when Sirdar is made to say, when asked to interfere between a python and its prey, "It is the business of the jungle gods, and not of pachyderms, to teach snakes vegetarianism." But for readers of the age which takes such snags in its stride the tale will be of constant and at times breathless interest.

> "Animal Lives," in The Times Literary Supplement, No. 1451, November 21, 1929, p. 969.*

RAMA, THE HERO OF INDIA: VALMIKI'S "RAMAYANA" DONE INTO A SHORT ENGLISH VERSION FOR BOYS AND GIRLS (1930)

AUTHOR'S COMMENTARY

The present English adaptation of Valmiki's Ramayana is the effect of many causes. Not the least of them is the fact that there is not a single good English version of it that is accessible to the young in the United States. The second factor that led us to write the Rama-story was the need for it among the children of the Dalton School where my wife teaches. Were it not giving away a real secret I should say that portions of the present work were tried on the children of the school. Some of them made a play and acted the story for our benefit.

The work that my wife has done on this book is much greater than the reader will ever know. If the Ramayana in its present form is clear it is due to her efforts. Without her insistence on lucidity we could not have attained our goal. Whatever clarity the book possesses is the result of her constant labour.

May the book succeed in meeting a real need among children of school-going age not only in the United States of America but throughout the English-speaking world.

> Dhan Gopal Mukerji, "A Word of Explanation," in his Rama: The Hero of India, E. P. Dutton & Co., Inc., 1930, p. vii.

Like the other great epics and hero cycles with which young people have been made familiar in adaptations and retellings, the Ramayana can claim an antiquity of thousands of years, but unlike them it still, in India, either in the original Sanskrit or in the vernacular, plays an active part in everyday life. Mr. Mukerji tells us that from babyhood on Hindus hear these tales, and when they are older learn to recite and chant them instead of reading them from the printed page; as a result they represent not only tradition and the past but form a living contribution to the life and speech of the Hindu people today.

Eastern legends because of their less familiar setting present more difficulties to the average reader than do the Greek epics, the Siegfried or King Arthur stories. Thus Mr. Mukerji's leisurely treatment is valuable, tending as it does to build up gradually a sense of familiarity. This whole volume devoted to the Ramayana succeeds better than Mrs. Steele's more condensed "Hero Tales of India" in making the reader aware of the grave and serious beauty of these legends.

The book is rich in imagery. There are "mountains like spears of sapphire," "rain like walls of moonstone between India and Ceylon," the sea "that echoes like a receding dream," "snow peaks that burnt at sunset like torches, then were lost to sight as the stars flung their silences upon the world." Besides these splendors of earth and sky we see King Janaka's palace with its tree-tall gates of beaten-gold, the diamond towers of Lanka, or Prince Indrajit's house of amethyst, ivory and onyx. Then, too, the austere beauty of the perfect life that we associate with Hindu ideals of conduct is suggested—"Untraveled though Rama was, the fragrance of his soul had blown with and against every wind to all the civilized countries of his time," and "good deeds follow a soul as evil actions do, even to the very Heaven where a soul seeks refuge and no man can change the result of his deeds, be he a beggar or a prince."

The first part of the book is better than the last, which seems slightly hurried, though the picture of Hanuman, the wise and noble monkey, in whom Pavana, the god of wind and storm, was incarnated, who leaps across the world to rescue Sita, Rama's wife, from the demon king, and plucks the sun from the sky to save the life of Rama's brother, is unforgettable.

> Anne T. Eaton, in a review of "Rama: The Hero of India," in The New York Times Book Review, September 28, 1930, p. 30.

In this story of the *Ramayana*, the great epic poem of India has been vividly and connectedly retold for young people. It will make its greatest appeal to the exceptional boy and girl and also to those adults who delight in Mr. Mukerji's poetic prose, for he has done a fine piece of work in retelling "these doings of Rama."

> T. C. B., in a review of "Rama: The Hero of India," in Library Journal, Vol. 55, No. 20, November 15, 1930, p. 925.

[This book] requires no particular maturity on the part of the reader; yet it puts him on terms of immediate intimacy with legendary India and its great hero, Rama, the "heart-ravisher." Rama's bride, Sita, kidnapped by the ten-necked demon Ravanna, that "loathing's very soul," and kept by him in captivity during all those years which count for so little in India's creed, his heroic brother Lakshmana, and the tremendous figure of Hanuman, the giant monkey, are all presented in such a way that Rama's message comes almost as a surprise to us. The Puritan tendency in Rama finds utterance in such a sentence as ''There is no escape for any soul from the jaws of duty until death shows him the secret passage of immortal life.''

A review of ''Rama: Hero of India,'' in The Nation, Vol. CXXXI, No. 3411, November 19, 1930, p. 558.

Dhan Gopal Mukerji's book is a retelling of the main incidents in the Ramayana—Rama's banishment from his kingdom through the treachery of his step-mother, the devotion of his brothers to him, his marriage with Sita and their lives together in the forest, the abduction of Sita and the war waged to rescue her from the King of Lanka, the alliance of Rama with Hanuman the Monkey King, and the rescue of Sita from the monsters who guard her and Rama's return to the kingship of his country— all these incidents are woven into a heroic and wonder-fraught narrative. Dhan Gopal Mukerji makes a mistake, I think, in permitting the flow of his narrative to be often broken by parenthetical explanation of Indian terms. I miss in this version of a great and beautiful story those episodes that give the atmosphere of Indian forests to the early books of the epic. But perhaps that atmosphere can hardly be rendered in a book intended for children of an alien civilization. (p. 23)

Padraic Colum, ''Animals, Fairies and Children,'' in The New Republic, Vol. LXV, No. 833, November 19, 1930, pp. 22-4.*

BUNNY, HOUND, AND CLOWN   (1931)

This book, designed for children between the ages of six and ten, . . . contains eleven stories. Many of them are very old and have been handed down by word of mouth from generation to generation in India. Although they are stories meant not merely to amuse but to ''teach the wise conduct of life,'' Mr. Mukerji's avowed ethical message does not assume the form of preachiness. If the moral of each tale is usually clearly stated it does naturally grow out of the story and is not tacked on or superimposed. Three of the tales give the book its title. **''The Dog of Paradise''** is a story of loyalty tried and rewarded; **''Holy Man and Frightened Bunny''** tells how a rabbit learned to conquer fear; **''The Clown of Heaven''** was transported there because in his earthly existence he had learned indifference and superiority to applause and derision. In other stories the undesirability of greed, conceit, stupidity, and deceit are illustrated, generally by making the possessors of those traits appear exceedingly ridiculous. Nevertheless, the mistake of sacrificing story interest to point a moral is never made. As a collection of stories about dogs and cats, rabbits, monkeys, tigers, flies, kings and clowns, the book will appeal to children. On the other hand, although the precepts behind some of these stories may be readily grasped by them, one suspects that the children for whom the book is intended will have to grow much older before they can understand the implications of others.

Gordon G. Hill, in a review of ''Bunny, Hound and Clown,'' in The Saturday Review of Literature, Vol. VIII, No. 11, October 3, 1931, p. 170.

In this book Mr. Mukerji retells for English-speaking children eleven fables from the folk-lore of India. Though much less successful in style than the author's version of the Ramayana for boys and girls, the Hindu philosophy and mysticism which the stories contain and the sincerity and earnestness with which the stories are retold give them a certain distinction and dignity. For children 9 to 12.

Anne T. Eaton, in a review of ''Bunny, Hound and Clown,'' in The New York Times Book Review, October 11, 1931, p. 17.

THE MASTER MONKEY   (1932)

[**The Master Monkey**] introduces us to the mythology of the East. The life story of a likable monkey-god, to-day the patron saint of every form of athletics among the Hindus, it is told in a style redolent of the calm brooding spirit of the Orient. There is plenty of action and adventure however, for Hanuman in his mission as liberator of the gods is born to deeds of heroism.

A review of ''The Master Monkey,'' in The Catholic World, Vol. CXXXVI, No. 813, December, 1932, p. 376.

Again, as in his fine version for young people of the Ramayana, the author is dealing with the legends and folklore of India. . . . Like the story of the Ramayana, this book has beauty of phrase and imagery; more simple in style and swifter in action, it will probably appeal to younger readers.

Anne T. Eaton, in a review of ''The Master Monkey,'' in The New York Times Book Review, March 5, 1933, p. 18.

FIERCE-FACE, THE STORY OF A TIGER   (1936)

Dhan Gopal Mukerji's animals always inspire respect and possess dignity. His convictions were always part of his work, and in so far as they are concerned the story might be read aloud to quite young children, for his convictions on the oneness of life in all its forms are those that little children instinctively hold. But the book belongs most to an age that takes kindly to the Jungle Books.

Fierce-Face, the tiger-kitten, is only just saved from the active dislike of his father—who like all tomcats resents the presence of his sons—by the resourceful devotion of his mother Bagni. She nurses him in secret, and even when her husband finds her and family life begins anew, stays always alert to keep the peace. It comes at length to a desperate family battle: Bagni and Fierce-Face go off together on their own. The care, loving prevision, and endless patience of Bagni stand by the truculent-looking but as yet inexperienced baby. He has to learn not only how to repel immediate dangers but to sense them afar off. He has to learn how villagers come out against the tiger with drums and swaying torches and how a man-eater is different from others of his tribe. He meets one of these outlaws, who is caught at length, to spend his time henceforth in a cage not too unhappy at a loss of freedom that insures food. But Bagni and her baby stay free. They meet with creeping killers and with forest fire, with white peacocks, the terrible boar, elephants, exquisite deer, monkeys, and a white cow like a crystal shape haloed in moonbeams. . . .

The preface says that ''the discerning adult reader will notice a unique presentation of reality'' in this information about the jungle conveyed through the life of a tiger. Without going so far as that precise adjective, one may well admit that this is a noble effort to show a tiger's own life through a tiger's own eyes in the intimate understanding that distinguishes all the animal stories that have come from this eminent author.

"The Prisoner of St. Helena and Tiger Ranging Free," in The New New York Herald Tribune Books, *November 15, 1936, p. 22.**

Save in Kipling's "Jungle Books" the magic of the Indian jungle is nowhere made so real and vivid as it is in the stories of Dhan Gopal Mukerji. He writes of animals in the same spirit in which children read or listen to animal stories. To this author, as to the child reader, nothing was more natural than that a tale should concern itself, and very seriously, with the doings of animals; he wins his audience through his entire lack of condescension. The animals in this, as in his other books, have the dignity of free wild creatures, and he treats them with the respect they deserve. . . .

Text and [Dorothy Lathrop's] illustrations together make a book of unusual truth and loveliness.

Anne T. Eaton, in a review of "Fierce-Face, the Story of a Tiger," in The New York Times Book Review, *November 29, 1936, p. 12.*

Jungle enchantment is warp and woof of this brilliant tale of animal lore. Bagni, the tigress mother, is the steady protector and patient guide for her young cub until his self-mastery equals the strongest of their kind. Written with rare understanding of children's interests in wild life. (pp. 361, 363)

A review of "Fierce-Face, the Story of a Tiger," in The Horn Book Magazine, *Vol. XII, No. 6, November-December, 1936, pp. 361, 363.*

This book deserves high commendation. In point of craftsmanship it comes near to being all that a book for children should be. "Spiritually," it is excellent. Those who have read *Gay-Neck* and other titles by this author will find in *Fierce-Face* the qualities they expect. A vigorous and beautiful prose, vividly re-creating the atmosphere of Indian jungle life and the never-ending warfare and watchfulness among its creatures, is the author's outstanding characteristic.

A review of "Fierce-Face," in The Junior Bookshelf, *Vol. 1, No. 2, February, 1937, p. 41.*

Antoine (Jean Baptiste Marie Roger) de Saint-Exupéry

1900-1944

French author/illustrator of fiction.

The following entry presents criticism of Saint-Exupéry's *Le Petit Prince (The Little Prince)*.

The author of reflective, often autobiographical adventure narratives for adults, Saint-Exupéry is perhaps best known as the creator of *The Little Prince,* **an allegorical fairy tale acknowledged as a classic of children's literature. Written in simple prose, the book is illustrated with childlike watercolors which are integral to the story.** *The Little Prince* **describes an imaginary encounter between Saint-Exupéry, who is stranded in the Sahara desert following a forced airplane landing, and a boy from a distant asteroid. The prince helps the narrator by sharing the knowledge he has gained since he left his tiny planet; on the first anniversary of his arrival on earth, the prince dies so that he can return home. Centering on themes of friendship and love while exploring what is truly important in life,** *The Little Prince* **contrasts inflexible adult thinking with the purity and innocence of children. The tale's philosophy is perhaps best expressed by a fox, who tells the prince that "it is only with the heart that one can see rightly; what is essential is invisible to the eye." A pioneer aviator, Saint-Exupéry published his only book for children in 1943 while in New York during the German occupation of France; observers note that the work reflects Saint-Exupéry's isolation and feelings of despair over the fate of his homeland.**

Reviewers have compared *The Little Prince* **with the works of such authors as Lewis Carroll, Jonathan Swift, and Charles Perrault; they remark, for example, that the book's pervading sense of loneliness and sad ending recall the tales of Hans Christian Andersen. While some critics debate the suitability of** *The Little Prince* **for children, most acclaim the book for its success in providing meaning on a spiritual and philosophical level while capturing the sense of wonder and imagination of childhood.**

(See also *Twentieth-Century Literary Criticism,* **Vol. 2;** *Something about the Author,* **Vol. 20; and** *Contemporary Authors,* **Vol. 108.)**

AUTHOR'S COMMENTARY

[Adèle Breaux tutored Saint-Exupéry in English while he lived on Long Island, New York. On November 17 and 20, 1942, she met with the author in his studio at the Bevin House. In the following excerpt from her book Saint-Exupéry in America, 1942-1943, *Breaux describes her reactions to seeing the drawings and reading the manuscript-in-progress for* The Little Prince.*]*

[On November 17,] the monastically bare room, where everything had a given place, was different. Sheets of onionskin paper haphazardly covered the worktable at the base of the tall, uncurtained window. Some were daubed and streaked with spots of varying colors; others represented figures and caricatures of personalities. A glass of tinted water and an open paint box with brushes stood at one end of the table. Just below it, a wastebasket overflowed with loosely wedged-in paper.

On the floor around the writing table lay crumpled sheets of the same paper. This part of the room curiously illustrated Saint-Exupéry's idea that intelligent disorder marks the presence of a personality.

Observing my obvious curiosity, Saint-Exupéry looked amused. All of a sudden the mask of reserve disappeared and with an open smile he asked very simply.

"Would you like to see what I have been doing?" He walked closer to the table. "As you observe, I have discarded a great deal. Some things here are acceptable. Some I am still considering. Examine what you wish!"

Here and there were penciled sketches of personalities, blocked in with water color, with just enough exaggeration of facial expression and dress to convey a definite idea. I picked up several pictures of a slender little boy with a scarf flowing about his neck as if to protect a delicate throat. Poses of this child against a variety of backgrounds predominated. Something in the posture, something in the grace of the scarf and the flow of the costume, even the carriage of the little figure reminded me of [Saint-Exupéry's wife] Consuelo. Something of his wife was present, a deep inescapable imprint of what he admired in her appearance. Were these sketches of a desired child, perhaps once dreamed about? These conjectures vanished as Saint-Exupéry, without waiting for me to make a comment, came nearer and began explaining.

> This is really ridiculous because I don't know anything about drawing or painting. I am doing a story about a little prince. My publishers have persuaded me that it will go over better if I do the illustrations myself, even if they are simple. Like that of most people, my training goes back to childhood days in school. I assure you that my talent never attracted attention. I was like any other child, doing more or less what he is told. I don't even remember if I liked it. But now the dabbling is amusing. I reject a drawing because the lines do not bring out what I want. Sometimes the color strikes a wrong note and I throw the sheet away.

He leaned down and began searching among the papers on one end of the table. Finding the desired water color, he handed it to me saying, "Here! See this old king in his dotage. His sky-blue cloak was not right for him, nor his ruddy face for his years." At this point he picked up another water color without having to search. "Look! In this second picture his skin color is better and I gave him a white cloak." As he handed it to me, he looked down with his face softened by a gentle smile. Then, as if sharing a love of fairy tales, he added with an amused, knowing expression, "Kings *always* wear ermine." (pp. 74-5)

Replacing on the table the picture of the king in the ermine robe, he lingered thoughtfully a moment and then picked up another water color, which he held at arm's length before my eyes. It revealed three strange brown bulbs sprouting luscious green foliage, joined together to form a triangle. With an air of complete satisfaction but with a humorous smile, he announced proudly, "This is my baobab!" I emitted a noncommittal "Oh." . . . Did a baobab really look like that? In my ignorance, I remained unimpressed. As it did not seem complimentary to question the artist, whose expression indicated a remarkable feat, the problem of reproducing a baobab on paper remained undisclosed.

Putting it down rather slowly, but always with his pleased eyes fixed on his masterpiece, he said, "You may have any of the other rejected drawings that please you. As you see, the wastebasket is full." (p. 76)

While glancing over the pictures on the table, I wondered how he managed to get his work done, for he was frequently away in Washington at the War Office and often in New York City.

"When do you do your work, Monsieur?"

> Mostly at night. I prefer to write then. Since the day often has its round of business, conferences, and other matters, and there are always social obligations, I usually begin around eleven o'clock, or even later, with a tray full of tall glasses of strong black coffee within reach. It is quiet at this time of day. No visits, no phone calls, no interruptions. I can concentrate. I write through the night without being aware of fatigue or sleepiness. I never have the slightest idea as to just when sleep overpowers me. Evidently I put my head down on my arm to think out a situation, and in the late morning I wake up in that position.

Perceiving my great interest, he continued speaking.

> It is the only way for me to accomplish anything. Once started, I am obsessed by the writing. I have to do it. I believe in it. I think it is as interesting to others as to myself. However, when it is really finished, I am sure it is no good. I am no longer a competent judge.

Momentarily stopping, he looked down at me very thoughtfully. We were still standing. My ears could hardly take in what he next said, "Why don't you try to write, Mademoiselle?"

"I don't believe I have that gift. You have no idea of how slowly words and expressions come to me."

With the utmost seriousness he answered,

> That is no criterion. No one could be slower than I am. I write by hand and choose thin paper because I use so many sheets to say very little. I keep on filling page after page until I come to an end. Then there is the inevitable boiling down. I often use a dictaphone in the shortening process. The typist takes it down but this is never the end. My work is usually revised from five to seven times before I consider the writing acceptable. When I believe I have finished, I get my friends to read parts of it and tell their reactions. Most of the time, there is further revision.

> (pp. 77-8)

[The following Thursday] the maid admitted me to the studio where Saint-Exupéry was standing before his table, apparently gazing out of the high, uncurtained window at the trees beyond. On hearing my footsteps, he quickly turned around and said with his customary directness, which never wasted words nor time, "I don't feel like doing any English today. Please do something else for me!" Immediately he turned back to his table, this time strewn with typewritten papers. Fingering them carefully, he selected some stapled pages. (pp. 79-80)

> "I would like you to read some of **Le Petit Prince,** which I have written in this house." After a slight pause, "My story is somewhat of a fantasy. By the way, there is a wonderful fantasy in English! Have you read *Mary Poppins*?"

> "No."

> "You should. It is the best children's story I have ever read. It is full of charm and quite appealing to grownups. I liked it so well that I read it several times. I consider it a real classic."

> (p. 80)

He arranged the chair, made me sit down, and proceeded to adjust a floor lamp to best advantage. Suddenly his tired face lighted up with animation.

> I had some trouble in persuading my publishers that the story could end with the little prince's death. *They* believe no story for children should end that way. I disagree with them. Children accept all natural things and adjust without harmful disturbances. The adults are the ones

who give them wrong attitudes, who distort their notions of the natural. I don't believe that death has to be morbid. No child is going to be upset by the going of the little prince. It's just a part of things as they are! Now read for yourself.

He spoke like a person bent on explaining his beliefs, for him unchangeable truths. Finally his rapid words revealing his ideas had brushed away the obvious film of his fatigue and discouragement. Saint-Exupéry sat again at his table but without any attempt to occupy himself. Immensely flattered and consumed with curiosity, I began to read with interest. While I was chuckling over his boa constrictor that looked like a hat, and his observations about grown-ups, he interrupted me to say, "I really did draw something like that in a similar situation as a child."

Aside from chuckling over his boa tale, I was struck by his creating immediately an intimacy with children through something they would accept as a matter of course in the world of make-believe. It was amusing to find him accenting the idea, as if it were a secret between him and small readers, that grown-ups just do not understand—they have to have complicated explanations. I noticed, too, that his language was explicit and that he used words beyond what most American educators consider the necessarily restricted vocabulary for a given age group. But then, for many years the French have believed that children accept new and even long words, for they usually ask questions about what they do not understand and assimilate with facility.

Soon I discovered that behind the façade for amusing children lay material for those who had lived long enough to be aware of individuals considered important, whose ideas and philosophy are far from ideal. However, the children would see only the funny, incongruous aspects. On the other hand, in a subtle way the adult reader would be amused, perhaps even comforted by shared opinions.

After reading a statement about who is acceptable in society, I asked, "Did you get this impression from observing rich and successful Americans? It sounds like that."

"No, I meant that nowadays a bank account largely determines anyone's importance and position in society in every corner of the globe."

In the publication that particular sentence was omitted.

As I read the first part, I felt that, like his previous books, this was peculiarly intimate writing, although in a different vein. He had more fully revealed himself, the man known by his family—his impatience at being interrupted in his work, his recognition of the unimportance of many accepted attitudes,

The Bevin House, where Saint-Exupéry wrote The Little Prince. *Alain Blanchet.*

and his lovable understanding of a sensitive child. Looking up I asked, "Is this not a story you wrote for the little boy you once were and who was not fully understood?"

A smile came as an answer, but it was an enigmatic smile within his reserve and seemed to contain a statement to himself of which I was to be left unaware. Still smiling, he stood up and turned his face toward the window as though thinking further, even seeing a friend in the distance. (pp. 81-3)

Quiet reigned until I had finished reading. In enthusiastic excitement I forgot all about being reserved and still. The reading had unleashed my tongue. Words toppled out.

> All the time you were writing this story, you were sharing truths discovered for yourself, even some disillusionments. You seem to be smiling most of the time and poking fun at types of people you don't like too well, but there's haunting sadness too. Something is out of reach, something never kept, or perhaps never attained!

I had not been looking at Saint-Exupéry. My eyes were fixed on the wall nearby while I tried to organize my reactions and express them clearly. I finished with,

> "Yes, the going of the little prince is beautiful, not at all morbid, and yet it is sad. Any child will accept his disappearance but will still feel sadness at the separation." I paused and then added slowly, "I suppose that, too, is a part of things as they are."
>
> (p. 84)

On the road back my eyes were fixed on the cement pavement but my mind was reliving the afternoon's proceedings, an unlooked-for honor, imperishable as a memory. It was the insight into a great man, fundamentally simple and direct, so dedicated to his gift that it was the essence of his being and the master of his life. (p. 85)

> *Adèle Breaux, in her* Saint-Exupéry in America, 1942-1943: A Memoir, *Fairleigh Dickinson University Press, 1971, 166 p.*

JOHN CHAMBERLAIN

What makes a good children's book? Is it simple motion? Or does the narrative have to be about things and persons and animals that a child has seen and known or heard about? As a father who blunders considerably when told to stand and deliver at the 7 o'clock bedtime hour, I wish I knew. The ability to answer such questions would also stand me in good stead in reviewing Antoine de Saint-Exupéry's **"The Little Prince,"** which is a fascinating fable for grown-ups but of conjectural value for boys and girls of 6, 8 and 10. **"The Little Prince"** may very well be a book on the order of "Gulliver's Travels," something that exists on two levels. But I won't know until I read it to my daughters a couple of years hence.

Saint-Exupéry's Little Prince walked up to him one day in the middle of the Sahara Desert. The French writer-aviator had made a forced landing in a desolate waste; something was radically wrong with the motor. He was having a devil of a time trying to be his own mechanic when the Little Prince, a golden-haired visitor from asteroid B-612, materialized out of nowhere and asked for a picture of a sheep.

Saint-Exupéry hadn't drawn anything since he was 6 years old. At that age he had made a picture of a boa constrictor digesting an elephant, but the grown-ups mistook the drawing for one of a hat, and the failure of adult comprehension had turned Saint-Exupéry away from the graphic arts. Rusty as he was, however, he tried drawing a sheep for the little visitor from outer space. Finally he succeeded in making a creditable picture of a box. To the Little Prince he explained that the sheep was inside the box. That seemed to satisfy everybody. And the Little Prince, although not precisely loquacious, began to tell Saint-Exupéry about life on the asteroids.

The asteroid from which the Little Prince came was so small that one could see a new sunset at any moment of the day merely by walking a few feet. Of the asteroid's three volcanos, one was extinct, but the Little Prince cleaned out all three of them each day just to be on the safe side. Flowers grew on the asteroid, and the Little Prince grew very fond of one flower in particular. But he had to be careful of the vegetation. If three baobab trees, for example, ever succeeded in getting a good growth on the asteroid they would tip it out of its orbit.

The Little Prince had come down to earth in search of a sheep to keep down the young baobab growths. But he also wanted a sheep that would not nibble the flowers. When Saint-Exupéry provides the Prince not only with a sheep in a box but also with a muzzle, the little boy's quest is ended.

Children will probably be amused by the sequence of events leading to the Little Prince's return to his tiny star. But this is only the fantastic outline of Saint-Exupéry's fairy tale. For along with his sheep in a box and his muzzle, the little boy returns home through interstellar space carrying with him a heavy cargo of philosophical wisdom.

To reach the earth in the first place, the Little Prince had to go from asteroid to asteroid. He discovered a king reigning on one of them, an absolute monarch who sustained the illusion of omnipotence by never ordering the sun to rise or set before its natural time. He found a drunkard cluttering up another asteroid. "Why do you drink?" he asked the sot. "To forget." "Forget what?" asked the Little Prince. "To forget that I'm ashamed." "Ashamed of what?" "Ashamed of drinking." Puzzled by this sequence of answers, the Little Prince mused: "These grown-ups are certainly very, very odd."

The business man who owned another asteroid reminded him of the drunkard, for all this man of affairs could do was to sit at a desk and add up columns of figures. The lamplighter on still another asteroid, one that turned on its axis each minute, had to light and to extinguish his lamps so often that he never had time to rest. "Orders are orders," he said. "I follow a terrible profession."

Yes, the adults among whom the Little Prince adventured were very odd indeed. So odd that they inevitably remind a reader of himself and his friends. The fox who counsels the Little Prince to love a specific flower instead of all flowers is more human. For the fox has a secret: only the individual relationship is interesting.

> "My life," he complains, "is very monotonous. I hunt chickens; men hunt me. All the chickens are just alike, and all the men are just alike. And, in consequence, I am a little bored. But if you tame me, it will be as if the sun came to shine on my life. I shall know the sound

of a step that will be different from all the others.''

Now, all of this foxy talk is quintessential wisdom. But is it for children? Can you clutter up a narrative with paradox and irony and still hope to hold the interest of 8 and 10 year olds? Maybe you can if the philosophy or the irony can be accepted as simple motion. . . .

Will Saint-Exupéry's philosophical passages captivate children who simply want to see people and animals in action? Personally, I can't visualize the colloquy with the drunkard provoking anything but blank incomprehension. And the business man adding up the numbers of planets and stars he claims to own probably illustrates too abstract a concept to appeal to the 10-year-old. However, large sections of **"The Little Prince"** ought to capture the imagination of any child. And I may be wrong about the drunkard and the business man. After all, who am I to say what children will or won't like? I can't even find a sure-fire formula for stories with which to amuse my own.

Anyway, **"The Little Prince"** will appeal to adults. And that is something.

> *John Chamberlain, in a review of "The Little Prince,"*
> *in* The New York Times, *April 6, 1943, p. 19.*

P. L. TRAVERS

[*Travers is an English author, journalist, and critic best known for her fantasy series about the magical nanny, Mary Poppins. Saint-Exupéry considered* Mary Poppins *"the best children's story I ever read."*]

In all fairy tales—and I mean fairy tales and not tarradiddies—the writer sooner or later gives away his secret. Sometimes he does it deliberately, sometimes unconsciously. But give it away he must, for that is a law of the fairy tale's being—you must provide the key. Antoine de St. Exupéry, in his new book **"The Little Prince"** has honorably obeyed the law. He makes us wait for the secret no longer than the second chapter.

"So I lived my life alone," he says, "without any one I could really talk to." There it is. A clear and unequivocal statement, a confession as bitter as aloes and familiar as the day. Most of us live our lives alone without anybody we can really talk to. We eat the indigestible stuff of our own hearts in silence, for we have not learnt to find the hidden companion within ourselves. Poets, and writers of fairy tales, are luckier. It may be that the substance of their minds is less dense than that of other men. Or perhaps they are more willing to slough its protective outer husk in order to get down to the essential bone. I don't know. I am only sure that you have to be bare and naked in some ultimate sense before you can hear the secret princely voice. Moreover, it is imperative that the prince should speak first. The etiquette of fairy tales and the court circles of the heart demand it. You may not command that voice. It will speak only to the ear that is humbly tuned to listen.

"Draw me a sheep!" cried St. Exupéry's prince in the silence of the desert. And so the friendship began.

Yet for us, if not for the author, there had been earlier intimations of his coming acquaintance with that royal boy. Was there not **"The Wild Garden"** with its proud delicate princesses and the snakes beneath the dinner table? And the sleeping child in the last chapter of **"Wind, Sand and Stars"** [**"Terre des hommes"**], that small Mozart indwelling in all men, whom all men consistently murder. Here, surely, were the first seeds of **"The Little Prince."** Indeed, it seems to me that each of his

books has been a path leading across the sand dunes to the prince's citadel. Whatever happens hereafter in St. Exupéry's external world will be clarified and sweetened for him by the memory of this desert meeting.

I cannot tell whether it is a book for children. Not that it matters, for children are like sponges. They soak into their pores the essence of any book they read, whether they understand it or not. **"The Little Prince"** certainly has the three essentials required by children's books. It is true in the most inward sense, it offers no explanations and it has a moral. But this particular moral attaches the book to the grown-up world rather than the nursery. To be understood it needs a heart stretched to the utmost by suffering and love, the kind of a heart that, luckily, is not often found in children. "Tame me," says the little fox to the prince, "so that I may accept the ties of love and be, for one single person, unique in all the world." "Mine," says the fox, "is a very simple secret. It is only with the heart that one can see rightly; what is essential is invisible to the eye." Indeed, yes. But children quite naturally see with the heart; the essential is clearly visible to them. The little fox will move them simply by being a fox. They will not need his secret until they have forgotten it and have to find it again. I think, therefore, that **"The Little Prince"** will shine upon children with a sidewise gleam. It will strike them in some place that is not the mind and glow there until the time comes for them to comprehend it.

Yet even in saying this I am conscious of drawing a line between grown-ups and children, in the same way that St. Exupéry himself has done. And I do not believe that line exists. It is as imaginary as the equator. Yet separate camps are here declared and the author stands with the children. He leans upon the barricades, gently and ironically sniping at the grown-ups, confident that the children are standing by to pass the ammunition. Yet children themselves draw no such line. They are too wise. They do not feel any more derisive toward grown-ups than they do toward animals. The child very seldom sits in judgment. To him the grown-ups are objects of wonder, often, even, of pity. He sees them as creatures not deliberately guilty but trapped, rather, by fatal circumstance. . . .

We cannot go back to the world of childhood. We are too tall now and must stay with our own kind. But perhaps there is a way of going forward to it. Or better still, of bearing it along with us, carrying the lost child in our arms so that we may measure all things in terms of that innocence. Everything St. Exupéry writes has that sense of heightened life that can be achieved only when the child is still held by the hand. In **"The Little Prince"** he has given the boy a habitation—Asteroid B-612—and a title. But the burning, freezing, golden face must have been with him as long as memory.

Delicately, with impish irony, the prince's journey is traced from star to star; his universe is mapped by St. Exupéry's own charming illustrations. He seeks his dream among the meteors but it is not until he arrives upon the planet, Earth, that his heart begins to glow. As he wanders in the empty desert there come to him the things he sought—the man, the fox and the serpent. Each of them out of his own nature brings him a gift—the man a drawing of a sheep, the fox a tamed and faithful heart, and the serpent the cruel loving stroke that frees him from mortality and returns him to his star. That is all. The gentle allegory is compressed into a few clear, colored pages. A short book, but long enough to remind us that we are all involved in its meaning. We, too, like the fox, have need to be tamed by love; we, too, must return to the desert to find our lonely princes. All fairy tales are portents, and life continually renews them in us. We have no need to mourn for the Brothers Grimm when fairy tales like **"The Little Prince"** may still be heard from the lips of airmen and all who steer by the stars.

> *P. L. Travers, "Across the Sand Dunes to the Prince's Star," in* New York Herald Tribune Weekly Book Review, *April 11, 1943, p. 5.*

BEATRICE SHERMAN

St. Exupery's new book is a very different one from his **"Night Flight," "Wind, Sand and Stars,"** or **"Flight to Arras"** [**"Pilote de guerre"**]. And yet it has the same fine, clear, rarefied quality of the high lonely spaces where a man's mind has the range to ponder and question and wonder about the meanings of things. **"The Little Prince"** is a parable for grown people in the guise of a simple story for children—a fable with delightful, delicate pictures of the little Prince on his adventurings. It is a lovely story in itself which covers a poetic, yearning philosophy—not the sort of fable that can be tacked down neatly at its four corners but rather reflections on what are real matters of consequence. . . .

For children the book will be as interesting as any of the best "Once upon a time" fairy stories, with its fine flights of fancy. The pictures in clean, clear watercolor, have the ethereal, fragile texture of wind and stars and flight. In their stark simplicity they have a sort of kinship with the things children like to draw.

The translation from the French [by Katherine Woods] is admirably done, preserving the surface simplicity of a lovely fable with significant undertones.

> *Beatrice Sherman, "A Prince of Lonely Space," in* The New York Times Book Review, *April 11, 1943, p. 9.*

COMMONWEAL

A story is inseparable from its form and if you try to re-tell a story that someone else has told the story disappears. . . . There is no use trying to tell the story of the little prince even when one is extremely anxious to tell enough of it so that people will want to read it.

There is even less use telling people how beautiful this story is because no one cares to read even a pretty list of adjectives. Imagine also the difficulty of trying to explain just how and why this story of a little prince from an impossible star who talks to snakes and foxes in the Sahara is not, is never whimsy. Imagine a grown man admitting in print that a story about a little boy who gets himself carried from star to star by holding on to strings attached to birds could possibly be the kind of a story that would deeply affect his emotions. And, too, there would have to be remarks about innocence, loneliness, truth and poetry which would be very difficult and embarrassing to write. Why, the book is printed as if it were a book for children—perhaps the publishers mean children to read it—imagine, then, the embarrassment of reviewing a book for children as if you thought it was a book for grown-ups. Imagine saying that to an adult the story is unforgettable, that it is the story of lost childhood, that it is so sad a story that only grown-ups can understand all that it means.

No, the best thing is to be strictly academic. That is lofty and safe ground to stand on. Thus. Saint-Exupéry in this fable follows in the long line of French moralists. As in Montesquieu's "Lettres Persanes," a character from a world we do not know is brought into the society in which we live. This character is innocent, intelligent and asks questions difficult to answer. Inevitably he is surprized at what he sees: inevitably we are brought to see ourselves as others see us. It is a classic method for laying bare the incongruities of a given civilization. But in **"The Little Prince"** the tone is no longer that of the eighteenth century moralist: witty, revolutionary and cerebral. The little boy who talks with Saint-Exupéry in the desert looks and laughs at our unchanged absurdities, but the story of his pitiful and brave excursion among us is told with a tenderness the eighteenth century never knew. (pp. 644-45)

We intend to keep both [the English and French] editions, and in no place where they might be mislaid. For no matter how certain we are that we will never forget the little prince, a story . . . exists in the telling; the little prince lives most brightly in the words to which he owes his existence, and we shall wish, certainly, to read these words again. (p. 645)

> *"With the Heart, Rightly," in* Commonweal, *Vol. XXXVII, No. 26, April 16, 1943, pp. 644-45.**

MARIA CIMINO

In considering some of the new children's books of this second year of war, it is interesting to note a number of good books that have their roots in the imagination. Fortunate, indeed, is the spring output in children's books, which may lay claim also to two adult books dealing with childhood, of such rare individuality as "The Human Comedy," by William Saroyan (Harcourt, Brace), and **"The Little Prince."** . . . **"The Little Prince"** confirms the surge of Saint Exupéry's poetic imagination which was so evident in his two earlier books. One is therefore not surprised to find here a fairy tale for which he has made the most appropriate water colors; a fairy tale that tells of the loneliness of life. . . . It is announced as a book for adults, but children will eventually make it theirs as they have done all the great fairy tales. They will understand it even though its allegory may not be clear to them, because they will approach it and accept its possibilities with the simplicity with which they meet all eternal things.

> *Maria Cimino, "The Spring Output," in* The Saturday Review of Literature, *Vol. XXVI, No. 16, April 17, 1943, p. 50.**

[KATHARINE S. WHITE]

The critics of children's books have a tendency to greet with joyous cries of welcome any juvenile written by an author who has a name in a wider field of writing. This is natural enough, considering the number of books they must read in a year by writers without talent, and often there is real cause for rejoicing over a great name on the title page. Not always, though. This spring, for example, the cries of welcome have been for **"The Little Prince."** . . . Whatever the merits of the book, it seems to be news: it has had a rush of publicity, it is on the bestseller lists, some reviewers announce that it has already taken its place among the children's classics, others call it a book only for subtle-minded adults, and all unite in praise and in rather solemn analysis of its overtones of meaning. I therefore feel strangely alone, since, to my mind, **"The Little Prince"** is not a book for children and is not even a good book. It can be described as a philosophical fairy tale, or, if you prefer the word so often used of Saint-Exupéry, a metaphysical one. The only youthful appraisal I can offer is that of a twelve-year-old boy, who likes almost all kinds of books and usually reads at top speed. After dragging through this one, he said, "He seems to be writing about grownup things in a childish way." Possibly this judgment has some merit because, when you come to think of it, the best children's books are those which treat childlike things in an adult way. "**The Little Prince**" unquestionably has its moments of charm and point and its naïve drawings have occasional humor and grace, but as a fairy tale, whether for adults or children, it seems to me to lack the simplicity and clarity all fairy tales must have in order to create their magic, and too often its charm turns into coyness and its point is lost in cloudy and boring elaboration.

> *Katharine S. White, in a review of "The Little Prince," in* The New Yorker, *Vol. XIX, No. 15, May 29, 1943, p. 65.*

ANNE CARROLL MOORE

By one of the happy chances of advance publication, Antoine de Saint-Exupéry's **The Little Prince** came to me on the eve of Hans Christian Andersen's birthday. I read it at once, not as a reviewer, but as a gift for a day which grows more significant every year that I live. . . .

If I were to be cast away, not on the proverbial desert island—there are no more desert islands—but in the dreariest of all places during this World War (which might be a schoolroom), I have always felt my one book would be Andersen's *Fairy Tales.* Now I should beg for a companion volume and its title is **The Little Prince.**

From its magical frontispiece, picturing the escape of the Little Prince from his tiny planet, with the aid of a migrating flock of wild birds, to his flowers and his volcanoes, I am held, as I believe many children will be, by the pictures—pictures which are an integral part of the dramatic and philosophic story; pictures so childlike and free, yet as suggestive of the ageless Primitives as the text, which, with all its fresh imagery and originality, is a reminder of Hans Christian Andersen and his supreme gift of giving life to the inanimate. "Saint-Exupéry has written a book to please the child he was and still is," I said to myself, "just as W. H. Hudson did in *A Little Boy Lost*." It may be disturbing to some readers that a snake should play a part in returning the Little Prince to his planet. Readers who feel that way may well reread *A Little Boy Lost* for a different attitude toward snakes. . . . (p. 164)

No one who has been as deeply moved as I have been by the recurrence of [Saint-Exupéry's] childhood memories as recorded in **Wind, Sand and Stars** and **Flight to Arras** can be expected to deal objectively with **The Little Prince.** I have been interested but not impressed by most of the adult reviewers and commentators who have attempted to place the book. Is it for adults or for children? they ask. Who shall say?

I look upon it as a book so fresh and different, so original yet so infused with wisdom as to take a new place among books in general. I predict that the children who like it will like it very much for its magical quality and the direct approach of the Little Prince to "matters of consequence." Children who have never held communication with the stars, with flowers, with desert foxes or with a stranded aviator may find it perplexing. The same holds good for adult readers who look upon philosophy as a subject for scholars rather than an experience of childhood. Those in whom the flower of imagination was never nourished and tended will probably wonder what it is all about when "reality" should be our first concern at this time.

That a fairy tale of such dimensions and permanent character has found an American publisher eager to give the careful attention to its translation and its format and to every detail so essential to the reproduction of the delicate water colors is worthy of special note. . . . [The illustrations] spring from a world of light and air and space, sun and stars as seen and felt by a child of France whose childhood has been the reserve strength of his adventurous manhood. (p. 165)

To the children of France the Little Prince should stand as a symbol of their deliverance from bondage in the 20th century. To many children of other countries the Little Prince will share the secret imparted to him by the fox he tamed in the desert. "It is only with the heart one can see rightly; what is essential is invisible to the eye." . . .

The Little Prince seems to me the most important book of many years. . . . (p. 166)

> *Anne Carroll Moore, in a review of "The Little Prince," in* The Horn Book Magazine, *Vol. XIX, No. 3, May-June, 1943, pp. 164-66.*

KATHERINE BRÉGY

There seems to be a slight controversy agitating both readers and critics as to whether this new and exquisite Saint-Exupéry volume is intended for children or grown-ups. It would be my own guess that anybody with imagination would welcome it as a kind of angelic visitation these stressful days. For, as the aviator-author reminds us, "All grown-ups were once children, although few of them remember it."

Not since Padraic Colum's delectable *White Sparrow* has there been anything which quite so unerringly hit a certain bull's-eye—that unique bull's-eye which is bounded on the north by irony and on the south by tenderness, on the east by a garden with one rosebush and on the west by stars that ring like little bells. (p. 326)

Personally, I long ago realized that Captain de Saint-Exupéry . . . was a poet and a mystic. But it had not occurred to me that he would be the one who could go far toward explaining that mysterious warning of our Lord that unless we become as little children we cannot enter the Kingdom of Heaven. (p. 327)

> *Katherine Brégy, in a review of "The Little Prince," in* The Catholic World, *Vol. 157, No. 939, June, 1943, pp. 326-27.*

FLORENCE BETHUNE SLOAN

Many grown-ups like ["**The Little Prince**"] very much, and we know boys and girls who have enjoyed it as a fairy tale. The author's unusual water colors of the Little Prince are a very important part of the strange story he tells. They are truly delightful and childlike, very much like boys' and girls' own drawings, we think. . . .

If you like imaginative books, beautiful pictures in words, and in line and color, you will like the story of the Little Prince, whatever your age may be, and will fall under the spell of this enchanting book. . . .

> *Florence Bethune Sloan, "Let's Read Now," in* The Christian Science Monitor, *August 30, 1943, p. 8.**

STANLEY WALKER

Children particularly interested [Saint-Exupéry], and he could talk to them for hours. His fondness for probing the minds and fancies of children probably accounts for his book **The Little Prince.** *Mary Poppins* was his favorite book, and he kept it at his bedside, to dip into as others do poetry. **The Little Prince** has been called autobiographical, and it was characteristic of his own mentality that the Little Prince, when he asked a question, could not rest or ask another till he got that one off his mind. (p. 64)

Stanley Walker, "Saint X," in Tricolor, Vol. II, No. 7, October, 1944, pp. 59-66.

THE JUNIOR BOOKSHELF

This is an outstanding book of a quality rare indeed. The question of its complete suitability for children will inevitably be raised because its full meaning will not be absorbed at a first reading nor indeed until the reader reaches more mature years, an age when he has come into closer contact with the sad realities of life. For sadness pervades this fairy story and the author reflects in it part of his philosophy. So indeed does Hans Andersen, and profound sadness pervades some of his best-known stories also. . . .

That the fantasy has the reality of truth there is no doubt. It is told in exquisite prose and with complete gravity, leaving in an adult reader's mind the feeling of satisfaction that only the best of stories can leave. The author's own illustrations are completely in harmony with the story, having the same delicacy, the same air of wonder.

A review of "The Little Prince," in The Junior Bookshelf, Vol. 9, No. 2, July, 1945, p. 73.

Saint-Exupéry and his mother, Countess Marie de Saint-Exupéry.

HENRI PEYRE

[*The following excerpt was originally published in 1955 in* The Contemporary French Novel.]

[*Le Petit Prince*] is a fairy tale of infinite charm, in which gentle satire of the dullness of grown-ups, of the pomposity of scientists, and of the aimless feverishness of businessmen is delicately blended with poetical evocations of the African desert and of cosmic wanderings among planets and stars. It illustrates the truth of Baudelaire's celebrated definition of genius as 'childhood recovered at will.' The Little Prince, whose fancy roams in interstellar spaces, also asks a few questions, intensely grave as children's questions can be. It incarnates Saint-Exupéry's passionate regret for the fervent faith of a child and his imaginative freedom, unspoiled by the hypocritical calculations of adults. The tale is written with a purity of outline and a terse simplicity of dialogue that recall the exquisite blending of reasonableness and supernaturalism that marks the seventeenth-century French fairy tales of Perrault. It makes no concessions to absurdity or cheapness of effect, as too many of our writings and films for children, unsuccessful imitations of *Alice in Wonderland* or of Walt Disney, are inclined to do. Its simple dialogue between a flier impatient with the evils of the world and a terse unsmiling child clinging to his dreams receives a tragic significance when read as the author's farewell to this gross earth over which millions of young men were then shedding their blood, their sweat, and their tears. (p. 176)

Henri Peyre, "Antoine de Saint-Exupéry," in his French Novelists of Today, revised edition, Oxford University Press, 1967, pp. 154-79.

RICHARD RUMBOLD AND LADY MARGARET STEWART

[*The Little Prince* was illustrated with Saint-Exupéry's] own water-colour drawings but, though remarkable for imaginativeness, they are no more than competent in execution. (p. 186)

The story is full of . . . charm, wit and fantasy. But underlying it is a note of sadness. . . . Both Saint-Exupéry and the little prince feel isolated and at loggerheads with the world, a world of 'grandes personnes' who have lost the secret of life. 'That secret is very simple. It is only the heart that can see rightly. . . . The essential is invisible to the eye.' (p. 187)

Richard Rumbold and Lady Margaret Stewart, in their The Winged Life: A Portrait of Antoine de Saint-Exupery, Poet and Airman, David McKay Company Inc., 1955, 224 p.

MAXWELL A. SMITH

One of the charms of Saint-Exupéry is that in some ways he never grew up but always kept [a] feeling of wonder, of eager anticipation in which the real world and the imaginary one blend. How else could he have written the inimitable *Little Prince*?

It is hardly possible, one feels, to exaggerate the role played by his early environment in the development of the sensitive, precocious child who later was to give us such a poetic transcription of our mysterious universe. Few writers have ever retained so vividly the charm of their early days, which can be flashed across the mind at will to comfort them in times of danger or lonely isolation. (pp. 15-16)

Unique among all of [Saint-Exupéry's writings, *The Little Prince*] is a delicate and ethereal fairy tale apparently addressed to children although its wide philosophical overtones as a parable will be understood only by adults. There has been much discussion concerning the author's purpose in writing this charming fable. Was it a brief relaxation from the anguish concerning his country which tormented him in his American exile, a bit of playful and poetic whimsy for the entertainment of children, particularly for the child he once had been and which in some respects he had fortunately never ceased to be? Was it chiefly a pretext for the lovely sketches and aquarelles which for years he had been drawing for his own delight? Was it rather like the *Lettre à un otage* intended primarily for the consolation of his beloved compatriots, an opportunity to lift them for a moment from their blackness of despair? To justify the latter theory, one might mention the dedication to his friend, Léon Werth, "This grown-up who lives in France where he is cold and hungry and has great need of being consoled."

It is possible, of course, for imaginative youngsters of all ages from eight to eighty to enjoy this delightful fantasy without bothering themselves too much concerning the motivation of the author. It would be pleasant for most readers to share the theory of the late Professor Eliot Fay, based on an interview with Consuelo de Saint-Exupéry, the author's wife, that this is an allegory of their love. Just as the Little Prince, tiring of his love for his beloved flower had left his tiny planet to wander through celestial space, so Saint-Ex, after seven years of married life, had suddenly informed his wife that he needed to be alone to travel and seek adventure throughout the world, but would some day return to her and settle down to a regular conjugal state. According to Consuelo, he did return three years later just as he had promised, a short time before the outbreak of the war. . . . Mr. Eugene Reynal, Saint-Exupéry's friend and American publisher, rejects completely, however, this romantic theory concerning the composition of *The Little Prince.*

According to a letter from Mr. Reynal, the book "had its origin in a little drawing made as a joke on the margin of Bernard Lamotte's original sketch for the illustrations in *Flight to Arras.* It was a little winged figure looking something like himself which he became intrigued with and which he kept drawing over and over again in different forms for his own amusement. As he played with it, it grew in form and I suppose set his mind to work with the little stories about the figure which finally emerged as a book. We kept after him to work on the drawings with a book in mind without having any more idea of the form the story might take than I am sure he had at that time. He would call us up excitedly at different times to show us how the drawings were coming along. When we suggested color, he started experimenting with that. I am quite sure the pictures and the book developed together in his mind and I am also sure they provided him with a new medium for expressing his own philosophy as well as a form of relaxation in this new departure for his work."

In many other ways, moreover, we may seek in *The Little Prince* a deeper revelation of the author's life and personality than is to be found in the purely factual references to his childhood and maturity of his other books. Guillain de Benouville, the famous leader of the Resistance Movement, tells in *Confluences* of his friendship with Saint-Ex in Algiers during May, 1944, and of the latter's handing to his friends a copy of *The Little Prince* which he evidently considered to be his autobiography. "He held it out with a smile, almost as if he had given us his photograph." Louis Barjon, who knew Saint-Ex well at this time, states in the same work that few books have given us a more faithful and profound picture of the real Saint-Ex, and even goes so far as to say that he could easily

show how the physiognomy of the little prince reproduces that of the author, feature by feature. (The reader thinks at once of the scarf which flew behind the little prince, and which was such an inseparable part of the author's attire.) Albérès likewise in his *Saint-Exupéry* finds in this autobiography "all his imagery and symbolism, the deserted planets and the marvelous flame of the man and his friendship, all this waking dream in which Saint-Exupéry lived and whose most touching image he gives us the day on which he assumed the paternity of the little prince. For in this book he has put the whole of himself."

Many readers likewise will have noticed in several of his earlier books premonitions or hints of the figure of the little prince. As early as *Southern Mail,* for instance, the hero, Bernis, was confronted with the "phantom of a tender urchin," the child which he had once been, and his death on the desert sands underneath the vertical star in which the treasure glittered resembles that of the little prince. In the chapter called **"The Secret Garden"** of *Wind, Sand and Stars* we encounter the little princesses with their tame snakes beneath the floor, and in the conclusion of the same volume we recall the episode in which the author feels compassion for the little Polish emigrant.

> I leaned over this smooth forehead, over these sweetly pouting lips and I said to myself: this is the face of a musician, this is the child-Mozart, this is a beautiful promise of life. The little princes of legends were not different from him.

So deeply a part of himself indeed is the concept of the little prince that P. L. Travers has written: "Each of his books has been a path leading across the sand dunes to the prince's citadel" [see excerpt above, 1943]. (pp. 189-93)

To analyze in detail so lovely and fragile a tale would be like removing the petals of a rose to try to discover its charm. . . . It is perhaps too early to predict what part of Saint-Exupéry's works will achieve immortality. Because of its poetic charm, however, its freshness of imagery, its whimsical fantasy, delicate irony and warm tenderness, it seems likely that *The Little Prince* will join that select company of books like La Fontaine's *Fables,* Swift's *Gulliver's Travels,* Carroll's *Alice in Wonderland* and Maeterlinck's *Blue Bird,* which have endeared themselves to children and grown-ups alike throughout the world. (pp. 199-200)

> *Maxwell A. Smith, in his* Knight of the Air: The Life and Works of Antoine de Saint-Exupery, *Pageant Press, Inc., 1956, 265 p.*

GERMAINE BRÉE AND MARGARET GUITON

Le Petit Prince, because it is a fairy story and ostensibly written for children, is the type of book immediately pigeonholed as "charming." And, in a sense, what could be more appropriate a vehicle for the poetry that Saint-Exupéry apprehended in his solitary flights than a fairy story about an astral prince! There is, nevertheless, more poetry in Saint-Exupéry's descriptions of his actual flights. And the charm of *Le Petit Prince* is sometimes blighted by a desperate, solitary sadness that no child would ever understand. It is also overshadowed at times by a series of rather ineffectual attacks upon the human race in general. That the human race is somewhat coyly referred to as "grown-ups" does little to relieve the sadness of the message. Indeed this very complicity with the world of childhood produces an uncomfortable impression. (pp. 201-02)

Germaine Brée and Margaret Guiton, "Return to Man," in their An Age of Fiction: The French Novel from Gide to Camus, *Rutgers University Press, 1957, pp. 180-233.* *

VICTOR E. GRAHAM

With its charming story enhancing rather pointed satire, Saint-Exupéry's **"Le Petit Prince"** resembles "Alice in Wonderland" and "Gulliver's Travels" which also can be read and appreciated at different levels by the child, the adult, and the scholar. A brief but penetrating analysis of the fantasy and mysticism in **"Le Petit Prince"** has recently been published by Yves Le Hir. With sure instinct, he examines the style of the work and points out the reasons for its different appeal to children and to adults.

In considering the symbolism of **"Le Petit Prince"**, Le Hir sees in the broken-down motor of the airplane the soul of the author. The diminishing water supply is spiritual grace which is drying up because of lack of sustenance. The desert as a symbol is not only a stage in spiritual development but the traditional setting for encounters with God. The theme of thirst is also traditional in mysticism and from material things one moves to the spiritual. . . .

Le Hir shows how Saint-Exupéry introduces in **"Le Petit Prince"** reminiscences of well-known fairy tales. When the little prince visits the planet of the king, for example, the monarch's command "Approche-toi que je te voie mieux" is like the wolf's invitation to Red Riding Hood when he is disguised as her grand-mother. Similarly, the interchange between the Vaniteux and the little prince makes one think of the same fairy tale: "Vous avez un drôle de chapeau"—"C'est pour, saluer." (p. 9)

Le Hir does not, however, show how many references there are in **"Le Petit Prince"** to the Gospels and the life of Christ. For Saint-Exupéry, **"Le Petit Prince"** is a statement of faith, and even though the analogy is not a perfect one, I do not think it is going too far to say that in many respects the little prince himself is like Christ and his revelation to the author parallel to the experience of the disciples with Christ.

It is in the desert at a time of great spiritual crisis that the "little prince" comes to the author. He is a prince, not of darkness but of light. Like Christ in the temple, he astounds the author with his precocity. Examples of his prescience are his immediate recognition of the author's drawing of an elephant inside a boa constrictor for what it is and his anticipation of the author's announcement that the airplane motor has been successfully repaired. (pp. 9-10)

It is significant, of course, that the little prince landed in the desert and that he met there, not only the author, but first of all the serpent which has always personified evil. Christ fought temptation in the desert and the little prince is in the throes of a struggle which the author cannot really comprehend. Even the serpent admits that the little prince is without sin, but the little prince is impelled to seek death from the serpent. The hour has come; the cycle is completed and the little prince's star (which like Christ's, was nearest the earth at the moment of his arrival) is again at its closest proximity. Even though the little prince is frightened, he knows that he is going to his "heavenly" home but, like Christ again, he promises to leave with his follower a sort of Holy Ghost—his star in the heavens and his memory. He tries to explain to the author how he will appear to die but assures him that his life will not end. At the last, then, the little prince seeks from the serpent a death which

he might easily have avoided. But, says the author, "je sais bien qu'il est revenu à sa planète, car, au lever du jour, je n'ai pas retrouvé son corps." . . .

On the night before he died, the little prince attempts to tell the author of the need for his approaching sacrifice. Together, at the suggestion of the little prince, they walk in the desert in search of a well. The author feels that it is absurd to seek water in such a place but, miraculously, they come on a well, not like typical Sahara desert wells, but similar in appearance to a village well. Here, together, they drink and this symbolical sort of communion is the emotional culmination of the whole story. (p. 10)

The very words of the little prince just before they set out on their quest—"J'ai soif aussi", suggest Christ, and the lesson the little prince leaves with the author after their "Last Supper" is just another variant of the Christian "Love one another."

After the little prince is gone, Saint-Exupéry leaves the desert but he is a changed individual. He has learned that it is not things which matter but their spirit. The corporeal form of the little prince was only "une écorce" and the author's belief in immortality, if you like, has been affirmed. The influence of the "little prince" whom he grew to love will continue to make itself felt on his life.

Now, it would be quite wrong to suggest that the little prince is in every respect like Christ. After all, he did not come to the earth to save men nor did he even sacrifice himself for the author. He wanted to return to his own planet and his beloved rose. The little prince does not have perfect knowledge when he reaches earth and he is no teacher except in the sense that the candour of a child can cause an adult to see with new eyes the idiosyncracies of the adult world.

But on the other hand, since the rose represents spiritual love in the life of the little prince, one might argue that he sacrificed himself for love of another and by his example inspired the author, who, by writing his "Gospel", is passing on to other children the story of the "little prince."

At any rate, I do not think it is too far-fetched to suggest that parts of the story of the little prince are remarkably like a fairy-tale transposition of certain episodes in the life of Christ and that this metaphorical sublimation accounts in part for the enduring popularity both with children and with adults of Saint-Exupéry's **"Le Petit Prince."** (p. 11)

Victor E. Graham, "Religion and Saint-Exupéry's 'Le Petit Prince'," in The Canadian Modern Language Review / La Revue canadienne des langues vivantes, *Vol. XV, No. 3, 1959, pp. 9-11.*

BETTINA HÜRLIMANN

[The following excerpt was originally published in German in 1959.]

Saint-Exupéry's *Little prince* is the most fragile and delicate of all those child-figures in children's literature (even though they may be for children in only a limited sense) whom we may set against the violent and conceited figures of the 'Superman', 'Mickey Mouse', 'Knatterton', and 'Globi' tradition. He is indeed so delicate that it may seem perverse to mention him in the same breath as this little bunch of storm-troopers who seek to attack all that is most humane on behalf of a pulp literature, which ranges from the swashbuckling to the downright brutal. But the little prince is a figure of courage. He has left the asteroid which is his home, has flown down to earth and has given up his life to save his soul, and that should be courageous enough for us. He has a certain innocence, a purity of heart, which is common to all the men of goodwill in children's literature, however differently they may otherwise express themselves.

The little prince may count himself first in their ranks. . . . Let us examine [Saint-Exupéry's] creation more closely. Is it rooted in fairy tale? Does the little prince represent one of those fairy-story characters that we know so well? To some extent he does, otherwise he would scarcely be a prince, for princes today are a dying race. But no prince in the fairy stories we know ever came down to us from outer space and none ever encountered before the figure that he met—an airman with his plane, forced down in the desert. This man is of the first importance, however, for it is up to him to tell the story; nobody except him, the airman with nine parched days in the desert behind him, has seen the prince or can say what happened. He talked to him every day and it is primarily their conversations which he has written down. With all the seriousness of an adult, but with the innocence of the child that he once was, Saint-Exupéry sets down these conversations and these events. (p. 93)

[It] is necessary for me now to touch on some of the factors which make *Le petit prince* in spite of everything a book for children. If publishers' figures are correct, then hundreds of thousands, not to say millions, of people must have read this book, among them a great many children and young people, and it was, after all, for them that it was written.

First of all there is the airman taking his engine to bits. For many children the story of the crashed airman, the final success of his repairs, the discovery of the well, and his return home, will be more interesting than the figure of the little prince, who is perhaps only some kind of Fata Morgana. He has to be accepted, because he leads the airman to the vital well.

But the more a child thinks about it, the more he will see the little prince as an important fellow actor. He will follow the dialogue between the two, without understanding all of it, and he will sense part of the great sadness which surrounds this eternally lonely little figure. But no child will understand the briefly recounted end of this little creature, which has every outward resemblance to a sacrifice. For if this were a proper fairy tale the prince would have to return to his asteroid and to his flower again, on whose account he got the airman to go through all that trouble of drawing a sheep with a muzzle on.

Saint-Exupéry the poet appends a comforting chapter to the end of his story. He says that he does believe that the little prince returned to his own planet. He himself loves to listen to the stars which are like five hundred million little bells and, 'full of wild surmise', he thinks of the desert as being the loveliest and saddest landscape in the world, where each of us may meet the little prince for ourselves. In this entrancing conclusion it is possible that he overestimates his audience of children in turning to them and only them in such an intimate way ('Et aucune grande personne ne comprendra jamais que ça a tellement d'importance!').

There may be some rare 'corrupted' adults and perhaps some quite uncorrupted children who hear the music of the stars. And perhaps they will remark some change in the heavens when, on an invisible planet high in the firmament, inside the picture of a box, the picture of a sheep (the strap of whose muzzle the airman has forgotten to draw) eats up the red rose belonging to a little prince.

This mental flight into the firmament will fascinate many children. For here is a universe which is different from that in Grimm's *Sterntaler*, different from that with its paved Milky Way in the book *Peterchens Mondfahrt (Little Peter's journey to the moon)*, which was the favourite of our own nurseries and is so still for many present-day children, different even from that of the bold adventurers in the books of Jules Verne. It is a universe which, despite the little golden-haired prince and his beloved flower, belongs to modern man with all the horrors and all the attractions of infinity—for some, nothing but fearful chaos, for others, an example of the most perfect order.

This is a book of pronounced individuality and the legacy of a writer tragically killed. Let us, nevertheless, try to place it in the context of great children's literature where, by reason of its conception and its unparalleled success, it truly belongs.

Saint-Exupéry, brought up in a kind and cultivated household, certainly knew the classic collections of fairy stories. He must surely have loved Andersen, for he has in common with him the rare courage to create a tragic ending. The little prince, bitten by the snake, 'fell as gently as a tree falls' and the little mermaid, whose destiny is fulfilled, dissolves into foam. Although a century separates them, they are both creations of the same temperament. They are even united in their courage and their final loneliness.

Is it possible that the author also knew the captivating nonsense of Carroll's *Alice in Wonderland*? Such a thing is easy to believe when you consider how the little prince put his planet in order, covering his flower with a glass globe, sweeping out his knee-high volcanoes, of which the two active ones were useful for cooking his breakfast on and the one extinct one served as a footstool. This little universe, so prosaic and yet so improbable, contains also the asteroid with the lamplighter on it, faced with a sun which rises and sets so quickly that he must be for ever lighting his lamp and putting it out again, with never a rest between; and the little prince need take only a couple of paces to enjoy the most beautiful sunset whenever he wishes to look at it. All such things belong to the realm which the English designate 'nonsense' and which, up to this time, was to be found chiefly in English children's books and most prominently of course in those of Lewis Carroll.

At one stage of his journey the little prince says to the businessman:

> Moi, je possède une fleur que j'arrose tous les jours. Je possède trois volcans que je ramone toutes les semaines. Car je ramone aussi celui qui est éteint. On ne sait jamais. C'est utile à mes volcans, et c'est utile à ma fleur, que je les possède.

This is but one place among many where in a childishly simple but by no means primitive way the moralists are shown the arguments for kindness and usefulness in the running of a state, even if it is a state on the smallest planet in the universe.

Whoever knows his way round the world of children and children's books may also recall an older contemporary of the little prince, again French, but this time four-legged, emerging from the brush-strokes of a kindly painter. It is, of course, Babar, that philanthropic monarch who provided his people with happiness and the blessings of peace and culture. . . . [It] is worth drawing attention here to the powerful support which he gives the little prince in today's peaceful battle over young children and their upbringing. Brunhoff's case indeed is simpler, in so far as he has already won the hearts of real children in many countries and in so far as his life is extensively the result of an optimism which still had faith in the progress of goodness. For Babar is a child of the thirties who has not experienced the Second World War. (pp. 94-6)

Saint-Exupéry's story of the prince appeared in 1943, although its conception dates back to 1940, the year when France lost her freedom. The little prince was therefore born in a year of darkest sadness—the year when his creator's country was occupied. . . . Where, therefore, could the little prince live except on a planet which had never been occupied, where could he go but to the desert?

From this we may understand the sadness which pervades this book and the feeling for humanity which radiates from this small, lonely child. The problems which the little prince argued with the airman are the problems of our own time—which the writer has now left for good.

The superficiality, the noise, and the harshness of our century, together with its cold reliance upon science and economics—all this is there. Its clearest symbol lies in the garden full of roses against which is set the one rose that is really treasured. It no longer has anything to do with children's books, or even with politics, and only to a limited extent with literature itself.

The lonely traveller in the skies, who passes hour upon hour alone with his wild machine, who has shut out all the voices of the outer world, has heard the voice within himself. The pilot, with death constantly before him, has listened to the voices of true life and from a keen love for just this life he has set down his 'little prince' on paper. The thing that moves us most is the extraordinarily delicate touch of this, the most masculine of modern writers; the tenderness which the big, coarse aviator feels for the small, charming creature who suddenly stands beside him and says: 'S'il vous plaît . . . dessinemoi un mouton.' But there is a similar tenderness in the little prince's feelings for his one rose and also for his huge, thirsty friend.

At the end of the book, shortly before their parting, the little prince speaks comfortingly about his approaching death, building up a bit of courage to face the yellow snake. He says that from now on the stars, which for some people are only lights and for others only golden coins, will be for the airman a firmament ringing with five hundred million little bells. With these words there enters, in this book for children, a sense of the transcendental, of the things which last for ever. It is presented so strikingly that we are made to forget that such an ending to this fairy tale, such an act of self-destruction on the part of the little prince, has no place in the world of Christian ideas, which has always been for us identical with the transcendental. Instead it comes from the questing spirit of an unbeliever (in the Christian sense) who finds himself face to face with death and infinity. He takes no comfort from God or from eternal life; there are no angels in this modern, fairy-tale heaven; there is just a single, lonely child whose cares have gone out, deep into limitless space, to a little red flower and three small volcanoes, one of which is extinct. (pp. 96-7)

In 1938 a forced landing in the Sahara, during which [Saint-Exupéry] had to struggle hard for his life, was undoubtedly the first cause for the writing of *Le petit prince*. His determination not to let himself or his friends go under in the profound pessimism of his time, which he felt so profoundly, led him to put words into the mouth of a child which would tell of

things no longer thought about by men—but things which Antoine de Saint-Exupéry hoped would offer some cure for the world. (p. 98)

Bettina Hürlimann, ''The Little Prince from Outer Space,'' in her Three Centuries of Children's Books in Europe, *edited and translated by Brian W. Alderson, Oxford University Press, Oxford, 1967, pp. 93-8.*

BONNER MITCHELL

Le Petit Prince may be considered to descend from an illustrious line of allegorical fairy tales which reached its French apogee in the eighteenth century *conte philosophique*. . . . *Le Petit Prince* is much more evidently a piece of creative literature than are **Pilote de guerre** or **Lettre à un otage** and its didacticism is correspondingly less frank. Expository devices are both more varied and more subtle. Like many marvelous and improbable tales, *e.g. Gulliver's Travels,* this one is put into the mouth of a normal, probable person, namely the real-life pilot Saint Exupéry. He speaks in an intimate, down-to-earth way, addressing himself directly to the reader on numerous occasions and explaining with care the more realistic circumstances of his experience. This literary pose is not meant to fool anyone, but it has a definite esthetic and didactic purpose. The narrator's tone constitutes in effect an invitation to reflect along with him upon a series of events which, it is pretended, he does not entirely understand. This is an old procedure for writers of allegory, being found, for example, even in the opening of the

"He carefully cleaned out his active volcanoes."

From The Little Prince, *written and illustrated by Antoine de Saint-Exupéry. Translated by Katherine Woods. Harcourt Brace Jovanovich, 1943. Copyright 1943 by Harcourt Brace Jovanovich, Inc. Reprinted by permission of the publisher.*

Divine Comedy. The device of reflecting aloud upon personal experiences was not, moreover, new to Saint Exupéry but had formed the very backbone of the autobiographical works [*Terre des hommes, Pilote de guerre,* and *Lettre à un otage. Le Petit Prince's*] main message is not contained, however, in the narrator's own remarks, though he does begin to interpret near the end, but must be sought in the actual events and characters which he describes. The book's didacticism is thus superficially covered over. The hero of the tale is not, either, consciously instructive, however inadvertently revealing his remarks may be. He is ever reluctant to answer questions, and it is only near the end that he, too, starts to talk directly about the meaning of his experiences. The story does contain two avowed teachers but both are minor characters. One of these is the Snake, who tells the Prince about death. The other, considerably more prominent, is the Fox, whose imaginatively expressed lessons to the hero are transmitted to the narrator and thence to the reader. These lessons are so closely connected to the events of the story, however, that they would be almost incomprehensible out of context. (pp. 454-55)

The Little Prince declares his scorn for pedestrian adult logic, and his attitude is reflected by certain qualities of the book itself. His remarks in conversations with the narrator often seem inconsequential, though his train of thought is, in another sense, unusually one-tracked. The occasional formal questions of *Pilote de guerre* and *Lettre à un otage,* followed by careful statements of opinion, are paralleled in *Le Petit Prince* by astonishing queries from the hero and the Fox. These questions are seldom answered right away, nor, indeed, are they answerable at all in objective terms. The events of the story, though not out of place in a fairy tale, are of course eminently unreasonable. Yet even in telling of the strangest occurrences the narrator continues to speak the language of a reasonable and practical man, and he provides numerous practical and chronological details. He suggests, as if this event needed a reasonable explanation, that the Prince must have left his planet by means of a migration of birds, and the episodes of the strange journey are kept in a careful sequence. (p. 457)

Le Petit Prince is farther from real life [than *Lettre à un otage*] and its symbols are accordingly both more in evidence and more obscure in meaning. The hero's planet, where he must live in constant relations with his volcanoes, his baobab trees, his rose and, later, with a sheep who may try to eat the rose, clearly represents social institutions, but the precise significance of all that is told about the planet is subject to interpretation. Besides grand symbols such as the planet and the serpent, the story has a host of symbolic details. Virtually everything the hero does, *e.g.* his drinking from a well in the desert, is susceptible of symbolic interpretation; indeed, it obviously requires such interpretation. The story itself, as distinguished from the narrator's "realistic" presentation, is almost pure allegory, much like that of *Le Roman de la rose,* with which it has in common a major symbol. (p. 459)

The author of *Pilote de guerre* and *Lettre à un otage* reasons constantly in a language full of metaphors and similes, but neither the narrator nor the other characters of *Le Petit Prince* habitually talk in such a way. In this work where virtually the whole narrative is symbolic the language of reasoning is markedly down-to-earth. Only the Fox, principal avowed teacher of the book, speaks by preference in metaphors. . . . Near the end, it is true, both the narrator and the Prince begin to summarize in metaphorical terms what they have learned, but these expressions are dependent upon narrative symbols already introduced. (pp. 459-60)

[In summary, *Le Petit Prince*] has an intimate tone and affects a superficial reasonableness, while the burden of its teaching is borne by an elaborate allegory which scorns logic and aims to charm instead of to convince by direct argument. (p. 461)

> *Bonner Mitchell, " 'Le Petit Prince' and 'Citadelle':*
> *Two Experiments in the Didactic Style," in* The French
> *Review, Vol. XXXIII, No. 5, April, 1960, pp. 454-61.*

JAMES E. HIGGINS

[Of *Night Flight, Wind, Sand and Stars,* and *Flight to Arras*] much has been said. They have been described as philosophical, poetic, mystical, rhythmic—and indeed they are. Nonetheless, given but one phrase to describe the essence of their enduring quality, it would have to be said of them that above all else they "disturb."

It is just this disturbing element in his writing which leads me to comment on a part of Saint-Exupéry's legacy which has been overlooked all too often, a slight volume published the year before his disappearance and titled, *The Little Prince,* a book which he said was intended for children.

This little book is one of those which just refuses to drop into a nice neat niche. Is it a fairy tale? A parable? Is it meant for children? Adults? Does the message outweigh the narrative? The list of questions goes on. But perhaps it is precisely here that the very power of the book is to be found. It is unique, it poses problems for the reader, no matter who he may be, and it never fails to respect the intelligence of the reader, no matter how young he may be.

Am I to recommend this book? If so, to whom? How am I going to introduce it? These are some of the special problems that Saint-Exupéry created for me as a librarian, when he introduced me to his Little Prince from Asteroid B-612.

Here is a book to which I am strongly attracted, but the reading experience has been so personal that I dare not recommend it without qualifying it. And what youngster wants a qualified recommendation?

So when I am asked for a good fantasy or fairy tale, now and then I slip in *The Little Prince* with one or two others, with a vague, "Here, try these, and let me know how you like them." I'm sorry to say that up until this time, the kids haven't been able to help me out of my dilemma either. Some liked it; others did not. From speaking to several of them I estimate that some of them found meaning; others did not.

Although the author hints in the dedication that this is a book for children, I still wonder if it is so. I have a hunch, and that's all it can be termed, that he is primarily interested in expressing himself in a new medium. I find the same things here that I found in his wonderful *Night Flight* and his other books, but here they are said in a new way. Perhaps they are said for a new audience; again, I cannot be sure.

Like the painter who turns from oils to water colors, he turns from his philosophical reminiscences to the fairy tale. He disciplines his writing so that the story unfolds in the simple, but poetic style of the traditional fairy tale. Every word seems essential in the telling.

In all of his books Saint-Exupéry expresses a mystical wonder about everyday life and common things. This book is no exception. His experiences as an aviator, his attraction to the culture of the East, and his philosophical outlook, all bring a rich quality of poetry to his work. He carries you away to places high above the clouds, your mind wandering among fields of thoughts, rich and provocative. When you look again, your feet have never left the ground. He has been speaking to you of ordinary things.

The Little Prince would challenge the term ''ordinary things''; to him they are ''matters of consequence.'' He would admonish me as he admonishes the author: ''I know—I, myself,'' he says, ''—one flower which is unique in the world, which grows nowhere but on my planet, but which one little sheep can destroy in a single bite . . . Oh! You think that is not important?''

Booth Tarkington spoofed the foibles of youngsters in *Seventeen*, and sometimes they resent it. But Saint-Exupéry has turned the trick, for here the adults are made the target for satire, and perhaps some of us will resent it. As he says to the children who will read this book, ''I have lived a great deal among grown-ups. I have seen them intimately, close at hand. And that hasn't much improved my opinion of them.''

He isn't making an attempt at being facetious either, for he proceeds to prove his theory that adults have no monopoly on wisdom.

The Little Prince has left his planet and his flower, to search for relief from his loneliness on other planets. (pp. 514-15)

When he first discovers that the flower which he has nurtured so carefully can be found by the millions on Earth, he becomes despondent. But slowly it is revealed to him that his flower is no less wonderful because of this, until he is finally able to say to a field of roses: ''You are not at all like my rose . . . in herself alone she is more important than all the hundreds of you other roses: because it is she that I have watered . . . because it is she that I have sheltered . . . because it is for her that I killed the caterpillars . . . because it is she that I have listened to when she grumbled or boasted, or even sometimes when she said nothing. Because she is *my* rose.''

This, therefore, is a love story. A love story in its own terms. Nor is it especially in terms for children, but rather in terms of universality; the same in which Hans Christian Andersen found himself so comfortable. (p. 515)

One reason why I find it difficult to categorize this little book of over 91 pages (the last two pages are left unnumbered for effect), is because it deals with the emotions rather than the intellect. Indeed, this is one of the messages it ticks out quietly to the reader; that even in this age of science, the poet sees far more than the analyst. The fox gives the Little Prince ''a very simple secret: It is only with the heart that one can see rightly; what is essential is invisible to the eye.'' More heresy!

The book is beautifully and simply illustrated by the author. The illustrations do not merely supplement the reading, but rather they are an integral part of the story. Several times during the narrative the reader is referred to the drawings. . . .

The sketch on the last page consists of a star and a few delicate lines representing an horizon. It says visually what the author has already said in language.

The language in the English translation, done by Katherine Woods, is so poetic that it made this reader wish that he were better equipped to read the original French.

Perhaps what I have said about this book, and the quotes which I have used, only give strength to the argument that Saint-Exupéry has taken on too much in attempting to communicate such ideas to children. Whether he has, or has not, is not of

prime importance to me. I thank him for making the attempt. More artists should have such faith in the capacities of young people. More writers should be ready to disturb the complacency of librarians like myself.

The Little Prince is an important part of the legacy which Antoine de Saint-Exupéry has left behind; a remembrance so strong and immediate that I cannot help but write of it in the present tense. Surely, this book lives today; so too does its author. (p. 572)

James E. Higgins, '' 'The Little Prince': A Legacy,'' in Elementary English, *Vol. XXXVIII, No. 8, December, 1960, pp. 514-15, 572.*

MARGERY FISHER

I suspect **The Little Prince** is something of a test piece (like the spinach story or *Alice*). To some people this piece of elaborate fancy about an aviator in the desert and a little prince from another planet, who comments artlessly on truth and beauty, mechanisation, greed and death, plumbs the deeps of human thought. To me, it is a piece of heavy, facetious and rather unpleasant whimsy; I wonder how many children would agree.

Margery Fisher, in a review of ''The Little Prince,'' in her Growing Point, *Vol. 1, No. 7, January, 1963, p. 107.*

ANDRÉ MAUROIS

[Maurois was a versatile French man of letters who made his most significant contribution to literature as a biographer. A friend of Saint-Exupéry, Maurois visited the author during the writing of The Little Prince.*]*

I shall certainly not try to ''explain'' **Le Petit Prince.** That children's book for grownups is alive with symbols which are beautiful because they seem, at the same time, both lucid and obscure. The essential virtue of a work of art is that it has its own significance, without reference to abstract concepts. A cathedral does not require commentaries, the starry vault does not require footnotes. I believe that **Le Petit Prince** may be an incarnation of Tonio [Saint-Exupéry] as a child. But as *Alice in Wonderland* was at the same time a tale for little girls and a satire on the Victorian world, **Le Petit Prince,** in its poetic melancholy, contains a whole philosophy. The king is obeyed only when he orders what would, in any case, occur. The lamplighter is respected because he is occupied with other things besides himself; the businessman is scoffed at because he thinks that stars or flowers can be ''possessed''; the fox lets himself be tamed in order to recognize a footstep that will be different from all others. ''One only knows the things that one tames, says the fox. Men buy things already made in the stores. But as there are no stores where friends can be bought, men no longer have friends.'' **Le Petit Prince** is the work of a wise and tender hero who did have friends. (pp. 215-16)

André Maurois, ''Antoine de Saint-Exupéry,'' translated by Renaud Bruce, in From Proust to Camus: Profiles of Modern French Writers *by André Maurois, translated by Carl Morse and Renaud Bruce, 1966. Reprint by Weidenfeld and Nicolson, 1967, pp. 201-23.*

ROBERT H. PRICE

Among all the French writers in the great tradition of the imaginary voyage, two seem to stand out as particularly kindred souls: Rabelais and Saint-Exupéry. What a fine case for literary influence could be made here if only Saint-Exupéry or one of his biographers mentioned Rabelais! We could then immediately ascribe the striking parallels to direct and conscious influence and thereby validate the internal evidence, just as it is possible to do with Pascal's *Pensées* and Saint-Exupéry's *Citadelle* [*The Wisdom of the Sands*] on the basis of Dr. Pélissier's first-hand knowledge of Saint-Exupéry's favorite authors. But there is no external evidence of any kind to support such a conjecture in the present instance and, however plausible it may seem, we cannot make the claim that Saint-Exupéry had Rabelais' fourth and fifth books of *Pantagruel* in mind when he wrote *Le Petit Prince*. We must content ourselves with seeing how the evident parallels in these works tend to throw into sharper relief certain otherwise enigmatic features of their shared theme of fanciful voyage and alienation from reality. The thematic and stylistic parallels also serve to underscore the essential spiritual kinship of these two profoundly humanistic authors, each of whom was a writer by avocation suffering in exile at the time he conceived of the work in question. The big prince, Pantagruel, at sea, and the little prince, in space, were seeking, as were their creators, reassurance and solid ground—a basis upon which to construct an ideal.

Both works can be read and enjoyed on two levels, and their authors insist that we not neglect the higher one. (pp. 264-65)

Saint-Exupéry, in order to stress the need to see beneath the surface of things, uses the device of the open and closed boa constrictor drawings at the beginning of *Le Petit Prince*. He also tells us of the Turkish astronomer who discovered in 1909 asteroid B 612, the little prince's home, but whom nobody believed at the International Congress of Astronomy because of his outlandish Turkish clothes. If, despite these examples and others, there is still any doubt left in the reader's mind about the author's intentions, he states unequivocally and with a touch of acerbity: "[. . .] je n'aime pas qu'on lise mon livre à la légère." (p. 265)

The dual nature of Rabelais' *Le Quart Livre* and of Saint-Exupéry's *Le Petit Prince* is probably a reflection of the very dual nature of life as experienced by the two authors in exile. There are, according to both these spiritual humanists, two levels of reality in life, and it is the deeper or, from the spiritual point of view, the higher level to which man must aspire if he is to arrive at ultimate truth. The conception of reality as expressed by Plato in his parable of the cave is analogous. But whereas for Plato, value exists independently of a valuator, for Saint-Exupéry, and doubtless for Rabelais, there is no such thing as *a priori* value. Rather, *man* is the measure of all things, and the world takes on meaning and value for him only insofar as he puts meaning and value into it by his involvement with, and contributions to, his fellow men. This conception is foreign neither to Renaissance thought nor to certain schools of twentieth-century French thought. Indeed, relativism is one of their basic characteristics and establishes an often overlooked affinity between two eras widely separated in time.

The peregrinations of the two princes illustrate the nature of this type of quest for individual truth. Rabelais chooses a long sea voyage . . . to symbolize his alienation from familiar reality and a quest for solid spiritual ground, for the trip was not undertaken solely for the purpose of finding out whether Panurge should marry or not; it was essentially a voyage of self-discovery. Whereas Saint-Exupéry, the aviator, naturally chooses the medium of space. . . . (pp. 265-66)

In reading these fanciful philosophical travel accounts we must always be aware of the fact that each author projects himself into a personified alter ego in which he mirrors his personal

growth. Pantagruel, whom Rabelais now rarely reminds us is a physical giant, gradually becomes during the course of the voyage a superior being—a giant in *moral* stature—the symbol of human potentiality. Likewise, the little prince through his encounter with the fox eventually discovers the answers to the great questions in life and rids his spirit of torment and uncertainty. In dealing with this process of spiritual growth, both authors use physical thirst as a symbol of spiritual thirst. (p. 266)

As seekers thirsting for ultimate truth, neither Rabelais nor Saint-Exupéry wrote from a dogmatic or even systematic point of view. Neither one was installed in a philosophical or theological system. They both insisted on freedom from preconceptions and prescriptions in their search for truth. And, likewise, it was in the very process of writing that their thoughts, and the form in which they expressed them took shape and direction. (pp. 266-67)

We know from the message of *Citadelle* that Saint-Exupéry was convinced that the future was unpredictable in life as well as in the artistic creative process—and so did Rabelais if we can take his scorn of fortunetellers in *Le Tiers Livre* as an indication.

Saint-Exupéry in maintaining that existence or creation precedes the plan is very close to existentialism. In all his works, it is evident that he insists on the vital need for man to grow and to define himself on the basis of his acts. And, according to Saint-Exupéry, man can meet this need only insofar as he establishes bonds of responsibility with his fellow men. The little prince learns that he is responsible for his rose and that it is the time and energy that he devotes to the care of his rose that endows it with value and meaning, thus giving him purpose and direction in life. It is unlikely that Rabelais, the dedicated and skilled physician, felt any differently about man's role in life. He detested the monastic ideal of withdrawal from life and everything else that he deemed to be a hindrance to man's physical, mental, and spiritual growth. The irrepressible Frère Jean des Entommeures is indication enough that Rabelais felt, as did Saint-Exupéry, that man, if he is to give meaning to his existence, must act in such a way as to be able to give meaning to his actions. Man is what he does, and if he can ascribe no significant and satisfying purpose to what he does, he can only drift aimlessly on the sea of life.

Pantagruel and the little prince do not drift during their voyages. They continually define themselves and become increasingly aware of their direction in life as they discover and disengage that "structure which alone matters." To be sure, Rabelais and Saint-Exupéry were seekers during their entire lifetime. But each one was, at the same time, quite clear in his own mind about what constituted obstacles to man's attempts to realize his full potential and promise as a human being. Neither Rabelais nor Saint-Exupéry had any patience with stupidity, superstition, preconceptions, and prejudices which thwart the growth of human dignity and rob man of his rightful equanimity and nobility of spirit. The *escales* or stopping-off places in both works (islands in one and planets in the other) afford the authors the opportunity to represent in the inhabitants the enemies of the ideal they had in mind. Allegorical social satire in the form of grotesque caricaturization shows how strongly the two authors felt about certain human preoccupations, attitudes, and vices. The reader is confronted with a series of ludicrous and frequently harmful cases of monomania which prevent man from extending his horizons. Constrained by intellectual and spiritual blinders, the various freaks fail even to glimpse the vision of their potential stature as men. The monomaniacs on the islands and planets are victims of their own simplistic and distorted views of life. Erich Auerbach sums it up nicely: "Thick-headedness, inability to adjust, one-track arrogance which blinds a man to the complexity of the real situation are vices to Rabelais. This is the form of stupidity which he mocks and pursues." The same appraisal, of course, holds true for Saint-Exupéry.

There can be little doubt that Rabelais believed self-discovery to be the most vital knowledge to which man can attain. Echos of Socrates are to be found throughout his writings. Besides mentioning the philosopher specifically in the prologue to *Gargantua* and elsewhere, Rabelais frequently alludes in various ways to the Socratic (or more properly, the Delphic) precept, "Know thyself." (pp. 267-69)

[According to Rabelais, self-knowledge] is the *sine qua non* of human endeavor, for to know one's own mind, it is necessary first to know one's own self. Man must make the attempt to find out what he is before he *can* know what he wants—before he *can* make meaningful and satisfying choices and thus live life to the fullest. The little prince after drinking from the well in the desert commented on its meaning to him and on the ultimate meaning of all things in life by repeating the lesson that the fox had taught him. . . . (p. 269)

The quest for self-knowledge and definition is perhaps one of the most salient commonly-shared features of sixteenth and twentieth-century French thought. (p. 270)

> Robert H. Price, " 'Pantagruel' and 'Le Petit Prince'," in Symposium, Vol. XXI, No. 3, Fall, 1967, pp. 264-70.*

PUBLISHERS WEEKLY

Back when we were courting, young men deluged us with copies of **"The Little Prince,"** that delicate, lovely and luminous story about a little prince who lived all alone on a star. . . . *Everybody* read and loved **"The Little Prince;"** it's been a steady seller since 1943, when . . . [it was first published] with little, delicate, lovely and luminous illustrations by the author. But we've waited 15 years to say this: we *hated* **"The Little Prince."**

> A review of "The Little Prince," in Publishers Weekly, Vol. 193, No. 9, February 26, 1968, p. 179.

ANNE W. DODD

The Little Prince is a short, charming book which lends itself well to an introduction of theme and symbolism in prose. Because *The Little Prince* is deceptively simple, the narrative can be easily read by seventh grade students, even many who are reading below grade level. Few students fail to fall in love with the little prince. . . . The people he meets in his travels are representative of many human characteristics that lead man astray and cause him to miss the essentials in life: beauty, love and friendship. (p. 772)

One major theme of *The Little Prince,* humanitarianism versus materialism, is one that is especially relevant in our world today. The teacher can easily direct the students to myriad examples of the little prince's ideas of grown-ups in the home, the school, and the community. The timelessness of the little prince's essentials in life (beauty, love and friendship) affords so many areas for inquiry that the teacher need not fear a lack of discussion material. No doubt you will notice how well a discussion of "flower children" ties in with *The Little Prince*! Perhaps he is unique in that he is an unspoiled flower child.

The little prince and the narrator of the story see mankind divided into two groups: grown-ups and children. Children recognize the important things in life because they have not adopted the materialistic outlook of grown-ups. Grown-ups always have to have things explained to them, but they never ask questions about essential matters. . . . Children, on the other hand, are concerned not with materialism, but with love, beauty, and friendship. . . . It is important to help the students realize that these categories are not all-inclusive: children may be materialistic; adults may be able to appreciate the beautiful and important things in life with no thoughts of money or acquiring status. A person's attitude, not his age, determines whether he is a "child" or a "grown-up".

Again and again in the book the differences between "grown-ups" and "children" are stressed. These differences constitute what we call the "generation gap". Grown-ups are portrayed as having no interests other than facts and figures, "matters of consequence". This phrase recurs as a key one describing grown-ups and their materialistic points-of-view. (pp. 772-73)

Although the narrative is simple, it is filled with symbols and philosophical material for discussion. (p. 773)

Philosophical problems, such as the meanings of life and death, are . . . explored in *The Little Prince*. Life and death can have significances quite different from those one usually associates with them; their importance is relative. One way in which this fact is pointed out is the method by which the little prince returns to his planet. The snake bites him; the little prince falls gently on the sand. The narrator, however, does not consider the little prince dead as we probably would. When he cannot find the little prince's body at daybreak, he assumes he has returned to his planet. . . . Death here is not final as far as the narrator is concerned. Life for the little prince has been given a meaning by the fox's secret. Because of the fox the little prince comes to understand why his rose is so valuable. If life can have more meaning, death, too, has another meaning here. Although it causes the little prince's body to disappear, the union of hearts has survived. Taking the time to tame someone in life makes this survival possible. Perhaps there is a hint here of a life after death, for the little prince does return to his planet and his rose; would that not be heaven for him?

There is so much that can be discussed in *The Little Prince* that I have only scratched the surface here. The combination in the book of fantasy, satire, philosophy, poetry, science, imagination, and childish gaiety can capture the hearts and minds of "grown-ups" as well as "children" in only ninety-two short pages. *The Little Prince* serves as an excellent introduction to interpreting literature for seventh graders; when studied in greater depth, it will certainly challenge older students also. (pp. 774-75)

> Anne W. Dodd, " 'The Little Prince': A Study for Seventh Grade in Interpretation of Literature," in Elementary English, Vol. XLVI, No. 6, October, 1969, pp. 772-76.

PHILIP MOONEY, S. J.

[*The Little Prince* is a] children's tale for adults—no one could mistake its basic meaning: Technology on its own can never bring human happiness because it can neither create human relationship nor reveal the person of another. The scientific approach, with its computerized classifications, is necessarily impersonal. Only the initiative of personal concern discloses the other to us, breaks down isolation and builds community among men. . . .

In the story the little Prince's quest is for friendship with man. ''Be my friend'' is the invitation he tenders when he arrives on earth. The invitation is shunted aside as the Prince encounters the impersonal, scientific, ''IBM'' posture in ''grown-ups who are no longer interested in anything but figures.''

The little Prince's overtures of friendship finally find a hearing in the person of the stranded aviator, Saint-Ex, as narrator of the tale. But even with this airman, to whom his machine is such a ''matter of consequence,'' the Prince must rehearse the wisdom of personhood through the parable of the fox. In a scientific age, scientific preoccupations tend to assume supreme significance. So it is that the aviator yields only sluggishly to the personal approach of the little Prince. But in the end it becomes his very own.

Saint-Ex acknowledges at the outset that he was all alone, without anyone he could really talk to, until he had an accident with his plane in the desert. But in responding to the little Prince's initiative of friendship, the pilot overcomes his isolation, ''establishes ties'' with the little Prince, and experiences anew the Christmas happiness of his childhood.... With the little Prince, Saint-Ex comes to be as a person ''in the impenetrable mystery of his presence.'' ...

Only another person's initial gesture of love can draw forth the personal response of concern, care, interest and love that *becomes a person so....* As John Macmurray so well says: ''To be an I is to be in the presence of You.'' But since I am a constant *I* as I go through life, there must be a constant *You* in whose totally concerned presence I am always coming to be as a person. This *You* must be in all the You's of my experience, yet transcendent of them all. This *You* is the Word become flesh as God's gift of total love for each man—''For God so loved the world that he gave his only-begotten Son.'' This *You* is Jesus Christ, Saint-Ex's little Prince.

Saint-Exupéry furnishes careful clues that identify the little Prince as the boy Jesus. (Christ comes as a boy, for who can be afraid to be himself in the presence of a child?) The little Prince first appears on earth in a sector of the Mediterranean desert beneath his particular star. His time on earth is preset, and when his hour of darkness comes for him to leave this world, it is the power of the ''serpent'' that sends him to his suffering and death. But the little Prince has confided to the aviator that he will prevail over death. ''I shall look as if I were dead, and that will not be true.'' The morning after the little Prince's death, his body is nowhere to be found. Saint-Ex knows that his Prince lives on; the Prince had told him....

Christ as the little Prince will always be a *responsible* friend to him. Of this Saint-Ex has no doubt: ''What moves me so deeply about this little prince who is sleeping here, is his loyalty to a flower—the image of a rose that shines through his whole being like the flame of a lamp, even when he is asleep.'' The little Prince had assured the flier he would be responsible for his rose.

The rose is the image in the heart of Christ of what Saint-Exupéry can become as a person in the sunshine of the presence of the little Prince. The little Prince as the constant *You* for Saint-Ex has tendered the initial grace of love, care and concern in his responsibility for his rose. But Saint-Ex must do his part. He too is responsible for the rose, for the person he can become. He must attend to the rose by virtue of his love for others. Saint-Ex will come to full flower as a person in the presence of the little Prince, even as he goes out in love to all those with whom Christ has identified Himself—''As long as

you did it for one of these, the least of my brethren, you did it for me.'' He must follow the wisdom of the little Prince: ''It is only with the heart that one can see rightly; what is essential is invisible to the eye.'' In this way the flier will never again be alone. He will create community and will experience the happiness ''born of the walk under the stars'' with the little Prince. (p. 611)

Philip Mooney, S. J., '' 'The Little Prince': A Story for Our Time,'' in America, *Vol. 121, No. 21, December 20, 1969, pp. 610-11, 614.*

ISABELLE JAN

[The following excerpt was originally published in French in 1969.]

Le petit prince is perplexing both for adults and children. It is the prototype of the work on two levels; it is about childhood yet apparently addressed to children. Children are shown as living in a world of their own and are therefore fundamentally different from grown-ups—they can see things the adult is no longer able to perceive. Thus it is the adult who plays at make-believe while the child is really living and dealing with serious matters such as the rose and the stars. The author, with one foot in each world, tries to explain the child to the adult and the child to himself. However, such a clear-cut demarcation between the two worlds is arbitrary, not to say misleading;

Saint-Exupéry beside the wreckage of his plane after crashing in the Libyan desert. Photograph by M. Racaud.

these are not, in fact, systematically opposed states but complementary ones whose interplay can be perceived by poets. *Le petit prince* is an essentially didactic work in that it is an exposition of Saint-Exupéry's thoughts on the subject of innocence—and is therefore mainly of interest to the Saint-Exupéry fan. However, children are informed in this statement addressed primarily to them, that they inhabit a distant, ideal planet where love is truly love and they cannot fail to be flattered by such a view. But this does not alter the fact that he expresses a rather superficially manichean and pessimistic conception of the world in a not very inspiring symbolism; pure, altruistic reactions are confined to the heavens—or more precisely to the star 'where love is forever' as the song goes. (pp. 76-7)

> Isabelle Jan, "Through the Looking Glass," in her
> On Children's Literature, *edited by Catherine Storr,*
> Schocken Books, 1974, pp. 56-78.*

CURTIS CATE

From *Pilote de Guerre*, strange as it might seem, it was but a short step to Saint-Exupéry's next work, *Le Petit Prince*, which he began writing in the summer of 1942. For the critique of collectivist thinking and western materialism which emerges in such exalted tones towards the end of *Flight to Arras* was more simply expressed in this later work. The Little Prince of this charming fable for adults is not simply the child Saint-Ex would have liked to father . . . ; in his solitary isolation he is a symbol of what modern man has become on a planet where increasingly there is no "gardener for men". "The important thing" as he had written in *Flight to Arras,* "is not exaltation. There is no hope of exaltation in defeat. The important thing is to get dressed, to climb aboard, to take off. What we may think of it ourselves is of no importance. The child who would derive a sense of exaltation from grammar lessons would strike me as suspect and pretentious. The important thing is to conduct oneself with reference to a goal which is not immediately visible." Invisible in just such a way is the goal which leads on K in Kafka's *The Castle,* a book which made a deep impression on Saint-Exupéry when he read it. Like K's, the universe of the Little Prince is full of baffling mysteries, and the frozen note of solitude which haunts it stems from an absence which had made of this lonely child an orphan. What that absence is is never explicitly stated in *The Little Prince,* but it is everywhere implied. As Saint-Ex had written years before in his notebook, à propos of Abbé Sertillanges' *Sources de la Croyance en Dieu* (Origins of the Belief in God): "Too soon deprived of God at an age when one still seeks refuge, here we must struggle for life like little solitary fellows."

For years, in countless letters written on restaurant menus and random sheets of paper, this "petit bonhomme solitaire" had been appearing in a variety of disguises: sometimes seated on a cloud with a crown on his head, sometimes posted on a mountain-top. . . . [Rare was the day at the Café Arnold] that Saint-Ex would not amuse his friends Hélène and Pierre Lazareff covering the paper napkins with pencil drawings of his Little Prince.

It is often difficult in the life of a writer to know at just what point and for what reason a diffuse nebula of ideas suddenly begins to solidify into the nucleus of a book. Such is not the case with *The Little Prince*, whose genesis . . . can be traced back to one of these napkin-drawing sessions. (pp. 457-58)

The idea of writing a children's fable was not originally Saint-Exupéry's at all. It all started one day over a lunch-table in a New York restaurant. Intrigued by Saint-Ex's doodlings on the white table cloth . . . [publisher] Curtice Hitchcock asked him what he was drawing.

"Oh nothing much," was the reply. "Just a little fellow I carry around in my heart."

Hitchcock treated the little fellow to a closer inspection and it gave him an idea. "Now look, this little fellow—what would you think of making up a story about him . . . for a children's book?"

The idea took Saint-Exupéry completely by surprise. He had never thought of himself as a professional writer, still less as an author of children's books. But once the seed of the idea had been planted, it kept steadily growing, nurtured as it was by the gentle prodding of his publisher. A children's book . . . for Christmas? The season of candles he had always loved . . . and children? He who seemed destined never to have any of his own, much as he had longed for them . . . Well, for lack of a real one, why not an imaginary little Antoine? . . . "Just think," he told Léon Wencelius a few days after this luncheon, "they're now asking me to write a book for children! . . . Accompany me to the stationer's would you? I want to buy some coloured pencils."

The pencils bought, Saint-Ex got to work on a few experimental drawings, which were probably intended to "fix" his still nebulous ideas. He then besought the assistance of his old Beaux-Arts colleague, Bernard Lamotte, whose illustrations for *Flight to Arras* had bowled him over for their "telepathic" accuracy of detail. Lamotte responded with a few sample sketches which left Saint-Ex dissatisfied: they were insufficiently naive and dream-like for the effect he wanted to convey. As the days passed and he became more absorbed by his tale, he began to realize that he would have to illustrate as well as write it himself. He continued to solicit his friend's expert advice, but his own ideas had now begun to jell, and one day, after a sleepless night spent painting a baobab tree uprooting a tiny planet, he refused to make the slightest alteration.

"You should straighten it up a bit here, darken it a bit there," began Lamotte.

"Impossible, *mon vieux*," answered Saint-Ex. "If this were a written text, all right—I would agree to modify it, for after all I'm a writer. That's my job. But I can't do better than this drawing. It's quite simply a miracle . . ." And that was that. (p. 461)

"Life" as Jonathan Swift once observed, "is a comedy for him who thinks and a tragedy for him who feels". Saint-Ex felt as deeply as he thought, and the resultant allegory in this case proved both humorous and sad. It was also occasionally sharp, as allegories are apt to be, which may partially (but only partially) explain the lack of an enthusiastic response comparable to that which *Flight to Arras* had enjoyed for weeks on end with the American reading public. Though Beatrice Sherman gave it a sympathetic treatment in the April 11, 1943 issue of *The New York Times Book Review* [see excerpt above], other reviewers seem to have been at a loss as to just how to interpret a book which could not easily be pigeon-holed. Writing some six months later in *The Commonweal* Harry Louis Binsse was forced to confess, a trifle wistfully, that he was one of the few American critics who regarded this little fable as something of a classic—"a sad classic to make the tears flow, but there is a joy in crying even for childhood, and childhood sometimes does not take as tragic what to me as an adult is tragic indeed.

But in this opinion I seem to be somewhat alone. The book has had no tremendous success though it was published last spring, and perhaps my judgment is wrong. What I suspect is that the public does not readily accept something from an author which does not fit into the category in which the public has placed that author, and for an imaginative airman to write what amounts to a fairy story—or at least a fanciful allegory—is perhaps too much for the public to swallow.''

It is also possible that certain critics were put off by the ironic digs at American civilization—as in the figure of the "businessman" (the word used in the French as well as the English text) too busy counting his millions of stars to be able to enjoy a single one, or in that of the pharmaceutical salesman whose thirst-curing pills allow one to save exactly fifty-three minutes per week. But they are only two of the protagonists whom the author mocked with a gentle humour which betrays no prejudice or "parti pris," since the others in this rogues' gallery include an ermine-robed king, a bearded pedant of a geographer, a humble lamp-lighter, a feather-hatted fop waiting for someone to admire the elegance of his attire, and even a lugubrious toper, who when asked by the Little Prince why he drinks, replies:

> "To forget."
>
> "To forget what?" inquired the Little Prince, already feeling sorry for him.
>
> "To forget that I am ashamed," confessed the drinker, bowing his head.
>
> "Ashamed of what?" asked the Little Prince who wanted to help him.
>
> "Ashamed of drinking!" concluded the drinker, shutting himself into a definitive silence.

This was the kind of circular, self-demonstrating syllogism which Saint-Exupéry in his spare moments liked to try out on friends and particularly on those who took pride in their "logical" turn of mind. It was a trait he shared with Charles Dodgson, better known as Lewis Carroll, an eminent mathematician who enjoyed devising theorems which had a baffling way of disproving their axioms.

Lewis Carroll patterned his Alice after a little girl he knew, and the Little Prince, of course, is Saint-Ex as a child. The Rose it is his duty to tend is a more complex creation, being first of all a symbol, but she is also very feminine and flighty, like Consuelo. . . . The Little Prince's three volcanoes, which he regularly sweeps like a chimney, were similarly inspired by the dead craters Saint-Ex had seen in southern Patagonia. Like all great fables, this one is as full of enchantment for a child as it is rich in nourishment for adults. . . . It echoes, on a purely lyric plane, many of the themes its author had most to heart: the fragility of joy ("A rose . . . is a somewhat melancholy fête.''), the primordial importance of love, without which one is blind—expressed in the little fox's secret. "One sees only with the heart. The essential is invisible to the eye." The importance of a mission, a duty, an obligation in life— exemplified by the lamp-lighter who lights and extinguishes his lamp because that is the way things are—"C'est la consigne" (Orders are orders). The vanity of riches and his abhorrence of the collective hurly-burly of metropolitan existence— symbolised by the train-switch operator, routing and rerouting passing expresses full of yawning and dozing passengers who have no idea whither they are bound, save for the little children with their noses pressed to the window-panes. The pleasure

which comes not because it is given or received but because it has been earned, like the sweet water of the well "born of the march under the stars, of the chant of the pulley, of the effort of my arms". And not least of all, the feeling that his broken-jointed carcass was done for. . . . "I can't carry off this body. It's too heavy," says the Little Prince as he prepared to return to his tiny star. "But it will be like an old discarded rind." Miraculously his old warhorse of a body had survived the hazards of the débâcle, but Saint-Ex could feel it creaking with every step he took—a battered carapace, a mortal coil he could not reel off and which his soaring spirit would have to drag around, like a prisoner's ball and chain, to the very end of his days. (pp. 464-66)

> *Curtis Cate, in his* Antoine de Saint-Exupéry, *G. P. Putnam's Sons, 1970, 608 p.*

JAMES E. HIGGINS

It is seldom considered that one of the basic needs of an author is to have an audience, not an audience who will buy his book after it is written, but rather one to whom he can speak during the lonely hours of his writing. (pp. 13-14)

In the years following the fall of France to Hitler in 1940, Antoine de Saint-Exupéry was in search of an audience. The famous French aviator-author had come to the United States in the hope that this would be the quickest way for him to rejoin his flying comrades in Tunis. His American publishers had established him in a New York apartment, where they hoped that he would write. He found it difficult. All biographical references indicate that he was experiencing a deep spiritual depression during this period. It was more than France's defeat that troubled him; he was bothered more by the fate of all mankind. Though his thoughts were grave, they were, at the same time, so simple in nature that he seriously doubted whether he would find anyone who might listen.

The adults he met were mostly concerned with "matters of consequence"—war bulletins, the stock market, golf, business, bridge, politics, fashions and such. He was looking for an audience who was more concerned with the blueness of the sky, the love for an animal, or the mystery of God. So he wrote *The Little Prince*.

Adult conversation concerning *The Little Prince* invariably leads to one question: Is it really a book for children? Underlying this question is an assumption that children aren't capable of grasping its spiritual meaning. (And indeed this may be true. Who shall say?) Paradoxically enough, Saint-Exupéry himself doubted the capability of most adults to grasp its meaning. It was this doubt that virtually forced him to select the genre of the fairy tale.

The difference between child and grown-up for Saint-Exupéry was more a matter of outlook than age; the former able to grasp things by faith; the latter relying upon reasonable evidence. Though he was speaking to a child-audience, obviously Saint-Exupéry hoped that many others would read his book. If it was meant solely for children his task would have been simpler. (pp. 14-15)

The chief quality which the child possesses, and which is so necessary for a good reading of this story, is an instantaneous and calm acceptance of mystery. The little prince is a mystical creature from the very outset; neither adult nor child will identify himself directly with him. He makes his entrance in the middle of the Sahara, a thousand miles from any inhabited region. Although later we are told of the little planet from which he emigrated, we never do discover his origin, or his family ties. He is a complete mystery from beginning to end.

To the question: "Is *The Little Prince* a story for children?"— one must answer: "Yes, it is a story for children, but not specifically for them alone."

Saint-Exupéry did not write directly to a flesh and blood audience of children. No doubt memory of his own childhood tastes helped him to fashion his story. . . . It was the genre of the fairy tale, not the children's story, which first attracted Saint-Exupéry's attention, because the fairy tale provided the form in which he could best encompass the ideas, feelings, and images that he wished to express.

However, the fairy tale, as such, is no more appropriate for children than it is for adults. *The Little Prince* is a children's story not because of its form, but because of its content. Saint-Exupéry succeeded in doing that which few writers have been able to do—he captured the innocence of childhood. When adults come away from a story, such as *The Little Prince,* wondering whether or not children are capable of grasping its meaning, they are in truth missing the essence of the story. They are assuming that Saint-Exupéry has written an allegory or a myth which permits the child-reader to become engrossed in the story, while his elders are free to busy themselves with the meanings which lie beneath the surface of the narrative— and that is all that there is to his story. *The Little Prince* is indeed satirically allegorical when it examines the *ways* of adults, but this is not the heart of the book. If it must be categorized, then it is best classified as a story *filled with mystery,* rather than as myth or allegory, and the mystery will healthfully perplex the adult as well as the child.

Saint-Exupéry's little book is not a mystery in the sense that modern readers have come to know the term—a mystery which excites the rational curiosity of the detective or the scientist. It is a child's mystery—a mystery which excites the awe and wonder of the child when a secret of the heart suddenly explodes in the sunlight of revelation. It is a mystery which has meaning not in the answers it provides, but in the wonder it reveals. It is the mystery of innocence—and therefore it has value and meaning for readers of all ages. (pp. 15-17)

Antoine de Saint-Exupéry, in *The Little Prince,* described his loneliness among grown-ups. (p. 88)

> So I lived my life alone, without anyone that I could really talk to, until I had an accident with my plane in the Desert of Sahara, six years ago. Something was broken in my engine. And as I had with me neither a mechanic nor any passengers, I set myself to attempt the difficult repairs alone. It was a question of life or death for me: I had scarcely enough drinking water to last a week.
>
> The first night, then, I went to sleep on the sand . . .

Outside of the fact that the desert itself possesses a spiritual awesomeness (at least for Saint-Exupéry it did), there is little to indicate that a fanciful tale is to follow. The setting is perfect for a true-to-life adventure yarn. The aviator's predicament suggests a tale of survival, similar to *Robinson Crusoe* perhaps. However, at sunrise (for sunrise will not confuse any reader into believing that this is a dream) the pilot is awakened by ". . . an odd little voice. It said: 'If you please—draw me a sheep!'''

With this strange request the reader is introduced to the little boy prince, and the story just as quickly belongs to him. The pilot joins the reader as a wonderer; he asks the questions the reader might ask. And he gets answers that only a little boy prince might give.

The story of the little prince cannot unfold until after the sheep has been drawn. The pilot will not have his questions answered by the little boy, because boys, be they real or fanciful, do not operate in this fashion. No, first the sheep must be drawn (that the picture is but a box with holes, and that the sheep is inside, is of no consequence), and then *he* will ask the questions, which after all, is a boy's prerogative. The pilot, and the reader, must be content to fashion the story from the brief glimpses provided by the little prince's conversation. (pp. 89-90)

It is the love of the little prince for his rose which eventually becomes the moving force of the book but Saint-Exupéry has more groundwork to lay before he begins to elaborate on it. For if the world of the little boy is to reveal any of its hidden secrets it must be seen in relation to the world of the adult.

The little prince has left his tiny planet of solitude in search of relief from his loneliness. His travels take him to seven planets, and on each of them he is introduced to another facet of the bewildering world of grown-ups. . . . (p. 90)

The seventh and final planet to be visited by the little prince is, of course, Earth, where kings, geographers, businessmen, tipplers, and conceited men can be found in great numbers, but where lamplighters, and others like them, have already become extinct, because no responsible task could be found for them to perform. It is not a human who is first encountered by the little prince, however (remember he was a thousand miles from any human habitation), but rather ". . . a coil of gold, the color of moonlight . . ."—a snake. His conversation with the snake is brief, but from it the reader learns that the innocence of the little prince must not be mistaken for naïveté. When the snake uses metaphor to describe its power to end life, the boy understands him perfectly.

When the snake and the boy part, the reader knows that they will meet again, and the inevitability of this future meeting changes the mood of the story. Actually a new story begins. The child-reader is introduced to the tale of tragedy; not like many of the wild emotional tragedies of adulthood, with the hero struggling valiantly, but hopelessly, against superimposing forces, but rather a calm, innocent, be it melancholic, acceptance of fate. Saint-Exupéry's narrative supposes that man has a hand in his own fate; that fate is not some demoniac joke perpetrated on him by scheming deities, but rather, it is the inevitable conclusion that adds nobility and meaning to the good life.

Tragedy gives a circular shape to a story; the reader becomes aware that there is a point along the way which must be returned to; true, the reader himself may wish against it, but in the end he knows that he too must accept it. And for all the sadness that may accompany this return, it is, nevertheless, right. The little prince, like the child-reader, knows that he will meet the snake again, and he both wishes and fears it.

Tragedy, then, is not a literary form which leads but to tears and the wringing of hands; rather it should quicken the pulse and set the nerves atingle, as the beholder feels himself drawn closer to other human beings through a tale that, although unique, is at the same time composed of experience that is common to all. Many adult tragedies revolve around the impossibility of a *return to innocence,* while the tragedy that has meaning for the child, as well as the adult, for the one through unconscious participation and for the other through retrospection, must deal with the painfulness—the loneliness—that accompanies the *preservation of innocence.* This is the tragedy of the little prince.

Saint-Exupéry's tiny hero does not cavort in a luxurious innocence of complete freedom. It is rather the innocent quality of his vision which strips away the superficialities of life and leads him always to the heart of the matter. What does he find there?—a love that commits him to the preservation of his innocence—a love which compels him to seek wisdom through open and honest inquiry—a love that restricts him to consideration of only "true matters of consequence"—a love that shoulders upon him the welfare of another.

Of course, when one reads a story of a little prince who descends to Earth, and there meets and converses with a serpent, the reader immediately is led to suspect that the author's intent may well be allegorical. In this case, however, the suspicion would be groundless. The reason for the protagonist being a little prince will be touched upon shortly. As for the snake, it is as natural as Hudson's vultures [in *A Little Boy Lost*], playing out its intended role in the scheme of things. At the same time, it is the one creature whose presence lends itself appropriately to the arena of mystery: the strangely beautiful creature with the cold silvery skin and the forked and flickering tongue; the creature that glides silently over the earth without the use of legs; the creature that has always fascinated men, especially the young. It is the epitome of those few things in the world that, when it is beheld, invites one to touch it because of its mysteriousness, and at the same time makes one fear the touch because of its differentness. (pp. 91-3)

The snake is an allusive symbol rather than an allegorical one, by the use of which the author hopes to induce a particular feeling within the reader, which will in turn make it possible for him to share intuitively in the spiritual experience of the protagonist. (p. 93)

[Before the little prince and the fox part, the fox leaves him with a secret:]

> "Goodbye," said the fox. "And now here is my secret, a very simple secret: It is only with the heart that one can see rightly; what is essential is invisible to the eye."
>
> "What is essential is invisible to the eye," the little prince repeated, so that he would be sure to remember.
>
> "It is the time you have wasted for your rose that makes your rose so important."
>
> "It is the time I have wasted for my rose—" said the little prince, so that he would be sure to remember.

Here one finds . . . an example which illustrates that mystical fancy for children leads not merely to escape from reality, but that, instead, it intensifies the realness of the child's surroundings, and gives him an awareness of the commutual quality of his own innermost feelings. For the child it is realism in its purest form. It strips away the artificial considerations of materialism, conformity, and convenience. It goes to the core of the matter, which exists in the realm of the spirit.

Saint-Exupéry considered this drawing to be his greatest artistic achievement. From The Little Prince, *written and illustrated by Antoine de Saint-Exupéry. Translated by Katherine Woods. Harcourt Brace Jovanovich, 1943. Copyright 1943 by Harcourt Brace Jovanovich, Inc. Reprinted by permission of the publisher.*

The little prince is a symbol of the innocence of childhood. He is not a cute figure, created through the sentimental process of personal reminiscence. If he represents Saint-Exupéry at all, he does so as Saint-Exupéry the child; not the child remembered, but the child as he was and would never be again. This makes the boy no less a creature than the adult, neither does the boy exist only in the metamorphic state of becoming an adult. The day comes for most children when they must cast off the cloak of innocence, and be children no more. This is not to be the fate of the little prince, for it has already been mentioned that he is a mystical being, and not like other boys in this respect. The reader is also aware, because of his encounter with the snake, of the price the little prince will pay for preserving his innocence by returning to his own planet.

The power of innocence is the power to grasp the simple truth, be it pleasant or not. This uniqueness doesn't divorce the boy from the adult, but rather it gives him a contributorial status in the lives of all men, be they young or old. The little prince seeks, after all, that truth which all men seek deep in their hearts: the meaning of love. His quest leads him to a simple answer, but the simplicity doesn't lessen its degree of gravity or validity. He is a tragic lover, aware of the great consequences of love once found, and he faces them squarely: "I am responsible for my rose," he says.

This is the simple discovery made by the little boy, and because of it, the appearance of all things is changed for him, and because of it, all his actions take on new meanings. It is an assertion that helps a child absorb the implications of another mystical statement, very familiar to most readers; the statement that commands: "Love thy neighbor"—a message which can dry up under adult illumination.

Saint-Exupéry recognized late in life that this commandment was at the very foundation of Western civilization. In *Flight to Arras* . . . he wrote:

> . . . I understand now for the first time the mystery of the religion whence was born the civilization I claim as my own: "To bear the sins of man." Each man bears the sins of all men.

Oddly enough this revelation came to Saint-Exupéry through his familiarity with the life of the desert people, and after he immersed himself deeply in Eastern thought and writing. It led him to include notions in his own works that are rarely entertained in Western schools and homes. The fox says: "It is the time you have wasted for your rose that makes your rose so important." This comes from a way of thought that rarely penetrates the American hide, nor is it likely that it would be accepted by many as a precept of good living for the young.

Saint-Exupéry comes back to the point again:

> "Only the children know what they are looking for," said the little prince. "They waste their time over a rag doll and it becomes very important to them; and if anybody takes it away from them, they cry . . ."

The value of *wastefulness,* to be sure, only has meaning in a world that also appreciates: "it is only with the heart that one can see rightly."

That the boy hero is a prince, of course, does have significance. It touches upon that aspect of Saint-Exupéry's thought and writing which stirs up most controversy among critics. Saint-Exupéry had little faith in the kind of freedom promised by democracy, probably because he had little faith in the grownups in whose hands democracy must rest. He was searching for someone who would answer affirmatively to the question: "Who will be responsible?" He was attracted by the tranquility of the East—and there he found the desert prince who ruled his people as a father rules his family. He was attracted by the nobility of the past—and there he found the knight errant dedicated to the chivalric code. (Forgetting, perhaps, that these too were grown-ups.)

André Gide, in the preface to *Night Flight,* compliments Saint-Exupéry for having stated so clearly the apparently paradoxical truth that man's happiness lies not in freedom, but in the acceptance of a duty. Some critics, Clifton Fadiman for one, warned readers of the grim totalitarianism that pervades such a line of thought. Nevertheless, for good or for bad, it is the line of thought which makes a prince of the little boy.

Love, after all, does demand total commitment. It does indeed curtail one's freedom. We find in *The Little Prince* the same implication that we find in so many of George MacDonald's stories: the beauty of love is to be found in the countenance of the lover, not necessarily in the object of affection. The rose of the little prince is little more than a vain, selfish little flower, until the reader discovers that she secretly returns his love. When it is time for him to leave she says:

> "Of course I love you . . . It is my fault that you have not known it all the while. . . .

> "Don't linger like this. You have decided to go away. Now go!"

> For she did not want him to see her crying. She was such a proud flower . . .

There is one way in which the little prince and Antoine de Saint-Exupéry, the man, are alike. They are both alone. And it is this aloneness which brings both sadness and gaiety to their lives; both mystery and clear vision to their dreams; both serenity and excitement to their hearts. It is their aloneness, strangely enough, that brings them closer to the essence of their fellow creatures.

The anniversary of the little prince's descent to Earth brings the story to its ending, because that is the only time in which the star will be in a position to make his return possible. Fearful though he is, and despite the pleas of the aviator, he keeps his appointment with the snake. He leaves behind a gift for the flyer that is as simple and mystical as the secret imparted to him by the fox. He leaves the sound of his laughter. (pp. 94-8)

The Little Prince is one of those rare books which leaves its readers always wondering what it is all about. And that is its peculiar contribution to children's literature. Some readers, young and old, may not be pleased by this quality of the book, for a book which evokes *wonder* is also sure to stir up a bit of confusion—and confusion, for these particular readers, is an intolerable disturbance to the mind and spirit. However, a good number of readers will find *The Little Prince* a book to which they will return from time to time, hoping to hear again its whispered secrets.

All of Saint-Exupéry's writing seems to be prefaced by: "I wonder"—and *The Little Prince* is no exception. It is a quiet adventure into the realm of the spirit, and therefore it needs readers who are not only willing to be disturbed, but eager to set forth on a journey into uncharted ways. It is a story of belief—not one of make-believe.

The little prince, of course, never strays from Saint-Exupéry's dictum: "What is essential is invisible to the eye." . . . Saint-Exupéry considers the visible things of the world to be only symbols, only hints, of the real beauty which lies hidden in the world of the spirit. . . . Saint-Exupéry cannot say for certain if this beauty has divine cause, but this, in a sense, makes his story more powerful, and certainly more universal, for, after all, not everyone has found God, but everyone knows of the search.

The little prince comes to realize that the wonder of the world is also the vast mystery of the world. He comes to realize: "The stars are beautiful, because of a flower that cannot be seen."

The entire tenor of *The Little Prince,* but especially the dialogue, is one of calm reasonableness blended with supernaturalism which is reminiscent of Perrault's fairy tales. Saint-Exupéry, like other writers of mystical fancy, deals with the wonderful, but he works in reverse. He doesn't start with the everyday experience and then show the wonder to be found in it if one will look with his heart. He begins with the marvelous and then shows how innocent, how childlike, how simple, how common it really is—again, if one will look with his heart. He never says specifically that it is God whom he is chasing, but . . . one wonders. (pp. 99-100)

Saint-Exupéry finds the spiritual world of adulthood to be impoverished, in a state of famine, mainly because grown-ups have forgotten that the heart is nourished by the invisible bond of love which brings man together. Love, for Saint-Exupéry, is not a matter of choice; it is a matter of consequence; indeed, it is a matter of survival. Men must learn to love one another or perish.

The little prince searches seven planets in quest of the marvelous and mysterious gift of love, only to find that he possessed it all along. Love had flourished on his own little planet, because he had committed himself to perform the everyday monotonous duties necessary to caring for his rose and his volcanoes. The little prince discovers the secret from the fox. Love is not some wonderful thing to be found in some fantastic world outside of reason. After one has discovered it, it will indeed be most reasonable—but one will not discover it through reason, for "it is only with the heart that one can see rightly."

And Saint-Exupéry does look with his heart—the heart of a child. For the adult, his little book is profound in its mysticism; for the child, it is simple in its innocence. (p. 100)

There is always something haunting about stories of mystical fancy. There is always something joyfully sad about their telling. There is the joy that the child finds in the secrets of the heart, and the sadness that he feels for not being able to fully share these secrets with others. Perhaps someday, when those who are charged with the education of the child can also share these secrets, the meaning of such books will take on more significance. When that day arrives, the joy to be found in a book like *The Little Prince* will be measurably increased, and the feeling of sadness will be gone forever. (p. 102)

The primary difference between writers of the mystical and other writers of fancy lies in the area of theme. Very often authors like Lewis and Saint-Exupéry are distinguished from other fantasists by their "seriousness." this is not to say that their books are necessarily somber and intense, but rather that they have selected themes as high as Heaven's door. The things about which they write—although presented in a fanciful form— are very real to these writers.

For instance, when he wrote *The Little Prince*, Saint-Exupéry used the same basic theme that he had already presented to adults in a variety of forms, but finally he had come to realize that this theme, the responsibility of love, was of such a universal nature that it encompassed the experience of children as well as grown-ups. He then proceeded not to reduce the theme to a child's understanding, but to shape it into a form that would give it a voice more attuned to the ear, the mind, and the heart of a child. (pp. 105-06)

> *James E. Higgins, in his* Beyond Words: Mystical Fancy in Children's Literature, *New York: Teachers College Press, 1970, 112 p.*

MAY HILL ARBUTHNOT AND ZENA SUTHERLAND

The Little Prince is a poetic fairy tale without a plot, whimsical and sophisticated in its concern with the inconsistencies of human behavior. . . . The lack of action and the allusiveness of the dialogue limit the book to those readers who can appreciate the spiritual values and the writing style—readers who include not only devoted children but many adults. (p. 222)

> *May Hill Arbuthnot and Zena Sutherland, "Modern Fantasy," in their* Children and Books, *fourth edition, Scott, Foresman and Company, 1972, pp. 210-77.*

LAURENCE GAGNON

Any literary work is susceptible to an indefinite variety of interpretations. In this respect works of literature are like formal systems. Our understanding of the sequences of words in a novel, poem, etc. or the sequences of symbols in a logico-mathematical system is not completely determined by those sequences of words or symbols, still less by any intentions of the author(s). We achieve an understanding of a literary work or a formal system when we associate with it some model of the way things are or, at least, of a way they could be. Sometimes in order to do this we may have to suspend (temporarily) some of our beliefs about what is the case. But such are the demands of imaginative interpretation.

One type of model which can be used with great success in interpreting works of children's literature and adult fantasy is a Heideggerian model. By associating parts of Martin Heidegger's philosophy with certain parts of these literary works, we can achieve a novel, if not profound, understanding of them. Two cases in point are *The Little Prince* by A. de Saint Exupéry and *Charlotte's Web* by E. B. White. It has even been reported that Heidegger himself once considered *The Little Prince* to be "one of the great existentialist books of this century."

Stated as simply and untechnically as possible, the particular Heideggarian model appealed to here is one concerned with persons and their capabilities. Now persons are capable of many things, of flying planes and watering flowers, of eating leftovers and killing insects. Yet these are rather superficial capabilities, not being characteristic of persons as such but rather only of persons as pilots or gardeners, omnivores or killers. Among the more fundamental capabilities are those of being aware of oneself, of being concerned about things in the world, of dreading one's death, and ultimately of living authentically. Since each person as such is unique and irreplaceable, this ultimate capability is also the ultimate personal obligation: to live authentically. Under the present interpretation, *The Little Prince* and *Charlotte's Web* are about various personal struggles to live authentically. In each of these works there are characters who find themselves thrown into existence, as it were, amidst other beings with whom they end up being concerned, all the while being confronted with the difficult and inescapable task of truly becoming what they alone can be—even unto death. This is precisely the task of living authentically. The ever-present danger here is that of losing one's sense of personal identity by becoming part of the crowd or by becoming overly concerned with other beings.

In *The Little Prince*, neither the stranded pilot nor the prince himself have succumbed to the temptation of becoming a people-self; i.e., a faceless, anonymous part of a crowd. Since he was six years old, the time at which he produced his famous drawings of a boa constrictor digesting an elephant, the stranded pilot has been of the opinion that grown-ups are not only concerned with inconsequential "matters of consequence," such as bridge and golf, politics and neckties, but also terribly dense when it comes to discussing such important matters as boa constrictors, primeval forests and stars. "So," he says, "I have lived my life alone, without anyone that I could really talk to . . ." . . . . (pp. 61-2)

The little prince has not been so lonely, having his flower to talk to. However, his opinion of grown ups is much the same as that of the stranded pilot. They are not merely strange, nor even "very, very odd," but rather "altogether extraordinary" in their denseness and their concerns. . . . [The king, the conceited man, the tippler, the businessman, the geographer]— none of these receives nor deserves the admiration of the little prince, for none are living authentically. Worse yet there is little hope that they will change, since they neither take care of things nor care for persons. What interest they take in the little visitor is selfish. Living on their respective planets, the little prince would at best be treated as an extension of themselves, not as a distinct individual worthy of their concern. It is not just physically that they lead isolated lives.

Only on asteroid 329 does the little prince find a man whom he could possibly befriend—the lamplighter—who at least takes care of his lamp. "But his planet is indeed too small. There is no room on it for two people." . . . On earth there is at least room. Here, of course, the little prince finds friendship. He tames the willing fox. He establishes ties with the not-so-willing, stranded pilot. He becomes forever responsible for them, and they in turn for him.

But there is always a danger here; one can lose oneself to the things one takes care of and the persons one cares for. One can become so concerned with other beings that one identifies with them rather than striving for the unique identity proper to oneself. As long as one does this, one cannot live authentically. Before he began his wanderings, the little prince was too concerned with his rose; in his conscientiousness he had become a slave to her and she in her vanity and pride encouraged his servitude. This was not good for either of them. At that time it was important to both that she be the only flower of her kind in the whole universe. Because of all this, his agony in the garden is inevitable, when he discovers that there are thousands upon thousands of roses like his own. Yet none are his rose. This the tamed fox enables him to see. What makes his rose precious is not its physical appearance but the time he has "wasted" on it. "It is only with the heart that one can see rightly; what is essential is invisible to the eye." . . . This truth, which men have forgotten, sets the little prince free; while he still has ties with his rose, he is no longer tied down to her.

In this regard the stranded pilot has much to learn. Although his initial concerns are taking care of his damaged plane and caring for himself, he eventually manages to become deeply concerned for his little visitor. But in this new concern, he becomes overly attached to his new friend. He understands that the little prince must leave but he cannot accept it as the fox has done. He asks for comfort and implores his readers to send him word of the little man's return. Yet this is understandable, for the stranded pilot is neither as wise and patient as the fox nor as young and innocent as the little prince. He requires more time.

The wisdom of the fox is not the only wisdom which the little prince discovers on earth. He also learns that while taking care of one's possessions and caring for others are necessary for one to live authentically, they alone are not sufficient, even when done without attachment. One must also recognize that life, especially one's own life, necessarily involves death, not as a termination of these concerns but rather as a culmination of them. This is the wisdom of the snake who always speaks in riddles. With a certain resoluteness, the little prince advances toward his own death, even though he is somewhat afraid and anxious. As the stranded pilot discovers, it was not by chance that little man was "strolling along like that, all alone, a thousand miles from any inhabited region." . . . Death is always a solitary experience.

But since the little prince is a star-child, innocent and true, there is a resurrection. His "was not such a heavy body" after all. . . . Yet even with the element of resurrection, the question of what comes after death ought not to arise. For dying is the ultimate individual act of which a person is capable. The stranded pilot cannot quite accept this. He still ponders the mystery of what happens afterwards: "What is happening on his planet?"; "Has the sheep eaten the flower?" (pp. 62-3)

These questions are not important in themselves, but only in so far as they symbolize the ties which have been established between the little prince and the stranded pilot. What is important is stated by the star-child:

> In one of the stars I shall be living. In one of
> them I shall be laughing. And so it will be as
> if all the stars were laughing, when you look
> at the sky at night . . . You—only you—will
> have stars that can laugh! . . . And when your
> sorrow is comforted (time soothes all sorrows)
> you will be content that you have known me.
> You will always be my friend. . . .

And this would be true, even if there were no resurrection. (p. 63)

Laurence Gagnon, "Webs of Concern: Heidegger, 'The Little Prince' and 'Charlotte's Web'," in Children's Literature: Annual of the Modern Language Association Seminar on Children's Literature and The Children's Literature Association, *Vol. 2, 1973, pp. 61-6.**

THE NEW YORKER

[*In celebration of the fortieth anniversary of the publication of* The Little Prince, *the working manuscript of the book was exhibited at the Pierpont Morgan Library in New York City. In the following excerpt, the critic describes his viewing of Saint-Exupéry's manuscript in the office of Herbert Cahoon, curator of autograph manuscripts, and reports his own observations and reflections as well as those of Cahoon.*]

Mr. Cahoon brought a blue cloth box with a red label on its side over to a small round table, opened it, and took out a thick bundle of onionskin paper. It was a heavy-looking manuscript for such a compact little book.

We knew that the manuscript had been acquired from Silvia Hamilton Reinhardt, to whom Saint-Exupéry gave it as a parting gift . . . when, in 1943, he left the United States. . . . (pp. 31-2)

[Saint-Exupéry's] handwriting in this manuscript is of the type the French describe as "legs of flies." It is minute and almost totally illegible. The manuscript of **"The Little Prince"** comprises a hundred and forty pages of text and preliminary drawings followed by thirty-five pages of drawings in pen and watercolor. The early drawings, incorporated into the text, differ from the final versions. For example, in its early version the sheep that the Little Prince asks the narrator to draw for him is barely recognizable as a sheep. "Here he looks like E.T.," Mr. Cahoon said, with a chuckle. And the long, rectangular box with the air holes which the narrator draws in despair after his three attempts at a sheep fail to satisfy the Little Prince is a simple cube to start with. . . .

The text does not flow. It goes by fits and starts. A paragraph is begun, abandoned, and begun again. At first, Saint-Ex writes in pencil—an extraordinarily well-sharpened pencil, for the writing is minute. Later, he switches to a very fine pen and brown ink. "There are portions that are left in here that do not appear in the book, and portions of the book that do not appear in the manuscript," said Mr. Cahoon. "And the wording shows marked differences." At a certain point in the manuscript, the paper becomes thicker and the author's handwriting larger; he is using a wider pen.... Saint-Ex must have been a careless smoker, for the manuscript is dotted with circular holes edged in rust-brown. And he must have prodded his working nights with coffee, for there are nearly as many beigy-brown stains, most often at the edges of a page. "This manuscript was really thought upon," said Mr. Cahoon. "You can see why it's one of our favorites. But *no* one will be able to read it." ...

Saint-Ex must have enjoyed drawing the baobab trees that threaten to overwhelm the Little Prince's asteroid, for there are three lovely detailed drawings of them in fine brown pen-and-ink. And, finally, there is an apotheosis of the Little Prince, in flight above an earthly landscape. "Looks as if someone rescued it from the wastepaper basket," Mr. Cahoon said, holding it up to the light. Sure enough, it had been crumpled into a ball and then smoothed out again. This drawing concluded the manuscript.... (p. 32)

Close to four million copies of **"The Little Prince"** have been sold to date, and it is now selling at a rate of more than two hundred thousand a year. It has been translated into fifty languages. It has been filmed twice—once in the Soviet Union, and once, as a musical, in the United States. (pp. 32-3)

It is amazing to think that during [Saint-Exupéry's] two years of exile in the United States he was able to work simultaneously on **"The Little Prince"** and **"Wisdom of the Sands,"** for if the latter is almost incomprehensible the former is the most lucid of fairy tales, written with crystalline delicacy and deep tenderness. The cadence of the prose, and of the dialogue between the Little Prince, the different characters he meets, and the narrator, is perfection. There is not a single false note in the French text. Inevitably, certain subtleties are lost in the English translation. In French, for example, when the Little Prince speaks his first words, "If you please, draw me a sheep," the "If you please" is said in the polite form and "draw me a sheep" in the familiar. Katherine Woods' translation is adequate most of the time, but she introduces into the English a note of gentility which is totally absent from the French. (She writes "tippler" for "drunkard," "adornment" for "dressing-up," and "charming" instead of "ravishing," and when the fox says "You see the grainfields down yonder?" he should be saying "See the wheat fields over there?") (p. 33)

A review of "The Little Prince," in The New Yorker, *Vol. LIX, No. 5, March 21, 1983, pp. 31-4.*

Kate Seredy

1899-1975

Hungarian-born American author/illustrator of fiction, re-teller, translator, and illustrator.

Seredy's belief in traditional values and universal harmony permeates her fiction for middle-graders. A gifted storyteller, she wrote warm-hearted narratives which frequently reflect the culture of her native land; her best-known work, *The Good Master*, depicts the vibrant cousins Kate and Jancsi and their adventures on a large Hungarian farm. Often utilizing pastoral settings in both Hungary and America, Seredy employed rhythmic prose and concrete imagery to explore the feelings of her child and adult protagonists. These characters, who include Hungarian peasants and aristocrats, American farm and city dwellers, and Russian prisoners of war, are generally courageous, hardworking, altruistic, and peace-loving individuals with faith in themselves. Seredy incorporates realism, rhythm, and softness into her usually monochromatic drawings. She is particularly cited for her powerful depictions of horses, and for the customary vitality and charm of her pictures.

Reviewers praise Seredy for the clarity and vividness of her prose, the beauty and drama of her well-designed art, and the integration of her texts and illustrations. While they find that her stories are occasionally didactic and border on sentimentality, critics appreciate the positive values she imparts to her readers as well as her sensitivity to diverse peoples and cultures.

The Good Master was named a Newbery Honor Book in 1936 as was *The Singing Tree* in 1940. *The White Stag* won the Newbery Medal in 1938 and received the Lewis Carroll Shelf Award in 1959.

(See also *Something about the Author*, Vols. 1, 24 [obituary]; *Contemporary Authors*, Vols. 5-8, rev. ed., Vols. 57-60 [obituary]; and *Dictionary of Literary Biography*, Vol. 22: *American Writers for Children, 1900-1960*.)

AUTHOR'S COMMENTARY

"Out of nowhere" sums up my own attitude toward my career as an author. I do not know anything about the craft of writing and the more I write, the less I know. Each time a story comes out of nowhere and—almost against my better judgment—I put it on paper and later see it in print, "Written and illustrated by Kate Seredy." I sigh: "This is the last. I can never write again—I don't know how."

They fill me with awe, these books bearing my name. Were I to climb into a jet plane without knowing anything about aircraft, take off, do daredevil stunts and land safely, I could be no more awed and surprised than I am every time I read the galleys of a new book of mine.

Every one of them—*The Good Master, The Singing Tree, The White Stag, Open Gate, Tree for Peter, Chestry Oak*, and *Gypsy*, started out to be picture books. *Gypsy* held her own and remained the story of a cat in pictures. All the others got out of

hand; people in them seemed to have ideas of their own and insisted on getting them on paper.

Never has this been more true than while I was writing **The White Stag**. I know I finished it in three weeks, writing almost mechanically, as if I had been taking dictation. Only when I read the galleys did I realize how little the conscious "I" had to do with writing that story. Perhaps tribal memory asserted itself—I do not know.

Oddly enough, I spent three years whittling down the story of Gypsy to the brief captions that appear in the book. She tended to be garrulous, too, but I managed to keep her from talking too much! (pp. 161-62)

[At] present, I am illustrating what I suspect will be my favorite book—the story of a sturdy little Bohemian peasant girl named "Philomena." (p. 162)

> Kate Seredy, "Concerning Myself," in Newbery Medal Books: 1922-1955, edited by Bertha Mahoney Miller and Elinor Whitney Field, The Horn Book, Inc., 1955, pp. 161-65.

GENERAL COMMENTARY

BLANCHE JENNINGS THOMPSON

[*Seredy dedicated* The Tenement Tree *to Thompson, calling her "my friend and relentless critic." Prior to writing the following essay, Thompson compiled a collection of poetry,* With Harp and Lute, *which Seredy illustrated. She later illustrated Thompson's* The Oldest Story *and* A Candle Burns for Frances.]

Miss Seredy (whose name, by the way sounds as if it began with Sh) looks like a changeling. She has a certain puckish humor that lends color to the theory, and she draws goblins, elves, and trolls with such a certainty that one knows she hears at times the horns of Faerie. . . .

Miss Seredy's most important education came from her father, an eminent and much-loved teacher of boys. From him came her self-discipline, her high ideals, sincerity, courage, and indomitable faith. Her hatred of intolerance, of war and cruelty came from him too. . . . (p. 217)

[One] of the things about her that I find most astonishing, particularly as a teacher, is the way she has mastered our difficult language and now writes a most beautiful clear, and vivid prose that native Americans might well envy. She still argues a bit about tenses, preferring the more arresting "historical present" when she is in the midst of an exciting passage and grumbling a little when it is ruled out by a matter-of-fact proof-reader. . . . (p. 218)

It was at Listening Hill [Miss Seredy's farm] that I read the **White Stag** in manuscript, with a sketch in color of the brilliant black and crimson jacket standing on the mantelpiece. I read it at one sitting, lost in the marvelous, moving prose and when I saw the double page picture with horses and riders in action (such horses!) I knew that here was a book. . . .

And now the **White Stag** has won the Newbery Medal for the most distinguished contribution to children's literature in 1937 and Kate Seredy is glad, but to her, I believe, it is not a goal but a stepping-stone and we all look forward to many more stories from her gifted hand. She has seen the White Stag and will follow it with unbroken faith in a great purpose. (p. 220)

> *Blanche Jennings Thompson, "On Listening Hill,"*
> *in* The Elementary English Review, *Vol. XV, No. 6,*
> *October, 1938, pp. 217-20.*

PETER PARLEY

[Kate Seredy's] two splendidly written and finely illustrated stories, **The Good Master** and **The Singing Tree,** must rank among the very best children's books of recent years. The background of farm life on the Hungarian Plains is vividly described and the two young heroes are alive and real, while the author's profound sense of human values runs throughout both stories like a warming summer sun. (p. 136)

> *Peter Parley, "A Five Years' Record: Recollections*
> *of Some Notable Books of the Years 1937 to 1941,"*
> *in* The Junior Bookshelf, *Vol. 5, No. 4, December,*
> *1941, pp. 131-39.**

MAY HILL ARBUTHNOT

[**The Good Master**] was an instantaneous favorite with children. If they were to be consulted, they would give this book the Newbery Medal rather than Miss Seredy's **White Stag. The Good Master** is the story of a Hungarian tomboy, Kate—a regular brat of a child. She is sent by her father to stay on her uncle's ranch. Her young cousin Jancsi imagines she will be a frail, dainty girl, and so he is horrified by the wild, impish Kate. . . . How Kate is gentled is a charming story. "The Good Master" is the understanding uncle. The aunt is just as patient with Kate, and Jancsi takes a hand, too, in the girl's reformation. But it is Kate's growing love of the horses and riding,

as well as her affection for her newly found relatives, that helps her learn gentler ways. Hungarian festivals and legends, the household crafts, the work of the ranch, the good food, and the warm family life add color and charm to a delightful story. The sequel to **The Good Master** is **The Singing Tree,** which sees Kate and Jancsi in their teens and the father gone to World War I. Anti-Semitism arises, but, in this story, it is happily banished. Here is no light-hearted tale for children but a story with a message. It comes perhaps too close to the didactic to be a popular story, but it is well worth reading and timely, too.

Kate Seredy . . . makes her illustrations a vital part of her books. Children give one look at the colored portraits of Kate and Jancsi at the beginning of **The Good Master** and wish to read the book immediately. In spite of the Hungarian clothes, these might be the children next door. These frank, look-you-in-the-eye children have fine heads, broad brows, and strongly modeled faces; Kate, with her dark blue eyes and saucy turned up nose, is particularly appealing. But throughout the books it is the movement in the pictures that holds the children. Kate Seredy draws splendid horses whose flashing legs you can almost see on the gallop, swirling skirts that make a dance come to life on the page, fairies that soar, dogs bounding or alert, and heroes who stride over the earth in power and might. These drawings of Miss Seredy's are alive with action and interpret the mood of the tale or the very essence of a character, whether a dog or horse or a human being. Children will try any book having Miss Seredy's illustrations. These are full of gaiety, vigorous action, and sheer beauty, but her writing is sometimes didactic. (pp. 418-19)

> *May Hill Arbuthnot, "Other Times and Places," in*
> *her* Children and Books, *Scott, Foresman and Com-*
> *pany, 1947, pp. 396-421.**

LOIS R. MARKEY

In 1951, Kate Seredy wrote and illustrated **Gypsy,** the life story of a cat. This seems an ordinary theme for a book. In fact, one can think of innumerable books about cats, good books. There is just one Gypsy. One must go back several years to discover why **Gypsy** is an incomparable book.

It starts in Budapest where a child sat listening to words well spoken, thoughts well chosen. In a room filled with books where good music was often heard sat Kate Seredy listening to the conversations of her family and their friends, listening now to words and music beyond her comprehension, but delighted in for their rhythm.

It was then that the wish must have been born in Kate Seredy's heart to translate those words and music and thoughts into something of her own creation, something that would be alive and something that would make other people know of these wonderful things. This wish became a desire to paint pictures and as soon as she was old enough, she went to the Academy of Art in Budapest.

Her art lessons taught her those truths that are so apparent in her best illustrations. One must know muscle and bone structure in order to draw an arm. One must be able to draw an arm well before one can paint the picture of a child. One must discipline oneself to absolute compliance with facts, faithfulness to reality, and conformity to the laws of nature and of life. (p. 451)

In 1935, the first book written and illustrated by Miss Seredy was published by the Viking Press. (p. 452)

From The Good Master, *written and illustrated by Kate Seredy. The Viking Press, 1944. Copyright 1935, renewed © 1963 by Kate Seredy. Reprinted by permission of Viking Penguin Inc.*

In the first few pages [of *The Good Master*], Jancsi is established as a real boy, a boy worth the consideration of any other child, when he brushes his teeth. "Squirting out the salty water, he set a new long-distance record; he even paused long enough to gaze at it admiringly and mark the spot with a stone. 'Can spit almost as far as Father,' he muttered with pride." And then came his temptation with the bottle of green stuff—perfumed hair oil which only grown men used. Quickly it was applied and with great self-satisfaction Jancsi was through the door and on his way to meet his city cousin Kate.

With two small incidents Kate Seredy forms a boy who immediately arouses reader interest. On the drive to town, the countryside is portrayed and the character of the Father emerges. Father is a man of few words, Father delights in teasing, and Father understands the nature of animals and of small boys—Father, the Good Master. "Jancsi heaved a sigh of relief. This was a man's world, and he was accepted!" The words secure a sense of warmth and love and sympathy which is sustained throughout the story.

While the character of Kate may be slightly overemphasized for the adult reader, this "miniature whirlwind" has her counterpart in real life, and she does delight the child reader. Kate's introduction to the ranch life of Hungary is the reader's introduction, too. The home, the animals, the customs, and the dress are a part of the story, not just descriptive words. Jancsi's costume will be remembered forever because Kate splits her own best blue dress in imitation. After her long riding lesson,

Kate seems more a real little girl as we read the words that tell us that she ate her supper standing and as we look at the picture of her clinging to the door, one foot rubbing the other, skirt split and pushed aside, exposing voluminous bloomers and saying, "Can't hurry and haven't any other dress. Can't sit either."

Here it is in *The Good Master* that Kate Seredy's unmistakable horses first appear. Since the horse is a most important part of the Hungarian rancher's life, many of the illustrations are devoted to the horse. Not only do they indicate the economic value, but also the historical and mythological importance of the Hungarian horse. This mythological background gives us a stylized horse, a magnificent animal, exciting and thrilling. The seed of *The White Stag* is here in *The Good Master,* here in the legend of the Milky Way told to Kate and Jancsi by Árpád.

Her interest in folklore is displayed in *The Good Master* by the inclusion of several Hungarian tales. They impede the progress of the story somewhat, but they heighten the Hungarian atmosphere of the book.

The most popular of her books, this, *The Good Master,* is deserving for its characterization, basic soundness, and beautiful illustrations. It includes that love for the good thought and word that was a part of her childhood.

The next year came *Listening,* a departure from *The Good Master* in that the story is laid in America and in that another strong interest of Miss Seredy's comes to light. Although a story of the first Dutch settlers in America is interwoven, essentially, *Listening* is a story dedicated to the simple country way of life with its hominess, its appreciation of woods animals and the domestic dog and cat.

This is the first time we have Miss Seredy's cat. Almost all the drawings show a preference for a triangular balance. The picture of the three cats with a teddy bear is a study in design. The suppleness and grace of the cat is used in an interesting fashion to form a softened triangle. One feels that the strength here is in design.

The prose of *Listening* does not show the same artistry of plot or characterization seen in *The Good Master,* but there is greater ease in the handling of conversational passages. It seems an experimental book and thus lacks the reader interest of *The Good Master.*

The White Stag . . . is the legend of the separation of the Huns and Magyars and the picture of the mighty conqueror, Attila. It is a terrifying and potent story of a powerful man who was the synthesis of the intense and compelling forces of conquest of the times. Its epic quality, its poetic elements give Miss Seredy full opportunity for artistry in illustration. The nobility of the man, the unearthliness of the stag, and the magnificence of the horses make a book of undisputed beauty. Old Testament in substance, despite its paganism, it should be read with that in mind. It is a substantiation of faith, faith in a pagan god, the only god they knew.

There is more excitement, more story value in *The White Stag* than in any of Miss Seredy's books. . . . Whether or not one is in sympathy with the ideologies hidden in *The White Stag,* it is a distinguished book, a fascinating story. (pp. 452-54)

[*The Singing Tree*] is a story of life and death and war. It is a story of individuals, of nationalities. It is an indictment of hatred, a plea for peace, a proclamation of faith in mankind. (p. 454)

Here the writing surpasses the illustrations. Dialogue and descriptive passages are well balanced. The words come effortlessly, they read quickly and well. If one episode in the plot is contrived, if there is some obvious preaching, it is not enough to spoil a good story. The true picture of adult-child relationships, the delightful play between Gregori, one of the Russian prisoners, and Kate, the understanding of the relationships between peoples of different backgrounds, and above all, the shining faith in the dignity and worth of man and beast make *The Singing Tree* a book worthy of young people everywhere.

In this book, there are hints of other themes running through Miss Seredy's mind. Kate's father, Sandor Nagy, says, "Home as no place in the city can ever be. There you are walled in like a prisoner, and your closest neighbors are strangers. Each family seems to live in a little cell, not knowing or caring what goes on next door. Here miles of the plains separate us from the nearest neighbor and yet I feel among friends." Her preference for the country life which was evident in *Listening* is here stated most definitely, for the reader feels that it is Miss Seredy speaking as well as Sandor Nagy. In *Listening* there was an indirect comparison of city and country life, but here the comparison is direct and emphatic in its conclusion. This alliance with country living was to form the theme of . . . *The Open Gate.*

To go back two years to 1941, a year after the publishing of *The Singing Tree,* brings us to *A Tree for Peter*—the very titles bespeak the nature lover. Although *A Tree for Peter* is a nature lover's book in that it treats of people longing for grass and flowers, it is not that alone. It has been called a modern miracle story. It is another statement of faith—faith in people and in the abilities of people.

A Tree for Peter tells the story of a small boy, who, because of his great longing for beauty grows up to become a builder, a man who transforms the ugliness of slums to homes of dignity and beauty.

Peter, the small lame boy, who feels the need for trees and grass and beauty finds a helper. His friend is a tramp, a stranger. Perhaps the tramp who helped Peter transform Shantytown into Peter's Landing was known only to Peter. Perhaps he could not have been known to anyone but Peter, but Peter knew him, and knew that he would come with his tree. He could have been an ordinary tramp, he could have been The Stranger. He was Peter's faith.

A Tree for Peter is a different release for Miss Seredy's recurring themes—love for the country and absolute faith, the first, to her, a natural sequence to the second. The rotogravures are not as successful as her other illustrations, and Peter seems younger than his six years. The art work as a whole is uneven, the foreshortened figures and faces of some of the illustrations are not in keeping with the beautifully done picture of the tramp clasping small Peter to him.

This story, a little sentimental, has not the strength of most of her other books, nor is Peter, his mother, or Pat as convincing as Kate, Jancsi, or the Good Master. It is however, inspirational in its message, has an unusual theme, and, of course, has its place in our Christmas literature.

The Open Gate . . . is the fulfillment, and completion of a theory hinted at in *Listening,* stated in *The Singing Tree.* The superiority of a country life over a city life is the argument of the book. The plot, deriving its interest less from exciting incidents and more from a quiet suspense, concerns a city-bred family who find themselves, through the contriving of Gran, the owners of an old farm. Will Gran be able to convince Father that here on the farm is the best way of life for them? (pp. 454-55)

Gran, in her dissertation on the life of the farmer says, "But a farmer, if he is worthy of the name, does not expect a reward that he can put in the bank, his real reward comes from the same source as his strength; from within himself." So here is the final statement on the best way of life. To be a part of the country, to plough the earth, to plant the seed, to harvest the crop, to tend the animals is to have the best of life—a dependence upon oneself and upon God, the real expression of faith.

Miss Seredy's great desire for understanding between peoples is apparent, too, in this her sixth book. When the family is listening over the car radio to the news of the Russian scorched earth policy, Father sighs, "Those people in Russia . . . Poland . . . China . . . Norway . . . oh, all of the little people with their beloved little farms and cherished little possessions, why THEY are the unsung heroes of wars." And then comes Mike, Slovak and victim of middle European troubles, who affirms, "Me, American." To Gran, "it was a hymn, a prayer, a salute to liberty . . . it was the most beautiful speech I ever heard in my life," concluding in her matter-of-fact way, "I am going to bed to think about all he said." An invitation to the family and to the reader to think about Mike.

Her reverence, too, becomes noticeable in *The Open Gate.* When Father and Mike are discussing using Mike's spring as water supply for Father's barn and Father suggests payment, Mike says, "Say t'ank you to He. He make water, He make friend in here." And then her point becomes very clear, "Say Mist' John, you city-man. You PAY for water in city ma'be? And for friend?" Father's reply is half-serious, half-laughing, "For water, always. For friend, well, most of the time."

Miss Seredy's regard for God's creatures, God's plants, and for God's gifts is evident in the scene when Mr. and Mrs. Van Keuran are told of the success of the boy Andy's sketches. Mrs. Van Keuran says, "It's the words you brought into this house . . . that Andy is blessed with a gift from God." Father's conclusion about the character of Mike sums up Miss Seredy's feeling about country living. "He is so close to Nature every moment that he has become a part of it. He is as honest as Nature itself, and as big and clean and as simple. He has grown, with roots deep in the soil, as naturally as that tree. He can't be wrong, he doesn't know HOW to be wrong—God bless him. . . .''

This book, as do several others, ends with a religious ceremony—Christmas—the festival of birth and hope. "An open door, an open gate, an open heart—you never can tell what minute happiness walks in, if we only keep them open."

The Chestry Oak takes us across the ocean to Hungary and back again to America, symbolically perhaps. Miss Seredy's artistry is without doubt at its best in her native Hungarian background. The illustrations, wonderfully drawn and design perfect, are presented in an unusual manner, placed as a series in the front of the book. Here, they do lose some of their story value, but they also whet the appetite for the story to follow. This story, woven around the legend of the planting of the acorn from the Chestry family oak is an interesting one. It is the story of a father and son, princes of Hungary, who must deal with the Nazi usurpation of their home and their lands.

Michael, prince of Chestry, nine years old, taught and cared for by his Nana, is ill prepared to withstand the part he must play in escape from the Nazis.

Despite the alarming and frightful events, the story drags and we cannot quite believe in either Michael's complete naiveté, or the reappearance at the end of the story of Midnight, Michael's beloved horse.

Passages are beautifully written. After Michael's wild ride on Midnight, trying to make his escape, he has been hurled through space to awaken to "the world made of leaves, grass, and spots of sunlight [which] spun around him . . . fast . . . fast . . . faster." This sentence and the ensuing passage show a style developed to more maturity and strength than before. The words rush, they paint and color, they lack only restraint.

Three years later, restraint, beauty, workmanship, and reverence are discernible in *Gypsy*. Here Miss Seredy is literally in her element. This is not precisely a religious ceremony or theme, but yet an epic event—birth. In her element she is, too, in subject,—a cat. Gypsy is God's creature and man's companion. The warmth and sureness, the dignity and reality wipe clear any vestige of sentimentality. Here is no cuteness, no design, no sloppy depiction of adorable kittens. Here is a cat with all her feline cunning, her knowledge, and her desires.

In text and picture with all the artistry possible Miss Seredy has made a book, a translation of those thoughts well chosen, those words well spoken, the music well played that she heard in her father's house. May we say that it might be as it was with Gypsy, "Now, indeed, she knew all there was to know. She was content"? (pp. 455-57)

Lois R. Markey, "Kate Seredy's World," in Elementary English, *Vol. XXIX, No. 8, December, 1952, pp. 451-57.*

THE JUNIOR BOOKSHELF

[*The Chestry Oak* and *Philomena*] are two welcome and worthy additions to the works of this fine author-artist. . . . (p. 151)

The two books illustrate different facets of Miss Seredy's genius, the heroic and the humane. *The Chestry Oak* is a story of Hungary during the war. The hero, Prince Michael, is the very small son of a Prince ruling wisely, if absolutely, over the valley which has been in his family for centuries. The Nazis use the father as their tool; he in turn supplies information of their plans to the Allies. In the climax of the story, the valley is devastated in an air-raid, father is killed, and Michael is adopted as a war-orphan by an American farmer. The *noblesse oblige* tone of the early chapters may trouble some readers, for Miss Seredy reverences the aristocracy as only a citizen of a democratic republic can, and the whole story is inevitably more highly charged with emotion than some children of the right age will bear. It is, however, a very worth-while book, lofty in theme and dignified in performance.

Philomena is very different. It is a story set vaguely in the mid-nineteenth century in Bohemia. Philomena is an enchanting little village girl who, on the death of her beloved Babushka, goes to Prague to find her aunt and to learn to work. With Babushka's posthumous assistance she accomplishes both tasks. This book is exactly right in tone. It treats of everyday trivialities and tragedies with the quiet seriousness which respects the child's point of view. There is no silliness, not a hint of the indulgent adult's grimaces. The nicest story for small children for a long time. The touch is surer than in Rumer Godden's stories, the nearest to a parallel. The book has gaiety,

the fluency which disguises art, and under the charm a rock-like strength. It belongs to a sturdy, healthy, peasant tradition.

Miss Seredy's lithographs are excellent in both books. *The Chestry Oak* gives her an opportunity to draw the horses she loves. In *Philomena* she delights in the homely charms of her heroine as well as in the baroque splendours of Prague. The whole design of the book is excellent, with pictures positively leaping from the page. (pp. 151-52)

A review of "The Chestry Oak" and "Philomena," in The Junior Bookshelf, *Vol. 21, No. 3, July, 1957, pp. 151-52.*

AILEEN M. KASSEN

Who is this woman who has shared her heart with us in stories, stories of faith and courage, stories alive with light and beauty, graced with her own wonderful illustrations? Kate Seredy is a daughter of Hungary, a transplanted foster-child to America. Her roots are part of the land. She stands unafraid, facing the time to come when all men shall truly love each other and peace and contentment shall reign over all. (p. 303)

The Good Master and *The White Stag* are for me her most enduring books. I feel *A Tree for Peter* has special value as a Christmas story; *Gypsy* as a satisfying picture story book focused on growth and birth. Her other seven have many merits to recommend them, but, for one reason or another, they do not achieve quite the same level of significance. Although all the books she has written are warm, attractive, and worthy of attention, it is the first two above that most richly deserve the accolade of "classic." Each of these, in its own way, is everlasting.

Of all Miss Seredy's books, *The Good Master* is the most popular, and deservedly so. Children love it! It gives them warm feelings of security and the goodness of life and presents a world they can easily accept. (pp. 306-07)

Permeating the story and unifying it is the belief that life at its best is simple—its rewards, love, peace, and happiness can be gained by honest work close to the soil—and that man must surely be eternally grateful to God for these blessings. In this belief, the author reflects the basic tenets of the Magyar—absolute faith coupled with a not unemotional attachment to the land and its fruits. (p. 307)

The Good Master offers more than a lesson. It is also real people, skillfully drawn, gentle humor, graphic pictures of a time and place now gone forever, drama and excitement, plus an introduction to Hungarian folklore. Without doubt, Miss Seredy's stunning color portraits of Jancsi and Kate that serve as a frontispiece help the reader initially to identify with the children. However, through the judicious use of telling incidents, the two children quickly stand on their own feet. Kate is first described as a delicate city cousin. Her introduction by the railroad guard nicely contrasts with the mental images Jancsi has built up. The guard says,

> Here, take this—this imp, this unspeakable little devil—take her and welcome . . . I'd rather travel with a bag of screaming monkeys than her, anytime.

The conflict of the book is set. Will The Good Master be able to tame her? How will he do it?

In the very first chapter, Kate, Jancsi, Father . . . , and the Hungarian plain itself are all established, partially through their own actions, and partially through what Miss Seredy as the

From Philomena, *written and illustrated by Kate Seredy. The Viking Press, 1955. Copyright 1955 by Kate Seredy. Renewed © 1983 by Thomas R. Hadaway, Executor of the Estate of Kate Seredy. Reprinted by permission of Viking Penguin Inc.*

omniscient narrator says about them. There is no introspection; what exists is open to any observer. Kate is like a chameleon. In these few pages she goes from just any kind of a little girl with plain black hair, a smudgy face, and skinny legs, to a bantam rooster tense and poised; to a miniature whirlwind; to a poor, sweet little kitten; to finally, a hellion, standing alone, bolt upright on the seat of the wagon, reins and whip in hand and grinning from ear to ear. She might be plain but she certainly isn't a sissy. The boy readers accept her and the girls adore her!

In the simple existence on the farm, it is the incongruities of life that make for laughter and Miss Seredy lightens the story with touches of humor. For instance, Jancsi, dreaming of rescuing the princess from a dragon, is knocked off his seat and back to reality by his sweet cow, and husky father angrily swings a broom as little Kate on the rafters above artfully and successfully dodges his swipes.

The book is liberally illustrated with graceful watercolor paintings tied perfectly to the text itself. They focus on the people or the horses, and background is rarely suggested. In shades

of black and grey, with white used as an important color, it is the posture of the characters that gives them life. As one child said, "They look like they would keep on moving. They don't look frozen." The pictures are simple, basically realistic, though at times they move toward the idealized concept. The lines are mainly curved and rhythmic, conveying roundness of form, and even in the midst of drama, softness. The folds of a dress, the attitude of a hand, or the sweep of a horse's back add movement and emphasis. Total placement of the paintings on the page varies considerably; some are framed in curves, some are round, triangular or square, but they all help the reader visualize the incidents and achieve immediacy.

Stylized designs are used as chapter headings and one-half and one-third page pictures are above them at the end and beginnings of the chapters. All these add richness and give the book much visual appeal. Repeated in the designs are the traditional symbols of peasant art.

Kate Seredy's knowledge and love of nature is highly developed in her style and use of imagery. "The air was drenched with their sweet, heady perfume," horses "glittering hoofs were made of diamonds," "The dark blue sky, cloudless, like an inverted blue bowl," are ways she invites the reader to visualize her scenes. Most often, the response suggested is a concrete, visual one. One would expect that from a writer who was first an artist. She leaves no setting incomplete; each is filled in and often embroidered. Short sentences stud the paragraphs which present relatively simple structure, and dialogue makes up a very large part of the book. Sometimes the figure of speech is unique, strikingly suggestive, as "fields of ripening wheat which looked like lakes of flowing honey, waving and billowing in the wind"; sometimes it is a common one, such as the ferry boat owner who looked "as white as a sheet." Repetition of words and of key phrases is frequent. This establishes patterns which are pleasant.

> The sleigh bells were cheerful; without them there would have been utter silence. The lanterns were comforting; without them there would have been utter darkness.

It is an easy book to read aloud and the total effect is natural.

Both from the pictures and from the words, costumes and countryside take on a life of their own. Give a reader crayons and he could color in Kate's dresses, or draw an interior floor plan of the farmhouse and furnish it with ease. The great Hungarian plain, in all its multitude of moods, and the villages it cradles, are recreated vividly.

Then, too, the relationship of The Good Master and the men who worked for him, the shepherds, and horse herders, the hired harvesters, is made quite clear. It is a relationship of dignity, not one of servitude. They admire each other and find pride in their respective roles. . . . [This] was hardly the typical situation in Hungary during those years. *The Good Master,* like the famous Laura Ingalls Wilder series, sets before its readers a simpler time, when men could leave small patches of wheat uncut in their freshly hand-mowed fields, patches that sheltered a partridge nest.

The drama of the book is largely connected to the incidents built around the horses. This device presages the almost legendary role that horses were to have in several of Miss Seredy's later books. The horse had great historical and mythological importance to the Magyars. In *The Good Master,* it is the horses that bring excitement and challenge, as in a horse race between Kate and Jancsi, in their successful leading of a stampede, and in Jancsi's thrilling riding-rescue of drowning Kate.

Woven skillfully through the book are four retellings of old legends, three Hungarian, one Turkish. . . . Although some critics might feel these tales impede the narrative flow, for me they add color and further illuminate the character of Hungarian life. (pp. 307-09)

[From] the ringing prose and the powerful illustrations [in *The White Stag*] there shines forth a vision of unparalleled determination, pride, and faith. As a retelling of a story that is the basis of a nation's heritage, it is excellent. The words are clear and strong and from the very beginning to the last line there is not an extra phrase. The integration of text and illustrations is remarkable. Almost every picture is sweeping, dramatic, and somehow bigger-than-life. This helps to convey the traditional atmosphere of wonder and excitement. The narrative leaps ahead, from episode to episode, unified by the goal and purpose of the migration. (p. 310)

What has been [Kate Seredy's] contribution to the field of children's literature? When one looks at a room of Rubens in the Louvre, or at a gallery in New York City whose every wall is covered with Rothkos, one comes away with a total impression of a man and an artist. The same can be said for the experience of reading the eleven books published by Kate Seredy. The values that are brought out in *The Good Master* and *The White Stag* reappear in almost every one of her books. As she restates them, she deepens their meaning and extends their significance, though never quite as successfully as in her two classics.

For her, the good man and the good life are inextricably intertwined. Happiness in life must be earned, and along with the necessity of hard work, go faith and hope. It is in a sense a double-sided image. As Father Matthias, the kindly old priest in *Philomena* says, "One must use both head and heart to make things come out right . . . one must make them work together like a team of horses." Peter, in *A Tree for Peter,* works hard to keep his garden and to plant his tree, waiting and hoping for the miracle to happen.

The miracle, or the dream, however, never is realized in Miss Seredy's works without cooperation and love; these are the essential ingredients. Success ultimately depends not on just an individual's heart and mind balancing each other, but on all the characters in her stories pulling together toward their goal. Love, as Papa, in *A Brand-New Uncle* explains, is not only important but necessary to everyone, for we all want to feel needed, and having a friend makes toting troubles easier.

The concept of interdependence is expanded in *The Singing Tree* and *The Chestry Oak* to include all the people in the world working together for peace and brotherhood. Grigori, the capable sweet Russian prisoner that Jancsi brings home to help, declares, "All same, Jancsi . . . Li'l' Russian, li'l' German, li'l' Hungarian," all men were brothers. With Nana, in *The Chestry Oak,* Miss Seredy seems to affirm that God has given men the means to conquer evil when they work together with a wall of prayers.

The greatest evil for mankind in Kate Seredy's books, is undoubtedly war, "that stampede . . . the mad whirlwind that sucks in man . . . and spits out crippled wrecks." In her view, the little people of the world do not make war. It is a terror forced on them. Again Grigori communicates this belief by stating that no *good* man can kill and laugh. It is interesting that both Father in *The Singing Tree* and Michael in *The Chestry Oak* are emotionally unable to stand the horror of the slaughter, and both react by completely blacking out their overwhelming experiences. Miss Seredy's nursing experience in the first World War had made her a confirmed pacifist and demonstrated to her the senselessness of war.

Looked at simply, she is an optimist, and her books confirm a positive world view. Gran, the central character in *The Open Gate,* believes that nothing bad ever happens without some good in it some place. Nana, the stalwart nurse in *The Chestry Oak,* teaches Michael, the hero, that nothing fine and noble will ever perish as long as there are hearts to remember. This optimism is tied to Miss Seredy's bond with the land, where there are always signs of renewal and hope. In *A Tree for Peter, The Chestry Oak,* and *The Singing Tree,* trees as objects in nature stand as true symbols of this affirmation of life and growth.

Opposing growth, besides the wickedness of war, is the crowded modern city. In all but one of the books, Miss Seredy sees the city as robbing man of his dignity, his initiative, his sense of values, his very identity. Farm and rural life alone hold a sense of permanency. There is no synthesis here. She does not, except in *The Tenement Tree,* see the vigor, excitement, and challenge of an urban way of life, nor does she see the limitations inherent in the world of the farmer. In *The Singing Tree* and in *The Open Gate,* this belief is so outspoken and romanticized as to raise questions for the modern reader. It is undoubtedly valuable for today's children to understand the wonders and rewards of living close to nature, an experience which is denied to most of them. But it is equally valuable, and it seems to me, very important, for these children also to see the possibilities for achieving selfhood in their mechanized, computerized world. Courage and faith, the two lanterns Miss Seredy gives man to light the way into the future, can be as effective in the city as they are on the farm.

Ideas are not, however, usually what children are looking for in their books, and Miss Seredy is aware of this. "Teach?" she says. "I wasn't trying to. I was only telling stories." Sometimes in *The Singing Tree, The Open Gate,* and even in *The Chestry Oak,* the teachings get in the way of the story. She seems to have some trouble in controlling her didactic impulse. The lessons are at times too pointed or a bit overdrawn. Their moral and religious overtones hint at preachiness. *A Tree for Peter, A Brand-New Uncle,* and *Philomena* are infused with an almost religious quality that comes precariously close to sentimentality.

Most often the story in Miss Seredy's books carries the reader along. Interest in the plot is achieved by the suspense built into it. The resolution is guessed at but not known; the problem grows naturally. *The Chestry Oak* contains many compelling incidents. It is structurally divided into three: the life of its hero, Michael, in Hungary before World War II; his period of relative amnesia (resulting from emotional trauma); and his refuge and new life in America. Michael's wild ride on the stallion is unforgettable. However, the book is flawed by a lack of clarity in the middle section and its relation and transition to the final section, and also by a contrived ending.

Parading through Miss Seredy's books are memorable characters. Nana, in *The Chestry Oak,* the epitome of peasant womanhood, is amazing. She is immensely wise and loving. Her teaching and understanding symbolize the ideal mother, one who can help her child develop to his fullest potential, who in no way holds too tight to his developing personality, and who is ready to relinquish the bond when the time is ripe. *The Chestry Oak* is as rich in fine characterization as is *The Good Master.* Somehow for me, the family in *The Open Gate* is hard to believe, and the personalities of Mama and Papa in *A Brand-New Uncle* come a bit too close to studied types. Most frequently, though, Miss Seredy is swift and skillful in establishing characters that talk and act like real people and not like puppets. A child reader commented, "Some characters do things in the order of the plot but these seem to really have to think about it and decide."

In reviewing Kate Seredy's style, it seems to me important to remember that English is her adopted language. Some of the greatest English writers have written in other than their native tongues. Joseph Conrad was acclaimed for his mastery, and today Vladimir Nabokov, thought by many to be the finest living author, is working in his third language. To conquer a second or a third language, to make it completely part of one, is without question a tremendous achievement. Hungarian is a Finnish-Ugrian language, not related to Indo-European tongues. It is considered particularly difficult for a Hungarian to make the very basic changes necessary for learning English.

In light of this, it is especially noteworthy that Miss Seredy has developed such skill and such a fine sense of language. Her stories seem to tumble out, the rhythm of their words closely allied with their meaning, and the dialogue and descriptive passages balanced. Children are well aware of her ability.

> I like the way she makes you see the pictures
> even though there is no illustration on the page.
> You have the picture in your mind and you
> know what it's like.

And another, "Her words are made into pictures even though they are not descriptions." Perhaps this is testimony to Miss Seredy's early training as an artist; certainly it underscores a sure understanding of the power of words.

Kate Seredy seems to be strongest in her handling of stories set against her native background. In *The Chestry Oak,* . . . her stylistic talents are seen in their full maturity, rich and eloquent. For me there are many passages that are immensely impressive. A scene at the beginning, of Nana in the great Chestry Palace, is Seredy fiction at its best, creating a world of the imagination yet a world well-understood. As one child added, "I do like the way she puts a feeling on you. It's sort of like a spell!"

Gypsy, a picture story of a cat, for the youngest reader, is the most controlled and reserved of her books. She says that she spent three years whittling down the story to the brief captions that appear, and the honing is clearly evident. *Gypsy* is a quiet book, to be read at quiet times, and its style is well suited to its story. In most of her other books this restraint and moderation is not so obvious or apparent.

It seems appropriate to end an appraisal of Miss Seredy with some thoughts on her illustrations. They give to children clear pictures of Hungary, of horses, of small animals, of honest, simple people. Only *Lazy Tinka* is printed in color; all the others are monochromatic.

> Even though they aren't in color, with the words,
> they fill the black and white sketches in and
> make them look colored,

was the way one little girl explained her reaction to the illustrations. The pictures always extend and decorate the text and seem well-placed. They contribute so much meaning to the stories that it is hard to consider them separately without doing an injustice to her creative power. The very best of them, in *The White Stag, The Good Master,* and *The Chestry Oak,* are strong and very beautiful; those of the animals in *The Tenement Tree* and *Gypsy* are alive and design perfect. As a whole group, they are of distinguished quality!

May Hill Arbuthnot, one of the deans of children's literature, sends us to find books for boys and girls to balance the speed and confusion of our modern world; books that build strength and steadfastness in the child, develop his faith in the essential decency and nobility of life, and give him feelings for the wonder and goodness of the universe. Kate Seredy's books do just this. She is a person worth knowing! (pp. 310-14)

> *Aileen M. Kassen, "Kate Seredy: A Person Worth Knowing," in* Elementary English, *Vol. XLV, No. 3, March, 1968, pp. 303-15.*

JAMES E. HIGGINS

Having been a Kate Seredy fan for many years, I have always been fascinated by her insistence that her books came from "out of nowhere" [see excerpt above in Author's Commen-

From A Tree for Peter, *written and illustrated by Kate Seredy. The Viking Press, 1941. Copyright 1941, renewed © 1968 by Kate Seredy. Reprinted by permission of Viking Penguin Inc.*

tary]. On first hearing such a statement, one takes it to be but a casual comment made by a modest woman, who is somewhat embarrassed by her own talent. I have heard or read similar statements made by several authors, only to find that they often follow them up with long dissertations, usually dwelling at some length upon such matters as style and syntax. As for Kate Seredy, there was something about her books that made me guess that she was being neither modest nor facetious, but rather that she was simply giving an honest description of herself.

If it was not literary training that had prepared her for a career in writing, then it must have been something about the woman herself, I hypothesized, and an interview with the lady would be the best way of finding out whether or not my hunches had any degree of validity.

After spending one of the most pleasant afternoons of plain talk that I can remember, I discovered what May Massee [children's editor at the Viking Press] had found so fascinating in this tough-fibered but gentle woman, and what had led Miss Massee after but one meeting to believe that it was not only possible but inevitable for Kate Seredy to become a writer. What for me had started out to be an interview became a conversation as if between two friends of long standing, and an afternoon of storytelling.

All my questions were answered, but not one of the answers was an explanation. Everything was *story*. If the conversation turned to one of her books, I was told a story; a query on

style—a story; on character or background—a story. Each story was so dramatic and so appropriate that no explanation was needed. (pp. 163-64)

Indeed, stories did seem to come from "out of nowhere," but only because they flowed so naturally from a mind that literally *thinks* story.

Kate Seredy's books, varied as they are in form, style, content, and characterization, all have one thing in common: each vividly reflects the person who is the author. She writes not only out of her own experience but out of her own feeling for life. The outer world of appearance is never distorted in the Seredy books. The true realism of the books, however, is not found in the way she depicts what is recorded by the senses, but rather in her ability to describe the encounter taking place between her imagination and her sensory impressions, which, in turn, results in the creation of a new image, just as real as the object that stimulated its creation.

The natural environment, people met, and incidents experienced are never described or reported directly to the reader by Kate, the author, unless they are first intuitively assimilated by Kate, the person. She takes possession of her world through the simple act of living, and her stories, in turn, take on life through this intimate process. She lives and then records out of her living, so that the reader discovers not only the world about her but the world within her as well.

Trees, for instance, play an important part in many of Miss Seredy's books (*The Tenement Tree* . . . , *The Singing Tree, The Chestry Oak, A Tree for Peter*). And it matters little to what biological species each of her trees belongs, because the distinguishing characteristic which gives them a common genus is that each one of them truly is a *Seredy* tree—just as there are *Wordsworth* daffodils and *Homer* dawns.

Although the reader of a Seredy book—it matters not whether he be reading print or picture—is free to read in any way he wishes, the author-illustrator sometimes, nonetheless, requests that he at least consider a point of view. It is as if she were saying: "This is how I see it, and I'm curious to see if you might be able to see it in the same way."

For instance, in *The Tenement Tree* the buildings that Tino sees from atop his dwelling place are accurately drawn, and one may view them as buildings. When Tino, however, asks the reader to *see* his "giants," one has no trouble finding them. They are there, too. Only a change of view is needed: "You're right, I can see them too, now that you mention it."

At other times, though Miss Seredy seems to have no particular point of view, she does, in fact, wonder out loud about things, people, and events, and as a result, she prods her readers to indulge in that all-too-infrequently-played game of *wondering* as well. For example, it surely does make a difference in *A Tree for Peter* how the reader accepts the appearance of the tramp in both text and illustration. To some readers *A Tree for Peter* is a straightforward realistic story; to others, it is a miracle story. The Seredy signature permits it to be both.

Now, when an author so chooses to draw deep from within himself, when he dares to tap the reservoir of self in order to bring forth his story, then he constantly runs the risk of being sentimental, egotistical, or—worse still—not completely honest. My own masculine bias would also suggest that this risk is doubly hazardous for the author who happens to be a woman. Books like *The Good Master* and *A Brand-New Uncle* have been occasionally criticized for hovering close to the edge of sentimentality; I cannot agree with the critics.

I believe it to be Kate Seredy's honest search to relive the emotion of the story experience that brings her bravely up to this thin but decisive edge. An author may choose to avoid the danger of sentimentality by throwing up a shield of objectivity and aloofness, but in doing so he must also forfeit the challenge of intuitive exploration. Seredy chooses to risk the danger (actually she has no choice, for this is her way of telling a story), and the result is most rewarding.

If there is a conscious method to Miss Seredy's style, I would guess that it comes through sound. Just as images are the usual beginnings of her stories and eventually the stuff of her stories, it is sound which determines how they will be told. Kate Seredy is not only skilled in accurately recording the sounds of the human voice in dialogue but she also tests her word pictures by their sound. Are the sounds appropriate for the image, the mood, the feeling? It is the human voice which serves as the prime determinant for such things as sentence length, vocabulary, punctuation, and syntax. The reader of a story like *The White Stag* can feel the words breaking the silence even if the sound remains within himself.

Yes, Kate Seredy's stories do come out of the "nowhere" of her heart. "She puts so much of herself into each one of her books" is the kind of oft-said phrase that has become rather trite in describing an author's work, but in this case it is literally true. Kate is in every one of her stories. Sometimes, of course, she is there in the flesh, as Kate herself in *The Good Master* and *The Singing Tree* or as Aunt Trina in *The Tenement Tree*. But she is a part of her other stories as well, just as she was a living part of the multitude of stories that she told me on that afternoon in early spring. (pp. 165-68)

> *James E. Higgins, "Kate Seredy: Storyteller," in* The Horn Book Magazine, *Vol. XLIV, No. 2, April, 1968, pp. 162-68.*

THE GOOD MASTER (1935)

AUTHOR'S COMMENTARY

Almost thirty years ago a few famous French artists and scientists came to Hungary to study peasant art and life. My father, who was doing research work along the same lines, was asked to join the party. It was summertime and it was decided that a few weeks in the country would be good for me, so I was taken along. I was about nine years old then, a typical pale, skinny city child and, being an only child, very much spoiled. I didn't want to go "with a lot of old men to look at old embroideries and stuff," but for once I couldn't have my own way. Of course, no one expected me to get interested in peasant art—and I didn't. I paid as little attention to the object of that trip as I possibly could. I went home from the trip very much healthier, with a creditable amount of escapades to my credit, but unharmed by ethnological or artistic knowledge. Or so I thought. Now I know that I went home full of impressions, deep, unforgettable impressions, only I didn't know it then, not for a long time. My mind was like a sensitive moving picture film, recording an incredible number of pictures. Films are worthless unless developed; my impressions were meaningless to me too, until passing years and new, conscious observations developed them.

We arrived in a small, remote village after sundown. I was too tired to notice how sleeping quarters were arranged for; I

only remember that a rosy cheeked, buxom, friendly peasant woman took charge of me. "You poor little scrawny chicken," she exclaimed over me, "what you need is a lot of milk, fresh from the cow, to put meat on your bones." She produced immense quantities of food for the party. I stubbornly refused to drink milk "fresh from the cow" and ate something thoroughly bad for me, hot, peppery sausages and big slabs of fresh bread. . . . Next morning a deep, mellow musical sound woke me up. . . . I struggled out of bed to investigate. A man (later I found out that he was the village herder) was walking slowly down the long street. He stopped by each house and blew his horn. From the yards came cows, one by one, and joined the growing herd. The village herder takes them to the pasture and brings them back at night. His horn marks the beginning and the end of each day. The ducks and geese are taken to the pasture later; one or two children are in charge of those. The men leave for the fields, and in the spring and summer the women stay home just long enough to cook a big meal. They carry it to their men at noontime and stay until dark, to help. In the afternoon the whole village is deserted. No one ever locks a door, the houses are open. "God gave us what we have," say the peasants, "if He sends a poor traveler this way, it is the Lord's will that he be fed and clothed." They are not fatalistic, but they have absolute confidence in divine providence. . . . They are hospitable, welcoming friends and strangers with a hearty "God brought you," and their last word to the parting guest is a sincere "God bless you."

They are very close to nature and have the innate gentleness of people who are in constant contact with growing things—plants and beasts. Their home craft—embroideries, carvings, pottery—is a mirror of their simple daily life. The designs are always pictures or symbols of animals and plants. Everything they produce is richly decorated. As inevitably as nature covers a barren patch of ground with vegetation, the Hungarian peasant will cover a plain surface with colorful, intricate designs. Clothes, household linen are embroidered. Cooking utensils and dishes are painted and glazed. Furniture, door and window frames, gates and fence posts, washboards and yokes, whips, plow-handles are carved, inlaid, painted. They are all born artists, but the greatest among them are the shepherds. Perhaps because they live far away even from the remote villages and modern civilization has not touched and confused their conceptions, their carvings show the perfect knowledge of essential form and understanding of structure that the Assyrian and Egyptian sculptors had. (pp. 167-68)

Years went by, war came, I had many interests, but as often as I could, I went back to the plains, with open eyes now. I had a mental picture of the life of the Hungarian peasant, a picture painted in bold, vivid colors, the red of wild poppies, blue of cornflowers, yellow of ripe wheat. A picture of generous, honest, hardworking people, whose feet are firmly planted in the soil and whose hearts and minds are open to all good things in life. . . .

So *The Good Master* was written—but I didn't really write it. All I did was to give a frame to the picture that many unknown Hungarian peasants painted for me, many years ago. (p. 168)

> *Kate Seredy, "The Country of 'The Good Master'," in* The Elementary English Review, *Vol. XIII, No. 5, May, 1936, pp. 167-68.*

In both appearance and content **"The Good Master"** is a genuinely joyous and beautiful book. The scene of the story is a farm on the great Hungarian plains, a farm where there were thousands of sheep, horses, cows and pigs, where there were chickens and ducks and geese, even donkeys, but only one boy, 10-year-old Jancsi. Jancsi would have given ten horses for a brother, he would have given a donkey even for a sister. Then a girl cousin of his own age arrived from the city.

They were wonderful outdoor experiences that the two children had; long rides across the plain with its solemn beauty, "its immense grassy expanses, unbroken by mountains or trees, shimmering under the Spring sun. The dark blue sky, cloudless, like an inverted blue bowl. Herds of grazing sheep, like patches of snow. At times these plains, called the 'puszta,' are the very essence of timeless calm." Then there were visits to the shepherds, who told them folktales and taught them carving; visits made by the gypsies to the farm that were less pleasant, the decorating of Easter eggs, fairs and round-ups and a Christmas celebration to end the book. . . .

[Miss Seredy] knows the country of which she writes. She knows people, too, and can make them so real and so alive that Jancsi, mischievous Kate, Jancsi's father, the lovable "good master" and Jancsi's mother, hospitable and protective, remain with us after the book is closed. The illustrations have beauty and vitality, the horses seem in motion and the children ready to speak. The crayon portraits of Jancsi and Kate are particularly charming, as is also the gracefully designed title page. "The Good Master" is a story that 9 to 12 year olds should not miss, and a lovely and distinguished piece of book making.

> Anne Thaxter Eaton, in a review of "The Good Master," in The New York Times Book Review, November 17, 1935, p. 25.

A glorious story. . . . [There is] serious charm in the telling of old legends by the herder under the clear, starry skies. The steady warm understanding of the wise father . . . is a shining quality throughout. The illustrations are closely and beautifully attuned to the text and the whole is a notable piece of creative work. (pp. 351-52)

> A review of "The Good Master," in The Horn Book Magazine, Vol. XI, No. 6, November-December, 1935, pp. 351-52.

Many a gay and brilliant bit of color has come out of Hungary to brighten America, but never a prettier piece of it, whether in picture or story, than this summer story. . . . It is by no means so strong a book as Alexander Finta's fine "Herdboy of Hungary," of whose illustrations these have a certain reminiscent tinge, but it is happier. Also it will please girls, being about a girl rather than about a boy, and this girl, one of those heroines of ten-year-old readers, a young person up to everything and generally in some kind of scrape. . . .

Hungarian customs and costumes brighten the pages, and though the tale has no special unity it will keep a ten-year-old well entertained.

> A review of "The Good Master," in New York Herald Tribune Books, December 22, 1935, p. 7.

This is a fine piece of creative work. . . . It belongs to that small group, of which Young Fu and Dobry are outstanding examples, of books for young readers that incidentally or essentially present a vivid picture of life in a foreign country. . . .

[The] headstrong, irresistibly mischievous child [Cousin Kate] enters like a whirlwind. Her first few days leave us breathless.

So much so indeed that one feels the picture to be rather overdrawn. . . .

In characterisation the book is outstanding. Cousin Kate is particularly vivid. Jancsi, her cousin, . . . is set quietly in contrast. The Good Master himself, loved by his men and sharing their problems, patient with his niece, stands clearly out as typical of his kind. Pisti the old shepherd is also typical. He represents the devotion to his calling, the closeness to the earth and the appreciation of nature's gifts that is so often found among shepherds. . . .

Miss Seredy is not only author, but is a children's book illustrator of established reputation. In this book she gives us pictures that march admirably with the story. Decorative in treatment, they give a fine impression of movement in horses, peasant dances or Hungarian legends.

> H. J. B. Woodfield, in a review of "The Good Master," in The Junior Bookshelf, Vol. 1, No. 3, May, 1937, p. 29.

Something makes this story unusually satisfying and wholesome (in the unpriggish sense of that word)—possibly the rhythmical background of farm life, but more probably the warm understanding between the children of the story and the adults in it, between the shepherds who tell tales to Kate and Jancsi, and between these two and . . . Jancsi's father, a magnificent peasant type. As the author of the story is also its illustrator, the book is a perfect unity, with pictures which are spirited as the tale grows spirited and become still as the pace of the story slackens. . . . [Kate Seredy] writes English prose of a fine simplicity with no trace of a foreign idiom. (p. 88)

> Dorothy Neal White, "Realistic Stories—Standards 5 and 6," in her About Books for Children, New Zealand Council for Educational Research, 1946, pp. 86-108.*

Kate is a fully realized character. Because she is a daredevil she has some exciting adventures: she disobeys instructions when she and Jancsi turn aside stampeding horses during a roundup; she goes away with the gypsies to try to save the livestock and grain they have stolen from the farm; she also exposes a fraudulent freak at the fair. All of these incidents—and others—are in accord with her character and contribute humor and drama. Beautiful traditions are observed by the dyeing of Easter eggs and the filling of shoes by Mikulas on the night of December sixth. Inserted stories—told by Jancsi's mother, the shepherds, and the miller—relate the folklore of the country. The theme of the superiority of life in the country over life in the city and of handcrafted articles over machine made ones is brought out. Kate Seredy's many graceful illustrations of the characters and horses contribute to the romantic interpretation that the text gives of a way of life. (p. 59)

> Marilyn Leathers Solt, "The Newbery Medal and Honor Books, 1922-1981: 'The Good Master'," in Newbery and Caldecott Medal and Honor Books: An Annotated Bibliography by Linda Kauffman Peterson and Marilyn Leathers Solt, G. K. Hall & Co., 1982, pp. 58-9.

LISTENING (1936)

Tucked away in the Ramapo Mountains is a house in a grove of pine trees, set close to a river. The only one in the valley, it might have been, as small Gail observed on her first sight of it, a lonesome house, but Uncle George assured her that it had plenty of friends, and no building could be lonely housing the charming Hunter family, with its two boys, its three cats and a beguiling dog named Viking.

The house held, too, a rich store of memories, and it was these memories which Uncle George interpreted to Gail on her first visit there, telling her the story of its growth, generation by generation from the first stone cottage which Joest Van Horn, newly arrived from Holland, built in 1656 for his wife, Katrina. . . .

In between the stories Gail has many good times with her cousins, frolicking on the river, helping to rebuild an old mill. Having learned to listen to the secrets of the old house, she learned, too, to hear and watch the secret life of the wild creatures in its surrounding woods. Thus, having briefly recaptured the romance of an American homestead, in a story for 8 to 12 year olds, Miss Seredy also sketches a fine portrayal of a modern American family, considerate, imaginative and gay. Not only the text but the format of the book as well appeals to the imagination. The author traces the growth of the house in pictures, interspersing them with many delightful drawings of animals, beautifully executed. . . .

Ellen Lewis Buell, in a review of "Listening," in The New York Times Book Review, October 25, 1936, p. 10.

Although the story in its construction offers incongruities of age appeal it will be enjoyed by many children of eight to thirteen to whom it will introduce new ideas and interests. Charming format and illustrations.

A review of "Listening," in The Booklist, Vol. 33, No. 4, December, 1936, p. 129.

[*Listening*] is most delightful . . . [in] illustrations. It attempts to combine the history of an old farmhouse from Dutch days to the present, with the story of the modern children who listen to the tale, but we feel that neither atmosphere is sustained. Chapter I. about the little girl arriving by bus in Hopkins Corner proves how well Miss Seredy can write.

A review of "Listening," in The Catholic World, Vol. CXLIV, No. 861, December, 1936, p. 378.

THE WHITE STAG (1937)

AUTHOR'S COMMENTARY

Soon after **"The White Stag"** was published, I sent a copy of it to a friend of mine, a teacher. In a few days I received a note from her in which, among other things, she said:

"How I envy you writers the ease with which you can present fine ideals to children without ever appearing to teach."

Teach? Why—I wasn't trying to! I was only telling stories! Hastily I glanced through my books, reading them a little apprehensively and, because of my friend's remark, with fresh eyes, as if I were reading someone else's writings.

That I did find fine ideals presented in my books, I can say now without conceit because those ideals are mine only through inheritance. And they are not mine alone; they govern the lives of many generations of people who have grown up under the same teacher—my father. And I know now why I receive countless letters from children of all ages; warm, spontaneous letters alive with eager response to those very ideals. I know

because I have seen eager response on the faces of countless children.

I remember the endless procession of boys coming to see my father after school; small boys with small problems, big boys with big problems. They came day after day with hunched shoulders and troubled eyes and the door of father's study closed upon them. After a while they left, shoulders straight, chin up and a brave, shining look in their eyes. They had found help and support in that short interval between the closing and opening of that door. Not financial help, not outside help; they had been shown how to help themselves. (pp. 2355-56)

Years later I asked one of those boys—a famous sculptor then— just what had made them come to father, only to him and not to the other teachers? For a long time he didn't answer. Then he said: "Your father told us stories . . . and somehow he made us think for ourselves." . . .

"He didn't teach, he didn't scold, he never told us what to do. He only told us stories but through those stories he taught us how to think, how to live. His creed was so simple that, without the magic of his words, it sounds almost trite. You must know all this, for you are his daughter."

"Yes, I know," I said. "Never run away from trouble but face it and it will disappear. Have faith in yourself and your work. . . ." The sculptor continued: "Finish what you have started. Try to make things instead of buying them. Give more than you take. Walk softly through the woods to watch the creatures instead of sneaking through with a gun in your hand. Your father hated guns. And, most of all, never give up. Don't ever quit. You know his favorite story, the legend of the White Stag, the story of unbroken faith in a great purpose. Through a lifetime he held that ideal up like a light for thousands of boys. You know."

Yes, I do know. He lived by the light of that legend and I was brought up to follow it. It is an ageless and immortal story; one of the great legends of mankind. Its appeal has no age limits. To a young child it is a fairy story, to a growing child it speaks of romance and adventure. To those of us, who are no longer children but have to make our way in the world as well as we can, the legend of the White Stag becomes truly a light; a light that shines with all the fine things which are the backbone of all religions; unshakable belief in a guiding hand from above and faith in one's purpose.

The legend comes to an end when that purpose is accomplished, when the Huns reach the land "between two rivers, surrounded by mountains." History takes up the thread and history, justly, condemns Attila. His subsequent conquests, his grasping for unlimited power over a whole continent are really the tragic story of his downfall. The story of a man who had ceased to look for guidance, who, drunk with power, believed in nothing but the might of his sword. I like to dream of the day when the light of faith (the White Stag)—will again outshine the flaming red light of intolerance. . . .

I, for one, brought up in the tradition of the immortal legend of the birth of a nation which has withstood the upheavals of centuries, can view today's happenings with more pity than abhorrence, more tolerance than hatred. In this spirit I pass on the legend of the White Stag, enriched by my father's philosophy, to new generations of children, not as a story to glorify war and conquest but as a great story of faith, courage and belief in a guiding hand. (p. 2356)

From The White Stag, *written and illustrated by Kate Seredy. The Viking Press, 1937. Copyright 1937, renewed © 1965 by Kate Seredy. Reprinted by permission of Viking Penguin Inc.*

Kate Seredy, " 'The White Stag,' an Immortal Legend," in Publishers Weekly, *Vol. CXXXIII, No. 25, June 18, 1938, pp. 2355-56.*

Against a background of velvet black, a cloud-white stag, an eagle of Hungarian red clutching a golden sword, sweep toward a sun in splendor. Thus at a glance the most beautiful cover of the season summarizes its most striking book for children. In tumultuous pictures and a prose driving like a storm-cloud, Kate Seredy, telling the story of Hun and Magyar emergence from the dim backward of legend into the half-light of history, tells, in the deepest sense of the word, her own story. This is her country, these her remote ancestors, this heroic legendry is in her blood. . . . Miss Seredy obeys a drive comparable to that of her subject, in setting down the story of the Hungarian drive out of Asia under the guidance of what we later come to call manifest destiny. In doing so she achieves a vocal prose that sets the story in a class by itself among the books of the year. Where the voice pauses come pictures that look as if the statues of the Millenium Memorial or the wild dusty shapes of the Historic Panorama in Budapest had been suddenly translated into another medium and infused with nervous energy. The book is Hungarian to the heart's core, and if Miss Seredy does not receive some sort of decorations from the government there's no gratitude along the Danube.

The story is called "a fragile thread; it cannot bear the weight of facts and dates," but it pulls like a wire cable. It cannot be sketched without incorporating its own phrases, even without quotation marks. Nimrod the mighty hunter killed his favorite horse and asked for a sign; an eagle was seen circling in the altar smoke and a storm drove its fire in a path to the westward burning high and bright. The old leader's sons, Hunor and Magyar, had been seven moons following a miraculous white stag outlined against the western sky as if it held the sun between its branching horns. The path of fire meets them beyond the hills and they return in time to take their father's command to build for him a mighty mound, the gigantic Tomb of Nimrod, and to lead their people westward. The tribe left the headlands of Asia; the untamed wilderness closed again upon their tracks. The two leaders married captive Moon Maidens; Hunor's son was Bendeguz, who married a Cimmerian princess caught up with her people along the way and capturing the hearts of her new people. Their son . . . was Attila the Scourge of God. It is he who is the blazing hero of the story. Not until the armies of Europe have become "panic-stricken rabble, wrecked, scattered, trodden down to the dirt by this merciless avalanche of horsemen," does it close.

Unless I am mistaken, it is the first time that Attila the Hun has been offered to English-speaking children as a culture-hero. He has, of course, been elsewhere recommended as such, outside Hungary, but that was before the Great War. Now he comes as he may have looked to the child who at the climax of the story comes running toward the golden conqueror, and stumbling, holds up her bruised hand for his comfort. As he does so, however, he catches sight of the hilt of Hadur's buried sword, and it is at this consecration of a hunger-drive to the spirit of destiny, and upon his oath upon the Hun sword to hold the land, that the tale ends. It is more than the setting of an ancient legend; it is the statement, at moments little less than magnificent, of an urge by no means peculiar to this time and tribe, recurring, like the swoop of some dark destroying angel, whenever and wherever the time for it has come in history.

A review of "The White Stag," in New York Herald Tribune Books, *November 21, 1937, p. 9.*

Boys and girls, in the early days of the world, who with their elders heard from the lips of bard and story-teller the legends of their tribe, were in one respect greatly privileged. They ran no danger, at least, of being surfeited with the mediocre; the tales to which they listened had gone through a selective process; they were great enough to endure and to be fresh with each repetition.

We are fortunate indeed to have such a retelling of an ancient legend as Kate Seredy gives us in **"The White Stag."** Reading it we realize once more the power of the epic tale, the thrill of high adventure splendidly set forth. For Miss Seredy's ear is tuned to the music of words, to the cadence of a sentence or a phrase, and her story . . . has caught something of the living quality imparted by the lips of the storyteller. As nearly as it is possible in this print-ridden world, we recapture, through **"The White Stag,"** the sensation of listening to a narrative that sweeps on in a rhythmic prose from its heroic beginning to a magnificent climax. . . .

Fortunately, Miss Seredy is her own illustrator. The drawings (the finest she has yet made) have the strength and grandeur of the legend. They are an integral part of the narrative, for it is by means of text and pictures together that we are able to [follow the story]. . . .

The White Stag leaps miraculously through the forests or in unearthly beauty stands luminously white against the white of the snow; moon maidens dance under the birch trees; white herons and great eagles fly through the twilight; there is high courage and steadfastness in every line of the tribal heroes as Miss Seredy draws them, and splendor in the horses who, in drawing after drawing, sweep magnificently into action.

This book will reach an older audience than **"The Good Master,"** Kate Seredy's fine story of child life on a farm in Hungary; in fact, **"The White Stag"** is a book with no age limits. Children will find in it the wonder of a fairy tale, to older boys and girls and adults it brings the stirring romance of heroic legend, and readers of any age will be grateful to see the scanty outlines of the history books rounded out with the color, atmosphere and poetry of this artist's retelling of the story of Attila.

Anne T. Eaton, in a review of "The White Stag," in The New York Times Book Review, *December 12, 1937, p. 10.*

The driving destiny of [the Huns and the Magyars], the sweep and power of the drawings, and the lofty, austere but breathless quality of the prose are all in complete harmony. It is simple enough for the age most stirred by myth and legend and there is a pleasant minimum of difficult proper names. A rare and beautiful book, but it would be a misfortune for any library to mistake it for something too fine for daily use. It will appeal to a child no less than it will nurture his reading taste. (p. 35)

Julia I. Sauer, in a review of "White Stag," in Library Journal, *Vol. 63, No. 1, January 1, 1938, pp. 34-5.*

On an evening of April, 1938, a group of boys and girls in or hovering upon their early teens met in the Childrens' Room of one of the public libraries in New York to listen to a story. . . . On the table there was just one book—Kate Seredy's **The White Stag.** The candlelight fell on the jacket design, on the burning red of the eagle, the shining white of the stag. . . .

From the very beginning, from that fine description of Old Nimrod, Mighty Hunter before the Lord, the story caught and held the listeners. As it went on the quiet of their bodies and the alertness, the intentness of their minds grew. . . .

You could have heard a pin drop in that room when the end came. A heroic story told in words that rang like bells had taken these young people completely "out of themselves." After the silence came applause, loud and hearty. Then the demand for the book, to look at it, to handle it. (p. 488)

Spirit and senses were both challenged by the significance of the story and by the bold beauty of the cover design. . . .

[*The White Stag*] calls to us all outwardly and satisfies us all inwardly, from the critic to the boys and girls whose silence when the tale was done is the greatest tribute that a creative artist can receive.

Before this latest "Newbery" book was put into the hands of the children, a number of critics questioned the wisdom of giving them a "glorified" version of the story of Attila the Hun. No one who watched them listening that spring evening could question it. Its integrity and beauty are such that they get from it just exactly what its creator intended them to get; human pride and courage and loyalty, human pain and failure and defeat and, shaping it all, the superhuman strength, the selfless purpose that marks a hero.

Any prize that is awarded, particularly to a book that is significant in relation to the past, the present and the future, is subject to the standards—one might almost say the prejudices—of a mature mind. That the childrens' librarians of North America should have awarded the John Newbery Medal to the story of Attila the Hun in this particular Year of Our Lord is a tribute both to them and to its author. To them because they recognized its enduring values, they listened for the young, hearty chorus of "Ayes." To her because the amazing actions of a practically insane world did not turn her from her purpose. . . .

One hundred years from now, perhaps, someone will take this book from a shelf and open it to one of the full-page drawings. To this person, our day will be a page in history, a record so confused and contradictory that he will wonder how such a book could have come out of it. Strong in purpose, clear in action, beautiful in wording and in pictures, it will do for him, this man of the future, just what it is doing for us. He will pause, as we pause, to salute it—the John Newbery Medal book for 1937, **The White Stag.** (p. 489)

Mary Gould Davis, "'The White Stag': Winner of the John Newbery Medal for 1937," in Library Journal, *Vol. 63, No. 12, June 15, 1938, pp. 488-89.*

In the last issue of this magazine, when making reference to the award of the Newbery Medal to **The White Stag,** we said, "For **The White Stag** we have nothing but the profoundest admiration; it is beautiful in every respect; writing, illustration, and format.'' After a second reading of the book we can but repeat that judgment with added emphasis. . . .

Miss Seredy has given us a fine piece of epic literature. She has given us, too, illustrations that are breathtaking in force. They illuminate essential points in the story and in themselves have a beauty and decorative treatment that is very rarely found in book illustration.

> *H. J. B. Woodfield, in a review of ''The White Stag,''*
> *in* The Junior Bookshelf, *Vol. 3, No. 1, October,*
> *1938, p. 39.*

[**The White Stag** is] a haunting retelling of the legend of the founding of the Hungarian nation, unique in literature for children. . . .

[Kate Seredy's] drawings of both children and animals in all of her stories are filled with vitality and a strong sense of movement, but the illustrations for **The White Stag** have even greater strength and sweep than those of any of her other books; they are entirely in keeping with the poetic majesty of the tale. Reading this story aloud makes manifest the poetic beauty of its language. (p. 337)

> *Bernice E. Cullinan with Mary K. Kerrer and Arlene*
> *M. Pillar, ''Historical Fiction and Biography,'' in*
> *their* Literature and the Child, *Harcourt Brace Jov-*
> *anovich, Inc., 1981, pp. 329-82.**

THE SINGING TREE   (1939)

Four years ago Kate Seredy's ''The Good Master'' was published, a spontaneous, lively tale of child life on a great ranch in the Hungarian plain. . . . [Children] in America promptly felt the tale's sincerity and took Jancsi and his tomboy cousin Kate to their hearts.

''The Singing Tree'' (though it can be read by itself) is about the same people and the same ranch four years later. Kate Seredy has handled the growing up of her characters with great skill. Jancsi and Kate are changed by the four years that have passed, but they are still the boy and girl we knew in ''The Good Master.'' We see them mature, too, in ''The Singing Tree,'' as new responsibilities come to them and are bravely accepted. For this story, which opens gayly with a wedding, begins in the year 1914, and one by one the men leave the ranch and the village to fight. Jancsi, ''the Young Master,'' is left by his father in charge of the farm, and the horse ranch; Kate and Mother Nagy carry on the household; Russian prisoners are sent to help with the harvest, German refugee children arrive to be nursed back to strength and all those who come to it find the farm a place of peace and kindness and hope for the future.

This is an uplifting book to read at a time when the world is torn by war, for it reminds us that human values transcend politics, and that everywhere individuals are ready to stretch out a hand of friendship to one another when the opportunity offers. The style has a lovely clarity and simplicity and the artist-author's drawings have their usual vitality and charm.

> *Anne T. Eaton, ''More about Jancsi,'' in* The New
> York Times Book Review, *November 12, 1939, p.*
> *10.*

[**The Singing Tree**] is a tender, thrilling story, and we can never have too many of Kate Seredy's lovely pictures. They are here in abundance, striking colored portraits of Kate and Jancsi,

From The Singing Tree, *written and illustrated by Kate Seredy. The Viking Press, 1939. Copyright 1939, renewed © 1966 by Kate Seredy. Reprinted by permission of Viking Penguin Inc.*

soft finished full page monotones and enchanting chapter headings and tail pieces. Miss Seredy has done her native land a service in so presenting it to American children.

> *A review of ''The Singing Tree,'' in* The Catholic
> World, *Vol. 150, No. 897, December, 1939, p. 377.*

The thesis of the book is summed up in a letter one of the German children writes his mother—''I do not hate Russians now, Mother, and I think that Jews are kind and good. . . . Grigori says that people are all the same in Russia and Germany and Hungary and that we are all brothers.'' A more serious story than **The Good Master,** yet there is fun and merriment. Kate and Jancsi are still high spirited and lovable. The book may not be as popular as its predecessor, as its more serious theme makes it older in interest, but it is an extremely worthwhile book, timely in its message, and sincere in treatment. Two gay frontispiece pictures of Kate and Jancsi and numerous black and white drawings by the author make the book attractive.

> *Marian Herr, in a review of ''The Singing Tree,''*
> *in* Library Journal, *Vol. 64, No. 22, December 15,*
> *1939, p. 1001.*

[This book] will be welcomed by a very large public. Its beauty of illustration . . . is of the same high quality as [**The Good Master**] and the story contains the same human qualities that were responsible for the earlier book's success.

It is concerned with deeper human emotions, hopes and fears. (p. 37)

The book has a propaganda value; propaganda for peace between nations and between races. I believe it was published in
America before the outbreak of the present war, but, appearing
here at the present time, it is like a voice crying in the wilderness. But children are not cynics and have no sense of
bitterness. They will welcome the book for the story and its
bearing on present events may give them cause to wonder and
to think. (p. 39)

> *A review of "The Singing Tree," in* The Junior Book-
> shelf, *Vol. 5, No. 1, October, 1940, pp. 37, 39.*

The themes of brotherhood and world peace are strongly emphasized. Aunt Sarah and Uncle Moses are initially the focus
for the concept of brotherhood which is greatly expanded with
the arrival of the six Russian prisoners of war and the six little
Germans.... A rounding out of this theme comes at the end
of the book when it is hinted that Kate's father will be bringing
home a Russian bride. Many references are made through the
characters to the evil of war.... Although possible, Kate's
finding Uncle Márton in the army hospital and his miraculous
recovery from amnesia seems contrived. The plentiful illustrations convey the vitality of the text. (pp. 74-5)

> *Marilyn Leathers Solt, "The Newbery Medal and
> Honor Books, 1922-1981: 'The Singing Tree'," in*
> Newbery and Caldecott Medal and Honor Books: An
> Annotated Bibliography *by Linda Kauffman Peterson
> and Marilyn Leathers Solt, G. K. Hall & Co., 1982,
> pp. 74-5.*

A TREE FOR PETER (1941)

The deep feeling that underlies all Miss Seredy's best work,
and is indeed the quality that provides its power, makes a story
whose elements have often appeared in fiction something new
to children and long to be remembered by those to whom this
year it will come at Christmas. The pictures ... are charged
with the same powerful emotion. The world is in trouble, the
whole book seems to say, but not in hopeless trouble; there is
an old security on which we can lay hold, a dream of beauty
that can bring order out of chaos.

It begins in a shanty town of dilapidated huts where only those
lived who had nowhere else to go. They huddled indoors, afraid
of everything: little lame Peter had no neighbors; no one looked
out. He was alone save on Sundays, when his mother did not
go out washing: happiness meant to him "the Sunday feeling."
But it came on weekdays when a ragged tramp [named King
Peter], whistling a lively tune, lit a bright fire in one of the
shacks, or took the child on the river in a rowboat, or showed
him the sunset on the dump, or gave him a red spade, or showed
him the trick of not being bashful, which is largely in remembering that the other fellow is probably just as afraid of you.
That made Peter friends with a big policeman, after the stranger
had gone on. The spade dug up the dump to make a secret
garden. At last, Peter had a tree for the garden, full of lights
that drew the squatters round it. They took courage from the
tiny flower-plot and made one so large that the Mayor—perhaps
his name may have been Fiorello—turned over the place to
them, to improve. And in a prologue and epilogue Peter Marsh,
a famous builder, shows his friend a little old red spade.

Who was the mysterious tramp? What was his lively song?
Try whistling "O come, all ye faithful, joyful and triumphant." ...

> *A review of "A Tree for Peter," in* New York Herald
> Tribune Books, *November 9, 1941, p. 8.*

A story of life in poverty and sordid surroundings, transformed
and transfigured by the glow of friendship and human kindliness....

The pictures on nearly every page make us feel that we know
not only the two Peters, but all the men, women and children
of Shantytown. Because the artist-author has felt deeply and
sincerely in making this book, both the text and the lovely
drawings have a moving quality for the reader.... [A] book
for parents and children to enjoy together at Christmas time.

> *Anne T. Eaton, "In Shantytown," in* The New York
> Times Book Review, *November 30, 1941, p. 10.*

Many a reader will find this story sentimental as they find Hans
Christian Andersen's The Little Match Girl sentimental, but to
me it is sound at the core. The author-illustrator has known
extreme poverty at first hand and she has realized childhood's
relation to it in terms of her own which ring true to my personal
relationship with children in similar circumstances.

> *Anne Carroll Moore, in a review of "A Tree for
> Peter," in* The Horn Book Magazine, *Vol. XVII, No.
> 6, November-December, 1941, p. 458.*

A candidate for the 1941 Newbery award should certainly be
Kate Seredy's utterly charming **A Tree for Peter** ..., which
we should like to put under every Christmas tree, not only for
its very appealing story, but for its very beautiful pictures.
Miss Seredy's is a rare art with a spiritual, ennobling quality
that will find ready response in her young readers and will help
to make them intolerant of the cheap and tawdry. (pp. 373-74)

> *A review of "A Tree for Peter," in* The Catholic
> World, *Vol. 154, No. 921, December, 1941, pp.
> 373-74.*

A moving story.... The spiritual significance and social implication of this modern miracle story should be apparent to
readers of all ages. The tender beauty of the illustrations in
addition to the text tends to create a surfeit of emotion.

> *A review of "A Tree for Peter," in* The Booklist,
> *Vol. 38, December 1, 1941, p. 117.*

Peter is a composite tragic hero. He arouses Aristotelian pity
and fear, and has the character defect of a disability. But he
is also close to the suffering saint. There is hubris in the people
of Shantytown—the hubris of self-centeredness and poverty of
spirit. The coming of the tramp is the catalyst that leads Peter
to find his center and with it the strength to cope with his
problems through his own enlarged view. The outward situation
is changed by the change in Peter, not as comedy might have
presented it by a physical change in surroundings coming first,
or a miraculous recovery for Peter.

The catharsis inherent in the story comes from the insight given
by the author of this inward-outward, rather than outward-
inward, transformation. Neither Peter's lameness, poverty, nor
loneliness could frighten him when the tramp showed him
"how to be."

Kate Seredy has written a timeless story—tragic, because it
presents the ever-recurrent problem of the difficulties created
by a physical disability; beautiful, because it is as simply and
powerfully told as a Biblical parable; mystical, because of the

indefinable quality of the tramp; realistic, because Peter's problem is not solved by a sudden cure of lameness.

The story communicates to all ages. It leaves the reader with a feeling of having been in a sanctuary and of being purified there of his pettiness, so that the world, seen from the great arched door as he prepares once more to return to mundane pursuits, seems more beautiful. (pp. 31-2)

> *Carolyn T. Kingston, "The Tragic Moment: Rejection," in her* The Tragic Mode in Children's Literature, *New York: Teacher's College Press, 1974, pp. 5-56.**

THE OPEN GATE (1943)

The lively and amusing experiences of an American city family who find satisfaction and happiness on a farm which they unexpectedly buy at auction. It was a determined grandmother with a pioneer spirit, whose secret plans brought joy of living to the Preston household. This is a warm-hearted story told with zest and jollity. It is full of the love of the earth and the animals and crops that grow on it, and is permeated with sympathy for people of diverse backgrounds. Kate Seredy's fine drawings add beauty to the book.

> *Alice M. Jordan, in a review of "The Open Gate," in* The Horn Book Magazine, *Vol. XX, No. 1, January, 1944, p. 40.*

There are a good many improbabilities in this story of a city family who stop in casually at a country auction and find themselves owners of a farm. Lively and full of action, it may be liked by boys and girls of around 12, but will not rank with the author's best.

> *A review of "The Open Gate," in* Wisconsin Library Bulletin, *Vol. 40, No. 1, January, 1944, p. 12.*

This is a rich book where, through moving and humorous happenings father, mother, Dick, and Janet and their neighbors, the Van Keurans, discover one another and a full life. The younger children gain a friend in Andrew Van Keuran and with him have strange and exciting adventures. . . . Through Mike—a character out of the Old World—the war comes into the story with its demands and loyalties. The author has expressed here, as in **"The Good Master"** and **"The Singing Tree,"** her deep love for the country and for all living things. The illustrations in black and white have the same warmth and humor as the story.

> *Blanche Weber Shaffer, "The Preston Family," in* The Saturday Review of Literature, *Vol. XXVII, No. 5, January 29, 1944, p. 32.*

There is genuine love of the land in this book. It is full, too, of warm-hearted human contacts and of friendly understanding between people of very different backgrounds.

The illustrations are as important as the text, for Kate Seredy has never shown more strength and understanding of human nature than in these drawings. They present loyal Mike Mogor and plump, jolly Lenka, his wife; the more austere Van Keurans, the Preston children and their neighbor Andy, and above all Gran herself with such vigor and characterization that the reader is entirely convinced of their reality.

> *Anne T. Eaton, "Some History, and Lighter Fare, for Younger Readers: 'The Open Gate'," in* The New York Times Book Review, *February 6, 1944, p. 18.*

The story is American in its writing and to many youngsters will be too sentimental in its whole outlook, especially in its approach to America's entry into the war. Gran dominates the scene, and if you do not like her you will find her a bit of a sententious trial. (p. 80)

> *A review of "The Open Gate," in* The Junior Bookshelf, *Vol. 11, No. 2, July, 1947, pp. 79-80.*

THE CHESTRY OAK (1948)

AUTHOR'S COMMENTARY

How did I happen to write [*The Chestry Oak*]? Because of Midnight, the horse that belongs to Michael in the story. It was because I met Midnight personally that I came to write the story. Two years ago I went to the Orange County Fair here in New York State, where the Army was showing cavalry horses. Among them were some that had been brought over from Europe, and the most beautiful of them all was a black stallion from Hungary. Looking at him, I thought how far away from home he was and yet how little difference it made to him

From The Chestry Oak, *written and illustrated by Kate Seredy. The Viking Press, 1948. Copyright 1948 by Kate Seredy. Renewed © 1975 by Thomas R. Hadaway, Executor of the Estate of Kate Seredy. Reprinted by permission of Viking Penguin Inc.*

what language people around him were speaking as long as they were kind. And I thought how wonderful it would be if human beings were as wise as horses; if we could stop building barriers of the differences in language, race, color, and creed, and learn the universal language of kindness and understanding.

When, later, I started to write about Midnight, the people who came into my story were those whom I have come to know in this new country of mine. And everything that happens to them in the story has happened. I don't mean that I've actually known them, one by one. But I've known boys like Michael, men like his father, and women like Nana; and I often meet people like Pop Brown and his family among my neighbors in Orange County. What happens to Michael in the story has happened to countless boys and girls all over the world. In a way, Michael's story is my own; it is the story of all who have had to leave their country, their family, and their friends, and make a new life for themselves in America. Yes, it's all real.

Stories, like plants, grow from one small seed that falls on fertile ground just at the right time. Seeing the Hungarian stallion Midnight at an American County Fair was the seed from which grew **The Chestry Oak**. While it grew, it took nourishment from all the things I remember of Hungary and strength from all the things I've learned of America and her people. (p. 286)

> *Kate Seredy, "A Golden Thread and One Small Seed,"* in Writing Books for Boys and Girls, *edited by Helen Ferris, Doubleday & Company, Inc., 1952, pp. 284-86.*

A beautifully written and compelling story of a little Hungarian prince caught in the maelstrom of World War II. Here are unforgettable characters: Michael, Prince of Chestry, reared in the tradition of courage, honor, and love of the soil; Nana, the peasant nurse whose wisdom shielded Michael from the disturbing changes, the violence and hatred of war; Michael's valiant patriot father; the GI who sent Michael to America from bombings had destroyed Chestry valley and castle; the American family who made Michael one of their own; and, not least, Midnight, the beautiful Chestry stallion. A moving, hands-across-the-sea experience for children and young people. Unfortunately, the fine illustrations appear, without page references, in a separate signature before the beginning of the story.

> *A review of "The Chestry Oak,"* in The Booklist, *Vol. 45, November 1, 1948, p. 93.*

There is a singing quality about Kate Seredy's writing that sets it apart from the hurried, clipped prose that is so often the rule today. In **"The Chestry Oak"** there's both beauty of writing and beauty of spirit, and there is an absorbing story for 9-to-12-year-olds that is sometimes sad enough to make you cry (without being sticky-sentimental). The stirring conclusion may make you cry, too—for happiness. . . .

As always, the Seredy drawings are a delightfully integrated part of the story, beautiful in themselves and as thoroughly a part of the book as only an author-artist could make them.

> *A review of "The Chestry Oak,"* in New York Herald Tribune Weekly Book Review, *November 14, 1948, p. 7.*

This book is a small work of art. Through the story of Michael, Prince of Chestry, Kate Seredy brings home to American chil-

dren what World War II has meant to Hungarian people, and to European children in general. The book is conceived as a sort of diptych: Michael in Hungary from 5 to 9, and from 9 to 12 in America. . . . The contrast of the two atmospheres is powerfully rendered by the story itself. It is to be hoped that the fine points on education of mind and heart displayed by young Michael and his Hungarian surroundings will be more than quaint foreign oddities.

> *Claire Huchet Bishop, in a review of "The Chestry Oak," in* Commonweal, *Vol. XLIX, No. 6, November 19, 1948, p. 156.*

One of the most beautiful books of the year is **The Chestry Oak**. . . . Miss Seredy's books do not appear so often as to dull the edge of a new one, and **The Chestry Oak** is not only enriched by her lovely drawings but distinguished by many passages of the kind of prose that won the Newbery Medal for **The White Stag**. The story of young Michael and the wonderful horse, Midnight, is an exciting blend of old Hungary and new America.

> *Blanche Jennings Thompson, in a review of "The Chestry Oak," in* The Catholic World, *Vol. 168, No. 1005, December, 1948, p. 222.*

Miss Seredy, Newbery Medal winner and among the most distinguished author-illustrators in the world, has written a sensitive and moving story of Hungary under the Nazis. (pp. 366, 369)

This is a fine story, written with style and extreme sensibility and illustrated with the author's exquisite lithographs. I think, however, that it may turn out to be one of those books which are *about*, rather than *for*, children. Children who are old enough to cope with its subtleties and its psychology may not be willing to interest themselves in the fate of a six-year-old. I hope, however, that teachers will try it on the exceptional reader. To the right child at the right time it may prove a profound experience. (p. 369)

> *M. S. Crouch, in a review of "The Chestry Oak," in* The School Librarian and School Library Review, *Vol. 8, No. 5, July, 1957, pp. 366, 369.*

GYPSY (1951)

A departure for Miss Seredy from her successful stories for older boys and girls, this picture story book about the kittenhood and maturity of a serene and beautiful cat has a very young format, although a distinctly adult slant. The illustrations—in full page—are at first glance breathtaking in their smooth detail and sheer massiveness, yet they seem too static, too unruffled to hold a child's interest for long; and the text which contains phrases like "her . . . kittens nursing within the gently curved crescent of herself" is a bit precious even for adults. Nevertheless this is spectacular arty merchandise.

> *A review of "Gypsy," in* Virginia Kirkus' Bookshop Service, *Vol. XIX, No. 15, August 1, 1951, p. 386.*

Although the format is that of a picture book, it is adults and older children who will most appreciate the rhythmic prose and lovely, sensitive drawings. . . . The slight tendency toward preciousness will surely be overlooked in view of the author-artist's ability to capture the moods and movements of cats.

> *A review of "Gypsy," in* The Booklist, *Vol. 48, No. 2, September 15, 1951, p. 38.*

Gypsy's discoveries of smells, sounds, movement, of friends and foe are described in prose which is expressive because it is so economical. The large pictures on every other page amplify the story as well as illustrate it. Some of these are a little sentimental, others oversoft, but the best have caught the gawkiness and the grace of a kitten on the move.

> *Ellen Lewis Buell, in a review of "Gypsy," in* The New York Times Book Review, *September 16, 1951, p. 28.*

["Gypsy" is] best taken as a sort of portrait gallery of the life of a kitten. Beginning and ending show the cat with her new kittens. The brief rhythmic prose is an odd sort of poetic interpretation of a cat's growth up to the moment of motherhood. The pictures, to my taste, are not very successful. Probably it will appeal to most cat lovers over ten, and as a gift for adults.

> *Louise S. Bechtel, "More Cats," in* New York Herald Tribune Book Review, *September 30, 1951, p. 10.**

Superb is the only word for these drawings of Gypsy the cat. The text is a simple, beautifully worded story. . . .

Only an artist who loves cats and has observed them for years could have made the drawings. As one turns the pages all the characteristics of a cat are revealed. There is warmth and grace in Gypsy herself—always. But the tall black cat who wooed her might have been carved out of black marble. He is magnificent.

This is a book for art lovers as well as cat lovers. Each page is a faithful study, each a triumph of design.

> *A review of "Gypsy," in* The Saturday Review of Literature, *Vol. XXXIV, No. 45, November 10, 1951, p. 70.*

Here at last is a book of beautiful drawings of cats that never verge on the sentimental or try to be "cute." Picturing Gypsy from babyhood to maturity, Miss Seredy has shown her exactly as she was—a mischievous, lovable kitten; an angular, awkward growing cat; a hunter stalking her prey; and a protective mother with kittens of her own. An immense amount of work must have gone into every perfect drawing, but the results will be worth it to all cat lovers.

> *A review of "Gypsy," in* The Horn Book Magazine, *Vol. XXVII, No. 6, December, 1951, p. 424.*

PHILOMENA (1955)

When Philomena was eleven her grandmother, Babushka, died, and she had to leave their Bohemian village to seek domestic service in Prague. She was not afraid, for Babushka had told her she would find there the beautiful aunt who had left home long ago; and, besides, she, Babushka, would be watching and listening up in Heaven, ready to help Philomena in time of need. Although this is not a fairytale, it has many of the characteristics of one. Children will love the story—with its happily-ever-after ending—of Philomena's search for her aunt; of the messages which come (she is sure) from Babushka; of the canary, the cat and the dog she acquires in the houses where she tries to learn to be a good servant. I have seen only a few of the many illustrations, but those are so lovely that this will be a book that is beautiful to look at as well as fun to read.

> *Jennie D. Lindquist, in a review of "Philomena," in* The Horn Book Magazine, *Vol. XXXI, No. 5, October, 1955, p. 367.*

The treatment of Babushka's death is remarkably skillful, making it beautiful and natural. . . . There is humor, common sense, loving kindness; there is deep appreciation of animals, of beautiful things, and of hard work, all carried gayly in a very real story.

It is based on the author-artist's memories of such a little servant in her own home in Prague. Her love for this young girl and her love for her native Bohemia have led her to lavish her best art on this little book. Girls of nine to twelve will enjoy it, but many others, for love of old Bohemian villages and of Prague, and for appreciation of a beautiful book, will treasure it. Children will gather a sense of the strange dignity of this great city, shown in dramatic backgrounds and in exquisite details. Philomena's costumes, even her nightgown (shown when for the first time she uses a bathtub with hot running water), are enchanting beyond words.

Miss Seredy may have written more important stories, as in her Newbery Medal book, **"The White Stag,"** and her even more popular **"The Good Master,"** but she has never created a character more appealing to younger children than Philomena. This little working girl from far away brings us an unforgettable message, as she talks to Babushka, and collects first an animal family, then a human one.

> *Louise S. Bechtel, in a review of "Philomena," in* New York Herald Tribune Book Review, *November 13, 1955, p. 6.*

The thousands of children who have voted Kate Seredy's **The Good Master** their favorite book will welcome her new **Philomena** which has a lively little heroine as clever and independent as the well loved Kate of **The Good Master**. The book is lavishly illustrated with some of Miss Seredy's best drawings and will be cherished by any little girl who gets it. . . .

> *Blanche Jennings Thompson, in a review of "Philomena," in* The Catholic World, *Vol. 182, No. 1089, December, 1955, p. 203.*

Philomena is not only a "strong country girl" who can hold her own in many an adventure, but she is the kind of heroine that readers will take to their hearts. Miss Seredy has told a friendly, humorous story that is as full of atmosphere as are her many lovely illustrations. . . . [It] is an appealing, beautiful book for girls of almost any age.

> *Ruth Hill Viguers, in a review of "Philomena," in* The Saturday Review, *New York, Vol. XXXVIII, No. 51, December 17, 1955, p. 34.*

THE TENEMENT TREE (1959)

A beautiful book, both in its conception and execution, this tells the story of imaginative, dreamy 8-year-old Tino, middle child of an Italian family living in a New York City tenement. Accustomed to the turmoil of city life, Tino found escape in imaginative flights of fancy. And when he went to spend a summer with his artist aunt on her farm, he found that he saw the life around him with creative vision. The great tree was conceivably a city tenement, with its fire escapes and inhabitants. The activities of the small animals had their parallels back home in the people he knew. With his aunt, Tino learned

From The Tenement Tree, *written and illustrated by Kate Seredy. The Viking Press, 1959. Copyright © 1959 by Kate Seredy. Reprinted by permission of Viking Penguin Inc.*

to create an expanding universe and when, at summer's end, he went home he was sensitive to his own most precious gift, a rich and responsive gift for seeing. Here is a might-be-true story, written with an evocative awareness of a child's encounter with nature, and given reality not only in the compassionate text but in the superb craftsmanship of her exquisite wash drawings, softly molded in rich blacks, grays and white. Kate Seredy . . . has been absent from the scene too long. This is an enchanting book. (pp. 322-23)

> *A review of "The Tenement Tree," in* Virginia Kirkus' Service, *Vol. XXVII, No. 9, May 1, 1959, pp. 322-23.*

["**The Tenement Tree**" has] beautiful pictures. Whether very many children who are not imaginative like Tino will read it is unimportant. They will *look* at it, and its beautiful patterns of country and city sights are an art education in themselves. Besides, there may be a host of grownups who can use it to help their Tinos to look with imagination on the wonders about them.

> *Margaret Sherwood Libby, in a review of "The Tenement Tree," in* New York Herald Tribune Book Review, *May 10, 1959, p. 26.*

This delightful and original book for the 7-10s is like a play within a play, for it is a story about a story which is exactly like the story you are reading! . . . The book has many beautiful and authentic drawings to go with a sparkling and swiftly paced text.

> *Silence Buck Bellows, "Forest of Imagination," in* The Christian Science Monitor, *May 14, 1959, p. 13.**

This is a beautiful and most unusual story which shows how a child with an imaginative mind can be helped to channel this imagination in the right direction. . . . Both text and pictures are knit together perfectly to bring enjoyment to a thoughtful child and his parents. Recommended.

> *Elsie T. Dobbins, in a review of "The Tenement Tree," in* Library Journal, *Vol. 84, No. 12, June 15, 1959, p. 2084.*

It is some time since there was a new book by Kate Seredy, and hopes run high. Certainly she has not drawn better, but the story is hardly worthy of the writer of the matchless prose of **The White Stag**. . . . With [Aunt Trina, Tino] learns to interpret imaginatively all he sees during a country holiday. The idea is clear enough, but is it sound? Is there a particular virtue in interpreting the creatures of the natural world in anthropomorphic terms? Tino might have seen the beauty and humour of snails without thinking of them as "women going to the laundromat."

Miss Seredy's illustrations are of quite exceptional beauty. Not even Dorothy Lathrop can surpass her in beauty of form and design. Her lithographs have the depth and luminosity of the mezzotint. (pp. 355-56)

> *A review of "The Tenement Tree," in* The Junior Bookshelf, *Vol. 24, No. 6, December, 1960, pp. 355-56.*

Seven- to ten-year-olds will find the contrasts in the complexities and marvels of city and country vividly portrayed by Kate Seredy's **The Tenement Tree**. . . . (p. 80)

The story can be read aloud, yet the beautiful pictures Kate Seredy has created for this book are an integral part of it. So provisions for showing the pictures must be made.

While Kate Seredy's telling of Tino's away-from-home summer has a casualness about it, this is not a book to be casually presented to children. Its very simplicity and openness enhance the subtleties that make the book memorable—memorable in terms of big ideas about creativity, its nurturing or its destruction; about the larger meaning of imagination; about the larger rewards of preserving one's fanciful ways of knowing. Too, this book presents most clearly how inextricably home is in the away-from-home; home is never left really except physically. Somehow, as one shares this book with children, he needs to see all this, and then without saying it directly, let the children catch the feeling for these big ideas about living. (pp. 80, 91)

> *Leland Jacobs, "Away from Home," in* Instructor, *Vol. LXXIV, No. 10, June, 1965, pp. 80, 91.**

A BRAND-NEW UNCLE (1961)

In the able hands of Kate Seredy . . . what might have been a straight sob story turns into a winning tale of two elderly people, who think they want to escape the responsibilities life has put upon them, and who learn that youth is recaptured best through sharing it with youth. It was Mr. Smith who had the idea of running away from his successful store and his seven sons and daughters and eleven- going on twelve- underfoot grandchildren. He wanted to have the childhood dreams he had missed— and of course Mrs. Smith went along. He saw the ocean for the first time—and New York—and he found an out of the way little house of four rooms—and he even went chasing butterflies. Instead, he came back with kittens—and news of a problem boy, ten and in a reformatory. The end was foreordained, but there are some nice bits en route—and Butch, and the Smiths, go home, gladder and wiser. It's all a bit too pat, too tailormade, but there is a kind of charm in the telling.

> *A review of "A Brand New Uncle," in* Virginia Kirkus' Service, *Vol. XXIX, No. 1, January 1, 1961, p. 11.*

The plot is not quite believable, the writing style is good and the attitudes of the Smiths warm and appealing. Although the action concerns a boy, the story will probably be enjoyed more by girls; some aspects of the writing have an appeal for adults that may escape young readers.

> *Zena Sutherland, in a review of "A Brand-New Uncle," in* Bulletin of the Center for Children's Books, *Vol. XIV, No. 9, May, 1961, p. 148.*

[Here is a book] labeled for the 9-12's that seems more suitable for grown-ups to own, teen-agers to borrow.... A deep affection permeates the pages of this book. But its problems are adult problems, its grandparents are its hero and heroine, its heartwarming sentiment an adult sentiment. If the 9-12's must wait a while before they can enjoy the text as well as the charming drawings, they will find this tender story one of growing-up's compensations.

> *Pamela Marsh, "Grownups," in* The Christian Science Monitor, *May 11, 1961, p. 2B.*

Not sophisticated enough for adult readers, this story about adults almost misses being for children. The lack of surprise in its predictable plot and characterizations keep the book from ranking with Miss Seredy's earlier and more substantial work. Illustrations by the author appropriately convey a soft mood.

> *Sarah Chokla Gross, "Caught in a Net," in* The New York Times Book Review, *May 14, 1961, p. 21.*

LAZY TINKA (1962)

A wise old woman instructs Lazy Tinka in the art of finding the Heavenly Father who clothes and feeds all his creatures. On her magical walk through the dark green forest, Tinka is surprised to find each of the animals, from spider to rabbit,

busily engaged in some form of work—a concept Tinka shuns. Inadvertently she helps each of her new friends in some small way and, when an enemy threatens to attack the little girl, they all band together to save her. Having learned the value of extending a helping hand and the tangible rewards of hard work, Tinka returns home, transformed, and ready to pitch in. Young children may find the logic somewhat difficult to follow, despite the inherent lesson in the story. Seven and up will love it. Pencil and pen illustrations in four colors not yet seen,— but Kate Seredy's lovely techniques insure their quality.

> *A review of "Lazy Tinka," in* Virginia Kirkus' Service, *Vol. XXX, No. 15, August 1, 1962, p. 683.*

A folk-like story.... The plot is not unusual, and the experiences in the forest seem long-drawn-out, but the author's style compensates considerably for these weaknesses; especially good are the bland and matter-of-fact conversations with animals. For example, well along in her wanderings, Tinka helps a rabbit rescue her brood, and when they get to the rabbit hole they find that father has left some cabbage and carrots. The rabbit comments that her mate is the best provider she's ever known. Tinka, thinking that the rabbit is talking of the Heavenly Father whom she is at last going to meet, says, "So this is where He lives! I've been looking for him since sunrise!" The mother rabbit, flattening her ears in suspicion: "What for? What has he done?" (pp. 64-5)

> *Zena Sutherland, in a review of "Lazy Tinka," in* Bulletin of the Center for Children's Books, *Vol. XVI, No. 4, December, 1962, pp. 64-5.*

One expects a high standard in text and illustration from Kate Seredy. This is not as good a story as *Philomena* and the colour illustrations are rather crude, although the black and white drawings retain their quality....

Much of this reads like a folk-tale, but it seems rather incongruous that Tinka should be given a passage from the Bible as a charm and should go through the forest asking for the "heavenly Father." This is surely a mixture of themes. The bright appearance of the book will attract children to read it, but it is not a worthy introduction to the work of this gifted author and artist.

> *A review of "Lazy Tinka," in* The Junior Bookshelf, *Vol. 28, No. 2, March, 1964, p. 89.*

[*Lazy Tinka*] is a gently gay and confiding version of a folk tale.... [The] repetitive pattern of narrative and dialogue link it pleasantly with a much older world of fireside tales, though the pictures, rather florid in colour and sophisticated in tone, are as spandy-new as a roll of wallpaper.

> *Margery Fisher, in a review of "Lazy Tinka," in her* Growing Point, *Vol. 3, No. 1, May, 1964, p. 323.*

Barbara (Claassen) Smucker

1915-

American-born Canadian author of fiction.

Smucker's distinctive contribution to Canadian children's literature is the creation of a body of realistic fiction, both historical and contemporary, that centers on ethnic and religious minorities. She writes with sensitivity and authority about the fight for freedom and dignity experienced by such diverse groups as persecuted Russian Mennonites, fugitive slaves, urbanized American Indians, and modern-day Amish farmers. Basing her stories on actual people and events, Smucker is noted for her meticulous research, which is evident in the authentic details that enhance her writing. She reveals the values of her Mennonite faith—compassion for the oppressed, selfless love, nonviolent action, trust in God—through her themes and characters. Smucker's earlier works were produced to teach ten- to fourteen-year-old Mennonite children about their heritage; her later books are directed more to the multicultural children of Canada. In actuality, Smucker's tales of fortitude, strong family relationships, and moral conviction have universal relevance.

Critics admire Smucker for focusing on little-known historical events and relating them with accuracy and drama. Although some reviewers feel that Smucker is more adept at plot and setting than literary style, other critics commend her portrayal of believable characters who prevail through the strength of their convictions and their inherent goodness.

Smucker won the Canada Council Children's Literature Prize in 1980 for *Days of Terror*. Her *Underground to Canada* was selected by the Canadian Children's Book Centre in 1978 as one of the fifty best books of all time in Canada, and also won the Brotherhood Award, National Conference of Christians and Jews, in 1980.

(See also *Something about the Author*, Vol. 29 and *Contemporary Authors*, Vol. 106.)

AUTHOR'S COMMENTARY

[In the following excerpt, Cory Bieman Davies interviews Smucker on her writing techniques, interest in historical fiction, and her works Underground to Canada *and* Days of Terror.*]*

[Cory Bieman Davies]: [Do] you ever think consciously, "I am writing a book for Canadian children?"

[Barbara Smucker]: When I started writing [*Underground to Canada*], I was working in the Children's Department at the Kitchener Library. A lot of kids came in working on projects on slavery. This was just one of their assignments then. But I could find very little material for them. We had this ancient book, *Uncle Tom's Cabin*, really out of date, and other materials on what happened to the slaves in the States. There really was nothing about what happened to them after they got here. I had been to Dresden, Ontario—there's a little exhibit there—where there's still a cabin that a slave built when he crossed the border, a school, a sawmill, and a little chapel. I was very interested in this. Then I read a book called *The Blacks in Canada: A History*, by R. W. Winks, a scholarly

Photograph by Stephen Epstein, for Mead Sound Filmstrips Ltd., Toronto, ON

book, which said that in 1850 there were 40,000 escaped slaves living in what is now Ontario. I realized I was dealing with a Canadian historical event that nobody had written about. Then I discovered material about Alexander Ross [an abolitionist featured in *Underground to Canada*]. It was really exciting when I found a line about him in the library. Mostly he was known as an ornithologist. The library here searched around to see if they could find something for me on him, and they found the original manuscripts at the University of Western Ontario. Western let me look at them.

[Davies]: I notice you include bibliographies for both *Underground* and *Days of Terror*. When you research a book, then, you try to read original documents?

[Smucker]: Yes, I read them if I can.

[Davies]: May we talk about the process of composition once you've completed your research? How do you work out the plot or find a main character?

[Smucker]: Somehow the stories just fall into place. In a way, it's easier to work out the plot if you're writing historical fiction because the plots are already taken care of by the event. Then it seems that the character kind of comes to fit into the story. As I began thinking about the slave story, I knew that I wanted it to happen to a child because I write for children. It should be a child of twelve or thirteen because younger would be too young, and when you write about older children then it's almost adult.

[Davies]: Why did you choose a girl to be the main character in *Underground*?

[Smucker]: I had read stories of Harriet Tubman, a slave woman who led all kinds of slaves up here so I knew a woman could do it.

[Davies]: You must feel very committed to making history come alive for a certain age group.

[Smucker]: Yes.

[Davies]: Why? Would you discuss the way you view historical fiction—as either valuable or significant?

[Smucker]: The first book I wrote was a little book called *Henry's Red Sea,* which is historical, and also about Mennonites who escaped from Russia after World War II and went to Paraguay. This was for very young children. It was told one evening at our home by a man who participated in the whole thing. It was so vivid, and as our children listened to it, I thought, "This is really a story that should be recorded for children. Why should it just be written down factually as history? If it is made into a story then children will read it." So I did that. That was twenty-five years ago, and that little thing is still in print.

[Davies]: You started writing fiction for children, then, because you thought children should have this story.

[Smucker]: Well, it's part of our heritage. Then I discovered that there are so many exciting things happening in history and that it doesn't have to be dull. I really love researching; I spend too much time on that.

[Davies]: What do you have to leave out because you are writing for children?

[Smucker]: In *Days of Terror,* for example, there were even more horrible things that happened to the Russian Mennonites. Rapes, for example. I didn't put that in because I thought there were enough horrible things in the murders, the starvation, the stealing from and the destruction of Mennonite homes and farms. You just do not put everything in. You don't avoid the violence, but certain things you don't have to put in. If I were writing this story for adults . . . it would be different.

[Davies]: The title of your most recent book, *Days of Terror,* is a rather violent title for a children's book. Is it your title or your publisher's title?

[Smucker]: It's my publisher's title. I called it *Immigrant Boy* originally. I thought that would be a better title. *Days of Terror* doesn't sound like a book for boys and girls, does it?

[Davies]: That didn't bother me, but I thought the title placed the emphasis on the terror in section two. I suspected you would rather place the real and final emphasis on the last section, **"Deliverance."**

[Smucker]: It's interesting that you say so, because that's what I felt. But the publishers said that my title was dull and wouldn't attract attention.

[Davies]: I did find your treatment of fear and terror in *Days of Terror* more immediate and convincing than your treatment of the same themes in *Underground*. Do you think that you are gaining strength as a writer with each book? Did you feel

more engaged with *Days of Terror* because of your own Mennonite heritage?

[Smucker]: I think so. Maybe *Days of Terror* is more powerful because I talked with the Mennonites who experienced this. They live around here. Mrs. Nickel, who lives only three blocks from here, told me her story, and when she is telling it, it's just as though it has happened to her yesterday. Then when I was in Winnipeg I talked with people, for instance a man whose wife had been raped, and he told me about this and got very dramatic. Maybe when you hear people tell about something that happened to them, it is more dramatic. The slave story I only read about.

[Davies]: I think your involvement comes through in the style of *Days of Terror.*

[Smucker]: Do you know, one of the Japanese boys [I met in a promotional tour arranged by my Japanese publisher] . . . said to me through an interpreter during my visit, "I didn't like Mr. Sims in your book [*Underground*]." I said, "Well, I didn't like him either. He was a very cruel man." The boy said, "That's not what I meant. The other characters were real characters, but Mr. Sims is like a stick." And so I thought, "He was sort of a stereotype bad man. I didn't take much time working out that character, Sims. It came through!"

I think I did get more involved in *Days of Terror.* But *Underground* is the one the Japanese children like. My Japanese publisher didn't think they would be interested in *Days of Terror.*

[Davies]: Why not?

[Smucker]: In Japan they don't have any immigrants. They would not be too interested in an immigrant story. All the time that I was writing *Days of Terror,* I thought about it being the story of immigrants, because there are so many immigrant stories in Canada now, ever so many—the Jewish, the Czechs, the Chinese people who came.

[Davies]: In your books there always seems to be a movement from one country to another; you take a character from one place to another.

[Smucker]: Yes . . . well, you know, we've moved quite a bit. We moved here from the States. (pp. 7-10)

[Davies]: Your Mennonite background helps to explain much about *Days of Terror.* Is there anything else in your own background which explains, in part, your interest in the Underground Railway and your personal reasons for writing *Underground to Canada*?

[Smucker]: I was born in Kansas. When I was very little my mother was quite ill with flu, and a black woman lived with us for about seven years. I think my ear became attuned to her kind of speaking. That may be where my interest started. I know she told a lot of stories to us. This would have been when I was between one and seven years old. I don't specifically remember the stories but she must have come out of slavery because most of them did. (pp. 10-11)

[Davies]: Do some of your strongest images and image patterns come from this past? You are always referring to the sun, for example, in *Underground*.

[Smucker]: The sun is important to me although I haven't really thought about that before. I remember as a child in Kansas that sometimes in the summer we would sleep outside. I remember how tremendous it was to wake up early and see the sun coming up. In the prairies it spreads all over the sky.

[Davies]: I have never seen that.

[Smucker]: Then, the sunsets are also tremendous in Kansas. That's the main thing you see because there are no trees to get in the way. There aren't any hills. You just see spreading colours. I think this has always impressed me—the sunrise and sunset.

[Davies]: Is your use of the sun deliberate, then?

[Smucker]: No. I've never really thought about it very much, but I suddenly remembered when you asked, how much I do like the sunrise and sunset.

[Davies]: I wondered, too, about images of chains and the movement from bondage to freedom in *Underground.*

[Smucker]: Yes, that need for freedom is important. [My husband] Don and I taught in an all-black college in Mississippi. He was president there for a while. This whole idea of bondage never leaves people whose ancestors grew up in the United States. We were there during the time Martin Luther King was killed. All the dislike for white people suddenly erupted. They wanted us to leave because they really did not want white people there. This whole black story has been a very important story to both of us, all our lives. If you grow up in the States you can hardly avoid having some feeling about it one way or the other—either having a tremendous prejudice, or feeling a burden that you have been a part of whatever caused this thing.

[Davies]: Let me change the topic somewhat, but still remain in your past. What books did you read as a child?

[Smucker]: When I was a child we didn't have many books to read. (pp. 11-12)

[Davies]: Did you read Kipling, for example?

[Smucker]: Yes, I had his books, but I think I started reading children's books more when my own children were growing up.

[Davies]: What did you read to them?

[Smucker]: We read all kinds of things to them. However, when I decided to be a Children's Librarian, then I added other kinds of books. In the class I took in Children's Literature, we had to read a hundred books—all the medal-winning books etc. I got really fascinated, especially with the books of historical fiction. (p. 12)

[Davies]: What writer do you like and read now?

[Smucker]: I like the English writers like Rosemary Sutcliff, Henry Treece, and Leon Garfield. I like Lucy Boston too. I also like to read fantasy very much. I like Susan Cooper, and Joan Aiken, who can churn out one book after another.

[Davies]: How do you like Madeleine L'Engle?

[Smucker]: I have read only one of her books. They are more scientific. Somehow science is not my thing.

[Davies]: Would you ever like to write a fantasy?

[Smucker]: I would surely like to try one. But I do like writers of historical fiction. At one point we lived in England for a year, and I wrote a book on Mediaeval history. It takes place in the 1300's.

[Davies]: How was it?

[Smucker]: It wasn't very good! I sent it to about ten different publishers, and it came back from all of them. Finally, I showed it to John Pearce, my present editor at Clarke, Irwin, and he said, "That's not your field." (pp. 12-13)

[Davies]: You seem to have found your fields in both *Underground* and *Days of Terror.* I have one final question about these books. In both of them, Canada is the place to which your characters come. They come to St. Catharines at the end of *Underground,* and to Manitoba at the end of *Days of Terror,* yet Canada is never fully realized as a setting in either book, is it? Have you ever wanted to write a sequel to either book?

[Smucker]: I have thought about it. When I was in Vancouver during Children's Book Week, in one of the schools I was in, all of the boys and girls in the room were from Hong Kong. They had read both of my books, and they said, "Mrs. Smucker, do you always write about people who come from one place to a new place?" They suggested, "Why don't you write about what happened to them after they lived in Canada?" because this is their situation. Here they are. What's going to happen to them now? Maybe I should write about this, but I haven't yet. (p. 13)

Cory Bieman Davies, in an interview with Barbara Smucker, in Canadian Children's Literature: A Journal of Criticism and Review, *No. 22, 1981, pp. 4-14.*

GENERAL COMMENTARY

BARBARA SMILEY

Volunteer work in the American Indian Center in Chicago provided [Barbara Smucker with] insight into the problems encountered by Indians leaving the reservation to seek employment in the city. In *Wigwam in the City* she looks with deep compassion and understanding at these problems, identifying with the Indian family as they try to adjust to the strange and alien city world, telling the story of their bewilderment with honesty and objectivity yet totally without sentimentality. (pp. 15-16)

Her latest book *Underground to Canada* has been developing over the last eight years. . . . Many hours of painstaking research have gone into it so that the historical background is absolutely authentic. The exciting story combined with Barbara Smucker's deeply felt sympathy for the slaves and understanding of their plight will live in the reader's memory for a long time. . . . [This is a] most gripping story and one that should not be missed by young people. (pp. 16-17)

As I talked to [Barbara Smucker] in her home about her life and her philosophy she gave me a feeling of great tranquility which lasted for many hours after I left. She has spent her life studying, helping, and writing about the oppressed and misunderstood people of this continent. Full of humour, kindliness and compassion, she is a wise ambassador and interpreter for those who have been less fortunate in the modern world. We are proud to number her among our Canadian children's authors. (p. 17)

Barbara Smiley, "Profile: Barbara Smucker," in In Review: Canadian Books for Children, *Vol. 11, No. 4, Fall, 1977, pp. 15-17.*

CORY BIEMAN DAVIES

[In *Days of Terror*] Barbara Claassen Smucker tells with characteristic compassion, simplicity and directness the story of the mass migration of Russian Mennonites to Canada in the early 1920's. *Days of Terror* represents Mrs. Smucker's attempt to keep strong within the larger Canadian community her own Mennonite heritage and faith, and to contribute strengthening Mennonite strands to multicultural Canadian peoplehood.

At the beginning of *Days of Terror,* during the peaceful days in Tiegen before the terror, Grandfather Penner tells Peter Neufeld, "We Mennonites have lived apart from Russian people. The price is too big to pay if we mix with them. Keeping our heritage and our faith has given us strength in a new land." However, during the years of his own imprisonment by the Russians, Grandfather rethinks the strengths of his heritage and faith, and the strengths which he grows to value no longer depend as heavily on Mennonite isolation or separation. He shares his hard-won wisdom first with Gerhardt, Peter's father, and then with Peter. About the past, he says to Peter . . . "We Mennonites lived too much apart and didn't know." . . . About the future in Canada, which will soon replace Russia as the "new land" for 20,000 Mennonites, he says to Gerhardt, "we must live among other Canadians. We must not withdraw from the native people as we have done in Russia." . . . Grandfather Penner finally has come, in the fiction, to a realization about Mennonite "peoplehood" which seems to correspond with Smucker's present interest in presenting the Mennonite heritage.

In maintaining, celebrating and sharing her Mennonite identity and history, Mrs. Smucker aligns herself with forward movements emerging in current Mennonite studies. In the last twenty-five years, Mennonite historians and theologians have departed from separatism and made advances in sharing their history, experiences, and values. (pp. 18-19)

For twenty-five years Mrs. Smucker has been committed to making history come alive for children. The significance of her current work may be demonstrated through comparison with her first book, *Henry's Red Sea,* which was also based on Mennonite history and themes. . . . The strong narrative line in *Henry's Red Sea* grew out of her oral source. Written specifically for Mennonite children . . . , the book addresses itself to Mennonite issues in a more direct and didactic way than does *Days of Terror.*

Days of Terror also began with specific details of a personal story, but it developed in different directions from those in *Henry's Red Sea* and grew to include several of the complex issues which modern Mennonite studies are now addressing. Smucker's social imagination responded again in *Days of Terror* to the oral transmission of events from the Russian past. A woman from Hespeler, Ontario told Smucker the story of apples given to her by an elder just before she boarded the emigrant train to Riga in the early 1920's. She was given ten apples, one for each day of the trans-Atlantic voyage. Originally, Smucker intended to write this story for young children, focussing it on a little girl. Later she decided to use an older child as her main character, and created Peter Neufeld, an older and more active hero. Katya became his younger sister. Smucker saved the story of the ten apples (which Aunt Lizzie gives to Katya) until the end of the larger story, where its telling achieves an emotional climax when it is joined to Katya's description of Aunt Lizzie's death. . . . (pp. 19-20)

Smucker also expanded and developed the character of Otto, Peter's older brother, and Otto's role in the Selbstschutz or Self Defense League. The sub-plot focussing on Otto's actions allows the author to explore the various kinds of conflict beyond the initial and obvious conflict between Russians and Men-

nonites during the civil war. Against the Mennonite principles of non-violence and non-resistance, Otto joins a Mennonite fighting unit (the First Halbstadt Company), formed to defend the Mennonite communities against Makhno's bandits in the terrifying days of anarchy. In the sub-plot, Smucker examines the conflicts caused within the Mennonite community, then within the Neufeld family, and finally within Peter. Choosing to keep Otto's secrets from his parents, Peter takes full responsibility for Otto's freedom by carrying a money belt past Russian guards into Riga. There Peter meets Otto, and gives him the money which will pay for the older brother's escape to the United States. Peter becomes a much more active and heroic character than his counterpart, Henry, in *Henry's Red Sea,* partly because the subplot in *Days of Terror* demands a more complex treatment of the themes of conflict and conscience without and also within the Mennonite community, the family and the individual. Peter has opportunities for action which Henry did not have. Peter and the Neufelds must make more complicated decisions than Henry and his family. The central characters in *Henry's Red Sea* remain essentially passive, however courageous, because of the nature of their refugee existence; only the Mennonite Central Committee acts.

Other differences point to the twenty-five years which stand between the writing of these two stories of conflict and conscience. Tina, the older sister in *Henry's Red Sea,* goes through a crisis in conscience, but she finally chooses to remain within the Mennonite family unit, affirming a faith in God which links her to her larger Mennonite community. Because it is an earlier book, *Henry's Red Sea* deals primarily with the conflicts between the Mennonites and their persecutors. Otto, however, does not return to his family unit once he and the Neufelds reach North America. Otto will never again "really fit" into the Neufeld family, although he can continue to love the family and stay in touch. Smucker's handling of the Self Defense League and her characterization of Otto point to the conflicts *within* the Mennonite community. . . . (pp. 20-1)

Smucker's treatment of Mennonite themes and history has followed changing patterns and impulses within the larger context of Mennonite self-understanding. While she does not choose to confront the complexities of separation or non-resistance in the same critical way that Rudy Wiebe has confronted them in *Peace Shall Destroy Many* and *The Blue Mountains of China,* or as some recent historians are confronting them in their studies of the Mennonites' years in Russia, she does place these controversial issues at the dramatic centres of her main plot and her sub-plot. She does allude to the very great wealth of some of the Mennonite landowners and their mistreatment of the Russian serfs, although she vindicates the Neufeld family from such charges of mistreatment and separatism by developing their relationships with their Russian servants, Tanya and Esch, and by leaving Grandfather Penner in the care of Igor, the Russian shepherd. Gerhardt mentions Uncle Herman's wealth: "One man should not own so much." Mrs. Neufeld's reply, "It is not for us to judge" . . . is significant, for it implies a kind of judgment (God's perhaps?) in the destruction of Herman's estates. For the most part, however, Smucker is sympathetic in her portrayal of the Mennonites' situation, and in her dramatization of their strengths.

Smucker's fiction for children written between *Henry's Red Sea* and *Days of Terror* maintained historical and social themes. Her novel about the underground railway for slaves from the Southern States to Central Canada, ***Underground to Canada,*** . . . has been very successful here and elsewhere. Over

Smucker working in her study. Photograph by Stephen Epstein, for Mead Sound Filmstrips Ltd., Toronto, ON.

the years her readership has moved out in ever-widening circles from the early Mennonite centre to include Canadians, Americans, British, Australians and Japanese of all faiths. In *Days of Terror* she returns after twenty-five years to specifically Mennonite themes and to Mennonite history as it merges this time with Canadian history.

Involved as she had been with the story of human dignity, survival and freedom in *Underground to Canada,* she confesses, "I got more involved" in writing *Days of Terror.* Again, she researched thoroughly. In addition to written sources of factual information—histories, manuscripts, diaries, other historical novels—she drew from interviews with many Russian Mennonites, now living in Ontario and Manitoba. As well, she drew from the experiences of her grandfather, C. F. Claassen, who worked with the relief committees in North America during these years, and of others in the Claassen family who gave shelter to a Russian Mennonite family for a time. (p. 22)

Barbara Smucker has written in *Days of Terror* a powerful novel capable of evoking emotional responses and of stimulating interest in another way of life. Much of the book's impact depends on the immediacy created through details in characterization and in dramatic incident. The characters and the incidents most real to Smucker either in her own remembered experiences or through those of other Mennonites emerge as

the most real and convincing for readers of the fictionalized version of the story. The characters of Aunt Lizzie and Makhno, for instance, are most effective. Mrs. Smucker remembers her own Aunt Lizzie: "she was really like this woman so maybe that came through. I really knew her. She was not pretty—stern—and when she smiled it was very warm. And she was abrupt and said exactly what she thought and her husband had been murdered. She was from one of these estates." Makhno, too, was real. There are many accounts in personal memoirs and anecdotal histories of Makhno, bandit and anarchist, who raided the villages of the Molotschna settlement from 1918 to 1919. Smucker has relied on the details in these memoirs to characterize Makhno in *Days of Terror.* Also, survivors of the exodus described Makhno to her: "He would ride in a carriage with a pillow sort of like he was an emperor of some kind. He was terribly perverted." . . . In Aunt Lizzie's description of Herman Klassen's murder by the Makhnovites . . . , Smucker combines the story of Makhno in the carriage and memories of her own Aunt Lizzie. From these historical and personal contexts, Makhno emerges in *Days of Terror* as a more convincing and complex villain than his counterpart, Mr. Sims, in *Underground.*

Immersion in received detail also stimulated Smucker's imagination as she was creating specific scenes in *Days of Terror.* She recreates details from Henry Rempel's *Passages Out of*

My Life in the scene depicting Peter's hatred for the Russian version of his name . . . , and in the symbolic descriptions of the ripe cherries in the orchards of Tiegen. . . . There are strong correspondences in detail between the railroad scenes in Lohrenz's *The Fateful Years* and in *Days of Terror.* (p. 23)

When I asked Mrs. Smucker during our interview to discuss her particular purpose in writing *Days of Terror* about the Mennonite communities in the Molotschna, and the exodus to Canada in the early 1920's, she paused for some time. To my second question asking whether she was trying to dramatize, through historical fiction, a particular aspect of Mennonite experience and/or to dramatize a more universal moment from bondage to freedom—since this, too, is the central theme in the non-Mennonite *Underground*—she replied that she was not conscious of trying to fulfill either of these purposes as I expressed them: "I just wanted to tell the story . . . I'd heard this story all my life . . . I wanted to write about it for children."

Barbara Smucker's social imagination responds to her historical material—most keenly and most empathetically when that material has come to her orally and personally—and it reaches out to touch her readers with the awareness of the gift of freedom and its attendant responsibilities. We remember and celebrate with her as we read "this story." (p. 24)

> *Cory Bieman Davies, "Remembrance and Celebration: Barbara Smucker's 'Days of Terror'," in Canadian Children's Literature: A Journal of Criticism and Review, No. 25, 1982, pp. 18-25.*

HENRY'S RED SEA   (1955)

The author has succeeded in giving us a vivid historical account of the Mennonite crossing of the "Red Sea" (the Russian territory encircling Berlin). . . . It's a delightful book with similes as fresh as the morning dew. Children will want to read it over again and even adults will try to finish it at one sitting. . . .

No one will want to miss the account of the brisk, efficient, and resourceful school teacher, Miss Epp, as she organizes her refugee school. . . .

It may appear somewhat strange that in the midst of the haunting fear of Communists . . . , there is also the longing of Henry to be back on their beautiful farm in Russia, and of his sister Tina for her teaching career. . . . [One] may wonder about a "beautiful farm home" in the midst of a collectivized state, or was that to have come into existence during the brief period of German occupation? The author might have explained this fact for the curious.

> *David Janzen, in a review of "Henry's Red Sea," in The Canadian Mennonite, Vol. 3, No. 4, October 21, 1955, p. 7.*

We read this poignant story to our children, and it completely absorbed their interest.

This account of a Mennonite refugee family will bring tears and lumps in the throat to the reader. The characters will be long remembered. . . .

Henry's Red Sea is a book that will make children and adults re-count their blessings. It will make an excellent family "read aloud" book.

> *Erling Nicolai Rolfsrud, in a review of "Henry's Red Sea," in Book News Letter, No. 241, December, 1955.*

[*Henry's Red Sea*] is a thrilling story. . . .

While the book is written for boys and girls of 10-15, yet its message is such that adults will find it interesting, enlightening, and inspiring. . . .

Don't miss having *Henry's Red Sea* in your home. It will be a blessing not only to the children but to the whole family as well.

> *A review of "Henry's Red Sea," in Missionary Challenge, December, 1955.*

Eleven-year-old Henry Bergen, Grandma, Mother, Tina who had hoped to finish her last year of study to be a teacher, and little lame Rudy, who joined the Bergens when his own mother died as they fled from their former homes, were among the thousand Mennonite refugees waiting in West Berlin for a way to open through Russian-occupied East Germany to the waiting Dutch ship *Volendam* in the harbor of Bremerhaven ready to sail to Paraguay and freedom. The story of how God moved through the Mennonite Central Committee and the American army in Berlin to bring deliverance is a marvelous episode in modern Mennonite history. To have heard it related in person by firsthand witnesses and masterful storytellers like C. F. Klassen and Peter Dyck is an unforgettable experience. Here it is preserved for children by Barbara Smucker in a deeply moving, profoundly spiritual story, *Henry's Red Sea,* an account of the miracle from the viewpoint of an eleven-year-old boy.

An important criterion of a good book for children is that it interest and challenge the respect of the adult reader. *Henry's Red Sea* passes this test both as to content and technique. It also meets the further requirement of appealing to children for whom it is intended. To catch and hold a child's attention a story must reach him through vivid characters, surprise, suspense, and fast-moving action. *Henry's Red Sea* is a good story for children because it includes these necessary elements in an effective plot which moves from episode to episode to a quick climax and to a conclusion which leaves the reader wishing for more story, and yet satisfied that this is the appropriate ending to the book. More than this, the plot contains important content, making Christian truth alive to boys and girls. The book is a powerful sermon on the strength and beauty of Christian love, bringing to children in a concrete, vivid manner the lessons of faith, salvation, forgiveness, peace, and good race relations, even though prayers are answered with both "yes" and "no." These teachings are included in a plot compellingly sketched with skillful reserve and yet with childlike clarity of detail. . . . (pp. 158-59)

It is difficult to evaluate one's response to this book apart from the context of the Klassen and Dyck accounts, and also apart from reports of the subsequent settlement in Paraguay. One constantly reads between the lines. How the book will speak to readers approaching it as strangers to the historical setting out of which it comes, remains to be seen; for the book is addressed to such an audience, children from nine to fourteen. From the comments of a number of adult and older child readers who did not previously know the background, the book promises to be a challenging story as it stands. Since it records a specific event in Mennonite history, on the other hand, might the information on the dust jacket, or similar factual background, be included as a footnote to the story in the book itself so as to tie the narrative even more closely to the actual historical setting? Or as a prelude, in the way Eric P. Kelly uses the powerful introduction "The Broken Note" to create the setting for the *Trumpeter of Krakow*? . . . How has the author been able to give such an amazingly convincing firsthand feeling throughout the entire book although she herself was not a part of this group? Or was she? A brief explanation from author to reader of how she came to write the story would enhance its value even more as the actual incident moves farther and farther into the past. (p. 160)

> *Mary Neuhauser Royer, in a review of "Henry's Red Sea," in* Mennonite Quarterly Review, *Vol. XXX, No. 2, April, 1956, pp. 158-60.*

CHEROKEE RUN (1957)

Boys and girls today are interested in stories of pioneer America. Too many books show the heroes as warriors courageous in battle. When I discovered that many Mennonites took part in the Cherokee Strip Run I knew that this was a story that could combine interest, church history, and demonstrations of courageous pioneers who did not kill and steal.

The incident of nonresistance in the face of a brazen land and house theft is a true story told by T. M. Erb, a pioneer Mennonite in Kansas who preached for the early pioneers in Oklahoma's Cherokee Run.

> *A review of "Cherokee Run," in* Missionary Light, *November-December, 1957.*

[*Cherokee Run*] will make a strong appeal to youthful readers in the church. . . .

The hardships of trying to provide a livelihood during the difficult times of drought and destruction of the crops by grasshoppers are vividly portrayed. The excitement of the "run" when on September 16, 1893, thousands of pioneers on horseback, in wagons, and on foot dashed into the state of Oklahoma to stake out claims for land is dramatically related.

Very impressively the account of the unscrupulous Jeb, who occupied the new sod house, and claimed their land, is told. Through the kindness shown to Jeb by Father Becker for the theft of which he had been guilty, he is won as a friend and becomes a Christian.

> *Ezra Beachy, in a review of "Cherokee Run," in* The Gospel Evangel, *January-February, 1958.*

WIGWAM IN THE CITY (1966; also published as *Susan*)

Susan Bearskin dreads the thought of leaving the Chippewa Reservation and moving to Chicago. . . . Her older brother has run away; the children in her school are cruel and hostile; the family has to make innumerable painful adjustments to an urban culture. Susan finds her brother hiding in Lincoln Park (a most contrived episode) and then she gets lost; she is sent by a policeman to the American Indian Center. With the help she receives there, and with encouragement from a loved uncle, Susan begins to feel at home in the city. The writing style is fairly pedestrian, and the instant hostility of her peers seems exaggerated, but Susan's story is important because there is such a paucity of material about the problems of the American Indian in a metropolis.

> *Zena Sutherland, in a review of "Wigwam in the City," in* Bulletin of the Center for Children's Books, *Vol. 20, No. 6, February, 1967, p. 98.*

The reader feels the fright and bewilderment of Susan and her mother as they face the physical adjustments to this strange and impersonal city, and he applauds Susan for the pride in her heritage which gives her the courage to face up to her problems. . . . The minor characters in the story, the people in the Indian Bureau, teachers, and the policeman are neither angels nor villains but believable people. This book will help fill the need for good stories of contemporary Indian life.

> *E. Louise Davis, in a review of "Wigwam in the City," in* School Library Journal, *an appendix to* Library Journal, *Vol. 13, No. 7, March, 1967, p. 131.*

The American Indians, a minority group whose problems only occasionally assume some prominence in the news, continue to have serious social and economic difficulties. The author's knowledge of contemporary reservation and urban Indian life has been well used in this sympathetic story about a Chippewa family that makes a difficult move to a large city. (p. 176)

This book explores the American Indian's increasing alienation from the mainstream of American life. It delineates clearly how traditional ideas of cooperation and sharing run counter to the white man's ethic of private ownership and industrialization. It also deals with the idea of individuality and pride in one's heritage. (p. 178)

> *John Gillespie and Diana Lembo, "Evaluating Contemporary Problems: 'Wigwam in the City'," in their* Introducing Books: A Guide for the Middle Grades, *R. R. Bowker Co., 1970, pp. 176-79.*

UNDERGROUND TO CANADA (1977; U.S. edition as *Runaway to Freedom: A Story of the Underground Railway*)

With a preachy tone, stiff dialogue, and thick characterizations that should have disappeared with Grandfather clauses, this lugubrious Underground Railroad story has its facts straight, its message perfectly clear. Julilly, separated from her Mammy Sally by a slave trader, clings to a goal of Canada and freedom. Alexander Ross, an abolitionist passing as an ornithologist, gets her away from her miserable Mississippi plantation along with equally determined friend Liza and two older boys. Their stops enroute are instructive, the overall risks repeatedly enunciated, but the wooden exchanges accumulate without relief. One notable feature: Canada, once reached, is no Promised Land, just a better place. A much more ambitious approach than Monjo's resonant *The Drinking Gourd* (1970) but less forceful and much less evocative.

> *A review of "Runaway to Freedom," in* Kirkus Reviews, *Vol. XLVI, No. 5, March 1, 1978, p. 245.*

There are some historical characters included in the novel, and there's evidence of solid research; what weakens the book is the writing style, which not infrequently becomes florid: "Her lips pinched firm and her eyes flamed with angry courage . . .".

> *Zena Sutherland, in a review of "Runaway to Freedom: A Story of the Underground Railway," in* Bulletin of the Center for Children's Books, *Vol. 31, No. 8, April, 1978, p. 135.*

Reading **"Runaway to Freedom,"** I wondered: Do we need another novel—rather like a slice of "Roots"—of human suffering and heroism midst the horror of slavery? Let me give a resounding "yes." We need scrupulously honest books like this one to inform subsequent generations that a grave crime was committed against a people, and that we must always be on guard against victimization and genocide....

Barbara Smucker's book is remarkable for its fine characterization and its insightful narrative; there isn't a false note. When the runaway, Lester, says, "No one is huntin' for us tonight. We got to cover a lot of ground," we *know* the hard miles the fugitives will travel before first light. Julilly and Liza, momentarily safe in an Underground "station," have a tub bath, and we *feel* their exquisite joy at being clean all over for the first time in their lives....

A partial bibliography of the Underground Railroad is given for the more curious student.

Jacket copy informs that Barbara Smucker has impeccable civil-rights credentials, and she appears to be of the white race—none of which has anything to do with her well-wrought book. *All* children should read it.

Virginia Hamilton, in a review of "Runaway to Freedom," in The New York Times Book Review, *April 30, 1978, p. 52.*

The action is immediate and the plot gripping, while characters fall entirely into the realm of archetypal representatives of the powers of good versus evil, and the style runs to clichés. Yet there is no question that the situation has been accurately researched and seldom so dramatically offered for the experience of readers this young.

Brad Hooper, in a review of "Runaway to Freedom: A Story of the Underground Railway," in Booklist, *Vol. 75, No. 1, September 1, 1978, p. 53.*

Smucker's story of her two fictitious characters sounds completely credible and serves as a tribute to those who hid in the "stations," and those who helped all along the way. While just skirting the sensational, the narrative compresses and attributes everything that could have happened to just two individuals. The "Canadian connection," not as well known in American children's fiction, deserves the attention it gets here. The sentimental ending, admittedly contrived, will satisfy younger readers.... The Acknowledgements and Partial Bibliography document a well-told tale. (p. 864)

Ruth M. Stein, in a review of "Runaway to Freedom—A Story of the Underground Railway," in Language Arts, *Vol. 55, No. 7, October, 1978, pp. 863-64.*

In this exciting work of historical fiction, the nightmare of slavery and the dream of freedom are made real and immediate to young readers. A strong sense of time and place, the intermixing of actual historical figures and fictional characters, and the vivid descriptions, enriched by authentic details, are successfully united. Only the final chapter is seriously flawed as Julilly is reunited with her mother and fellow escapee in a forced and melodramatic conclusion. Liza's disability, caused by a vicious beating after her unsuccessful escape, is realistically treated. (p. 423)

Barbara H. Baskin and Karen H. Harris, "An Annotated Guide to Juvenile Fiction Portraying the Disabled, 1976-1981: 'Runaway to Freedom'," in their More Notes from a Different Drummer: A Guide to Juvenile Fiction Portraying the Disabled, *R. R. Bowker Company, 1984, pp. 423-24.*

DAYS OF TERROR   (1979)

[Barbara Smucker's presentation of heroism in *Days of Terror*] is thoroughly researched and excellently developed. *Days of Terror* ... is fiction, telling the story of Peter Neufeld, a Mennonite boy living in the Ukraine during the Russian Revolution. But the horrors that eventually led his family to emigrate to Canada with so many other Mennonites in that period are straight history. Smucker does not hesitate to describe unpleasant reality—children die from malnutrition; lice-covered, plague-ridden revolutionaries billet themselves in the Mennonite homes. But the strength and courage of the characters—particularly Peter's father and grandfather—and the warmth of their family relationships make it a very moving book to read. When those members of the Neufeld family who were allowed to emigrate are finally reunited in Canada, Smucker evokes feelings even stronger than those felt when the two girls in her *Underground to Canada* ... reached their freedom. One feeling is pride that such people made Canada their home. Encouraging kids to read Canadian writing of this sort could have all kinds of benefits. (p. 14)

Mary Ainslie Smith, "Small Wonders," in Books in Canada, *Vol. 8, No. 10, December, 1979, pp. 12-14.**

Sparing few horrifying details, Smucker focuses on the heroism of a family uprooted, a nonviolent group suffering the indignities of war. As in *Underground to Canada,* Smucker's characters manage to put the heart back into history. (p. 49)

Ann Johnston, "Bringing Up Baby on Homegrown Heroes," in Maclean's Magazine, *Vol. 92, No. 51, December 17, 1979, pp. 46-9.**

As in her *Underground to Canada, Days of Terror* is historical fiction that comes complete with bibliography and footnotes, not too many footnotes and just enough books on the bibliography to encourage the interested reader to learn more about the Mennonites. (pp. 139-40)

Days of Terror demonstrates how superior fiction can be at telling truth. Although the novel follows an ordered time sequence, Smucker imposes a tripartite structure, Peace, Terror, Deliverance, to sharpen our awareness of how a particular Mennonite family perceived the Russian Revolution....

Peter grows up in a society threatened on all sides. He puzzles about the evil of the bandits and sees a man killed. He worries about the fate of his brother, Otto, and tries to protect his younger sister, Katya. He catches typhus, starves, and is finally fed through the efforts of North American and European Mennonites. This list of horrors is incomplete yet the book does not seem melodramatic since Smucker also makes Peter think about the more ordinary problems of growing up—his longing to be treated as a man, not a boy. His wish that his father could understand his interest in art. (p. 140)

Adrienne Kertzer, in a review of "Days of Terror," in Canadian Ethnic Studies, *Vol. XII, No. 1, 1980, pp. 139-41.*

This direct, uncompromising tale gives full credit to individual courage and full value to the faith which sustained the Neufelds and families like them in adversity. Precise in social detail and clear in the issues it raises, it is the kind of book which brings history out of the textbooks without diluting or romanticising it.

*Margery Fisher, in a review of "Days of Terror,"
in her* Growing Point, *Vol. 20, No. 4, November,
1981, p. 3965.*

AMISH ADVENTURE (1983)

[*Amish Adventure* could] be called a problem novel in some respects. The central character, Ian McDonald, is almost an orphan: his mother is dead and his father has left for the winter to work on an oil rig. On his way to Toronto to stay with his shrill Aunt Clem, the Volkswagen in which Ian is driving hits an Amish family's horse and buggy. The Amish, always ready to try to love their enemies, take him under their wing. Smucker grinds her literary gears a bit in the novel. A reader can plainly see the moral of the story (tolerance) and Smucker's ecological concerns (Amish-style farming does not abuse the land as much as corporate farms do). But at heart, *Amish Adventure* is about a contemporary child confronting part of the world that has remained resolutely uncontemporary—and people who live lives sometimes as puzzling as Job's. (pp. 50, 52)

*Anne Collins, "Driving Home the Moral of the Story,"
in* Maclean's Magazine, *Vol. 96, No. 27, July 4,
1983, pp. 50, 52.**

This story lives up to the high standards the public has come to expect of prize-winning author Barbara Smucker; it is well written and interesting, with enough action to keep young readers eagerly turning the pages. But above all, it is warm and deeply understanding of both the strengths and weaknesses of the human heart. The author knows the Amish folk, and never has their way of life been better or more sympathetically explained to youngsters attuned to a faster, flashier, and in many ways emptier life than theirs. Highly recommended for all junior readers.

*Joan McGrath, in a review of "Amish Adventure,"
in* Quill and Quire, *Vol. 49, No. 8, August, 1983,
p. 39.*

Barbara Smucker is an admirable writer of children's books, best known for two excellent historical novels: *Underground to Canada* . . . [and *Days of Terror*]. Both are well-told, exciting, based on sound research, and challenging to their young readers' intelligence and sensibilities. Smucker's latest book, *Amish Adventure* . . . , falls somewhat short of her own high standards.

It's still a good story, founded on an interesting premise. Ian McDonald, a city boy, finds himself transplanted from a high-rise apartment in Chicago to the traditional farm home of an old-order Amish family in rural Ontario. . . .

Smucker had to find a way to get Ian into this new environment, and although the chain of circumstances accomplishing the transition is rather complex, she does pull it off pretty well. . . . The technical description of [the car/buggy] accident, by the way, is not entirely convincing. (p. 34)

But although Smucker deserves high marks for plot, her characterization falls rather flat. While the reader learns a great deal about Amish beliefs and their way of life in general, we don't find out very much about the Bender family as individuals—certainly not as much as we would like to know. Jonah, the grandfather, and Reuben [a boy Ian's age] talk to Ian a lot, but their characters are only what we would expect: Jonah is a wise and kindly old man, while Reuben is a boy who likes working on the land and taking care of animals. The three adult women in the Bender household are sympathetic and capable people, but that's all we learn about them. We know that John, the older son, faces a conflict because he can't decide whether to commit himself to the Amish way of life, but we see nothing of the way he resolves his dilemma. We learn that the Benders are peaceful and forgiving, that they won't press criminal charges even after their barn is burned, but we learn little of the impervious streak that caused them to cast aside their daughter Hannah because she went to university and then became a nurse.

At least the Benders are presented sympathetically. Representing the alternative to their way of life are two characters so unpleasant as to be quite unbelievable. Jack Turner, the driver of the car that caused the accident, runs away rather than accept any responsibility. Ian's Aunt Clem is cold and unresponsive and scorns Ian's affection for his Amish friends.

The story also contains an important underlying theme—concern for the environment—but this is rather meagerly developed. Ian's father has strong feelings about preserving the natural environment—this, we are told, is part of his job with the oil company. But we are never told exactly what he does. Ian shares his father's interests, and one argument he uses for staying with the Benders is that he will learn from them how to use and still preserve the land. We learn that the Benders rotate crops and plough in manure. We know that they love their farms. But beyond that there is no elaboration on their traditional relationship with the land. Environmental protection is a worthy issue for Smucker to raise, but her readers would be able to handle more than the superficial treatment she gives it. (pp. 34-5)

Mary Ainslie Smith, in a review of "Amish Adventure," in Books in Canada, *Vol. 12, No. 7, August-September, 1983, pp. 34-6.*

This is a briskly-moving story. . . . The Amish way of life and the frequently harsh demands of their religion are explained in sympathetic detail, as are the endless chores of tending a farm without any modern machinery, electricity or plumbing. Ian is the most fully-developed character—he is believable as he struggles with his feelings and identity. . . . [The] book is both a good story and an honest discussion of a minority faith.

Phyllis Ingram, in a review of "Amish Adventure," in School Library Journal, *Vol. 30, No. 3, November, 1983, p. 97.*

Ian is developed as a believable character. Reuben is more a counterpart than a real person. . . . While the main characters are boys, the rest of the children in the family are girls. This is not strictly a boy's story; rather it is a family's story. It is also for young adults rather than children because the reader has to think to understand the grandfather's answers to Ian's questions. On the surface, the answers won't make much more sense to the average reader than they do to Ian. The point of the book seems to be: Yes, the Amish are different, but they don't bother us, so let's not bother them. Let's just accept them the way they are.

If there are Amish or other "plain people" in your area, or your students have questions about these groups, the book is recommended. Otherwise, consider it an optional purchase. (p. 37)

*Sharon Howell, in a review of "Amish Adventure,"
in* The Book Report, *Vol. 2, No. 5, March-April,
1984, pp. 36-7.*

In *Amish Adventure* Mrs. Smucker stimulates our interest in
another way of life, as she stimulated it earlier in *Underground
to Canada* and *Days of terror*. She stimulates also strong emotional responses. This is a fine book: suspenseful, tough, and
compassionate all at once.

I find *Amish Adventure* to be Mrs. Smucker's most skilfully
presented book to date. She exercises good control, for the
most part, over her structure: she juxtaposes scenes and setting
to good effect (contrasting city and rural especially); she develops themes consciously but easily, often opposing isolation
and community, hate and love, violence and peace; she uses
symbolism with more skill and sensitivity than in her previous
books. There are some weaknesses in characterization—Aunt
Clem and Pete Moss, the antagonists, are not entirely convincing. The treatment of some scenes seems contrived to fit
necessities of plot—see Aunt Clem's kidnapping of Ian; a few
scenes are heavy-handed in their didacticism—see Ian's meeting with Pete Moss in jail. Smucker includes, as in her other
books, helpful documentation and bibliography for readers who
wish to acquaint themselves with the factual background of the
book. (p. 138)

The readers learn, with Ian, about the history of the Old Order
Amish people. More importantly, we learn about a different
way of living: we experience life within that community with
Ian, the welcomed outsider, a Canadian child of Presbyterian
background.

Because there were no outside perspectives in her two previous
novels, the effects were one-dimensional. Mrs. Smucker . . .
told a Mennonite story of escape in *Days of terror* from the
point of view of a persecuted Mennonite family fleeing from
the Ukraine in the 1920s to come to Canada. In *Underground
to Canada,* she told of an escape to Canada on the Underground
railway from the point of view of a black slave girl. In *Amish
Adventure,* Smucker is doing several new things. Her time
frame here is contemporary, not historical as in the other two;
her setting now is for the most part Canadian, not American
as in *Underground,* or European, as in *Terror.* Now Canada is
a fully realized place—not just a haven at the end of a journey.
And now the story of those who have found the haven is told
from the outsider's perspective. Two points of view, then,
coexist in this book as Smucker tells two stories: of the modern

Canadian boy and of the established Canadian Amish community.

Ian needs the Benders' warmth and rootedness as he struggles
with his many problems. . . . Through Ian's search for positive
senses of home and identity, Smucker's narrative enacts the
psychological journey towards understanding. (pp. 138-39)

The quiet strengths of the Amish—perseverance, temperance,
love, forgiveness—become his. In return the strengths he brings
from the outside, his initiative and pragmatism, help the Benders.

This interdependence of cultures, however, is shown to be hard-
won. Smucker does not ignore the inevitable conflicts, the
antagonism and persecution which the Amish face in rural
Ontario. They are spelled out in Jack Turner's belligerence
after the accident, in the bullying by Peter Moss (an alienated
teenager), in his vandalism of the Amish schoolhouse, and in
his burning of the Benders' barn. Nor does Smucker ignore
the conflicts within the Amish culture. Ezra's daughter has
permanently exiled herself from the family to become a nurse
in the city and to marry an outsider. John Bender has left
because there is no room for non-conformity in the Amish
faith. (p. 139)

[In] the barn-raising scene at the end of *Amish Adventure,*
Smucker weaves all of the threads of this novel together into
the kind of powerful resolution that her two previous works
have lacked. All of the characters join in a new-found understanding: John Bender, the prodigal son returned, affirms his
Amish identity by "swinging his hammer from the centre of
the highest rafter: he seemed to be holding the whole structure
together" . . . ; Pete Moss, forgiven by Ezra and paroled by
the courts, will help Ezra in subsequent barn-raisings; Ian and
Reuben carry nails and hammers together. Rebuilding the barn
coincides symbolically with the rebuilding of relationships—
between Ezra and John, and Ezra and Pete Moss; with the
rebuilding of a healthy farm; and with the rebuilding of Ezra's
faith in life. For Ian, the life of cooperation here has replaced
the life of isolation.

Amish Adventure dramatizes a belief in the inherent ability of
goodness to overcome and reform evil. (p. 140)

*Cory Bieman Davies, "Quiet Strength: Barbara
Smucker's 'Amish Adventure'," in* Canadian Chil-
dren's Literature: A Journal of Criticism and Review,
Nos. 35 & 36, 1984, pp. 137-40.

Robert Louis (Balfour) Stevenson

1850-1894

(Born Robert Lewis Balfour Stevenson; also wrote under the pseudonym of Captain George North) Scottish author of fiction and poet.

The following entry presents criticism of Stevenson's *Treasure Island*.

Stevenson is the author of several works which are considered distinguished contributions to literature for young people. Perhaps foremost among these books is *Treasure Island*, his first novel, first historical romance, and first popular success. An essayist and short story writer before he composed *Treasure Island*, Stevenson began his classic adventure after being challenged by his twelve-year-old stepson, Lloyd Osbourne, to create a story based on a map the boy had drawn with Stevenson. Filled with danger, mutiny, violence, and murder, the novel relates the tale of Jim Hawkins, a resourceful eighteenth-century English adolescent whose search for treasure on a desert island in the Caribbean changes his attitude towards himself and human nature. At Lloyd Osbourne's request, *Treasure Island* omits major female characters; it does, however, introduce one of literature's most notorious villains, the morally ambivalent one-legged pirate Long John Silver, who is recognized as the real hero of the story and its ultimate reason for success. Although Stevenson wrote *Treasure Island* specifically as a novel for boys which would emphasize action rather than motive, the work is frequently explored for such themes as greed, moral choice, and the presence of good and evil within the individual. *Treasure Island* was originally titled "The Sea Cook," a reference to Silver. Published in *Young Folks* magazine from October 1, 1881 through January 28, 1882 under the pseudonym of Captain George North, the work was unsuccessful with children until it appeared in book form in 1883 under Stevenson's name.

Over the last century, critics have acclaimed nearly every aspect of *Treasure Island*; "it seemed to me," commented Stevenson, "as original as sin," a sentiment with which most reviewers agree. They also praise the excellence of the novel's construction and characterization, the clarity and vividness of its style, and its natural dialogue. A work considered limited in scope but nearly flawless in execution, *Treasure Island* is lauded as one of the greatest books ever written, one which continues to attract both children and adults through the power of Stevenson's storytelling and the skill of his approach.

(See also *Nineteenth-Century Literature Criticism*, Vol. 5; *Yesterday's Authors of Books for Children*, Vol. 2; and *Dictionary of Literary Biography*, Vol. 18: *Victorian Novelists after 1885*.)

AUTHOR'S COMMENTARY

[The following essay originally appeared in the Idler *in August, 1894.]*

[*Treasure Island*] was far indeed from being my first book, for I am not a novelist alone. But I am well aware that my paymaster, the Great Public, regards what else I have written with indifference, if not aversion; if it call upon me at all, it calls

on me in the familiar and indelible character; and when I am asked to talk of my first book, no question in the world but what is meant is my first novel.

Sooner or later, somehow, anyhow, I was bound to write a novel. It seems vain to ask why. Men are born with various manias: from my earliest childhood, it was mine to make a plaything of imaginary series of events; and as soon as I was able to write, I became a good friend to the papermakers. Reams upon reams must have gone to the making of 'Rathillet,' 'The Pentland Rising,' 'The King's Pardon' (otherwise 'Park Whitehead'), 'Edward Daven,' 'A Country Dance,' and 'A Vendetta in the West'; and it is consolatory to remember that these reams are now all ashes, and have been received again into the soil. I have named but a few of my ill-fated efforts, only such indeed as came to a fair bulk ere they were desisted from; and even so they cover a long vista of years. 'Rathillet' was attempted before fifteen, 'The Vendetta' at twenty-nine, and the succession of defeats lasted unbroken till I was thirty-one. By that time, I had written little books and little essays and short stories; and had got patted on the back and paid for them—though not enough to live upon. I had quite a reputation, I was the successful man; I passed my days in toil, the futility of which would sometimes make my cheek to burn—that I should spend a man's energy upon this business, and yet could not earn a livelihood: and still there shone ahead of me an unattained ideal: although I had attempted the thing with vigour not less than ten or twelve times, I had not yet written a novel. All—all my pretty ones—had gone for a little, and then stopped inexorably like a schoolboy's watch. I might be compared to a cricketer of many years' standing who should never have made a run. Anybody can write a short story—a bad one, I mean—who has industry and paper and time enough; but not every one may hope to write even a bad novel. It is the length that kills. (pp. 111-13)

In the fated year I came to live with my father and mother at Kinnaird, above Pitlochry. Then I walked on the red moors and by the side of the golden burn; the rude, pure air of our mountains inspirited, if it did not inspire us, and my wife and I projected a joint volume of logic stories, for which she wrote 'The Shadow on the Bed,' and I turned out **'Thrawn Janet,'** and a first draft of **'The Merry Men.'** I love my native air, but it does not love me; and the end of this delightful period was a cold, a fly-blister, and a migration by Strathairdle and Glenshee to the Castleton of Braemar. There it blew a good deal and rained in a proportion; my native air was more unkind than man's ingratitude, and I must consent to pass a good deal of my time between four walls in a house lugubriously known as the Late Miss McGregor's Cottage. And now admire the finger of predestination. There was a schoolboy in the Late Miss McGregor's Cottage, home from the holidays, and much in want of 'something craggy to break his mind upon.' He had no thought of literature; it was the art of Raphael that received his fleeting suffrages; and with the aid of pen and ink and a shilling box of water colours, he had soon turned one of the rooms into a picture gallery. My more immediate duty towards the gallery was to be showman; but I would sometimes unbend a little, join the artist (so to speak) at the easel, and pass the afternoon with him in a generous emulation, making coloured drawings. On one of these occasions, I made the map of an island; it was elaborately and (I thought) beautifully coloured; the shape of it took my fancy beyond expression; it contained harbours that pleased me like sonnets; and with the unconsciousness of the predestined, I ticketed my performance 'Treasure Island.' I am told there are people who do not care for maps, and find it hard to believe. The names, the shapes of the woodlands, the courses of the roads and rivers, the prehistoric footsteps of man still distinctly traceable up hill and down dale, the mills and the ruins, the ponds and the ferries, perhaps the *Standing Stone* or the *Druidic Circle* on the heath; here is an inexhaustible fund of interest for any man with eyes to see or twopence-worth of imagination to understand with! No child but must remember laying his head in the grass, staring into the infinitesimal forest and seeing it grow populous with fairy armies. Somewhat in this way, as I paused upon my map of 'Treasure Island,' the future character of the book began to appear there visibly among imaginary woods; and their brown faces and bright weapons peeped out upon me from unexpected quarters, as they passed to and fro, fighting and hunting treasure, on these few square inches of a flat projection. The next thing I knew I had some papers before me and was writing out a list of chapters. How often have I done so, and the thing gone no further! But there seemed elements of success about this enterprise. It was to be a story for boys; no need of psychology or fine writing; and I had a boy at hand to be a touchstone. Women were excluded. I was unable to handle a brig (which the *Hispaniola* should have been), but I thought I could make shift to sail her as a schooner without public shame. And then I had an idea for John Silver from which I promised myself funds of entertainment; to take an admired friend of mine [W. E. Henley] . . . , to deprive him of all his finer qualities and higher graces of temperament, to leave him with nothing but his strength, his courage, his quickness, and his magnificent geniality, and to try to express these in terms of the culture of a raw tarpaulin. Such psychical surgery is, I think, a common way of 'making character'; perhaps it is, indeed, the only way. We can put in the quaint figure that spoke a hundred words with us yesterday by the wayside; but do we know him? Our friend, with his infinite variety and flexibility, we know—but can we put him in? Upon the first, we must engraft secondary and imaginary qualities, possibly all wrong; from the second, knife in hand, we must cut away and deduct the needless arborescence of his nature, but the trunk and the few branches that remain we may at least be fairly sure of.

On a chill September morning, by the cheek of a brisk fire, and the rain drumming on the window, I began *The Sea Cook*, for that was the original title. I have begun (and finished) a number of other books, but I cannot remember to have sat down to one of them with more complacency. It is not to be wondered at, for stolen waters are proverbially sweet. I am now upon a painful chapter. No doubt the parrot once belonged to Robinson Crusoe. No doubt the skeleton is conveyed from Poe. I think little of these, they are trifles and details; and no man can hope to have a monopoly of skeletons or make a corner in talking birds. The stockade, I am told, is from *Masterman Ready*. It may be, I care not a jot. These useful writers had fulfilled the poet's saying: departing, they had left behind them Footprints on the sands of time, Footprints which perhaps another—and I was the other! It is my debt to Washington Irving that exercises my conscience, and justly so, for I believe plagiarism was rarely carried farther. I chanced to pick up the *Tales of a Traveller* some years ago with a view to an anthology of prose narrative, and the book flew up and struck me: Billy Bones, his chest, the company in the parlour, the whole inner spirit, and a good deal of the material detail of my first chapters—all were there, all were the property of Washington Irving. But I had no guess of it then as I sat writing by the fireside, in what seemed the springtides of a somewhat pedestrian inspiration; nor yet day by day, after lunch, as I read aloud my morning's work to the family. It seemed to me original as sin; it seemed to belong to me like my right eye. I had counted on one boy, I found I had two in my audience. My father caught fire at once with all the romance and childishness of his original nature. His own stories, that every night of his life he put himself to sleep with, dealt perpetually with ships, roadside inns, robbers, old sailors, and commercial travellers before the era of steam. He never finished one of these romances; the lucky man did not require to! But in *Treasure Island* he recognised something kindred to his own imagination; it was *his* kind of picturesque; and he not only heard with delight the daily chapter, but set himself acting to collaborate. When the time came for Billy Bones's chest to be ransacked, he must have passed the better part of a day preparing, on the back of a legal envelope, an inventory of its contents, which I exactly followed; and the name of 'Flint's old ship'—the *Walrus*—was given at his particular request. And now who should come dropping in, *ex machinâ*, but Dr. Japp, like the disguised prince who is to bring down the curtain upon peace and happiness in the last act; for he carried in his pocket, not a horn or a talisman, but a publisher—had, in fact, been charged . . . , to unearth new writers for *Young Folks*. . . . [When] he left us, he carried away the manuscript in his portmanteau.

Here, then, was everything to keep me up, sympathy, help, and now a positive engagement. I had chosen besides a very easy style. Compare it with the almost contemporary **'Merry Men'**; one reader may prefer the one style, one the other—'tis an affair of character, perhaps of mood; but no expert can fail to see that the one is much more difficult, and the other much easier to maintain. It seems as though a full-grown experienced man of letters might engage to turn out *Treasure Island* at so many pages a day, and keep his pipe alight. But alas! this was not my case. Fifteen days I stuck to it, and turned out fifteen chapters; and then, in the early paragraphs of the sixteenth, ignominiously lost hold. My mouth was empty; there was not one word of *Treasure Island* in my bosom; and here were the proofs of the beginning already waiting me at the 'Hand and Spear'! Then I corrected them, living for the most part alone, walking on the heath at Weybridge in dewy autumn mornings, a good deal pleased with what I had done, and more appalled than I can depict to you in words at what remained for me to do. I was thirty-one; I was the head of a family; I had lost my health; I had never yet paid my way, never yet made £200 a year; my father had quite recently bought back and cancelled a book that was judged a failure: was this to be another and last fiasco? I was indeed very close on despair; but I shut my mouth hard, and during the journey to Davos, where I was to pass the winter, had the resolution to think of other things and bury myself in the novels of M. de Boisgobey. Arrived at my destination, down I sat one morning to the unfinished tale; and behold! it flowed from me like small talk; and in a second tide of delighted industry, and again at a rate of a chapter a day, I finished *Treasure Island*. It had to be transcribed almost exactly; my wife was ill; the schoolboy remained alone of the faithful; and John Addington Symonds (to whom I timidly mentioned what I was engaged on) looked on me askance. He was at that time very eager I should write on the characters of Theophrastus: so far out may be the judgments of the wisest men. But Symonds (to be sure) was scarce the confidant to go to for sympathy on a boy's story. He was large-minded; 'a full man,' if there was one; but the very name of my enterprise would suggest to him only capitulations of sincerity and solecisms of style. Well! he was not far wrong.

Treasure Island—it was Mr. Henderson who deleted the first title, *The Sea Cook*—appeared duly in the story paper, where it figured in the ignoble midst, without woodcuts, and attracted not the least attention. I did not care. I liked the tale myself, for much the same reason as my father liked the beginning: it was my kind of picturesque. I was not a little proud of John Silver, also; and to this day rather admire that smooth and formidable adventurer. What was infinitely more exhilarating, I had passed a landmark; I had finished a tale, and written 'The End' upon my manuscript, as I had not done since **'The Pentland Rising,'** when I was a boy of sixteen not yet at college. In truth it was so by a set of lucky accidents; had not Dr. Japp come on his visit, had not the tale flowed from me with singular ease, it must have been laid aside like its predecessors, and found a circuitous and unlamented way to the fire. Purists may suggest it would have been better so. I am not of that mind. The tale seems to have given much pleasure, and it brought (or was the means of bringing) fire and food and wine to a deserving family in which I took an interest. I need scarcely say I mean my own.

But the adventures of *Treasure Island* are not yet quite at an end. I had written it up to the map. The map was the chief part of my plot. For instance, I had called an islet 'Skeleton Island,' not knowing what I meant, seeking only for the immediate picturesque, and it was to justify this name that I broke into the gallery of Mr. Poe and stole Flint's pointer. And in

the same way, it was because I had made two harbours that the *Hispaniola* was sent on her wanderings with Israel Hands. The time came when it was decided to republish, and I sent in my manuscript, and the map along with it, to Messrs. Cassell. The proofs came, they were corrected, but I heard nothing of the map. I wrote and asked; was told it had never been received, and sat aghast. It is one thing to draw a map at random, set a scale in one corner of it at a venture, and write up a story to the measurements. It is quite another to have to examine a whole book, make an inventory of all the allusions contained in it, and with a pair of compasses, painfully design a map to suit the data. I did it; and the map was drawn again in my father's office, with embellishments of blowing whales and sailing ships, and my father himself brought into service a knack he had of various writing, and elaborately *forged* the signature of Captain Flint, and the sailing directions of Billy Bones. But somehow it was never *Treasure Island* to me.

I have said the map was the most of the plot. I might almost say it was the whole. A few reminiscences of Poe, Defoe, and Washington Irving, a copy of Johnson's *Buccaneers,* the name of the Dead Man's Chest from Kinglsey's *At Last,* some recollections of canoeing on the high seas, and the map itself, with its infinite, eloquent suggestion, made up the whole of my materials. It is, perhaps, not often that a map figures so largely in a tale, yet it is always important. The author must know his countryside, whether real or imaginary, like his hand; the distances, the points of the compass, the place of the sun's rising, the behaviour of the moon, should all be beyond cavil. (pp. 115-30)

[It] is my contention—my superstition, if you like—that who is faithful to his map, and consults it, and draws from it his inspiration, daily and hourly, gains positive support, and not mere negative immunity from accident. The tale has a root there; it grows in that soil; it has a spine of its own behind the words. Better if the country be real, and he has walked every foot of it and knows every milestone. But even with imaginary places, he will do well in the beginning to provide a map; as he studies it, relations will appear that he had not thought upon; he will discover obvious, though unsuspected, shortcuts and footprints for his messengers; and even when a map is not all the plot, as it was in *Treasure Island*, it will be found to be a mine of suggestion. (p. 131)

> *Robert Louis Stevenson, "My First Book: 'Treasure Island',"* in his Essays in the Art of Writing, *Chatto & Windus, 1905, pp. 111-31.*

THE ACADEMY

[The following review was originally published in the Academy *on December 1, 1883.]*

Mr. Stevenson has treated a well-worn theme with freshness. His story is skilfully constructed, and related with untiring vivacity and genuine dramatic power. It is calculated to fascinate the old boy as well as the young, the reader of Smollett and Dr. Moore and Marryat as well as the admirer of the dexterous ingenuity of Poe. It deals with a mysterious island, a buried treasure, the bold buccaneer, and all the stirring incidents of a merry life on the Main. . . . [Mr. Stevenson's buccaneers] are, for the most part, superlative and consistent villains. They cannot inspire the most enthusiastic youth with a desire for the return of the glorious age of buccaneering. Their profession is not set forth in a dangerous halo of romance, nor are their deeds made alluring through a familiar moral process by which crimes are mitigated with the milk of sophistry. Mr. Stevenson deserves praise not alone for this. He has dared to depict an island the sole attraction of which lies in its hidden treasure. With a healthy realism he has avoided that false and specious luxuriance which denaturalises the action of a story by placing its actors out of harmony with their surroundings. His island is no garden of Eden, where all the products of all the zones thrive in happy ignorance, and where the modern representatives of the Swiss Family Robinson may find all to their liking and life certainly worth living. It has its drawbacks as well as its piratical hoard, but it is portrayed in several vivid pictures with the truth and precision of nature. In the opening chapters only may be detected a discordant touch. Here the events are a little too melodramatic and the narrative somewhat strained. The affray with the revenue officers and the discovery of the chart of the island are cleverly managed and form an ingenious prelude. The blind sailor, Pew, is an exception to the author's otherwise excellent delineations. After we have recovered from the thrilling shudder he causes, we feel that he is an anomaly, monstrous, irrelevant—a transitory spasm of nightmare in a coherent story. This, however, is a slight matter. The dramatic verse of the narrative is not less striking than its unflagging spirit. The invention is rich and ready, the dialogue abounds in pith and humour, while the characters—particularly the sailors—are drawn with great force and distinction. Among these is one who stands out with the prominence of one of Cooper's or Marryat's heroes. Long John Silver is a creation. There is not so much of the salt about him as might be desired, but there is no gainsaying his merit. We may long to hang him, or wish him a bad end, in the final chapter, but it is impossible not to be interested in him. With all our knowledge of this abandoned ruffian, of his treachery, his craft, and his abominable wickedness, it is surprising how his humour and cynicism move us to admiration. There is not a false touch in the portrait; the character has all the complexity of a humorist, and is painted with unerring consistency. The scheme by which this cold-blooded villain seduces the crew to mutiny is detailed with admirable irony and humour. . . . [We] shall be surprised if '**Treasure Island**' does not satisfy the most exacting lover of perilous adventures and thrilling situation; he can scarcely fail to share in the anticipations of Jim Hawkins, the relater of this sea yarn, when he finds himself on board the *Hispaniola*, 'with a piping boatswain and pig-tailed singing seamen, bound for an unknown island and to seek for buried treasure.' (pp. 128-29)

> *"Unsigned Notice, 'Academy',"* in Robert Louis Stevenson: The Critical Heritage, *edited by Paul Maixner, Routledge & Kegan Paul, 1981, pp. 128-29.*

[ARTHUR JOHN BUTLER]

[*The following review originally appeared in the* Athenaeum *on December 1, 1883.*]

Any one who has read '**The New Arabian Nights**' will recognize at once Mr. Stevenson's qualifications for telling a good buccaneer story. The blending of the ludicrous with the ghastly, the commonplace with the romantic, of which that book offered examples in plenty, is just what a tale of the search for a pirate's treasure demands. Mr. Stevenson's genius is not wholly unlike that of Poe, and one might almost suspect that the germ of '**Treasure Island**' is to be found in the Gold Beetle, and especially in its last sentence; but it is Poe strongly impregnated with Capt. Marryat. Yet we doubt if either of those writers ever succeeded in making a reader identify himself with the

supposed narrator of a story, as he cannot fail to do in the present case. As we follow the narrative of the boy Jim Hawkins we hold our breath in his dangers, and breathe again at his escapes. The artifice is so well managed that when, for a few chapters, Jim disappears, and the story is taken up by a shrewd doctor, who is never in much danger, the change is felt as a sensible relief. And yet, artistic as the book is, one cannot help feeling that the art is a little too patent. Partly, no doubt, this arises from the fact of the story being laid in the last century. It is given to very few people so to throw themselves into a past age as to avoid all appearance of unreality. In the heroic style this does not matter; but the more real the characters, the more does the difference between the views of one age and another show itself. To take an author already named, 'Snarleyvow' is one of the feeblest of Marryat's novels. In the common phrase, a story of this kind is seldom wholly free from the 'smell of the lamp.' To a reader who can discount this (if one can discount a smell!) it matters little; but it may be doubted whether Mr. Stevenson will succeed as well as inferior artists in pleasing the public whom his story might seem best adapted to reach—the boys. Even if they do not feel the difficulty already indicated, they will demur to his too philosophic rejection of poetical justice in allowing the arch-scoundrel to escape the fate which overtakes all his accomplices. In real life John Silver would hardly have got off; he certainly ought not to do so in fiction. (pp. 130-31)

> [Arthur John Butler], *"Unsigned Review, 'Athenaeum',"* in Robert Louis Stevenson: The Critical Heritage, *edited by Paul Maixner, Routledge & Kegan Paul, 1981, pp. 130-31.*

[W. E. HENLEY]

[*Henley was an English poet, dramatist, and editor of several periodicals, including the* National Observer *and the* New Review. *His most famous poem, "Invictus," demonstrates his braggadocio style and optimistic spirit. Henley and Stevenson became professional partners as well as friends, collaborating on four plays and often turning to each other for encouragement. In 1875, Henley had a foot amputated. Stevenson wrote to him, "It was the sight of your maimed strength and masterfulness that begot Long John Silver . . . the idea of the maimed man (was) entirely taken from you." The following review appeared in the* Saturday Review *(London) on December 8, 1883. Later that month, Stevenson wrote a letter to Henley stating: "I'm glad to think I owe you the review that pleased me best of all the reviews I ever had . . . To live reading such reviews and die eating ortolans—sich (sic) is my aspiration."*]

['**Treasure Island**'] is a book for boys which will be delightful to all grown men who have the sentiment of treasure-hunting and are touched with the true spirit of the Spanish Main. It is the story of the monstrous pile which Flint, the great pirate, buried, with extraordinary circumstances of secrecy and ferocity, on an unknown islet; and it sets forth, with uncommon directness and dexterity, the adventures of certain persons who went in search of the cache, and returned to Bristol city with seven hundred thousand pounds in all the coinages of the world. It contains a delightful map (a legacy from Flint himself), a hoard that will bear comparison with Monte Cristo's own, a fort, a stockade, a maroon, and one of the most remarkable pirates in fiction. Like all Mr. Stevenson's good work, it is touched with genius. It is written—in that crisp, choice, nervous English of which he has the secret—with such a union of measure and force as to be in its way a masterpiece of narrative. It is rich in excellent characterization, in an abundant invention, in a certain grim romance, in a vein of what must, for want of a better word, be described as melodrama, which is both thrilling and peculiar. It is the work of one who knows all there is to be known about 'Robinson Crusoe,' and to whom Dumas is something more than a great *amateur*; and it is in some ways the best thing he has produced. (p. 132)

[John Silver's] wickedness is the wickedness of a man of genius; he has no heart, but he has any amount of character and brains; he is a desperado of the worst type, but entirely passionless—a kind of buccaneering Borgia; in victory and defeat alike he maintains a magnificent intellectual superiority—to himself, his comrades, and his circumstances; and when at last he disappears from the story, you are glad that he has not gone the way of his companions (shot, drowned, stabbed, marooned), but has got off to his old negress with a whole skin and a bagful of pieces-of-eight. There are many good characters and sketches of character in the book—Dr. Livesey, Squire Trelawney, Captain Smollett, Billy Bones, Ben Gunn the maroon (a study of singular freshness and originality), the horrible blind pirate, Jim Hawkins himself; but Long John, called Barbecue, is incomparably the best of all. He, and not Jim Hawkins, nor Flint's treasure, is Mr. Stevenson's real hero; and you feel, when the story is done, that the right name of it is not **'Treasure Island,'** but 'John Silver, Pirate.' (pp. 135-36)

> [W. E. Henley], "Unsigned Review, 'Saturday Review'," *in* Robert Louis Stevenson: The Critical Heritage, *edited by Paul Maixner, Routledge & Kegan Paul, 1981, pp. 131-36.*

GRAPHIC

[*The following review originally appeared in* Graphic *on December 15, 1883.*]

The warmest admirer of Mr. Robert Louis Stevenson would probably find it difficult to say what precise quality in his writings it is which gives them such keen and peculiar pleasure. It is not only his perfect mastery of style,—a mastery which entitles Mr. Stevenson almost alone among living writers to be called classic,—it is something more than his unique imaginative power. These are things one can name; but in their combination something further suggests itself to the mind, something for which it would almost appear criticism has yet to find a name. There is no need to inquire why, after giving us such a rare piece of fiction as **'The New Arabian Nights,'** Mr. Stevenson should choose to present us with a story for boys. It seems whimsical—but it would be grudging to resent an apparent decline in choice of subject when the story for boys is such a one as **'Treasure Island.'** It is a tale, says Mr. Stevenson, in his introductory stanzas 'To The Hesitating Purchaser,' of 'storm and adventure, heat and cold, of schooners, islands, and maroons, and buccaneers and buried gold, and all the old romance, retold exactly in the ancient way,' and further on he suggests a comparison between himself and 'Kingston and Ballantyne the Brave, or Cooper of the Wood and Wave.' Needless to say there is no resemblance between Mr. Stevenson and any other boys' writer, and this romance is told in anything but the ancient way. In **'Treasure Island'** there is combined with an imagination far stronger than that of any of the writers named, a power of expression unique in the literature of our day, and an insight into character, and a capacity to depict it, unsurpassed, and almost unsurpassable. This was a bold experiment, this resuscitation of tales of buried treasure in the Spanish Main, the mutiny, the buccaneer, the stockade, and the miraculous boy who does everything and always succeeds. Yet under Mr. Stevenson's masterly touch everything becomes new. We can think of no other writer who possesses such an

extraordinary power of filling the reader with a sense of coming danger. As in **'The Pavilion on the Links'** the air seemed thick with Italians, so in the opening of **'Treasure Island'** it seems thick with buccaneers. Pew, the horrible blind man, whose stick came tap-tapping along the frosty road; Billy Bones, the captain 'who blew through his nose so loudly that you might say he roared;' Ben Gunn, the marooned sailor, whose heart was 'sore for Christian diet,' who many a long night on his lonely island 'dreamed of cheese—toasted mostly—and woke up again;' and Long John Silver, the wooden-legged miscreant, 'his eye,' at certain times, 'a mere pin-point in his big face, but gleaming like a crumb of glass' (an ordinary writer would have said a bead)—these are all creations, living, lying, swearing, murderous miscreants, as different from the sailors of Marryat and Ballantyne as any suit of clothes from a breathing man. There are passages in this romance surpassing in power anything that Mr. Stevenson has yet done; there are characters that deserve to live among literary creations; there are adventures as rapid and breathless as any ever imagined or experienced; for all this we must be thankful. Yet we want no more boys' books from Mr. Stevenson. We want him to employ his unique gifts in the highest department of literature now open to him—contemporary fiction. (pp. 140-41)

> "Unsigned Review, 'Graphic'," *in* Robert Louis Stevenson: The Critical Heritage, *edited by Paul Maixner, Routledge & Kegan Paul, 1981, pp. 140-41.*

THE LITERARY WORLD

[**Treasure Island** is] as extraordinary a story of pirates and piracy as ever was written—a book which in its way is almost as good as anything would be that Defoe, Capt. Maryatt, and Clark Russell could write if they were to put their heads and hands together. (p. 51)

[The story] begins somewhere along in the last century with the arrival at the Admiral Benbow inn on the Bristol coast, England, of a grim old sea-dog with a sea-chest and a tarry pig-tail. . . . [After] one or two mysterious visits it turned out that he was an old pirate. Then came his death, by apoplexy and rum, and the opening of his sea-chest, and the discovery of the chart of the island, where he had killed his six shipmates, one by one, and buried his gold—seven hundred thousand pounds of it—with no one but himself and the chart to tell the tale.

Of course with this discovery an expedition is fitted out to recover the treasure. Squire Trelawney and Dr. Livesey are at the head of it; Jim Hawkins, cabin boy, tells the story; and among the crew there ship, unbeknown to the Captain and the owners, some of the dead pirate's old gang. Secretly they are after the treasure too! The hero of them is Long John Silver, the cook, a man of prodigious mental force and physical power, who has lost his left leg close to the hip, but can do as much with his right leg and his crutch as most men who are not crippled, and who becomes a foremost figure in the adventures which follow. (pp. 51-2)

By the time Treasure Island is sighted, mutiny is on foot among the crew of the "Walrus," the knowing ones among the crew being bent on getting possession of Captain Flint's money themselves. Long John is at the head of the plot. Battle, murder, and sudden death ensue on ship and on island; the air is full of the lingo of the pirates and the smoke of fire-arms, a temporary truce ends in a dire tragedy, the buried treasure is found and recovered, and Jim Hawkins lives to tell as exciting and dramatic a story as often finds its way into print.

Considering the coarseness and brutality of some of the characters, the shocking nature of some of the incidents, and the horrible colors of the whole business, Mr. Stevenson has succeeded in avoiding what is objectionable. He gets along without any profaneness to speak of, which we may be sure is more than his pirates could do; the delineation of character and incident is remarkable for verisimilitude and vividness; the eighteenth century flavor is effectively imparted; and as a dramatic romance of bloody adventure on the high seas we must give the book high praise. Not everybody, to be sure, cares to read such romances, and not everybody ought to; but those who are at liberty so to do will find this one admirable in form. Though there is rough talk in it, and rum, and murder, and assassination in cold blood, and suggestions of horrors untold, yet the materials are so subordinated to the treatment, and the art of the writer is so perfect, that the effect does not become shocking. It would seem heartless to say of such a book that it is capital, for that would imply a relish for one of the darkest chapters of events in human history; but piracy is a fact, and this picture of it is graphic and obviously true. At any rate, we would rather it were read twice over than some of the current novels we have. Nobody can be much the worse for such a book, even though there are places in it which may make one shudder. As for ourselves we will confess that, though with a head full of Hesiodic Legends, and Addison, and Wendell Phillips, and a dozen other far weightier matters, having read the first few pages of this book, we did not lay it down till we had finished it. So easy is it on the slightest provocation to be "a boy again." (p. 52)

> *"Mr. Stevenson's New Books," in* The Literary World, *Vol. XV, No. 4, February 23, 1884, pp. 51-2.*

THE DIAL

[*The following review was originally published in the* Dial *in May, 1884.*]

Mr. Stevenson's romance of **'Treasure Island'** is a tissue of highly improbable incidents which do not for a moment throw the spell of reality around the reader, and yet constrain him to acknowledge the skill with which they are worked up. The author shows considerable strength of invention in unfolding the plot and delineating the characters, which are life-like and well-sustained. But beyond this exhibition of his power in the line of fiction, there is no appreciable good accomplished by the book. It is a picture of the roughest phases of sea-life. The effort to recover a pirate's buried treasure from a desolate island in the mid-ocean, by a couple of gentlemen whose followers comprise cutthroats, mutineers, and a sprinkling of honest mariners, is neither dignified nor edifying. It will be relished by adventure-loving boys, but whether it will be wholesome reading for them is more than doubtful.

> *"Unsigned Notice, 'Dial'," in* Robert Louis Stevenson: The Critical Heritage, *edited by Paul Maixner, Routledge & Kegan Paul, 1981, p. 142.*

WILLIAM ARCHER

[*A Scottish dramatist and critic, Archer is best known as one of the earliest and most important translators of Henrik Ibsen's plays and as a drama critic of the London stage. The following excerpt is from an essay which is the first general assessment of Stevenson's work; it is also the first to elucidate several critical points that are repeated throughout Stevenson criticism.*]

There are fashions in style as in everything else, and, for the moment, we are all agreed that the one great saving grace is

Lloyd Osbourne.

"lightness of touch." Of this virtue Mr. Stevenson is the accomplished model. He keeps it always before his eyes, and cultivates in everything a buoyant, staccato, touch-and-go elasticity. In description he jots effects rather than composes pictures. He has a Dickens-like knack of giving life and motion to objects the most inanimate. (p. 583)

In character-drawing, or rather sketching, Mr. Stevenson's effort is the same. Here he forswears analysis as in description he has forsworn synthesis. A few crisp, clean strokes and a wash of transparent colour, and the oddity stands before us as though fresh from the pencil of Mr. Caldecott. For Mr. Stevenson's characters are all oddities. It is to the quaintly abnormal that this method of presentation applies. To draw the normal, to make a revelation of the commonplace, is a task which demands insight quite other than Mr. Stevenson's, labour quite foreign to his scheme. Richardson knew nothing of lightness of touch; it was at some sacrifice of this supreme quality that George Eliot made Rosamond Vincy live not only as a phantasm before the mind's eye, but as a piece of flesh and blood, solid in three dimensions, to whose reality every fibre of our moral being bears witness with a thrill. All Mr. Stevenson's personages have hitherto been either wayside silhouettes taken in the course of his wanderings, or figures invented to help out the action of tales whose very essence lies in their unreality. "Long John Silver" is perhaps his most sustained effort in character-drawing, brilliantly successful as far as vividness of presentation is concerned, but conceived outside of all observation, a creature of tradition, a sort of nautical were-wolf. To apply analysis to such a character would merely be to let out the sawdust. (pp. 584-85)

William Archer, "Robert Louis Stevenson: His Style and His Thought," in Time, London, n.s. Vol. XIII, No. 11, November, 1885, pp. 581-91.

HENRY JAMES

[*James was an American novelist and critic who was a close friend and correspondent of Stevenson's as well as an admirer of his work. Janet Adam Smith writes, "They were the two most conscious novelists of their time in England; they thought more profoundly about their art, and cared more intensely for it, than any of their contemporaries. . . . Their criticism of each other's work was acute and technical." In his* Robert Louis Stevenson and the Fiction of Adventure, *Robert Kiely notes that James's essays on Stevenson are "the finest criticism written on that author." In 1891, James published "The Pupil," a story which belongs to the "boy's book" category he refers to in the following essay; critics conclude that James was probably influenced by* Treasure Island *and* Kidnapped *when he wrote "The Pupil."*]

"**The New Arabian Nights**" offers us, as the title indicates, the wonderful in the frankest, most delectable form. Partly extravagant, and partly very specious, they are the result of a very happy idea, that of placing a series of adventures which are pure adventures in the setting of contemporary English life, and relating them in the placidly ingenious tone of Scheherezade. This device is carried to perfection in "**The Dynamiter**," where the manner takes on more of a kind of high-flown serenity in proportion as the incidents are more "steep." In this line "**The Suicide Club**" is Mr. Stevenson's greatest success; and the first two pages of it, not to mention others, live in the memory. For reasons which I am conscious of not being able to represent as sufficient, I find something ineffaceably impressive—something really haunting—in the incident of Prince Florizel and Colonel Geraldine, who, one evening in March, are "driven by a sharp fall of sleet into an Oyster Bar in the immediate neighborhood of Leicester Square," and there have occasion to observe the entrance of a young man followed by a couple of commissionaires, each of whom carries a large dish of cream-tarts under a cover—a young man who "pressed these confections on every one's acceptance with exaggerated courtesy." There is no effort at a picture here, but the imagination makes one of the lighted interior, the London sleet outside, the company that we guess, given the locality, and the strange politeness of the young man, leading on to circumstances stranger still. This is what may be called putting one in the mood for a story. But Mr. Stevenson's most brilliant stroke of that kind is the opening episode of "**Treasure Island**"—the arrival of the brown old seaman, with the sabercut, at the "Admiral Benbow," and the advent, not long after, of the blind sailor, with a green shade over his eyes, who comes tapping down the road, in quest of him, with his stick. "**Treasure Island**" is a "boy's book," in the sense that it embodies a boy's vision of the extraordinary; but it is unique in this, and calculated to fascinate the weary mind of experience, that what we see in it is not only the ideal fable, but, as part and parcel of that, as it were, the young reader himself and his state of mind: we seem to read it over his shoulder, with an arm around his neck. It is all as perfect as a well-played boy's game, and nothing can exceed the spirit and skill, the humor and the open-air feeling, with which the whole thing is kept at the critical pitch. It is not only a record of queer chances, but a study of young feelings; there is a moral side

in it, and the figures are not puppets with vague faces. If Jim Hawkins illustrates successful daring, he does so with a delightful, rosy good-boyishness, and a conscious, modest liability to error. His luck is tremendous, but it doesn't make him proud; and his manner is refreshingly provincial and human. So is that, even more, of the admirable John Silver, one of the most picturesque, and, indeed, in every way, most genially presented, villains in the whole literature of romance. He has a singularly distinct and expressive countenance, which, of course, turns out to be a grimacing mask. Never was a mask more knowingly, vividly painted. "**Treasure Island**" will surely become—it must already have become, and will remain—in its way a classic; thanks to this indescribable mixture of the prodigious and the human, of surprising coincidences and familiar feelings. The language in which Mr. Stevenson has chosen to tell his story is an admirable vehicle for these feelings; with its humorous braveries and quaintnesses, its echoes of old ballads and yarns, it touches all kinds of sympathetic chords. (p. 877)

Henry James, "Robert Louis Stevenson," in The Century, Vol. XXXV, No. 6, April, 1888, pp. 869-79.

ARTHUR CONAN DOYLE

[*The following excerpt is taken from an essay originally published in the* National Review *in January, 1890.*]

A very singular mental reaction took Mr Stevenson from one pole to the other of imaginative work, from the subtle, dainty lines of **Prince Otto** to the direct, matter-of-fact, eminently practical and Defoe-like narratives of **Treasure Island** and of **Kidnapped**. Both are admirable pieces of English, well conceived, well told, striking the reader at every turn with some novel situation, some new combination of words which just fits the sense as a cap fits a nipple. **Treasure Island** is perhaps the better story, while **Kidnapped** may have the longer lease of life as being an excellent and graphic sketch of the state of the Highlands after the last Jacobite insurrection. Each contains one novel and admirable character, Alan Breck in the one, and Long John in the other. Surely John Silver, with his face the size of a ham, and his little gleaming eyes like crumbs of glass in the centre of it, is the king of all seafaring desperadoes. Observe how the strong effect is produced in his case, seldom by direct assertion on the part of the story-teller, but usually by comparison, innuendo, or indirect reference. The objectionable Billy Bones is haunted by the dread of 'a seafaring man with one leg.' Captain Flint, we are told, was a brave man; 'He was afraid of none, not he, only Silver—*Silver was that genteel.*' . . . [By] a touch here and a hint there, there grows upon us the individuality of this smooth-tongued, ruthless, masterful, one-legged devil. He is to us not a creation of fiction, but an organic living reality with whom we have come into contact; such is the effect of the fine suggestive strokes with which he is drawn. And the buccaneers themselves, how simple and yet how effective are the little touches which indicate their ways of thinking and of acting. 'I want to go into that cabin, I do; I want their pickles and wine and that.' 'Now if you had sailed along o' Bill you wouldn't have stood there to be spoke to twice—not you. That was never Bill's way, nor the way of sich as sailed with him.' Scott's buccaneers in *The Pirate* are admirable, but they lack something human which we find here. It will be long before John Silver loses his place in sea fiction—'and you may lay to that.'

There is still a touch of the Meredithian manner in these books, different as they are in general scope from anything which he has attempted. There is the apt use of an occasional archaic or unusual word, the short strong descriptions, the striking metaphors, the somewhat staccato fashion of speech. Yet, in spite of this flavour, they have quite individuality enough to constitute a school of their own. Their faults, or rather perhaps their limitations, lie never in the execution, but entirely in the original conception. They picture only one side of life, and that a strange and exceptional one. There is no female interest. We feel that it is an apotheosis of the boy's story—the penny number of our youth *in excelsis.* But it is all so good, so fresh, so picturesque, that, however limited its scope, it still retains a definite and well-assured place in literature. There is no reason why *Treasure Island* should not be to the rising generation of the twenty-first century what *Robinson Crusoe* has been to that of the nineteenth. The balance of probability is all in that direction. (pp. 396-97)

Arthur Conan Doyle, "Mr. Stevenson's Methods in Fiction," in A Peculiar Gift: Nineteenth Century Writings on Books for Children, *edited by Lance Salway, Kestrel Books, 1976, pp. 391-403.*

THE CHURCH QUARTERLY REVIEW

Scott is assuredly the supreme master of combination of incident and character, and it is therefore eminently satisfactory to observe that Mr. Stevenson appears to be a disciple of this greatest of novelists. He is certainly not wanting in the power to invent a striking plot. *Treasure Island* alone is evidence of this; but it is also seen in *Kidnapped* and *The Master of Ballantrae,* to say nothing of some of the minor stories. In all these, however, the story is not the whole object; except in the first-named there is no danger of its being taken for the principal object. The chief interest in all these works lies in the characters described in them; and it is this which essentially differentiates *Treasure Island* from its contemporary in appearance, *King Solomon's Mines,* and from the multitude of boys' books in which pirates and treasure and hair-breadth escapes equally play a part. Silver, Captain Smollett, Dr. Livesey, and Mr. Trelawney are all living persons, clearly imagined and vividly portrayed, both in word and action. It is in the conversations that Mr. Stevenson's genius for the creation of character especially appears. The speeches of the various personages of his stories have the naturalness, the inevitableness, which are the best signs of the characters having been well and truly conceived. The dialogue between Silver and Captain Smollett before the attack on the blockhouse, and the scene when Jim Hawkins falls into the hands of the mutineers, are admirably told, and have a life and probability which could hardly be bettered. (pp. 204-05)

"Mr. R. L. Stevenson's Novels," in The Church Quarterly Review, *Vol. XXXI, No. LXI, October, 1890, pp. 195-211.*

ANDREW LANG

[*A Scottish critic, poet, and fiction writer, Lang was one of Britain's most powerful men of letters during the closing decades of the nineteenth century. He is chiefly remembered today as the editor of the "color fairy books," a twelve-volume series of fairy tales from various world cultures. Throughout his literary criticism, Lang espoused a strong preference for romantic adventure novels. He wrote to Stevenson soon after the publication of* Treasure Island *that "I don't know, except for* Tom Sawyer *and the* Odyssey, *that I ever liked any romance so well." In the following excerpt, Lang continues his laudatory evaluation of* Treasure Island.]

It was probably by way of mere diversion and child's play that Mr. Stevenson began **"Treasure Island."** He is an amateur of boyish pleasures of masterpieces at a penny plain and twopence coloured. Probably he had looked at the stories of adventure in penny papers which only boys read, and he determined sportively to compete with their unknown authors. **"Treasure Island"** came out in such a periodical, with the emphatic woodcuts which adorn them. It is said that the puerile public was not greatly stirred. A story is a story, and they rather preferred the regular purveyors. The very faint archaism of the style may have alienated them. But, when **"Treasure Island"** appeared as a real book, then every one who had a smack of youth left was a boy again for some happy hours. Mr. Stevenson had entered into another province of his realm: the king had come to his own again.

They say the seamanship is inaccurate; I care no more than I do for the year 30. They say too many people are killed. They all died in fair fight, except a victim of John Silver's. The conclusion is a little too like part of Poe's most celebrated tale, but nobody has bellowed "Plagiarist!" Some people may not look over a fence: Mr. Stevenson, if he liked, might steal a horse,—the animal in this case is only a skeleton. A very sober student might add that the hero is impossibly clever; but, then, the hero is a boy, and this is a boy's book. For the rest, the characters live. Only genius could have invented John Silver, that terribly smooth-spoken mariner. Nothing but genius could have drawn that simple yokel on the island. . . . The blustering Billy Bones is a little masterpiece: the blind Pew, with his tapping stick (there are three such blind tappers in Mr. Stevenson's books), strikes terror into the boldest. Then, the treasure is thoroughly satisfactory in kind, and there is plenty of it. The landscape, as in the feverish, fog-smothered flat, is gallantly painted. And there are no interfering petticoats in the story. (pp. 29-30)

Andrew Lang, "Mr. Stevenson's Works," in his Essays in Little, *Charles Scribner's Sons, 1891, pp. 24-35.*

S. R. CROCKETT

[*An ordained minister before he turned to literature, Crockett wrote many historical romances and several children's books. He is perhaps best known for* The Raiders *and* The Black Douglas *as well as for two stories based on his Scottish childhood,* Sir Toady Lion *and* Sir Toady Crusoe. *An admirer of Stevenson, Crockett dedicated* The Stickit Minister *to him.*]

I love Jim Hawkins. On my soul I love him more even than Alan Breck. He is the boy we should all like to have been, though no doubt David Balfour is much more like the boys we were—without the piety and the adventures. I read Stevenson in every line of **"Treasure Island."** It is of course mixed of Erraid and the island discovered by Mr. Daniel Defoe. But we love anything of such excellent breed, and the crossing only improves it. Our hearts dance when Mr. Stevenson lands his cut-throats, with one part of himself as hero and the other as villain. John Silver is an admirable villain, for he is just the author genially cutting throats. Even when he pants three times as he sends the knife home, we do not entirely believe in his villainy. We expect to see the murdered seaman about again and hearty at his meals in the course of a chapter or two. John is a villain at great expense and trouble to himself; but we like him personally, and are prepared to sit down and suck an apple with him, even when he threatens to stove in our "thundering old blockhouse and them as dies will be the lucky ones." In our hearts we think the captain was a little hard on him. We know that it is Mr. Stevenson all the time, and are terrified exactly like a three-year-old who sees his father take a rug over his head and ''be a bear.'' The thrill is delicious, for there is just an off chance that after all the thing may turn out to be a bear; but still we are pretty easy that at the play's end the bearskin will be tossed aside, the villain repent, and John Silver get off with a comfortable tale of pieces of eight.

No book has charted more authentically the topographical features of the kingdom of Romance than **"Treasure Island."** Is that island in the South or in the North Atlantic? Is it in the ''Spanish main''? What *is* the Spanish main? Is it in the Atlantic at all? Or set a jewel somewhere in the wide Pacific, or strung on some fringe of the Indian Ocean? Who knows or cares? Jim Hawkins is there. His luck, it is true, is something remarkable. His chances are phenomenal. His imagination, like ours, is running free, and we could go on for ever hearing about Jim. We can trust Jim Hawkins, and void of care we follow his star.

O for one hour of Jim in the **"Wrecker"** to clear up the mystery of the many captains, or honest and reputable John Silver to do for the poor Scot down below in a workman-like manner when he came running to him, instead of firing as it were ''into the brown'' till that crying stopped—a touch for which we find it hard to forgive Mr. Stevenson—pardon, Mr. Lloyd Osbourne.

Again, Alan Breck is ever Alan, and bright shines his sword; but he is never quite Jim Hawkins to me. Nor does he seem even so point-device in **"Catriona"** as he was in the round house or with his foot on the heather. But wherever Alan Breck goes or David Balfour follows, thither I am ready to fare forth, unquestioning and all-believing.

But when I do not care very much for any one of Mr. Stevenson's books, it is chiefly the lack of Mr. James Hawkins that I regret. Jim in doublet and hose—how differently he would have sped **"The Black Arrow"**! Jim in trousers and top hat—he would never have been found in the **"Black Box,"** never have gone out with Huish upon the **"Ebb Tide."** John Silver never threw vitriol, but did his needs with a kinfe in a gentlemanly way, and that was because Jim Hawkins was there to see that he was worthy of himself. Jim would never have let things get to such a pass as to require Attwater's bullets splashing like hail in a pond over the last two pages to settle matters in any sort of way.

I often think of getting up a petition to Mr. Stevenson . . . , beseeching ''with sobs and tears'' that he will sort out all his beach-combers and Yankee captains, charter a rakish saucy-sailing schooner, ship Jim Hawkins as ship's boy or captain (we are not particular), and then up anchor with a Yo-Ho-Cheerily for the Isle of our Heart's Desire, where they load Long Toms with pieces of eight, and, dead or alive, nobody minds Ben Gunn. (pp. 110-11)

> *S. R. Crockett, ''Mr. Stevenson's Books,'' in* The Bookman, *London, Vol. VII, No. 40, January, 1895, pp. 109-11.*

J. M. BARRIE

[Certainly one of literature's most infamous pirates is Captain Hook, the villain of Barrie's play Peter Pan. *A Scottish dramatist and novelist, Barrie modeled Hook and his crew after Long John Silver and his band of buccaneers. The following excerpt from* Margaret Ogilvy, *Barrie's biographical tribute to his mother, describes the reaction of both mother and son to Stevenson's works, most notably* Treasure Island.*]*

These familiar initials [R.L.S.] are, I suppose, the best beloved in recent literature, certainly they are the sweetest to me, but there was a time when my mother could not abide them. She said 'That Stevenson man' with a sneer, and it was never easy to her to sneer. At thought of him her face would become almost hard, which seems incredible, and she would knit her lips and fold her arms, and reply with a stiff 'oh' if you mentioned his aggravating name. In the novels we have a way of writing of our heroine, 'she drew herself up haughtily,' and when mine draw themselves up haughtily I see my mother thinking of Robert Louis Stevenson. He knew her opinion of him, and would write, 'My ears tingled yesterday; I sair doubt she has been miscalling me again.' But the more she miscalled him the more he delighted in her, and she was informed of this, and at once said 'The scoundrel!' If you would know what was his unpardonable crime, it was this, he wrote better books than mine.

I remember the day she found it out, which was not, however, the day she admitted it. That day, when I should have been at my work, she came upon me in the kitchen, **'The Master of Ballantrae'** beside me, but I was not reading: my head lay heavy on the table and to her anxious eyes, I doubt not, I was the picture of woe. 'Not writing!' I echoed, no, I was not writing, I saw no use in ever trying to write again. And down, I suppose, went my head once more. She misunderstood, and thought the blow had fallen; I had awakened to the discovery, always dreaded by her, that I had written myself dry; I was no better than an empty ink-bottle. She wrung her hands, but indignation came to her with my explanation, which was that while R.L.S. was at it we others were only 'prentices cutting our fingers on his tools. 'I could never thole his books,' said my mother immediately, and indeed vindictively.

'You have not read any of them,' I reminded her.

'And never will,' said she with spirit.

And I have no doubt that she called him a dark character that very day. For weeks too, if not for months, she adhered to her determination not to read him, though I, having come to my senses and seen that there is a place for the 'prentice, was taking a pleasure, almost malicious, in putting **'The Master of Ballantrae'** in her way. I would place it on her table so that it said good-morning to her when she rose. She would frown, and carrying it downstairs, as if she had it in the tongs, replace it on its book-shelf. I would wrap it up in the cover she had made for the latest Carlyle: she would skin it contemptuously and again bring it down. I would hide her spectacles in it, and lay it on top of the clothes-basket and prop it up invitingly open against her tea-pot. And at last I got her, though I forget by which of many contrivances. What I recall vividly is a key-hole view, to which another member of the family invited me. Then I saw my mother wrapped up in **'The Master of Ballantrae'** and muttering the music to herself, nodding her head in approval, and taking a stealthy glance at the foot of each page before she began at the top. (pp. 131-35)

'The Master of Ballantrae' is not the best. Conceive the glory, which was my mother's, of knowing from a trustworthy source that there are at least three better awaiting you on the same shelf. She did not know Alan Breck yet, and he was as anxious to step down as Mr. Bally himself. John Silver was there, getting into his leg, so that she should not have to wait a moment, and roaring, 'I'll lay to that!' when she told me consolingly that she could not thole pirate stories. Not to know these gentlemen, what is it like? It is like never having been in love. But they are in the house! That is like knowing that you will fall in love to-morrow morning. With one word, by drawing one mournful face, I could have got my mother to abjure the jam-shelf—nay, I might have managed it by merely saying that she had enjoyed 'The Master of Ballantrae.' For you must remember that she only read it to persuade herself (and me) of its unworthiness, and that the reason she wanted to read the others was to get further proof. All this she made plain to me, eyeing me a little anxiously the while, and of course I accepted the explanation. Alan is the biggest child of them all, and I doubt not that she thought so, but curiously enough her views of him are among the things I have forgotten. But how enamoured she was of 'Treasure Island,' and how faithful she tried to be to me all the time she was reading it! I had to put my hands over her eyes to let her know that I had entered the room, and even then she might try to read between my fingers, coming to herself presently, however, to say 'It's a haver of a book.'

'Those pirate stories are so uninteresting,' I would reply without fear, for she was too engrossed to see through me. 'Do you think you will finish this one?'

'I may as well go on with it since I have begun it,' my mother says, so slily that my sister and I shake our heads at each other to imply, 'Was there ever such a woman!'

'There are none of those one-legged scoundrels in my books,' I say.

'Better without them,' she replies promptly.

'I wonder, mother, what it is about the man that so infatuates the public?

'He takes no hold of me,' she insists. 'I would a hantle rather read your books.'

I offer obligingly to bring one of them to her, and now she looks at me suspiciously. 'You surely believe I like yours best,' she says with instant anxiety, and I soothe her by assurances, and retire advising her to read on, just to see if she can find out how he misleads the public. 'Oh, I may take a look at it again by and by,' she says indifferently, but nevertheless the probability is that as the door shuts the book opens, as if by some mechanical contrivance. I remember how she read 'Treasure Island,' holding it close to the ribs of the fire (because she could not spare a moment to rise and light the gas), and how, when bed-time came, and we coaxed, remonstrated, scolded, she said quite fiercely, clinging to the book, 'I dinna lay my head on a pillow this night till I see how that laddie got out of the barrel.' (pp. 142-45)

> J. M. Barrie, "R.L.S." in his Margaret Ogilvy, Charles Scribner's Sons, 1896, pp. 131-49.

H. BELLYSE BAILDON

["Treasure Island"] rapidly made its author famous, and remains, with the possible exception of "Dr. Jekyll and Mr. Hyde," his most popular work. Nor is it difficult to understand its attraction, combining as it does charm of style, vividness and compactness of narration, and the supreme fascination of one evil but masterful character, Long John Silver, who rivets the reader's attention throughout, even as the eyes of the Ancient Mariner held the Wedding Guest. Writing, as Stevenson did, purely to entertain and interest young people, there is little of his rather perplexing philosophy which, in a book like "Prince Otto," seems to mock and baffle our interest, and in others like "Dr. Jekyll," "The Master of Ballantrae," and "Ebb-

tide," distresses us with a sense of moral and spiritual defeat and disaster. (pp. 52-3)

For terse and vigorous and unflagging narrative power "Treasure Island" may be equalled, but cannot be excelled. As a mere piece of literature it is of course head and shoulders over the ordinary book of adventure; but its distinctive merit which seems to me to put it into a higher category than even "Robinson Crusoe," is the masterly delineation of the almost Napoleonic villain "Long John Silver." I say Napoleonic, because it seems to me that in John Silver we have qualities which on a higher and greater stage might have made such a Jupiter Scapin. The same superb indifference to right and wrong marks the ex-buccaneer and the quondam "Scourge of Europe." And John Silver meets his Wellington in Dr. Livesey and is beaten, and yet carries, as Napoleon did, what we may call all the stage honours. The doctor, like Wellington, seems rather the agent in the hands of a vindicating Providence, an embodiment of justice, and bulks no more in comparison with Silver than a David compared in stature with a Goliath. Like Milton's Satan, Silver takes with him the suffrages of the reader. He fascinates us, as he does Jim Hawkins, not only by his masterly villainy, but by a certain urbanity that is almost Olympian, and he seems to play with the lives of men with the same light unabashed enjoyment with which a child kills flies. In spite of his crutch and stump he seems to tower over the others like a bad god, who jovially plays at skittles with human lives. Revolting as Silver's actions are, we never quite hate him as we ought. His *aplomb* keeps us in perpetual good humour. Whether a man can be as bad as Silver, so to speak, with such a good grace, one may well doubt. But that he, like the Master of Ballantrae, is one of the most striking figures in fiction, admits, I think, of no cavil. And, strange as it may seem, the more one studies these masterly and masterful villains, the more one tends to class them with such high company as Iago, Mephistopheles, and Milton's Satan. I know that is a great deal to say, but I say it with conviction. There is certainly nothing in Scott that comes into the same class. His Bertrams and Roderick Dhus and Bois Gilberts seem melodramatic and conventional in comparison. This I know is treason, but I believe it to be true. One sometimes thinks Stevenson must have signed a new kind of pact with the devil and been made a burgess of hell, so alarming an intimacy he seems to have with evil.

But then comes the limitation. John Silver is really the one character of the book, the Hamlet of the play. The other characters are all carefully differentiated, but they fall almost as far short in degree of real vitality in comparison with Silver, as they do in point of importance and bulk in the reader's eye. Jim Hawkins, the nominal hero, is just in Chadband's phrase a "human boy," except when he is rather supernaturally cool and acute. Even Dr. Livesey is somewhat wooden, and the other characters are like planets revolving round the resplendent villainy of Silver. Of course the blind Pew, with the almost sepulchral tapping of his stick, and Captain Flint himself, to a less degree, are ineffaceable images and memories for the reader.

At first sight it may seem curious that Stevenson, who so despised the modern racing and toiling for wealth, should have been so fascinated by the notion of treasure-hunting that he not only devotes the whole of this, certainly one of his best books, entirely to this pursuit, but frequently harks back upon the same idea. I cannot but think it is in part the inveterate moralist that lies in his fibre that makes such themes attractive to him.

As in the story of "The Rajah's Diamond" there lies in **"Treasure Island"** the moral that the desire and pursuit of great wealth reduces man to a savage, a criminal, and a ruffian. Yet I cannot say that the moral is very impressively driven home, and the escape of John Silver scot-free, after all his hideous crimes, seems a notable defeat of earthly justice. Yet his escape seems to me truer to life and art than his condign punishment would have been. It is these supreme rascals that sometimes seem finally to dodge the punishment that seems so surely to befall lesser criminals. A man of his adroitness could play the rôle of respectability and innocence to perfection, and might well die in the odour of sanctity, and face death and judgment with the same effrontery with which he confronted danger and perpetrated crime in his life. One asks oneself, what could God Himself make of such an indomitably bad soul; and one even fancies the devil regarding him askance and fearing to be juggled out of his bad pre-eminence. (pp. 107-09)

If some fairy or genius were to offer one the opportunity of appropriating any one work published during this last generation, merely with the view of being remembered a century hence, I am not sure that I would not choose **"Treasure Island."** There are many things, as an artist and man of letters, I would be prouder of having written, but, if it were a question of mere literary survival, I would as soon risk myself in this bark on the rapids of Time as in any other. It is not a perfect book, and yet it has a curious fascination. . . . Whether we can analyse it or no, there must be some peculiar magnetism about a book of adventure which grown men and even women can read again and again. I re-read lately, after a long interval, the greatest classic, except the "Odyssey," of all books of adventure, the original of a thousand imitations here and on the Continent, especially in Germany, "Robinson Crusoe." One saw clearly the merits of Defoe's achievement, the pre-Raphaelite detail of treatment, so convincing to the reader, and so useful to Swift in rendering credible and interesting his more fanciful "Gulliver's Travels." But Crusoe himself—and this is no doubt one cause of the continued acceptance this wonderful book meets with—is hopelessly commonplace, what we now call "the man in the street." What a deaf-mute is he, for instance, regarding natural beauty!—early eighteenth century at its worst; the whole colour of the story is grey as a Platinotype photograph. In **"Treasure Island"** we are in a world glowing with colour, rich in romantic *chiaroscuro*. Yet the book has no pretence to originality, is professedly a *rechauffé* of a number of its predecessors, but it has a combination of attractions which few of its predecessors had achieved. True enduring originality consists, not in doing what no one has ever done before, but in doing what many have attempted, in a better way. "Hamlet," "Faust," "Paradise Lost," and "The Fairy Queen," are the aloe-flowers crowning a series of previous efforts. So in its way is **"Treasure Island."** It will be a strange, dull, bloodless, if highly superior, generation that ceases to find interest and pleasure in **"Treasure Island"**! (pp. 229-30)

> *H. Bellyse Baildon, in his* Robert Louis Stevenson: A Life Study in Criticism, *A. Wessels Company, 1901, 244 p.*

LAFCADIO HEARN

[The following excerpt is taken from a collection of Hearn's lectures delivered from September 1900 to March 1903.]

It is not surprising that such a man [as Stevenson] should have produced the best boys' book of adventure ever written, **"Treasure Island."** Certainly the mere story here would not give the book the unequalled merit which it has. The plan of the story reminds us a little of various tales by Washington Irving. But not even Irving could have written with such wonderful style and realistic colour. You read Irving or Maryatt, and remember the story—that is all. But when you read Stevenson you remember the very words: sentences and paragraphs remain in imagination as if they had been burnt into it. That is what the difference of style means. For example, as I speak to you, there comes immediately to memory Stevenson's description of the cunning look of the one-legged conspirator whose eye glittered under his half-closed lids "like a clump of glass." Hundreds of expressions like this, conveying exactly the impression of a picture, can not be forgotten. (pp. 788-89)

> *Lafcadio Hearn, "Victorian Fiction," in his* A History of English Literature in a Series of Lectures, *Vol. II, edited by R. Tanabe and T. Ochiai, The Hokuseido Press, 1927, pp. 735-809.**

RICHARD MIDDLETON

What was it in **"Treasure Island"** that the readers of *Young Folks* did not like? If we could find a satisfactory answer to the question we should be nearer to an understanding of juvenile standards of criticism. Offhand, though we should not have thought of bracketing it with "Tom Sawyer" and the "Iliad," like Mr. Andrew Lang, we should have said that **"Treasure Island"** was the best boys' book that had ever been written. Pirates, treasure, a desert island, some good fighting and a boy hero are the elements that we should seek in a model work of that description; and though we do not credit the young with any taste for style, they should surely appreciate the romantic spirit and unfailing energy with which Stevenson's tale is told. He avoided, too, the heavy-handed morality that proved the undoing of Dean Farrar, and even, from a boy's point of view, of Thomas Hughes. Virtue triumphs, but so, to a minor extent, does the principal villain—that very finished ruffian John Silver. . . . An omission in the story that the author lamented would not probably occur to the mind of a boy. "The trouble is," he wrote, "to work it off without oaths. Buccaneers without oaths—bricks without straw. But youth and the fond parent have to be consulted." Another omission, that of female characters, was in joyful obedience to the wishes of the boy on whom he tried the earlier chapters, and here he was undoubtedly right. Yet the readers of *Young Folks*, those bizarre and nameless critics, refused to hear the charmer's voice till he changed his pipe and gave them the **"Black Arrow."**

Boys are ineloquent critics, and this heightens the difficulty of understanding their literary preferences; so that we are forced to fall back on theory to account for the failure of **"Treasure Island"** in serial form. Perhaps the most notable difference between that and the average book for boys lies in the fact that Stevenson's characterization is more than skin deep. His hero, Jim Hawkins, is a real boy, and not one of the super-boys who lead armies and drive motor-cars across the pages of most boys' books. Admitting that Jim does heroic things, it is nevertheless true that Stevenson has robbed him of the normal heroic glamour. The grown-ups in the book do not turn to him for orders or acclaim him as a genius. We are made to feel, indeed we are told—that his splendid achievements are due to luck rather than judgment, and he emerges from his adventures without a halo. Now, doubtless, this study of a boy is faithful in terms of life, but this is not the kind of part that a boy would choose to play in his dreams. In the imaginary world of youth a boy triumphs over difficulties by superior skill and intellect, and not by luck, and his triumph is immediately recognized by old and young alike. Instead of adding a new kingdom to this world, "Treasure Island" is a shrewd blow at this fundamental law. It suggests that it is possible for a boy hero to be thoughtless and even foolish, and is a manifest denial of the truth that a boy can do no wrong in the world of adventure.

Again, though the adult mind finds John Silver a convincing and sufficient villain, it may be doubted whether he is acceptable to the young as a type of pirate captain. He is smooth-tongued and hypocritical, and he achieved by guile the ends that a proper pirate captain would have attained by force. It is a pity, for it cannot be denied that his ferocity is genuine when he doffs his ignoble mask. Flint or William Bones must have played the part with a better grace; in fact, from all we learn of Flint he must have been a model pirate, and all the lesser ruffians of "Treasure Island" fall to talking of him when they want to make our flesh creep. Their villainy is merely the shadow of Flint's, and tender youth, with a mind tuned for deeds of violence, may well imagine that the book begins too late. "Treasure Island" is well enough, but where is the tale of Flint's adventures? That is the book that a healthy-minded, blood-thirsty boy would wish to read.

Doubtless in humanizing his characters, in making his boy-hero a mere lifelike boy, in sketching his pirates as the cowardly, clumsy ruffians they were in real life, Stevenson was at variance with juvenile conceptions of adventure; and yet the story is so good that the coldness of those early readers remains a mystery. (pp. 250-51)

> *Richard Middleton, "'Treasure Island' as a Book for Boys," in* The Living Age, *Vol. 271, No. 3511, October 21, 1911, pp. 249-51.*

FRANK SWINNERTON

[*Swinnerton was an English novelist and critic whose* R. L. Stevenson: A Critical Study *is recognized as perhaps the best and most controversial twentieth-century criticism on Stevenson. Rating him as "a writer of the second class," Swinnerton charges that Stevenson's romances are merely a series of picturesque and exciting incidents that lack unifying themes or realistic characters. After the book's publication in 1914, fewer critics defined Stevenson as a major writer. Although Swinnerton says, "If (Romance as an art) is dead, Stevenson killed it," he does approve of* Treasure Island, *as the following excerpt indicates.*]

By Stevenson's own account [see excerpt above in Author's Commentary] the first fifteen chapters of *Treasure Island* were written in as many days. He explains that he consciously and intentionally adopted an "easy" style. "I liked the tale myself," he says; "it was my kind of picturesque." Well, it was the simplest kind of picturesque, a sort of real enjoyment of the thing for its own sake; and our own enjoyment of it is of the same kind. It is extraordinarily superior to the imitations which have followed it, for this reason if for no other, that it was the product of an enjoying imagination. It is possible to read *Treasure Island* over and over again, because it is good fun. There is a constant flow of checkered incident, there is enough simple character to stand the treasure-seekers on their legs, and the book is a book in its own right. It does not need defence or analysis; it sustains its own note, and it is as natural and jolly an adventure story as one could wish. Moreover, the observation throughout is exceedingly good, as well as unaffected. It is interesting to notice how vividly one catches a picture from such a brief passage as this (in Chap. XXVII):

> As the water settled I could see him lying huddled together on the clean, bright sand in the

shadow of the vessel's sides. A fish or two whipped past his body.

Or again, on the following page, when Jim Hawkins has thrown overboard another of the mutineers:

> He went in with a sounding plunge; the red cap came off, and remained floating on the surface; and as soon as the splash subsided I could see him and Israel lying side by side, both wavering with the tremulous movement of the water.

Such slight passages really indicate an unusual quality in the book. They convey a distinct impression of the scene which one may feel trembling within one's own vision and hearing. The fact that *Treasure Island* has so clear a manner, unaffectedly setting out in simple terms incidents which have the bare convincingness of real romance, gives that book a singular position among the romances of Stevenson. The further fact that the incidents have some more coherence in themselves than incidents have in some of our author's romances serves to add to the book's effect. Something of this coherence (I except from the range of this term the doctor's sudden irruption into authorship, and the picturesque but arbitrary introduction of the castaway) may have resulted from the quickness with which the tale was written. (pp. 149-51)

> *Frank Swinnerton, in his* R. L. Stevenson: A Critical Study, *revised edition, George H. Doran Company, 1923, 195 p.*

J. E. G. de MONTMORENCY

Stevenson has given us in John Silver a figure of romance possibly unequalled in its subtlety by any creator since Shakespeare and Webster. A wonderful creature is John Silver. . . . Ask any boy if Silver is wholly bad and he will instantly answer "No," and the boy is right. Jim in the story saw through him and loved him. Yet Silver from one point of view is a monster and a ruthless murderer, from another he is a self-seeker and disloyal to his own men, and he is undoubtedly afraid not of death on the field or on the sea, but of death in Execution Dock. He is almost as bad as David, that great Romantic Semitic figure. Yet, like David, he is a figure that no one will hear a word against. Why? Because he is, in a sense, the incarnation of Romance. He has a great brain and a greater personality. He is capable of service in the largest degree and willing service in any field. He is perfectly efficient. On the other hand, he is as great a commander as he is a servant. There is no pettiness in him. He looks far ahead and sees something that no one else sees. He has self-control, and yet he is a king of Romance. He can be generous, he can be just, he is always wise even in his crimes, but above all, he sees visions, and dreams dreams at the very time that he flings aside superstitions and fears. That there have been such men, and that they have won the hearts of men there can be no doubt, and they are the products of Romance, of that hunger for the unknown, which is above all treasure and constitutes in itself a hope and a splendour. (pp. 526-27)

> *J. E. G. de Montmorency, "Romance," in* Contemporary Review, *Vol. CXXIII, No. 187, April, 1923, pp. 525-527.**

LEONARD WOOLF

Stevenson was quite a good imitator of great writers, but he was not a great writer or artist himself. His ear for verbal music was not fine, and his phrases are rather laboured. He is, indeed, at his best where he is sufficiently interested in his subject to

"The Late Miss McGregor's cottage" in Braemar, Scotland, where Stevenson wrote the majority of Treasure Island *in August-September, 1881.*

forget about his style. He can then write good, plain, honest English which makes no pretensions to be great literature. This is the case in *Treasure Island* and in some of his other stories. I must have read *Treasure Island* many times, but, when I read it again . . . , it still carried me along with it, and was thoroughly entertaining. It is preeminently a day-dream type of story, and Stevenson always remained a typical day-dream writer. He appeals to the child or to the primitively childish in grown men and women. There is nothing against him in that; a good story is rare, and personally I hope that I shall never grow too old to enjoy one. *Treasure Island, Kidnapped, The Master of Ballantrae* are all good stories, and the more Stevenson forgets himself and his style in them and becomes absorbed in telling the tale, the better they are. (pp. 42-3)

> *Leonard Woolf, "The Fall of Stevenson," in his* Essays on Literature, History, Politics, Etc., *L. and Virginia Woolf, 1927, pp. 39-43.*

JAMES O'DONNELL BENNETT

It all started with a fanciful map and it ended in a fame that bids fair to last as long as any of the glories which literature has bestowed upon her children since that time Homer sat down in the agora to tell a good story of perilous ventures by land and sea. (p. 15)

[From] a map drawn to while a rainy hour away, and from a boy's hectoring, sprang a tale that for nearly half a century has put crimson spots into the cheeks of succeeding decades of

boys and made their eyes shine, and put fiber into their fancy. Like this:

> I began to be horribly frightened, but I kept my
> head, for all that.

Young James Hawkins, in a dreadful plight surely . . . , said that. All right, let us be like young Hawkins, who was the second boy involved in the affair of **"Treasure Island."** Let us keep our heads. That is the moral of Stevenson's best seller. (p. 16)

[Mr. Richard Le Gallienne] tells in one of his books—very precise and proper-like—how he "ventured to regret that Mr. Stevenson should continue . . . to squander his great gifts upon the British boy, who cares as much about style as a pig about asparagus."

Don't we, though! British or native, mates, I'll tell 'e we do care about style, and sense it relishingly, too, even though we could not define the difference between style and asparagus. It is this very style of **"Treasure Island"** that has kept it glowing in the hearts of nearly fifty years of boys and boys of more than fifty years—aye, of sixty, and more. (pp. 17-18)

A thousand tales as dashingly conceived as **"Treasure Island"** long since have gone to Davy Jones' locker for the lack of the sinewy, marrowy (one of Stevenson's pet words), swift-moving, simple yet boldly colored and nervously atmospheric style of **"Treasure Island."** Nervously atmospheric, you might say, means naught. What I mean is that, when Stevenson wanted it to, his style shimmered like the heat-waves over the island or glistered like slipping heaps of coin.... (p. 18)

To prevent that treasure from coming into the possession of men who are legitimately and gallantly seeking it is the aim of John Silver, the one-legged sea cook with the heart of Lucifer and the tongue of a Billingsgate fishmonger. Silver's Billingsgate possesses these elements of originality and genius: It is Billingsgate without a profane or filthy word in it....

It has been remarked by many who have made particular examination of **"Treasure Island"** that, unfolding though it does the violent adventures of many violent men, it contains not one oath, and yet its vituperation is blistering. The fact is worth noting for the lesson it conveys. The lesson is that the true artist can without the sacrifice of power observe a decent reticence in all things—the true artist. (p. 19)

> *James O'Donnell Bennett, "Stevenson's 'Treasure Island'," in his* Much Loved Books: Best Sellers of the Ages, *Boni and Liveright, Publishers, 1927, pp. 15-22.*

G. K. CHESTERTON

Treasure Island was written as a boy's book; perhaps it is not always read as a boy's book. I sometimes fancy that a real boy could read it better if he could read it backwards. The end, which is full of skeletons and ancient crime, is in the fullest sense beautiful; it is even idealistic. For it is the realisation of an ideal, that which is promised in its provocative and beckoning map; a vision not only of white skeletons but also green palm trees and sapphire seas. But the beginning of the book, considered as a boy's book, can hardly be called idealistic; and is found in practice to be rather too realistic. I may make an egotistical confession here, which I think is not unique and not without its universal inference about the spirit of youth. When I read the book as a child, I was not horrified by what are called the horrors. Something did indeed shock me, just a little more than a child should be shocked; for of course he would have no fun if he were never shocked at all. But what shook me was not the dead man's chest or the live man's crimes or the information that "Drink and the devil have done for the rest"; all that seemed to me quite cheery and comforting. What did seem to me ugly was exactly what might happen in any inn-parlour, if there were no pirates in the world. It was that business about apoplexy; or some sort of alcoholic poisoning. It was the sailor having a mysterious thing called a stroke; so much more terrifying than any sabre-stroke. I was ready to wade in seas of gore; for all that gore was crimson lake; and indeed I always imagined it as a lake of crimson. Exactly what I was not ready for were those few drops of blood drawn from the arm of the insensible sailor, when he was bled by the surgeon. That blood is not crimson lake. Thus we have the paradox that I was horrified by the act of healing; while all the rowdy business of hitting and hurting did not hurt me at all. I was disgusted with an act of mercy, because it took the form of medicine. I will not pause to draw the many morals of this paradox; especially in relation to a common fallacy of pacifism. I will content myself with saying, whether I make my meaning clear or not, that a child is not wicked enough to disapprove of war.

But whatever be the case with most boys, there was certainly one boy who enjoyed *Treasure Island;* and his name was Robert Louis Stevenson. He really had very much of the feeling of one who had got away to great waters and outlandish lands; perhaps even more vividly than he had it later, when he made

that voyage not metaphorically but materially, and found his own Treasure Island in the South Seas. But just as in the second case he was fleeing to clear skies from unhealthy climates, so he was in reviving the adventure story escaping from an exceedingly unhealthy climate. The microbe of morbidity may have been within him, as well as the germ of phthisis; but in the cities he had left behind pessimism was raging like a pestilence. Multitudes of pale-faced poets, formless and forgotten, sat crowded at those café tables like ghosts in Hades, worshipping "la sorcière glauque," like that one of them whose mortality has been immortalised by Max [Beerbohm]. It is too often forgotten that if Stevenson had really been only a pale young man making wax flowers, he would have found plenty of pale young men to make them with him; and the flowers and flower-makers would long have withered together. But he alone escaped, as from a city of the dead; he cut the painter as Jim Hawkins stole the boat, and went on his own voyage, following the sun. Drink and the devil have done for the rest, especially the devil; but then they were drinking absinthe and not with a "Yo ho ho"; consuming it without the most feeble attempt at any "Yo ho ho"—a defect which was, of course, the most serious and important part of the affair. For "Yo ho ho" was precisely what Stevenson, with his exact choice of words, particularly desired to say just then. It was for the present his most articulate message to mankind. (pp. 84-7)

> *G. K. Chesterton, in his* Robert Louis Stevenson, *Dodd, Mead & Company, 1928, 211 p.*

F. J. HARVEY DARTON

[The following excerpt is taken from an essay that appeared in the original edition of Children's Books in England *published in 1932.]*

In 1868 [when Charles Dickens's *Holiday Romance* appeared in serial form], though it might not be suspected from what was supplied to them by austere adults, children really did know a good deal about piracy and bloodshed—on paper. Dickens's William Tinkling, Esq., aged eight, and Lieut.-Col. Robin Redforth, aged nine, might very well have been regular subscribers to *The Boys of England* ..., so easy was the nonchalance of their desperate conduct. What is more, a still greater authority on frightfulness was about that very time engaged in his earliest investigations. James Barrie, in the preface to the first book-form edition of the play of *Peter Pan* (1928), has confessed that as a boy he was terribly addicted to 'penny dreadfuls'. (p. 294)

Lawless adventure was the feat that haunted the advocates of manliness. As Satan was sometimes considered the hero of *Paradise Lost,* so the Pirate King might almost be given a romantic halo. If the manly and righteous hero were too tame, the author would be accused of writing a disguised sermon. If, on the other hand, excitement was achieved by a heightening or empurpling of the literary style, the charge of sensationalism would be preferred. 'Adult' romance itself was even then beginning to be thought a little too heavy in manner. It was therefore a new and joyful experience for readers to find real literature concerning itself with reckless ferocity, as happened when *Treasure Island* in 1882 and *King Solomon's Mines* in 1885 carried both fathers and sons clean away and stirred their blood without any qualms.

One of the books was an historical throw-back, the other a product of then modern exploration. But in essence they were alike, in that, as books read by boys, they were different from anything that had been composed before, and different, at that, in the way in which they rekindled genuine romance. They did not furbish lumber. They caught the sudden freshness which is the very heart of an adventure-story in a way previously unknown, except perhaps in that one brief moment when Friday's footmark startled Crusoe and all readers of his story. Here, in Treasure Island and Kukuanaland, was surprise upon surprise, each one sudden, but each one also natural, capable of rational and brave explanation when you knew all the facts.

The publication of *Treasure Island* is a matter of historical as well as personal importance. For one thing, it made Stevenson's reputation. In terms of the market, 'I was thirty-one; I was the head of a family; I had lost my health; I had never yet paid my way, never yet made two hundred pounds a year.' In terms of moral strength to the writer, it meant that though he circumscribed his art within a style ostensibly suited to Jim Hawkins, he thoroughly enjoyed being himself over a tale which made him a boy again.

He had always been a boy at heart. He had adored Mayne Reid, Fenimore Cooper, Jules Verne and Marryat, and had had a passion for maps. He knew now that other grown men wanted to remain young. He read his manuscript in the early stages to his father and his twelve-year-old stepson Lloyd Osbourne, and made the discovery that 'it seemed to me original as sin; it seemed to belong to me like my right eye. I had counted on one boy, I found I had two in my audience. My father caught fire at once.' That was the real secret: not that boys delighted in tales meant for men, like *Robinson Crusoe* and *Midshipman Easy*, but that men—Victorian men—were eager for tales meant for boys, like *Treasure Island.*

So far as the younger half of Stevenson's audience was concerned, there was everything in the story which romantic boy-hood ought to expect: buried treasure, pirates, strange noises, seafaring, a resourceful but quite fallible young hero, and a 'smooth and formidable' villain who has passed into the gallery of immortals. On the other hand, there was also nearly everything which most boys even then were guarded against: plenty of blood, plenty of rum, and that grim song, 'Fifteen men on the dead man's chest'. It was the very apotheosis of the 'penny dreadful' which the virtuous and healthy magazines had been founded to dethrone. Not even the heroic shrill splendour of the boy Jim's defiance: 'the laugh's on my side; I've had the top of this business from the first; I no more fear you than I fear a fly. Kill me, if you please, or spare me'; not even that courageous grasp of morality could hide the fact that the expedition was launched by greed and decorated with murder and treachery, and concluded by luck rather than righteousness. (pp. 294-95)

[Both Stevenson and Rider Haggard] employed the trick of emphasis on one or two abnormal characters. That was not a modern invention, though it has become a common modern practice. But it was powerfully used. Long John Silver, Pew the horrible blind beggar, Ben Gunn, Israel Hands, the three English diamond-seekers, Gagool, and (according to the reader's fancy) Umbopa or Twala, all stand out independently complete, without special aid from the plot of the stories. . . . Stevenson and Haggard both realized consciously or unconsciously, the need of something more than adventure undertaken in an atmosphere of 'manliness'. The events must be swift and stirring, but that is not enough. The persons must be such as the reader, young or old, would either earnestly desire or earnestly hate to be himself, or else (like Capt. Good, R.N., or Ben Gunn) companionably eccentric. They must *not* be tailors' models of good and bad male bipeds. They must have marked idio-syncrasies. But equally they must not be grotesques, suddenly triumphant or cast down with no reason given but their exceptional physique or intellect or vileness. They must in short be probable impossibilities—a necessity of romance as well as of Aristotelean tragedy.

That was an entirely new note in fiction for the young, just as was the deliberate fusion of father and son into one reader. The scenes and properties of the two stories were not new. Stevenson admits his theft of the parrot, for instance, from Defoe. . . . Neither pirate treasure nor Ophir was a novelty in history, let alone romance, nor was the desire for them a Victorian inspiration. But it was a fresh thing to have them treated with so careless a rapture. There is a certain difference in the raptures themselves. Stevenson appealed to a past which had in his day only a literary reality. There were no buccaneers left in 1882, and, though he could easily have invented a treasure-hunt for that very year, his bent lay otherwise, and he preferred the revival of the past. But Haggard was dealing with something like a genuine possibility: indeed, it is a history lesson in itself to realize that the districts of Solomon's Mines and of Milosis (beyond Kenya; in *Allan Quatermain*) were sufficiently unexplored in 1885 for his stories to be wholly plausible. He gave English boys a better idea of the potential wonders of the Empire than could be had from any school-task. Stevenson, in a way, did the same kind of service in colouring history, but it had been performed more often and more laboriously before. (pp. 296-97)

Not every adventure-novelist can invent a Jim Hawkins (much less a John Silver) or an Allan Quatermain. And if the hero is not to become a twopence-coloured Jack Harkaway (the 'blood and thunder' hero invented by Bracebridge Hemyng, and appearing in *Boys of England* from 1871 onward), he is apt to be colourless—a mere peg for events. He too often had no imagination or temperament of his own, and was only a type, conducting himself fearlessly, resourcefully and modestly in moments of great practical danger—which were the true point of the stories. In England, of course, he was emphatically British, in the United States as emphatically American. The hero was the plain boy, who dislikes singularity, and eventually becomes a bore.

That was his ultimate fate from the creative point of view, so to speak. He passed into currency and had face-value; and the money so minted was very plentiful, until a new standard had to be set up: until the grown-up novel ousted the boys' book. *Treasure Island* and *King Solomon's Mines* were the first signs of that change, but they were also, at the moment of their first appearance, the very stimulus which the boys' book proper needed. They made it grow up into greater maturity, but in doing so gave it also the chance of growing clean out of boy-hood. To put it contrariwise, they increased the youthward frontier of the novelist's kingdom. (p. 300)

F. J. Harvey Darton, "The Eighties and Today: Freedom," in his Children's Books in England: Five Centuries of Social Life, *revised edition, edited by Brian Alderson, Cambridge University Press, 1982, pp. 293-315.**

STEPHEN GWYNN

[*Treasure Island*] is first and foremost that very rare thing, a really good piece of narrative fiction—not of the highest kind by any means, for that deals with passions that have a certain nobility; and the most to be said for pirates is that their proceedings have a certain picturesqueness. But since, beyond doubt, pirates existed, a story of pirate adventure is a fair subject for art, provided that over and above the merely exciting elements it shows us human nature. Stevenson so compounded his tale that the lawless desperadoes should be seen in company and in conflict with valiant and honourable men; but the success of his work lay in the inspiration which made him conceive as the leader of the pirate gang a man of such ability that he could, when it suited his purpose, become a decent, orderly citizen, prudent in his affairs. It is a boys' book certainly; when women are left out, problems of conduct are greatly simplified; but any boy who reads it will learn, knowingly or not, a deal about the mastery of men. It is a boys' book, but in a tissue of highly coloured invention the whole action is determined by characters. Jim Hawkins is throughout an instrument of lucky chance; he never controls the situation. The things that he does are done on a boyish impulse, though he does them courageously and competently, and by doing them gains valuable information for the chiefs of the expedition. But at one point, after his vagrant activities appear to have been crowned with triumph, he blunders into the hands of the pirates and is only saved because John Silver, the pirate leader, recognising that the game is lost, sees a chance to make terms for himself by saving the boy. That scene in which Silver, by a mixture of cunning and audacity, establishes his authority over angry ruffians who want to wring the boy's neck for thwarting their plans is really the centre of the book. What follows rises in key, as it should in a tale of violence, up to the final discharge of weapons over the rifled hiding-place; but . . . the real hero of the book is John Silver, and it is in that conflict of wills that Silver saves the life of Jim Hawkins and his own. (pp. 98-9)

[John Silver's killing of one of the crew who had not belonged to the pirate ship] has never in fifty years gone out of my mind. Most of the story had slipped from my memory; but not the blind man's evil presence, nor his death under the trampling feet of horses; still less the swift terrible action of the crippled man who hurls his crutch like a spear at the retreating sailor, catching him full in the back, and then with a one-legged leap is on the body and drives a knife home again and again. Nothing could be better imagined to convey the formidable nature of this treacherous ruffian who can make his very disability at once a trap and an engine to slay.

Certainly this is not the highest kind of imagination, but it is powerful as a Daumier picture; we see and we hear the pant that accompanies the murderer's leap and the stab. The same quality lasts through the story; Stevenson lived the adventure, and wherever it took him, a map of the country was present to his mind. Almost without exception, too, he preserves the key of his style, avoiding words or turns of thought which are not dramatically appropriate to an intelligent boy. An exception comes as the story approaches its climax, when Jim Hawkins, towed on a rope by Silver, accompanies the mutineers on their way to the cache—to which they have now the map for a guide. A "Tall Tree" is the final indication, and as they scramble over wooded hills, at last one huge pine towers above all: "a giant of a vegetable, with a red column as big as a cottage, and a wide shadow around it in which a company could have manoeuvred". Now "giant of a vegetable" is the expression of a trained seeker after words that shall give a shock of surprise; this is the author of *Virginibus Puerisque* speaking, and not Jim Hawkins; and alliteration tempted him to "column" instead of trunk because he wanted to say that a company could have manoeuvred in the shadow. Stevenson had become so excited by his own narrative that he forgot Jim Hawkins for the moment and wrote as he might have written to Gosse or

any sympathetic man of letters. For indeed just here there is more than a boy's mind in the observation of Silver, made drunk for a moment in spite of his wariness by the possible presence of some huge mass of gold. Still it would be tedious to insist on exact verisimilitude; and an intelligent boy might have noticed, as Hawkins does, Silver's instant rallying of his faculties when he and the others stand before an already ransacked pit. In the surprise of the ambush that follows, he alone is braced for action, and it comes characteristically when he fires his pistol into the body of one fellow who had attempted revolt against his rule. There is a touch of genuine irony too when he recognises the real agent of his defeat—Ben Gunn, the half-imbecile seaman whom other pirates had marooned on this island three years before: "Ah, Ben Gunn, to think as how you've done me!" (pp. 101-03)

[In] this piece of happy invention, conceived almost as a game, Stevenson utilises all his resources—all that he had read and all that he had observed. Much of it seems to be work of sheer fancy; but wherever fancy can be solidly buttressed up with fact, he props and pins the structure. Perhaps the secret of its success is that it was in the last resort a piece of play rather than a piece of work. He went at it as a good player goes into a game of Rugby football, with all his faculties jubilantly at stretch. (pp. 103-04)

> *Stephen Gwynn, in his* Robert Louis Stevenson, *Macmillan and Co., Limited, 1939, 267 p.*

KATE FRIEDLAENDER

[*Dr. Friedlaender's essay explores why children, particularly in the latency period, come to read books and stories of their own free will. In the following excerpt, she regards* Treasure Island *as an adventure story which helps boys resolve the Oedipus conflict. For a response to Friedlaender's essay, see the excerpt by A. C. Capey (1974).*]

[What] is, in the ordinary course of events, the psychic situation of children about the age of thirteen? Naturally, conflicts and phantasies are no longer the same as at the begining of latency. Under the pressure of physiological maturing, and, thereby, of the renewed flaring-up of sexual desires, conflicts which were repressed during latency, now receive fresh impetus. Whilst during the earlier stage of latency, the psychical task for children of either sex, from the viewpoint of psychic economy, is the same, that is to say, the repression of conflicts, the sublimation of instincts, and the building up of defence-mechanisms, with the approach of prepuberty and the attendant rekindling of the instinctual life, come once more to the fore. Latency, for the boy, follows the dissolution of the Oedipus complex, effected by means of the castration fear. The strong sexual strivings for the possession of the mother, and the aggressive tendencies against the father are in part repressed, in part sublimated, while they have undergone certain transformations through the workings of the defence-mechanisms. The remainder of the old instinctual situation, however it may have shaped itself, becomes freshly imbued with energy in prepuberty. In the phantasies, which now emerge, one can recognize in what way the Oedipus complex has been dealt with.

"Treasure Island" stands for the typical adventure story whose phantasies suggest a possible denouement of the Oedipus conflict, or rather be it said, whose phantasies answer to a definite phase in the dissolution of the Oedipus complex. The boy, who is about fifteen, leaves his mother to be taken on by a party of men in their hunt for treasure. Owing to good luck, bravery, disobedience to orders, no matter what, he learns of the treasure's whereabouts, discovers the conspiracy among the pirates, comes repeatedly to the rescue of his fellows, and outwits the most dreaded of the pirates. He saves his own life by intimidating the pirate ringleader—this slip of a boy—with the news of how he, the youngest of them all, has been the one, right from the start, to see through and to foil his plottings. The boy, in these ways, measures his strength with his father's, the father image being represented by various good and bad characters in the story, and so becomes acknowledged by all as a rival on an equal footing. This phantasy overshadows everything else, the original cause of the rivalry, the competition for the mother, getting altogether pushed into the background. The homosexual attitude to the father which constitutes a significant phase in the dissolution of the Oedipus complex, seems to be the unconscious content of many adventure stories. (pp. 139-40)

> Kate Friedlaender, "Children's Books and Their Function in Latency and Prepuberty," in American Imago, Vol. 3, Nos. 1 & 2, April, 1942, pp. 129-50.*

DAVID DAICHES

[*An English-born Scottish critic and educator, Daiches is considered a pioneer in reassessing Stevenson's life and career following the relative critical neglect caused by Frank Swinnerton's* R. L. Stevenson: A Critical Study. *Daiches's* Robert Louis Stevenson *(1947) and* Stevenson and the Art of Fiction *(1951) along with J. C. Furnas's* Voyage to Windward *(see excerpt dated 1951) are credited with sparking a renewed interest in and a more positive critical approach to Stevenson.*]

It was perhaps natural that [Stevenson] . . . should, at least in his prose, abandon the autobiographical and semi-autobiographical kinds of writing which had hitherto constituted his principal work and turn to the pure adventure story. He was no longer quite so preoccupied with himself; he had established a happy *modus vivendi* with both his parents and his wife, and his imagination could roam more freely as a result. In finishing his stepson's map and romantically labelling it "Treasure Island" he entered on his second stage as a writer: up till now he had been primarily an essayist and bellelettrist, but from now on his principal task was to be the writing of adventure stories.

First the map and then the story: the procedure was appropriate enough. In a story of this kind you start with the romantic idea and then proceed to embody it in a suitable narrative. "Treasure Island" was the title of the map long before it was the title of the story. . . . If "Treasure Island" existed, it existed obviously as an object of desire, picturesque, remote, and shrouded in mystery. The story must, therefore, be cast in one of the oldest of all narrative moulds—the quest.

This basic pattern—the quest for something desirable—can be used in a great variety of ways. The object of the quest may be of itself something of such transcendent importance that it sheds its light, as it were, continuously over the whole narrative, and every episode takes on its appropriate meaning only in the light of the meaning of the object sought. Or the thing sought may be in itself of no importance whatsoever, introduced only as an excuse for the narration of the adventures which accompany its search. Between these two extremes an infinite number of gradations are possible. Ulysses sought his home, Jason sought the Golden Fleece, King Arthur's knights sought the Holy Grail, and innumerable adventurers of fact and fiction have sought simply hidden treasure. The difference between this basic pattern of the quest as used in the epic or other "serious" type of fiction and as used in the pure adven-

ture story such as *Treasure Island* is just that in the former the object of the quest is itself something of supreme importance, whose possession will wholly change the life of the possessor and whose nature determines both the character and the behaviour of the searchers. In the pure adventure story, however, the thing sought has no such influence over the story as a whole. The treasure of *Treasure Island* does not attract only pirates or swaggering adventurers; it attracts both good men and bad, pirates, honest sailors, a doctor, a squire, and a respectable youngster. The treasure is neither good nor evil; it is in itself, in fact, of no importance whatsoever. It serves only as an excuse for the story, as a supreme motivation. Its final attainment comes as something of an anti-climax—part of it (the bar silver) is even deliberately left behind. And as for the disposal of the treasure, the matter is dismissed by the author in a sentence: "All of us had ample share of the treasure, and used it wisely or foolishly according to our natures."

It is essential to a story of this kind—a boy's story, told with a constant eye on a boy's imagination and desires—that the reader have from the beginning the assurance that in spite of all the breath-taking chances and hair-breadth escapes things are going to turn out all right for the hero and his friends. There must, of course, be an element of risk—the greater the better—but the main problem must always be *how* the hero escapes, not *whether* he escapes. If his ultimate success is known in advance, no danger can be too terrific, no threat too sinister. But that ultimate success must be foreknown; for in a story of this kind the reader is meant to identify himself with the hero, and this cannot be done with assurance unless the possibility of the hero's failure and death is removed from the beginning.

Stevenson achieves this essential requirement of a boy's story very simply and effectively by the device of having the story told by the hero himself, in the first person. If the hero survived to tell the tale, then, whatever the perils he encountered, we can be sure that he escaped them. We can safely identify ourselves with him. (pp. 32-5)

[The first paragraph of *Treasure Island*] is a masterly opening. It fulfils simultaneously three separate functions: it makes clear that the hero and his party survived to tell the tale, thus confining the suspense within the limits necessary in a boy's adventure story; it strikes at once the note of romance and adventure by names such as "Squire Trelawney," "Treasure Island" and "Admiral Benbow," images like "the *brown* old seaman with the *sabre-cut*," and phrases like "there is still treasure not yet lifted"; and it sets the actual story going at once by narrating, in the concluding part of the sentence—". . . first took up his lodging under our roof"—the first of the series of incidents which constitute the story. The story is thus set going in the very first sentence, with the proper note struck and the proper anticipations aroused. (pp. 35-6)

Stevenson's choice of images in the opening paragraphs of *Treasure Island* is worth noting. After the opening sentence, with its immediate introduction of the "brown old seaman," the story proceeds:

> I remember him as if it were yesterday, as he came plodding to the inn door, his sea-chest following behind him in a hand-barrow; a tall, strong, heavy, nut-brown man; his tarry pigtail falling over the shoulders of his soiled blue coat; his hands ragged and scarred, with black, broken nails; and the sabre-cut across one cheek,

a dirty, livid white. I remember him looking round the cove and whistling to himself as he did so, and then breaking out in that old sea-song that he sang so often afterwards:—

> "Fifteen men on the dead man's chest—
> Yo-ho-ho, and a bottle of rum!"

in the high, old tottering voice that seemed to have been tuned and broken at the capstan bars. . . .

Though the effects here are obvious . . . the technique is by no means unsubtle. The device of reminiscence is used to enhance the vividness of the images, and the images themselves are very carefully chosen, moving to a climax from "inn door," "sea-chest," "nut-brown," "tarry pigtail," "hands ragged and scarred," "sabre cut across one cheek," to the sinister words of the "old sea-song" which are to ring like a *leit-motiv* through the book. After these two lines of song the images die away to an intriguing suggestion of decay and secrecy:

> "This is a handy cove," says he, at length; "and a pleasant sittyated grog-shop.—Much company, mate?"

> My father told him no,—very little company, the more was the pity.

> "Well, then," said he, "this is the berth for me."

We are barely past the first page and the story is well under way—not so much in terms of actual incidents, though the first of these has been told, as of anticipation, suggestion and setting. It is as difficult to remove the attention from the book at this point as at any point later on. Many a writer of mystery stories could study with profit Stevenson's method of arresting the attention of the reader at the very beginning of the book. . . . (pp. 36-7)

Images suggestive of danger, suspicion, mystery and the picturesque having been presented to us right away, Stevenson proceeds to point out the contrast—so important to him as to so many of his predecessors in Scottish literature—between interior and exterior, between the warm inn parlour and the wind and waves outside. This gives the reader a sense of danger threatening from outside, and no sooner has this suggestion been conveyed than it is punched home with the reference to "the seafaring man with one leg" whom the sailor at the inn is half expecting with apprehension.

That contrast between interior and exterior is the only hint we are given of the difference between the normal life of the hero, Jim Hawkins, and his parents at the inn, and the new life which (though at first they do not know it) begins with the arrival of the sailor. We are told very little of the "Admiral Benbow" in normal times—that is, before the story opens. The only point that must be made is that Jim, a normal boy with nothing unusual in his background, is involved, first slowly and then precipitately, in a series of adventures in which he equips himself manfully in the midst of danger and excitement. An adventure story of this kind has little time for retrospect, for its whole effectiveness depends on its steadily gathering speed from the very first sentence, moving forward at an ever increasing pace until the climax is reached. There is another reason why it would not do to emphasize the normal routine of Jim Hawkins' life. The "Admiral Benbow," a picturesque eighteenth century inn situated in a lonely cove, is even without

the intrusion of suspicious seamen an object of romance and glamour in the nineteenth and twentieth centuries. It is one of those scenes, so dear to Stevenson, which call out for an appropriate adventure story. Life at the "Admiral Benbow" even in the quietest of times could therefore hardly be held up as the most effective foil to the adventurous life led by the hero after the story commences. The "Admiral Benbow" by its very existence adds the first note of color and adventure to the story. The contrast, therefore, between Jim's life after the arrival of the seaman and his previous life can only be made implicitly, by the sense of sudden intrusion with which the seaman's arrival is presented, and by the gradual fading out, throughout the rest of the early part of the book, of the domestic images (associated with Jim's parents) which might suggest normal life. Jim's father has to die so as to give Jim that combination of independence and responsibility without which he could not appropriately take a central part in a narrative of this kind: his mother can be put away in a less drastic manner, to take care of the inn until the hero comes home.

Bill Bones, the seaman who arrived at the "Admiral Benbow" in the first paragraph, not only provides the opening incident in the chain of events which leads to Treasure Island; he is also to foreshadow the subsequent events in a manner calculated to produce the right kind of suspense, and to arouse in the reader the emotions appropriate to a "pure" adventure story. He unites in his own person the past, present and future. His present dread of encountering "the seafaring man with one leg" is the result of his past association with Treasure Island and at the same time points forward to those future events which involve Jim and his friends in Bill Bones's past. As a technical device, Bill is a perfectly conceived character. It is he who makes the connection between the normal and the abnormal, the everyday and the picturesque, the humdrum and the adventurous, providing the bridge which enables Jim Hawkins (and therefore the reader) to cross with plausibility from the one to the other. And when Bill dies—which is not until he has brought adventure to the "Admiral Benbow" with a vengeance—his death both marks the end of the first movement of the story and motivates the second part. For it is Bill's death which enables Jim and his mother to acquire the map of Treasure Island.

Bill Bones's stay at the "Admiral Benbow" is thus a kind of overture to the story, anticipating the main themes that are to be fully brought forward later. He even produces in the good folk of the neighbourhood an emotion which is symbolic of the aim of every adventure story of this kind: "People were frightened at the time, but on looking back they rather liked it: it was a fine excitement in a quiet country life." This is one of the few suggestions of that contrast between the normal and the adventurous life which, as we have seen, is for the most part hinted at rather than directly expressed.

After Chapter I—which is not allowed to conclude without an appearance by Dr. Livesey, whose character is built up in an admirable little incident, thus foreshadowing another aspect of the future—the pace begins to quicken. With the arrival of Black Dog it is clear that the rush of events is beyond the hero's control (it is characteristic of the adventure story that the hero does not take control until a fairly late stage in the story: at first he is *swept* into the story, and only later is he able—since he is the hero—to establish a measure of control); and with the appearance of the blind and sinister Pew in Chapter III, with his tapping stick and "cruel, cold and ugly" voice, we know that there is no turning back for Jim Hawkins: he has been manoeuvred by chance right into the midst of a dangerous and complicated situation, and if he is to come out alive and with credit it is certainly by a different route from the one which brought him in. In the adventure story you enter purely by chance, but you get out in large measure as a result of your own contrivance.

The speed in Chapter III is terrific: we are swept along with all the emotions of suspense and excitement until Pew has handed Bill the "black spot" and Bill has responded by falling down dead, "struck . . . by thundering apoplexy." The story is rapidly moving clear of the limited environs of the "Admiral Benbow," and with Chapter IV danger and suspense ooze from every line: domestic images are now definitely finished with, and they are used only to suggest contrast—contrast between Jim's situation and the normal situation of other people:

> It was already candle light when I reached the hamlet, and I shall never forget how much I was cheered to see the yellow shine in doors and windows; but that, as it proved, was the best of the help we were likely to get in that quarter. For—you would have thought men would have been ashamed of themselves—no soul would consent to return with us to the "Admiral Benbow." The more we told of our troubles, the more—man, woman and child— they clung to the shelter of their houses. The name of Captain Flint, though it was strange to me, was well enough known to some there, and carried a great weight of terror. Some of the men who had been to field-work on the far side of the "Admiral Benbow" remembered, besides, to have seen several strangers on the road, and, taking them to be smugglers, to have bolted away; and one at least had seen a little lugger in what we called Kitt's Hole.

In this skilful passage Stevenson not only points the contrast between domestic images of warmth and security and the terror outside in which the hero is involved; he also succeeds in linking up the feeling of terror with the already ominous name of Captain Flint, and, with the vague report of the smugglers and the "little lugger," conveys the effective suggestion that these external and normally remote forces of piracy and evil are slowly but surely closing in on Jim Hawkins. The return to the inn and the searching of the dead sailor's body become, under these circumstances, acts of heroism or at least of courage, calculated to begin the transformation of Jim from a passive to an active character. This transformation, which is most important for the structure and pattern of the story, reaches its climax in Part V, where Jim slips away from his companions and for a while plays a lone hand. In Chapter XXVI Jim achieves his full stature as hero, and henceforth he need play no major part in the story.

Chapter V gives a preliminary skirmish between the forces of good and evil—presented rather as "our side" versus the others, in true adventure story style—which serves both to heighten the already excited atmosphere and to foreshadow the future. The aura of romance is deftly thrown over the incident to prevent it from appearing as a mere brawl:

> The window of the captain's room was thrown open with a slam and a jingle of broken glass; and a man leaned out into the moonlight, head

An undated letter by Stevenson to Dr. Alexander H. Japp, a Scottish author and journalist. The letter refers to the progress of the manuscript of Treasure Island *and the map that prompted the story.*

and shoulders, and addressed the blind beggar on the road below him.

Pew, the blind beggar, having served his purpose, is killed off, and in the following chapter Jim is brought together with Dr. Livesey and the Squire in order to provide the proper machinery for moving the story into the more picturesque environment of Treasure Island itself. The map of the island that had been found on the dead captain's body, the evidence that treasure is hidden there, the determination of the Squire to fit out a ship and find it, accompanied by the doctor and Jim, provide the means of gracefully leaving the first part of the story behind and moving out smoothly to greater adventures.

There is a final brief return to a domestic interior as the Squire, Dr. Livesey and Jim talk things over at the Hall, and this serves to emphasize once again the contrast between comfortable life at home and the adventurous life on which Jim and his friends are about to embark, so that the reader has no chance of missing the significance of the structural watershed that divides the dangerous quest for treasure from the comfortable activities of ordinary folk in England: "The servant led us down a matted passage, and showed us at the end into a great library, all lined with bookcases and busts upon the tops of them, where the squire and Dr. Livesey sat, pipe in hand, on either side of a bright fire.'' The fire and Dr. Livesey's pipe are characteristic Stevensonian symbols of the good life (domestic variety), just as lonely inns by the coast, ships, maps, and pirates are symbols of the good life (department of romantic adventure). (pp. 38-44)

In the scene at Bristol which follows, Stevenson cunningly puts the reader into the possession of significant information which is withheld from the chief characters—namely, knowledge of the real nature of the crew and of Long John Silver's true intentions. This is achieved quite simply by sketching in the character of the Squire as unsuspicious, boyish, and good-naturedly egotistical, and at the same time making use of Jim's youth and lack of knowledge of the world in letting him experience something which is revealing to the reader but not to Jim. In other words, in accordance with Stevenson's doctrine of the function of character drawing in a romance (as distinct from a dramatic novel or a novel of character), he gives his actors only as much individualization as will provide them with the necessary motives for key actions.

The fact that the reader now knows what neither Jim nor his friends know provides him with the necessary suspense to make the otherwise rather dull journey out of Bristol full of excitement. It is only when the voyage is almost over that Jim, hiding in the apple barrel, overhears the conversation of the pirates, and the truth about Long John Silver and his fellow adventurers is finally out. The hints that had been provided by Billy Bones and his adventures at the ''Admiral Benbow'' now take on, in retrospect, a new meaning; past and present are joined together to promise an exciting and dangerous future. In this game of balancing knowledge against ignorance Stevenson shows himself very adroit. First the reader and Long John Silver's gang know the truth, while Jim and his friends remain in ignorance; then Jim and his friends learn the truth about Silver's gang, but Silver and his gang do not know that Jim and his friends know. It is only very much later, when the action on the island is rapidly reaching its climax, that Jim in a fit of desperate bravado blurts out to the pirates the truth about his overhearing their conversation in the apple-barrel. This careful balancing of knowledge and ignorance greatly enriches the possibilities of suspense, and Stevenson makes good use of the opportunities he thus provides for himself.

The whole texture and atmosphere of the story changes once Treasure Island has been reached. No longer is the sense of adventure conveyed by the impinging of the picturesque and the unfamiliar on the familiar: everyday life has now been left altogether behind, and the story can now be told simply in terms of the rise and fall in the fortunes of either side. The arena has been cleared of all superfluous characters and scenery. We are told enough of the physical features of the island to provide an adequate setting for the drama that is being played out against it, and that is all the author now requires. Stevenson has used one of the favourite recipes of writers of adventure stories: he has set the protagonists alone on an uninhabited island. The recipe requires, however, that one new character be introduced on the island, some unexpected and unpredictable character who will be able to play a *deus ex machina* part in the plot if necessary. Such a character is Ben Gunn, who plays a minor yet decisive role in the story. His unknown history and unforeseeable actions prevent the story from degenerating into a mere conflict between good and bad characters of which the outcome can be calculated in advance.

In keeping Jim moving back and forth between the two groups—the Squire's group and Long John Silver's—Stevenson man-

ages to keep a bi-focal view on the action, as it were. It is important that the pirates are not considered altogether as villains, for they, after all, provide the principal romantic interest and in a boy's story are bound to be in some degree and in some sense sympathetic characters. Stevenson solves this problem in part by the character of Long John Silver, a cunning combination of charm, strength and black villainy (W. E. Henley without Henley's virtue, Stevenson asserted) and reinforces this solution by keeping Jim in closer touch with Long John than with the ''good'' party. What is at stake is thus not simply the finding of the treasure by Jim and his friends, nor even their successful escape from the pirates. A much more complicated pattern of suspense is set up, which, while leaving the issue of the physical safety of the hero in doubt long enough to get some excitement out of it (though, as we have seen, not absolutely in doubt, for we knew in advance that Jim, the Squire and Dr. Livesey have all come safely out of the adventure), at the same time poses the subtler problem of the fate and intentions of Long John.

The problem to be faced by any writer of a boys' adventure story of this kind is that, while the struggle has to be essentially between the good and the bad, the real romantic interest tends to lie with the bad. Picturesque villainy is naturally more appealing in such a context than everyday virtue, and the author's task is to enlist the sympathies of the reader at the same time on the side of virtue and of the picturesque. This can be done, as it has been done in recent American popular boys' fiction and films, by substituting the G-man for the gangster and insisting that to live virtuously is often to live picturesquely and dangerously at the same time, but it makes for a much richer narrative texture if the problem is faced by shading the gradations of virtue and vice from the completely unsympathetic villain (like Israel Hands) to the complete hero (like Dr. Livesey) and by keeping in the centre of the picture a character like Long John who, though villainous in intention, is often admirable in action. It becomes important, when such a technique is employed, to detach this half-way character from the side of evil, to which he originally belongs, and, by some development of the plot, to put him in a relation with the other side which none of his companions can achieve. Stevenson has managed all this very deftly, and the part played by Silver in the latter part of the book is sufficient to arouse the reader's admiration for certain aspects of his character unmixed with any approval of villainy as such. The non-committal end of Silver—neither full fortune, like Jim and his friends, nor full misfortune, like the other pirates—lays the final emphasis on his special function in the plot.

Jim's adventure with Israel Hands, and his final success in saving the *Hispaniola,* gives him sufficient stature to enable him to stand for the reader in a boy's adventure story—to serve, that is, as the character with which the reader identifies himself as he reads—without removing him too far into the realm of the heroic so that he ceases to be recognizable as an ordinary boy. His good fortune is due as much to luck as to skill. . . . Jim has courage and resourcefulness, but it is not these qualities alone that enable him to save himself and his friends. He has a kind of beginner's luck. There are several reasons why Stevenson should have deliberately kept Jim from achieving too impressive a heroic stature. The obvious one is that he is to stand for the boy reader and must not therefore move too far above such a reader's conceivable accomplishment. Another reason is that he must not compete in picturesque bravado with Long John Silver nor in calm adult competence with Dr. Livesey. He is the ordinary boy thrown into the midst of adventure by pure chance and acquitting himself very creditably. In the course of the story he develops from a purely passive character into an experienced and resourceful campaigner. This development takes place under the reader's eyes, and the reader can see it as natural and inevitable in the circumstances. With his outwitting of Israel Hands Jim achieves his full stature as a man of action, just as in his refusal to go back on his word and escape from Silver and his men with Dr. Livesey he achieves his full moral stature.

It is a standard and necessary device in this kind of adventure story that the fortunes of the hero should be at their most critical point at the very moment when help arrives. Jim and Long John Silver face the wrath of the five pirates alone, and their fate seems sealed, but a last minute rescue is effected by the Doctor, seaman Gray, and Ben Gunn, whose action is, of course, appropriately prepared for and explained. It is important that at this critical juncture in the story Jim and Long John Silver are joined together against the five pirates, even though Silver is—or was—himself the leader of the pirates. The careful way in which Stevenson manoeuvres Silver into this position is another of his devices for keeping the reader's sympathy on the side of the picturesque, even though the picturesque is bound up with evil. Circumstances force Long John Silver to range himself on the side of Jim and his friends against the others, and thus we are able to contemplate and enjoy the good points in Silver's character without feeling that we are letting our sympathies fall on the wrong side.

The book ends, as it begins, with a deliberate pushing of the whole story into the past: it is a retrospect, a thing finished and done with, something to be talked over by the fire on a winter's night. . . . (pp. 44-9)

The story begins and ends as a recollection, from the comfort of the present, of the adventures and discomforts of the past. (p. 50)

David Daiches, in his Robert Louis Stevenson, *New Directions Books, 1947, 196 p.*

J. C. FURNAS

[*Furnas is an American biographer, historian, novelist, and journalist whose* Voyage to Windward: The Life of Robert Louis Stevenson *is considered the most balanced and authoritative of Stevenson biographies. David Daiches calls it "the definitive life . . . accurate, perceptive, understanding, drawing on much unpublished material, the product of indefatigable research and clear intelligence." Hayden W. Ward calls Furnas "Stevenson's most dependable biographer."*]

I know of no more striking example [than *Treasure Island*] of an artist's taking a cheap, artificial set of commercialized values—which is fair enough to the Victorian "boys' story"—and doing work of everlasting quality by changing nothing, transmuting everything, as if Jane Austen had ennobled soap-opera. It is dizzying to jump from *Don Zalva the Brave*, rich with inky cuts, to a bit from the next column of *Young Folks* doing Pew on the highway or Silver negotiating with Captain Smollett. The ingredients are utterly nonoriginal—even Billy Bones at the Admiral Benbow was half stolen, as Louis ruefully admitted some years later, by unconscious memory from Washington Irving. But anybody needing example of the difference between fuzzy and hard-twist writing should read the original Irving and then what Louis did with the same materials filtered through discipline. He was clearly showing what it was to be steeped in Bunyan and Defoe, his masters in monosyllabic English narrative. The free, clear run of *Treasure Island*—the

string pulling with a readiness that, to a writer, feels almost eager—first acknowledged him master of his craft. (p. 199)

J. C. Furnas, in his Voyage to Windward: The Life of Robert Louis Stevenson, *William Sloane Associates, Inc., 1951, 566 p.*

ELIZABETH NESBITT

[*The following essay was originally published in 1953.*]

[*Treasure Island*] is an event in the development not only of romance but of children's literature as a whole. There had been adventure tales before, but in them the element of adventure had been watered down by ulterior motives of piety or morality, or crudity of style had rendered unacceptable the quality of "brute incident—not mere bloodshed or wonder," which Stevenson so stressed. *Treasure Island* is that increasingly rare thing, an excellent story written for story's sake and written with a craftsmanship that raises it to the level of art. In its beginning and its climax, in its incidents and its characters, in its settings and situations, the book demonstrates the rightness of Stevenson's conception of the true nature of romance.

In considering *Treasure Island* the emphasis must be on narrative method and style, since the interest is held, not by conduct, not by effect of character upon circumstance, but by sheer adventure appropriate to situation and setting and therefore, in Stevenson's estimation, romantic. Certain situations demand certain events, certain settings call aloud for a certain sort of story, he writes in **"A Gossip on Romance."** From the beginning to the end the story marches with rapid inevitability from incident to incident, with action so predetermined by quick-moving events that morality in the sense of hesitations and doubts of the human conscience is irrelevant.

No story of its kind has ever had better opening chapters, as one by one, vividly, and with a gripping quality of mystery, the characters who are to precipitate the action are introduced [Billy Bones, Black Dog, and the blind beggar]. . . . Not least among the merits of the book are the word drawings of these villains. Stevenson holds true to his theory that sufficient character portrayal can be admitted to make real the sense of danger and to arouse the sense of fear. As each arrival increasingly threatens the sheltered, uneventful life of the inn and countryside, filling the bitter cold winter days with a terrible atmosphere of dark deeds and emotions, past and present, the sense of fear and unavoidable involvement mounts. Unforgettable as these early characters are, the figure of Long John Silver overshadows them, with his slyness and cunning, his seeming geniality and innate cruelty. The most effective scenes of the book, and those which constitute the true climax of the tale are those in which Silver saves Jim Hawkins from the vengeance of the crew and at the same time insures that he himself will be saved. Here again, Stevenson fulfills his own requirement—that the "characters should fall from time to time into some attitude to each other or to nature, which stamps the story home like an illustration." This is, however, not so much a result of character analysis or portrayal as of narrative technique. Essentially, the characters are type characters, types necessary to the nature of the story—on the one hand, Jim and the doctor and the squire, simple, average, uncomplicated, undistinguished; on the other hand, Long John Silver and his companions, animated by lust and greed, true and typical ruffians and villains. In both cases it is situation that reveals character, rather than character controlling and creating situation.

The reminiscent point of view and the use of the first person play a large part in inducing in the reader the right mood of suspense and anticipation. It is a well-known fact that children dislike the use of the first person, realizing instinctively that often the "I" introduces too much of the subjective and introspective. In *Treasure Island,* as in *Robinson Crusoe* and *Gulliver's Travels,* they accept it, since in these books the emphasis is on action, not on thought and feeling. Emotion may be and is present, but it is made apparent by being inherent in situation, rather than by analytical dissection of a character's response to situation. Consequently, there is no hindrance to the reader's identification of himself with "I"; in this case, Jim Hawkins. The sense of ineradicable memories, strongly felt in the opening phrase of the true story, "I remember him as if it were yesterday," is sustained to the last paragraph, where it is again forcibly expressed. Throughout, it does much to deepen the convincingness of the story and to heighten its reality. This effect is strengthened by the character of Jim and the place he occupies. Standing between Dr. Livesey, an ordinary able and calm adult, and the devious and cunning Long John Silver, he is a boy with a normal boy's courage and resourcefulness. Again, it is circumstance and situation and the accident of being in a certain place at a certain time which call forth these qualities in Jim and which make him the central moving figure in many of the episodes. He is the victim of circumstance, not the instigator of it.

A prime requisite of adventure fiction is obviously continuity and rapidity of action. To create a story which mounts steadily in intensity, to invent successive incidents which shall be varied and plausible, to draw background and scene as inherent parts of the action, is in itself an art, an art compounded of storytelling ability and power of style, an art produced by a creative imagination, disciplining itself by reality. Stevenson may not have created the tale of adventure as a type, but he is one of the few to tell it as it should be told, as a story which must stand or fall on its merits, as a story untrammeled by other motives. He was, above all things, a storyteller and a lover of good tales. . . . To have a good tale to tell is, however, not enough. It must be told with a power of style which makes it credible, which sustains the initial interest aroused by the type of story, which enables the reader to immerse himself in the setting and to participate in the action.

Stevenson was not only a lover of tales, but equally a lover of words and phrases. He was a meticulous searcher for the right word for the right thing, a builder of phrases precise and exact. He had two of the greatest gifts a writer may possess, the gift of selectivity and the gift of stressing of essentials. The tight economy of detail and word, the strict adherence to the relevant, the fine precision of phrase, combine with a faculty for observation, a sense of the relationship between scene and mood, and a facility in harnessing imagination to reality to make a story that wholly absorbs the reader. Characters and scenes are etched upon the memory forever because of the fine clarity of description, the emphasis upon distinguishing and distinctive characteristics. Background is drawn sparingly, with a keen awareness of the part it plays in enhancing mood. The romantic, the dramatic, and the picturesque are so tempered by realism as to enable the reader to be convinced of any event, no matter how remarkable. The story progresses unimpeded, each sentence carrying the action forward, each chapter offering a faultlessly motivated episode, each bit of the amazingly actual dialogue contributing its share. The very matter-of-factness and objectivity with which the passions of greed and lust are treated make the story wholesome and rid it of any tinge of morbidity; for here the interest is concentrated, not on the problem of good and evil in man, but on the pitting of strength against strength, of wits against wits, in healthy combat.

It is no wonder this book made Stevenson a popular author. It appealed to boys and to the eternal boy in men; to the story-loving spirit which had treasured the chapbooks and perpetuated folk literature by word of mouth for generation after generation. In Stevenson's own day, the combination of robust, vigorous adventure and artistry of execution must have been a shock. Consequently Stevenson, like Howard Pyle, fostered the recognition that writing for children is a field of writing which should call for the best in technical excellence. To us, in retrospect, *Treasure Island* anticipates the escape from previous limitations of Puritanism and didacticism into complete freedom of form, idea, and substance. (pp. 303-06)

Elizabeth Nesbitt, "A New Impulse in Romance: Robert Louis Stevenson," in A Critical History of Children's Literature by Cornelia Meigs, Anne Thaxter Eaton, Elizabeth Nesbitt, and Ruth Hill Viguers, edited by Cornelia Meigs, revised edition, Macmillan Publishing Company, 1969, pp. 302-09.

LILLIAN H. SMITH

When Robert Louis Stevenson blazed a new trail with his story of *Treasure Island* he not only wrote a great pirate story, he also influenced much subsequent writing for children, giving it a trend toward an ever widening field of high adventure. Many writers who followed in this field failed to grasp the important fact that it is not alone the *adventure* of *Treasure Island* that has made it so beloved by children. Its inherent qualities are those of a writer whose creative imagination is joined with a masterly prose style, an association which has given the book its staying power.

Let us see what an analysis of *Treasure Island* will reveal. The story is told in the first person by Jim Hawkins, a boy whom chance involves in a strange adventure. By the device of the first person Stevenson gives his story a plausibility, an appearance of truth necessary to all romance. It also gives a consistent and unified point of view—Jim's—which throws the events into sharper relief. Jim himself reports his experience. It fills his memory with strong and vivid pictures full of color. (p. 136)

Jim himself is not a memorable character, although he has substance enough to be credible. There is no need for more. He is there to tell the story. Because he sees it as a boy would see it, a child can identify himself with Jim, live through the stirring scenes he describes, and come to know the strange company aboard the "Hispaniola." The story itself is not a mere string of exciting events. Stevenson is a master at constructing plot and *Treasure Island* is one of his best. We not only know what happens, we know why it happens. The events move logically and inexorably to a climax. Although a child's interest, while reading *Treasure Island,* is mainly in the tense, swiftly moving narrative, it is the larger-than-life size characters of the story which live in his memory. Children like strong, colorful characters as much as adults do. In the smooth-tongued, ruthless pirate, Long John Silver, they meet a terrifying, yet somehow likeable buccaneer. His individuality grows in their minds until he takes on a reality that makes pirates in other books seem mere pieces of stage property in comparison. The characters in many pirate stories seem unreal because while they are shown in action, the reader has no clue to the motivation which governs their conduct and actions. The events of the story, while they may be dramatic and exciting, seem to take place without regard to the kind of people involved. The reader has no way of getting inside the minds of the characters, no way of knowing them as he comes to know Long John Silver, because the author is writing about his characters from the outside and sees them only as stage properties necessary to carry the action of the story.

This is not Stevenson's method. The reader comes to know the characters not only through their own revealing speech, but by direct and indirect hints and suggestions. The characters come alive for the reader because he knows *how* they think and what effect this has on events. Nothing happens that is not related to the individuality of the characters.

And how simple, vigorous, and eloquent is the telling of the story of *Treasure Island;* the apt, unusual word, the pictorial phrase, the striking similes which effectively suggest a picture to the imagination. The story is so fresh, brushed in with such sure, suggestive strokes, that it is impressed on the reader as a concentrated essence of experience etched forever on the mind. No wonder it has passed into the permanent literature of childhood. (pp. 136-37)

> *Lillian H. Smith, "Stories," in her* The Unreluctant Years: A Critical Approach to Children's Literature, *American Library Association, 1953, pp. 130-148.**

LESLIE A. FIEDLER

[*The following excerpt is taken from Fiedler's introduction to the 1954 Rinehart edition of* The Master of Ballantrae.]

One hundred years after the birth of Stevenson, the question of his worth as a writer remains still very much at issue. Unless we are willing to surrender him completely to children or to indulge a sneaking fondness for him as unanalytically as if we were ourselves children, we must make a really critical assessment of his work. We must meet the question: Is a liking for *Treasure Island* a literary enthusiasm or a minor subliterary vice, like reading detective stories? The enthusiasm of the first generation of Stevensonians found a critical approach to what seemed to them all charm and magic impertinent; but today we are inclined to be suspicious of the easy triumphs of the R.L.S. style; and the genre of Romance to which Stevenson's reputation is tied has been relegated among us to the shelves of the circulating library. (p. 77)

If we remember that Long John Silver appeared for years in the "Katzenjammer Kids," we will, I think, begin to see the possibilities of a quite different approach. Imagine Anna Karenina or Stephen Dedalus appropriated by the comic strips! It could be done only in vulgar burlesque; but the Sea-Cook can be kidnapped without impertinence. Like other Stevensonian characters (Jekyll and Hyde, for instance), he exists, as it were, in the public domain—along with Thor and Loki, Hansel and Gretel. The characters of Stevenson seem to have an objective existence, a being prior to and independent of any particular formal realization. They are, in short, not merely literary creations, but also embodiments of archetypal themes—and it is in the realm of myth, which sometimes overlaps but is not identical with literature, that we must look for clues to the meaning and unity of Stevenson's work.

Modern prose fiction has handled the myth in two quite different ways, one sophisticated, one naïve; the former, that of James Joyce, for instance, leads from the inward novel of character, through psychological naturalism, to symbolism and beyond to the conscious manipulation of the mythic; the latter begins with the outward Romance of incident, the boys' story

or thriller, and moves through allegory, often elusive, to the naïve or unconscious evocation of myth. To the latter group belong such varied writers as Melville, Arthur Conan Doyle, Graham Greene—and Robert Louis Stevenson. They are possessed of a double ambiguity: on the one hand, they are likely to deny point-blank the symbolic intent which the critic can not help seeing in them; and on the other, they tend to define a wavering line between literature and subliterature—falling sometimes to the side of achieved formal statement and sometimes to that of a shoddy and cheaply popular evocation of archetypal themes.

Sophisticated exploiters of the mythic (Joyce, Mann) are inevitably limited in their appeal, and in their work the traditional "story" plotted in time tends to be replaced by the timeless movement of archetypes in the psyche. Such naïve exploiters of the mythic as Greene and Stevenson, on the contrary, preserve the "story" and its appeal intact; in them the picturesque never yields completely to the metaphysical—and they can always be read on one level as boys' books or circulating-library thrillers. (pp. 77-8)

Over and over again since his reputation was first questioned, critics have asked: Is there in Stevenson's work a single motivating force, beyond the obvious desire to be charming, to please, to exact admiration—that seems to us now a little shallow and more than a little coquettish? Frank Swinnerton, who led the first reaction against the uncritical adulation of R.L.S. [see excerpt dated 1923] found in only one book, *Jekyll and Hyde,* a "unifying idea." But "idea" is a misleading word; a single felt myth gives coherence, individually and as a group, to several of Stevenson's long fictions—and it is the very myth explicitly stated in *Jekyll and Hyde.* The books besides the latter are *Treasure Island, Kidnapped, The Master of Ballantrae* and the *Weir of Hermiston;* the organizing mythic concept might be called the Beloved Scoundrel or the Devil as Angel, and the books make a series of variations of the theme of the beauty of evil—and conversely the unloveliness of good. The Beloved Scoundrel makes his debut as Long John Silver in *Treasure Island,* a tale first printed, it is worth noticing, in a boys' magazine, and written to explain circumstantially a treasure map drawn for a child's game that Stevenson had been playing with his young stepson.

There can be little doubt that one of Stevenson's motives in marrying was to become a child—and finding himself at the age of thirty at long last a child enabled him unexpectedly to become for the first time a real creative writer; that is, to sustain a successful long fiction. All of Stevenson's major loves had been older, once-married women—which is to say, mothers. (pp. 79-80)

His marriage to Mrs. Osbourne not only gave him a mother to replace his own, from whom he felt estranged and to whom he could not utterly commit himself without feelings of guilt toward his father, but provided him for the first time with a brother in the form of his twelve-year-old stepson, Lloyd. An only child and one isolated by illness, Stevenson had never been able to feel himself anything but a small adult . . . ; against the boy Lloyd he was able to define himself as a boy. Together they *played* at many things; toy soldiers, printing . . .—even writing. Before Lloyd had fully matured, he and Stevenson had begun their collaboration with *The Wrong Box.* Writing to R.L.S. seemed always a kind of childish sport; "to play at home with paper like a child," he once described his life's work, a glance over his shoulder at his disapproving forebears, good engineers and unequivocal adults. But there is in such a concept of art, not only the troubled touch of guilt, but the naïve surge of joy; and Stevenson's abandonment to childhood meant his first release as an artist—produced *Treasure Island, Kidnapped* and *A Child's Garden of Verses.*

Long John Silver is described through a boy's eye, the first of those fictional first-person-singulars who are a detached aspect of the author. It is Jim Hawkins who is the chief narrator of the tale, as it is Jim who saves the Sea-Cook from the gallows. For the boy, the scoundrel par excellence is the Pirate: an elemental ferocity belonging to the unfamiliar sea and uncharted islands hiding bloodstained gold. And yet there is an astonishing innocence about it all—a world without sex and without business—where the source of wealth is buried treasure, clean gold in sand, for which only murder has been done, but which implies no grimy sweat in offices, no manipulating of stock, none of the quiet betrayals of capitalist competition. The very embodiment of this world, vain, cruel, but astonishingly courageous and immune to self-deprecation, able to compel respect, obedience—and even love—is John Silver; and set against him for a foil is Captain Smollett, in whom virtue is joined to a certain dourness, an immediate unattractiveness. Not only Jim, but Stevenson, too, finds the Pirate more lovable than the good Captain. In one of his *Fables* written afterwards, he sets before us Alexander Smollett and John Silver, debating with each other while thier author rests between Chapters XXXII and XXXIII; and Captain Smollett is embarrassed by the Sea-Cook's boast that their common creator loves him more, keeps him in the center of the scene, but keeps the virtuous Captain "measling in the hold."

Kidnapped, like *Treasure Island,* was written for a boys' magazine, and in both all important relationships are between males. In *Kidnapped,* however, the relation of the Boy and the Scoundrel, treated as a flirtation in the earlier book, becomes almost a full-fledged love affair, a pre-sexual romance; the antagonists fall into lovers' quarrels and make up, swear to part forever, and remain together. (pp. 80-1)

> Leslie A. Fiedler, "R.L.S. Revisited," in his No! in Thunder: Essays on Myth and Literature, *Beacon Press, 1960, pp. 77-91.*

DOUGLAS BROWN

[*The following essay originally appeared in the* Journal of Education *in August, 1957.*]

It is part of Stevenson's admirable side that, at times, his notion of his talent and of his deficiencies was so acute. A gifted writer, but not a great one: an important novelist for boys, but for adults only a novelist interesting in certain ways. The sustained attempt of his later years, dogged by ill health, to transmute the gift manifest in *Treasure Island* and *Kidnapped* and qualify as an artist, a serious imaginative novelist, ought to command respect. But I do not find that even *Weir of Hermiston* stands up to the claims often made for it and for its promise. And I make little doubt that *The Master of Ballantrae,* and even the best of the shorter tales, have neither classical status in adult literature nor any significant claim as stories for boys. The narratives are nervous and fitful, they haven't the 'buoyancy of vitality' Stevenson hoped for, there is nothing distinct at the centre while there life might flow into the parts. The warmth, in fact (to use his own terms), and the dash of the picturesque, the little dose of inspiration, the trick of style, and the industry, sufficed to make *Treasure Island* and *Kidnapped* the fine things they are—together with certain other qualities. But there was nothing that might suffice to produce work able to stand beside

Conrad's; and it is to Conrad's novels that Stevenson points on, whether you take him as a boy's novelist or a man's.

The proper context for a discussion of Stevenson's real achievement, then, might include the best work of Marryat and Rider Haggard and Conan Doyle and perhaps Buchan. In that framework he is indeed secure. Probably no novelist, at present, holds a more secure place in the Establishment of English teaching. It seems a pleasant duty therefore, when the Establishment's values and backings are constantly and rightly up for checking, to confirm after reconsideration the propriety of his standing. It should, I think, rest absolutely on those two books. (pp. 123-24)

I do not see, on reflection, an overriding reason for backing these two books, but a gathering of many congenial ones. To begin with, there is the deep but sensible respect for youthful personality, for will and conscience and mind at the point of growth. Henry James writes of 'the singular maturity of the expression that he has given to young sentiments; he judges them, measures them, sees them from outside as well as entertains them. He describes credulity with all the resources of experience, and represents a crude stage with infinite ripeness.' James often overrated Stevenson. But here he defines a real source of strength, shown particularly in the handling of the two boy protagonists. The reflective notations tend to give the 'I' a quality of responsibility as a person that one misses in most romantic narratives so presented. Their moral sense of themselves or others (even where deficient) seems to *matter.*

The heroic industry implies that respect too, the sheer hard work to get authenticity of scope and detail, the grain of experience, into the island, and into the historic Scotland of David and Alan's encounter. Stevenson draws, for the rendering of that Scotland, upon his deepest personal commitments and loyalties, and upon a kind of impassioned research: it is a whole dimension removed from 'local colour'. That he should do so, for a boys' story, is his tribute of respect.

There is more than respect, of course, in his attitude to boyhood. It was romantic, nostalgic and an imaginative evasion of the special tribulations of his own lot as an adult. So he puts up a protective screen about his protagonists from time to time; his sentiment is not free-standingly an artist's. But it works out as fact that even the protective indulgence implies a statement of the dignity and the obligations of boyhood; or sends a current of tenderness flowing about a boy's mistakes, misjudgments, vanities or wilfulness.

The way a nascent moral sense is kept alert and pushing inside the narrative of romantic adventure is important. 'Stevenson's habit of mind,' remarks Swinnerton . . . , 'was moral and practical; the highest and lowest alike were strange to it; it had excellent equipoise and admirable sanity. It had not normally a very wide range of sympathy or interest.' This is the impression I take from the novels. If such habits of mind incapacitate for the finest adult fiction, they also qualify admirably for the finest youthful. Here, the range of experience to be addressed is limited, and the moral feeling to be developed sensitive and sane rather than subtle and profound. The last third of *Treasure Island,* Chapter XVIII of *Kidnapped* and the later sequence of **'The Flight in the Heather'**—these are the places to feel how his sense of the moral order youth must come to terms with invigorates his imaginative writing.

This clear, responsible, uncomplicated moral feeling lends its edge to another strength, perhaps of a more immediate potency. I mean Stevenson's gift for implying alteration and growth, the inward sensation of growing up, in the relations of characters and in the impact of events upon characters. Here again, it is a gift almost restricted to the area of adolescence, and the terms of its expression are terms adolescence can respond to. His two best novels draw their sustenance, I think, in large part from the connections set up between their narratives and three fundamental and ancient ceremonies of the process from youth to maturity: the quest, the ordeal and the initiation. Those connections are close and continual: one of the three deep centres of youthful experience is almost always present. Stevenson's isolations and emphases are finely contrived to this end. Jim's refusal to break his word and so escape from Silver and the pirates, and his final triumph in the skills of irregular warfare, act as submerged images of moral and physical emergence into manhood. In such a spirit ordeals are endured. ('I felt somehow grown-up' wrote a thirteen-year-old in the last sentence of an imaginative composition about a train accident he had watched. That is the sensation Stevenson gets into art.) (pp. 125-27)

Stevenson subordinates interest in character to the solidifying and validating of scene and episode as a sequence of events. Yet he does draw not only his protagonists, but also the two central figures they encounter in the external romantic world— Silver and Alan—with the kind of authority that at once interests and involves young readers. And he draws them from a deeper layer of personal experience and the play of memory than boys' writers ordinarily do. Not only the 'maimed strength' of Silver, but also his mask, and the suggestions of reserves of dark vitality, are the effect of imagination working upon Stevenson's relation with Henley, his perceptions about him, his failure to penetrate him. It is a commonplace that the invention of Silver, with his ambiguous moral stature and the accumulation of authoritative perceptions about him, imparts extraordinary vitality to *Treasure Island.*The slow discovery of his 'identity', the ensuing realization that still the 'identity' is not morally simple, the sense of ties—affection, fear, honour, fascination—that bind Jim to him, collaborate to leave the impression of perhaps the most telling character-study in boys' fiction. Stevenson has drawn on deep recesses of knowledge, yet perfectly adapted his creation to the potentialities of boys and of the world of boyhood's adventures.

Lastly, what ought to be said of that 'pretty trick of style' improved by such industry? 'A tremendous vain Scots savour of language and retort' is Swinnerton's neat summary of the rhetoric. Here at least is skill, here is industry, care to write well. More, there is a real flair for the detail that etches a whole scene upon the mind; for the visually indelible; and for the locking together of romantic adventure and homely experience, each in the sort of phrase that carries confidence. What hard work, and a good ear, and a narrative manner plausible and substantial with corroborative detail, yet sufficiently terse and spare—what these could do, they did. And the industry as well as the style is itself a tribute to the genre and to its readers. The adult critic may discover falsities and idiosyncrasies that distract and pall and seem to call attention to themselves. The young reader is differently affected. If the style does call attention to itself, he will be less ready to notice the call; he gives himself more readily to what the words say. He finds Stevenson's style, in fact, wonderfully functional: it entirely convinces. Its glitter is like the eye of the Ancient Mariner.

If and when a young reader does become aware of Stevenson's 'style', I still think that little but good comes of it: a recognition

The frontispiece of the first edition of Treasure Island.

that writing *can be* 'fine', that narrative prose can do more than say the obvious thing in the obvious way. This recognition of the very possibility of 'fine writing' is a useful and necessary stage. It matters little that Stevenson's springs from no deep centre, but from an honourable determination to do what by 'heroic industry' he could do, according to his lights. (pp. 128-29)

Treasure Island and ***Kidnapped*** may do rather more. They may generate some respect for the kind of experience communicated in the literature of the past. So doing, they may shake a little the exaggerated regard our children are bound to have for the ephemeralities of the present, and of the potent mass media of the present: such a shaking is a necessary preliminary to the appreciation of literature. And second, by their own virtues they may prepare young readers for *Youth* and *The Nigger of the Narcissus*. These have an advaantage lacking in Stevenson's work, and essential to adolescence: they lead on to tales as fully adult as any in the language: to *Typhoon* and *The*

Shadow-Line, and the full-length masterpieces of Conrad. (p. 129)

Douglas Brown, ''R.L.S.: Inspiration and Industry,'' in Young Writers, Young Readers: An Anthology of Children's Reading and Writing, edited by Boris Ford, revised edition, Hutchinson, 1963, pp. 123-29.

WILLIAM GOLDING

When one turns to *Treasure Island,* one sees immediately that Stevenson was the professional knowing precisely what effects he wanted and how he was going to get them. Every chapter is shaped and fitted into the general structure like the timbers of a ship. There are moments of lambent actuality which only come to a writer at full, dedicated stretch. Who can forget the notch in the sign of the Admiral Benbow, or the musket shot that spat like a curse through the mainsail of the departing ship? (p. 844)

So much praise has been poured out on *Treasure Island* that I tried to find something to carp at; and found precious little. The book remains sharp and swift as I remember it. Surprisingly enough, however, since I left the nursery and went to sea myself, the topsail-schooner Hispaniola—an unusual rig for the eighteenth century—has become a little fuzzy round the edges. This is a pity, as she used to be my favourite ship. Stevenson chose her because he thought himself unable to handle square-rig; but she never lies before us in one convincing piece. Her tonnage remains in doubt. She was big enough to carry thirty people or more to the Pacific. We have Captain Smollett's own word for it that she was splendid at sea; she 'lay a point closer to the wind than a man has a right to expect of his own wife.' Yet later he anchors her in nine feet of water.

A small, frivolous point, that one. But dare I say, in the teeth of the applauding generations, that I do not find *Treasure Island,* the physical patch of land itself, wholly in focus? We get glimpses that are superb; that sandy gash with the two-guinea piece lying in the middle of it where the treasure had been, the fort and stockade, the glade where Silver murdered Tom so horribly. But the island as it stuck out of the sea, the reason for it being there, and the relationship between the parts, escapes me even when I use the overrated chart. An island must be built, and have an organic structure, like a tooth.

There my carping ends. (pp. 844-45)

Characterisation remains vivid. The bluff and unsubtle Squire Trelawney, forthright and minatory Captain Smollett, mature Doctor Livesey, honest Redruth and feckless Ben Gunn—they all stand up to close examination. Even the remainder are not without substance. They were, I should think, fugitives from the disbanded Hawkhurst Gang. Their talk strikes the perfect middle way between the literal and the emasculated. (p. 845)

But the lifeblood of the book is Long John Silver. Most writers can invent a Baddy, and a few of them a Goody. But there are some characters in books who live their own abundant life beyond the threshold of our business of moral judgments. Here we are, they seem to say, and now what are you going to make of us? Despite their authors they are outside good and evil. They exist by right of their own joy in life. They are as naturally and brilliantly alive as a swallow diving on a cat. Who can doubt that Silver enjoys his villainy, likes to be liked, finds success and failure a huge joke? For the other mutineers are small-time crooks, doomed from the beginning. But Silver disappears at the end with a modest competence, to start all over again. He goes, having delighted in the murders, the turning of coats, the devious treacheries. When he vanishes from our sight in port, good and evil have become irrelevant standards of judgment. One can almost hear him quoting from another book as he goes—'What larks, Pip, eh? What larks!' (p. 846)

William Golding, ''Islands,'' in The Spectator, Vol. 204, No. 6885, June 10, 1960, pp. 844-46.*

ROBERT KIELY

Treasure Island is one of the most satisfying adventure stories ever told primarily because it is the most unhampered. The great pleasure in reading the first few chapters depends not only on the gathering mystery, but on the exhilarating sense of *casting off* which Stevenson gives us. I mean casting off both in the nautical sense of leaving port and in the conventional sense of throwing off encumbrances. It is the perennial thrill of the schoolboy tossing away his books on the last day of the term or the youth flinging off his sticky clothes for the first swim of the season. What this amounts to is a temporary change of roles, a peeling down to what seems for the moment our least complicated and perhaps our most essential self.

Stevenson begins the process in *Treasure Island* with shameless dispatch by getting rid first of geographical place and time present and all the demands that go with them. We are relieved of place in the first sentence when Jim Hawkins explains that he will keep ''nothing back but the bearings of the island, and that only because there is treasure not yet lifted.'' He then speaks of taking up his pen to write the story ''in the year 17—,'' but, like other ''historical romanticists,'' fails to fill in the last two numbers or to say how long before 17— the adventure actually occurred. He says at the beginning of the second paragraph, in introducing Billy Bones, ''I remember him as if it were yesterday,'' and here we have another notch in our release from time. Not only are we well removed historically, but we are offered as our only authority the imperfect memory of a boy who assures us casually that he recalls past events as though they had all happened the previous day.

We become aware almost at once that Jim Hawkins' memory is anything but flawless. He recalls his first impression of Bones upon his arrival at the Admiral Benbow:

> . . . a tall, strong, heavy, nut-brown man; his tarry pigtail falling over the shoulders of his soiled blue coat; his hands ragged and scarred, with black, broken nails; and the saber cut across one cheek, a dirty, livid white.

And, of course, the stranger immediately breaks into a chorus of ''Fifteen men on the dead man's chest.'' There seem to be a great number of details here, but they would hardly help distinguish Bones, tanned, scarred, and pigtailed, from the general run of disreputable seamen, especially as conceived in the mind of a child who has never seen one. ''Character to the boy is a sealed book,'' Stevenson wrote in **''A Humble Remonstrance.''** ''For him a pirate is a beard, a pair of wide trousers, and a liberal complement of pistols.'' Here then is the next item dismissed from the book. We are early relieved of personality except as a costume or disguise which may be put on and off at will.

Before the *Hispaniola* can sail in search of the treasure, the characters must all shed their old selves, determined up until then only by the faintly vocational fact that one is an innkeeper's boy, one a doctor, one a squire, and so forth, and assume the new roles required by the nature of the adventure. As in any game, the assumed roles should and do have some connection with the original talents or inclinations of the character. Just as a strong arm and a straight eye make the best "pitcher" and the smallest boy the best "cox," so the characters of *Treasure Island* are assigned roles which best fit their previously if sketchily established selves. Even the selecting is accomplished, as in a boy's game, by a self-appointed leader who achieves the desired transformation merely by stating it:

> "Livesey," said the squire (to the doctor), "you will give up this wretched practice at once . . . we'll have the best ship, sir, and the choicest crew in England. Hawkins shall come as cabin-boy. You'll make a famous cabin-boy, Hawkins. You, Livesey, are ship's doctor; I am admiral."

Only Long John Silver takes on a role not befitting his pre-established character as buccaneer. When he becomes sea-cook aboard the *Hispaniola*, the first ominous rumblings begin which threaten to spoil the game, but really make it interesting.

Perhaps a corollary to the dismissal from the novel of historically measurable time and the complexity of human personality is Stevenson's cavalier casting off of the serious consequences of mortality. It is not that people do not die in *Treasure Island*. They drop on all sides throughout most of the book. There are, of course, the expected casualties among the pirates and the loyal but minor members of the crew, once the fighting gets under way on the island. But the fatalities before that are rather different and particularly indicative of the efficient purpose death serves the story. The first demise, which takes place in Chapter III, is that of Jim's sick father, who we know is ailing somewhere in an upstairs bedroom, but whom we never meet face to face. Jim's account of the event is characteristically matter-of-fact and inaccurate. "But as things fell out, my poor father died quite suddenly that evening, which put all other matters on one side."

Actually, the death of Jim's father puts nothing aside at all. He is buried in the next paragraph and not mentioned again, while the incidents of the mystery continue to accumulate at the same headlong rate which had been established while he was still alive and ailing. The only thing the death of Jim's father puts aside is Jim's father. Critics are forever trying to read something of Stevenson's youthful difficulties with his own father into the recurring theme of filial isolation in his fiction. (pp. 68-71)

[We] need not reach very far into an author's private relationships to recognize the universal truth that boyish adventures, especially games involving danger, are possible only when the limiting authority symbolized by the male parent is absent. . . . A mother may be overridden, convinced, left temporarily behind. But the father must give way altogether so that his place may be taken by a kind of romantic opposite, dusky and disreputable, a Nigger Jim, a Queequeg, a Long John Silver.

The next two deaths, occurring in fairly rapid succession before Treasure Island is reached and the main part of the story begins, efficiently eliminate characters who had served as narrative and psychological preliminaries to Long John Silver. Billy Bones and Blind Pew are the first to intrude seriously on the life of the inn at Black Hill Cove as representatives and messengers from a vast and mysterious other world where terror prevails; they also introduce separately the two apparently contradictory aspects of personality combined in Long John Silver.

One role we first see played by Billy Bones, the browned and burly pirate, lusty, loud, and frightening to behold, but basically good-natured and kind. His strong exterior hides not only a kind heart, but a weak one, which is the eventual cause of his death by apoplexy when he receives the black spot. This is the bogieman who turns out to be less of a threat than he had seemed, both kinder *and weaker* than he looked. When Bones dies of a stroke he has served the narrative purpose of bearing the sea chest containing the chart of Treasure Island into the story and the psychological purpose of presenting Jim and the reader with half of what we can expect from Long John Silver. Jim dispenses with Bones quickly, and interestingly enough associates his tearful reaction to his death with left-over emotion from the death of his father.

The other half of Long John Silver and the next character to threaten the order of the Admiral Benbow Inn from a faraway renegade world is Blind Pew. He is the nightmare of every child, and perhaps of every adult—the deformed stranger, apparently harmless, even feeble, offering friendship and requesting help, and suddenly demonstrating unexpected reserves of cruel strength. (pp. 72-3)

When Blind Pew has delivered the black spot, a warning of doom, to Bones, he too has served his narrative purpose and may die. He is stamped to death by horses, but the scene is too swift to be gory. . . . (pp. 73-4)

Death in *Treasure Island* is quick, clean, and above all, efficient for the rapid advancement of the plot. It never provokes a sense of real pathos even in the case of Jim's father, and it is not an impediment in the lives of the surviving characters. On the contrary, especially in the early part of the book, removal of characters by natural or "accidental" means is another step in the process of casting off the potential obstacles to free movement in the adventure to come. Bones and Pew could perhaps have wandered off, run away, disappeared from the plot without dying, when their respective missions were completed. But they would then have lurked in the background of the rest of the story, complicating its essential simplicity with minor but unanswered questions. It is appropriate anyway that these two advance guards from the pirate world, these two preludes to the character of Long John Silver, should die before that legendary and duplex buccaneer is born into the novel twenty pages later.

Long John Silver is the kind of character critics like to give hyphenated names to: villain-as-hero, devil-as-angel, and so forth. Certainly the duplicity of the man justifies these labels even if it does not seem adequately explained by the clichés they have become. Silver appears to be physically weak because of the loss of one of his legs, yet Jim repeatedly notes what a husky man he is and how well he maneuvers even aboard ship. He is capable of being generous, kind, and reasonable, as he demonstrates on the voyage out and at the end of the story when his position on the island is weakened. But he is also capable of uncomplicated cruelty. In both moods he holds a kind of parental sway over Jim. In the early chapters Jim attaches himself to Silver and obeys him for much the same reasons he obeyed Billy Bones, partly out of curiosity, partly out of admiration, and partly out of pity for his physical disability. As for Long John, there is no doubt that he regards Jim Hawkins with paternal affection. "'Come away, Hawkins,' he would say; 'come and have a yarn with John. Nobody more welcome than yourself, my son.'" And much later, on the island, Silver offers Jim a kind of partnership in piracy in words not unlike those of a self-made man inviting his son to join the family business: "I've always liked you, I have, for a lad of spirit, and the picter of my own self when I was young and handsome. I always wanted you to jine and take your share." . . . (pp. 74-5)

But Jim has also seen Silver, like Pew, reveal startling physical power in spite of his debility, and brutality, in spite of his previous kindness. Jim is watching when Tom Morgan, a loyal member of the crew, refuses Silver's invitation to mutiny. The sailor stretches his hand out to Long John: "'Hands off,' cried Silver, leaping back a yard, as it seemed to me, with the speed and security of the trained gymnast." And when the sailor turns his back and begins to walk away,

> John seized the branch of a tree, whipped the crutch out of his armpit, and sent that uncouth missile hurtling through the air . . . Silver, agile as a monkey, even without leg or crutch, was on top of him next moment, and had twice buried his knife up to the hilt in that defenceless body.

At moments like this it is obviously fear mixed with awe at the athleticism of this supposed cripple that compels Jim. (pp. 75-6)

What, finally, are we to make of Long John Silver? Is he after all the heroic villain or the angelic devil? In a general way he is both. But this anxious reaching out for a permanent judgment overemphasizes the moral dimension of Silver's character and of the whole novel. David Daiches, in an excellent essay, "Stevenson and the Art of Fiction," suggests that

> all of Stevenson's novels have a highly sensitive moral pattern . . . Consider even *Treasure Island,* that admirable adventure story . . . What we admire is not always what we approve of . . . That Stevenson was here consciously exploring the desperate ambiguity of man as a moral animal is perhaps too much to say.

I would agree that the structural design of Stevenson's later moral tales is visible in *Treasure Island,* but the "desperate ambiguity of man" seems to me to have been left deliberately—and successfully—unexplored. We should take Stevenson at his word when he explains to Henry James that the luxury in reading a good adventure novel, *Treasure Island* in particular, "is to lay by our judgment, to be submerged by the tale as by a billow."

Silver is a player with two faces, that of the blustering buccaneer with a good heart (like Bones) and that of the cripple with a vicious heart and almost superhuman strength (like Pew). For us to ask which is the "real" Silver, to push aside the whiskers and try to see which of the two roles is better suited to the countenance is unfair, irrelevant to the spirit of the novel, and not worth the trouble because it is impossible to do. It is also unconvincing to attempt integrating Bones and Pew in order to show Silver's double nature as springing from a single psychological source. The contradictory tendencies are not presented as part of a complex personality fraught with tension and paradox. Such a union of traits is not impossible for a novelist to achieve in a seadog. Melville and Conrad both accomplish it. But Stevenson does not do it in *Treasure Island.* And that is another reason for questioning the value of the hyphenated labels. Not only do they stress moral issues where they barely exist, but they imply an integration of Silver's dual

roles whereas Stevenson seems to have taken some pains to keep them apart.

One of the pleasures in reading *Treasure Island* is in observing Long John Silver making his repeated "quick changes," alternating rather than growing or developing, bounding back and forth between "Bones" and "Pew." Stevenson again and again allows him to assume his most Pew-like part, unctuous and perfidious, only to be defied and shattered by a verbal barrage from a loyal member of the crew which transforms him into "Bones," a roaring but impotent husk. One of the best examples of Silver's capacity for rapid change is when Captain Smollett replies to his treacherous offer of "protection" if the pirates are given the treasure chart:

> "You can't find the treasure," (said Smollett). "You can't sail the ship—there's not a man among you fit to sail the ship. You can't fight us—Gray, there, got away from five of you. Your ship's in irons, Master Silver . . . and they're the last good words you'll get from me; for, in the name of heaven, I'll put a bullet in your back when next I meet you. Tramp, my lad. Bundle out of this, please, hand over hand, and double quick."

Smollett speaks to Silver as though he were a bad boy, not only naughty, but bungling in his attempts at villainy. And at once, the fearsome and oleaginous enemy becomes a comic, almost pathetic, buffoon, bellowing hollow threats. Retreating without dignity, he literally "crawled along the sand" to safety.

Jim, too, gets in his verbal "licks" against the pirate chief when he falls into the enemy's hands and things are looking blackest for him. He pelts the Pew-disguise with a furious tirade and concludes by shouting: "I no more fear you than I fear a fly."

What self-respecting pirate would take this kind of talk from a child? None at all, of course, but then as we have pointed out, Silver is given no self to respect. There is no basic personality from which he may derive strength when challenged or to which the reader may assign responsibility when Silver himself is doing the threatening. He is a weed that flourishes in ideal conditions but shrivels without resistance at the first sign of opposition. The point of the story as well as the pleasure in reading it is in the active conflict, not in its cause or even its final result. To try to speak seriously of good or evil in *Treasure Island* is almost as irrelevant as attempting to assign moral value in a baseball game, even though a presumable requisite to enjoying the contest involves a temporary if arbitrary preference for one side or the other.

The fuss that some critics have made over Silver's escape with a small part of the treasure at the end of the book as a sign of Stevenson's moral softness or of his "liberation" from strict Calvinist dogma seems rather foolish. Silver has murdered, robbed, and lied, but he has also been a good cook, a remarkable physical specimen in spite of his lost leg, and a rather affectionate if irresponsible replacement for Jim's dead father. Above all, he has been entertaining, and in a timeless, placeless, nearly conscienceless world, Stevenson seems justified in paying him off and sending him packing. To have killed him would have implied a punishment, a moral judgment Stevenson apparently did not want to make in this book. By the same token, to have rewarded him too generously or to have brought about his conversion would also have introduced a moral element not anticipated by anything earlier in the novel and therefore hardly appropriate at the conclusion. (pp. 76-9)

Later on, most obviously in *Dr. Jekyll and Mr. Hyde* and in *The Master of Ballantrae,* Stevenson returns to the theme of the double personality and tries with varying success to raise in the midst of melodrama serious moral and psychological questions. But it is important to see that his first impulse is to play a game and to teach us nothing more or less than how to play it with him. *Treasure Island* belongs not in the ironic mold of *Huckleberry Finn,* in which the adult world is seen through the eyes of a boy for what it really is. Without the transcendental overtones, it follows more closely in the tradition of Blake's *Songs of Innocence* and Wordsworth's "We Are Seven." The child is isolated from the adult world, protected from it by his own lack of experience, and does not really see it at all except in imperfect and distorted glimpses. We learn precious little about the psychology of evil from Long John Silver and nothing of real consequence about nineteenth-century morality from reading *Treasure Island.*

William Golding's *Lord of the Flies,* as a serious variation on the theme of boys' adventure, may make twentieth-century readers suspicious of the ingenuousness of a *Treasure Island* or a *Swiss Family Robinson.* In fact, it must have been intended, in part, as an antiromantic antidote to that "escapist" genre. But it ought to be remembered that, unlike *Treasure Island* and despite its popularity among adolescents, *Lord of the Flies* depends almost entirely on adult assumptions for its effectiveness as a novel. Moreover, one of the ironies of the book is that, for any of the youngest participants, the whole ghastly episode might have been regarded, even to the end, as little more than an exciting (if bewildering) romp on a desert island. It is this limited attitude toward reality, without benefit of adult insinuation, which Stevenson sought to capture in *Treasure Island.* His extraordinary success depended largely on his early conviction that, with respect to certain areas of experience, the child's amoral view was perfectly valid. (pp. 79-80)

> *Robert Kiely, in his* Robert Louis Stevenson and the Fiction of Adventure, *Cambridge, Mass.: Harvard University Press, 1964, 285 p.*

EDWIN M. EIGNER

Stevenson's characters do not usually end as whole men, but either as paralytics or as monsters, depending on which side of the disaggregated mind wins the perennial war in the members.

The protagonists . . . end always as paralytics, as men spiritually disqualified from the life of action. These characters come from novels belonging to the realistic tradition—from Thackeray and from Trollope—but they live in surroundings and face problems which are more appropriate to works of the romantic tradition. Stevenson's most characteristic technique, after that of the *Doppelgänger,* is to place an essentially unromantic man in an inherently romantic situation. The best of the realistic novels, especially after *Madame Bovary,* had done precisely the opposite. The great realists believed in man, but not in his possibilities, and their heroes go nobly to defeat. Stevenson always maintained at least a hunger for life, but he could not bring himself to create characters strong enough to live it; *his* heroes go tamely into retirement.

Even *Treasure Island,* the "elementary novel of adventure," shows some aspects of this same problem. Stevenson wrote that for the sake of "circumstantiation" and because he was himself more or less grown up, he "admitted character, within

certain limits, into his design." Morton Zabel reads the book as a *Bildungsroman,* and so to some extent it is; Jim Hawkins must gain his maturity by rejecting Long John Silver in spite of the latter's charm and vitality. His development is like that of the narrator in Conrad's "The Secret Sharer," who must not only accept the violent man as his double, but must let him go when the proper time comes. Maturity, however, is not always presented as a good thing in Stevenson, and the rejection of Silver involves also a rejection of what is young and alive in Jim's own character. Stevenson, of course, is not about to labor such a chilling point in a work of this type, and so Jim's vitality is allowed to pass away with no protest louder than a sigh. The only voice raised against the process is Silver's own. "Ah, you that's young," he says—"you and me might have done a power of good together!" . . . by which, no doubt, he means a power of bad. But Stevenson does not necessarily mean this. For in *his* fictional world there is no Agincourt to follow the banishment of plump Jack Silver; rather, . . . there is only the tortuous futility of the Battle of Shoreby, and Jim Hawkins, content with his treasure, is primed for a life of quiet and inglorious retirement; oxen and wain-ropes, as he concludes, could not drag him away from it. (pp. 75-6)

> *Edwin M. Eigner, in his* Robert Louis Stevenson and Romantic Tradition, *Princeton University Press, 1966, 258 p.*

W. W. ROBSON

[What] is our feeling at the end of *Treasure Island*? The conventions of youthful romance are preserved. The good are rewarded and the evil punished. Silver's escape ingeniously solves a technical problem, and is in keeping with his ambiguous role throughout. (Ben Gunn, who engineers his escape, is once more used adroitly.) He is allowed to take away a *little* of the treasure.

But what *is* the treasure? Some might say that it is no more than a necessary ingredient of the plot, in itself morally neutral: good men as well as bad go in search of it. Others might feel, as Jim does, that it is contaminated by the blood that has been shed for it, and the evil of Flint who buried it there. Others again might feel that this is *innocent* gold, not like the gold of commerce, or of Balzac's novels. A pirate as the symbol of a scoundrel is a boyish, innocent imagining, and this is piratical gold. Personally, I do not think the treasure has much more of a symbolic role than the Maltese Falcon (in Hammett's story, not in the film). Like the Falcon, it is a token of greed rather than the 'stuff as dreams are made on'. It has little emotional significance. There is almost nothing of the inward, sensuous excitement we feel in Legrand and the Negro at the climax of Poe's *The Gold Bug* (to which Stevenson was admittedly indebted). The attainment of the treasure is almost an anti-climax. Part of it is even left behind (the bar *silver*—is this a mere coincidence?) At any rate, the book closes on a curiously *sad* note ('Oxen and wain-ropes would not bring me back again to that accursed island.'). This makes me think that the book has a serious core, in Silver's relationship with Jim, and that that 'real' elements—that is to say, elements of personal significance to Stevenson—went into the creation of that relationship.

There is an absence of emotional pressure in the winning of the treasure. Many readers may agree that Stevenson's first title, *The Sea Cook,* is better than the one he finally chose. We must respect his intuitive decision that he could not accommodate *two* such powerful archetypes as the Sea Cook and Buried Treasure. (There is more suggestion of a latent meaning in buried treasure—the mother's body?—in the corresponding scene in *The Gold Bug*.) Or perhaps there is a still deeper reason. Perhaps Stevenson could not accommodate, at this period of his life, a tale of which the latent meaning was the struggle of a child with his father for the possession of his mother. We might bear in mind some background psychological considerations which, being psychological, are merely speculative. The avoidance of the 'treasure' theme of *Treasure Island* may have something to do with Stevenson's personal stabilization at that time. After his marriage to a motherly type of woman, he had achieved a degree of resolution of his difficult relationship with his father (warm affection and passionate disagreement). *Treasure Island* was written with the enthusiastic collaboration of his father—himself a lover of romantic adventures—and of Stevenson's stepson, the boy Lloyd Osbourne. It was the first book in which he was really fulfilled as a writer. And yet there is that curious note of sadness at the end. There are some disturbing touches, like the marooning of the three pirates: 'Coming through the narrows, we had to lie very near the southern point, and there we saw all three of them kneeling together on a spit of sand, with their arms raised in supplication.' This seems very poignant for a boys' story. Where is the 'happy ending'? (pp. 72-4)

[On] its own plane *Treasure Island* fulfills the primary purpose of all fiction: to provide the reader with imaginative understanding of human nature, in ideal conditions for the existence of that understanding. Even by itself it suggests doubts about the view, still quite common, that Stevenson was not really a creative writer at all, but an essayist who occasionally graced the lighter forms of fiction with a characteristic touch. And taken in the context of Stevenson's developing art, we may see it as a preliminary sketch of his main theme: the theme, or insight, he indicates in these words from *Dr. Jekyll and Mr. Hyde:* 'I saw that of the two natures that contended in the field of my consciousness, if I could rightly be said to be either, it was only because I was radically both.' At a less profound level, we might conclude our revisiting of *Treasure Island* by remarking that it is the commonplace and yet (to Stevenson) astounding co-presence of good and evil qualities in the same person—rather than the simpler human problem of reconciling personal liking with moral disapproval—which gives a tinge of serious interest to this yarn about pirates; which reappears in the bold morality art of *Jekyll and Hyde;* and which finally reached an extra dimension of significance in the subtler art of *The Master of Ballantrae* and *Weir of Hermiston*. (p. 74)

W. W. Robson, "'The Sea Cook': A Study in the Art of Robert Louis Stevenson," in On the Novel: A Present for Walter Allen on His 60th Birthday from His Friends and Colleagues, edited by B. S. Benedikz, J. M. Dent & Sons Ltd., 1971, pp. 57-74.

A. C. CAPEY

[Kate Friedlaender's analysis of *Treasure Island*] in terms of its appeal to the prepubertal boy depends upon certain general characteristics which enable her to speak of a 'typical adventure story . . . whose fantasies answer to a definite phase in the dissolution of the Oedipus complex' [see excerpt dated 1942]. . . . (p. 229)

By dwelling on the general and the typical (the 'ingredients it has in common with ephemeral yarning'), Dr. Friedlaender blurs the distinction of *Treasure Island;* but if her account in places is crude and misdirected it does provide us with a valuable insight which repays prolonged examination. The rivalry of the boy with various grown men is of central significance in the book (cf Jim's 'envious' emulation of the doctor in

'taking French leave' from the stockade), and it is true too that 'the original cause of the rivalry' (if we accept for the moment Dr. Friedlaender's assumptions) is 'pushed into the background' by Jim's departure for sea—and, we should add, by his father's death earlier. Perhaps a false stress is put on the boy's leaving his mother, if the implication is that 'competition' for her is about to be dissolved by 'the homosexual attitude to the father' or father-figures Jim meets among the crew. The only competition for the mother evinced by the book—the real father's death having been hastened by one of the associated father-figures, Billy Bones—is that between Jim and the apprentice tap-boy appointed to replace him and/or his father at the Admiral Benbow Inn; to ignore the psychological implications of Jim's hostility to the 'clumsy stranger who was to stay here in my place beside my mother', while emphasising 'the dissolution of the Oedipus complex' through the practised 'rivalry' and achieved 'equality' with adults on the expedition, is to miss an opportunity to make the required point in Stevenson's distinctive way.

Jim's growing up in the course of the book is rather more than a matter of 'rivalry' leading to acknowledged 'equality' with the father-figures, so that the terms require some qualification and elaboration. Consider the incidents they apparently refer to. Jim is not 'taken on by a party of men in their hunt for treasure': the expedition is launched by his elders and betters after he, alone (for his mother is preoccupied with settling 'the captain's score'), has provided its compelling motive in the form of 'Flint's Fist'—though 'the treasure's whereabouts' is something 'he learns of' while looking, uncomprehending, over the doctor's shoulder at the map of the island. It is true that, 'owing to good luck' (and it *does* matter that it is that and not something else), he 'discovers the conspiracy among the pirates' and is able immediately to forewarn his friends. But it is not true, despite the warm testimony of the doctor, that he 'comes repeatedly to the rescue of his fellows': on the contrary, Ben Gunn directs him to the safety of the stockade, Gray saves his life in the ensuing battle, Gray, Livesey and Gunn at the final test when he and Silver face the enraged mutineers across the empty treasure-pit; Jim's navigation of the *Hispaniola* to North Inlet, under the indispensable direction of Israel Hands, is his single conscious contribution to the salvation of his friends after he has imparted to them the news of what he heard in the apple barrel.

Stevenson goes to some trouble, in fact, to show that Jim is a boy, with a boy's limitations and particular qualities in the company of adults; there are few concessions to the heroic rôle exemplified, in its incomparably cruder form, by the three lads in *Coral Island*, and even 'the cruise of the coracle' shows Jim subject to wind and waves and dependent on luck as well as skill in boarding the *Hispaniola*. It is true that he 'measures his strength' with Israel Hands in 'rivalry' culminating in the boy's ascendancy, but the significance of the psychological opposition between them is achieved through Stevenson's 'imaginative handling' of the sequence on board the rolling schooner. The boy and the man are deadly enemies, but the limitations of the one are set against the infirmity of the other, the rivals share for their different purposes the same desire to beach the ship safely, guile is matched by guile, the armed man by the quicker boy and by the ironic encumbrance of O'Brien's corpse, and finally two near misses with the knife by two accidental pistol-shots. That Jim should fire 'without a conscious aim' is necessary and right in the context, an instinctive reaction to 'pain and surprise' felt by one who believes himself unassailable in the shrouds and sits there 'smiling away, as conceited as a cock upon a wall'.

> One more step, Mr. Hands, . . . and I'll blow
> your brains out!

shows Jim resuming the pretentious rôle of his initial approach to him:

> I've come aboard to take possession of this
> ship, Mr. Hands; and you'll please regard me
> as your captain until further notice;

but the moment Jim is 'acknowledged by [Hands] as a rival on an equal footing'—

> . . . I reckon I'll have to strike, which comes
> hard, you see, for a master mariner to a ship's
> younker like you, Jim

—is in fact the prelude to the pirate's last attempt to assert his mastery and his almost simultaneous overthrow:

> . . . both my pistols went off, and both escaped
> out of my hands. They did not fall alone; with
> a choked cry, the coxswain loosed his grasp

"Right in front of me, not half a mile away, I beheld the Hispaniola *under sail." Illustration by Walter S. Paget, an English figure painter who created pictures for the first edition of* Treasure Island.

upon the shrouds, and plunged head-first into the water.

Stevenson's ability to create the limitations and the arrogance of the 'ship's younker' at the same time as he shows himself successful has its origins far back in the book, in the creation of feckless brutality, leaderlessness and cowardice among the buccaneers who sack the Admiral Benbow. 'You can't find the treasure,' says Smollett to Silver in the stockade. 'You can't sail the ship . . . You can't fight us—Gray, there, got away from five of you.' Hands may have been Flint's gunner, but his bombardment of the block-house is ineffective; while the futility of the mutineers' assault on the stockade is crystallised in the inability of Red Cap to get off the fence. However fierce and treacherous the mutineers may be, they are fundamentally as incompetent as Silver describes them—too insubordinate to mutiny intelligently, too drunk to notice Ben Gunn settle an old score with one of them, so riven with faction as to make the glimpse Jim has of Hands and O'Brien at each other's throat not wholly surprising. The fate of Billy Bones, paralysed by rum in the manner of Flint himself, is seen to extend eventually to the remnant:

> . . the wind brought us a noise between shriek-
> ing and singing . . . 'Heaven forgive them,'
> said the doctor; ''tis the mutineers!' 'All drunk,
> sir,' struck in the voice of Silver from behind
> us.

It is into such company that Jim stumbles on his return to the stockade, where he boasts:

> . . . your whole business gone to wreck; and if
> you want to know who did it—it was I! I was
> in the apple barrel . . . and I heard you, John
> . . . and told every word you said before the
> hour was out. And as for the schooner, it was
> I who cut her cable and it was I that killed the
> men you had aboard of her, and it was I who
> brought her where you'll never see her more,
> not one of you. The laugh's on my side; I've
> had the top of this business from the first; I no
> more fear you than I fear a fly.

—The reader, of course, is in a position to assess the exaggeration in Jim's claims and to see more clearly than the dumbfounded audience what Stevenson is actually doing here. In his passage of sustained rhetoric Jim is explicitly 'measuring his strength' with the pirates', vindicating his triumphant right to be 'acknowledged by all as a rival on an equal footing'. What can the pirates say? They cannot check the facts; they can only add further illustrations of Jim's ascendancy. Morgan recalls, fatuously, that 'it was him that knowed Black Dog', and Silver adds the scarcely more pertinent point that 'it was this same lad that faked the chart from Billy Bones'. Silver speaks for all in saying,

> First and last, we've split on Jim Hawkins!

Jim's prowess, real and imagined, deliberate and accidental, makes him the gigantic excuse the humiliated pirates need ('You came crawling on your knees to me to make [a bargain with the doctor],' retorts Silver when presented with the Black Spot, '—on your knees you came, you was that downhearted'). As the scales fall from their eyes, the pirates simply hoodwink themselves differently, driven to do so by Jim's rhetorically selective self-advertisement.

That is the psychological point of interest. Dr Friedlaender, however, takes Jim's account at its own valuation, assumes that it carries the author's imprimatur, and provides further exaggerations of her own:

> [Jim] outwits the most dreaded of the pirates. He saves his own life by intimidating the pirate ringleader . . . with the news of how he, the youngest of them all, has been the one, right from the start, to see through and to foil his plottings.

—Silver has not been 'outwitted', nor is he now 'intimidated'; the words do not apply to the case. It is true that Jim has been a major instrument in foiling Silver's plot, but by going AWOL ashore after breaking the news to his friends he has helped to deprive them of the opportunity to weigh anchor and maroon the bulk of the mutineers. Even Jim hasn't claimed to have 'seen through' Silver's plottings 'from the start' (uniquely he might have done so, having been paid to look out for the man): Dr. Friedlaender's Jim is her own and Jim's invention, and her misreading of the character's relation to Silver—a misreading occasioned by the demands of her thesis—compels her to refer to their association in terms too general to account satisfactorily for what Stevenson offers us.

'A proper realisation of Silver' will be a necessary element in our 'proper participation in Jim Hawkins' adventures'; in fact the boy's growth in the course of the book to the point where he is 'glad to be so cheaply quit of him' is a growth in understanding of the complex character of Silver and of himself in relation to him. The relationship begins with the dreams consequent on keeping a 'weather-eye open for a seafaring man with one leg'. . . . and it ends in dreams after the 'formidable seafaring man with one leg has at last gone clean out of [Jim's] life',

> . . . when I hear the surf booming about [the accursed island's] coasts, or start upright in bed, with the sharp voice of Captain Flint still ringing in my ears: 'Pieces of eight! pieces of eight!'

The later nightmares refer to a specific frightening incident, when Jim returns to the stockade expecting to find his friends and is caught by the mutineers:

> All was dark within, so that I could distinguish nothing by the eye. As for sounds, there was the steady drone of the snorers and a small occasional noise, a flickering or pecking that I could in no way account for . . . And then, all of a sudden, a shrill voice broke forth out of the darkness: 'Pieces of eight! pieces of eight!' . . . without pause or change, like the clacking of a tiny mill.

The earlier nightmares, not quite without foundation in that Billy Bones' preoccupation and fear have infected Jim his 'weather-eye', simultaneously create and discredit the reader's expectations, so that the first encounter with Silver is a welcome relief from the imagined horror:

> His left leg was cut off close by the hip, and under the left shoulder he carried a crutch, which he managed with wonderful dexterity, hopping about on it like a bird. He was very tall and strong, with a face as big as a ham—plain and pale, but intelligent and smiling. Indeed, he

> seemed in the most cheerful spirits, whistling as he moved among the tables, with a merry word or a slap on the shoulder for the more favoured of his guests.

The reality is so different from the dream that Jim's fears lest Silver should 'prove to be the very one-legged sailor whom [he has] watched for' are immediately allayed. There are connections between the two descriptions: the dream-figure's deformity loses its hideousness in the precise observation of the waking boy, who remarks the cripple's 'wonderful dexterity', manliness and strength, qualities which correspond to the 'monstrous' capacity to 'leap and run' shown in the dream (and which are shown for fearless admiration in the final chase across the plateau—'The work that man went through, leaping on his crutch till the muscles of his chest were fit to burst, was work no sound man ever equalled'). But the connections are there for the reader, not for Jim, for whom the reassuring largeness of the 'intelligent and smiling' face before him bears no resemblance to the 'diabolical expressions' of his dreams. The conscious terror which the nightmare is subsequently understood to have prefigured comes with the murder of 'poor Tom' and the boy's aimless flight from the scene, a sequence which stands in relation to the nightmare rather as Silver's parrot 'clacking' in the block-house stands towards Jim's final dreams. Silver, now 'resting lightly on his crutch', now 'leaping back . . . with the speed and security of a trained gymnast', 'smiling away . . . , his eye a mere pin-point in his big face', is transformed from genial publican to 'monster':

> . . . John seized the branch of a tree, whipped the crutch out of his armpit, and sent that uncouth missile hurtling through the air. It struck poor Tom, . . . [who] had no time given him to recover. Silver, agile as a monkey, even without leg or crutch, was on the top of him next moment . . .

It is tempting to say that the murderous Silver is the real man, and the 'bland, polite, obsequious seaman of the voyage out' the mask. Certainly Silver employs his beaming countenance as a mask, but to see it as only that is to miss the point of Stevenson's creation. Silver has made of his quayside inn a freshly painted, neat and 'bright enough little place of entertainment', and if the sailors he attracts are rough and loud he is himself 'a very different creature', 'clean and pleasant-tempered'. That is the man to whom Jim responds and who is the boy's father-figure on the voyage . . . and it is appropriate, therefore, and not a mere matter of engineering, that it should be Jim who hears the pregnant words:

> 'No, not I,' said Silver, 'Flint was cap'n; I was quartermaster . . .'

and who realises (not taking, at this stage, the full significance of Silver's disclaimer) that the 'capital fellow' is not what he has seemed to be. But neither is Silver all that a pirate seems to be, if (as Jim notes) Pew, Black Dog and Billy Bones are to be thought of as representative. He is a gentleman of fortune, certainly, but he also has aspirations to being a gentleman and is quite at home eating pork with the squire's party. Moreover, although he is as ruthless as the other mutineers, he has 'a head on his shoulders': he knows the limitations of the crew, and if he could have his way would delay the mutiny to the last possible moment; he murders Tom only when he has failed to persuade him to join the mutiny, and is incomparably more discreet about the job than the murderers of Alan, whose cry disturbs the marsh birds and (we learn in due course) helps to recall the invaluable Gray to the colours. Indeed, Tom's forth-right praise reveals the quandary Silver is in:

> ... you're old, and you're honest, or has the name for it; and you've money, too, which lots of poor sailors hasn't; and you're brave, or I'm mistook. And will you tell me you'll let your-self be led away with that kind of a mess of swabs?

Tom does not know, nor do Jim and the reader at this stage, that more lies behind Silver's efforts to recruit him than the characteristic flattery and that with the urgent appeal—

> All's up—you can't make nor mend; it's to save your neck that I'm a-speaking, and if one of the wild 'uns knew it, where 'ud I be, Tom—now, tell me. where 'ud I be?

—is implied the menace of the Black Spot, 'tipped' by the 'wild 'uns'. Silver's fortunes are at stake, as they have been since the apple barrel conversation, with Hands itching to get at the pickles and wines in the cabin, the boatswain 'grumbling as loud as the worst' at the 'dreary morning's work' of berthing the ship, and the whole crew 'tired and out of sorts'. 'Silver was the captain,' observes Jim of the scene on board when the men are given shore leave, 'and a mighty rebellious crew he had of it.' A double-mutiny is impending, to avert which Silver 'outstripped himself in willingness and civility . . . , all smiles to everyone'; and how close it remains is signified by the murder of Alan, for which Anderson and Merry (we may suppose) are responsible. Tom's murder is thus not the action simply of a coward but an attempt to salvage something from the wreck of an intelligent scheme; and when Smollett dis-misses him under the flag of truce he is furious not so much at his rebuff (surely?) as at hearing home truths. When Jim returns to the stockade we see Silver still fighting his dual battle, trying to ease himself from a trap in which the 'wild 'uns' are largely responsible for placing him: there would have been nothing for Jim to hear in the apple barrel if the patrons of the Sign of the Spy-Glass had been suited to its landlord.

Jim is as exceptional among the cabin party as Silver is among the mutineers. Of each it may be said (with whatever different implications) that he has 'a foot in either camp'. Neither can be relied on to do what his side expect of them, and is conse-quently rejected by them. Jim's friendship with the men on the voyage out, his labouring with them to 'warp' the ship and his slipping ashore with them make both his accidental eaves-dropping and his misdirected return to the stockade appropriate. But the resumed relationship, as he and Silver await the result of the council of war outside the block-house, shows the two friendless ones inevitably relying on each other, not their erst-while wholesome friendship but a marriage of convenience which each would renounce if he could. 'The homosexual attitude to the father' which Stevenson may be 'unconsciously' presenting at this point is not of primary importance. The rope that binds Jim to Silver on the trek for the treasure signifies his captivity rather than their association, even if it ensures that the pair keep together as the doctor has recommended. The turns Jim's fortunes take between his capture and his rescue are correlated with various facets of Silver's character, man of honour and buccaneer, one-legged monster and fearful depen-dant; the rope acts for Silver as both lifeline and gaoler's key.

That 'squire's side' should finally accept the humbled Silver has its origins deep inside the book—it represents no concession

to sentiment. There are no loose ends or gratuitous 'arrange-ments' in *Treasure Island,* no sudden pumping up of a failing balloon such as we get in *Coral Island* or *Jack Holborn;* rather an economy and an inevitability that prompt comparison with *Nostromo.* And by 'no loose ends' is meant such important effects, for any reader who is disposed to elevate Jim above his station, as the boy's task of sorting the treasure, his two scalings of the stockade—the first cautious, the second thought-less—and the rôle of Ben Gunn. If the reader is enabled to identify himself with Jim and enjoy the range of his perils and excitements, he is offered much more than 'a typical adventure story'—he is encouraged to evaluate the purposes and achieve-ments of the hero, and to acquire a larger vision than is open to Jim alone; and as he ponders the tale with its particular marks of Stevenson's 'inspiration and industry' he may find that even the routine title signifies more than the 'ephemeral yarning' it ostensibly advertises. (pp. 230-38)

> *A. C. Capey, "'Treasure Island' and the Young Reader," in* The Use of English, *Vol. 25, No. 3, Spring, 1974, pp. 228-38.*

HAYDEN W. WARD

A clue to [the reasons for the broad appeal of *Treasure Island*] is to be found in a remark Stevenson made to W. E. Henley at the time he was writing *Treasure Island:* "It's awful fun boys' stories; you just indulge the pleasure of your heart, that's all; no trouble, no pain." Setting forth an aesthetic justification of adventure fiction in **"A Humble Remonstrance,"** Stevenson says that the writer of boys' stories reproduces the substances of his own "youthful daydreams." And in **"A Gossip About Romance,"** written in February, 1882, just as *Treasure Island* was concluding its serial appearance in *Young Folks,* he says that providing the pleasurable substance of daydreams is the chief purpose of the writer of romance. . . . (p. 305)

From *Treasure Island* on, the central purpose of Stevenson the writer was . . . to represent an increasingly complex body of romantic fiction, which would be "to a grown man what play is to the child."

As he tells the story of how *Treasure Island* was written, Ste-venson makes us realize that its peculiar appeal to both juvenile and adult readers is, in part, the result of the interplay of boyish and mature sensibilities that produced it. He recounts the well-known story of his making a map of "Treasure Island" with the help of his thirteen-year-old stepson, Lloyd Osbourne. From the features of the map, Stevenson's preeminently concrete imagination (he was from a family of distinguished civil en-gineers) developed the incidents of the plot, according to Lloyd's "classical tastes" in adventure—which included, as he wrote to Henley, not allowing women in the story, a condition which he himself was "blythe to obey." The later works upon which he collaborated with Stevenson, such as *The Wrong Box, The Ebb-Tide,* and *The Wrecker,* reveal, in the early draft stages, that Lloyd Osbourne had considerable skill in contriving plots, and, although Stevenson himself rewrote these novels to a considerable extent before publication, he generally preserved the core of Lloyd's earlier work. The vigor and fecundity of Stevenson the writer's late years owe much not merely to Lloyd Osbourne's collaborative hand, but to his helpful suggestions and criticism as well. It seems that his presence at Braemar and Davos, while Stevenson was writing *Treasure Island* at the rate of a chapter a day, was a powerful stimulus. Indeed, Stevenson told Henley that the book was "purely owing to Lloyd." (p. 306)

In addition to Lloyd, Stevenson had the occasional but enthusiastic help of his father. . . . According to Stevenson, his father provided the inventory of Billy Bones's sea chest and suggested *Walrus* as the name of Captain Flint's ship. J. C. Furnas notes that Thomas Stevenson also suggested the device of the apple barrel and wrote the elaborate signatures on the redrawn map that was used in the book edition [see excerpt dated 1951]. It would have been more accurate for Stevenson to have said that his father's "own stories" were often recited as bedtime stories to Louis himself, and probably did as much as any direct literary influence to whet his taste for adventure yarns.

Thomas Stevenson's "collaboration" with his son was incidental, but it had its origin in Louis's early youth. One is struck by the circumstantial parallel between his telling stories to amuse his sick son and Stevenson's writing *Treasure Island* for Lloyd. Thomas Stevenson seems to have had, as one of his many facets, a talent for relating empathically to the imagination of a boy. In *Treasure Island,* for the first time, his son was able to embed that seemingly inherited talent in the crisp, concise, vivid style that he had developed only after a literary apprenticeship going back to his teens.

From the unusual "collaborative" circumstances of its composition derives, quite probably, the most notable characteristic of *Treasure Island:* the continuity and compatibility of boyish and adult experience, and the freedom from a moral sense that is the consequence of the adult characters' adherence to a boy's point of view. Squire Trelawney, Dr. Livesey, and Captain Smollett trust Jim Hawkins to tell their joint adventures to the world, a trust predicated, one supposes, on their faith that his powers of memory and articulation are equal or superior to their own. From the very beginning, Jim seems indispensable to, a collaborator in, their treasure-seeking enterprise: when he has related to his friends what he has heard in the apple barrel, Dr. Livesey says, "Jim here . . . can help us more than anyone. The men are not shy with him, and Jim is a noticing lad." By this point in the novel, Jim has given ample evidence of the truth of this observation: he has found and saved the map, and discovered the plans for mutiny; by the book's end, he will have contributed greatly to preserving both the treasure and the safety of his friends. Whose way of "noticing" better qualifies him to tell the story?

Although giving an account of the adventure is an adult responsibility, Jim gains the experience to do so as a result, not of his acquired knowledge, but of his boyish innocence, which makes even Billy Bones, Ben Gunn, and Long John Silver trust him without the long acquaintance that accounts more readily for the trust of the doctor and the squire. Billy Bones depends upon Jim to be a nurse and confidant, telling him of Flint's treasure and offering to share it with him (as Silver does at another crisis in the story). After only a brief interview, Ben Gunn, who has not seen another man for three years, trusts Jim to be the agent of his being rescued and tells him the location of his precious boat. And Silver readily makes Jim his partner in the ad hoc conspiracy to outwit the other pirates in seeking the treasure.

Grown men feel impelled to tell Jim their private affairs with the assumption that he will assist them in the realization of their ambitions as no adult can, with the belief that his honesty, courage, and perspicacity are more conducive to effective action because they have not been weakened by the corruption that is understood, but never expressly stated, to be the inevitable consequence of growing up. It is as though, in making

Jim their collaborator, they are trying to summon up these lost powers of youth's integrity in themselves. (pp. 307-08)

The implication, one supposes, is that in this world of boy's fantasy, a man cannot do much good by or for himself. Jim's narrative makes us believe that the inclinations of a boy can be so compatible with the needs and enthusiasms of men that they willingly and immediately cast off their adult consciousness—indeed, the entire burden of their experience and years—to share in a boy's way of conceiving and enacting his desires. Squire Trelawney's outburst, when plans have been made for the voyage, exemplifies the point:

> To-morrow I start for Bristol. In three weeks' time—three weeks!—two weeks—ten days— we'll have the best ship, sir, and the choicest crew in England. Hawkins shall come as cabin-boy. You'll make a famous cabin-boy, Hawkins. You, Livesey, are ship's doctor; I am admiral. We'll take Redruth, Joyce, and Hunter. We'll have favourable winds, a quick passage, and not the least difficulty in finding the spot, with money to eat—to roll in—to play duck and drake with ever after. . . .

It proves ironic in the event that the first member of this "choicest crew" that the squire mentions is the cabin boy. The very order of his spontaneous remarks, early in the book, implies the primacy of the boy as controlling agent of the situation in this pleasurable world of "day-dream." Using coins to play ducks and drakes (or chuck-farthing, poor Ben Gunn's favorite boyhood game), while it surely implies irresponsibility from an adult perspective, also implies acceptance of a view of life in which the symbolic power of money has not yet destroyed the power of innocent, unintellectual physical pleasure. One thinks more of throwing pennies in a wishing-well as the squire speaks than of that fantasy of economic power, lighting cigars with twenty dollar bills.

Jim comes to full consciousness of the supremacy of boyish power over the ineptitude of corrupt men when, after he has been captured by the pirates, he catalogs his triumphs over them. . . . In addition to the triumph of a boy's will, this speech asserts implicitly the premise that once the action is over, the boy's moral strength is sufficient for him to forgive his enemies, as men seldom do, in a spirit of good sportsmanship, and also for him to protect his defeated grown-up antagonists from harsh punishment at the hands of government authorites, who doubtless do not take the same sporting attitude. For Jim, once the adventure is done, it ought to be "shake hands all around." And Silver, at least, is willing to act provisionally on that premise, not only because it is expedient, but because he believes it, because he sees in Jim's generosity the spirit of the gentleman, a status to which he professes aspirations all through the book. Fortunately for Jim, the other pirates, who are mere "sheep," are docile enough to go along with the fantasy that they have been bested in a game. Sullenly, they hope for a few extra innings.

In this romantically idealized world, the effect of boy and men on one another is reciprocal: Jim gets responsibility, respect, and treasure; and his grown friends and adversaries get a chance, or are forced, to play life's dangerous game on his terms, without any of the troublingly complex psychological or moral awareness that paralyze the mature will to action (in the episode with Israel Hands, we see attempted murder reduced to a game of dodge-and-seek on the listing deck of the *Hispaniola*).

At the same time that he is made a collaborator in grown-up enterprises, Jim has the opportunity to exercise his boyish penchant for adventure, for exposing himself to seemingly gratuitous danger simply because the sport satisfies his curiosity: boredom is to be avoided at all costs, and as most adults know, it is a major condition of doing one's duty, of being "grown up," a state generally measured by one's capacity to sit motionless for long periods of time.

On two occasions, Jim leaves his friends: he goes ashore with the jolly boat full of mutineers and runs away into the woods, where he finds Ben Gunn. Later, he leaves the stockade and, using Gunn's little boat, eventually manages to capture the *Hispaniola*. In each of these episodes, Jim's dereliction of duty and following of his own boyish impulses lead to great benefits for his mature friends. One of the conditions of the romance of boyish adventure is the hero's freedom to act according to his own instincts, without being too restrained by adult supervision.

In order to make Jim's dereliction seem less serious, Stevenson makes Long John Silver the expositor of adult ethics, during the long speech that Jim overhears from the apple barrel. Throughout the book, in fact, Silver has a way of invoking "dooty" when he is on the point of violence or treachery. And this irony, obvious as it is, has the effect upon the reader of lessening the influence of Captain Smollet, who is Silver's reputable counterpart, a man of duty and prudence, a man whom Silver admires. Captain Smollett's being seriously wounded gives Jim the freedom to act. When he returns to the stockade, expecting to see his friends, his conscience is quite relaxed: "Possibly I might be blamed a bit for my truantry, but the recapture of the *Hispaniola* was a clenching answer, and I hoped that even Captain Smollett would confess that I had not lost my time." . . . (pp. 308-11)

"Truantry" suggests an analogy with absence from school: that is, from the dull and disagreeable duty of a boy to learn the adult way of acting and thinking. That disregard for this duty should be a condition of effective action is one of the underlying assumptions of *Treasure Island* that makes it distinct from most other boys' adventure stories, in which the hero becomes competent only when he ceases being a child and begins to act like a man.

Instead of adult knowledge to help him in his adventures, Jim has luck, a sense that circumstances conduce ultimately to his benefit. Stevenson depicts luck not as a blindly operative cosmic force but as an attribute of character. It enables one who has courage, practical intelligence, and moral principles—in a word, pluck—to survive and prosper with only occasional help from Providence.

The process is demonstrated when Jim voyages in Ben Gunn's boat and recaptures the *Hispaniola*. First of all, he is favored by a dark night, when "the fog had buried all heaven," and by an ebbing tide that carries him out toward the ship, where he discovers that the pirates have left her virtually unmanned. The next morning, when the sea gets rough, he tries to paddle the coracle to safer waters and, instead, nearly tips over. . . . The passage demonstrates the exploratory, pragmatic attitude of the boy hero in meeting a series of demanding physical situations, a pragmatism that complements his innocent moral idealism. In boys' adventure fiction, Christian values of good and evil are assumed to operate, usually without explicit statement. Even the villains accept these values, quite without reflection, and go about their crimes with a guilty sense of their depravity, even as the friends of the boy hero have a sense of their salvation.

Jim is, indeed, a kind of providential agent, a character initially implied by Squire Trelawney:

> "Hawkins, I put prodigious faith in you," added the squire.
>
> I began to feel pretty desperate at this, for I felt altogether helpless; and yet, by an odd train of circumstances, it was indeed through me that safety came. . . .

Silver shares the squire's "faith" by the book's end, when he literally fastens himself to Jim by a rope that strongly recalls the symbolic "monkey-rope" of Ishmael and Queequeg in *Moby-Dick*. As Silver says, imparting almost supernatural efficacy to Jim's testimony on his behalf, "You speak up plucky and, by thunder! I've a chance." . . . Dr. Livesey, Jim's closest adult friend, epitomizes the feelings of the men in the book when, outside the stockade, talking to Jim about his marvellously successful exploits, he says, "There is a kind of fate in this. . . . Every step it's you that saves our lives." . . . Silver puts the same idea from the defeated pirates' perspective: "First and last, we've split upon Jim Hawkins!" . . . (pp. 311-12)

That Silver is not killed off at the end, as are most vanquished master-villains, is one of the intriguing facts of the book. The reasons are to be found, in part, in Stevenson's relation with Henley, Long John's original. Just as, several years later, he could not bear to sever altogether a friendship that had become an intolerable psychological burden, and asked his lawyer and friend, Charles Baxter, to set up a disguised allowance for Henley, even though he wanted never to communicate with him again, so Stevenson has Jim sigh with relief that Long John Silver has escaped with part of the treasure and will trouble him no more. The pattern of fiction is repeated in Stevenson's life: he could not kill off a character he really liked.

Silver's treachery and murderousness are not much held against him, either by Jim or by his adult friends; after all, Silver kills only underlings. What disgusts Jim is Silver's ambivalence, his seeming continually to switch sides in the game that his vivid, histrionic character does much to create. Disloyalty is a serious offense in a boy's view. But Silver has always a gleam of awareness that the game is not self-contained, as the other characters, with less experience, believe; his memory of "many brisk lads drying in the sun at Execution Dock" recalls to him that the game has an unhappy way of spilling over into real life, where the result is poverty and shameful death. Silver is trying to use the treasure-hunting game as a hedge against the hideous possibilities of life; the other major characters are playing it for fun. To play for real, as both Silver and another charming outlaw of Victorian fiction, Becky Sharp, so well understand, is to cheat of necessity.

Silver is, of course, the darker, seamier side of Jim's potential adult character, as Dr. Livesey is the respectable side. Silver turns up, under other names, in Stevenson's later fiction, his nature darkened finally, in *The Master of Ballantrae*, into satanic evil. And there, the protracted game of hide-and-seek ends in death for both the hero and his antagonist. In *Treasure Island*, the boy's daydream, as Jim says in closing, never turns to waking nightmare. (pp. 312-13)

Stevenson [believed] that pleasure exists, perhaps ecstasy, in mastering physical difficulties; in enduring bravely, as though it were a matter of little consequence in the event and yet well worth the telling afterwards, the pain that attends this mastery (or failure to master, as the case may be). This continuity of belief can be seen from *Treasure Island* to *St. Ives,* in which Stevenson has the hero escape from imprisonment in Edinburgh Castle by scaling down its walls in the dead of night, only to become involved in a series of dangerous adventures. As the other late, unfinished writings suggest, Stevenson never lost his feeling about the pleasure to be derived from the romance of boys' fiction. But *Treasure Island* is the seminal work, in which Stevenson fused in its purest form the central theme of his work, the possibility of combining moral order with individual freedom, and the clarity and ease of style that became characteristic of most of his later writings. . . . (pp. 315-16)

To understand why grown men still "indulge the pleasure of their hearts" with *Treasure Island,* we cannot read about Huck Finn or Holden Caulfield, who experience the poignant loss of the efficacy of boys' dreams. Rather, we need to consider that, long after the dream has faded as a practical reality, Hemingway's old Santiago continues to fish, and Updike's Rabbit Angstrom stops to play pick-up basketball with a group of boys. (p. 316)

Hayden W. Ward, "'The Pleasure of Your Heart': 'Treasure Island' and the Appeal of Boys' Adventure Fiction," in Studies in the Novel, Vol. VI, No. 3, Fall, 1974, pp. 304-17.

IRVING S. SAPOSNIK

As the narrator of *Treasure Island,* Jim Hawkins is in many ways the prototype of Stevenson's youthful adventurers. He is not only the first, but the least complex; and his story is without many of the intricacies which are found in the subsequent adventures of Richard Shelton in *The Black Arrow* and David Balfour in *Kidnapped.* Although Jim Hawkins's story in *Treasure Island* is not without its structural subtleties and moral ambiguities, Stevenson has him present his adventures in a great rush, with a maximum of excitement and with a minimum of analysis. The object is immediacy of detail to insure immediacy of recognition. Jim is carried upon his voyage by a series of events whose rapidity leave both him and the reader little time for reflection. Both character and reader are captivated by the fascination of treasure, the crude equivalent of the idealized romantic quest, and both board the *Hispaniola* with eager and suspicious anticipation. In Jim, Stevenson creates an archetypal boy—lonely, impressionable, honest, fearful—and constructs a narrative of his adventures whose success depends upon that lightninglike concision which is the hallmark of the Stevenson style. (pp. 105-06)

[The] richness of *Treasure Island* goes beyond exciting action and narrative rapidity, essential as these are to its success. Within its narrative directness, it raises questions of social conduct and moral concern which do not usually appear in conventional adventure tales. The real measure of Stevenson's success is his ability to introduce these considerations without upsetting the delicate balance of make-believe. The people of *Treasure Island* are real and unreal; for the most part, they exist in a timeless, spaceless world removed from the incursions of a shattering reality; they are the "puppets" Stevenson intended them to be. On the other hand, they are motivated by all-too-human passions, and they enact a paradigm of that commercial spirit which has become the basis of modern capitalism. (pp. 106-07)

As popular as it has become, *Treasure Island* is possibly the strangest adventure story ever written, for it is a boy's book

without a hero and without a satisfying conclusion. Furthermore, it recalls for young and old the truths about themselves and their society which they may wish to forget. The young reader cannot shy away from the suggestions of youth's limitations: its nightmarish loneliness; its tangential relationship to the adult society; its impulsive action only sometimes successful, often foolish; and its inability to know others and especially itself. The adult reader faces more painful truths: he must confront the emptiness of that which he has striven to achieve, and he must acknowledge the valid analogy of the treasure hunt with the competitive society from which he draws his values.

From the very beginning the metaphor of money dominates the action: Billy Bones is fearful of discovery because he is privy to the secret of the treasure; Jim's mother is a combination of honesty and greed (as he describes her) as she forages the dead Billy's seaman's chest so that she may take her rightful due; Squire Trelawny dreams of "money to eat—to roll in—to play duck-and-drake with ever after"; and Dr. Livesey commends the death of Pew while rapaciously pocketing the oilskin packet whose contents spell unearned riches. As if this delineation were not sufficient, there is Long John Silver, whose surname embellishes the narrative with visions of monetary pursuit and material gain. Money is the ruling principle of *Treasure Island,* and the reader is hardly surprised to discover at the end of the book that the treasure is an epitome of all the world's currency. . . . (pp. 107-08)

Viewing *Treasure Island* as an economic myth serves to extend its psychological and social implications. By using the ingredients of conventional romance, it reconstructs with diagrammatic precision the ethical bones of Western society. Little distinction is drawn between the established possessors of respectable position and the cutthroat have-nots who lust for fame and power: both are motivated by the same underlying greed, a compulsive desire for material acquisition and self-aggrandizement. Moral lines are difficult to draw in such a world, and values are measured only by individual achievement. Its central figure is Silver who represents in his conduct the best possible method of survival. A utilitarian of the first order, he recognizes that he must survive by his wit and by his bluff. (p. 108)

Always calculating, Long John Silver wins over even the cautious Livesey and the fearful Jim; ever mercurial, he sways between allegiance to Jim and an unsatiable desire for wealth. Silver's ambition goes beyond material gain, for he recognizes the power of money and hopes to invest it so that he may one day be a member of Parliament and ride through the streets in a coach. His whole being is directed toward the use of money to achieve reputation. A thorough pragmatist, he combats the difficulties of existence with whatever means at his disposal; a total individualist, he never forgets that his primary loyalty is to himself. Appropriately, he is the only one in the novel to emerge unscathed, to escape to a presumed life of comfort. While condemnation in the next world may well be his lot, his secular achievement is hardly impaired.

John Silver's complement is Jim Hawkins. Silver lives by his wits, but Jim moves in a world where luck is his protection; Silver is crafty, but Jim survives by accident and instinct. The best indication of their difference is in their individual reactions to the treasure hunt: Silver finds it a rousing adventure and a means to security; Jim sees the events as tragic and is condemned to such nightmares as he dreamt before. While Silver counts his gold, Jim reckons the lives lost upon the chase and forswears a like adventure. Just as Silver anticipates Stevenson's James Durie, Jim resembles his young David Balfour; both are the two faces of the Stevenson man. If Silver is the first of Stevenson's magnificent villains, Jim is the forerunner of his unheroic heroes. Unable to escape, he must make the best of his world, but only after realizing his inadequacies. At the end of his adventure, Jim is as much a prisoner as he was at Squire Trelawney's. Compelled to recount a story which he would rather forget, he serves as the voice of those who live his adventure with him and who, like him, are imprisoned in their memories.

The only true survivor of the treasure hunt is Silver, who leaves the known world and its aspirations for some supposed paradise with an old Negress and a pet parrot. In *Treasure Island,* such escape remains a remote possibility. The difficulty for romance occurs later when materialism shatters the purity of idealism and egoism brutalizes the charm of innocence. As an early romance, *Treasure Island* not only allows fantasy but spells out its ingredients with an artistry unparalleled in other works of its kind. Yet it neither sentimentalizes nor avoids the uglier aspects of the world it depicts. Like its author, it stands midway between a fanciful impulse toward romantic adventure and a necessary acknowledgement that the greatest adventure is the life we endure. (pp. 108-09)

> *Irving S. Saposnik, in his* Robert Louis Stevenson,
> *Twayne Publishers, Inc., 1974, 164 p.*

JENNI CALDER

[*An American-born British critic and educator, Calder is the daughter of critic David Daiches, whose works on Stevenson are among the most respected in the field.*]

[*Treasure Island*] established Stevenson as a writer who was able to produce a kind of story for which there was a hungry readership, a hungry readership of adults who had seen the Victorian age eat away at fantasy, at dreams, at romance, at heroics, and longed for a legitimate adventure fiction. Stevenson was lucky; not lucky that his talent should be recognised, for it was manifest and accessible, but lucky that his talent should coincide so creatively with a need of the time.

Treasure Island has lasted as a children's adventure story. It rests uneasily in that genre. It has always been a story that adults have relished perhaps more than children, in fact it may be adult favour that has kept it so very much alive. Stevenson was more concerned with writing out of his system certain elemental fantasies than in deliberately putting together a story that would appeal to boys, and it tends to be this aspect that attracts critical attention. A neutral, unformed hero (a borrowing from Scott) enters an anarchic world, uncovers but scarcely discovers some vivid truths about human nature, and returns none the worse but none the better either to normality. If the story is read by children sometimes with impatience it may be because the hero, the character with whom they are asked to identify, has so little personality. Jim Hawkins does not seem to be of any great importance. The memorable characters are those surrounded by moral ambiguity, Billy Bones and Long John Silver, and the characters in whom greed and deceit, fear and violence are an integral part of their substance. There is no doubt that Long John Silver, based with his loud flourishes and one-leggedness on Henley, is the hero of the book. Jim Hawkins slides out of the memory. Stevenson was to do much better with a 'neutral' character when he created David Balfour. Significantly, poor Jim fades through a superabundance of equivocal father figures. (p. 173)

> *Jenni Calder, in her* RLS: A Life Study, *Hamish Hamilton, 1980, 362 p.*

PERRY NODELMAN

[*The following excerpt is taken from a paper delivered at the Boston Public Library on October 23, 1982.*]

In his *Anatomy of Criticism,* Northrup Frye distinguishes between two important types of characters: the *eiron,* the self-effacing speaker of truth, and the *alazon,* the self-centered imposter or hypocrite. For Frye, the traditional heroism of the heroes of romances and of comedies with happy endings makes them into *eirons:* they are modest, they are brave, and they are right, and that's why they have happy endings. Meanwhile, tragic heroes, who tend to trust themselves too much, or to misunderstand the world they live in and therefore must suffer, are *alazons.*

Now Peter Rabbit and Anne of Green Gables and Jim Hawkins of my own favorite children's classic, *Treasure Island,* are not tragic heroes. But if they have anything in common, it's their lack of heroic perfection. . . . If anything, they are *alazons,* imposters, people who've got caught up in the sort of events that always happen to heroes in romances or adventures, and who therefore ought to be heroic, but who somehow never seem quite able to manage it. (p. 46)

In *The Coral Island,* Ralph Rover tells how, before his shipwreck, he loved to hear "wild adventures in foreign lands."

"'One more step, Mr. Hands,' said I, 'and I'll blow your brains out!'" Illustration by N. C. Wyeth, an American artist whose paintings for the 1911 Scribner's edition are perhaps most closely associated with Treasure Island.

In *Treasure Island,* Jim Hawkins tells how, before his adventure, he was "full of sea dreams and the most charming anticipations of strange islands and adventures." Well, Ralph goes on to have lots of wild adventures; but for all his constantly professed Christianity, for all his constantly professed hatred of the violent savagery and cannibalism he finds so fascinating that he can't seem to stop talking about it, Ralph never loses his love of interesting places and strenuous action. But when Jim Hawkins speaks of his anticipation of strange adventures, he quickly adds, "In all my fancies nothing occurred to me quite so strange and tragic as our actual adventures." "Tragic" is an interesting word; after actually having been on Treasure Island, Jim Hawkins can find nothing good to say about it, or pirates, or adventures. In retrospect, and as unlikely as his behavior on the island makes it seem, he claims that "from the first look onward, I hated the very thought of Treasure Island." And finally, he says, "Oxen and wain-ropes would not bring me back to that accursed island." Jim wants us to know he's changed his mind, learned from his bad experiences; yet for all his gloomy I-told-you-so's, all his dampening of the spirits of adventure, the story Jim tells is a lot more interesting than the story the enthusiastic Ralph Rover tells. Why?

I think the answer is that Jim's sour grapes make him an inadequate hero: [an] imposter. As the hero of an adventure, there are three things he ought to be able to do. He ought to be able to believe that what he does is right, and he ought to be able to enjoy doing it, and he ought to do it very well indeed. Now the young Jim the adventures of *Treasure Island* actually happen to manages all three; but Stevenson cleverly gives us *another* Jim Hawkins also, the older one who tells the story. And this other Jim constantly tries to undermine our enthusiasm for his younger self's actions. The younger Jim tells the pirates about what a terrific hero he's been: "if you want to know who did it . . . it was I. I was in the apple barrel the night we sighted land . . . and as for the schooner, it was I who cut her cable, I who killed the men aboard her." But the older Jim interprets the exact same events quite differently, sees them as evidence of youthful rashness and thoughtlessness and ignorance: "I was full of folly, if you like." In saying things like that, this older Jim announces himself as an inadequate hero; anyone who makes such sanctimonious comments about the stupidity of being adventurous surely doesn't belong in an adventure. But he also *does* make his point: what allowed the younger Jim to become a hero was nothing truly great nor admirable, but mere folly, mere human weakness. He was simply not good enough nor great enough. He was inadequate.

Now I assume that most readers respond to the older Jim's sanctimonious superiority to his younger self the same way I do: we'd like him to just shut up. If we're reading this book, then we're reading it because we *like* pirates and adventures, and we aren't going to have much patience with someone telling us how foolish such things are. In fact, I suspect it's our rejection of the older Jim's spoilsport attitudes that lets us enjoy and embrace the younger Jim's folly so wholeheartedly; we like the inadequate rash kid better than the boring prig he grew up into. Furthermore, and like the apparently inadequate Anne at Green Gables, Jim *does* end up saving the day in *Treasure Island,* and as his older self points out, he does it by being rash and foolish. In both books we have it both ways at once: the thrill of adventure and romance and happy endings as accomplished by perfectly unheroic, perfectly normal people like you and me. (pp. 48-9)

Perry Nodelman, "Some Heroes Have Freckles," in Children and Their Literature: A Readings Book,

edited by Jill P. May, ChLA Publications, 1983, pp. 41-52.*

FERNANDO SAVATER

The purest piece of storytelling I know, the one that most perfectly combines the initiatory and the epic, shadows of violence, and the macabre with the incomparable splendor of triumphant audacity, the scent of seagoing adventure—which is always the most perfect, the most absolute adventure—with the subtle complexity of a boy's first and decisive moral choice; in short, the most beautiful story that has ever been told me, is *Treasure Island.* Rarely does the year pass that I do not reread it at least once; and more than six months never pass without having thought about it or dreamed of it. It is not easy to put one's finger on the source of this book's inexhaustible magic, for like all good stories it aspires only to be told and retold, not explained or commented on. Mind you, I am not saying that it is impossible to comment on it or explain it; I am only stating that this is not what it aspires to, what it requires of its hearer's or reader's generosity. Yet nothing is simpler than to point out several of its obvious partial charms: its impeccable sobriety of style, the narrative rhythm that seems to sum up all perfection in the art of storytelling, the vigorous depiction of its characters, the shrewd complexity of an extremely simple plot.

A first reading might give the impression that it is the story of one fabulous figure, John Silver; but then we notice that the really disconcerting character, the hero of the tale in every sense of the word, is Jim Hawkins, whose view of Silver is what constitutes the latter's whole enigma. It is tempting to compare the relationship of the *Hispaniola*'s cabin boy and its cook with that which connects Ishmael and Ahab; but it would be a mistake to think of them as similar. It is true that both Ishmael and Jim are forced to make the fundamental moral choice when they confront an exhibition of untamable energy from the two ferocious cripples who threaten them; it is true that both Ahab and Silver utterly crush the soft substance of everyday corporate morality, demonstrating the invulnerable reality of authentic free will; and it is no less true that both succeed in terrorizing and repelling the civilized, almost mother-ridden Ishmael and Jim. But the positive aspect of the comparison ends here, for the reactions of Ishmael and Jim are diametrically opposite when they are faced with the challenge of their overpowering tempters. Ishmael chooses sides against Ahab from the very first moment; his fascinated attraction to the *Pequod*'s captain is based precisely on the nostalgic feeling of knowing that he is everything Ahab is not; Ishmael loves the sea as a terrible, though exciting, alternative to his real everyday world, the land; Ahab knows nothing of the land, to which he does not belong; and he *is* the sea, the white monster and the deep abyss. In Ahab's ocean, Ishmael disappears; he comes to the surface only for an instant, to recount his anti-Ahabian joy in fondling the sperm whale's delicious softness; when he finally reappears it is because Ahab, the whale, and all that they represent have disappeared in the welcome blackness of memory, out of which he begins to tell the tale: "Call me Ishmael. . . ." But Jim accepts Silver's challenge and fights on the pirate's own ground; in fact, as the one-legged cook reminds him, he becomes the only real buccaneer in addition to Silver—the vigorous whelp of an extinct breed. This is why Jim does not weaken when he enters the pirates' dangerous terrain—the sea, the gloomy, swampy island, the schooner's secret depths—but acquires more and more strength, changes from narrator into protagonist, tells the story to himself (while

Ishmael tells it to Ahab) and at the end of the book splits in two: part of him, part of the treasure, goes with Silver and part remains with the representatives of the established order. And there is more, for Jim's last thought at the end of the novel is for the bar silver that still remains on the island, and which, as he coolly says, "certainly . . . shall lie there for me." A dangerous coolness, and profoundly ambiguous, like everything else in this disconcerting story.

This radical ambiguity is the secret, or the treasure if you like, of this peerless tale. The many-faceted world of adolescence, that is, the world of the moment immediately previous to the invention of necessity, here achieves its finest literary crystallization (leaving out Henry James' *The Turn of the Screw*, if you wish). The unhesitating and definite judgment which morality always thinks it is ready to dictate has never been so hopelessly frustrated.

John Silver, hypocrite, murderer, and traitor, struggles to take possession of a treasure which belongs much more to the pirates who had striven and suffered for that gold than to the prosperous adventurers who are trying to take it over thanks to fortuitous circumstances. His attitude toward Jim is always perfectly loyal, even when he deceives him, just as the serpent's was toward Adam and Eve; and finally, Silver saves Jim's life, the murderer's and thief's life Jim has decided to create for himself on the pirates' isle.

The intriguing figure of Jim Hawkins piles up endless ambivalences; a spy who sees and hears everything, he passes from one side to another in a rapid and equivocal kind of traffic, incapable of staying quietly in one camp or the other, faithful only to himself as a fugitive, an infiltrator. His apparently frail figure is revealed at every turn as the strongest one in the story, the cleverest and most implacable, but also as obviously childish; he is the catalyst of the action, the one who throws the dice anew every time the story bogs down in apparent equilibrium, the inexorable inciter of adventure.

And what shall we say of other, minor paradoxes, such as Ben Gunn, that ragged millionaire, a repentant pirate, the scarecrow figure who is inescapably master of the situation? He is the most inept and ridiculous of all Flint's henchmen, but the only one who can pass himself off as Flint, as a spectral voice among the trees, because he is the owner of the pirates' hoard. Captain Flint's true heir is this pitiable ghost, whom his companions do not respect living or dead! And those most worthy squires Trelawney, Dr. Livesey, and the others reveal a suspicious talent for deception and for alliances that are more opportunist than opportune, in addition to other traits whose morality is decidedly pragmatic, such as their truly buccaneerish greed for the island's treasures.

Although in the strict sense it cannot be said that anyone steps out of his role (except Jim?), and all the characters more or less respect the convention of their respective positions in life, the course of the story implicitly undermines the confidence each character has in his own logic. All of them know how to make good speeches rationalizing their behavior, but from time to time a small revealing sigh slips out, such as that moment when Trelawney, at the beginning of the treasure voyage, confesses that he admired old Flint and "was sometimes proud he was an Englishman."

The Spanish word *peripecia*, a sudden reversal of circumstances, comes from the Greek *peripeteia*, an unexpected turning of tables. In this etymological sense, the reversals of Jim

and John Silver are truly dizzying. Jim changes, almost unconsciously, from the good son of a modest family, helping his parents to run the family business, into first the confidant and then the legatee of an old pirate from the great Flint's crew. However, he is the accomplice of another buccaneer, a blind man, who delivers to the first pirate the "black spot," a buccaneer-style ultimatum, and the way he collects the inheritance which implicitly belongs to him rather closely resembles theft. From there he goes on to be the one who sets off the expedition by discovering the map and making it public; the complete break with his former life is made clear when he returns to the inn to say goodbye to his mother, and finds that she has brought in a boy of his own age to help her in the work of the place. This intruder who is occupying his niche in normal life definitely uproots him, propels him toward adventure. He becomes the *Hispaniola*'s cabin boy and the scullion of Silver the cook— becomes his friend and faithful listener to Silver's tales of pirates, in which Jim's own experiences are prefigured. But he is the one who listens to and warns of the buccaneers' plot, crouched in the apple barrel as if he were the ship's good spirit, a seagoing—and quiet—poltergeist.

As soon as they reach the treasure island, Jim goes into a frenzy of escapes. First he jumps into Silver's boat even though he has discovered his plot, thus escaping from those who presumably are on his side (Trelawney, Livesey, etc.). As soon as he sets foot on land he also flees from Silver and the rest of the pirates to wander alone on the island. He encounters the hermit Ben Gunn, whose lack of confidence in this disconcerting fugitive is matched by the reader's excited uneasiness in the face of such confusing behavior. He again joins his former companions, the "good guys," in the old stockade, fights along with them like one of their own, and again surreptitiously abandons them when night falls. And what is his objective? To take over the *Hispaniola*! The innkeeper's boy, the cabin boy, the spy, the friend of Bill Bones and John Silver, now finally turned into a pirate, sets out to board the schooner. And he wins it, steers it to a distant cove, and is its commander; now he is Captain Jim Hawkins. Of the Royal Navy? Despite the fact that he strikes the black flag, his actions are more those of a buccaneer than of an officer of His Gracious Majesty; let us leave him as a pirate, to be fair to him. In any case, he shows himself to be an energetic captain, who does not hesitate to kill the mutinous Israel Hands in order to maintain control in the conquered ship. Now where is the timid, pious servant of the *Admiral Benbow*? He returns to the stockade and by sheer chance finds himself in the midst of the pirate camp, again John Silver's accomplice and confidant. Next morning Dr. Livesey bitterly reproaches him for his behavior and urges Jim to escape with him, despite his having given Silver his word of honor not to do so. But Jim refuses, he *cannot* leave; he, who unhesitatingly breaks all the promises of obedience he had made to Captain Smollett and Trelawney, gives unbreakable precedence to the oath sworn to a pirate, thus implicitly respecting the *omertà* of the Brothers of the Coast. In the end it is with John Silver that he sets off in search of the treasure, and it is legitimate to ask what would have happened if it had been the pirate who had found Flint's gold; in any case, the patient greed of Ben Gunn, the marooned pirate, had already placed it in safety, perhaps preventing Jim from doing another about-face.

On his side, the figure of John Silver suffers no fewer sudden reversals. The first has occurred before the story's beginning and has carried him from quartermaster of Flint's *Walrus* to innkeeper of *The Spyglass* in Bristol, as we learn when we listen with Jim from inside the apple barrel. From there he becomes cook of the *Hispaniola,* an "official" job which he carries on simultaneously with his role as leader of the pirates' mutiny that is being planned on the schooner. Implacable murderer of the sailors loyal to Captain Smollett, no sooner does he reach the island than he assumes the title of "Captain" Silver, being, together with Smollett himself and Jim, the third person of this rank to appear in the novel at one point or another. He soon changes roles, from the vicious attacker of the stockade to the one responsible for converting it into a refuge, leaving the "good guys" the role of marauders without a camp. His ambiguous actions, as he protects and uses Jim, place him at odds with the rest of the pirates, who send him the black spot; but he smothers the rebellion by showing the treasure map which the "good guys" have given him with suspicious ease. Does he really believe that he has a chance to find Flint's wealth, or does he perform the ritual of search to the very end as a means of escaping from his dangerous and disillusioned companions, whom he leads into a trap? Certainly, in the final ambush he cooperates with the "good guys" by killing the ringleader of the recent rebellion against his authority. Finally, Silver quietly rejoins the winning group and responds to Smollett's question with "Come back to my dooty, sir," to which the legitimate captain either cannot or will not reply. Completely transformed, he even joins in celebrating their departure from the island like one more member of the victorious group. . . . (pp. 29-34)

He still gets a chance to show one last side when he flees with a modest part of the treasure, thanks to Ben Gunn's complicity and the tacit compliance of the rest of the "good guys," who are happy to be free of him and the knotty problem of bringing him to justice. In the last chapter there is a particularly impressive moment when, before they finally embark from the island, the night breeze brings to Dr. Livesey and Jim a noise of laughter or distant shrieking. It is the surviving pirates, wandering ghostlike on the island, already mingling with the other ghosts of Flint's crew. Their cries are the result of despairing drunkenness or the delirium of fever, and Dr. Livesey feels pity for them and even wonders if it is not his duty to offer them the services of his profession. Silver, very much at home in his new role, as he had been in all the previous ones, dissuades him from doing so, for those men, he says, can neither keep their word nor believe that anyone else can. Livesey replies indignantly that his case is not exactly different, to which Silver makes no reply, though evidence of the difference leaps to the eye: Silver is there and not with the ghosts, which proves that he knows very well which promises he must keep. His old associates must also have arrived at this same conclusion, as is significantly proved by the bullet that a vengeful pirate fires on the departing schooner, which passes a few inches over Silver's head.

But what particularly intrigues the thoughtful reader, the one who reads the book for the second time (and who is not always the best reader), is the relationship between Jim and Silver. If some psychoanalyst has studied this novel—and I don't know whether one has—he would not have failed to notice that the story begins with the death of Jim's father and ends with the disappearance of Silver, who acts as a father image for the boy throughout the novel. Seen in these terms, the whole story can be understood as a meditation on orphanhood, or, if you like, as that acceptance of solitude which marks the adolescent's entrance into adulthood. Silver, unworthy but stimulating, dan-

gerous but also a helper if his aid can be gained, such a virtuoso of hypocrisy that he succeeds in making it an unusual form of frankness, is the father who shows how to renounce parents, the father whose astonishing strength and freedom establishes a law which refutes all attempts at legislation. Only by demonstrating in his own person the most radical independence and the most unconditional courage does Jim win the right to be helped by Silver and to help him; the strongest man sells the right to his complicity by courage and freedom. But I do not want to speak in a language that is not mine, and so I leave the familiar metaphors for the professionals of such pastimes. I would rather couch the question in moral terms, if the adjective serves. Jim has to decide whether his field of activity is that of the pirates, or, as a child would brutally put it, whether John Silver is good or bad. And there is no use here in retreating to the holier-than-thou superiority of adult relativism, which knows already that it all depends, mind you, and that all of us are both good and bad. For we are inside the greatest adventure of all, among pirates and in mortal danger, with an incalculable treasure at stake, and we must make the right choice or perish in the attempt. Jim is aware that there are two ways of doing things, two opposite ways—Captain Smollett's and Captain Silver's—and that both ways, if the cards are played right, can offer unsuspected resources of strength and admirable victories. All his initial education, all the language he has been given, inclines him to respect and imitate Captain Smollett's way and not to seek salvation outside it; but, and this is the story's hidden plot, events point him toward the pirates' world, offering him the profound temptation of piracy; that is, the suggestion that, to win a real buccaneer's treasure, one must in some sense become a buccaneer. At this point John Silver, master buccaneer, appears and gratuitously offers him his irresistible lesson. Smollett's way does not lead to the treasure, for he has no sympathetic relationship with the treasure; Silver's way is the constant promise of it. In the end Silver escapes with the most precious part of the treasure, that is, with his spirit and panache—these are riches that no one can steal from the pirate. There is a crucial moment in the story when Jim and Silver are as honest with each other as their respective roles permit. When Jim climbs into the stockade after hiding the *Hispaniola* and falls unexpectedly into the pirates' hands, he believes himself lost and blurts out all his activities against them—his spying in the barrel, stealing the schooner, and so on—and admits to having played a leading role in the action at every moment, offering with breathtaking audacity to intercede for them if they spare his life. Then he turns to Silver and says,

> "And now, Mr. Silver, I believe you're the best man here, and if things go to the worst, I'll take it kind of you to let the doctor know the way I took it."

> "I'll bear it in mind," said Silver, with an accent so curious that I could not, for the life of me, decide whether he were laughing at my request or had been favourably affected by my courage.

This short dialogue is particularly significant. Jim has just explained his piratical behavior, has ratified Silver's teachings, and asks him, the man most likely to understand him, to explain to the "good guys" the inevitability of that behavior in view of the enterprise they had undertaken. If one really wants to experience a search for treasure, then one must experience it as a pirate. Now Jim, who has sufficiently demonstrated his buccaneering aptitudes both to Silver and himself, has also really earned, and not in the form of resentment or timidity, the right to reject piracy, which is what he solemnly does at that moment, and even offers the possibility of repentance to his hearers. From that time onward Jim begins to disengage himself from the treasure, until his final declaration that nothing in the world would bring him back to seek the rest of the riches hidden on the island. His proving is over, his choice is made. Or is it? Because he still studies Silver to see if he is laughing at him or approves his actions; because, the next day, he will not escape with the doctor so as not to break his sworn word to the pirate; because, after all, what would have happened if John Silver had been the one to find the treasure? Neither Stevenson nor anyone else can know that; fortunately, the story has no other ending than the events themselves which form it, and which resist to the end any conclusive interpretation.

To summarize, I have read and still read *Treasure Island* as a reflection on audacity. Jim Hawkins is undoubtedly audacious from his first appearance in the novel, but left to himself he would not be capable of exploring all the aspects of his gift, especially that moment of transgression without which it cannot be said that true audacity exists. This is John Silver's virtue, to show audacity's *demonic* face to Jim. And there is no doubt that Jim takes full advantage of the lesson, recoiling from none of the violent, rapacious, or destructive aspects of demoniacal audacity. And this continues to the end, until his domesticated and soothing final return to the "good guys." This twist of the plot is also an audacious act, perhaps the greatest of the whole tale, the one that was being carefully prepared in all the previous reversals. In the end, is it not the demoniacal John Silver himself who teaches Jim the tactical virtues of a timely reunion with the side of the law? "Come back to my dooty, sir." Oh, the old fox! And what matchless audacity, what a splendid lesson in freedom! Desperate and disillusioned audacity of freedom! Jim accepts the challenge like a true pirate, ready to go on to the end of the adventure. In a fight without quarter, by trickery and by death, he has won the ship, the island, and the treasure; now comes the most difficult test, the hour of renunciation, and in this predicament his audacity does not flag either. Now John Silver can disappear in the hurly-burly of the port, for the game has been played, and well played, to the very end. And so boldness has imposed its own order, and perhaps Jim will become a squire; but the dream, ah, the dream is uncontrollable. There another legend goes on uninterruptedly. There the waves break forever on the shores of the remote island, and the parrot voice of Flint's unquiet ghost keeps on crying "Pieces of eight! Pieces of eight!" as if it were calling us to new adventures. (pp. 34-8)

> *Fernando Savater, "A Treasure of Ambiguity," in his* Childhood Regained: The Art of the Storyteller, *translated by Frances M. López-Morillas, Columbia University Press, 1982, pp. 29-38.*

PAUL HEINS

In his essay on Stevenson Henry James . . . called *Treasure Island* a classic [see excerpt above, 1888]. He tells how the mood of the story was set from the very beginning. . . . Certainly, the first third of *Treasure Island* still strikes the reader as powerfully as it did Henry James, compounding mystery with suspense and culminating in the revelation of the true nature of John Silver as Jim lay hidden in the apple barrel.

The rest of the story depends in great part on the working out of the original premises. The sea voyage and its nautical terminology and the desert island with its Crusoe-like derelict Ben Gunn are, of course, the normal stuff of this kind of adventure story. But Jim, the frank, objective narrator, imperceptibly develops new facets of character. Imprudently, as well as impulsively, he makes two excursions unbeknown to his party—narrated in **"My Shore Adventure"** and **"My Sea Adventure"**—and when he accidentally finds himself in the clutches of John Silver and his men, he displays astonishing bravado. (p. 198)

Seen from this point of view, Jim can be considered, along with John Silver, a richly portrayed character. The ambivalence of John Silver has long been recognized as a master stroke of characterization in keeping with the intuitions of the author of *The Strange Case of Dr. Jekyll and Mr. Hyde.* Jim, on the other hand, has long been submerged as the witnessing protagonist of an adventure story. In the final paragraph of the book, however, he states, "Oxen and wain-ropes would not bring me back again to that accursed island; and the worst dreams that ever I have are when I hear the surf booming about its coasts, or start upright in bed, with the sharp voice of Captain Flint still ringing in my ears: 'Pieces of eight! pieces of eight!' " Here we have no account of joyous adventure but the terrors of memory poignantly expressed.

In our own day, another kind of sea voyage—that of *The Slave Dancer* (Bradbury)—also ends with a powerful epiphany of memory. Not that Paula Fox consciously imitated Stevenson; but it is noteworthy that she ended her novel with a similar kind of emotional cadence. Stevenson, as is well known, was a conscious stylist and in writing a boy's book did not forsake his conscious devotion to his own way of choosing words and forming sentences. In *Treasure Island,* except for the deliberate use of expressions such as "wain-ropes" or a bit of dialect to flavor his prose, Stevenson generally used direct, concrete words for his protagonist's narrative, at the same time elaborating the sentence structure to accommodate many of the possibilities of syntactical subordination. Consequently, in writing a juvenile novel, he was able to combine richness of narrative with conversational eloquence. (pp. 198-200)

> *Paul Heins, "A Centenary Look: 'Treasure Island'," in* The Horn Book Magazine, *Vol. LIX, No. 2, April, 1983, pp. 197-200.*

WILLIAM BLACKBURN

Robinson Crusoe establishes a basic paradigm: European man, stranded in the wilderness, subdues it to his needs and eventually returns home in triumph. This is not to say the hero is unchanged by his adventures, but the emphasis is on the struggle against external threats. The essential point is that the changes in Crusoe—his piety and industry—simultaneously fit him to survive on the island and also to take his proper place in European society upon his return. The desert island, that landscape so rich with symbolic possibilities, merely provides the arena in which Crusoe—as he so interminably insists on reminding the reader—can subdue the natural man in himself by subduing nature. Though many later novels will find darker possibilities on desert islands, *Robinson Crusoe* is serenely dedicated to the triumph of civilization over savagery, and the hero's commitment to the values of that civilization remains unshaken. In essence, all that Crusoe learns from his sojourn on the island is that he can and must subdue it, and Defoe's limited internalization of nature characterizes the island-romance until we come to a book which internalizes the island in quite a different way, Robert Louis Stevenson's *Treasure Island*.

Though Stevenson gleefully described *Treasure Island* as being "as original as sin," he was in fact well aware of his debt to his predecessors, and to Defoe in particular. . . . Nevertheless, despite his declared intention to revive "all the old romance, retold / Exactly in the ancient way," Stevenson's island does not reflect the triumphant imperial self displayed in *Robinson Crusoe*. Their superficial resemblance notwithstanding, the adventures of Jim Hawkins do not produce the same effect as those of Robinson Crusoe, and the lessons Jim learns from his experience are radically different from those gleaned by Defoe's hero. (p. 10)

Stevenson follows Defoe's paradigm: hero voyages to island, has various heart-in-mouth adventures, and returns home. But everything Crusoe learns confirms the wisdom of his society and his father. . . . Everything Hawkins learns calls into question the unshakeable certainties of his childhood, and he is thrown on his own resources in a way in which Crusoe never was. And, as one might well expect in a romance—and especially in one which had its genesis in a map—the treatment of landscape is particularly significant. The island bulks large in Jim's daydreams:

> I approached that island in my fancy, from every possible direction; I explored every acre of its surface; I climbed a thousand times to that tall hill they call the Spyglass, and from the top enjoyed the most wonderful and changing prospects. Sometimes the isle was thick with savages, with whom we fought; sometimes full of dangerous animals that hunted us; but in all my fancies nothing occurred to me so strange and tragic as our actual adventures.

Jim's first sight of the island contrasts the daydream with the reality in a way typical of the novel's continual undermining of the boy's expectations. The foliage

> had a kind of poisonous brightness. . . . A peculiar stagnant smell hung over the anchorage—a smell of sodden leaves and rotting tree trunks. I observed the doctor sniffing and sniffing, like someone tasting a bad egg.
>
> "I don't know about treasure," he said, "but I'll stake my wig there's fever here."

In the novel's last paragraph, we meet a Jim Hawkins very different from the lad who once dreamed of going treasure hunting: "Oxen and wainropes would not bring me back again to that accursed island; and the worst dreams that ever I have are when I hear the surf booming about its coasts, or start upright in bed with the sharp voice of Captain Flint still ringing in my ears. . . ." These three visions of the island sum up Jim's experience; the movement from daydream to nightmare is a pattern central to the novel.

I do not wish to accuse Stevenson of modern morbidity; the author of *Treasure Island* was not trying to be J. D. Salinger. He was well aware of the limitations imposed by his intended audience—a letter records his dismay in writing the novel and having "to work it off without oaths. Buccaneers without oaths—bricks without straw. But youth and the fond parent have to be consulted"—but this did not impede his deft and quiet marking of Jim's fall from innocence to experience. Crusoe's

father was an infallible guide, but Jim's father is too sick and weak to deal with Billy Bones. Other adults are likewise unreliable: his mother, failing utterly to understand their situation, insists on having her due and not a farthing over, and promptly faints when her myopic rectitude gives the pirates time to overtake them; or Squire Trelawney, who is simply Jim writ large. . . . The obligatory rattlesnake Jim blunders across on the island is deplorably obvious: Jim learns many things more happily left unknown. One of his more educational experiences comes when, after a deadly parody of a child's game . . . , Jim is cornered by Israel Hands. Confident in the civilizing power of his brace of pistols, Jim

> was drinking in his words and smiling away as conceited as a cock upon a wall, when . . . back went his right hand over his shoulder. . . . I felt a blow and then a sharp pang, and there I was pinned by the shoulder to the mast. In the horrid pain and surprise of the moment—I scarce can say it was by my own volition, and I am sure it was without a conscious aim—both my pistols went off . . . the cockswain loosed his grasp upon the shrouds, and plunged head first into the water.

Stevenson artfully spares the sensibilities of his readers, but there can be little question that here we touch one of the sources of the boy's nightmares. Like Nick Adams and Huck Finn, Jim has reason to have bad dreams.

The ambiguity of the island also reflects the pervasive moral ambiguity of the novel. F. J. H. Darton—who really should have known better—castigates Stevenson's novel because "the expedition was launched by greed and decorated with murder and treachery, and concluded by luck rather than righteousness" [see excerpt above, 1932]. What Darton fails utterly to realize is that the moral ambiguity he so energetically deplores is central to the novel. On his island, Crusoe learned that man is the monarch of all he surveys, that he is indeed the master of his fate. Crusoe is justified by his success—but the success of Hawkins and his friends, as Darton notes, proves nothing at all. Unlike Crusoe, Jim Hawkins is not justified by his works; material success does not resolve moral uncertainty. Nowhere is Stevenson's deliberate ambiguity more apparent than in his handling of Long John Silver. Silver is a liar, a cheat, and a thief; he commits murder before our eyes and—what must have been little less reprehensible in the eyes of many of Stevenson's contemporaries—he lives with "a woman of color." Yet Silver has intelligence and courage—the preeminent virtues of the Doctor Livesey Jim so admires—and this makes his case problematical. So much so, that when this blackest of villains escapes scot-free at the novel's close (and four hundred guineas to the good), few readers can be so heartless as to wish the case otherwise.

Thus we see that the ambiguous landscape of the island designedly mirrors the ambiguity of the novel as a whole. The unreliability of adults, winning "by luck rather than righteousness" (the accident of the apple barrel; the fact that Jim's friends triumph through his disobedience and desertion of his post, not through Jim's being a good bunny), and the complexity of Long John Silver all emphasize "the limits of the human will and the fragility of fortune . . . as patrons of reality." Crusoe's island was merely an elaborate commentary on the wisdom of his father and his society; Jim's island continually corrodes the bright certainties of his childhood. Just as the island is not what he imagined it to be, neither is anything else; the ambiguity of the landscape figures the larger ambiguity of which Jim has become so nightmarishly aware. Stevenson, by his internalization of landscape, enriches and extends the tradition he inherits from Defoe—and breaks the trail which will be followed by the serious juvenile romances of the twentieth century. Stevenson is not their only begetter, but he determined the direction they could not choose but follow. (pp. 10-11)

> *William Blackburn, "Mirror in the Sea: 'Treasure Island' and the Internalization of Juvenile Romance," in* Children's Literature Association Quarterly, *Vol. 8, No. 3, Fall, 1983, pp. 7-12.**

APPENDIX

The following is a listing of all sources used in Volume 10 of *Children's Literature Review*. Included in this list are all copyright and reprint rights and acknowledgments for those essays for which permission was obtained. Every effort has been made to trace copyright, but if omissions have been made, please let us know.

THE EXCERPTS IN CLR, VOLUME 10, WERE REPRINTED FROM THE FOLLOWING PERIODICALS:

The Academy, v. XXIV, December 1, 1883.

America, v. 137, December 3, 1977 for a review of "And This Is Laura" by Ethna Sheehan. © 1977. All rights reserved. Reprinted by permission of the author./ v. 112, June 26, 1965; v. 121, December 20, 1969. © 1965, 1969. All rights reserved. Both reprinted with permission of America Press, Inc., 106 West 56th Street, New York, NY 10019.

American Imago, v. 3, April, 1942.

Appraisal: Children's Science Books, v. 4, Spring, 1971. Copyright © 1971 by the Children's Science Book Review Committee. Both reprinted by permission.

Arizona English Bulletin, April, 1976. Reprinted by permission.

The Athenaeum, n. 2927, December 1, 1883.

The Atlantic Bookshelf, a section of *The Atlantic Monthly,* v. 180, December, 1947. Copyright 1947, renewed 1975, by The Atlantic Monthly Company, Boston, MA. Reprinted by permission.

The Atlantic Monthly, v. 192, December, 1953. Copyright 1953, renewed 1981, by The Atlantic Monthly Company, Boston, MA. Reprinted by permission.

Best Sellers, v. 36, July, 1976; v. 42, February, 1983; v. 43, May, 1983; v. 44, January, 1985. Copyright © 1976, 1983, 1985 Helen Dwight Educational Foundation. All reprinted by permission.

Book News Letter, n. 241, December, 1955.

The Book Report, v. 2, September-October, 1983; v. 2, March-April, 1984. © copyright 1983, 1984 by Linworth Publishing Co. Both reprinted by permission.

Book Week—World Journal Tribune, April 9, 1967. © 1967, *The Washington Post.* Reprinted by permission.

Arbuthnot, May Hill. From *Children and Books*. Scott, Foresman, 1947. Copyright, 1947, renewed 1974, by Scott, Foresman and Company. Reprinted by permission.

Arbuthnot, May Hill. From *Children and Books*. Third edition. Scott, Foresman, 1964. Copyright © by Scott, Foresman and Company, Glenview, IL 60025. All rights reserved. Reprinted by permission.

Arbuthnot, May Hill and Sutherland, Zena. From *Children and Books*.Fourth edition. Scott, Foresman, 1972. Copyright © 1972, 1964, 1957, 1947 by Scott, Foresman and Company. All rights reserved. Reprinted by permission.

Bader, Barbara. From *American Picture Books from Noah's Ark to the Beast Within*. Macmillan, 1976. Copyright © 1976 by Barbara Bader. All rights reserved. Reprinted with permission of Macmillan Publishing Company.

Baildon, H. Bellyse. From *Robert Louis Stevenson: A Life Study in Criticism*. A. Wessels Company, 1901.

Barrie, J. M. From *Margaret Ogilvy*. Charles Scribner's Sons, 1896.

Baskin, Barbara H. and Karen H. Harris. From *More Notes from a Different Drummer: A Guide to Juvenile Fiction Portraying the Disabled*. Bowker, 1984. Copyright © 1984 by Barbara H. Baskin and Karen H. Harris. All rights reserved. Reprinted with permission of the R. R. Bowker Company.

Bennett, James O'Donnell. From *Much Loved Books: Best Sellers of the Ages*. Boni & Liveright, 1927. Copyright 1927, by Boni & Liveright, Inc. Renewed 1954 by Liveright Publishing Corp. Reprinted by permission.

Breaux, Adèle. From *Saint-Exupéry in America, 1942-1943: A Memoir*. Fairleigh Dickinson University Press, 1971. © 1971 by Associated University Presses, Inc. Reprinted by permission.

Brée, Germaine and Margaret Guiton. From *An Age of Fiction: The French Novel from Gide to Camus*. Rutgers University Press, 1957. Copyright © 1957 by Rutgers, The State University. Reprinted by permission of Rutgers University Press.

Brown, Margaret Wise. From comments from the dust jacket to *The Fish with the Deep Sea Smile*. By Margaret Wise Brown. Dutton, 1938. Copyright 1938 by E. P. Dutton & Co., Inc. Renewed 1965 by Roberta Brown Rauch. All rights reserved. Reprinted by permission of Roberta Rauch.

Butler, Dorothy. From *Cushla and Her Books*. The Horn Book, Inc., 1980. Copyright © 1975 and 1979 by Dorothy Butler. Reprinted by permission of the author.

Calder, Jenni. From *RLS: A Life Study*. Hamish Hamilton, 1980. Copyright © 1980 by Jenni Calder. Reprinted by permission of A. D. Peters & Co. Ltd.

Cate, Curtis. From *Antoine de Saint-Exupéry*. Putnam's, 1970. Copyright © 1970 by Curtis Cate. All rights reserved. Reprinted by permission of the Putnam Publishing Group.

Chesterton, G. K. From *Robert Louis Stevenson*. Dodd, Mead, 1928. Copyright, 1928 by Dodd, Mead and Company, Inc. Renewed 1955 by Oliver Chesterton. Reprinted by permission of Miss D. E. Collins.

Conford, Ellen. From ''Nobody Dies in My Books,'' a promotional piece by Little, Brown, 1977. Reprinted by permission of Little, Brown and Company, Inc.

Cullinan, Bernice E. with Mary Karrer and Arlene M. Pillar. From *Literature and the Child*. Harcourt Brace Jovanovich, 1981. Copyright © 1981 by Harcourt Brace Jovanovich, Inc. All rights reserved. Reprinted by permission of the publisher.

Daiches, David. From *Robert Louis Stevenson*. New Directions Books, 1947. Copyright 1947 by New Directions. Renewed 1975 by David Daiches. Reprinted by permission of the author.

Darton, F. J. Harvey. From *Children's Books in England: Five Centuries of Social Life*. Edited by Brian Alderson. Revised edition. Cambridge University Press, 1982. © Cambridge University Press 1958, 1982. Reprinted by permission.

Davis, Enid. From *The Liberty Cap: A Catalogue of Non-Sexist Materials for Children*. Academy Chicago Publishers, 1977. Copyright © 1977 by Academy Chicago Publishers. All rights reserved. Reprinted by permission.

Donelson, Kenneth L. and Alleen Pace Nilsen. From *Literature for Today's Young Adults*. Scott, Foresman, 1980. Copyright © 1980 Scott, Foresman and Company. All rights reserved. Reprinted by permission.

Dreyer, Sharon Spredemann. From *The Bookfinder, a Guide to Children's Literature about the Needs and Problems of Youth Aged 2-15: Annotations of Books Published 1975 through 1978, Vol. 2*. American Guidance Service, Inc., 1981. © 1981 American Guidance Service, Inc. All rights reserved. Reprinted by permission.

Eigner, Edwin M. From *Robert Louis Stevenson and Romantic Tradition*. Princeton University Press, 1966. Copyright © 1966 by Princeton University Press. All rights reserved. Excerpts reprinted by permission of Princeton University Press.

Fiedler, Leslie A. From an introduction to *The Master of Ballantrae: A Winter's Tale*. By Robert Louis Stevenson. Rinehart, 1954. Copyright © 1954, renewed 1982 by Leslie A. Fiedler. Reprinted by permission of Leslie A. Fiedler.

Furnas, J. C. From *Voyage to Windward: The Life of Robert Louis Stevenson*. William Sloane Associates, Inc., 1951. Copyright © 1951 by J. C. Furnas. Copyright renewed, 1979 by J. C. Furnas. Reprinted by permission of Brandt & Brandt Literary Agents Inc.

Gillespie, John and Diana Lembo. From *Introducing Books: A Guide for the Middle Grades*. R. R. Bowker Co., 1970. Copyright © 1970 by Xerox Corp. Reprinted by permission.

Gillespie, John T. From *More Juniorplots: A Guide for Teachers and Librarians*. Bowker, 1977. Copyright © 1977 by John Gillespie. All rights reserved. Reprinted by permission of the R. R. Bowker Company.

Gwynn, Stephen. From *Robert Louis Stevenson*. Macmillan and Co., Limited, 1939.

Hearn, Lafcadio. From *A History of English Literature in a Series of Lectures, Vol. II*. Edited by R. Tanabe and T. Ochiai. The Hokuseido Press, 1927.

Higgins, James E. From *Beyond Words: Mystical Fancy in Children's Literature*. New York: Teachers College Press, 1970. © 1970 by Teachers College, Columbia University. Reprinted by permission of the publisher.

Huck, Charlotte S. and Doris Young Kuhn. From *Children's Literature in the Elementary School*. Second edition. Holt, Rinehart and Winston, 1968. Copyright © 1961, 1968 by Holt, Rinehart and Winston, Inc. All rights reserved. Reprinted by permission of CBS College Publishing.

Human—And Anti-Human—Values in Children's Books: A Content Rating Instrument for Educators and Concerned Parents. Edited by the Council on Interracial Books for Children, Inc. Racism and Sexism Resource Center for Educators, 1976. Copyright © 1976 by the Council on Interracial Books for Children, Inc. All rights reserved. Reprinted by permission.

Hürlimann, Bettina. From *Three Centuries of Children's Books in Europe*. Edited and translated by Brian W. Alderson. Oxford University Press, Oxford, 1967. © Oxford University Press 1967. Reprinted by permission.

Jan, Isabelle. From *On Children's Literature*. Edited by Catherine Storr. Allen Lane, 1973. Copyright © Les Editions ouvrieres, 1969. Translation copyright © Allen Lane, 1973. Reproduced by permission of Penguin Books Ltd.

Kiely, Robert. From *Robert Louis Stevenson and the Fiction of Adventure*. Cambridge, Mass.: Harvard University Press, 1964. Copyright © 1964 by the President and Fellows of Harvard College. All rights reserved. Excerpted by permission.

Kingston, Carolyn T. From *The Tragic Mode in Children's Literature*. New York: Teachers College Press, 1974. Copyright © 1974 by Teachers College, Columbia University. Reprinted by permission of the publisher.

Lang, Andrew. From *Essays in Little*. Charles Scribner's Sons, 1891.

Matthias, Margaret and Garciela Italiano. From "Louder than a Thousand Words," in *Signposts to Criticism of Children's Literature*. Edited by Robert Bator. American Library Association, 1983. Copyright © 1983 by the American Library Association. All rights reserved. Reprinted by permission.

Maurois, André. From "Antoine de Saint-Exupéry," translated by Renaud Bruce, in *From Proust to Camus: Profiles of Modern French Writers*. By André Maurois, translated by Carl Morse and Renaud Bruce. Doubleday & Company, 1966. Copyright © 1966 by André Maurois. Reprinted by permission of the author and the author's agents, Scott Meredith Literary Agency, Inc., 845 Third Avenue, New York, NY 10022.

Moss, Elaine. From *Picture Books for Young People 9-13*. The Thimble Press, 1981. Copyright © 1981 Elaine Moss. Reprinted by permission.

Appendix

CUMULATIVE INDEX TO AUTHORS

This index lists all author entries in *Children's Literature Review* and includes cross-references to them in other Gale sources. References in the index are identified as follows:

AITN: *Authors in the News*, Volumes 1-2
CA: *Contemporary Authors* (original series), Volumes 1-116
CANR: *Contemporary Authors New Revision Series*, Volumes 1-17
CAP: *Contemporary Authors Permanent Series*, Volumes 1-2
CA-R: *Contemporary Authors* (revised editions), Volumes 1-44
CLC: *Contemporary Literary Criticism*, Volumes 1-36
CLR: *Children's Literature Review*, Volumes 1-10
DLB: *Dictionary of Literary Biography*, Volumes 1-45
DLB-DS: *Dictionary of Literary Biography Documentary Series*, Volumes 1-4
DLB-Y: *Dictionary of Literary Biography Yearbook*, Volumes 1980-1984
NCLC: *Nineteenth-Century Literature Criticism*, Volumes 1-10
SAAS: *Something about the Author Autobiography Series*, Volume 1
SATA: *Something about the Author*, Volumes 1-42
TCLC: *Twentieth-Century Literary Criticism*, Volumes 1-18
YABC: *Yesterday's Authors of Books for Children*, Volumes 1-2

Farmer, Penelope (Jane) 1939- 8
  See also SATA 39, 40
  See also CANR 9
  See also CA 13-16R

Feelings, Muriel (Grey) 1938-
  See Feelings, Muriel L.
  See also SATA 16
  See also CA 93-96

Feelings, Muriel L. 1938- 5
  See also Feelings, Muriel (Grey)

Feelings, Muriel L. 1938- and
    Tom Feelings 1933- 5

Feelings, Thomas 1933-
  See Feelings, Tom
  See also SATA 8
  See also CA 49-52

Feelings, Tom 1933- 5
  See also Feelings, Thomas

Feelings, Tom 1933- and
    Muriel L. Feelings 1938- 5

Fitzgerald, John D(ennis) 1907- 1
  See also SATA 20
  See also CA 93-96

Fitzhardinge, Joan Margaret 1912-
  See Joan Phipson
  See also SATA 2
  See also CANR 6
  See also CA 13-16R

Fitzhugh, Louise 1928-1974 1
  See also SATA 1
  See also obituary SATA 24
  See also CAP 2
  See also CA 29-32
  See also obituary CA 53-56

Fleischman, (Albert) Sid(ney) 1920- 1
  See also SATA 8
  See also CANR 5
  See also CA 1-4R

Foster, Genevieve (Stump) 1893-1979 7
  See also SATA 2
  See also obituary SATA 23
  See also CANR 4
  See also CA 5-8R
  See also obituary CA 89-92

Fox, Paula 1923- 1
  See also CLC 2, 8
  See also SATA 17
  See also CA 73-76

Fritz, Jean (Guttery) 1915- 2
  See also SATA 1, 29
  See also CANR 5, 16
  See also CA 1-4R

Gág, Wanda (Hazel) 1893-1946 4
  See also YABC 1
  See also CA 113
  See also DLB 22

Geisel, Theodor Seuss 1904- 1
  See Seuss, Dr.
  See also SATA 1, 28
  See also CANR 13
  See also CA 13-16R

George, Jean Craighead 1919- 1
  See also CLC 35
  See also SATA 2
  See also CA 5-8R

Gibbons, Gail (Gretchen) 1944- 8
  See also SATA 23
  See also CANR 12
  See also CA 69-72

Giovanni, Nikki 1943- 6
  See also CLC 2, 4, 19
  See also SATA 24
  See also CA 29-32R
  See also DLB 5, 41
  See also AITN 1

Glubok, Shirley (Astor) 1933- 1
  See also SATA 6
  See also CANR 4
  See also CA 5-8R

Goffstein, M(arilyn) B(rooke) 1940- 3
  See also SATA 8
  See also CANR 9
  See also CA 21-24R

Graham, Lorenz B(ell) 1902- 10
  See also SATA 2
  See also CA 9-12R

Grahame, Kenneth 1859-1932 5
  See also YABC 1
  See also CA 108
  See also DLB 34

Greenaway, Catherine 1846-1901
  See Greenaway, Kate
  See also CA 113

Greenaway, Kate 1846-1901 6
  See also Greenaway, Catherine
  See also YABC 2

Greene, Bette 1934- 2
  See also CLC 30
  See also SATA 8
  See also CANR 4
  See also CA 53-56

Greenfield, Eloise 1929- 4
  See also SATA 19
  See also CANR 1
  See also CA 49-52

Gripe, Maria (Kristina) 1923- 5
  See also SATA 2
  See also CANR 17
  See also CA 29-32R

Hamilton, Virginia (Edith) 1936- 1
  See also CLC 26
  See also SATA 4
  See also CA 25-28R
  See also DLB 33

Haskins, James 1941- 3
  See also SATA 9
  See also CA 33-36R

Hay, Timothy 1910-1952
  See Brown, Margaret Wise

Henry, Marguerite 1902- 4
  See also SATA 11
  See also CANR 9
  See also CA 17-20R
  See also DLB 22

Hentoff, Nat(han Irving) 1925- 1
  See also CLC 26
  See also SATA 27, 42
  See also CANR 5
  See also CA 1-4R

Hergé 1907-1983 6
  See also Rémi, Georges

Hinton, S(usan) E(loise) 1950- 3
  See also CLC 30
  See also SATA 19
  See also CA 81-84

Hoban, Russell (Conwell) 1925- 3
  See also CLC 7, 25
  See also SATA 1, 40
  See also CA 5-8R

Hogrogian, Nonny 1932- 2
  See also SAAS 1
  See also SATA 7
  See also CANR 2
  See also CA 45-48

Houston, James A(rchibald) 1921- 3
  See also SATA 13
  See also CA 65-68

Howe, James 1946- 9
  See also SATA 29
  See also CA 105

Hughes, Monica (Ince) 1925- 9
  See also SATA 15
  See also CA 77-80

Hughes, Ted 1930- .3
  See also CLC 2, 4, 9, 14
  See also SATA 27
  See also CANR 1
  See also CA 1-4R
  See also DLB 40

Hunt, Irene 1907- 1
  See also SATA 2
  See also CANR 8
  See also CA 17-20R

Hunter, Kristin (Eggleston) 1931- 3
  See also CLC 35
  See also SATA 12
  See also CANR 13
  See also CA 13-16R
  See also DLB 33
  See also AITN 1

Isadora, Rachel 1953(?)- 7
  See also SATA 32
  See also CA 111

Iwamatsu, Jun Atsushi 1908-
  See Yashima, Taro
  See also SATA 14
  See also CA 73-76

Jansson, Tove (Marika) 1914- 2
  See also SATA 3, 41
  See also CA 17-20R

Jarrell, Randall 1914-1965 6
  See also CLC 1, 2, 6, 9, 13
  See also SATA 7
  See also CANR 6
  See also CA 5-8R
  See also obituary CA 25-28R

Jordan, June 1936- 10
  See also CLC 5, 11, 23
  See also SATA 4
  See also CA 33-36R
  See also DLB 38

Kark, Nina Mary (Mabey) 1925-
  See Bawden, Nina
  See also SATA 4
  See also CANR 8
  See also CA 17-20R

Kästner, Erich 1899-1974 4
  See also SATA 14
  See also CA 73-76
  See also obituary CA 49-52

Author Index

Author Index

CUMULATIVE INDEX TO NATIONALITIES

AMERICAN

Adkins, Jan **7**
Adoff, Arnold **7**
Alcott, Louisa May **1**
Alexander, Lloyd **1, 5**
Aliki **9**
Anglund, Joan Walsh **1**
Armstrong, William H. **1**
Aruego, Jose **5**
Aylesworth, Thomas G. **6**
Babbitt, Natalie **2**
Bacon, Martha **3**
Bang, Molly **8**
Baylor, Byrd **3**
Bemelmans, Ludwig **6**
Bendick, Jeanne **5**
Bethancourt, T. Ernesto **3**
Blume, Judy **2**
Bontemps, Arna **6**
Bova, Ben **3**
Brown, Margaret Wise **10**
Byars, Betsy **1**
Cameron, Eleanor **1**
Carle, Eric **10**
Charlip, Remy **8**
Cleary, Beverly **2, 8**
Cleaver, Bill **6**
Cleaver, Vera **6**
Clifton, Lucille **5**
Coatsworth, Elizabeth **2**
Cobb, Vicki **2**
Cohen, Daniel **3**
Cole, Joanna **5**
Collier, James Lincoln **3**
Conford, Ellen **10**
Corbett, Scott **1**
Crews, Donald **7**
de Angeli, Marguerite **1**
DeJong, Meindert **1**

de Paola, Tomie **4**
Donovan, John **3**
du Bois, William Pène **1**
Emberley, Barbara **5**
Emberley, Ed **5**
Engdahl, Sylvia Louise **2**
Enright, Elizabeth **4**
Estes, Eleanor **2**
Feelings, Muriel L. **5**
Feelings, Tom **5**
Fitzgerald, John D. **1**
Fitzhugh, Louise **1**
Fleischman, Sid **1**
Foster, Genevieve **7**
Fox, Paula **1**
Fritz, Jean **2**
Gág, Wanda **4**
Geisel, Theodor Seuss **1**
George, Jean Craighead **1**
Gibbons, Gail **8**
Giovanni, Nikki **6**
Glubok, Shirley **1**
Goffstein, M. B. **3**
Graham, Lorenz B. **10**
Greene, Bette **2**
Greenfield, Eloise **4**
Hamilton, Virginia **1**
Haskins, James **3**
Henry, Marguerite **4**
Hentoff, Nat **1**
Hinton, S. E. **3**
Hoban, Russell **3**
Hogrogian, Nonny **2**
Howe, James **9**
Hunt, Irene **1**
Hunter, Kristin **3**
Isadora, Rachel **7**
Jarrell, Randall **6**
Jordan, June **10**

Keats, Ezra Jack **1**
Kellogg, Steven **6**
Klein, Norma **2**
Konigsburg, E. L. **1**
Kotzwinkle, William **6**
Krementz, Jill **5**
Kuskin, Karla **4**
Langstaff, John **3**
Lawson, Robert **2**
Le Guin, Ursula K. **3**
L'Engle, Madeleine **1**
LeShan, Eda J. **6**
Lester, Julius **2**
Lionni, Leo **7**
Livingston, Myra Cohn **7**
Lobel, Arnold **5**
Lowry, Lois **6**
Manley, Seon **3**
Mathis, Sharon Bell **3**
McCloskey, Robert **7**
McCord, David **9**
McDermott, Gerald **9**
McHargue, Georgess **2**
McKinley, Robin **10**
Monjo, F. N. **2**
Mukerji, Dhan Gopal **10**
Myers, Walter Dean **4**
Ness, Evaline **6**
O'Brien, Robert C. **2**
O'Dell, Scott **1**
Paterson, Katherine **7**
Pinkwater, D. Manus **4**
Pringle, Laurence **4**
Raskin, Ellen **1**
Rau, Margaret **8**
Rey, H. A. **5**
Rey, Margret **5**
Rockwell, Thomas **6**
Sachs, Marilyn **2**

Scarry, Richard **3**
Schwartz, Alvin **3**
Selden, George **8**
Selsam, Millicent E. **1**
Sendak, Maurice **1**
Seredy, Kate **10**
Seuss, Dr. **9**
Showers, Paul **6**
Shulevitz, Uri **5**
Silverstein, Shel **5**
Simon, Seymour **9**
Singer, Isaac Bashevis **1**
Slote, Alfred **4**
Smucker, Barbara **10**
Sneve, Virginia Driving Hawk **2**
Sobol, Donald J. **4**
Speare, Elizabeth George **8**
Spier, Peter **5**
Steig, William **2**
Steptoe, John **2**
Sterling, Dorothy **1**
Suhl, Yuri **2**
Taylor, Mildred D. **9**
Thomas, Ianthe **8**
Tobias, Tobi **4**
Tunis, Edwin **2**
Uchida, Yoshiko **6**
Van Allsburg, Chris **5**
Viorst, Judith **3**
Watson, Clyde **3**
Weiss, Harvey **4**
Wersba, Barbara **3**
White, E. B. **1**
White, Robb **3**
Wibberley, Leonard **3**
Wilder, Laura Ingalls **2**
Willard, Nancy **5**
Williams, Jay **8**

Williams, Vera B. 9
Wojciechowska, Maia 1
Yashima, Taro 4
Yep, Laurence 3
Yolen, Jane 4
Zim, Herbert S. 2
Zindel, Paul 3
Zolotow, Charlotte 2

AUSTRALIAN
Chauncy, Nan 6
Lindsay, Norman 8
Phipson, Joan 5
Southall, Ivan 2
Travers, P. L. 2
Wrightson, Patricia 4

AUSTRIAN
Bemelmans, Ludwig 6

BELGIAN
Hergé 6

CANADIAN
Burnford, Sheila 2
Houston, James 3
Hughes, Monica 9
Kurelek, William 2
Lee, Dennis 3
Little, Jean 4
Montgomery, L. M. 8
Smucker, Barbara 10
Stren, Patti 5

CHILEAN
Krahn, Fernando 3

CZECHOSLOVAKIAN
Sasek, M. 4

DANISH
Andersen, Hans Christian 6

DUTCH
Bruna, Dick 7
DeJong, Meindert 1
Lionni, Leo 7
Spier, Peter 5

ENGLISH
Aiken, Joan 1
Ardizzone, Edward 3
Ashley, Bernard 4
Bawden, Nina 2
Bond, Michael 1
Boston, L. M. 3
Briggs, Raymond 10
Burningham, John 9
Burton, Hester 1
Carroll, Lewis 2
Chauncy, Nan 6
Christopher, John 2
Cooper, Susan 4
Dahl, Roald 1, 7
Farmer, Penelope 8
Greenaway, Kate 6
Grahame, Kenneth 5
Hughes, Monica 9
Hughes, Ted 3
Lear, Edward 1
Lewis, C. S. 3
Lively, Penelope 7
Macaulay, David 3
Milne, A. A. 1
Nesbit, E. 3
Norton, Mary 6
Oakley, Graham 7
Pearce, Philippa 9
Peyton, K. M. 3

Pieńkowski, Jan 6
Potter, Beatrix 1
Ransome, Arthur 8
Serraillier, Ian 2
Sutcliff, Rosemary 1
Townsend, John Rowe 2
Travers, P. L. 2
Treece, Henry 2
Walsh, Jill Paton 2
Wildsmith, Brian 2
Willard, Barbara 2
Williams, Kit 4

FILIPINO
Aruego, Jose 5

FINNISH
Jansson, Tove 2

FRENCH
Brunhoff, Jean de 4
Brunhoff, Laurent de 4
Saint-Exupéry, Antoine de 10
Ungerer, Tomi 3

GERMAN
Kästner, Erich 4
Krüss, James 9
Rey, H. A. 5
Rey, Margret 5
Zimnik, Reiner 3

GREEK
Zei, Alki 6

HUNGARIAN
Seredy, Kate 10

INDIAN
Mukerji, Dhan Gopal 10

ISRAELI
Shulevitz, Uri 5

ITALIAN
Collodi, Carlo 5
Munari, Bruno 9

JAPANESE
Anno, Mitsumasa 2
Watanabe, Shigeo 8
Yashima, Taro 4

NEW ZEALAND
Mahy, Margaret 7

POLISH
Pieńkowski, Jan 6
Shulevitz, Uri 5
Singer, Isaac Bashevis 1
Suhl, Yuri 2
Wojciechowska, Maia 1

RUSSIAN
Korinetz, Yuri 4

SCOTTISH
Burnford, Sheila 2
Stevenson, Robert Louis 10

SOUTH AFRICAN
Lewin, Hugh 9

SWEDISH
Gripe, Maria 5
Lagerlöf, Selma 7
Lindgren, Astrid 1

WELSH
Dahl, Roald 1, 7

CUMULATIVE INDEX TO TITLES

Title Index

Title Index